D1327794

SULTAN QABOOS AND MODERN OMAN

SULTAN QABOOS AND MODERN OMAN

1970–2020

Edited by Allen James Fromherz and Abdulrahman al-Salimi

EDINBURGH
University Press

Edinburgh University Press is one of the leading university presses in the UK. We publish academic books and journals in our selected subject areas across the humanities and social sciences, combining cutting-edge scholarship with high editorial and production values to produce academic works of lasting importance. For more information visit our website: edinburghuniversitypress.com

Edinburgh University Press Ltd
The Tun—Holyrood Road
12(2f) Jackson's Entry
Edinburgh EH8 8PJ

Typeset in 11/15 Adobe Garamond by
IDSUK (DataConnection) Ltd, and
printed and bound in Great Britain

A CIP record for this book is available from the British Library

ISBN 978 1 4744 9346 8 (hardback)
ISBN 978 1 4744 9348 2 (webready PDF)
ISBN 978 1 4744 9349 9 (epub)

CONTENTS

FIGURES AND TABLES

Figures

Tables

CONTRIBUTORS

Calvin H. Allen Jr. is Emeritus Dean of the College of Arts and Sciences at Shenandoah University, Virginia where he was also Professor of Middle East History.

Javier Guirado Alonso is a PhD Student and Teaching Assistant in Gulf and Middle East History at Georgia State University.

Juan Cole is Richard P. Mitchell Collegiate Professor of History at the University of Michigan.

Maria F. Curtis is Associate Professor of Anthropology and Cross-Cultural Studies at the University of Houston, Clear Lake, Texas.

Sean Foley is Professor of History at Middle Tennessee State University.

Allen James Fromherz is Director of the Middle East Studies Center and Professor of Gulf, Mediterranean and Middle East History at Georgia State University, Atlanta.

Victoria Penziner Hightower is Professor of Middle East and Gulf History at the University of North Georgia.

Valerie J. Hoffman is Emerita Professor of Religion at the University of Illinois at Urbana-Champaign.

Jonathan Mark Kenoyer is George and Barbara Dales Professor of Anthropology at the University of Wisconsin, Madison.

Salim al-Kharusi is Assistant Professor of Law at the College of Law, Sultan Qaboos University, Muscat.

Jeffrey R. Kinnier is a PhD student in Indian Ocean History at Georgia State University.

Krista Lewis is Chair of the Department of Anthropology at Appalachian State University in North Carolina.

Mandana E. Limbert is Associate Professor of Anthropology at Queens College and The Graduate Center, City University of New York.

Francis Owtram is Honorary Research Fellow at the University of Exeter, UK.

J. E. Peterson is Historian and Political Analyst on the Contemporary Arabian Peninsula and the Gulf.

Barbara Michalak-Pikulska is Professor of Arabic Literature and the Head of the Arabic Department, Jagiellonian University in Krakow.

Jody Pritt is Director of International Student and Scholar Services at Georgia State University in Atlanta.

Uzi Rabi is Director of the Moshe Dayan Center for Middle East Studies at Tel Aviv University.

Abdulrahman al-Salimi is an Omani scholar and the author of several works on Ibadi and Omani history.

James Worrall is Associate Professor in International Relations and Middle East Studies at the University of Leeds, United Kingdom.

ACKNOWLEDGMENTS

This book resulted from the combined effort of an international team of scholars, administrative leaders, and editors all persevering through a global pandemic. We want to thank the Ministry of Endowments and Religious Affairs in Oman for their support of this book and "Sultan Qaboos and Modern Oman: 1970–2020": a conference taking place at Georgia State University in 2022. In particular, we are grateful for the support of HE Sheikh Abdullah b. Muhammad al-Salmi, the Minister of Endowments and Religious Affairs. We also want to thank the editors at Edinburgh University Press, including Emma Rees, who is one of the finest commissioning editors in history, as well as Louise Hutton, Eddie Clark, and Bekah Dey for their work in bringing this book to production. Also, we are grateful to Nicola Ramsey, newly appointed as CEO of EUP in 2021. NYU Abu Dhabi Humanities Center deserves credit for a fellowship and conference in 2016 that brought Dr. Fromherz and Dr. al-Salimi together to start discussions on this volume. At Georgia State University, Ahu Kostak-Bulat, Marla Meredith, Jeff Irwin, and Michelle Robinson worked tirelessly with authors and presenters, and Wolfgang Schloer has provided excellent leadership at the Office of International Initiatives. In Oman, we want to thank Mrs. Basma al-Bassami, Mr. Hamid al-Salami, Mr. Mohammed al-Sinani, and Mr. Moatasim Al-Busaidi for their important work on this project. The GSU History Department and College of Arts and Sciences supported the project.

We are especially grateful to the Middle East Studies Center and its faculty affiliates and thank Dean Sara Rosen, Associate Dean Dan Deocampo, and James Taylor. Finally, we want to thank each of our authors for their patience, their debate, their conversation, and their compelling contributions to this volume on the reign and impact of Sultan Qaboos (1970–2020).

INTRODUCTION
SULTAN QABOOS, OMANI SOCIETY, AND THE "BLESSED RENAISSANCE", 1970–2020

Allen James Fromherz

Sultan Qaboos made nearly 100 official speeches and various pronounce-ments throughout his reign from 1970 to 2020. These were awaited, social events, especially in the early years, with Omanis gathering around the one TV in town or hearing his voice over the radio.[1] In addition to moments of soaring rhetoric, his conversational style and engagement, detailing means of increasing oil production, or drip irrigation systems for date palms, seemed to involve the public even in the minutiae of governing. He reached out to Omanis on both a practical and emotional level by speaking to the people, addressing their concerns in their everyday lives, much as he would during his many driving trips around the country when he met with Omanis from various backgrounds one-on-one. He also created a sense of a shared plan, a common framework, especially during longer national day speeches that went into great detail, committing government departments in ways that would be remembered by the people. A message seemed to unite all his speeches: he could not do this alone. He empowered Omanis in the building of mod-ern Oman a process of social transformation that he and Omanis labeled "The Blessed Renaissance." In 1974, "the success we see in the sectors of both our local and international policies is the true reflection of the efforts of our people . . ."[2] Sometimes, his speech seemed familiar, relatable. In 1975, as if to speak directly to Omanis who were experiencing the marvels of color vision, he said, "Today I am happy to be addressing you on Oman Color TV . . ."[3] In 1980, on the tenth anniversary of National Day, he reiterated that the achievements of the Omani Renaissance, the building of roads, schools, and hospitals, the creation of opportunities when "we were poor in everything except in the strength of our Omani traditions . . ." was not his effort, or that of his government alone. Rather, "every Omani can hold up his head with pride at our achievements. The benefits of modern medicine are available to everyone; schools have been built. We now have 100,000 boys and girls receiving education."[4] In 2001, "Shura (consultation) is firmly rooted in the life of the Omani community . . . Nations are being built solely by the hands of the citizens . . ." In 2009, he made clear the involvement of women, "Since the beginning of this era we have given absolute priority to the participation of Omani women in the Blessed Renaissance."[5] The message was clear each time. Omanis could not be passive recipients of the state's largess, or mere subjects of the Sultan. Instead of merely imposing change from above, the Sultan sought their cooperation in the building of modern Oman.

Figure I.1 Oman's Sultan Qaboos chairs the opening session of the annual summit of the Gulf Cooperation Council (GCC) in Muscat on December 29, 2008. Credit MARWAN NAAMANI/AFP via Getty Images.

Through these speeches and his moderate and peaceful demeanor, Sultan Qaboos became, to Omanis, the embodiment of an integrated Omani ideal. He modeled pursuing change, and choosing elements of European society, while preserving Omani tradition and identity. He spoke in various venues, from universities, to consultative council chambers, to police academies and the United Nations. Even his style of dress, wearing the traditional Omani headdress, the *muzzar*, which distinguished him as an Omani, set him apart from other Gulf leaders as seen here at his opening of the Gulf Cooperation Council in 2008 (Figure I.1). Other Arab rulers commonly wore the *bisht*, a black robe with gold trim, over *dishdasha* (white inner robe) with a checkered *shumagh* (often red and white) head covering. Sultan Qaboos, in contrast, wore the *bisht*, the *dishdasha* as well as his muzzar, not the checkered shumagh. This visually proclaimed his Arab and distinctively Omani identities simultaneously. In other speeches, he was in full military uniform (1990 National Day). In still others he wore a simple and humble, white *dishdasha* at his desk (2007 after a massive storm, Bait al-Barakah). Finally, he was seen "at ease," but still militarily ready, wearing army combat camouflage during one address (1981 National Day). Choice of dress reflected the subject and audience addressed. Through his multiplicity of roles, Sultan Qaboos bin Said also saw himself as a bridge between the cultural, religious, and ideological divides in Oman; divides that were tearing apart other regions of the Middle East.

In 1970, the year he came to power, Oman was, like many of its neighbors, riven by geographical, religious, and social chasms. Of course, there were still supporters of his father and the world itself was vulnerable to turf wars between Soviet and U.S. cold warriors. In 1980, ten years after he came to power, the Sultan cited "unbridled ambitions of the Soviet Union" as one of the main threats facing the region and the world.[6] A split along any one of Oman's many divides could have threatened insurrection, civil war, and intervention by outside powers, especially those in the region hungry to take advantage of Oman's new-found petroleum resources which were only beginning to be fully exploited in the late 1960s. The Sultan maintained a baseline of order and defended the borders of the Sultanate during a crucial period when borders were only just being drawn through sand and sea. He used force effectively when it was seen as necessary, putting down Oman's many insurgencies that were funded to a large extent by outside powers. The Omani Renaissance was about more than building bridges, it was proclaimed as a way to defeat the threat of communism. In 1972, on the second national day, he noted:

> We are waging a battle for building our country in various fields of development, we are also waging a sacred and armed battle against the enemy of Islam and the country, supported by Marxist Aden . . . active international communism is working there to achieve its ambition in the Arab Peninsula to transform it into a huge communist camp . . . Oman is not a target (of the so-called Popular Front for the Liberation of Oman and the Arabian Gulf) in itself but is the door to the rest of the countries in the region, to sink them in a sea of blood, subversion, chaos, poverty, atheism and looting, as the Popular Front has done to the people of South Yemen.[7]

Development projects in Oman were part of a strategy encouraging the people of Dhofar and the Southern Province to join "their brothers, men of our Armed Forces, to fight for the sake of their faith, country, and dignity." After all, as the Sultan stated in 1971, "we clearly affirm that Dhofar is an integral part of the Sultanate of Oman, to precisely the same extent that Muscat [the capital] is part of this dear Omani land."[8] As such, the expansion of infrastructure and development outside the capital was a matter of national survival and urgency. The acts of building and defending the nation were equated in 1975 in one of the Sultan's main speeches addressed not to a council, but "to the people." In speaking to the armed forces, he praised the situation of Dhofar and the remote mountain villages where healthcare and education infrastructure was being built. The Salalah–Thumrait road over the mountains became a "vital artery" in the region and helped to stabilize the gains against rebels in the region.[9] Yemen was not the only source of trouble for Oman. Sultan Qaboos also defended Oman against attempts to consume valuable territory, such as at the border in al-Buraimi.

Emerging out of the 1970s with few of the immediate threats that had once destabilized its borders, Oman built an experienced, highly respected military, navy, and security system that helps to maintain its neutrality. Oman, however, was very careful about deploying its armed forces, rarely used outside national borders; Operation Desert Storm to liberate Kuwait being the major exception.[10] Consensus, not force, was his most convincing, and most important, tool. Even as fighting raged in Dhofar, Sultan Qaboos focused on creating and supporting a new vision of Oman's modernization, the Omani Renaissance (Ar. *Nahda*), which sought to repair existing social dichotomies. This creation of a stable social and governmental infrastructure, more than any military success alone, caused a domino effect that helped even in areas of fighting. Prioritizing development created a virtuous cycle. Oman's modernization program was implemented through consensus in a way that fed stability throughout Oman. That stability, in turn, led to more opportunities for careful modernization. He chose a path of moderation tailored to Oman's specific circumstances. This was a policy, in effect, that allowed pragmatic integration, the construction of a new Omani way between two opposing paths of change and continuity.

There were many choices and opportunities, as well as many limitations and existential risks, before the new Sultan on July 23, 1970, the date of his accession. His father, although he made important steps toward unification, including ending a parallel Imamate state, relied often on force and personal acquisition, not on building coalitions. Said bin Taimur was from a different generation of rulers. He seemed to see oil wealth as his to keep and he resisted the full deployment of new resources. He lacked a vision of modern Oman that involved the Omani people themselves. Sultan Qaboos, unlike his father, immediately began a program of distributing resources, including society in the process, and building webs of consensus and consultation based on new and traditional institutions and means of communication. Avoiding some of the downsides of so-called rentier states where oil wealth is merely given out and there is no, or little, investment in the state by those who receive that wealth passively, Sultan Qaboos actively and consistently called for the sustained involvement of Omani society and the Omani people. The concept of the "Blessed Renaissance", one that would keep aspects of both the past and the future, allowed the Sultan and his government to frame modernization in a way that avoided the backlash seen in other parts of the Middle East.

While his father saw the state as an extension of himself, and while some other rulers in the region distributed resources mainly to their own family, Sultan Qaboos, with no children of his own, made the Omani people his heirs. Sultan Qaboos and Omanis, through the Renaissance program, achieved what many outside observers considered impossible: a stable multisectarian, multiethnic, multi-religious state in the Middle East based on a balance of tradition and modernity, local heritage and external ideas. Often-times, he made decisions for the benefit of his country, such as the nationaliza-tion of oil, that were diametrically opposed to the external interests of major Western oil companies. Other times, he encouraged new interpretations and modernizations of Islamic law that caused some rumblings of opposition within. Each time, these decisions were portrayed as a social effort, justified by a mission he laid out at the beginning of his reign: to create the social, governmental, and cultural conditions necessary for a stable and prosperous country. Like every good bridge-builder, he knew the importance of stabiliz-ing the foundations of both banks, both sides of the bridge. Only when both sides are supported can the infrastructure of understanding bridge the span between them. Instead of choosing between East or West, modernization or tradition, Ibadi Islam or Sunni Islam, the interior of Oman or the ports, traditional Omani culture or European culture, Sultan Qaboos, with the backing of Omani society, supported the use of elements from each, turning dichotomies into opportunities for bridge-building. Sultan Qaboos actively sought out the consensus, something that went beyond the mere obedience or reverence of the Omani people. He realized that a sustainable, peaceful modernization could not occur without the distribution of the country's wealth to its people and the active and interested involvement of those people in the process of development. The Omani Renaissance, the name given by Qaboos to this program of modernization and renewal, was not a program imposed or distributed only from above, but a new and Omani-specific social attitude to modernization, an approach to the future, a national ideal that required Omanis from all backgrounds to come on board.

The social and cultural history of modern Oman, the change and adapta-tion within the many layers of Omani society from 1970 to 2020, the reign of Sultan Qaboos, is the focus of the studies in this book. With chapters on changes and continuities Omani society, law, health, religion, and even litera-ture and poetry during the reign of Qaboos and based on the active efforts of Omanis at every level, not just a mandate from on high, this volume explores the extent and depth of Oman's successful modernization process. In addi-tion to being a new approach with new perspectives, the book also serves as a corrective to certain trends in most studies of the Middle East. Oftentimes, Western observers have viewed Middle Eastern and, in particular, Gulf states as "black boxes." The exterior-facing sides of the boxes, the form of government, the source of their resources, their external alliances being prioritized as the most important aspect. The contents of the box, that is, the actual nuances of Gulf and Middle Eastern societies themselves, are treated as more or less irrelevant or even unknowable. This categorizing method, when taken to the extreme, has led to serious misunderstandings and highly inaccurate predictions. This book calls for looking inside the box, and a more nuanced understanding, one that puts the society and culture at the forefront, not as passive recipients of change but as active participants in modern history.

In addition to social factors, the specific character, decisions, and policies of the Sultan himself were also crucial to the rapid success of Oman. Aspects of the Sultan's public image were tailored to a program of pragmatic integration between change and continuity. Here was a man rooted proudly in Oman and Arabia, but also educated in the West, capable of appreciating and fostering beauty from many cultures. Anecdotes about the Sultan from those who met him confirmed this remarkable aspect of the Sultan's character. He embodied and bridged many worlds and possibilities.

One example of this bridging was Sultan Qaboos' interest in classical music. Sultan Qaboos, thoughout his reign from 1970 to 2020, loved Western classical music. In 1985, the Royal Oman Symphony Orchestra (ROSO) was established as the first of its kind: composed of Omani musicians trained in classical music.[11] When he sponsored the playing of Mozart or Verdi, he also wore the clothes of a respected Ibadi Omani. In 2011, long before other Gulf states would open similar world-class cultural institutions, Sultan Qaboos inaugurated the Royal Opera House Muscat, the first in the Gulf open to the public. (Riyadh had an opera house, but it was private.) Although the project was met with some protests by Islamic scholars, the Opera House, a project close to the Sultan, opened after a decade of careful craftsmanship. Building it required a program of training in the lost arts of traditional Arabic woodworking and stonemasonry. The message communicated by the Arab–Western architecture of the Royal Opera House was both subtle and convincing. At first glance, the building has some of the same design features of a typical, European concert hall. Looking closer at the extensive and elaborate designs, traditional Arabic patterns from Oman and around the Middle East emerge. The building is a combination and celebration of the traditions of Arabia and Europe and their capacity for dialogue. Opera House programming, which includes concerts from traditional Omani dance and music to the famed youth symphony orchestra of Venezuela, reflected Oman's status as a showcase of culture in a part of the world, the Gulf, more famous for skyscrapers and oil wells. A philosophy of diversity through unity, and change through continuity applied to the highly varied contours of Omani society, geography, and religion.

The Opera House, although opposed by some more conservative voices at first, was only one architectural legacy of the integration of cultures and styles during the Sultan Qaboos period. The Sultan Qaboos Grand Mosque, a modern, architectural highlight of Muscat, Oman's capital, symbolized unity within the Islamic community as well a desire by the Sultan to follow a modernizing approach within his faith as an Ibadi Muslim. Sultan Qaboos ordered the construction of the Opera House only after 2001, the year of the official opening of the Sultan Qaboos Grand Mosque. The mosque was built purposefully as a celebration of many different Islamic styles, Islamic arts, and heritage from around the world, with multiple niches representing typical mosque decorative designs from Al-Andalus to Central Asia. For Sultan Qaboos, this was not just an Ibadi or an Omani mosque, even if he and most Omanis were Ibadi Muslims. Instead, the mosque was dedicated both to Islamic unity and to modernizing Islamic thought: ". . . We decided to make this blessed mosque a center of culture and thought that, with God's good grace and assistance, would contribute to the revival of the Islamic heritage—God willing—and highlight the civilized values of the Muslim nation while modernizing its approach to dealing with Islamic affairs and issues."[12]

The Sultan Qaboos Grand Mosque and the Royal Opera House, despite initially being challenged by some more conservative religious opinions in Oman, now stand as symbols of Sultan Qaboos' explicit, rhetorical program of unity across divisions pursued from the beginning of his reign. In each case, the message is both clear and subtle, divisions and diversities within Islam and within Oman need not be a source of intractable divisions. The Royal Opera House and the Sultan Qaboos Mosque are emblematic of a deeper, difficult, and challenging process of integration, unification, and bridge-building, pursued quietly, but persistently, throughout the reign of Qaboos.

From the beginning, in the far more turbulent 1970s, Qaboos realized he could not pursue this process of integrating supposed dichotomies on his own; a sustainable project of national renewal could not be based on symbols or buildings alone. When he first arrived in Muscat after coming to power in 1970, Sultan Qaboos did not pursue an ideological approach, or make a pledge to a particular power or influence, even though southern Arabia was then a battlefield for the Cold War. Instead, he appealed to the people of Oman—calling for a program of integration and development that would require Omanis, and not just their ruler or new government, to participate. This Omani program of pragmatic integration and modernization would soon be called the Renaissance, or Rebirth. Of course, at an early stage many Omanis may have been apprehensive. What did this program of rebirth really mean? Will we need to abandon our culture, our identities and way of life as this new ruler opens the gates of our country to the outside world? Will the government really provide the services we need or will resources mainly be held by a few? What will happen to those who once fought against the Sultan's father? By the end of the 1970s, however, enthusiasm among Omanis for "the Renaissance" was so strong that it became known as the "Blessed Renaissance." There are several reasons for this; as the name "Renaissance" implies, the modernization of Oman and the power of the Sultan was not about forcing Oman and Omanis into the modern age from the top down. Unlike other Middle Eastern states where modernization was primarily a destructive process of secularization that pitted the state against society and religion, modernization in Oman did not mean the destruction of the particularities of Omani society and history. Instead of an imposed system or program brought in from outside and instituted purely from above, Sultan Qaboos explicitly encouraged all Omanis to join in a rebirth of Oman's historical heritage, harkening back to an idealized history when Oman was a global center and crossroads of diversity. Importantly, Qaboos did not simply "take power" from his father or from the oil companies, who famously wanted to hoard the wealth of Oman's oil reserves, which he later nationalized. Instead, he also handed power over to Omanis as a whole. He knew meaningful change could emerge from the cooperation of Omanis themselves. He admitted, from the beginning, the limits of his own power. In his first official address he stated:

> We hope that this day will mark the beginning of a new age and a great future for us all . . . unless there is cooperation between the government and the people, we will not be able to build our country with the speed required to

free her from the backwardness she has endured for so long. The government and the people are as one body. If one of its limbs fails to do its duty, the other parts of the body suffer.

In his way of appealing to the power of the people, and in creating a particularly Omani program of Renaissance, a program that was not controlled by outside, ideological influences, but was homegrown, Sultan Qaboos did not hoard power or try to force Oman into a preordained ideological vision. The first address was brief, perhaps one of the shortest of his reign. But it was also one of the most important. The message was clear. This was the start of a new era for Oman that could be built only by Omanis themselves, not by intervention by outside powers, not by a process brought in from the outside or managed purely from above. By focusing on Oman and the Omani people, not on the British or the Soviets, not just on communism or capitalism, not on a false dichotomy of Islam or on Western ways, he avoided the typical conflicts between identity and unity, tradition and modernity, Islam and the West, ruler and ruled, that inflicted other states in the Middle East. Of course, there may have been some who may have wanted him to act more like a traditional strongman, to establish military rule, to force over the divisions within his country. Instead, the Sultan appealed not to the West or to technocratic secularization but to an Islamic, Arab, and particularly Omani tradition of authority through consensus. In the 1970s, there were tremendous pressures to impose either Soviet-supported and state-sponsored communism or Western-supported capital-sponsored democracy. Either choice was often a losing bargain for states forced to choose between the extraction of their resources by multinational corporations or the relinquishing of their sovereignty and identity to communist ideologies. Oman, instead, created its own system or model of modernity, called the Omani Renaissance.

Oman's modernization deserves study as a potential model of careful planning and pragmatic integration that avoided the ideological ruptures and upheavals of other modernization projects. By proclaiming the Renaissance as a bridge between memory and desire, past and present, Oman was not simply following the West or abandoning its own culture. Since the end of the Second World War, Western political scientists and sociologists alike have predicted the inevitable end of traditional government systems. As societies became more educated and economies more developed, and as the end of the Cold War in the late 1980s seemed to lay bare the limits of Soviet-style communism, the assumption was that the "Washington Consensus," a term for a set of policy proscriptions based on neoliberal ideas coined by Carnegie Endowment fellow Moisés Naím, would prevail. Francis Fukuyama famously called this the "end of history."[13] Capitalist democracy based fundamentally on superior Western ideas and the liberal model, with perhaps some local flavor or culture allowed, was believed to be the only and inevitable way forward. In the 1990s and early 2000s, the assumption was that Western-style, democratic systems based on modern, liberal capitalism were inherently superior and more stable. These systems would inevitably replace kings, sultans, and sheikhs. Neoconservatives in the United States and Europe, as during the George W. Bush administration, even favored direct intervention against some rulers and regimes to speed what they viewed as an inevitable process along. By 2002, Naím himself, however, was calling the Washington Consensus, a "damaged brand."[14] Later, the approach to democratization became much more subtle. In an address to the University of Cairo, President Obama promised support for democratic movements and, at least according to some interpretations, the United States became less concerned with the risks of Islamist democracy. In 2011, the so-called "Arab Spring" erupted in Tunisia and spread throughout the Middle East. In the end, however, only Tunisia itself was profoundly transformed from a dictatorship to a functioning democracy where power was, for a time, shared by Islamic and secular parties. Non-monarchies and dictatorships where power was based on force and fear and where social divisions and inequalities are much more prevalent, such as Libya and Syria, fell into periods of profound instability and their divisions became bait for outside powers to fight destructive proxy wars. Traditional monarchies, although rattled somewhat, remained relatively unscathed. Along with the kingdoms of Morocco and Jordan and the sheikdoms of the Gulf, the Omani Sultanate remained and even strengthened in the midst of these external destabilizing influences. The Sultan did not seek to divide and conquer his people into camps, or to crush dissent as the military-based dictators Assad or Mubarak tried to do. He listened to concerns from cities such as Sunni-majority Sohar, which was a center of protest during the Arab Spring. Instead of tanks or bombs to crush dissent, he sent resources to Sohar and to other parts of Oman that felt less included in recent development and opportunities. The Sultan also kept open a steady program of gradual, constitutional, and governmental reform throughout his reign, culminating in the writing of a formal constitution and the promise of more representative rights and democratic governance. For some, this process is too slow. There was dissent within Oman under Sultan Qaboos about the speed and extent of institutional reforms and power-sharing. However, instead of merely suppressing that dissent, the Sultan's informal bridge-building and quiet, albeit often secret and informal, consultation and negotiation, reached out, listened to concerns and tried to bring dissenters into the fold as happened at the beginning of the Sultan's rule. Of course, there remain groups within Oman that still do not accept this contract, who demand further reforms and Western democracy at a more rapid pace. Or, on the other side, there are some who want to see the establishment of a pure, Islamic state. Nonetheless, they are not driving Oman into an abyss of civil war or intractable conflict due not only to the unifying message of the Sultan or his leadership, but by the genuine social cohesion he built around the idea of the Renaissance as a bridge between tradition and modernity, Islam and the West.

Wrongly conflating absolutism with monarchy, and assuming that Arabia's monarchs are in many ways the same as Western ones, scholars in the West have puzzled over this "persistence of monarchy" in the Middle East.[15] As I argued in *Qatar: A Modern History*, a new model needs to emerge to understand the success of the Gulf states and other monarchies such as Jordan and Morocco, one that acknowledges the power and persistence of local traditions of consultation between tribes, social groups, and governments.[16] The traditions of the *majlis* (tribal council) and the *diwan* (place for locals and others to meet with the ruler) were not merely seen as window-dressing. Qataris themselves mattered for the success of Qatar's Emiri system. For Oman, the need for consultation was even greater. Unlike Qataris, who are primary Sunni Muslims and a relatively small population of merchant and nomadic tribes, Oman is an even more complex mosaic of cultures, interpretations of Islam, geographies, and even faiths. Nonetheless, the Sultan, through a program of active social engagement, not top-down rule, was able to recruit Oman's highly diverse population in the distinctively Omani Renaissance. This social engagement, more than the form of government itself, explains the success and persistence of Sultan Qaboos. Unlike Western monarchs, before constitutional monarchy, who believed "I am the state" and who created state institutions as a means of centralizing power, the Sultan shared the resources of Oman and built a state in cooperation with many sectors of society even as he remained, legally, a final arbiter.

One reason for Western befuddlement over the "persistence of monarchy" in countries such as Oman is a profound case of cultural and historical confusion about the meaning of monarchy and traditions of rulership, especially among many Western political scientists who study the Middle East. First, Western monarchy is profoundly different from Arabian monarchy. Western monarchy was established in agricultural, land-based economies. The centralization of kingdoms and their transformation into nations was based in medieval history, in Europe's long, contentious history of controlling land as the source of power and economic resources.[17] European monarchy and its institutions created the modern Western state, which grew out of an ever-expanding process of centralizing land grabs by local notables, becoming lords, becoming monarchs. Until well into the Industrial Revolution, agriculture, not trade, comprised most of the Western economy and basis of power. The sultan in Muscat, Oman, however, almost always relied on trade and duties from the customs house, not on agricultural or land-based taxation. In Europe, eventually, the Western monarch became Hobbes' *Leviathan*. Louis XIV, the Sun King, created an apparatus of central power and control over estates. Napoleon showed a path that could metastasize, over several wars and upheavals and imperial breakups, into the dictatorial, nationalistic, military or technocratic regimes of the twentieth century. Industrialization, although it brought people from the farms to the cities, and lowered the importance of agricultural revenue, did not effectively limit the potential power of Western-style rulers, who were increasingly hobbled as constitutional monarchs. Hitler used many old tools and symbols to consolidate power, to eliminate diversity, and to concentrate a national socialist ideology around himself. Later, dictatorial rulers in the Middle East, some supported by the Soviets, others by the United States, used the apparatus of the modern state and military as a personal extension of themselves, forcing modernization, industrialization, and centralized state-building on their people. Some non-Western, Middle Eastern monarchs, however, grounded themselves in deeper, local traditions of consensus and rule that predated the modern state. The counterexample of the Shah of Iran, who was also technically a monarch and who fell in 1979, only reaffirmed the need for other Middle Eastern monarchies to share their resources and modernization process with their societies.

Several writers, many reading from Marxist theory, have assumed that Middle Eastern monarchies, with modernization, would fail. The idea of a sultanistic, oriental, or patrimonial state has dominated conceptual categories. Some historians and political scientists have labeled the system of government in Oman, and elsewhere in the Middle East, as merely a species of this same, imposed state.[18] Many of these studies provide important insights, and Uzi Rabi addresses these contributions and approaches in his literature review. Nonetheless, a misunderstanding of the specific realities of Oman persists in many studies of the modern Omani Sultanate, even in some of the more serious studies of Oman's history. Western sociological and political models, from Marx to Durkheim to Weber, might need to be abandoned to fully understand the nature of the modern Omani Sultanate.

While studies of modern Oman have noted the development of infrastructure, literal bridge-building and modern services, or focused on external diplomatic overtures and peacemaking by the Sultan, the main accomplishment of Qaboos was far less tangible and visible. It was his reconciliation of the different tribes, interpretations, ways of living and being that defined Omanis and their histories in separate ways from Salalah to Musandam. In a matter of a few short years, Sultan Qaboos unified the Sultanate and brought stability. He brought the Ibadi religious establishment into the fold as supporters of the Sultan, as well as those who once supported a rival imam in Nizwa. As the studies in this volume confirm, commitment to modernization of Islamic law often happened without the full prodding of the state. He went out into the country regularly and established constant means of communication through his governors with local tribes and leaders. The government compiled information about his people, a list of tribes and names, not for the purposes of imperial control, as Britain had often done in India, but to ensure that various traditional leaders would have a voice and be heard as modernization rapidly brought new services into the vast hinterlands.[19] Of course, there were limits to this process and resistance by those who felt left out of the government's sorting. Even so, by identifying them the state did not try to eliminate dissent or division by the tribes. Rather, the effort was focused on bringing different tribal groups into the fold, to provide them with access to services, education, and healthcare. This, in turn, allowed many tribal groups to coexist with state and government authority. The Sultan also appeared as a symbol of unity himself, on the new media of television and on radio, a regular voice that could form the basis of a new social contract. Instead of sending in modernizing bulldozers to tear down the past he actively preserved the built cultural environment, and intangible heritage, even as people were often desperate for services after decades of isolation from the outside world under his father. While some elements of traditional life were inevitably impacted, previous ways of life and heritage were never vilified as enemies of progress. Unlike the models of the Pahlavi Shah in Iran or the Ataturk in Turkey, the Omani Renaissance project was not based on military enforcement of modernity that pitted the state against Islamic or traditional elements of society. Instead, it embraced a type of heritage modernism that actively sought the support and involvement of many social sectors. Why destroy the benefits of tradition for the sake of modernity or the benefits of modernity for the sake of tradition when both can be had at once? Instead of rejecting Islam, or Ibadism, the Sultan highlighted its modern elements and quickly gained the support of both Ibadi and non-Ibadi Muslim leaders. He did not use Ibadi identity as a wedge issue or try to favor Ibadis as loyalists. The fact that Ibadis are the majority, but not an overwhelming majority in Oman, may have helped him since Ibadi leaders would not welcome a take-over or external intervention in Islamic matters by Sunni states. Of course, not all development, and not all reconciliation of different elements of Omani society was easy or perfect. Some initiatives failed. Some attempts to bring services were not implemented as quickly as needed. Some heritage was not preserved as well, or as perfectly, as it could have been. But these shortcomings became the basis of doing things better in other parts of the Sultanate. The main lesson from Oman's success is that states and societies cannot be fit easily into taxonomies. The particularities of Omani culture and history and the specific decisions of its ruler matter as much as, if not more than, the formal category of government: Sultanate. Oman's particularities explain the success of Sultan Qaboos in modernizing Oman.

Monarchy in Oman has a different etiology from that in the West, or even from other Middle Eastern states such as Iran or Jordan. First, there was a very different relationship between land and economy in Oman. Although there are fertile regions, known for date-growing, such as the Batinah, much of the Omani economy and most of the revenue provided to the sultans who ruled from the ports, was based on international trade. Instead of centralizing land power and increasing taxation to accumulate more power, as was the pattern of the monarchs in the West, the Sultan's wealth was based on the setting of reasonable customs duties that did not drive trade or merchants away to other ports. The interior of Oman, in contrast, was ruled mainly by Ibadi Imams. In Ibadi tradition, these were elected, religious rulers who governed only through consensus and often through very light and decentralized means of control. Even if, in practice, the Imamate became hereditary, in the mountainous regions, tribes, chiefs, and families maintained a great deal of independence from the imam, scattered and sheltered in dispersed valleys of the interior. A primary way for the imam to gain influence was through *hikma* or the traditional role as arbiter of disputes between different tribal chiefs and families that saw themselves as equals. Occasionally, a head chief or even an imam would emerge, someone who could rally Omanis when their independence was challenged by outside powers. The Persians or the Portuguese barely made a dent in the deeper, interior history of Oman. At the same time, the Omanis of the interior did not stay in the hinterland, locked in a box. During Oman's first, nineteenth-century period of reform, also called a "Renaissance," Omanis left the mountains and internationalized Omani culture and Ibadi law. They ventured far abroad, taking advantage of commercial opportunities throughout the Indian Ocean and forming cooperative networks with other Muslims and non-Muslims alike. Peoples from throughout the Indian Ocean formed the navy of the Sultan and Omanis effortlessly blended into the cosmopolitan markets and ports of the Indian Ocean littoral. Omani merchants relied on cooperation with members of the Banyan Hindu merchant community, for instance, who often manned the custom's house for the Sultan—then a main source of revenue. At the same time, the Ibadi Omanis maintained their cultural particularities in far off ports, becoming a migrant merchant community. There was a consolidation of Ibadi Islamic law within this community, a profoundly global process based on letters across the sea.[20] In the first half of the nineteenth century, the Sultan Sayyid Said bin Sultan (d. 1856) embraced his role as chief merchant and first among equals, building his capital in Zanzibar. Consensus, not centralized power, consultation, not monopoly of violence, was the means to influence. As much as Western monarchs encouraged exploration and became the heads of expanding empires, it would be hard to imagine the King of England transferring his main palace and capital to Virginia or Australia. Crucially, although Britain was always a major influence and various treaties did give the British a great deal of leverage, Oman was not under the direct control of an outside power. It was not a colony, mandate, or protectorate. The father of Sultan Qaboos was famously upset if the proper diplomatic protocol, which should have treated him as an equal or peer to the monarch of England, was not properly followed. The building of modern Oman and the national program of integration pursued by Sultan Qaboos, cannot be seen as merely a predictable postcolonial process, as a reaction to or embrace of an outside, imperial power. His father, with the help of British forces, had defeated the imam and consolidated claims over the interior. Sultan Qaboos, however, knew it was necessary to create a unified nation based upon both the historical traditions of Oman and those aspects of the Western economic, social, and educational model that were most useful. Remarkably, and building off its global history, Oman's policy of integrative pragmatism and building of bridges between dichotomies worked not just for resolving disputes within Oman, but as a means for dissipating conflict between Oman's neighbors as well. After securing stability at home through consensus, Sultan Qaboos became a peace-builder abroad, using his skills at mediation, which ultimately is the traditional source of power and respect in an Arabian cultural context, to lower the temperature of conflict between regional adversaries.

Sultan Qaboos, drawing on the positive aspects of the Ibadi Imamate of the interior, its basis on consensus, and the Sultanate of the ports, its openness in reaching toward the outside world to establish a new, combined Imamate and Sultanate models of rulership and brought both into the modern world. While many other Middle Eastern states languished in ideological battles between Islamists and secularists, Shiites and Sunnis, rural tribes and central governments, Oman through those divisions, emerging from profound poverty to become one of the most successful and stable states in the world. What explains the persistence of the Omani system of government, which has steadily liberalized and shared more legal, constitutional power formally, is a network of historical, cultural, and informal factors that made the Omani Renaissance possible. In fact, as the Omani Renaissance implied, it was through the continuation of Omani traditions of consensual, cooperative governance and that the Sultanate found success.

By April 2000, Sultan Qaboos and Omanis had much to celebrate. It had been three decades of the Omani Renaissance that began when the Sultan came to power in 1970: ". . . We have endeavored to ensure that every step taken by Oman's Renaissance springs from our deepest reality, that it is inspired by our heritage, religion and values, and that incorporates those aspects of modern civilization that are useful. That has been our aim, whether this means involving citizens in public affairs in which they take part . . . or whether it means improving our economy and raising the living standards of our people."[21] The Sultan was making it clear to all who heard his speeches that the Omani Renaissance could not be about him alone. It had to involve Omani society. It also had to combine elements both intrinsic to Oman and from the outside world. Through the rhetoric of Renaissance, Sultan Qaboos linked and harmonized otherwise competing forces of tradition and modernity, conservatism and progressivism, diversity and unity, Islam and the West, central planning and individual capital. Other groups throughout the world were embracing ideologies of liberalism versus communism, Salafism versus military secularism, monarchy versus democracy. Sultan Qaboos and Omanis turned their focus not on external ideology but on what Omanis have called the "Blessed Renaissance." This may sound nationalistic to Western ears. In many ways there was a profound sense of national purpose, especially during the first decades of the Renaissance when progress on infrastructure, in education, health, and other areas was happening at an exponential pace, transforming the landscape of Oman in profound ways, seemingly overnight. However, this was not an ethno-nationalism based on one group or people who alone held the keys to Omani identity or Omaniness. In downplaying divisions, both in himself and in Oman, and in representing the Renaissance as a program of national renewal, Sultan Qaboos helped to provide the glue necessary for keeping Oman together.

Although there were issues, challenges, and conflicts throughout his reign, even his Opera House and Mosque had detractors, Sultan Qaboos did not deal with dissent or difference by merely attempting to crush it or any alternatives to the state. While some in his government may have attempted to suppress some dissent, Sultan Qaboos himself was clear when it came to freedom of thought. In 2000 he stated that: "The suppression of ideas, thought and intellectual effort is a major sin . . . Ideas cannot be suppressed. Our religion stands for ideas and the intellect, the suppression of thought. Never. Our religion is tolerant, ethical and receptive to ideas . . ."[22]

The Omani Renaissance, as a bridge identity between tradition and modernity, helped to build an overarching sense of "Omaniness," of being Omani. There is a genuine belief and pride among Omanis that the Omani Renaissance was possible not only because of the Sultan alone, but also because of a combined effort by Omanis as a whole. Omaniness is a bridge identity within Oman, one with the capacity to expand and include multiple premodernization or non-national identities. Omaniness is also about more than the past, even as the past is not rejected. Omaniness embraces of modernity and tradition, of Western and Arab, of Ibadi, Sunni, and Shia, and African Swahili, there are Muslim and non-Muslim citizens. The oldest surviving Hindu temple in Arabia is still in Old Muscat, not far from the Royal Palace. Several hundred Hindus are citizens of Oman. While Yemen is riven by conflict, Saudi Arabia has wrestled with dynastic challenges, and the Gulf is split between those who want to call it Persian and those who want to call it Arabian, Oman stands apart as an island of unity and a keystone of stability. Since the mid-2000s, the world has seen the rise of new, decentralized media and cultural environments in which categories and subcategories of fractured identities are privileged over integrative ones such as nations. The succession to His Majesty Sultan Haitham bin Tariq Al-Said in 2020 and the embrace of a new set of steady reforms show that the current generation of Omani society is on board with the program or pragmatic integration established by Sultan Qaboos and his generation of Omanis.

Chapter Summaries

In 1972, a United Nations Children's Fund (UNICEF) team of four young women researchers arrived in Oman in the midst of transformation. They flew into Othaiba Airport, which, before Seeb International Airport, was just a gravel runway and a terminal, which "consisted of a large hangar that provided basic services . . .," to conduct a field study in Oman on the conditions of children and families in the Sultanate.[23] They stayed at al-Falaj Hotel, "one of only two hotels in the city." They had to buy supplies in Muscat since they were on their way through the mountains. The dirt road to Nizwa required a Land Rover and when they arrived in that capital of the interior, they were covered in a layer of dust after almost four hours of driving. There was not yet a bridge over the Wadi Abydah, so they were required to cross the riverbed. During rains, it seemed, the city was virtually cut off from the road to Muscat. Little did they know that in a few short years, the country and the people they came to help would transform into a stable, unified nation that formed a pillar of progress in the heart of a troubled region. When the UNICEF workers arrived, it had been only two years since the accession of a new, young Sultan, who had been educated in the West, but who was also acutely aware of the value and potential of his own culture. When they returned thirty years later in 2003, Oman was a different world. It had rocketed from near the bottom to the top rankings in the UN Human Development Index. Instead of steamrolling or forcing Oman into the future, the Sultan and his government made the Omani Renaissance a national project, seeking the cooperation and mutual effort of a variety of tribes, cities, and peoples throughout the Sultanate. He focused on relationships and coalitions, schools and hospitals, as well as just roads and bridges, preserving heritage sites instead of simply tearing them down for everything new, the social and cultural heritage and, in marked contrast to his predecessor, eagerly embraced investment in education, infrastructure, healthcare, and social development. What these UNICEF visitors did not fully realize was that they were witnessing one of the most rapid, extraordinary, and, for some observers, unexpected, social changes in the history of the modern Middle East. When they came back to Oman thirty years later, they were astonished, like modern Rip Van Winkles, at the visible and less tangible transformations. The chapters of this volume are organized to highlight the impact of those changes, as seen on the ground by outside observers and Omanis themselves.

The first chapter addresses the important work already done by scholars of modern Oman. Uzi Rabi discusses the existing, Western literature on the Sultan Qaboos era. While recognizing the valuable insights of various scholars and observers, Rabi, in his overview of works by prominent political scientists, historians, anthropologists, and observers of Oman, argues against the "black box" approach to modern Omani history. Explaining how the Sultan created a "national ethos" through the Renaissance, Uzi Rabi shows that Omani society, not just the Sultan, was involved at many levels in the sustained success of Oman's modernization process from 1970 to 2020. Unlike regimes in other parts of the Middle East, Sultan Qaboos did not concentrate all power in himself or rely primarily on the monopoly of violence. The successful and stable transition to Sultan Haitham is presented as further proof of this deeper social consensus around shared ideas such as the preservation of heritage.

Heritage

As new resources poured into historical research, archaeology, and heritage development, Oman's balanced modernization project led not only to the creation of future possibilities, it also lengthened the chronological imagination, the sense of a shared past stretching deep into the historical archeological record. The Omani Renaissance, based on the concept of rebirth not on destructive modernization, sought to bridge tradition and modernity, heritage and development. The next chapters show how archaeological discoveries sponsored by the reign of Sultan Qaboos deepened and lengthened Oman's and Omanis' conception of their own past. J. Mark Kenoyer, an archaeologist who specializes in the Indus civilization as well as southern Arabia and Oman, shows how a vast new corpus of scholarship about the deep past of Oman emerged after 1970. Even 4,000 years ago, global interactions between Oman and distant cultures were common. By opening Oman to international trade, the message was that Sultan Qaboos was simply returning Oman to ancient roots. Of course, archaeologists and historians are fully aware that aspects of ancient trade were very different from modern systems, but the symbolism was still important. Krista Lewis, another archaeologist, focuses on an ancient Omani commodity that was traded throughout

Eurasia: frankincense. The establishment of UNESCO recognition and the creation and modern administration of heritage sites in Dhofar have provided opportunities to link heritage with economic development. Victoria Hightower and James Worrall's chapter provides a periodization of heritage activities pursued during the era of Qaboos. Preserving heritage while providing for the divergent needs of tourists and local stakeholders is not always an easy process. Sultan Qaboos, his ministries and the bureaucracy developed heritage policies that changed over time becoming more inclusive and flexible, celebrating local traditions while also telling a national story. Private non-state institutions, working from the ground up, such as Bait al-Zubair, emerged and linked themselves to the heritage narrative.

The Sultan had a nuanced view of history and discouraged an uncritical approach to the past or to any received information. In one of his speeches, he noted that "history which was written down centuries ago is sometimes highly embroidered and distorted . . . History needs to be looked at critically, so that when we read history, we read it thinkingly and apply our intellects . . ." Sounding like a modern Ibn Khaldun (d. 1406) the North African historian who encouraged a critical reading of the past, the Sultan directly encouraged reading sources. "Turning to Omani history, when they talk about aspects of history and say there were ninety thousand—or a hundred thousand—horsemen, where did they all come from? Where did they get their food? Should we accept these things at face value? No . . . I say to students of history: be critical . . ."[24] For Sultan Qaboos, heritage, history, and even religion, should not be accepted blindly, "You must avoid letting anyone take away your freedom of thought in any way. People must use their minds and think . . ."[25]

Certain types of infrastructure rapidly facilitated the ability of Omanis in isolated areas to think differently, to quickly realize much broader horizons. The establishment of modern postal services, for example, allowed for a massive expansion of the geography of information, the speed and extent by which messages could be sent and received. In their book, the UNICEF researchers described how important supplies originally arrived in Nizwa via horseback. The post office was close to the sidr tree where merchants gathered. It was in an old building outside the city wall. The postman came only three times a week and post was not delivered to houses but to the post office where residents picked up their mail. The only telex machines were in the *wali*'s office and urgent messages were sent by horse or, later, by Land Rover. By the middle of the 1970s a transitional office had been built. By 2003, a brand-new post office had been built, with a traditional Omani wooden door and architecture. It also contained all the modern amenities and means of communicating with the outside world.[26] Links to Nizwa from Muscat were particularly important since the town was once the capital of the imam and is considered the most important town in Ibadi tradition. The Omani postal service revolutionized communication and commerce, connecting parts of Oman that had previously required long and arduous journeys. Messages could also be sent and received from throughout the world, an extraordinary change from the profound isolation of inner Oman under the Sultan's father. In 1972, the Sultan celebrated Oman becoming a full member the Arab Postal Union, the Arab Telecommunications Union, and the International Postal Union in the same list as UNESCO, the World Health Organization, and the Islamic Conference.[27] Chapter 5 shows how stamps and the official images used on them became a way of celebrating the heritage of Oman and portraying the Omani Renaissance as an effort led by the Sultan but shared by various sectors of society. The stamps used by Omanis during the Renaissance were symbols of a new, competent system, assured by the government, and government institutions, which was only just beginning to reach into villages and towns outside the main centers. The colorful and diverse images described by Calvin Allen, many from his own collection, were like small windows, used to glimpse the hundreds of exciting changes and developments occurring not only in their backyard but also throughout the Sultanate. Sultan Qaboos took a keen in interest in the establishment of new post offices, even mentioning specific locations in his national addresses, for example, the Central Post office in Ruwi was announced in 1975. He knew they would be the first step in creating an efficient communications infrastructure. He reflected on this opening of Omani society in his 1975 speech, "Oman today is not the Oman of yesterday. Its lackluster face has changed. It has shaken off the dust of isolation and stagnation, opened its doors and windows to the light and declared to the world it is ready to communicate directly with it, interact with the changes taking place in it . . ."[28]

Religion and Society

One of the remarkable characteristics of modern Oman is the relatively apolitical nature of religion in the Sultanate. While the postage stamps and archaeological sites described above might be easily used to unify and create a sense of national purpose, religious differences are often harder to shape into bridge identities. Remarkably, and unlike most Middle Eastern states where there is an explicit and an implicit tension between the religious establishment and the state, Sultan Qaboos and his government was able to achieve the cooperation of the Ibadi religious establishment quickly and in a sustained way. The stabilizing role of religion in Oman is even more extraordinary considering that Oman had been divided just decades before into two systems of rule, with the Ibadi Imam in power in Nizwa and the Sultan in power in Muscat. Also, Oman is divided by Shiite, Sunni, and Ibadi interpretations of Islam, as well as a minority of Hindu citizens, let alone the multifarious religions, from Catholicism to Buddhism, practiced by Oman's non-citizen resident population. The ministry in charge of religious affairs eventually evolved from one dedicated to Islam to one that embraced all the varied religions practiced within Oman. Three chapters in this volume address the question of religion in Oman and the successful integration of religious leaders and religious reforms in the Omani Renaissance agenda.

First, Abdulrahman al-Salimi, co-editor of this volume, provides an in-depth, historical account of the Sultanate–Imamate system in Oman. Tracing the history of Oman from the Islamic period to the first "Ibadi Renaissance" in the nineteenth century, Abdulrahman al-Salimi makes a compelling argument that Sultan Qaboos successfully combined elements of both the Sultanate and the Imamate, creating a fusion rooted in Omani tradition and history but also allowing for a bridge between old dichotomies. Valerie Hoffman, a scholar of Ibadism, provides a useful guide and summary of history of Ibadi Islam before showing how Ibadism under Sultan Qaboos became a part of the Renaissance agenda. Specifically, Ibadi leaders, such as Sheikh al-Khalili, did not always agree with everything the government proposed. Nevertheless, and perhaps as a result of being given leeway to express differences, many scholars came on board with the Sultan's modernization agenda, modifying aspects of Ibadism and responding to external accusations, mainly from the mufti in Saudi Arabia. In this way, the Ibadi leadership became defenders not only of Ibadism but of Oman and the Sultanate. The anthropologist Mandana Limbert, in her study of Ibadism in the Omani town of Bahla in the "Middle of a Reign" in the 1990s, discusses the growing interest in elaborating religious heritage at the time. With the opening of a local library and the popular circulation of everyday *fatwa*s or legal opinions, she explores how Ibadi religious scholars were also engaging in a form of heritage work, cognizant too of the complex generational relationships and transformations they were addressing and shaping.

Law, National Identity, and Literature

A main reason for the success of Sultan Qaboos was the establishment of the rule of law and the gradual opening of governance and governing decisions to Omanis as education slowly spread throughout the Sultanate. Salim al-Kharusi, an assistant professor of law at Sultan Qaboos University, outlines the constitutional history of the reign of Sultan Qaboos. From an "unwritten constitution" to the establishment of the first Omani constitution in 1996, the middle of the Sultan's reign, and its subsequent updates, Omani constitutional law integrated what was useful from multiple models and sources, from modern law to Ibadi and non-Ibadi Sharia. This legal approach was achieved alongside the building of national identity in Oman. John Peterson, in his chapter, provides an excellent overview of the challenges of creating a sense of Omaniness and the way the Sultan, with the involvement of society, created the necessary conditions for a stable, national identity that pragmatically integrated internal divisions.

The Omani renaissance influenced far more than religion or the creation of an overarching national identity, it also transformed cultural expression, leading to a burst of literary creativity with many authors addressing modern, challenging topics. Sultan Qaboos repeatedly supported freedom of thought and expression, rejecting many of the assumptions and structures of more traditional, patriarchal culture. While still recognizing the Sultan as a symbol of their country's progress, Omani poets and writers wrote past the panegyric style typical in other Middle Eastern states. Barbara Michalak-Pikulska writes a fascinating chapter on the cultural and literary flourishing in Oman from 1970 to 2020, showing how Sultan Qaboos' education, literacy, and freedom of thought allowed writers to explore issues of family, identity, and change that may have been hidden or suppressed elsewhere. Not all of the culture of Oman was sponsored from above. While the state provided support, literary and cultural civil society, in the form of clubs and publications, flourished in Oman.

Infrastructure and the Environment

Many of these cultural achievements would not have occurred without a stable and functioning health infrastructure. Sean Foley, in his chapter, shows how the founding of hospitals and the creation of healthcare infrastructure, often from scratch, throughout the Sultanate had a dramatic impact on wellbeing. This remarkable healthcare system, which increased life expectancy dramatically, was built with the support of Ibadi religious leaders and all sectors of society. Higher education requires a critical approach that welcomes international scholarship. Establishing Sultan Qaboos University and other institutions throughout the Sultanate, was a keystone achievement of Sultan Qaboos. Jody Pritt demonstrates how Sultan Qaboos also envisioned higher education opportunities for Omanis beyond the immediate horizon in Oman. In her interviews with Omani scholars in the United States on exchange programs she shows how their experiences and training are being used to contribute to Oman after their return to the Sultanate. In fact, as early as 1975 Sultan Qaboos spoke of sending Omanis "abroad to gain expertise" with fifty-nine students completing English-language courses in Britain to allow them to study in the United States.[29] Education at all levels was a major concern of the Sultan and the Renaissance project.

In addition to literature, healthcare and education, the building of practical infrastructure was crucial, especially in the ports, was crucial to the economic success of Oman. Javier Guirado examines the role of Muscat, which became the center of the web of communication and transportation for the whole Sultanate. Greater Muscat, with its various neighborhoods, was a symbol of the unification of the Sultanate. In 1975, a renewed road between Muscat and Mutrah was expanded with street lighting. A dual carriageway was being built between Ruwi and Seeb as well as the Bidbid road and the Mutrah, Quriyat road and the Qurm road were a part of the second five-year plan laid out by the Sultan in 1975.[30] No longer were passengers arriving on a gravel track as the UNICEF workers had experienced in 1972. The runway at Seeb

International Airport was extended. Also, a seawater desalination plant and power plant were built at Ghubrah to meet rapidly growing energy needs in the Muscat region. Land distribution and reform was a crucial part of the Sultan's planning. The Sultan discussed the ways land was being divided and distributed to citizens. This required the creation of a legal structure for land and property rights almost from scratch. Land would no longer be acquired via force or be subject to amorphous claims. Reflecting the importance of land distribution, this was a highly regulated process requiring several departments. "Land is distributed to citizens via six main departments—the Land Distribution Department, the Property Register Department, the Survey Department, the Town Planning Department, the Judicial Committee and the Technical Committee. Each of these departments has specific responsibilities and each of them is designated to regulate distribution, protect the citizen's legal title and define the boundaries of his property . . ."[31] This building of institutional legal systems, meant to create fairness and transparency, was almost as monumental as the bridges across the mountains. Sultan Qaboos was careful to add that there should be buffers between houses and factories, schools and suqs. The Social Affairs department was tasked with building 500 new houses for citizens in the Muscat–Mutrah area, with the Sultan proposing that "those on limited incomes will be provided with large housing units."[32]

Even after basic needs were met, infrastructure planning continued unabated into the twenty-first century. Jeffrey Kinnier provides an economic and technical analysis of the great port infrastructure projects of Sultan Qaboos, at Salalah and Duqm, showing how "free trade zones" have provided Oman with opportunities to reach out into the trade networks of the Indian Ocean. Maria Curtis shows how the environment was not neglected in the pursuit of economic development. Instead, Sultan Qaboos equated the environment with national heritage and identity and encouraged the Omani people to preserve a fragile balance.

Diplomacy

The final two chapters examine the ways in which Sultan Qaboos extended his bridge-building skills to the outside world, expanding the reach of his stabilizing influence. Juan Cole focuses on the last decade of the Sultan's reign showing how the personality and convictions of the Sultan, which were also shared by his people, allowed him the flexibility to reach across divides and sponsor agreements between adversaries. Unlike the 1970s, when the Sultan was clearly on the side of the United States and Britain versus the Soviets, in the last few decades Oman has been able to pursue an independent foreign policy due to its relative social cohesion and the fact that it faced no serious internal threats. Although not unconditional, the support and trust of most Omani people toward the Sultan freed him and his diplomats from many of the restraints and prejudices that prevented other leaders from pursuing peace. Francis Owtram examines the history of Oman's "quiet diplomacy," a strategy that allowed the Sultan and the Sultanate to maintain open channels of communication between rival powers while ensuring the security of Oman's borders.

According only to internationally recognized data, the modernization of Oman since 1970 has been a major success. In 2019, the last year of Sultan Qaboos' reign, Oman had a high UN Human Development Index of .813, a great improvement from the early 1970s when Omanis faced low quality of life, high infant mortality, and lack of access to education and basic services. Other measures of success are less tangible, but also important. Early commitment to culture and heritage in Oman, for example, has made Oman stand apart from its neighbors. Also, Oman achieved a level of unity and national identity despite internal divisions that have troubled other, wealthier states in existential ways. The Omani Renaissance was about more than just the building of hospitals, roads, and schools. In terms of cultural expression, literature, preservation, embrace and preservation of traditions and intangible heritage, recognition of environmental standards, even diplomacy, it has been Omanis, not just their government, who have invested in the renaissance project—a way that bridges change and continuity. The development of Oman from 1970 to 2020 was not simply the result of top-down government imposition by a rentier state. Instead, the Sultan tried, at every opportunity, to call for the cooperation of Omanis. Ultimately, much of the success of the Omani Renaissance was due to the actions of the Omani people themselves.

Notes

1. Mandana Limbert discusses the social aspect of Qaboos' speeches in Bahla. Mandana Limbert, *In a Time of Oil: Piety, Memory and Social Life in an Omani*

Town (Stanford, CA: Stanford University Press, 2010). By 1990, most homes had televisions and it was not necessary to go to the one television in town or to the *wali*'s office to hear national pronouncements and speeches.

2. Sultan Qaboos bin Said, *The Royal Speeches of his Majesty Sultan Qaboos bin Said 1970–2010* (Muscat: Ministry of Information, 2010), 36.

3. Ibid., 45.

4. Ibid., 105–106.

5 Ibid., 522.

6. Ibid., 108.

7. Ibid., 20.

8. Ibid., 14.

9. Ibid., 45.

10. Oman provided Masirah Island as a base and contributed to the Arab contingent of Joint Forces Command East.

11. The ROSO Facebook page mentions 1985 as the date of founding, available at: https://www.facebook.com/royalomansymphonyorchestra, last accessed June 30, 2021.

12. Ibid., 436.

13. Francis Fukuyama, *The End of History and the Last Man* (New York: Free Press, 1992).

14. Moisés Naím, "Washington Consensus: A Damaged Brand," *Financial Times*, October 28, 2002.

15. Lisa Anderson asked it most succinctly and directly, in her highly cited article, "Absolutism and the Resilience of Monarchy in the Middle East," *Political Science Quarterly*, 106(1) (1991): 1–15.

16. Allen J. Fromherz, *Qatar: A Modern History* (Washington, DC: Georgetown University Press, 2016).

17. Joseph Strayer, *On the Medieval Origins of the Modern State* (Princeton, NJ: Princeton University Press, 2005).

18. These studies also acknowledge, however, the nuances of Omani culture and society, but see Western-based predictive models as predominant. Fred Halliday's tendency to emphasize a Western-style centralization, and inevitable instability of sultanic power in *Arabia Without Sultans* (London: Penguin, 1974), was followed more recently by Marc Valeri's, *Oman: Politics and Society in the Qaboos State* (Oxford: Oxford University Press, 2014). The question of the persistence of Arab monarchies remains largely unanswered by these approaches.

19. See Dale Eickelman, "Counting and Surveying an 'Inner' Omani Community: Hamra al-'Abriyin," in Richard Pennell (ed.), *Tribe and State: Essays in Honour of David Montgomery Hart* (Wisbech: menas Press, 1991), 253–277.

20. There now are several works on the *waraka* or papers and network of rules of trade and life, and accommodations of Ibadi law, that formed the basis of the Omani Indian Ocean and networks beyond. See Amal Ghazal, *Islamic Reform and Arab Nationalism: Expanding the Crescent from the Mediterranean to the Indian Ocean (1880s–1930s)* (New York: Routledge, 2010); Fahad Bishara, *A Sea of Debt: Law and Economic Life in the Western Indian Ocean* (Cambridge: Cambridge University Press, 2017).

21. *The Royal Speeches*, 421.

22. Ibid., 411.

23. Nouhad Kanawati et al., *Nizwa and Sohar 30 Years Ago: A Glimpse of the Past* (Beirut: Lebanon, 2003).

24. *The Royal Speeches*, 411.

25. Ibid., 411.

26. Kanawati et al., *Nizwa and Sohar*, 123–124.

27. *The Royal Speeches*, 20.

28 Ibid., 49.

29 Ibid., 47.

30 Ibid., 49.

31 Ibid., 51.

32 Ibid., 51

1

THE LEGACY OF SULTAN QABOOS: A HISTORIOGRAPHICAL NOTE

Uzi Rabi

This chapter provides a synthesis and overview of the literature about Oman under the rule of Sultan Qaboos bin Said (1970–2020). It aims to bring the leadership of Sultan Qaboos and his successful modernization of Oman into the proper context, while engaging with substantial scholarly works on the Sultanate during this period.

It would be natural to start with the legendary scholar and analyst of Middle Eastern politics, Fred Halliday. Halliday's wide knowledge of southern Arabia, particularly Oman, was expressed in his work *Arabia Without Sultans*.[1] The book dealt with the peculiarities of "Arabian regimes" and the opposition movements ranged against them. Halliday's intellectual outlook was grounded by the "new left," which was in vogue among academic circles in London, and by his considerable travels in Arabia, particularly in the Democratic People's Republic of Yemen (South Yemen). He supported the Dhofari rebels, objecting to the military backing that Sultan Qaboos, the young Sultan who replaced his backward-thinking father, Sultan Said, received from the late Shah of Iran and Britain's Royal Air Force (from its base in Salalah). However, Halliday was comfortable changing his ideas when findings contradicted his beliefs. Two decades later, Halliday realized that Qaboos, who modernized Oman, brought it prosperity, and continued to move it steadily towards the twenty-first century, was on the right side of history.[2] He also provided political unity and secure borders. When Sultan

Qaboos overthrew his father in July 1970, few expected him to survive long. Educated at the Royal Military Academy Sandhurst, and backed by the British, the young and relatively unknown Sultan took the throne of an extremely underdeveloped country which was plagued by civil war. The "New Oman" (*Uman al-Jadida*) that was created was a united country. Until then, Omani society was split between the Imamate of Oman and the Sultanate of Muscat, and was relatively isolated until Sultan Qaboos' seizure of power in 1970.

General treatments of post-1970 developments in Oman include studies by John Towsend (1977), Calvin H. Allen, Jr. (1987), and Ian Skeet (1992).[3] These studies were well-detailed and served as a point of departure for later studies. They elaborated on the contingent processes that drove the dramatic developmental changes since 1970, and are crucial to providing an answer as to how the young Sultanate coped with the challenges of the time. These studies focus on the transformation of Oman under Qaboos from an impoverished state into a wealthy country with first-world infrastructure, a vibrant tourism industry, and a military alliance with both Britain and the United States.

Later studies on Oman's politics and economy include those by Mohamed bin Musa al-Yousef (1995) and Calvin H. Allen and W. Lynn Rigsbee II (2000).[4] These books produced an effective contribution to the scholarly literature. Their writing was on firmer ground while looking at oil as the factor that broke the political balance, serving as the catalyst for economic development. Based on extensive sources, they skillfully illustrated how the Sultan built his power base and constantly renewed them to meet internal as well as external challenges that threatened its perceived stability. Indeed, Sultan Qaboos' strategies on the international stage have secured Oman's integrity. The Sultanate has prioritized maintaining autonomy from Saudi Arabia far more than the other smaller Gulf Cooperation Council (GCC) states. Such positions were demonstrative of the Sultanate's guideline of not compromising its geopolitical independence and its ability to maintain a neutral position on regional conflicts. Yet, almost all of these studies treated Oman under Qaboos as a postcolonial laboratory in an attempt to better understand the social and political mechanisms of authoritarianism.

Marc Valeri's *Oman: Politics and Society in the Qaboos State*, at times, fits into this pattern. Valeri produced a comprehensive, well-written book which is based on extensive local research and many interviews. Valeri touched on important topics and carefully investigated some concerns facing the Sultanate, such as inter-generational conflict; the young population's expectations in a transitory period in which privileges enjoyed by their parents are no longer guaranteed; or, broadly speaking, the challenges of a welfare state which can no longer provide the same benefits for every segment of the population.

Valeri's main insights can be summed up in what he dubbed as the "Sultanistic Regime" (pp. 171–181), which is based on a "combination of arbitrariness and tradition." Drawing on theories gleaned from the work of Houchang Chehabi and Juan Linz's 1998 edited volume, which focuses on states like the Dominican Republic, Cuba, Nicaragua, Haiti, and Iran,[5] Valeri adopted this idiom ("Sultanistic Regime") and fully implemented it on the Sultanate of Oman. Accommodating his writings with a Western-style agenda, or the seeking of democratic participatory politics, Valeri concluded, "Social and demographic changes in Oman for the last decade have not led the regime to give the impression of being ready to concede even a piece of political power".[6] The mechanisms used by scholars to analyze the Middle East, adhering to the Euro-centric model of the state as a "black box," failed to account for many particularistic characteristics that are prevalent within Middle Eastern societies, the Sultanate of Oman in particular. For Valeri, as for others who seek to better understand Oman's political culture, it might have been much more effective to extrapolate, for example, with Hussein al-Ghubash's *Oman: A Thousand Years of Democratic Tradition*, a thorough study that draws on both Western and Islamic political theory, and brings an in-depth examination of the ingredients that comprise Omani political culture.[7] Ghubash argues that Oman, with its long tradition of adherence to the institution of the Ibadi Imamate, as well as its geographic isolation from the rest of the Arabian Peninsula, went through a different process of national identity formation than other parts of the Arabian Peninsula. Oman is not a black box. Ibadism and other cultural and religious particularities continue to shape the formal and informal political expectations and structures of the Sultanate.

Foreign experts, nonetheless, have wondered from time to time if the Sultanate had permanently crushed the Ibadi Imamate, especially as, in 2005, the Omani authorities accused a faction of "Ibadi activists" of pursuing plans to restore the Ibadi Imamate.[8] Some observers jumped to the conclusion that this event might signal the start of infiltration of extremist ideas, with rumors circulating that al-Qaeda had already entered Oman by hijacking Ibadi thinking. Delving into Ghubash's arguments and the dialectical process through which the Omani political ethos was to evolve would suggest that extremist groups may not find fertile ground in this country. Although there are some important non-Omani contributions to the study of Oman, including John Peterson's *Oman in the 20th Century*,[9] which does provide important perspectives.[10] But, until recently, very few books were written (in English) from an Arab perspective, and indeed very little even in Arabic. Hussein al-Ghubash managed to put this deficit right. His book is firmly rooted in Western scholarship, but at the same time he sheds a refreshing light on his subject. Persuasive, thorough, and drawing on Western as well as Islamic political theory, this book analyzes the different historical and geopolitical roles of this unique country. Oman's millennial tradition serves as a background against which Ghubash explains the solid national culture of the Sultanate and its unique sociopolitical situation.

The Sultanate's norms of non-violence and dialogue should be attributed to Sultan Qaboos and most Omanis who adhere to the Ibadi branch of Islam, also known as the "third branch," which was established over 1,300 years ago, predating Islam's split between Sunna and Shia after the Prophet Muhammad's death. Ibadis represent only 0.03 percent of Muslims worldwide, and their brand of Islam is thus unknown to most Sunnis and Shiites in the Islamic world. Ibadism is characteristically tolerant. The Ibadis stress the "rule of the just" and condemn violence in pursuit of political objectives. The influence of such cultural and religious norms in the Sultanate's political and social structures is evident by the extensive protections that the Omani legal system offers to religious minorities, such as Hindus, Christians, Sikhs, and Buddhists. Oman has historically maintained a sizeable presence of South Asian minorities, which has contributed to its tolerant culture. Authorities in the country imprison and fine people found guilty of "defaming" any religion or promoting sectarian strife.[11]

Monarchies and sultanates are not, by definition, parliamentary democracies. The Sultanate of Oman stands as a prime example of a country that has sought a middle ground between "top-down" and "bottom-up" revolutions.

Sultan Qaboos realized that Oman would not be able to depend indefinitely on oil revenues to incentivize the docility of its subjects, at least to the extent of Saudi Arabia and elsewhere. Instead, he sought out a different formula, which provided a symbiotic relationship between ruler and the ruled, where change and improvements emerge steadily as part of their tacit understanding. Although Qaboos' rule drew on traditional modes of tribal paternalism, the Sultanate introduced mechanisms to gradually promote limited political participation among Omanis. The reasoning behind these attempts derives from the very nature of the Sultanate's socioeconomic structure. As the Omani government gradually lost the advantages of a rentier state, in which power attained through oil revenues is vested only in the hands of the ruling elite and the people's right to political participation is exchanged for welfare, the state is no longer capable of sustaining the population in this manner and must compensate for reduced material benefits by expanding its citizens' role in the political arena. This was an integral and inherent dimension of the "Omani Renaissance." Only few were to observe the inner rhythm of the "Omani Renaissance" and follow the vision Qaboos was portraying from his early days as Sultan. J. E. Peterson (2004) and Joseph A. Kechichian (2005) are worth mentioning in this regard.[12] Following a different perspective, Valeri ends his book with the ultimate question of whether and how the Omani fragility (both politically and economically) is linked to the practice of the politics of survival. To be sure, challenges still lie ahead, as is the case with every state and society, but Valeri's provocative declarations regarding the Sultanate were accompanied by gloomy predictions, as if it is a failed state. Such predictions were to get an ultimate answer throughout the post-"Arab Spring" decade. One need only look at Oman's neighbor, Yemen, for a cautionary example as to what Oman might have been.

A highly important and timely contribution was brought in by anthropologists and ethnographers in the three recent decades. Starting with Dawn Chatty's *Mobile Pastoralists* (1996) and ending up with Mandana Limbert's *In the Time of Oil* (2010), this literature has highlighted the power of ethnography to engage questions that cut across scale and national boundaries and focus on notions of mobility and belonging that exceed national frames.[13] Limbert's book is certainly a case to the point. A richly textured ethnographic analysis of the transformations and tensions of everyday life in Bahla, a small town in the interior of Oman (*al-Dakhiliyya*) serves to eschew the simple narrative of rupture and radical change that dominates popular accounts of the oil boom. It also contributed to later debates on the nature of social memory and subjectivity. It therefore paved the way for more voices and plurality and for a better understanding of Omani history through an added field of scholarship on the Indian Ocean, the Arabian Peninsula, and other fluid transregional spaces.

The Arab Spring served as the catalyst for the breakdown of the Middle East's colonial-created states. Iraq and Syria, whose boundaries were drawn by the Sykes–Picot Agreement at the end of the First World War (and implemented during the San Remo Conference in April 1920), experienced a painful dismantling of their various components. In Iraq, the government failed to fuse the fragmented society and in Syria, the bloody civil war exacerbated tensions between the minority Alawite government and their allies and the Sunni majority throughout the country. But it was not the Fertile Crescent alone that experienced disintegration and de-territorialization: Libya and Yemen, countries with a tribal–sectarian divide, also witnessed the overthrow of autocratic rulers during the events of the "Arab Spring," and similar processes of state collapse were put in motion.

Some Western observers believed the Sultanate was about to experience a "spring." They portrayed scenes of ongoing protests and growing discontent as if the Sultan was on the brink of a revolution. While there were slogans such as "The people want the fall of corruption" (*isqat al-fasad*) or "Yes to a new Oman," there were not the cries of "The people want the fall of the regime" as was the case in Tahrir Square in Cairo. Protesters also called on the Sultan to personally intervene to provide more job opportunities and measures to curb rising prices and inequalities. To be sure, discontent around the country was primarily motivated by social and economic issues, but, for the most part, it fizzled out rapidly. This may be explained in large part by the responsiveness of Sultan Qaboos' government. The Omani state took several steps to appease the protesters. In mid-February 2011 it was announced that the private sector minimum wage for nationals would be increased by 200 Omani riyals to about $520 (an increase of 43 percent). These steps were followed up by the introduction of a monthly allowance (150 Omani riyals) for job seekers and the creation of 50,000 new jobs for Omanis in the public sector, the doubling of the monthly social security allowance for eligible needy families, and an increase in student allowances.

In early March, in the largest ever cabinet reshuffle, the Sultan dismissed one-third of his cabinet, including 'Ali al-Ma'amri, the minister of national economy, Ahmad Makki, and the minister of commerce and industry, Maqbul al-Sultan. These decisions were another indication of the state's responsiveness and creativity when it comes to embodying both national unity and the struggle against corruption. In retrospect, these steps were to alleviate much of the protesters' complaints, in much the same way that gestures toward Islamists, including the Sultan's approval of the establishment of Islamic banks in May 2011, had their own effect. Sultan Qaboos also announced his intention to expand the powers of the advisory Council of Oman, namely, the elected Consultative Council (*Majlis al-Shura*) and the appointed State Council (*Majlis al-Dawla*). Despite positive steps toward liberalization over the last three decades, these observers kept pointing to the country's constrained political climate which creates a power imbalance in favor of the state, and thereby makes it difficult for contestation to take place as political freedoms remain limited.

The expectation that a "repressive Sultanistic regime" would be corroborated by a full-scale "Omani Spring," some external observers were quick to gather information in order to put some teeth to their "unique, in-depth insights." One report described the 2011 events, as "Several hundred protesters, journalists, and human rights activists were arrested all over the country."[14] A creeping militarization was imposed, with a drastic increase in police controls and checkpoints on roads to the UAE. In June and July 2011, more than 100 individuals received jail terms, some for up to five years, on charges such as "possessing material with the intention of making explosives to spread terror," "illegal gathering," and "sabotaging and destroying public and private properties."[15] Many of these conclusions misread Omani realities, or took short-term evidence as proof of long-term trends. As time has shown, the protests did not develop with the same intensity and were small-scale in comparison with other parts of the Arab Middle East.

Some protesters in Sur, Salalah, and Sohar tried to channel discontent and run their protest along sectarian lines. The influence of Muslim Brotherhood cells and networks was partially visible in these protests, and that of

Salafi–jihadi movements, though meagre, was seen in several Batinah protests, particularly those in the port cities of Sohar and Shinas. At times, these
extremists managed to coordinate their activities with some young secular
intellectuals. A report from July 2014 estimated that 200 Omanis had joined
Salafi–jihadi military groups in Syria,[16] encouraging some observers to mis-
takenly argue for the re-emergence of the Ibadi Imamate or the penetration
of extremist radical ideologies into the Sultanate. However, by any standard,
these protests were few and far between and were fizzled out in no time.

Instead of being a repressive, Sultanistic regime or a failed Middle Eastern
state, Oman serves as a counterexample. Under the leadership of Sultan
Qaboos, the Sultanate created a national ethos, which has been capable of
incorporating under one roof disparate creeds, and a social fabric which
respects the differences of the "other." The Omani formula has incorporated
economic, cultural, educational, and foreign policy components. Thus, the
Sultanate stands to become an example of the "other Middle East," where
"Omaniness" develops as an inclusive identifier, in a way that "Iraqiness" or
"Syrianess" was unable to do so.

The peaceful transition of power following the death of Oman's Sultan
Qaboos bin Said in January 2020 must have surprised many observers who
had long believed Oman would face a state of chaos upon the death of the
longest-serving Sultan. Simon Henderson, a most knowledgeable scholar of
the Gulf states' ruling systems titled his piece in his edited volume *Sudden
Succession* as follows: "Oman after Qaboos: A National and Regional Void."
In his opening remark Henderson further elaborates on this notion: "The
ailing Sultan Qaboos bin Said Al-Said, now seventy-nine years old, has no
children and no announced successor, with only an ambiguous mechanism
in place for the family council to choose one. This study considers the most
likely candidates to succeed the Sultan, Oman's domestic economic challenges, and whether the country's neutral foreign policy can survive Qaboos'
passing."[17] In fact, the transition was less disruptive than many had expected.
This is likely due to the careful preparations for succession made by Sultan
Qaboos during his reign.

Omani history could attest that a smooth transition of power is rare after
the death of long-serving leaders such as Sultan Qaboos who governed Oman
for fifty years. Historically, Oman witnessed fierce power struggles following

the death of sultans, most notably that of 1856 which resulted in the division of the Omani empire among the late Sultan's two sons. However, in this most recent transition, the al-Said ruling family council was quick to announce Haitham as the next Sultan based on a recommendation left by Sultan Qaboos himself in a sealed will.

Sultan Qaboos encouraged the drafting of an updated Omani constitution to provide the royal family with three days to choose a successor. Under the new law, if the ruling al-Said family fails to reach a decision, a council of military and security authorities, Supreme Court chiefs, and members of Oman's two quasi-parliamentary advisory assemblies (one being the *Majlis al-Dawla*, which is the upper house of the Council of Oman, and the *Majlis al-Shura*, which is its lower house) are to open and read a letter containing the name of the monarch's personal choice penned by Qaboos.[18] This procedure was perceived by some observers as a recipe for mixed messages. Marc Valeri, questioning this, wrote:

> If the royal family cannot make a decision, up to what point is it ready to be deprived of supreme decision making by individuals who do not belong to the Al-Said family and who owe their position to Qaboos only? Moreover, in spite of the precautions taken by the ruler, is there not a risk of contradictory messages emerging, a situation which would involve political confusion? In Qaboos' absence, there does not seem to be any patriarchal figure in the Al-Said family who could oversee the succession process and ensure that disagreements remain contained.[19]

In fact, none of these issues arose as serious factors in maintaining the continuity of the Sultanate. Other observers noted that a succession crisis could result from a potential power vacuum in Muscat, prompting tribes of the interior to push for a restoration of the Ibadi Imamate.[20] In this case, too, the immediate post-Qaboos era has shown that Qaboos' careful preparation prevented the restoration of the Ibadi Imamate or other destabilizing possibilities.

The peaceful power transition was facilitated by the stable political environment Sultan Qaboos left behind. The new Sultan has gained immediate legitimacy and allegiance among key state actors like the Sultan's Armed Forces (SAF), the Royal Oman Police, the national intelligence community, and the Supreme Court. Sultan Qaboos pursued balanced and neutral policies during his fifty-year rule, an exception to the rule in the boiling Middle East region. Since the end of the Dhofar rebellion in 1975, there have been no armed revolutionary movements in Oman. In sharp contrast to some gloomy predictions raised by several writers, the post-Qaboos era was to paradoxically reveal that the more successful a leader has been in fostering a strategy and defining the main goals, the less consequential his exit.

Sultan Haitham promised, in his first speech on January 11, 2020, to continue to pursue Qaboos' balanced domestic policy and neutral, peace-making focused foreign policy. While Sultan Haitham must show apprecia-tion for the achievements of his predecessor he should in tandem establish his own public image and portray his era as independent from that of Qaboos'. The Sultanate of Oman faces mammoth domestic challenges, including the remarkable slump in oil prices (which constitute the source of 75 percent of Oman's revenues), weak economic growth, and high youth unemployment, which were further bolstered by the Covid-19 pandemic side-effects). Oman has also reduced its 2020 financial budget by US$1.3 billion to accommo-date the decline in revenues from oil exports

Sultan Haitham will succeed in this critical period by overcoming cur-rent economic obstacles and solving youth unemployment. If so, he will be perceived as an initiator rather than simply as a follower of the late Sultan. He must craft his own image and not risk comparison with his accomplished predecessor. As a result, Omanis will differentiate between both Sultans' lega-cies and acknowledge their achievements in successfully leading their country during different periods. This will naturally be a difficult task as the era of Sultan Qaboos will remain a vital part of the history of Oman and the memo-ries of Omanis.

Notes

1. Fred Halliday, *Arabia Without Sultans* (London: Penguin, 1974). The book was conceived of, and written, in the early 1970s, and published in 1974 in Brit-ain and in 1975 by Random House in the United States. Subsequent transla-tions appeared in Arabic (Kazima: Kuwait), Persian (Kitabsira: Tehran), Turkish (Evren: Yayinlari) and Japanese (Hosei University Press). In a 1977 *New Yorker* article, Joseph Kraft reported that he found a room full of unread copies in the Saudi Foreign Ministry.

2. Adel Darwish, "Professor Fred Halliday: Celebrated Scholar of Middle Eastern Politics," *Independent*, October 23, 2011, available at: https://www.independent.co.uk/news/obituaries/professor-fred-halliday-celebrated-scholar-middle-eastern-politics-1972887.html.

3. John Towsend, *Oman: The Making of the Modern State* (New York: St. Martin's Press, 1977); Calvin H. Allen, Jr., *Oman: The Modernization of the Sultanate* (Boulder, CO and London: Westview Press and Croom Helm, 1987); Ian Skeet, *Oman: Politics and Development* (London: Macmillan, 1992)

4. Mohamed bin Musa al-Yousef, *Oil and the Transformation of Oman, 1970–1995: The Socio-Economic Impact* (London: Stacey International, 1995); Calvin H. Allen and W. Lynn Rigsbee, II, *Oman under Qaboos: From Coup to Constitution, 1970–1996* (London: Frank Cass, 2000).

5. Houchang E. Chehabi and Juan J. Linz (eds.), *Sultanistic Regimes* (Baltimore, MD: Johns Hopkins University Press, 1998)

6. Marc Valeri, *Oman: Politics and Society in the Qaboos State* (New York: Columbia University Press, 2009), 175, 225,

7. Hussein al-Ghubash, *Oman: A Thousand Years of Democratic Tradition* (Abingdon: Routledge, 2006).

8. See, for example, "Fi Bid' al-Muhakama Dafa Mutahamun Bi-Ann Himayat al-Madhhab al-Ibadi Ahad Ahdafahum" ("At the Beginning of the Trial, Defenders Declared that Protection of the Ibadi Doctrine is One of Their Goals"), *al-Hayat*, April 19, 2005.

9. John Peterson, *Oman in the 20th Century: Political Foundations of an Emerging State* (London: Croom Helm, 1978).

10. John Peterson, *Oman in the 20th Century: Political Foundations of an Emerging State* (London: Croom Helm, 1978).

11. As appeared in Giorgio Cafiero and Theodore Karasik, "Can Oman's Stability Outlive Sultan Qaboos?" April 27, 2016, available at: https://www.mei.edu/publications/can-omans-stability-outlive-sultan-qaboos.

12. J. E. Peterson, "Oman: Three and a Half Decades of Change and Development," *Middle East Policy* 6(2) (2004): 125–137; Joseph A. Kechichian, "Political Participation and Stability in the Sultanate of Oman," research paper (Dubai: Gulf Research Center, November 2005).

13. Dawn Chatty, *Mobile Pastoralists: Development Planning and Social Change in Oman* (New York: Columbia University Press, 1996); Mandana Limbert, *In the Time of Oil: Piety, Memory, and Social Life in an Omani Town* (Stanford, CA: Stanford University Press, 2010).

14. See, for instance, the U.S. Department of State Country Reports for Oman on Human Rights Practices 2012, 1.usa.gov/URP0Gp, and 2013, 1.usa. gov/1s8ym3S; Gulf Center for Human Rights, "Torture in Oman," January 29, 2014, available at: http://gc4hr.org/report/view/20. Such practices continue today. See "Oman: Rights Routinely Trampled," Human Rights Watch, December 19, 2014, and as appeared in Marc Valeri, "Simmering Unrest and Succession Challenges in Oman," January 28, 2015, available at: https://carnegieendowment.org/2015/01/28/simmering-unrest-and-succession-challenges-in-oman-pub-58843.

15. Ibid.

16. See Turki al-Balushi, "Umaniyun Yuqatilun fi Suria" ("Omani Fighting in Syria"), *al-Balad*, July 20, 2014, available at: http://albaladoman.com/?p=20361.

17. Simon Henderson, "Oman after Qaboos: A National and Regional Void," *Sudden Succession* (Washington, DC: Washington Institute, 2019), December 30, 2019, available at: https://www.washingtoninstitute.org/policy-analysis/oman-after-qaboos-national-and-regional-void-sudden-succession-essay-series.

18. Martin Dokoupil, "Succession Question Fuels Uncertainty in Oman," *Reuters*, May 24, 2012, available at: http://www.reuters.com/article/us-oman-succession-idUSBRE84N0K420120524, last accessed December 6, 2016.

19. Marc Valeri, "Oman and the Succession of Sultan Qaboos," *Hurst*, December 3, 2014, available at: http://www.hurstpublishers.com/oman-succession-sultan-qaboos, last accessed May 10, 2016.

20. As noted in Giorgio Cafiero and Theodore Karasik , "Can Oman's Stability Outlive Sultan Qaboos?" MEI@75: Peace, Prosperity, Partnership, April 27, 2016.

2

PREHISTORIC INTERACTIONS BETWEEN OMAN AND THE INDUS CIVILIZATION: PROJECTING THE PAST IN THE PRESENT

Jonathan Mark Kenoyer

The Omani Renaissance was a "rebirth" of Oman's past. As such, heritage and preservation of the past were a part of Oman's development goals. Ancient communities living in the geographical regions encompassed by the Sultanate of Oman have long played a key role in the development of cultural traditions and trade networks that link Eastern Arabia to the regions further to the east and west (Figure 2.1). The history of these communities and their contributions to world history are well documented and represented in the recently opened National Museum in Muscat. This museum has well-articulated introductions in Arabic and English relating to the archaeological and cultural heritage of Oman and Eastern Arabia as a whole. Many other museums have also been established in different major cities and form part of the legacy that can be directly attributed to the vision of His Majesty the late Sultan Qaboos bin Said Al-Said who began his rule in 1970. Archaeological surveys and excavations were occasionally carried out prior to this time, but he issued formal decrees regarding the importance of heritage preservation (Al-Busaidi 2004: 35) and established important institutions to carry out the formidable task of investigating, preserving, and presenting the cultural heritage of the nation. The Ministry of Heritage and Culture was established in 1976, the National Heritage Protection Law was set up in 1980, and many other heritage projects were undertaken under the Office of the Adviser to

His Majesty the Sultan for Cultural Affairs. In addition, Sultan Qaboos University enrolled its first students in 1986 and today includes departments of Archaeology, History, Geography, Tourism, and Earth Sciences that all contribute to the documentation and preservation of national heritage sites and buildings. The previous Minister of Heritage and Culture, His Majesty Sultan Haitham bin Tariq Al-Said was selected by the late Sultan to be his successor and in 2020 the new ruler combined the first two institutions under a single entity now titled the Ministry of Heritage and Tourism. Because of the long-term continuities of vision and leadership, the Sultanate of Oman stands out as a unique example of how the heritage of a nation can be studied, preserved, and presented to its own population as well as the whole world. This achievement has taken place in conjunction with the construction of new roads, factories, cities, dams, and other essential aspects of national development that often encroach on and destroy the record of past human

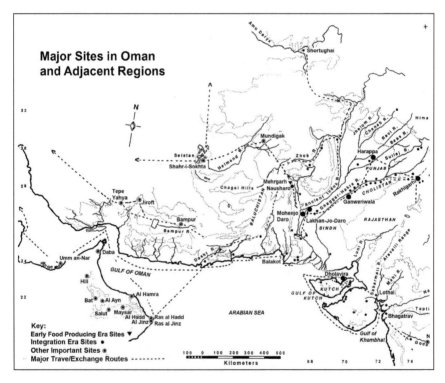

Figure 2.1 Map of Oman and selected sites mentioned in text. All maps and photos by J. M. Kenoyer.

activities. Major conservation efforts have been carried out at the larger world heritage sites as well as at numerous smaller sites and forts located in different parts of the country. The overall result of the heritage management in Oman has been very positive, and the management of sites and archaeological finds has been greatly enhanced through local and international collaborations (Al-Belushi 2008: 149–173).

Ongoing excavations and new publications by local and international scholars continue to increase our understanding of the importance of Oman for the social and cultural evolution of humankind in the region. Numerous coastal and inland sites dating from the mid-fourth to the second millennia BCE provide important evidence of early overland and maritime trade that linked this part of Arabia to many other adjacent regions. Archaeological sites in Oman's highly distinct geographical regions provide evidence for the local development and adaptation of various techniques that were used to obtain and capture water and sustain local agriculture and settlements (Cleuziou et al. 2018: 247–250). This chapter focuses on the important archaeological discoveries from 1970 to 2020 during the reign of Sultan Qaboos, relating to early interactions between prehistoric communities living in various parts of Oman and the regions of West and South Asia. These are often connected to early civilizations in Mesopotamia (Iraq, Syria), the Iranian plateau (Iran), Baluchistan and the greater Indus River Valley region (Pakistan and western India). We will also include some discussion of links to other regions of the Arabian Peninsula and North Africa. The time period selected for this chapter represents the first major period of "global" interaction between Oman and other contemporaneous civilizations. The importance of Oman's role in trade and economic exchange during this period ensures that the contributions of Oman to world history is well represented in museums in Oman as well as throughout the world.

Chronological Context

The burst in archaeology in Oman from 1970 to 2020 has revolutionized our understanding of human history in the southeast corner of Arabia. For instance, we now know that human occupation in Southeast Arabia occurred during the earliest periods of hominid dispersal out of Africa between 2.5 million and 300,0000 years ago for the Lower Paleolithic, and from 300,000 to 100,000 years ago for the Middle Paleolithic (Rose et al. 2019: 17ff). The site of Aybut Al-Auwal in Dhofar, Oman dated to 106,000 years ago or earlier, indicates that early humans were already definitely in the region (Rose 2018: 35–36). Evidence for later Upper Paleolithic communities are also reported in various locations of Eastern Arabia, but there appears to have been a break in occupation before the regions were gradually occupied by Neolithic foragers and fisher folk as well as some pastoralists around 6000 BCE or slightly earlier (Uerpmann, Potts, and Uerpmann 2009: 212).

Knowledge of the Copper/Bronze Age in Oman (3200–1300 BCE) has boomed since 1970. For the later time periods, the common chronological framework provided to the public in regional museums and brochures produced by the Ministry of Heritage and Culture, Oman follows a traditional cultural historical model beginning with the Neolithic, followed by the Bronze and Iron Age. On the basis of more precise dating from specific sites in Oman and neighboring UAE, archaeologists have established a relative chronology (Table 2.1) that is linear in structure. Early agro-pastoral communities, commonly referred to as "Neolithic" appear as early as 6000 BCE, but continue in some regions to much later. A gradual transition is seen around 3200 BCE with the establishment of permanent burial monuments associated with what is called the Hafit period. The Umm an-Nar period (2700–2000 BCE) is also referred to as the Magan Civilization (Charpentier et al. 2013: 85–98). It is distinguished by the emergence of large agricultural settlements, some with stone towers and elaborate stone burial monuments. The Magan Civilization is roughly contemporaneous with the main urban phases of the Indus Tradition (2600–1900 BCE) (Indus Valley Civilization) of modern Pakistan and western India and also with the Early Dynastic and Akkadian periods of Mesopotamia to the west. It had links to development in southeastern Iran to the north, and with Yemen and Saudi Arabia to the south and southwest, a pattern of linkages to distant cultures and ports around the Indian Ocean that repeated several times in Oman's history. It reflects the intense, maritime tendency of its human geography. Sultan Qaboos' opening of the region to international trade, starting in 1970, is just the latest manifestation of Oman's long history of global interconnectedness.

Table 2.1 Indus, Oman, Mesopotamia chronology

Indus	UAE/Oman	Mesopotamia
Localization era	Wadi Suq period	Isin–Larsa dynasties
Late Harappa phase	2000–1300 BCE	2000–1800 BCE
1900–1300 BCE		
Integration era	Umm an-Nar period "Magan Civilization"	Ur III, 2113–2000 BCE
Harappa phase	2700–2000 BCE	Akkadian period 2350–2200 BCE
2600–1900 BCE		Early Dynastic period 2900–2350 (2371) BCE
Regionalization era Early Harappan Kot Diji, Ravi, Hakra phases	Hafit period	Jemdet Nasr period 3100–2900 BCE
5000–2600 BCE	3200–2700 BCE	Uruk period 3900–3100 BCE
Early food producing era	Neolithic foraging–pastoral	Ubaid and Chalcolithic, Neolithic periods
c. + 7000–5000 BCE	6000–3000 BCE	>4000 BCE

Due to the history of excavations in adjacent regions and new discoveries in Oman itself, the names for different periods and the periodization of the archaeological chronology of Oman has undergone several modifications. It is not unlikely that new subperiods and terms will be introduced as more sites are excavated in Oman. Brief summaries of the Neolithic and Hafit periods are necessary before discussing the Umm an-Nar period or Magan Civilization and its links to the urban centers of the Indus Civilization and Mesopotamia.

Neolithic Period

The cultural and socioeconomic foundations of later Bronze Age cultures in what is now Oman can be traced to the early marine foragers and pastoral communities during the Neolithic period. Understanding the depth of this history is important as this linkage is particularly relevant to the many people who still rely on the sea for their livelihood, and is well represented in all the major archaeological museums and the Natural History Museum in Muscat. The importance of marine resources as a major adaptive strategy in the past is highlighted in displays of fishing gear, boats, and marine shell ornaments found in the Neolithic galleries at the National Museum as well as in the small museum at Ras al-Jinz, and will form an important part of new museums being constructed in other coastal cities.

Large shell middens and associated settlements dating to the Neolithic period are found along the Batinah coastal region north of Muscat (Kennet, Deadman, and Al-Jahwari 2016: 155–168), as well as the eastern and southeastern coasts of Oman (Méry and Charpentier 2013: 73–78). These communities were relatively sedentary and focused on the exploitation of local marine and lagoon resources (Charpentier et al. 2012: 59; Charpentier et al. 2013: 89), and to some extent the hunting of terrestrial wild animals (Uerpmann, Potts, and Uerpmann 2009: 205–214). There is no evidence for sustained agriculture, but some of these Neolithic communities further to the north in the UAE used domestic animals such as sheep/goats and cattle (Uerpmann et al. 2012: 385–400).

In addition to shell middens, some sites have clusters of burials with various types of grave goods, including stone tools as well as ornaments made of shell, bone, and locally available soft stone. Pearls were often placed in the mouth of the dead and some of them were perforated as ornaments (Carter 2005: 162). Local fishermen still collect the large *Pinctada* molluscs and send them off to markets in the larger cities where their meat is prized as an aphrodisiac. Although the harvesting of natural pearls is rare today, they are still recovered occasionally and are highly valued. Because of its continued importance today modern museum visitors can easily understand why the Neolithic fishing communities used pearls as ornaments and in special burial rituals.

One of the most important localities for early Neolithic fisher communities is located at Ras al-Hamra, which is now an important suburb of modern Muscat. One site, RH5, has both a settlement area and a cemetery that was used for over 500 years, from between 3800 and 3300 BCE (Marcucci et al. 2011: 201–222). The site has been protected from destruction with the long-term goal of making it into an open-air museum and major tourist attraction. Excavations revealed evidence for circular huts that were made using small wooden posts and covered with branches (Cleuziou et al. 2018: 81–86). A wide range of ornaments were made at the site, including shell bracelets made from local *Conus* shells (Figure 2.2), ornaments made from *Pinctada* (pearl shell), soft stone beads and pendants, and ornaments made from black basalt with white spots collected from local river beds. Many other Neolithic coastal sites, with similar ornament styles have been found all along the coastal regions extending to the south to Ras al-Hadd and beyond (Buta et al. 2018: 147–153).

Figure 2.2 Shell bracelet made from *Conus* shells, RH5.

The site of RH5 at Ras al-Hamra also has evidence for the earliest copper tools in Oman, including a complete knife that may have been used in processing fish (Giardino 2017: 34). Most of the other objects were relatively small hooks and awls made from hammered copper. Other sites further south along the coast and all the way to Ras al-Jinz also have evidence for small fragments of copper tools, so this was clearly a technology that was widespread during middle to late Neolithic period in this region. The lack of primary evidence for local mining and smelting of copper at this time period has led some scholars to suggest that the copper found in Oman during the Neolithic was traded from outside regions, either from Mesopotamia (Giardino 2017: 38) or possibly from across the Gulf in Eastern Iran or Baluchistan where copper-working has a much earlier history (Thornton 2009: 301–327). However, other studies of early copper objects in Mesopotamia have determined that six out of twenty-three sampled artifacts dating to the Uruk period (end of the fourth millennium BCE) have chemical signatures that can be correlated with the copper ore and metal objects found in Oman (Begemann et al. 2010: 159). Because of the long history of interaction between Iran/Baluchistan and Eastern Arabia it would not be surprising if local communities were involved in copper smelting and local tool production, but more studies are needed to clarify the situation. The most complete objects from these sites are on display in the National Museum and attract considerable attention due to their exquisite design and the fact that many similar copper tools, stone, and shell ornaments continue to be produced and used in Oman today.

Although the main Neolithic social and economic networks may have been along the coast or in local inland regions, the discovery of grey ware pottery at RH5, Ras al-Hamra that has its origins in southeastern Iran, indicates that there was long-distance interaction between communities living on both sides of the Hormuz Strait and Gulf of Oman (Marcucci et al. 2011: 201–222). The important use of boats to move along the coast and between different regions is confirmed with direct evidence for the use of boats made of bundled reeds coated with bitumen from the site of as-Sabiyah in Kuwait (Carter 2002: 13–30; Carter and Crawford 2003: 83–88) (Figure 2.3). The discovery of an early Neolithic settlement on the island of Mazirah, 20 km off

Figure 2.3 Replica reed boat, National Museum, Muscat.

the eastern coast of Oman, is also direct evidence for the movement of people who were using boats to navigate the coastal waters (Charpentier et al. 2013: 89). Indirect evidence for the use of boats is demonstrated by the discovery of pottery from southern Mesopotamia and Iran at numerous sites in Eastern Arabia (Méry and Charpentier 2013: 73). Many of the modern communities in Oman today have links with regions across the Gulf, and the ancient links between Oman and the Makran coast, Baluchistan, and Iran provide an important historical depth to those linkages.

Unlike the Neolithic period of the Fertile Crescent, regions of the Levant and Anatolia, this time period in Oman and Eastern Arabia did not see the indigenous domestication of any specific plants or animals. Wild camels, gazelle, ibex, and oryx were hunted, but the camel was not domesticated until much later (Curci, Carletti, and Tosi 2014: 207–222). The site of Buhais 18 in the UAE has evidence for cattle, sheep, and goats (Uerpmann et al. 2008; Uerpmann and Uerpmann 2018: 64–65), but the herding of domestic animals was not common in most regions of what is now Oman. Evidence for the use of grains such as sorghum, wheat, and barley have been discovered at some sites, and it is possible that small-scale cultivation was carried out in some localities, but domestication of these plants took place in more distant regions of North Africa (sorghum) and West Asia (wheat and barley) (Cleuziou et al. 2018: 247). The date palm and its fruits was also important in the region, but it is not known if it was domesticated locally or brought to the region from Iran or Mesopotamia (Gros-Balthazard et al. 2017: 2211–2218). Date seeds have been found from the site of Dalma 11 (*c.* 5290–4540 calBC) located on an island off the north coast of the UAE (Beech 2000: 83–89), but the dates may have been brought to the site with other trade items arriving by boat, either from Mesopotamia (Tengberg 2012: 142) or Iran (Cleuziou et al. 2018: 247). The subsistence patterns and trade networks established during the Neolithic continued throughout the later Bronze Age even though there is evidence for the gradual increase in the reliance on cultivated plants and external trade contacts during the subsequent Hafit and Umm an-Nar periods.

Hafit Period, 3200–2700 BCE

During the Hafit period (3200–2700 BCE) there is evidence for the establishment of larger sedentary communities in areas where there was sufficient water, either through seasonal rainfall or permanent springs. Although hunting of wild animals was still widely practiced, some of these communities developed small-scale agriculture, primarily cultivating wheat, barley, and dates (Cleuziou et al. 2018: 243). Evidence for the early use of dates is also found in the coastal regions of Baluchistan, extending from Iran to Pakistan (Méry and Tengberg 2009: 2012–2017; Tengberg 2012: 139–147; Cleuziou et al. 2018: 247), and further studies are needed to determine if there were perhaps multiple regions where domestication occurred. Other Hafit communities are found in local environments that were not conducive to agriculture and it is possible that they were primarily herders, predominantly of sheep and goats (Deadman and Al-Jahwari 2016: 27). Marine subsistence was also very important for some communities and the excavations at the coastal site of HD-6, Ras al-Hadd, demonstrates the presence of permanent settlements that were focused primarily on marine resources (Azzarà and Cattani 2018: 146–150). HD-6 also has evidence for many different craft activities, such as shell ornament manufacture, fired steatite bead-making, and local stone tool production. The local production of shell and stone ornaments may have been important for local and regional trade, with agro-pastoralists located further inland and possibly to more distant communities in the south (Yemen), north (Baluchistan, Iran/Pakistan), and west (Mesopotamia, Kuwait, and Iraq).

The Hafit communities established a distinctive burial tradition where the dead were buried in small truncated conical rock cairns with openings facing to the east (Figure 2.4). The tower-like tombs were built with semi-dressed stone and located on prominent ridges or plateaus overlooking the river valleys and oases as well as along major trade routes (Madsen 2017: 235–238). The name for this period derives from the excavation of tombs located on a prominent plateau, Jebel Hafit, that straddles the border between Oman and the United Arab Emirates (Madsen 2017). These cairns were often reused repeatedly and were even used by other communities in subsequent periods. Their position and distribution suggest that they were a form of marker to establish hereditary ownership of the land. Objects included as burial offerings include locally produced ornaments of marine shells, but also imported exotic pottery and copper/bronze objects that have links with the Jemdet Nasr period in Mesopotamia (Madsen 2017: 237). Mesopotamian pottery from other Hafit tombs at the site of Hili 8 UAE may date even later to the Early Dynastic period (Madsen 2017: 237). The discovery of imported Jemdet Nasr

Figure 2.4 Hafit tombs, Al-Ayn.

pottery in a Hafit burial at the coastal site of RJ-6, Ras al-Jinz, located at the eastern tip of Oman, indicates that these trade goods were widely distributed at both inland and coastal sites (Cleuziou et al. 2018: 205, fig. 95). The burial goods in Hafit tombs also included imported beads made from faience, fired steatite, and carnelian, which may have been obtained through trade with Mesopotamia, Iran, or even the Indus Valley region (Law 2018: 160–188).

While there is no doubt that there were strong connections with Mesopotamia, to the west there also appear to have been important linkages with regions north of the Gulf, such as Baluchistan, and interior regions of the Makran coast and southeastern Iran. One main link to the north may have been through the Musandam Peninsula and across the Hormuz Strait, which would provide direct access to the communities of the Halil Rud Civilization that has been discovered at the sites of Konar Sandal, Jiroft (Majidzadeh and Pittman 2008: 69–103), and Tepe Yahya in Kerman Province, Iran (Lamberg-Karlovsky and Potts 2001) (see Figure 2.1). To the east along the Makran coast traders could travel up the Dasht River to link with Indus sites such as Sutkagen Dor (Dales and Lipo 1992) and Miri Kalat (Besenval 2005: 1–10). It is possible that more direct maritime links between eastern parts of Oman

and the core regions of the Indus Valley region and Gujarat were also beginning at this time, but this is still not confirmed (Frenez et al. 2016: 107–124;
Méry et al. 2017: 163–184).

The Hafit period also saw the early development of copper extraction
from the rich ores scattered throughout the Al-Hajar mountain range. The
gradual intensification of copper production for trade with Mesopotamia
may have been one of the economic stimuli that led to the establishment of
Hafit settlements throughout the region (Cleuziou 1996: 159–165; Laursen
and Steinkeller 2017: 14). Copper ornaments and pins are occasionally found
in Hafit tombs, but the most important direct evidence for local manufacture
of copper objects comes from the site of HD-6, Ras al-Hadd (Giardino 2017:
42–43). The discovery of copper tools, hooks, rods, and chisels in different
stages of production, along with a fragment of a copper ingot suggests that
the site was linked to inland copper smelting centers. Chemical analysis of
the copper objects found at HD-6 reveals the use of arsenic as an important
alloy used to create stronger and harder tools, and all of the artifacts also have
trace amounts of nickel. Arsenical copper ores and the presence of nickel as
well as traces of silver are characteristic of the inland ore bodies and suggests
that the copper objects at HD-6, RJ-6, and other Hafit sites was being produced in Oman itself (Giardino 2017: 44, 61–62). Other evidence for local
copper production has been reported from the inland site of Kasr Al-Khafaji
(Tower 1146), Bat, dating to around 3000 BCE (Thornton 2016: 25–47, 230)
and the site of Al-Khashbah (Schmidt and Döpper 2014: 187–230).

Most scholars assume that the impetus for local copper smelting in Oman
is the result of trade opportunities that were emerging with the large urban
centers in Mesopotamia (Giardino 2017: 20ff). However, the emergence of
Oman as an important copper-producing region might have also been due to
increased local demand for copper to supply the needs of expanding populations involved in fishing and farming. It is also possible that there may
have been a gradual decrease in production in regions to the north across the
Gulf due to deforestation and overexploitation of the easily accessible ores.
Intensive production of copper had been going on since the fifth millennium
BCE at sites such as Tal-i-Iblis in the copper-rich regions of southeastern Iran
(Thornton 2009: 310). There is also considerable evidence for fourth–third
millennium smelting in other regions of Iran (Matthews and Fazeli 2004:

61–75) and Afghanistan (Hauptmann and Weisgerber 1980: 120–127; Dales 1992: 19–32). It is possible that the depletion of forests needed to produce charcoal for smelting in these regions and also the problems of overland trade between Afghanistan/southeastern Iran and Mesopotamia (Dales 1976: 67–78) may have contributed to the rise of intensive copper smelting activities in Oman and the UAE. These regions south of the Gulf would have had abundant uncut forests of suitable wood for producing charcoal (i.e., acacia and jujube), as well as rich and previously unexploited copper ores. Current studies related the massive copper slag deposits in the inland regions of Oman to calculate the amount of wood needed to produce charcoal may provide some insight into the environmental impact copper smelting had on the ancient environment (Sivitskis et al. 2019: 1–24). It is not unlikely that the deforestation of the interior regions of Oman as well as the coastal foothills of the Al-Hajar mountain range is directly linked to Bronze Age and later Iron Age copper smelting. Current strategies for water harvesting and reforestation in many parts of Oman may eventually result in landscapes that are more similar to those that would have been present during the earlier Bronze and Iron Ages.

Umm an-Nar

During the Umm an-Nar period (2700–2000 BCE), named after a style of communal burial first documented at the site of Umm an-Nar near Abu Dhabi, numerous large settlements were established along the interior overland trade routes linking easternmost Arabia (Oman) with the central gulf regions (UAE and Bahrain). Other large settlements were established along routes that linked the Batinah coast to the interior and on islands in the central Gulf itself. The cultural and sociopolitical developments in the Umm an-Nar period reflect the emergence of what some scholars have called tribal alliances and kinship networks, rather than hierarchical state-level society (Cleuziou and Tosi 2018: 108). The name for this period derives from the excavations at the site of Umm an-Nar, located on an island off the northern coast of the UAE (Tosi 1976: 81-92; Frifelt 1991; Frifelt 1995). The most prominent features of the inland settlements in Oman and the UAE are circular stone towers, often with a well in the center, and sometimes with deep circular channels for collecting and storing seasonal rainwater (Frenez et al.

Figure 2.5 Salut Bronze Age tower (ST1) and water channels.

2016: 107–124) (Figure 2.5). Rectangular houses constructed of dressed and undressed stone along with mud-brick super structures were built adjacent to and surrounding the towers (Thornton, Cable and Possehl 2016). These sites were supported by irrigation systems bringing rainwater and possibly subsurface water from springs and wells to intensively cultivated fields of grain (primarily wheat and barley), lentils and date palms (Al-Jahwari 2009: 122–133; Cremaschi et al. 2018: 123–140).

The monumental developments in settlement architecture coincided with the construction of large circular burial monuments using local rock for the inner structure but with finely dressed white stone facing on the exterior (Figure 2.6). These large tombs were erected in locations adjacent to the major settlements and in locations that were highly visible from throughout inhabited region (Degli Esposti and Phillips 2012: 87–100). The burial towers had internal subdivisions that were used repeatedly over many generations. In some instances the accumulated burials and burial goods were taken out and redeposited in large pits associated with the monuments. The burial goods included various pottery vessels that were locally produced as well as some imported vessels from Mesopotamia and from the Indus Valley

Figure 2.6 Umm an-Nar period tombs, Bat, Oman.

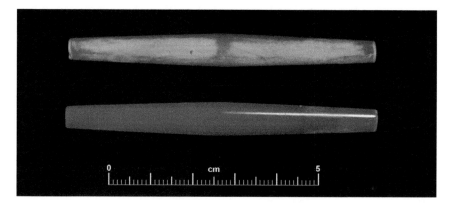

Figure 2.7 Long biconical Indus carnelian bead, Bat, Oman.

region. Many beads from both the Indus and possibly Iran were also found in the tombs, along with bronze artifacts, carved chlorite vessels, and occasionally seals. A complete long biconical bead was found in association with one of the Umm an-Nar tombs in Bat (Grave 155) (Figure 2.7) excavated by the German Archaeological mission (Döpper and Schmidt 2014: fig. 14e).

Many coastal sites dating to this time period have been discovered along the Batinah coast as well as the eastern and southeastern coastal regions. Excavations at various sites in the locality of Ras al-Jinz and Ras al-Hadd provide important evidence for the nature of coastal adaptations that focused on local marine resources as well as on both regional and long distance trade (Figure 2.1). The sites of RJ-2 (Tosi 1982; Cleuziou and Tosi 1988: 11–27) and RJ-3 (De Rorre et al. 2020: 109–126) at Ras al-Jinz have revealed the presence of large multi-roomed mud-brick buildings that contained distinctive artifacts from the Indus Valley region. The most important objects include a small copper bronze Indus seal, large black slipped jars with Indus writing, decorated pottery from the Indus as well as an ivory comb (Cleuziou et al. 2018: 269–296). In addition, large amounts of bitumen that were part of the exterior coating of reed boats were found in some of the rooms. The bitumen and associated shells could be traced to a region south of modern Mosul, which was a major source of bitumen for Mesopotamia (Cleuziou, 2018: #11778, 292). All of these discoveries indicate that people living at the site were linked to both of these distant regions through trade. Another site, HD-1 at Ras al-Hadd, also has evidence for Indus pottery and a rare example of an Indus vessel with painted Indus script (Figure 2.8) (Cattani et al. 2019: 69–84; Cattani and Kenoyer 2021). All of these discoveries, which occurred under the auspices of the ministry from 1970 to 2020, confirm the links between Oman and distant trading partners to the east and to the west.

Figure 2.8 Pottery with painted Indus script, HD1, Ras al-Hadd.

The major economic development associated with the emergence of these large settlements has been linked to trade, both internally between the coastal and inland regions and also with more distant regions in southern Mesopotamia, Iran, and the Indus Valley (Potts 1993: 323–333; Frenez 2020: 7–47). Copper may have been one of the most important commodities that was produced for both regional and external trade (Weisgerber 1984: 196–201), but other items may have included dried fish (Cleuziou et al. 2018: 351) and ornaments made from local marine shells (Gensheimer 1984: 65–73; Marucci 2012: 443–450). In addition, this region may have played a significant role in the transshipment of goods coming from the southern Indus Valley and Gujarat that were destined for the cities of southern Mesopotamia. The presence of Indus pottery (Méry and Blackman 1996), carnelian beads (Kenoyer and Frenez 2018: 397–410), and other diagnostic artifacts (Frenez et al. 2016: 107–124; Frenez 2020: 7–47) at coastal and inland sites provides direct evidence that some Indus-related materials were traded to eastern Arabia during this time period. There is also evidence that some Indus communities may have been living at inland sites (Frenez et al. 2016: 107–124) and that some Indus-style pottery was being made at sites in eastern Arabia (Méry et al. 2017: 163–184). It should be noted, however, that no Indus-derived copper objects have been identified at the major stopping points along this route such as Bahrain and Tel Abraq (Begemann et al. 2010: 162). Although there is less evidence for the trade of pottery from Mesopotamia to eastern Arabia (Thornton 2013: 598–617, 608; Frenez 2020: 15) the trade from east to west was quite important and the region of Magan is specifically mentioned as a source of copper and other exotic items in Mesopotamian texts. Evidence for this trade with Mesopotamia is supported by the identification of copper objects that can be correlated to ores and metals produced in Oman and the UAE. During the height of trade with Mesopotamia in the Early Dynastic III period (c. 2500–2320 BCE) and the Akkadian period (2350–2150 BCE), 48 percent to 55 percent of the copper objects studied appear to derive from Oman (Begemann et al. 2010: 159). It is also important to note that a large percentage of the copper/bronze artifacts in Mesopotamia were made from copper coming the Indus (Meluhha) related copper sources areas in the southern Aravalli Range, Rajasthan/Gujarat (Begemann et al. 2010: 159).

Overall the Umm an-Nar period represents an important phase of both internal development and long-distance exchange that was the culmination of both local and regional processes of cultural interaction. Communities living on the coasts and interior of eastern Arabia, specifically the copper-producing regions of central Oman and UAE, played an important role in linking the cities of the Indus Valley and Mesopotamia to Iran and the rest of Arabia.

At the end of the Umm an-Nar period the intensity of trade with the Indus and Mesopotamia begins to decline until new political and economic developments emerge during the Iron Age and the subsequent historical period, *c.* 600 BCE (Cleuzieu and Tosi 2018: 480). Although this chapter is focused on the Bronze Age, all of the subsequent periods are well represented in the form of museum exhibits and profusely illustrated scientific publications. The comprehensive coverage of Oman's past has made it possible for foreign visitors and the general public to appreciate the complex history of the region and the continuing role that Oman is playing in the modern context.

Conclusion

The archaeological history of Oman continues after the Umm an-Nar period with the later Bronze Age Wadi Suq period and Early Iron Age developments that link the region to a much larger world and more complex social and political networks that are beyond the scope of this chapter. The most challenging issue that still needs to be addressed is how to preserve the most important sites and still continue with economic development and modernization. As Sultan Qaboos understood during his reign, 1970–2020, educating the public, particularly the younger generation, about the importance of these sites, and of Oman's deep heritage of global connectivity and trade is one of the main mechanisms for long-term preservation and conservation. Teaching the archaeology of Oman in public schools and universities, for example, has been an important first step in this direction. Further, incorporating the study of prehistoric archaeology, including technology, economics, and trade, into curricula for tourism and other disciplines will help students to realize how important this region has been in the past and could help to direct development in the future of modern Oman.

References

Al-Belushi, M. A. K., "Managing Oman's Archaeological Resource: Historical Perspectives," *Public Archaeology* , 7(3) (2008): 149–173.

Al-Busaidi, Y., "The Protection and Management of Historic Monuments in the Sultanate of Oman: the Historic Buildings of Oman," *Proceedings of the Seminar for Arabian Studies* 34 (2004): 35–44.

Al-Jahwari, N. S., "The Agricultural Basis of Umm an-Nar Society in the Northern Oman Peninsula (2500–2000 BC)," *Arabian Archaeology and Epigraphy* 20 (2009): 122–133.

Azzarà, V. and M. Cattani, "The Beginning of a New Era in the Ja'alan: The Hafit Settlement HD-6 at Ras Al-Hadd," in S. Cleuziou and M. Tosi (eds.), *In the Shadow of the Ancestors: The Prehistoric Foundations of the Early Arabian Civilization in Oman,* 2nd expanded edn. (Muscat: Ministry of Heritage and Culture of the Sultanate of Oman, 2018), 146–150.

Beech, M., "Archaeobotanical Evidence for Early Date Consumption in the Arabian Gulf," *Antiquity* 75 (2000): 83–89.

Begemann, F., A. Hauptmann, S. Schmitt-Strecker, and G. Weisgerber, "Lead Isotope and Chemical Signature of Copper from Oman and its Occurrence in Mesopotamia and Sites on the Arabian Gulf Coast," *Arabian Archaeology and Epigraphy* 21 (2010): 135–169.

Besenval, R., "Chronology of Protohistoric Kech-Makran," in C. Jarrige and V. Lefèvre (eds.), *South Asian Archaeology 2001*, vol. 1 (Paris: CNRS, 2005), 1–10.

Buta, M., D. Frenez, E. Bortolini, V. Charpentier, and J. M. Kenoyer, "Bead Production in the Late Neolithic Communities of Coastal Oman," in S. Cleuziou and M. Tosi (eds.), *In the Shadow of the Ancestors: The Prehistoric Foundations of the Early Arabian Civilization in Oman. Second Expanded Edition* (Muscat: Ministry of Heritage & Culture, Sultanate of Oman, 2018), 147–153.

Carter, R., "Ubaid-period Boat Remains from As-Sabiyah: Excavations by the British Archaeological Expedition to Kuwait," *Proceedings of the Seminar for Arabian Studies* 32 (2002): 13–30.

Carter, R., "The History and Prehistory of Pearling in the Persian Gulf," *Journal of the Economic and Social History of the Orient* 48(2) (2005): 139–209.

Carter, R. and H. E. W. Crawford, "The Kuwait–British Archaeological Expedition to As-Sabiyah: Report on the Fourth Season's Work," *Iraq* 65 (2003): 77–90.

Cattani, M. and J. M. Kenoyer, "Ras Al-Hadd HD-1 Preliminary Report, Field Season 2019–2020," Bologna/Madison, 2021.

Cattani, M., J. M. Kenoyer, D. Frenez, R. W. Law, and S. Méry, "New Excavations at the Umm an-Nar Site Ras al-Hadd HD-1, Sultanate of Oman (Seasons 2016–2018): Insights on Cultural Interaction and Long-Distance Trade," *Seminar for Arabian Studies* 49 (2019): 69–84.

Charpentier, V., J.-F. Berger, R. Crassard, M. Lacaze, and G. Davtian, "Prehistory and Palaeo-geography of the Coastal Fringes of the Wahiba Sands and Bar al-Hikman, Sultanate of Oman," *Proceedings of the Seminar for Arabian Studies* 42 (2012): 57–78.

Charpentier, V., J.-F. Berger, R. Crassard, F. Borgi, G. Davtian, S. Méry, and C. S. Phillips, "Conquering New Territories: When the First Black Boats Sailed to Masirah Island," *Proceedings of the Seminar for Arabian Studies* 43 (2013): 85–98.

Cleuziou, S., "The Emergence of Oases and Towns in Eastern and Southern Arabia," in G. Afanasev, S. Cleuziou, J. R. Lukacs, and M. Tosi (eds.), *The Prehistory of Asia and Oceania (Colloquia of the XIII International Congress of Prehistoric and Protohistoric Sciences 16)* (Forlì: ABACO Edizioni, 1996), 159–165.

Cleuziou, S. and M. Tosi, "The Third Campaign at RJ-2: Preliminary Report," in S. Cleuziou, J. Reade, and M. Tosi (eds.), *The Joint Hadd Project Summary Report on the Season October 1987– February 1988* (Paris/Rome: ERA30/IsMEO, 1988), 11–27.

Cleuziou, S., M. Tosi, D. Frenez and R. Garba (eds.) *In the Shadow of the Ancestors: The Prehistoric Foundations of the Early Arabian Civilization in Oman* (Muscat: Ministry of Heritage and Culture of the Sultanate of Oman, 2018).

Cremaschi, M., M. Degli Esposti, D. Fleitmann, A. Perego, E. Sibilia, and A. Zerboni, "Late Holocene Onset of Intensive Cultivation and Introduction of the Falaj Irrigation System in the Salut Oasis (Sultanate of Oman)," *Quaternary Science Reviews* 200 (2018): 123–140.

Curci, A., M. Carletti, and M. Tosi, "The Camel Remains from Site HD-6 (Ras al-Hadd, Sultanate of Oman): An Opportunity for a Critical Review of Dromedary Findings in Eastern arabia," *Anthropozoologica* 49(2) (2014): 207–222.

Dales, G. F., "Shifting Trade Patterns Between the Iranian Plateau and the Indus Valley in the Third Millennium B.C.," in J. Deshayes (ed.), *Le plateau iranien et l'Asie Centrale des origines à la conquête islamique* (Paris: CNRS, 1976), 67–78.

Dales, G. F., "A Line in the Sand: Explorations in Afghan Sistan," in G. L. Possehl (ed.), *South Asian Archaeology Studies* (New Delhi: Oxford University Press and IBH, 1992), 19–32.

Dales, G. F. and C. Lipo, *The Makran Coast of Pakistan: A Search for Ancient Seaports* (Berkeley: Archaeological Research Facility, University of California,1992).

De Rorre, A. P., J.-F. Berger, M. Delfino, J. M. Kenoyer, E. Maini, and V. M. Azzarà, "The Ras al-Jinz Reloaded: Resuming Excavations at the Edge of Arabia," *Seminar for Arabian Studies* 50 (2020): 109–126.

Deadman, W. and N. S. Al-Jahwari, "Hafit Tombs in ash-Sharqiyah, Oman: Assessing the Accuracy and Precision of Google Earth Remote-sensing Survey and Analysing Their Distribution in the Landscape," *Arabian Archaeology and Epigraphy* 27 (2016): 19–30.

Degli Esposti, M. and C. Phillips, "Iron Age Impact on a Bronze Age Archaeological Landscape: Results from the Italian Mission to Oman Excavations at Salūt, Sultanate of Oman," *Proceedings of the Seminar for Arabian Studies* 42 (2012): 87–100.

Döpper, S. and C. Schmidt, German Expedition to Bāt and Al-Ayn, Sultanate of Oman: The field seasons 2010 to 2013, University of Tübingen, 2014.

Frenez, D., "Cross-Cultural Trade and Socio-Technical Developments in the Oman Peninsula during the Bronze Age, ca. 3200 to 1600 BC," *OCNUS* 27 (2020): 7–47.

Frenez, D., M. Degli Esposti, S. Méry, and J. M. Kenoyer, "Bronze Age Salut (ST1) and the Indus Civilization: Recent Discoveries and New Insights on Regional Interaction," *Seminar for Arabian Studies* 46 (2016): 107–124.

Frifelt, K., *The Island of Umm An-Nar: Third Millennium Graves* (Aarhus: Aarhus University Press,1991).

Frifelt, K., *The Island of Umm An-Nar: The Third Millennium Settlement* (Aarhus: Jutland Archaeological Society Publications,1995).

Gensheimer, T. R., "The Role of Shell in Mesopotamia: Evidence for Trade Exchange with Oman and the Indus Valley," *Paléorient* 10(1) (1984): 65–73.

Giardino, C., *Magan: the land of Copper, Prehistoric Metallurgy of Oman* Muscat: Ministry of Heritage and Culture of the, Sultanate of Oman, 2017).

Gros-Balthazard, M., M. Galimberti, A. Kousathanas, C. Newton, S. Ivorra, L. Paradis, Y. Vigouroux, R. Carter, M. Tengberg, V. Battesti, S. Santoni, L. Falquet, J.-C. Pintaud, J.-F. Terral, and D. Wegmann, "The Discovery of Wild Date Palms in Oman Reveals a Complex Domestication History Involving Centers in the Middle East and Africa," *Current Biology* 27(14) (2017): 2211–2218.

Hauptmann, A. and G. Weisgerber, "The Early Bronze Age Copper Metallurgy of Shahr-i-Sokhta (Iran)," *Paléorient* 6 (1980): 120–127.

Kennet, D., W. M. Deadman, and N. S. Al-Jahwari, "The Rustaq–Batinah Archaeological Survey," *Proceedings of the Seminar for Arabian Studies* 46 (2016): 155–168.

Kenoyer, J. M. and D. Frenez, "Carnelian and Agate Beads in the Oman Peninsula during the Third to Second millennia BC," in M. Tosi, S. Cleuziou, D. Frenez, and R. Garba (eds.), *In the Shadow of the Ancestors: The Prehistoric Foundations of the Early Arabian Civilization in Oman*, 2nd expanded edn. (Muscat: Ministry of Heritage and Culture of the Sultanate of Oman, 2018), 397–410.

Lamberg-Karlovsky, C. C. and D. Potts (eds.), *Excavations at Tepe Yahya: The Third Millennium* (Cambridge, MA: Peabody Museum of Archaeology and Ethnology, 2001).

Laursen, S. and P. Steinkeller, *Babylonia, the Gulf Region, and the Indus. Archaeological and Textual Evidence for Contact in the Third and Early Second Millennium B.C.* (Winona Lake, IN: Eisenbrauns, 2017).

Law, R. W., "Analysis of Stone and Metal Artifacts from HD-6, HD-10 and HD-1, Ras Al-Hadd, Sultanate of Oman," in S. Cleuziou and M. Tosi (eds.), *In the Shadow of the Ancestors: The Prehistoric Foundations of the Early Arabian Civilization in Oman*, 2nd expanded edn. (Muscat: Ministry of Heritage and Culture of the Sultanate of Oman, 2018), 160–188.

Madsen, B., *The Early Bronze Age Tombs of Jebel Hafit* (Abu Dhabi: Jutlang Archaeological Society Publications and Abu Dhabi Tourism and Culture Authority, 2017).

Majidzadeh, Y. and H. Pittman, "Excavations at Konar Sandal in the Region of Jiroft in the Halil Basin: First Preliminary Report (2002–2008)," *Iran* 46 (2008): 69–103.

Marcucci, L. G., F. Genchi, É. Badel, and M. Tosi, "Recent Investigations at the Prehistoric Site RH-5 (Ra' s al-Hamra, Muscat, Sultanate of Oman)," *Proceedings of the Seminar for Arabian Studies* 41 (2011): 201–222.

Marucci, L. G., "Exploration of HD60, a Large Bronze Age Deposit of Conus sp. at Ras al-Hadd, Sultanate of Oman," in J. Giraud, G. Gernez, and V. d. Castéja (eds.), *Aux Marges de l'archéologie: Hommage à Serge Cleuziou* (Paris: De Boccard, 2012), 443–450.

Matthews, R. and H. Fazeli, "Copper and Complexity: Iran and Mesopotamia in the Fourth Millennium B.C.," *Iran* 42 (2004): 61–75.

Méry, S. and M. J. Blackman, "Black-Jars of Meluhha: Production and Diffusion of Indus Pottery Ware During the Second Half of the 3rd Millennium B. C.," *Harappan Studies* 3 (1996): 2–18.

Méry, S. and V. Charpentier, "Neolithic Material Cultures of Oman and the Gulf Seashores from 5500–4500 BCE," *Arabian Archaeology and Epigraphy* 24(1) (2013): 73–78.

Méry, S., M. Degli Esposti, D. Frenez and J. M. Kenoyer, "Indus Potters in Central Oman in the Second Half of the Third Millennium BC. First Results of a Technological and Archaeometric Study," *Seminar for Arabian Studies* 47 (2017): 163–184.

Méry, S. and M. Tengberg, "Food for Eternity? The Analysis of a Date Offering from a 3rd-millennium BC Grave at Hili N, Abu Dhabi (United Arab Emirates)," *Journal of Archaeological Science* 39(6) (2009): 2012–2017.

Potts, D. T., "Tell Abraq and the Harappan Tradition in Southeastern Arabia," in G. L. Possehl (ed.), *Harappan Civilization: A Recent Perspective* (New Delhi: Oxford & IBH Co. Pvt. Ltd., 1993), 323–333.

Rose, J. I. "On the Trail of the First Humans in Oman," in S. Cleuziou, M. Tosi, D. Frenez, and R. Garba (eds.), *In the Shadow of the Ancestors: The Prehistoric Foundations of the Early Arabian Civilization in Oman* (Muscat: Ministry of Heritage and Culture of the Sultanate of Oman, 2018), 32–36.

Rose, J. I., Y. H. Hilbert, A. E. Marks, and V. I. Usik, *The First Peoples of Oman: Palaeolithic Archaeology of the Nejd Plateau* Oxford: Archaeopress, 2019).

Schmidt, C. and S. Döpper, "German Expedition to Bāt and Al-Ayn, Sultanate of Oman: The Field Seasons 2010 to 2013," *Journal of Oman Studies* 18 (2014): 187–230.

Sivitskis, A. J., J. W. Lehner, M. J. Harrower, I. A. Dumitru, P. E. Paulsen, S. Nathan, D. R. Viete, S. Al-Jabri, B. Helwing, F. Wiig, D. Moraetis, and B. Pracejus, "Detecting and Mapping Slag Heaps at Ancient Copper Production Sites in Oman," *Remote Sensing* 11(3014) (2019): 1–24.

Tengberg, M. "Beginnings and Early History of Date Palm Garden Cultivation in the Middle East," *Journal of Arid Environments* 86(1) (2012): 139–147.

Thornton, C. P. "The Emergence of Complex Metallurgy on the Iranian Plateau: Escaping the Levantine Paradigm," *Journal of World Prehistory* 22 (2009): 301–327.

Thornton, C. P. "Mesopotamia, Meluhha, and Those in Between," in H. E. W. Crawford (ed.), *The Sumerian World* (Abingdon: Routledge. 2013), 598–617.

Thornton, C. P. "Excavations at Kasr al-Khafaji (Tower 1146) (Chapter 3)," in C. P. Thornton, C. M. Cable, and G. L. Possehl (eds.), *The Bronze Age Towers at Bat, Sultanate of Oman Research by the Bat Archaeological Project, 2007–12* (Philadelphia: University of Pennsylvania Press, 2016), 25–47.

Thornton, C. P., C. M. Cable, and G. L. Possehl (eds.), *The Bronze Age Towers at Bat, Sultanate of Oman Research by the Bat Archaeological Project, 2007–12* (Philadelphia: University of Pennsylvania Press, 2016).

Tosi, M., "The Dating of the Umm an-Nar Culture and a Proposed Sequence for Oman in the Third Millennium BC," *Journal of Oman Studies* 2 (1976): 81–92.

Tosi, M., *A Possible Harappan Seaport in Eastern Arabia: Ra's Al-Junayz in the Sultanate of Oman*, in *First International Conference on Pakistan Archaeology*, Peshawar, March 1–4, 1982.

Uerpmann, M., R. d. Beauclair, M. Händel, A. Kutterer, E. Noack, and H.-P. Uerpmann "The Neolithic Site FAY-NE15 in the Central Region of the Emirate of Sharjah (UAE)," *Proceedings of the Seminar for Arabian Studies* 42 (2012): 385–400.

Uerpmann, H.-P., D. T. Potts, and M. Uerpmann, "Holocene (Re-)Occupation of Eastern Arabia," in M. D. Petraglia and J. I. Rose (eds.), *The Evolution of Human*

Populations in Arabia, Vertebrate Paleobiology and Paleoanthropology (New York: Springer Science, 2009), 205–214.

Uerpmann, H.-P., M. Uerpmann, and S. A. Jasim (eds.), *The Archaeology of Jebel al-Buhais, v*ol. 2. (Tübingen, Kerns, 2008).

Uerpmann, M. and H.-P. Uerpmann, "Early Herders at Al-Buhais 18," in S. Cleuziou and M. Tosi (eds.), *In the Shadow of the Ancestors: The Prehistoric Foundations of the Early Arabian Civilization in Oman*, 2nd expanded edn. (Muscat: Ministry of Heritage and Culture of the Sultanate of Oman, 2018), 64–65.

Weisgerber, G., "Makkan and Meluhha: Third Millennium B.C. Copper Production in Oman and the Evidence of Contact with the Indus Valley," in B. Allchin (ed.), *South Asian Archaeology 1981* (Cambridge: Cambridge University Press, 1984), 196–201.

3

THE LAND OF FRANKINCENSE: DHOFARI SITES AS NATIONAL AND WORLD HERITAGE

Krista Lewis

Frankincense is one of Oman's most recognizable and celebrated cultural symbols. The modern rise in visibility of frankincense as a part of Omani identity and economy is closely tied to the history of archaeological research in Oman's southern region of Dhofar. Over the course of Sultan Qaboos' reign, the archaeological and cultural heritage of southern Oman, where frankincense trees grow, went from virtually unknown to a backbone of the Sultanate's national identity and tourism industry due to strategic promotion of its association with frankincense.

In securing a place on the UNESCO World Heritage list for a group of sites in Dhofar, Oman under Sultan Qaboos was able to capitalize on frankincense's romantic history and heady scent for a range of strategic purposes. Foremost among these were attracting tourism and nurturing a distinctive Omani cultural ideology surrounding the ancient frankincense trade and the modern use of the aromatic. The "Land of Frankincense," as it is officially known today, is a group of four geographically distinct heritage locations across Dhofar. It was inscribed on the UNESCO World Heritage list in 2000.[1] Three of the sites included in the Land of Frankincense World Heritage listing are archaeological parks and the fourth is a nature reserve for frankincense trees. Al-Baleed is a large late ancient to medieval trading port city on the outskirts of Salalah, the regional capital of Dhofar. Khor Rori (ancient Sumhuram) is a fortified South Arabian Iron Age town on the eastern side of the Salalah coastal plan. Wubar

(Ubar) is a small walled settlement at Shisr in the inland desert.[2] Al-Baleed and Sumhuram are famed for their role in the sea transport of frankincense. Wubar is located at a permanent water source and served as a junction between key caravan routes.

The development of the "Land of Frankincense" as not only a UNESCO World Heritage site in Dhofar but also a symbolic "brand" for Oman as a whole occurred in four overlapping phases: awareness and protection of resources; the rise of scientific archaeological research; acquiring UNESCO World Heritage status; and increasing focus on the expansion of high-end tourism. It is not just a story of the quest for scientific advancement or economic gain, but also of an intentional crafting of a heritage narrative linking Oman's rich past to its modern and changing identities. The pathway was not direct nor without challenges, including administrative, financial, and social issues. This chapter describes how the heritage identity of Oman in "The Land of Frankincense" was shaped, where it stands at the passing of Sultan Qaboos, and what role it might continue to play in Oman's future.

Frankincense

The frankincense tree (*Boswellia sacra*) produces a gum-resin with a strong, distinctive aroma. Frankincense resin has been internationally famous since ancient times for use as an incense on its own or as an ingredient in incense mixes, perfumes, and other beauty and health products. Frankincense's use and meaning differed from place to place and over time as it was adapted into the cultural repertoires of far-flung societies across global trade routes. Within southern Arabia, frankincense resin and other parts of the plant are used for a wide range of traditional practices, including as part of social and protective rituals, as a dye, a beauty aid, food additive, and many medicinal remedies and prophylactics for humans and animals.[3] Today, it is common to encounter the scent of burning frankincense throughout Oman in prominent public places such as government office buildings, shopping malls, and hotel lobbies.

Frankincense trees require highly specific environmental conditions to thrive. They grow in only a few places in the world, namely Oman's southern Dhofar region, adjacent eastern Yemen, and part of Somalia. Related species also grow in other areas of east Africa and India. Dhofar is an ecologically distinct region of the Arabian Peninsula, rendered remarkably tropical and comparatively lush by the influence of the Indian Ocean southwest monsoon and divided from northern Oman by extensive deserts. This unique geography and ecology creates the mountain-slope microclimates that allow frankincense trees to thrive.

Since prehistory, the climate of southwest Arabia (Dhofar and adjacent parts of Yemen) has also supported local cultural lifeways that differ significantly from most others on the Arabian Peninsula. The distinctive cultural makeup of the population of Dhofar in modern times was among the challenges faced by a young Sultan Qaboos when he first came to power. Among the strategies Sultan Qaboos used to unify the country ideologically were cultural heritage and a sense of unity rooted in a distant archaeological past. The case of the Land of Frankincense sites is one example of the many and diverse efforts of Qaboos and his government to establish a sense of national cultural unity.

Protection of Cultural Heritage in Oman

Prior to the start of the Sultan Qaboos era little concentrated effort had been made to recognize, investigate, or celebrate the archaeological and cultural heritage of Oman. During the first two decades of Sultan Qaboos' reign, he asserted a foundational vision that cultural heritage would be of central importance to the future of the country. Such a decision to prioritize culture cannot be taken for granted especially in the case of new, politically fragile, and economically underdeveloped countries such as Oman was at the time that Qaboos took over from his father. As the new Sultan established his governmental structure over the years, provisions for cultural heritage were developed and refined.

A Department for Antiquities was created within the Ministry of Information and Culture in 1973. As the governmental structure unfolded, in 1976 a separate Ministry of Omani Heritage was established. By the end of the 1970s, it was already becoming clear that the increased pace of development brought by Sultan Qaboos' efforts and increased oil revenues was a threat to the preservation of Oman's past and that additional policy guidelines were needed.[4] The primary legislation in the Sultanate regarding archaeological resources is the 1980 National Heritage Protection Law (NHPL). The law has ten sections that address defining, registering, conserving, and protecting historic buildings, monuments, archaeological resources and movable heritage, as well as managing excavation works. The responsibility for implementing the conditions set out in the legislation is placed upon the Ministry of Culture and Heritage.[5] Although the Ministry of Heritage and Culture is ostensibly the only authority on matters of archaeology and cultural heritage, in practice this has not turned out to be completely true, for example, regarding the case of the Land of Frankincense sites, as we will see below.

Joining UNESCO early and supporting its activities helped to set the stage for the declaration of the Land of Frankincense. Oman under Sultan Qaboos became a member of UNESCO in 1974, just four years after he came to power. Oman signed several key UNESCO agreements in the area of cultural heritage. In 1977, Oman became a signatory to both the 1954 UNESCO Convention for the Protection of Cultural Property in the Event of an Armed Conflict and the 1970 UNESCO Convention on the Means of Prohibiting and Preventing the Illicit Import, Export and Transfer of Ownership of Cultural Property. In 1981, Oman became a party to the 1972 UNESCO Convention Concerning the Protection of the World Cultural and Natural Heritage. This commitment to playing a role in the global protection of heritage was an essential step toward the eventual acceptance of Omani properties on the World Heritage list.

Oman's first two properties inscribed on the UNESCO World Heritage list acquired their status in 1987 and 1988. Both were cultural properties in northern Oman, the first being Bahla Fort, and the second a group of prehistoric tomb sites.[6] Following those two early successes, the Land of Frankincense was added to the register over a decade later. Today, Oman has five entries on the UNESCO World Heritage list, but arguably the Land of Frankincense is one of the most well-known and internationally celebrated of those.[7] Of all the UNESCO listed properties in Oman, the scope of the Land of Frankincense is the broadest chronologically, geographically, and culturally.

The site of Al-Baleed illustrates of Qaboos' forethought for preservation of cultural resources. The sizeable ruins of Al-Baleed are located in a prime beach location on the outskirts of Salalah, but were expressly protected from the outset of Qaboos' reign. It is said that because he was the son of a Dhofari woman, he recognized and respected the mostly Islamic period town as an ancestral space for the Salalah community. The site also includes substantial numbers of Islamic period graves that, according to Muslim belief, should not be disturbed. Whether initially for sentimental or shrewd reasons, or a mixture of both, the choice to save Al-Baleed rather than bulldoze it for development has turned out to be a masterful one. Al-Baleed is now is now the centerpiece of the Land of Frankincense and the home of the Land of Frankincense Museum. The site and museum attract large numbers of international and local visitors, reaching into the tens of thousands per month during the high tourist season.

Early Archaeological Research in Dhofar

Archaeological research in the Dhofar region has most often been conducted by foreign archaeologists, but the agenda of much of that work was carefully guided by Qaboos. Some of the earliest archaeological investigations in Dhofar were carried out in 1952–3 and 1960 by Frank P. Albright, R. L. Cleveland, and Wendell Phillips of the American Foundation for the Study of Man (AFSM). AFSM conducted initial surveys and excavations at two of the sites that would eventually become part of the Land of Frankincense, Khor Rori and Al-Baleed.[8] Qaboos was aware of the existence of this early archaeological work and the international connections afforded by the presence of foreign archaeologists. For example, oil magnate turned archaeologist Wendell Phillips was a friend of Sultan Said bin Taimur. Phillips' sister, the late Merilyn Phillips Hodgson, reminisced about having played with a young Qaboos at the palace in Salalah while both were children.[9]

Although there were some occasional visits by foreign archaeologists to the region following the AFSM work, there was a relative dearth of archaeological work in Dhofar for many years. In general, international archaeological research in southern Arabia was sparse until the late 1970s and 1980s when interest grew rapidly, except in Dhofar. Archaeology in that period was at first largely focused on the grander archaeological sites of the caravan cities of Yemen and the prehistoric sites of northern Oman.[10] In Dhofar, archaeological research in the 1970s and 1980s was limited to a very few projects, including a prehistoric survey in the Nejd, work by Paolo Costa at the site of Al-Baleed, and some documentation of Islamic period monuments and cemeteries on the Salalah plain.[11] More focused attention to the archaeology of Dhofar began in the 1990s. The renewed interest was largely an unintentional offshoot of the activities of a new round of foreign adventurers who decided to pick up the perennial quest for the so-called "Lost City of Ubar."

The "Lost City of Ubar"

In the medieval period, there were a wealth of stories in Arabic literature that elaborated on Qur'anic references to an ill-fated desert city called Iram or Ubar (Wubar). This lost city was said to have existed in the unlikely location of the extreme environment of Arabia's Rub al-Khalil. Ubar, according to the varied tales, was inhabited by the tribe of ʿAd, a wicked and decadent people who were destroyed in a cataclysmic night in punishment for their many sins. The tantalizing tale of Ubar eventually caught the imagination of European explorers, adventurers, and political agents working in the region, especially in the first half of the twentieth century.[12]

A new modern quest for Ubar came to Oman in the early 1990s in the form of a highly publicized expedition.[13] In 1989, two Americans, Nicholas Clapp and George Hedges, were granted permission to make a documentary about the so-called lost city. They were successful in their bid to work in the Sultanate at least in part because they had acquired the partnership and Oman connections of Sir Ranulph Fiennes, famed adventure expedition leader. Fiennes was a former British officer who had served in the Omani army under both Sultan Said bin Taimur and the new Sultan Qaboos, including years of service during the Dhofar rebellion. The lost city project also had the offer of financial backing from the Oman International Bank. In order to gain archaeological validity for the pursuit, archaeologist Juris Zarins was recruited onto the team. Zarins had decades of experience in the region and was one the very few Arabian archaeology specialists in the United States at the time.

The TransArabia Expedition gained a significant amount of international press attention during its run from 1992 to 1995, especially in the first two seasons of its work. Alongside the allure of a lost city in the sands, the main attraction in the media was a collaboration with scientists at NASA to employ satellite imagery in the search for archaeological remains.[14] The use of satellite images for archaeological site discovery and documentation is almost routine today, but at that time it was a cutting-edge approach. The combination of a dramatic desert setting, lost cities, and hi-tech from outer space proved an irresistible combination and the project was covered in news stories and magazines worldwide.[15]

Once in Oman, Clapp decided that an archaeological site adjacent to the Bedouin oasis town of Shisr must be the location of the Lost City. Excavations began in search of proof, but regardless of the outcome it seems that, in the eye of the public at least, the die was cast. The site certainly has some features which, although not proof of the legend, made for compelling storytelling. The site is a walled enclosure ringed with a series of towers surrounding a collapsed sinkhole. The dramatic large hollow in the middle of the site is seen by some as proof of the destruction of its sinful inhabitants as told in the tales of Ubar. Despite the enthusiastic assertions of the filmmakers and adventurers, there is no evidence that the site at Shisr can be identified as the infamous lost city. In a review of the question, Edgell concluded that not only is the site at Shisr not a candidate to be "Ubar," but that "There are no prospects of there ever having been a legendary city called Ubar (or Wabar) within the Rub al-Khalil, or Arabian Sands."[16] More recently, the team involved in the 1990s expedition wrote that the Shisr site is a likely the inspiration for "some elements of the Ubar legend, but it is not the 'Ubar' of legend."[17]

The most important legacy of the TransArabia project was that it would pave the way for work that had an enduring impact on Oman's archaeology as well as the creation of the Land of Frankincense. In terms of cultural policy, development, and state interests, how the TransArabia Expedition was administratively handled is fascinating. Sultan Qaboos quickly saw the unique public relations value in encouraging a high-profile international expedition to the country. Of particular note in discerning the Sultan's interest in this project was the 1991 creation of a special supervisory authority, the National Committee for Supervision of Archaeological Survey, to manage the project. In a watershed moment that would decisively shape the future Land of Frankincense, the committee was established outside the Ministry of Heritage. The Committee was chaired by H.E. Abdul Aziz bin Mohammed Al-Rowas, who was then Minister of Information.[18] From this point onwards Al-Rowas took direct and personal interest in the management of the antiquities of Dhofar, especially Shisr and Zarins' work, followed a little later by Khor Rori, and eventually also Al-Baleed. Al-Rowas would take this portfolio of responsibility with him when he became the Adviser to H.M. the Sultan for Cultural Affairs in 2001 and continue to manage it until his retirement after the death of Sultan Qaboos.[19]

Scientific Archaeological Research in Dhofar

In the latter seasons of the TransArabia Expedition, the work at Shisr was oriented mainly toward the routine process of scientific archaeological research. The slow process of excavating a limited, mostly destroyed, and moderately-sized site in the desert gained less press than the earlier phase, but generated more useful archaeological information. Beyond the site at Shisr, Zarin's work in the first half of the 1990s included a reconnaissance of other ancient sites in the area.[20] Later, this would lead to an important regional survey that ultimately recorded hundreds of archaeological sites in Dhofar. The Dhofar archaeological survey might never have happened without the fanfare of the TransArabia Expedition, but ultimately it was the survey that fundamentally transformed our understanding of the prehistory and early history of the region, establishing a record of Dhofar's long occupation timeline.[21]

As the TransArabia project and the initial Dhofar Survey wound down, the region attracted additional foreign archaeological interest. In what eventually became the longest running archaeological project in Dhofar, an Italian team from the University of Pisa began work on the site of Sumhuram at Khor Rori in 1996. Sumhuram is a third century BC to fifth century AD South Arabian period fortified town in a lovely setting overlooking a freshwater drainage into the sea. This project was headed up throughout its duration not by an archaeologist, but by an epigrapher, Alexandra Avanzini, a specialist in ancient South Arabian languages. Avanzini's professional interest in the site stemmed from the presence of inscriptions in the Ancient South Arabian script. She staffed the site with a series of capable trained archaeologists as field directors running up to five months of excavations each year throughout the duration of the project, which continued until 2019.[22]

The third archaeological jewel of the Land of Frankincense, Al-Baleed, is the largest of the three archaeological sites in the group. Al-Baleed was a major late ancient to medieval trading port city famous for its export of Arabian horses as well as frankincense.[23] Al-Baleed was the earliest of the three sites to be subject to substantial modern scientific investigation. In the late 1970s, Paolo Costa, an Italian archaeologist who at the time was serving as the head of the Omani Antiquities Department, conducted a series of excavations there. His work laid the foundation for all future work at Al-Baleed by establishing a permanent archaeological grid and investigating several major features, including the town's large congregational mosque.[24]

Archaeological Parks and UNESCO World Heritage Status

By the time the TransArabia expedition was catapulting into international news, Sultan Qaboos and H.E. Abdul Aziz bin Mohammed Al-Rowas clearly saw the tourism potential for Dhofar and moved to push it ahead. By 1993, the Sultanate reached out to UNESCO for help with a cultural tourism plan, and the following year an evaluation and technical report were made by Michael Jansen of RWTH Aachen University. As a result, from 1995 to 2000, Oman partnered with Aachen to develop Al-Baleed as an archaeological park. The site was mapped, overall documentation conducted, and tourist paths through the site were installed. In addition, some minimal intervention archaeological excavations were conducted in order to better understand the site and, more importantly, to reveal some architectural features to make the area more attractive to tourists.[25] During this same period, a funerary mosque in the middle of Al-Baleed was documented and excavated for two seasons in 1996–97 by an Omani team from Sultan Qaboos University.[26]

The long steady pace of work at Sumhuram formed another stable foundation for the Land of Frankincense from an archaeological research perspective. Even more relevant for the development of the archaeological park at Khor Rori and its tourism prospects, Avanzini and the Italian team played central roles in developing the on-site museum and preparing the site to receive visitors. For years, alongside the ongoing excavations, the Italian team supervised the consolidation and restoration of the excavated parts of the city. Over the years, Avanzini and her team were also major players in the establishment of museums, visitor centers, and restoration work elsewhere throughout the Land of Frankincense.

With the assistance of the Italian and German projects, Al-Rowas and the staff of the Office of the Adviser to the Sultan for Cultural Affairs had everything they needed to apply for and secure the UNESCO World Heritage status for the Land of Frankincense. At the dawn of the twenty-first century, not only was the UNESCO listing accomplished, Al-Baleed and Khor Rori were the first and only archaeological parks in the Arabian Peninsula.

Tourism in the Land of Frankincense

Over the last two decades, Oman has steadily continued to develop the tourism appeal, physical landscapes, and projects associated with the Land of Frankincense sites. Continued archaeological research during this time has taken place mainly at Al-Baleed and Sumhuram, with many of the excavated areas of both sites now open for tourists to explore or view. Both sites also have associated museums and other activities for visitors to engage in while on their visits.

Most of the archaeological work at Al-Baleed has focused on the major architectural features of the site, including the city defensive wall with its stout towers and monumental gates, the administrative citadel-fort area, and a selection of the many mosques in the town. Investigation of those features was important to expand scientific understanding of the city, but also was paired with restoration and consolidation work that made the site more comprehensible to visitors. At Al-Baleed, the most extensive archaeological work to date was directed by Juris Zarins and Lynne Newton from 2005 to 2012. Zarins was personally invited by Al-Rowas to take on the project and was an employee of the government of Oman during those years. Zarins and Newton's efforts established a detailed chronological sequence for Al-Baleed and revealed much of the city's layout and key features. From a tourism perspective, the work of Zarins and Newton greatly expanded the number of walls and features that were visible, giving visitors a sense of the historic cityscape.[27]

Al-Baleed, with its prime location in Salalah and impressive monumental character, sees the vast majority of the tourist volume of all the locations in the Land of Frankincense. Since 2007, the Al-Baleed Archeological Park has also been home to the Land of Frankincense Museum, the largest cultural institution in Dhofar. Its galleries present the full scope of history in Dhofar from prehistory through to the Omani Renaissance of Sultan Qaboos. Due to its proximity to the modern port terminal of Salalah, Al-Baleed has garnered large numbers of visitors who are bussed to the site from large cruise ships. In addition to being able to peruse the museum and stroll or take a golf cart tour through the ruins of the very large walled city site, the park offers other activities for visitors. For the more recreation-minded, the Al-Baleed park today has small boats for rent to cruise the lagoon-moat that circles most of the ancient town and a lovely lawn area next to the water where families can relax and picnic. The beach in front of the site is also open to the public and is a popular spot for locals.

Because of Al-Baleed's relaxed setting and its convenient location for school groups, of all of the frankincense sites, it is the only one of the properties that regularly attracts significant numbers of local visitors in addition to foreign tourists. Engaging and serving local populations living in or near World Heritage and other protected cultural zones is a persistent and very real ethical question that is not unique to Oman. To encourage local visitation, the entry fee for Omanis to the ticketed Land of Frankincense sites is much lower than it is for outside visitors.

The site of Sumhuram at Khor Rori is a lovely site in a scenic location with good tourist appeal, so it sees many more visitors than Shisr or the Wadi Dawkah Frankincense Tree Park. Reaching Khor Rori does require about an hour round trip drive from Salalah, though, so it is visited by far fewer tourists than Al-Baleed. The Museum at Khor Rori is smaller than the larger Land of Frankincense Museum at Al-Baleed. Rather than duplicating what can be seen at the other museum, it is focused on displaying key information specifically about Sumhuram and the natural environment of Dhofar.

Although Wubar was not initially intended to be extensively developed for tourism in the way that Al-Baleed and Sumhuram were, the site has regularly attracted small numbers of visitors.[28] The location of Wubar is not convenient for casual tourism. It takes a long drive through a flat sand desert to reach Shisr, and there were, until recently, almost no public facilities there. For the last two decades, Wubar has mainly been visited by tourist groups as a short stop on the way to the desert dunes for Rub Al-Khali camping. The archaeological site of Wubar also continues to have a relatively small but enthusiastic following due to the lingering fame of the Ubar project. In response to the continued interest, some tourist-focused developments were conducted in recent years, including consolidation of the walls of the site. A modern visitor center presenting site information and a multilingual animated film about the Ubar legend was opened at Shisr in 2016.

The Wadi Dawkah Frankincense Park was established to protect a portion of the natural habitat of frankincense trees. Dawkah has not been discussed extensively in this chapter because it does not have the long history of development and research of the other three elements of the Land of Frankincense;

it does, however, serve a vital role. Due to the combined forces of changing climate and increased animal herds, frankincense trees throughout Dhofar are under severe threat. Today, there are relatively few large, mature, and healthy frankincense trees left in the wild. With a frankincense nursery at the al-Baleed archaeological park to start new trees and a protected place to reintroduce the plantings at Wadi Dawkah, the Land of Frankincense also serves a critical conservation mission. Visitors can freely visit Wadi Dawkah, but the location currently provides little beyond a sign, a scenic overlook to view the valley's frankincense groves, and some modest outdoor picnic structures.

Challenges and Opportunities

Managing four geographically distant and logistically varied properties such as those that comprise the Land of Frankincense would be a tall order anywhere in the world. Each of the properties have faced a number of anticipated and unexpected challenges over the years and undoubtedly will continue to do so. Challenges have included the types of routine headaches associated with bureaucratic management, lack of sufficient training for and involvement by staff, poorly planned and executed building projects, environmental impacts, and the mixed inherent appeal of the sites.

Compared with most of its neighboring countries in the Arabian Peninsula, Oman was a relatively early entry into the international heritage arena. Although Yemen had two still-inhabited historic cities inscribed on the UNESCO World Heritage list before Oman's earliest listings, no other Arabian Gulf country accomplished this until 2005 and later. In recent years, Oman has been joined by other GCC countries in a focus on cultural heritage and especially archaeology. This has been described as an Arabian Gulf "Heritage Boom."[29] Like the other Gulf states, Oman's antiquities, including the Land of Frankincense sites, are subject to the tensions inherent in balancing rapid economic development with the desire to preserve heritage.[30] There are a number of ways in which this issue has impacted the Land of Frankincense, including loss of elements of the historic landscape around the protected park area of Al-Baleed and the damage that blowing dust from a nearby rock quarry does to the frankincense trees at Wadi Dawkah.

Perhaps the single greatest current challenge faced by the Land of Frankincense is the fundamental and enduring issue of funding. The Land of

Frankincense, especially the development of its tourist infrastructure, has been a very expensive investment by the Omani government. In recent years, a major goal has been to find ways to make the Land of Frankincense financially self-sustainable.[31] This is a tall order considering not only the expense of the facilities that must be maintained, but also the large number of Omanis who have full-time employment at the sites, parks, and museums associated with the four properties.[32] Strategies for generating funding have included not just efforts to increase tourism numbers, but also creating associated profit-generating business partnerships. A striking example of this is the luxury seaside Al-Baleed Resort by Anatara which opened in 2016 right next to the Al-Baleed Archaeological Park and site. Although such forms of direct income may not cover the costs of running and maintaining the Land of Frankincense enterprise, its role as part of the package of Salalah tourism is an important element of the overall strategy for bringing outside revenue into to the region.

The future of the Land of Frankincense will be determined by how Oman continues to address these challenges as well as the fact that the endeavor has to serve a number of constituencies with different expectations and needs. Foreign tourists coming to the region can be divided into two main groups based on their origin and their season of visit. Arab tourists, mostly from other Gulf states, flock to Salalah in the summer for the cool and green landscapes during the monsoon season. Their habits, interests, and demands are quite different from the global tourists, mostly from Europe, who come during the winter to enjoy the warm, mild weather and beaches. To secure a sustainable future for its heritage, Oman must continue to seek not just tourism revenues, but also the continued engagement and support of the local population who could connect to these places as a part of their past.[33] A related critical issue for heritage in Oman is that there are still very few highly trained Omani archaeologists.[34]

Conclusion

When Sultan Qaboos came to power he took on a culturally diverse and politically divided territory that had not yet fully taken the form of a modern state. The Dhofar region was arguably the most problematic, an area initially in open rebellion both before and after his overthrow of his father.[35] Dhofar is inhabited by culturally and tribally diverse groups including indigenous speakers of non-Arabic languages.[36] Historically, Dhofar was also culturally and politically distinct from the populations of northern Oman, amplifying the challenges of bringing its peoples into alignment with a national identity. Although the country was firmly defined and the Dhofar war ended relatively early in Qaboos' reign, the project of developing a true national consciousness was a much more extended and multifaceted endeavor. The span of time and space captured by creating a unified Land of Frankincense out of these diverse sites across Dhofar created an unparalleled opportunity to craft and reinforce a heritage narrative connecting Oman's past to its present and its diverse people together into one nation.[37]

Today, Dhofar's frankincense and its archaeological, historic, and ecological landscapes, in particular the sites of the UNESCO World Heritage Land of Frankincense, are among the highlights of the Sultanate's tourism industry. The Land of Frankincense as a concept, as an administrative unit, and as a UNESCO World Heritage listing illustrates Sultan Qaboos' long-term investment in cultural heritage as well as developing a diversified economy for a country facing a future increasingly less dependent on oil revenues. At his death, Sultan Qaboos' last move to continue to protect and advance Omani heritage was in his choice of successor, Haitham bin Tariq Al-Said. With the new Sultan's long experience as the Minister of Culture and Heritage in his background, we can predict that cultural heritage will remain a priority for the country well into the future, although exactly what role the Land of Frankincense sites in particular will play under the new administration remains to be seen.[38]

Notes

1. See at: https://whc.unesco.org/en/list/1010. The UNESCO listing was originally called "The Frankincense Trail", but the title was officially changed in 2005, perhaps in part to further distinguish Oman's relationship to frankincense from other neighboring countries, especially Yemen, where frankincense also grows and/or through which the ancient trade routes passed.

2. In most English-language sources, the legendary desert city is referred to as Ubar. Recently, the Omani government has decided to standardize the spelling in Latin characters to Wubar, which is a better approximation of the Arabic

spelling and pronunciation of the word. In the remainder of this chapter, the spelling Ubar is used when referring to the subject of legendary stories, while the term Wubar will be used to refer to the modern tourist destination in the Land of Frankincense that is located alongside the modern desert village of Shisr.

3. M. Raffaelli et al., "Dhofar, the Land of Frankincense," in Alessandra Avanzani (ed.), *Along the Aroma and Spice Routes: The Harbour of Sumhuram, its Territory and the Trade between the Mediterranean, Arabia and India* (Pontedera: MB Vision, Bardecci & Vivaldi, 2011); Nigel Groom, "Trade, Incense, and Perfume," in St John Simpson (ed.), *Queen of Sheba: Treasures from Ancient Yemen* (London: The British Museum Press, 2002); A. G. Miller and M. Morris, *Plants of Dhofar, the Southern Region of Oman: Traditional, Economic, and Medicinal Uses* (Muscat: The Office of the Adviser for Conservation of the Environment, Diwan of the Royal Court, Sultanate of Oman, 1988), 78–81, 298–304; Tim Mackintosh-Smith, "Scents of Place: Frankincense in Oman," *Saudi Aramco World*, 2000.

4. Mohammed Al-Belushi, "Archaeological Legislation in the Sultanate of Oman," *International Journal of Heritage Studies* 20(1) (2012): 1–18.

5. There have been a number of renaming episodes of this ministry throughout its short history. The ministry was, at the time the NHPL was passed, called the Ministry of National Heritage and Culture. Even before that, it was first named the Ministry of Omani Heritage.

6. See Kenoyer, Chapter 2, this volume

7. See at: http://whc.unesco.org/en/statesparties/OM. A sixth Omani World Heritage site, a natural resource property dedicated to the Arabian Oryx, was accepted and then later delisted.

8. Alessandro de Maigret, *Arabia Felix: An Exploration of the Archaeological History of Yemen*, trans. Rebecca Thompson (London: Stacey International, 2002), 105–106; Brian Doe, *Southern Arabia: New Aspects of Antiquity* (London: Thames & Hudson, 1971), 10; Ray L. Cleveland, "The 1960 American Archaeological Expedition to Dhofar," *Bulletin of the American Schools of Oriental Research* 159 (1960); Frank P. Albright, *The American Archaeological Expedition in Dhofar, Oman, 1952–1953* (Washington, DC: The American Foundation for the Study of Man, 1982); Wendell Phillips, "History and Archaeology of Dhofar," University of Brussels, 1972.

9. Personal communication from Merilyn Phillips Hodgson.

10. For Yemen, see Doe, *Southern Arabia*, 11; de Maigret, *Arabia Felix*, 110–112; Jean-François Breton, *Arabia Felix from the Time of the Queen of Sheba Eighth Century B.C. to First Century A.D.*, trans. Albert LaFarge (Notre Dame, Indiana:

University of Notre Dame Press, 1999), 7. For prehistory in northern Oman, see Doe, *Southern Arabia*, 11; Maurizio Tosi, "The Emerging Picture of Prehistoric Arabia," *Annual Review of Anthropology* 15 (1986): 464–469; Mohammed Al-Belushi, "Managing Oman's Archaeological Resource: Historical Perspectives," *Public Archaeology* 7(3) (2008): 154–155.

11. For prehistory, see J. Pular and B. Jackli, "Some Aceramic Sites in Oman," *Journal of Oman Studies* 4 (1978). For Al-Baleed, see P. M. Costa, "The Study of the City of Zafar (Al-Balid)," *Journal of Oman Studies* 5 (1979). For Islamic monuments, see Paolo M. Costa, *Historic Mosques and Shrines of Oman*, vol. 938, Bar International Series (Oxford: Archaeopress, 2001); Paolo M. Costa and S. Kite, "The Architecture of Salalah and the Dhofar Littoral," *Journal of Oman Studies* 7 (1985); G. Oman, "Preliminary Epigraphic Survey of Islamic Material in Dhofar," *Journal of Oman Studies* 6(2) (1983); G. Oman, "Arabic–Islamic Epigraphy in Dhofar in the Sultanate of Oman," in P. M. Costa and M. Tosi (eds.), *Oman Studies: Papers on the Archaeology and History of Oman*, Serie Orientale Roma (Rome: IsMEO, 1989). For a more thorough discussion of the history of archaeological research in Oman see Al-Belushi, "Managing Oman's Archaeological Resource," 152–155.

12. H. Stewart Edgell, "The Myth of the 'Lost City of the Arabian Sands,'" *Proceedings of the Seminar for Arabian Studies* 34 (2004); Nicholas Clapp, *The Road to Ubar: Finding the Atlantis of the Sands* (Boston, MA: Houghton Mifflin, 1998).

13. R. Fiennes, *Atlantis of the Sands: The Search for the Lost City of Ubar* (London: Signet, 1992); Clapp, *The Road to Ubar*.

14. Ronald G. Blom et al., "Southern Arabian Desert Trade Routes, Frankincense, Myrrh, and the Ubar Legend," in James Wiseman and Farouk El-Baz (eds.), *Remote Sensing in Archaeology* (New York: Springer, 2007).

15. See, for example, John Noble Wilford, "On the Trail from the Sky: Roads Point to a Lost City," *The New York Times*, February 5, 1992. The documentary about the search for Ubar was titled "Lost City of Arabia." It aired as part of the PBS series NOVA on October 8, 1996, see at: https://www.pbs.org/wgbh/nova/ubar/index.html.

16. Edgell, "The Myth of the 'Lost City of the Arabian Sands'", 105.

17. Blom et al., "Southern Arabian Desert Trade Routes, Frankincense, Myrrh, and the Ubar Legend," 86.

18. J. Zarins, *The Land of Incense: Archaeological Work in the Governate of Dhofar, Sultanate of Oman 1990–1995*, ed. Moawiyah Ibrahim, vol. 1, Archaeology and Cultural Heritage Series (Musqat: Sultan Qaboos University Publications, 2001), Acknowledgements.

19. The way that the Land of Frankincense was built and administered is also an example of one of Qaboos' key political strategies in Dhofar: that of working through trusted aides from important Dhofari families. The Director of the Land of Frankincense under Al-Rowas was from the Shanfari family. See Marc Valeri, *Oman: Politics and Society in the Qaboos State* (Oxford: Oxford University Press, 2013), for further discussion of this tactic.

20. Zarins, *The Land of Incense*, 1.

21. *Atlas of Archaeological Survey in Governorate of Dhofar Sultanate of Oman* (Muscat: Office of the Adviser to His Majesty the Sultan for Cultural Affairs, 2013); N. Al-Jahwari, "Long-Term Settlement Patterns in the Southern Oman Peninsula: Quantified Analysis of the Archaeological Evidence," *Adumatu* 29 (2014); Lynne Newton and Juris Zarins, "Preliminary Results of the Dhofar Archaeological Survey," *Proceedings of the Seminar for Arabian Studies* 40 (2010).

22. Alessandra Avanzini (ed.), *A Port in Arabia between Rome and the Indian Ocean (3rd C. BC–5th C. AD) Khor Rori Report 2*, vol. 5, Arabia Antica (Pisa: Univeristà di Pisa, 2008); *Khor Rori Report I*, vol. 1, Arabia Antica (Pisa: Univeristà di Pisa, 2002); Alessandra Avanzani and Alexia Pavan, "Sumhuram, a South Arabian Port," in Alessandra Avanzini (ed.), *Along the Aroma and Spice Routes: The Harbour of Sumhuram, Its Territory and the Trade between the Mediterranean, Arabia, and India* ((Pontedera: MB Vision, Bardecci & Vivaldi, 2011).

23. Juris Zarins, "Aspects of Recent Archaeological Work at Al-Balid (Zafar), Sultanate of Oman," *Proceedings of the Seminar for Arabian Studies* 37 (2007); Lynne Newton and Juris Zarins, *Dhofar through the Ages: An Ecological, Archaeological and Historical Landscape*, The Archaeological Heritage of Oman (Oxford: Archaeopress, 2019).

24. Costa, "The Study of the City of Zafar (Al-Balid)."

25. Michael Jansen (ed.), *Documenting Al-Baleed, Site Atlas 1996–2001* (Aachen: RWTH-Aachen University, 2003).

26. M. Ibrahim and A. al-Tigani, "A Report on Two Seasons of Sultan Qaboos University Excavations at Al-Balid, Dhofar 1996–7," Office of the Adviser to HM the Sultan for Cultural Affairs, Muscat, 1997.

27. Newton and Zarins, *Dhofar through the Ages*; Zarins, "Aspects of Recent Archaeological Work at Al-Balid (Zafar), Sultanate of Oman." Recent excavations at Al-Baleed, conducted by a team based at the University of Arkansas at Little Rock and directed by the author, have begun to fill in quotidian information about the daily life of inhabitants of the city.

28. Michael Jansen, "Foreward and General Introduction (2000)," in Michael Jansen (ed.), *Documenting Al-Baleed, Site Atlas 1996–2001* (Aachen: RWTH-

Aachen University, 2003); Abdul Aziz bin Mohammed al-Rowas, "Foreward," ibid.

29. Gerd Nonneman and Marc Valeri, "The 'Heritage' Boom in the Gulf: Critical and Interdisciplinary Perspectives," *Journal of Arabian Studies* 7(2) (2017); William G. Zimmerle, "From History to Heritage: The Arabian Incense Burner," in Allen James Fromherz (ed.), *The Gulf in World History*, Arabian, Persian and Global Connections (Edinburgh: Edinburgh University Press, 2018).

30. Mohammed Ali Al-Belushi, "Archaeology and Development in the GCC States," *Journal of Arabian Studies* 5(1) (2015).

31. Ghanem al-Shanfari, the Director of the Land of Frankincense sites under Al-Rowas up until 2020, personal communication.

32. As pointed out by Valeri, *Oman: Politics and Society in the Qaboos State,*and other authors, a significant part of Sultan Qaboos' strategy to legitimize and secure his rule was welfare programs, including providing jobs to its citizens.

33. The issue of the diverse constituencies of heritage in Dhofar is too vast an issue to tackle adequately in this chapter. Suffice it to say for the moment that even the concept of "local" constituents is also complex, composed of the various eth-nolinguistic groups indigenous to Dhofar, communities of differing economic status, large numbers of guest workers largely from south Asia, and also Omanis from the north.

34. Here, too, is a situation which requires its own study. While museum-based jobs are considered acceptable professional situations, archaeology seems to be tainted as a less desirable career path for most Omanis for a number of cultural and economic reasons.

35. Valeri, *Oman: Politics and Society in the Qaboos State*, 58–64; Jeremy Jones and Nicholas Ridout, *A History of Modern Oman* (New York: Cambridge University Press, 2015), 132–160.

36. Kaltham Al-Ghanim and Janet C. E. Watson, "Language and Nature in South-ern and Eastern Arabia," *European Journal of Social Sciences* 3(2) (2020); Janet C. E. Watson et al., "Modern South Arabian: Conducting Fieldwork in Dhofar, Mahrah and Eastern Saudi Arabia" (2019); J. E. Peterson, "Oman's Diverse Society: Southern Oman," *Middle East Journal* 58(2) (2004); Miranda Morris, "Dhofar: What Made It Different?" in Brian R. Pridham (ed.), *Oman: Economic, Social and Strategic Development* (London: Croon Helm, 1987).

37. See Valeri's extensive discussion of national identity building under Qaboos. Among other factors he notes the importance of archaeology, especially regard-ing prehistory and medieval trade, as way of asserting a shared Omani heritage

while eliding mention of modern Omani history prior to 1970 (*Oman: Politics and Society in the Qaboos State*, 119–147).

38. Under Sultan Haitham, the Land of Frankincense is beginning a new administrative chapter as it has now been incorporated into the Ministry of Culture and Heritage. Previously, the sites of the Land of Frankincense had been managed more directly through the sultan via the Office of the Adviser to H.M. the Sultan for Cultural Affairs.

References

Al-Belushi, Mohammed, "Managing Oman's Archaeological Resource: Historical Perspectives," *Public Archaeology* 7(3) (2008): 149–173.

Al-Belushi, Mohammed, "Archaeological Legislation in the Sultanate of Oman," *International Journal of Heritage Studies* 20 (2012): 1–18.

Al-Belushi, Mohammed Ali, "Archaeology and Development in the GCC States," *Journal of Arabian Studies* 5(1) (2015): 37–66.

Al-Ghanim, Kaltham and Janet C. E. Watson, "Language and Nature in Southern and Eastern Arabia," *European Journal of Social Sciences* 3(2) (2020): 10–18.

al-Rowas, Abdul Aziz bin Mohammed, "Foreward," in Michael Jansen (ed.), *Documenting Al-Baleed, Site Atlas 1996–2001* (Aachen: RWTH-Aachen University, 2003), vii.

Albright, Frank P., *The American Archaeological Expedition in Dhofar, Oman, 1952–1953* (Washington, DC: The American Foundation for the Study of Man, 1982).

Al-Jahwari, N., "Long-Term Settlement Patterns in the Southern Oman Peninsula: Quantified Analysis of the Archaeological Evidence," *Adumatu* 29 (2014): 7–38.

Atlas of Archaeological Survey in Governorate of Dhofar Sultanate of Oman (Muscat: Office of the Adviser to His Majesty the Sultan for Cultural Affairs, 2013).

Avanzini, Alessandra (ed.), *Khor Rori Report I*, vol. 1, Arabia Antica (Pisa: Univeristà di Pisa, 2002).

Avanzini, Alessandra (ed.), *A Port in Arabia between Rome and the Indian Ocean (3rd C. BC–5th C. AD) Khor Rori Report 2*, vol. 5, Arabia Antica (Pisa: Univeristà di Pisa, 2008).

Avanzani, Alessandra and Alexia Pavan, "Sumhuram, a South Arabian Port," in Alessandra Avanzani (ed.), *Along the Aroma and Spice Routes: The Harbour of Sumhuram, its Territory and the Trade between the Mediterranean, Arabia, and India* (Pontedera: MB Vision, Bardecci & Vivaldi, 2011), 43–56.

Blom, Ronald G., Robert Crippen, Charles Elachi, Nicholas Clapp, George R. Hedges, and Juris Zarins, "Southern Arabian Desert Trade Routes, Frankincense, Myrrh, and the Ubar Legend," in James Wiseman and Farouk El-Baz (eds.), *Remote Sensing in Archaeology* (New York: Springer, 2007), 71–87.

Breton, Jean-François. *Arabia Felix from the Time of the Queen of Sheba Eighth Century B.C. to First Century A.D*, trans. Albert LaFarge (Notre Dame, IN: University of Notre Dame Press, 1999).

Clapp, Nicholas, *The Road to Ubar: Finding the Atlantis of the Sands* (Boston, MA: Houghton Mifflin, 1998).

Cleveland, Ray L., "The 1960 American Archaeological Expedition to Dhofar," *Bulletin of the American Schools of Oriental Research* 159 (1960): 14–26.

Costa, P. M., "The Study of the City of Zafar (Al-Balid)," *Journal of Oman Studies* 5 (1979): 115–150.

Costa, Paolo M., *Historic Mosques and Shrines of Oman*, Bar International Series, vol. 938 (Oxford: Archaeopress, 2001).

Costa, Paolo M. and S. Kite, "The Architecture of Salalah and the Dhofar Littoral," *Journal of Oman Studies* 7 (1985): 131–158.

de Maigret, Alessandro, *Arabia Felix: An Exploration of the Archaeological History of Yemen*, trans. Rebecca Thompson (London: Stacey International, 2002).

Doe, Brian, *Southern Arabia*, New Aspects of Antiquity (London: Thames & Hudson, 1971).

Edgell, H. Stewart, "The Myth of the 'Lost City of the Arabian Sands,'" *Proceedings of the Seminar for Arabian Studies* 34 (2004): 105–120.

Fiennes, R., *Atlantis of the Sands: The Search for the Lost City of Ubar* (London: Signet, 1992).

Groom, Nigel, "Trade, Incense, and Perfume,"in St John Simpson (ed.), *Queen of Sheba: Treasures from Ancient Yemen* (London: The British Museum Press, 2002), 88–94.

Ibrahim, M. and A. al-Tigani, "A Report on Two Seasons of Sultan Qaboos University Excavations at Al-Balid, Dhofar 1996–7," Office of the Adviser to HM the Sultan for Cultural Affairs, Muscat, 1997.

Jansen, Michael (ed.), *Documenting Al-Baleed, Site Atlas 1996–2001* (Aachen: RWTH-Aachen University, 2003).

Jansen, Michael, "Foreward and General Introduction (2000)," in Michael Jansen (ed.), *Documenting Al-Baleed, Site Atlas 1996–2001* (Aachen: RWTH-Aachen University, 2003), ix–x.

Jones, Jeremy and Nicholas Ridout, *A History of Modern Oman* (New York: Cambridge University Press, 2015).

Mackintosh-Smith, Tim, "Scents of Place: Frankincense in Oman," *Saudi Aramco World* (2000): 16–23.

Miller, A. G. and M. Morris, *Plants of Dhofar, the Southern Region of Oman: Traditional, Economic, and Medicinal Uses* (Muscat: The Office of the Adviser for Conservation of the Environment, Diwan of the Royal Court, Sultanate of Oman, 1988).

Morris, Miranda, "Dhofar: What Made it Different?" in Brian R. Pridham (ed.), *Oman: Economic, Social and Strategic Development* (London: Croon Helm, 1987), 51–78.

Newton, Lynne and Juris Zarins, "Preliminary Results of the Dhofar Archaeological Survey," *Proceedings of the Seminar for Arabian Studies* 40 (2010): 247–266.

Newton, Lynne and Juris Zarins, *Dhofar through the Ages: An Ecological, Archaeological and Historical Landscape.*, The Archaeological Heritage of Oman (Oxford: Archaeopress, 2019).

Nonneman, Gerd and Marc Valeri, "The 'Heritage' Boom in the Gulf: Critical and Interdisciplinary Perspectives," *Journal of Arabian Studies* 7(2) (2017): 155–156.

Oman, G., "Preliminary Epigraphic Survey of Islamic Material in Dhofar," *Journal of Oman Studies* 6(2) (1983): 277–289.

Oman, G., "Arabic–Islamic Epigraphy in Dhofar in the Sultanate of Oman," in P. M. Costa and M. Tosi (eds.), *Oman Studies: Papers on the Archaeology and History of Oman*, Serie Orientale Roma (Rome: IsMEO, 1989), 193–198.

Peterson, J. E. . "Oman's Diverse Society: Southern Oman." *Middle East Journal* 58, no. 2 (2004): 254–269.

Phillips, Wendell, "History and Archaeology of Dhofar," University of Brussels, 1972.

Pular, J. and B. Jackli, "Some Aceramic Sites in Oman," *Journal of Oman Studies* 4 (1978): 53–74.

Raffaelli, M., S. Mosti, C. Bellini, and M. Mariotti Lippi, "Dhofar, the Land of Frankincense," in Alessandra Avanzani (ed.), *Along the Aroma and Spice Routes: The Harbour of Sumhuram, its Territory and the Trade between the Mediterranean, Arabia and India* (Pontedera: MB Vision, Bardecci & Vivaldi, 2011), 117–139.

Tosi, Maurizio, "The Emerging Picture of Prehistoric Arabia," *Annual Review of Anthropology* 15 (1986): 461–490.

Valeri, Marc, *Oman: Politics and Society in the Qaboos State* (Oxford: Oxford University Press, 2013).

Watson, Janet C. E., Miranda J. Morris, Abdullah al-Mahri, Munira A. al-Azraqi, Saeed al-Mahri, and Ali al-Mahri, "Modern South Arabian: Conducting Fieldwork in Dhofar, Mahrah and Eastern Saudi Arabia" (2019).

Wilford, John Noble, "On the Trail from the Sky: Roads Point to a Lost City," *The New York Times*, February 5, 1992, 1.

Zarins, J., *The Land of Incense: Archaeological Work in the Governate of Dhofar, Sultanate of Oman 1990–1995*, Archaeology and Cultural Heritage Series, ed. Moawiyah Ibrahim, vol. 1 (Muscat: Sultan Qaboos University Publications, 2001).

Zarins, Juris, "Aspects of Recent Archaeological Work at Al-Balid (Zafar), Sultanate of Oman," *Proceedings of the Seminar for Arabian Studies* 37 (2007): 309–324.

Zimmerle, William G., "From History to Heritage: The Arabian Incense Burner," in Allen James Fromherz (ed.), *The Gulf in World History*, Arabian, Persian and Global Connections (Edinburgh: Edinburgh University Press, 2018), 295–312.

4

THE MULTIPLE LEGACIES OF
SULTAN QABOOS: HERITAGE AND
OMANI NATION-BUILDING

Victoria Penziner Hightower and James Worrall

Slated to open in 2020 and postponed due to the Covid pandemic, the Oman Across the Ages Museum, formerly the Oman Renaissance Museum, represents a culmination of Sultan Qaboos' heritage agenda initiated in 1970.[1] Despite a report on national identity in the Gulf that ignored Oman's heritage achievements, heritage investment held economic and rhetorical significance within Sultan Qaboos' campaign to build Omaniness: the modern sense of being Omani that unfolded over his reign (1970–2020) and attempted to supplant the more local, tribal, ethnic, or religious identities previously present prior to the modern state.[2] Qaboos drew on historic structures, cultural symbols, and narratives about the past to support his broader modernization campaigns in ways that evolved and developed over five decades.

No evaluation of Oman since 1970 can start without discussing the contested role of Sultan Qaboos himself. For some scholars, Qaboos was the fount of legitimacy and authority, an idea reinforced by the 1996 Basic Law in which the Sultan was declared "the symbol of national unity and the guardian of its preservation and protection."[3] Other scholars have taken a less Qaboos-centric approach and recognized additional factors in his decision making.[4] In fact, heritage institutions and programs did not emerge fully formed from the mind of Sultan Qaboos, nor were they entirely independent of his influence. Oman's heritage development reflects Qaboos' broader attitudes and approaches to his sultanic authority in that it was not fully centralized and reflected an evolving vision.

This chapter outlines the development of heritage policy and outcomes over the course of Qaboos' reign by tracing Oman's heritage structures, institutions, and narratives by period. Qaboos used heritage to create a more inclusive, flexible, and unifying Omani identity, one that made space for religious, sectarian, and tribal differences as a bulwark against division and conflict.

His agenda created an authorized heritage discourse (AHD) that acted as a legitimating force for the state. It was not simply about the consolidation of Qaboos' authority, the simple legitimation of his dynasty's rule or naive self-aggrandizement.[5] His Omani AHD reinforced the very idea of being an Omani, celebrating a glorious past while naturalizing a shared present and future.[6] While this goal was identified early in Sultan Qaboos' state-building campaign, its fulfillment reveals a more pragmatic and reactive reality. The best example of acceptance of the AHD and the need to renegotiate its construction occurs in the proliferation of private museums, including Bait al-Zubair, which, until the Omani National Museum opened in 2016, was *the* most preeminent and visited museum in the Sultanate. Many other families have followed a similar trend, creating family–national museums in order to display their own and their region's history as part of the broader Omani national past (see Table 4.1, below). This chapter demonstrates the contingent nature of Oman's heritage program. The development of both public and private initiatives were clearly governed by the vagaries of resources, attention, opportunities, and threats more than any specific vision over the long arc of Qaboos' reign.

Heritagization

Not all history becomes heritage. The process by which practices, structures, and ideas become useful for heritage narratives is called heritagization.[7] Oman is under-represented in the proliferating discussion of Gulf heritage because Oman's heritage was, until recently, not aimed at establishing a global brand along the lines of Dubai or Qatar.[8] This meant that scholars rarely recognized the products or process of heritage development in Oman, and it is only recently that some have begun questioning the global aspirations of Gulf museum narratives, allowing space for heritagization processes like Oman's to be acknowledged.[9]

Oman's interest and investment in heritage, the construction of its institutions and narratives was incremental, starting with select fort restorations and increasing archaeological excavations in the 1970s, accelerating after the 1990s with the expansion of tourism, and experiencing another boost in 2016 following the opening of the Oman Museum and the adoption of the Tanfeedh Initiative on economic diversification which demonstrates how Oman's heritagization process is adaptable, unfolding over the course of Qaboos' reign.[10]

As Qaboos and his government set the heritage agenda, he could draw on Oman's hundreds of forts, castles, towers, and archaeological sites dating back thousands of years, and written documents to produce a rich AHD and "a common Omani ethos."[11] Oman has more standing historic buildings than most countries in the Arab world, and Oman's Ministry of Heritage and Culture maintains the *Dar al-Makhtutat wa al-Watha'iq* (Omani Documents and Manuscripts House) that includes 4,700–5,000 manuscripts dating back centuries.[12] Qaboos had "therefore" a built environment and documentation to draw on as he pieced together a narrative of Omaniness that was timeless, stretching to a distant Omani past and that attempted to include all inhabitants of the contemporary territory under a single national identity.[13] Although some, like anthropologists Amal Sachedina and Mandana Limbert, question this AHD's representativeness, and political economists, like Marc Valeri, criticized it as "cultural engineering," it nonetheless has created a flexible "common grammar" through which Omanis incorporate their voices with increasing frequency in the twenty-first century.[14]

Qaboos and his government used heritage to help construct a deeper Omani identity beyond the royal family and to downplay recent fractiousness.[15] Just as modernization and governing processes responded to complex, contradictory, and dynamic domestic and international pressures, so too did heritage, creating a process of heritagization that, while encouraged by Qaboos, was not always controlled by him.[16]

1970–1980: Building Heritage One Fort at a Time

Upon his accession in 1970, Sultan Qaboos dramatically accelerated the development of infrastructure and the provision of services, especially in education and healthcare. Not far behind these pressing development priorities was investment in heritage. The Omani economy underwent dramatic income changes in the 1970s but spending regularly exceeded income. In 1973, income topped 68.5 million OMR and in 1974, this jumped to 303.2 million OMR with a 23 million OMR and a 9 million OMR budget deficit.[17] The modest investment in heritage restoration reveals Qaboos' recognition that it could support his other priorities, and his measured approach to heritage reflects his financial constraints.

Nonetheless, he invested in fort restoration for a different purpose than his predecessors. While other sultans and sayyids restored forts primarily for defensive purposes, Sultan Said was encouraged by his British advisors to do so late in his reign. Qaboos' initiation of fort restoration supported his broader campaign of renewal that, much later, became known as the Omani Renaissance.[18] Qaboos initiated restorations very early in his reign, and, while politically motivated, they were not meant to garrison troops or overtly pacify the vicinity.[19] Sultan Qaboos identified heritage as significant for reinforcing his broader modernization campaigns. He used speeches to reinforce Oman's deep historical roots in its territory to inculcate through repetition Oman's unity and spread the message through education.[20] He referenced "the heritage of his forefathers, and the civilization they achieved," and later noted, "we are just as keen to hold on to our traditions and our heritage" as to develop the state.[21] These claims had to be reinforced and he and his government used heritage to knit Oman's fractious regions together and achieve broader national goals.

According to a UNESCO report, the Oman Ministry of National Heritage and Culture (MNHC) prioritized investment in three specific restoration projects in the 1970s: one wall, one fort, and one house. They allocated funds to restore the Bahla *sur* (wall), bombarded during the Imamate War, and Jibreen Castle (Qal'a Jibreen) in the interior in recognition of their architectural signifiances and as a political tool to curry favor within a recently rebellious region.[22] They also allocated funds to restore the recently opened Oman Museum in Bait Nadir for its transformation into a national museum to display archaeological artifacts.[23] This report downplays other more quietly restored structures, prioritized by precursors of the MNHC which restored Bait al-Rudaydah in Birkat al-Mouz and Bait Greiza and Rawiyah Fort in Muscat in the 1970s. As Limbert asserts in her anthropology of Bahla, "in

Oman, fort restoration takes precedence over any other type of restoration work."[24] Fort restoration not only formed the basis of Qaboos' attempts to demonstrate the presence of the state throughout the territory, it also served to establish selection criteria for inclusion into the narrative of Omaniness.

Sultan Qaboos also created new institutions that could help manage and provide expertise for heritage projects, but the budget necessitated these be small or outsourced entirely. In 1972, the Oman Historical Association was formed by private Omani and non-Omani citizens with Sultan Qaboos' permission and patronage.[25] The Sultanate also invested in archaeological investigations to demonstrate long-term, significant inhabitation.[26] The prominence of archeological excavation and fort restoration in the first decade of Qaboos' rule is striking. He supported several, pre-existing archeological digs in the Sultanate and funded new ones, many undertaken by foreign archaeological teams.[27] In 1973, he established the Department of Antiquities within the Ministry of Information and Culture (MIC), calling it a "mirror" reflecting Oman's achievements.[28] The MIC became the MNHC in 1975, reflecting an evolving institutionalization and formalization of heritage preservation and investment. Alongside institutionalization, on February 10, 1972, less than six months after gaining UN membership, Oman joined the United Nations Educational, Scientific, and Cultural Organization (UNESCO). A few years later, in 1978, Oman ratified conventions against smuggling and to protect cultural heritage during war.[29]

Despite this institutionalization and the embedding of heritage into Qaboos' rhetorical agenda, Oman's heritage program was plagued with challenges. Qaboos undertook capital investment in heritage, occasionally without accurate estimates or recognition of inflationary forces.[30] Even in the showpiece of Jibreen Castle, "realistic proposals" to restore the site were not implemented due to budgetary considerations.[31] A. G. Walls, the UNESCO observer, noted the government did not have a "well defined and clear image" of the MNHC's function, had insufficient funds to "fulfill even the most basic of duties," and little legislation to provide force to its recommendations.[32] At times, a lack of expertise led to improper restoration, best exemplified by the Omani Museum in Bait Nadir.[33] The UNESCO report criticizes Bait Nadir for being tendered to the lowest bidder who was unsupervised by the MNHC, used mediocre materials and improper techniques such that the cement walls spawled (chipped off), the exterior paint used was unsuitable for a saline climate and thus blistered, and the interior painting was erratic. Further, improper sealing of the bitumen on the roof enabled leaks to damage collections and the timber roof structure. Put more directly, the report explains, "One would expect that any restoration work carried out would be to the highest possible standard to impress and to project a public image the Ministry could be proud of. This has not happened . . . The final product is unsightly and crudely finished."[34] Despite these early challenges, Oman's investment in heritage projects brought about dividends in later decades.

In prioritizing building and fort restoration, the creation of a National Museum, and investment in archaeological investigations in Sohar and Dhofar, Qaboos revealed his intentions to project state power beyond Muscat while also naturalizing Oman's existence through the historical record. His attempts to create an Omani AHD supplemented and supported his broader campaign to use the past to create a sense of unity.

1980s–1990s: Sustaining Heritage Narratives

During the second and third decades of his reign, the Sultan's heritage rhetoric shifted from constructing the Omani AHD to sustaining it through a continued institutionalization in heritage infrastructure. He continued fort restoration, established museums, and reinforced the rhetoric and infrastructure of heritage. Nontheless, Oman was still constrained by finances, rising expectations, and urbanization.

Qaboos responded to rising political pressure by expanding the role of consultative bodies. His meet-the-people tours of the country of the 1970s continued in the 1980s, and were augmented by the creation of a more formal structures for consultation. The *Majlis al-Istishari al-Dawla* (State Consultative Council) was replaced in 1990 by the *Majlis al-Shura* and *Majlis al-Dawla* (State Council) in 1996.[35] Although heritage dropped out of the Fifth Five Year Plan (1996–2000), it was embedded in the Basic Law of 1996 as an important government function.[36] Qaboos' rhetoric further cemented the link between the distant past and glorious future in this period.[37] Heritage explained Omanis' duty "to serve their country by carrying forward what has been achieved in the past,"[38] and "not to desert the traditional professions" of agriculture, fisheries, animal husbandry, and handicrafts.[39] He argued that Oman "has consistently combined this heritage with its modernization," and to underline his point declared 1994 the year of Oman's heritage.[40] This era reveals the evolving nature of the AHD as Qaboos responded to new challenges and opportunities in the Omani heritagization process.

In continuing the institutionalization of heritage, he introduced the National Heritage Protection Law (NHPL) by Royal Decree, 6/1980 which specified the rights and duties of property owners toward significant sites.[41] This law, significantly, established a broad understanding of national heritage as being both the mobile and immobile cultural properties along with criteria for establishing heritage sites based on age and significance.[42] Oman reached a further milestone in 1987 as Bahla Fort was inscribed on the World Heritage list,[43] followed by sites at Bat, al-Khutm, and al-Ayn (1988), the Frankincense Trail (2000), and the ancient site of Qalhat (2018).[44] The inscription of these sites represented a recognition of Oman's significance to world history and culture; for Qaboos, they represented "the contribution made by Omanis throughout the ages in building civilisations [sic] and in interacting with other countries."[45] Additionally, the government invested in a series of museums within and beyond Muscat (see Table 4.1).

Table 4.1 Museums opened by date, place, and funding source

Museum name	Place	Government or private	Opened
National Museum/Heritage and Culture Museum	Muscat	MHC	1974/1988
Omani Museum	Muscat Information City	MIC	1978
Oman Oil and Gas Exhibition Centre	Muscat	PDO	1979/1995
Oman Natural History Museum	Muscat	MHC	1985
Omani Aquarium and Marine Science and Fisheries Centre	Muscat	Government	1986

Museum name	Place	Government or private	Opened
Maritime Museum	Sur	Government	1987
Sultan's Armed Forces Museum Bait al-Falaj Museum	Muscat	Ministry of Defense	1988
Oman Children's Museum	Muscat	MHC	1990
Omani French Museum	Muscat	MHC	1992
Sohar Fort Museum	Sohar	Government	1992/1993
Bait al-Zubair	Muscat	Private	1998
Currency Museum	Muscat	Central Bank of Oman	1998
Planetarium	Muscat	PDO	2000
Al-Saidia School Museum of Education	Muscat	Government	2000, 2016
Old Castle Museum	Al-Kamil WalWafi	Private by Khalfan al-Hashimi	2000
Land of Frankincense Museum	Dhofar	Government	2001
Muscat Gate Museum	Mutrah	Government	2001
Bait al-Safah (Safaah)	al-Hamra	Private by Rashid bin Saif al-Abri	2005
Bait al-Baranda Museum	Muscat	Muscat Governorate	2006
House Museum Adam	Muscat	Private by Latif al-Bulushi	shortly before 2006
Sayyid Faisal bin Ali Museum	Muscat	MHC	2008
Turtles Museum	Ras al-Had	Omran	2008, 2017
Khasab Castle Museum	Musandam	MT	2009
Ghalya's Museum of Modern Art, now Place and People Museum	Muscat/ Mutrah	Private	2011/2013

Museum name	Place	Government or private	Opened
EcOman Centre	Muscat	PDO	2011
Ibna Majan Museum	Sohar	Private	2014
Bidiyah Museum	Bidiyah	Private	Before 2015
Bait al-Ghasham	Al-Shali'li Village in Wadi Maawil	Private	2016
National Museum in Oman	Muscat	Government	2016
Museum of Illusions	Muscat Grand Mall Bushar	Private	2018
Al-Bait al-Gharbi Museum	Qasra near Rustaq	Private by Zakia Al-Lamki	Opened by 2018
Madha Museum	Madha in Musandam	Private with support by MHC	2018
Bait al-Rudaydah	Birkat al-Mouz	MT	2019
Oman Across the Ages Museum	Manah/Nizwa	Royal *Diwan*	Expected 2022
Hila Alazwani's House	Nizwa	Private	n.d.
Mathaf 'Afiyya al-Turathi	Sohar	Private	n.d.
al-Qurya al-Turathiyya Bahla	Bahla	Private	n.d.

Qaboos' heritage agenda also began to expand beyond Oman's borders, capturing local and international imaginations. The 1980 Voyage of Sindbad demonstrated Oman's commitment to an Arab-focused agenda by taking the story from *1001 Arabian Nights* and demonstrating its salience.[46] The ship, the *Sohar*, was later placed in a position of prominence on the roundabout leading to the al-Bustan Palace Hotel and at one end of the broad sweep of the processional way running through Muscat and Mutrah. During the later 1980s, the expeditions to find the lost city of Ubar in the Empty Quarter of Dhofar attracted significant attention, and after its discovery Sultan Qaboos personally sponsored the excavations at Shisr.[47]

To move beyond rhetoric and create the heritage vernacular, the government invested the designation of mundane items as having national significance in a process similar to that seen in other Gulf states. The installation of iconic heritage items on roundabouts, including *dallas* (coffeepots), dhows, *khanjar*s, incense burners, forts, castles, and Qaboos' own visage helped to create "super trademarks" of Omani national identity.[48] The iconic Burj al-Sahwa (Renaissance Tower) commemorates twenty-five years of the Renaissance and features juxtaposed symbols of Oman's past and present.[49] The increasing complexity of National Day celebrations and the addition of the Muscat and Salalah Festivals celebrated and commodified heritage.[50] Building standards encouraged an architectural language meant to echo historic structures.[51] There was a growing Qaboos-ization of iconic structures and buildings, solidifying his role in modernization and as symbol and paterfamilias of the Omani nation and its glorious past.[52] Qaboos' attempts at public heritage displays were aimed at creating a common narrative of heritage. These displays are rarely criticized by Omanis publicly, but Sachedina reports that some of her informants were critical of the secularization or sanitization of heritage objects that divorced them from their social contexts.[53]

A sign of the public's acceptance of the national narrative is how it permeates the private sector and coexists with the public sector. The *Nadi al-Thaqafi al-'Omani* (Oman Heritage Club) was established by citizens in 1983, initially under the Ministry of Development and Education and Children's Issues, moved in 2008 to the Ministry of Heritage and Culture to strengthen cultural ties between Omanis and spread knowledge of Omani culture.[54] Perhaps the most famous private museum in the country is Bait al-Zubair, opened in 1998 to showcase Omani daily life through quotidian objects.[55] It functioned as a national museum despite the existence of two other state-funded institutions that existed for the same purpose (the Bait Nadir/National Museum and Omani Museum). It is Bait al-Zubair's "scale" that makes it approachable, while its responsiveness makes it well visited.[56] It became an important early node within Oman's nascent tourist industry. Sarah White notes that early in the 1990s, Mohammad al-Zubair wanted to display Omani heritage and ethnographic items in the Zubair Corporation headquarters, but after consultation with the museum's experts they realized the "national and global significance" of the collection and transformed his family's former residence into the museum. From this, he was able to create a complex of ultimately five buildings which house artifacts and train Omanis in partnership with Sultan Qaboos University to interpret and act as guides.[57] This museum began as a way to glorify a single family within the history of Oman, but quickly expanded to glorify all of Oman's history. While it demonstrates the power of the AHD as guided by Qaboos, it also reinforces the reality that not all institutions emanated either from him or from his government. Despite accepting the broad outlines of Qaboos' heritage narrative, the establishment of private heritage organizations also reflects a tacit acceptance of space for different narratives under the AHD that had been constructed.

Underlining the contingent nature of heritage development in Oman is the fact that not all initiatives came to fruition. In the 1980s, Qaboos envisioned creating an Oman Cultural Foundation to include archives, a national museum, a theater, and library near the airport to welcome arrivals and impress them with Oman's culture and heritage.[58] Although this did not come to fruition, it seeded success in the twenty-first century with a subsequent clustering of institutions around the airport. This demonstrates the vitality of heritage investment as well as the continued recognition by Qaboos and his government that not all projects could be realized.

The 1980s and 1990s were an important period of consolidation, marked in particular by 1994 as the Year of Heritage. There were significant improvements in the quality, scope, and scale of the investments in heritage. The transfer from immovable castles and forts, to daily objects of personal significance to all Omanis expanded the AHD to encompass most Omanis' experiences. Heritage rhetoric and the Omani AHD was envisioned to act as a counterbalance to development, modernization, and the perceived loss of identity this entailed. However, heritagization in this period was often plagued by constrained resources and fragmented responsibilities which resulted in private initiatives.

The 2000s: The Heritage Business

From the 1970s to the 1990s, Oman's heritage industry focused squarely on Omanis, constructing a legible heritage discourse that was authorized and, for some, representative. In the twenty-first century, the audience shifted as funding bodies for heritage projects diversified to include the Royal *Diwan*, the Ministry of Heritage and Culture, the Ministry of Tourism, and more private citizens. For instance, Petroleum Development Oman (PDO) created Knowledge World and has gifted three museums and attractions: the Oil and Gas Museum (1995), the Planetarium (2000), and, most recently, the EcOman Centre (2011).[59] Heritage institutions and projects ceased to have simply rhetorical value for Omanis or for constructing an Omani AHD, but were harnessed for economic diversification and the projection of a national brand onto the international marketplace. The proliferation of museums (see Table 4.1), public and private, the investment in restoration and marketing are testiments to this shift.

Although the government sporadically encouraged tourism in earlier decades; after 1999 it became a national priority and heritage became an important way to boost it. In his National Day speech in 1999, Qaboos called for tourism to aid economic diversification, just a decade after establishing the Ministry of Tourism and nine after opening the country up to international tourists.[60] In 2011, Oman launched a global awareness campaign to attract tourists.[61] Additionally, with the Ninth Five Year Plan (2016–2020), heritage returned to prominence in national planning through a section titled "Enriching Cultural Life and Promoting the Role of Citizenship and Identity." It envisaged an expansion of the fort restoration program to include more forts and heritage structures throughout the country; the completion of surveys of historic buildings and sites; the protection of urban heritage from development; and "developing and upgrading existing museums to be in line with recent international development in the museum system."[62] In 2007, Royal Decree 60/2007 established the National Records and Archives Authority.[63] Shortly thereafter, Ministerial Decree 23/2008 governing document preservation was issued.[64] Heritage institutions were uniquely poised to enhance the Sultan's agenda, building on the prior attempts to create an AHD, and, as of August 2020, the Ministry of Heritage and Culture had restored eighty-two forts, citadels, walls, and towers in Oman.[65] It also has invested in museums, including, for instance, in Birkat al-Mouz where the MT created a global small-arms museum in the Bayt al-Rudayda, attempting to capitalize on Birkat Al-Mouz's proximity to Nizwa.[66] This era brought Oman's heritage development into line with many other Arab Gulf States that used the past as spectacle.

To achieve these goals, increased institutionalization provided coherence and direction, though Sultan Qaboos kept a sharper eye on some projects. For instance, the establishment of the Sultan Qaboos Higher Center for Culture and Science in 2005 coordinated several institutions, domestic and international, previously under direct control of the *diwan*.[67] Additionally, in 2016, the Tanfeedh Initiative (the National Programme for Enhancing Economic Diversification) under the *Diwan* of the Royal Court, established a tourism strategy creating fourteen tourism clusters throughout Oman with the first being Muscat, the Frankincense trail, coastal Musandam, Dakhiliya forts and villages, and Sharqiya.[68] These laws and initiatives represent the continuing consolidation of key bureaucratic and institutional structures for the promotion and management of heritage in the Sultanate.

Reorganizations expanded the Directorate of Tourism's role in heritage. The initial tourism slogan "Oman—the Essence of Arabia" demonstrates the success of Qaboos' quest to create an AHD that is useful for Omanis, rooted in ideas of authenticity and which could contribute to the international image of the Sultanate.[69] In 2010, the tourism slogan shifted to "Beauty has an address" to expand the audience of Oman's tourist campaigns. This campaign was aimed specifically at attracting tourists from the "Sultanate's key source markets," including India, the United Kingdom, Germany, France, the Netherlands, Belgium, the UAE and Australia.[70] By 2014, the by then-Ministry of Tourism (MT) directly operated over fifty forts, castles, and museums.[71] Moreover, after 2016, the Tanfeedh Initiative brought development and implementation beyond the government even further. "Tanfeedh labs" brought 160 organizations, public and private, along with private citizens together to work "on identifying and examining obstacles and limitations and try to overcome the challenges by making the necessary amendments to laws and regulations, prioritizing goals, providing funding for projects, agree on the assigned tasks, responsibilities and timeframes, and prepare detailed roadmaps to achieve the goals of the Ninth Five Year Development Plan."[72] The ultimate recognition of the intertwining of heritage and culture with tourism came in 2020 with the formation of the Ministry of Heritage and Tourism.

Building on the campaign from the 1980s to recognize the heritage significance of mundane objects, Qaboos led attempts to formalize recognition for intangible heritage within and beyond the Sultanate.[73] In 2005, Oman signed the UNESCO convention protecting intangible heritage inscribing ten music, food, dances, pastimes, and practices on it, building on the engagement with UNESCO in the 1970s.[74] In 2007, Oman signed the 2005 UNESCO International Fund for Cultural Diversity, instituting several conferences and initiatives aimed at recognizing and promoting cultural diversity.[75] In 2017, the MHC published an *Omani Encyclopedia*, cataloging Omani heritage elements.

In the last decade of Qaboos' reign, Oman established itself as a leading facilitator of international dialogue on heritage issues, the 2015 Salalah Recommendation on Archeological Parks Sites and the 2017 Muscat Declaration on Tourism and Culture being particularly important signifiers of the Sultanate's growing international role in heritage governance. In line with Tanfeedh's notion of clusters, in 2019, Oman hosted a four-day "International Workshop of the Practical Management of the Salalah Guidelines for the Management of Public Archaeological Sites," in Nizwa. Commenting on the workshop's location, Nasser bin Said al-Jahwari noted that it was "in order to allow everyone to see and experience the Salut site, and to also gain an appreciation of how UNESCO status, infrastructure, facilities, and the tourism and hospitality sectors can all be brought together to benefit local communities."[76]

Further enhancing Oman's international stature are its spectacular museums. The Oman National Museum opened in 2016, and positions itself as inheritor to the 1970s national museum. It has fourteen galleries which emphasize the territoriality of Oman historically and the diversity of Omani society today, including a room with replicas of the country's major forts by region, various clothing displays, and an intangible heritage gallery.[77] Beyond this, it has further galleries that convey Oman's enduring connection to the world and to its recent and distant past.

Additionally, the as-yet-unopened Oman Across the Ages Museum (formerly the Oman Renaissance Museum) is a truely spectacular museum in the Arab Gulf model. Funded by the Royal *Diwan* with exhibits curated by the U.K. curatorial firm BarkerLangham, this museum's purpose was to reinforce the AHD constructed by Qaboos. H.E. Jamal al-Moosawi, Secretary-General of the National Museum explained the two museums' purposes: "while the experience a visitor gets from Oman's National Museum is based on original artefacts, along with other supporting digital interactive elements, Oman Across Ages Museum will be a high-tech monument aimed mainly at attracting the youth."[78] The spectacularization of Omani heritage marks a new chapter in Oman's heritage agenda while also acting as a continuation of Oman's particular style of heritagization, focusing on education and an AHD that emphasizes the importance of the state. By focusing on the youth, who have little personal frame of reference for the 1970s, this museum is aimed at shaping their understandings of the state's role in their lives, which seems particularly salient in light of the periodic protests and criticism that have emerged since 2011.[79]

This heritage agenda is not without criticism. Some have claimed that the expansion of heritage institutions in the twenty-first century was chaotic and occasionally destructive.[80] The 2011 renovation plans for Port Sultan Qaboos created an aesthetic that some considered inauthentic and disconnected from the Omani past.[81] Causevic and Neal noted versions of history presented to tourists are explained through a recitation of chronology rather than through an exploration of the richness of narratives associated with the site.[82] Sachedina criticizes the AHD constructed by Qaboos and the Omani government as creating a "regime of historicity" that divorced Omanis' lived experiences from the versions presented to tourists.[83]

It is not only to tourists or academics that these structures can appear to be divorced from human experience. As Abdul Sheriff has noted in Stone Town in Zanzibar, heritagization often dehumanizes a place, by presenting a pristine, sanitized experience that focuses on the non-human elements of a space, including its architecture, aesthetics, and spatialization.[84] In Limbert's visit to Jibreen Castle with Omani friends, she recalled how some of her older Omani friends found the building's restoration hollow because it did not have the sounds of a household that they remembered. The younger Omanis accompanying her, however, accepted this structural presentation as a true representation of heritage, having no memory of Jibreen as a functioning home and administrative center.[85]

Often criticisms leveled at heritage development in this era raise the question, who is visiting?[86] In official fort visitation statistics, Omani visitors increased between 2009 and 2018 from 51,000 to 71,000 visitors per year, suggesting that there is a market for Omani domestic heritage tourism.[87]

But questions of accessibility and interest remain.[88] Hassan al-Shukaili noted that increasing entertainment options are competing with museum-going, so the Tanfeedh Initiative's attempts to package cultural tourism with broader entertainment experiences could appeal to both Omani and non-Omani visitors and reveals a shift within the Omani government to serve both Omanis and tourists.

Despite its pervasiveness, the AHD in Oman is not stiflingly exclusive. Limbert notes that the restoration of Bahla Fort created an opportunity for the local community to showcase its own past.[89] In Khasab Castle (Qal'a Khasab) the MT coordinated with the Khasab branch of the Omani Women's Association to establish a museum and a gift shop that displayed locally made crafts. The project pumped 25 percent of its 600,000 OMR budget into the local community, employed largely local artisans, included training programs for local Omanis, and is partly run by the Omani Woman's Association today.[90]

As tourism gained momentum and broader space opened for non-governmental heritage investment, more families began to insert themselves into the heritage narrative by creating private, family museums, building on the success of Bait al-Zubair. For instance, Bait al-Safah (Hamra), Ibna Majan (Sohar), Hila Alawani House (Nizwa), the Qusra Museum (Rustaq), and the Bidiya Museum (Bidiya). Karen Exell and Matthew MacLean have examined the role of private collections in the complementary construction of national identity.[91] As happens in their examples from Doha and Dibba, these museums demonstrate the families' desires to be incorporated into the narrative of the Omani past and to show *their* distinct history to visitors, thereby humanizing the experience for visitors, revealing an alternative presentation of the Omani past, and one that harmonizes with the existing AHD. These museums reveal both the power of the AHD as constructed by Sultan Qaboos, and its flexibility. For instance, the Bait al-Safah Museum in Hamra emphasizes Hamra's deep role in Oman's past with only the scarcest reference to the modern Omani narrative.

In the twenty-first century, heritage became an important element of economic diversification, resulting in a higher degree of investment and institutionalization at the governmental level. There has certainly been a dramatic increase in visitors. In 1999, Oman's forts and castles received 206,588 visitors, by 2019 they received 426,505 visitors. Museum visits doubled from

198,000 visitors in 2012 to 408,040 in 2019.[92] The funding of heritage institutions by private interests or through public–private partnerships, as well as their location beyond the capital, in areas which historically were hostile to Muscat, suggests a tolerance, within limits, for variations on the main AHD theme.[93] For Sultan Qaboos, the twenty-first century was a period in which the vision he constructed expanded and proved enduring, but also began to face greater challenges to its voracity and its organization.

Conclusion: Omani Heritage after Qaboos

As Oman struggles in the twenty-first century to fully acknowledge and incorporate its diverse populations, heritage institutions and their multivocality provide a way to both reinforce state authority and allow for public representation.[94] This is already happening to a small degree in the Oman National Museum where the country's forts are displayed with an account of their histories and displays of Omani national dress incorporate versions of Swahili fashion, reflecting limited acceptance of diversity in the AHD. Further, the Tanfeedh Initiative nodes have the potential to create opportunities for other families and communities to tell their own stories as we are already seeing in the establishment of private, family museums, which could undoubtedly address elements of the families' lived experiences.

There is much work yet to be done to assess the depth to which Omaniness is felt by citizens, understood by visitors, and how the role of private museums affects the feeling and experience of a homogeneous Omani identity. A true test of the strength of the Sultanate's AHD will come as families begin to display experiences within living memory that are currently excluded from public, open discussion except in patterned and superficial ways. For instance, the Sultan's Armed Forces Museum is one of the few to partially tackle, or even acknowledge, the mid-twentieth-century conflicts, such as the Imamate Rebellion or Dhofar War. As time passes, these more sensitive episodes in the Omani recent past will open for discussion.

Oman's heritagization process might look different from its neighbors in the Arab Gulf, but it nonetheless follows similar purpose: creating an Omani national identity, one that can be embraced by all Omanis and one that emphasizes and legitimates the current state and its rulers. It unfolded incrementally and, while there was a goal of using heritage to create unity, the plan was constantly mediated by Qaboos' and his government's priorities and resources. Yet there are clear consistencies: the increasing institutionalization of heritage administration, the quest for international recognition, the expanded funding for the projects, and the tolerance for private initiatives.

Oman's and Qaboos' attitude toward heritage and its utility for Oman shifted over the course of Qaboos' rule. In the 1970s, the Sultan's speeches were peppered with specific references to heritage in order to create that shared national consciousness through the construction of an AHD that posited all Omani citizens as being part of an eternal and glorious Omani nation. These references fell out of favor in the 1990s, but returned in the 2000s with the linking of heritage to tourism. The available evidence suggests that Qaboos set an agenda and occasionally took a personal interest in particular projects. Our assessment of Qaboos' heritage agenda challenges the image of Qaboos as omnipotent Sultan. The increasing institutionalization and bureaucratization created layers of distance between Qaboos and the projects undertaken in his name. Although he might have been the instigator of projects and the visionary for the ideals of Omaniness, he was far from the sole controller of all aspects of this agenda. Further assessment would shed further light on his degree of influence in his personal role in constructing the AHD and direction of heritage institutions to this end.

The strength of the wider national narrative does not preclude its evolution; indeed, the spectacular projects have already shown a considerable shift in the country's strategy as these came to fruition late in his reign. Qaboos envisioned a narrative of the Omani past that naturalized and institutionalized Omaniness spatially within the territory of Oman, its government structure, legal code, and people's daily lives, constructing a notion of Omani identity that many could embrace. As the Sultanate moves into the post-Qaboos era it does so with clear legacies but ones which must continue to adapt to the range of challenges the nation faces, balancing the pressures of tourism and representation, while maintaining a unifying national narrative.

Notes

1. Samuel Kutty, "Oman Across the Ages Museum: A Cultural and Educational Hallmark," *The Oman Observer*, May 1, 2021, see at: https://www.omanobserver.om/article/8407/Main/oman-across-ages-museum-a-cultural-educational-hallmark, last accessed May 1, 2021.

2. Kristin Smith Diwan (ed.), "AGSIW Workshop Report: Gulf Societies in Transition: National Identity and National Projects in the Gulf States," Arab Gulf States Institute in Washington, June 10, 2016, available at: https://agsiw.org/wp-content/uploads/2016/06/National-Identity_Web-1.pdf, last accessed February 12, 2021; Marc Valeri, *Oman: Politics and Society in the Qaboos State* (London: Hurst, 2013), 5.

3. Basic Law Article 41; Valeri, *Politics and Society*, 5; Michael Herb, *All in the Family: Absolutism, Revolution and Democracy in the Middle Eastern Monarchies* (Albany, NY: State University of New York Press, 1999), 145.

4. miriam cooke's work did not address Oman because it fundamentally did not fit with her understanding of tribalism. Nonetheless, her idea that "tribal is not the traditional and certainly not the primitive" can be useful in the Omani context because the traditional is the modern and does not represent any notion of primitivity. miriam cooke, *Tribal Modern: Branding New Nations in the Arab Gulf* (Oakland, CA: University of California Press, 2014).

5. Laurajane Smith, *The Uses of Heritage* (Abingdon: Routledge, 2006), 3, 12–42; Valeri, *Politics and Society*.

6. Smith, *The Uses of Heritage*, 3, 12–42.

7. Walsh argues that heritagization is a process that creates acceptable heritage narratives that are national that take into account regional idiosyncrasies, but result in a "denying the uniqueness" of local histories because of the sanitization, beautification, and commodification of heritage. Poria and Ashworth suggest that heritage resources aim "to legitimize a specific social reality" and that "*Heritagization* is a process in which heritage is used as a resource to achieve certain social goals," among them creating solidarity by highlighting differences to "legitimize a certain social order." They define heritagization as a way of using the past to educate the present. Schnepel suggests that heritagization is prone to contestation because of the politics of cultural heritage and that both remembering and forgetting plays "a vital role" in "strategies of identification, providing legitimacy and meaning to the present, as well as direction and goals for the future." Kevin Walsh, *The Representation of the Past: Museums and Heritage in the Post-Modern World* (London: Routledge, 1992), 135–139; Yaniv Poria and Gregory Ashworth, "Heritage Tourism: Current Resource for Conflict," *Annals of Tourism Research* 36(3) (2009): 522–525; Burkhard Schnepel, "Travelling Pasts: An Introduction," in Burkhard Schnepel and Tansen Sen (eds.), *Travelling Pasts: The Politics of Cultural Heritage in the Indian Ocean World* (Leiden: Brill, 2021), 3–4.

8. National Museum of Saudi Arabia (1998); Museum of Islamic Art (2008); King Abdulaziz Center for World Culture (2017); Louvre Abu Dhabi (2017); National

Museum of Qatar (2019). Expected/planned museums include Zayed National Museum (2025) and Dubai's Museum of the Future (2022). Pamela Erskine-Loftus (ed.), *Reimagining Museums: Practice in the Arabian Peninsula* (Edinburgh/Boston: MuseumsEtc, 2013); Karen Exell and Trinidad Rico (eds.), *Cultural Heritage in the Arabian Peninsula: Debates, Discourses and Practices* (Burlington, VT: Ashgate, 2014); Karen Exell and Sarina Wakefield (eds.), *Museums in Arabia: Transnational Practices and Regional Processes* (Abingdon: Routledge, 2014); Pamela Erskine-Loftus, Victoria Penziner Hightower and Mariam al-Mulla (eds.), *Representing the Nation: Heritage, Museums, National Narratives and Identity in the Arab Gulf States* (Abingdon: Routledge, 2016); Sarina Wakefield, *Cultural Heritage, Transnational Narratives and Museum Franchising in Abu Dhabi* (Abingdon: Routledge, 2020); Jean Nouvel, "The Flying Saucers Have Landed: Qatar's Thrilling New Supersized Museum," *The Guardian*, available at: https://www.theguardian.com/artanddesign/2019/mar/27/flying-saucers-have-landed-qatar-supersized-national-museum, last accessed February 12, 2021.

9. Sarah Kneebone, "Engaging Visitors, Without an Attraction!," 346–391; Sarah White. "The Relationship between Museum Architecture, Exhibits and Audience, 392–431; Marcia Dorr, Abdullah ibn Salem al-Zahli, Aisha bint Abdullah al-Thanawi, and Sif bin Khamis al-Rawahi, "Khasab Castle: A Museum for the Material Culture of the Musandam Peninsula in the Sultanate of Oman," 284–321, all articles in Pamela Erskine-Loftus (ed.), *Reimagining Museums: Practice in the Arabian Peninsula* (Edinburgh/Boston: MuseumsEtc, 2013); Amal Sachedina's work on religious heritage, "Transfiguring Islam, Ethics and Politics Through Museum Practices to Forge the Sultanate of Oman," in Sarina Wakefield (ed.), *Museums of the Arabian Peninsula: Historical Developments and Contemporary Discourses* (Abingdon: Routledge, 2021), 47–64; Pamela Erskine-Loftus, "Does it Matter if Museum Practices are Thought of as 'Global'?" in Sarina Wakefield (ed.), *Museums of the Arabian Peninsula: Historical Developments and Contemporary Practices* (Abingdon: Routledge, 2021), 209–223.

10. This has echoes in other processes such as decentralization efforts, see James Worrall, "Power and Process: Decentralisation in Oman," Program on Governance and Local Development (GLD), Working Paper No. 32 (July 2020), 20.

11. Uzi Rabi, *Tribes and States in a Changing Middle East* (London: Hurst, 2016), 86.

12. "'Ardh Mara'" Oman Ministry of Heritage and Culture, 2013, available at: https://manuscripts.mhc.gov.om/ar/%d8%b9%d8%b1%d8%b6-%d9%85%d8%b1%d8%a6%d9%8a/, last accessed February 12, 2021.

13. Valeri, *Politics and Society*, 28, 119–120; Aasem al-Sheedi, "Kayf bana al-Sultan Qaboos dawla wa Azinat bayn al-Asala wa al-Ma'asira" ("How did Sultan Qaboos Build the State and Balance between Authenticity and Contemporaneity"), *Oman Daily*, January 20, 2020, available at: https://www.omandaily.om/?p=760669, last accessed February 12, 2021.

14. Amal Sachedina, "Of Living Traces and Revived Legacies: Unfolding Futures in the Sultanate of Oman," PhD dissertation, University of California, Berkeley, 2013, 7–8; Valeri, *Politics and Society*, 132.

15. Herb, *All in the Family*; Mohammed Ali K. Al-Belushi, "Managing Oman's Archaeological Resource: Historical Perspectives," *Public Archaeology* 7(3) (2008): 153–154; Mohammed Ali K. Al-Belushi, "Archaeology and Development in the GCC States," *Journal of Arabian Studies* 5(1) (2015): 42–43; Roby Barrett, *Oman: The Present in the Context of a Fractured Past* (Tampa, FL: Joint Special Operations University, 2011); Karen Exell and Trinidad Rico, "'There Is No Heritage in Qatar': Orientalism, Colonialism, and Other Problematic Histories," *World Archaeology* 45(4) (2013): 671.

16. Dawn Chatty, "Rituals of Royalty and the Elaboration of Ceremony in Oman: View from the Edge," *International Journal of Middle East Studies* 41(1) (2009): 39, 52, 53; Jeremy Jones and Nicholas Ridout, *A History of Modern Oman* (Cambridge: Cambridge University Press, 2015).

17. John Townsend, *Oman: The Making of a Modern State* (London: Croon Helm, 1977), 149–151.

18. Letter from W. N. Monteith, British Consul General, Muscat, to A. T. Lamb, Bahrain, April 24, 1960, FO 371/149018, 91; Letter from E. A. W. Bullock, Foreign Office, to B. R. Pridham, Esq. Muscat, May 9, 1960, FO 371/149018, 93; Mandana Limbert, *In the Time of Oil: Piety, Memory and Social Life in an Omani Town* (Stanford, CA: Stanford University Press, 2010), 23; Townsend, *Oman*, 122–152.

19. Limbert, *In the Time of Oil*, 23.

20. "Speech of His Majesty on the Occasion on the 7th National Day," November 18, 1977, in *The Royal Speeches of His Majesty Sultan Qaboos bin Said, 1970– 2010* (Muscat: Ministry of Information, 2010), 78.

21. "Speech of His Majesty on the Occasion of the 4th National Day," November 18, 1974, 35; "Speech of His Majesty to the People," November 26, 1975, 54.

22. Before being bombarded, Bahla Fort and its wall were among the most complete fort and town wall complexes in Oman. Jibreen Castle included some of the more unique architecture features found in Oman, and by the 1970s

was recently enough inhabited to be investigated and used for future restorations throughout the country. A. G. Walls, "Preservation of Monuments and Sites: Report Prepared for the Government of the Sultanate of Oman" (Paris: UNESCO, 1978), 5.

23. The Ministry of Heritage and Culture has undergone a number of name changes since 1970: Ministry of Oman Heritage (1975); Ministry of Information and Culture (1975); Ministry of National Heritage and Culture (1976); Ministry of Heritage and Culture (2002); Ministry of Heritage and Tourism (2020). "Qaboos Speech, November 26, 1975," 54.

24. Limbert, *In the Time of Oil*, 21–23, 27; Walls, "Preservation of Monuments and Sites," 5.

25. Al-Belushi, "Managing Oman's Archaeological Resource," 153–154; Tridwip K. Das, "The Future's in the Past: The Historical Association of Oman Resuscitated with Appointment of New Chairman," *Muscat Daily*, December 30, 2020, available at: https://www.pressreader.com/oman/muscat-daily/20201230/282157883863978, last accessed February 12, 2021.

26. Al-Belushi, "Managing Oman's Archaeological Resource," 153–154; Al-Belushi, "Archaeology and Development in the GCC States," 42–43.

27. Letter from Monteith to Lamb, April 24, 1960, FO 371/149018, 91; Letter from Bullock to Pridham, May 9, 1960, FO 371/149018, 93; Mohammed Ali K. Al-Belushi, "Oman's Archaeological Resource," 155; Al-Belushi, "Archaeological Legislation in the Sultanate of Oman," *International Journal of Heritage Studies* 20(1) (2014): 50; Lynne S. Newton and Juris Zarins, "Preliminary Results of the Dhofar Archaeological Survey," *Proceedings of the Seminar for Arabian Studies* 40 (2010): 248; Andrew Williamson, "Harvard Archeological Survey in Oman, 1973: III—Sohar and the Sea Trade of Oman in the Tenth Century A.D.," *Proceedings of the Seminar for Arabian Studies* 4 (1974): 78–96; Al-Belushi, "Managing Oman's Archaeological Resource," 149, 152–154.

28. Al-Belushi, "Managing Oman's Archaeological Resource," 155; Al-Belushi, "Archaeological Legislation," 50; "Speech of His Majesty to the People," November 26, 1975, 55–56.

29. Alessandr Gugolz, "The Protection of Cultural Heritage in the Sultanate of Oman," *International Journal of Cultural Property* 5(2) (2007): 291.

30. Ronald Lewcock, "Three Problems in Conservation: Egypt, Oman and Yemen," in R. Holod (ed.), *Conservation as Cultural Survival* (Philadelphia, PA: Aga Khan Award for Architecture, 1980), 66–68; Dale F. Eickelman, "Kings and People: Oman's State Consultative Council," *Middle East Journal* 38(1) (1984): 55; Townsend, *Oman*, 149–151.

31. Walls, "Preservation of Monuments and Sites," p.4.
32. Ibid., 1.
33. Ibid., 33–34.
34. Ibid., 5, 33.
35. Jones and Ridout, *History of Modern Oman*, 48–51; Eickelman, "Kings and People," 51–71.
36. Ministry of National Economy, "Fifth Five Year Plan," 1996–2000, available at: http://extwprlegs1.fao.org/docs/pdf/oma151055.pdf, last accessed February 12, 2021; Royal Decree No. 101/96 Promulgating the Basic Statute of the State, available at: https://mjla.gov.om/eng/basicstatute.aspx, last accessed February 12, 2021] Valeri, *Politics and Society*, 149.
37. "Speech of His Majesty on the Occasion of the 16th National Day," November 18, 1986, 185
38. "Speech of His Majesty at the Opening Ceremony of the Sultan Qaboos University," November 18, 1986, 180.
39. "Speech of His Majesty on the Occasion of the 16th National Day," November 18, 1986, 185
40. "Speech of His Majesty on the Occasion of the 23 National Day," November 18, 1993, 301
41. Al-Belushi, "Archaeological Legislation," 38.
42. Al-Belushi, "Archaeological Legislation," 38–39; Al-Belushi, "Managing Oman's Archaeological Resource," 158; Yaqoub Salim Al-Busaidi, "The Protection and Management of Historic Monuments in the Sultanate of Oman: The Historic Buildings of Oman," *Proceedings of the Seminar for Arabian Studies* 34 (2004): 35–44 at 35–36.
43. "Bahla Fort," UNESCO, available at: http://whc.unesco.org/en/list/433, last accessed February 12, 2021.
44. The Arabian Oryx Sanctuary was inscribed (1994) and delisted (2007) for the reduction in its size. "Oman," UNESCO World Heritage Convention, available at: http://whc.unesco.org/en/statesparties/om, last accessed February 12, 2021; "Arabian Oryx Sanctuary," UNESCO World Heritage Convention, available at: http://whc.unesco.org/en/list/654, last accessed February 12, 2021.
45. "Speech of His Majesty to the 33rd Session of the General Conference of UNESCO," October 4, 2005, 479.
46. Tim Severin, *The Voyage of Sinbad* (London: Hutchinson, 1982).
47. Nicholas Clapp, *The Road to Ubar: Finding the Atlantis of the Sands* (Boston, MA: Houghton Mifflin, 1998); Ranulph Fiennes, *Atlantis of the Sands* (London: Bloomsbury, 1992).

48. Michael E. Geisler, "Introduction: What are National Symbols: and What Do They Do For Us?" in Michael E. Geisler (ed.), *National Symbols, Fractured Identities: Contesting the National Narrative* (Middlebury, VT: Middlebury College Press, 2005), xvii.

49. Sachedina, "Of Living Traces," 5; Marc Valeri, "State-Building, Liberalization from Above and Legitimacy in the Sultanate of Oman," in Oliver Schlumberger (ed.), *Debating Arab Authoritarianism: Dynamics and Durability in Nondemocratic Regimes* (Stanford, CA: Stanford University Press, 2007), 145.

50. Anne K. Rasmussen, "The Musical Design of National Space and Time in Oman," *The World of Music* 1(2) (2012): 63–96.

51. Soheir M. Hegazy, "The Omani Architectural Heritage: Identity and Continuity," *Heritage and Sustainable Development* 2: 1341–1451, available at: https://www.cpas-egypt.com/pdf/Sohair_Mohamed_Hegazy/Researches/04-The%20Omani%20Architectural%20Heritage%20-Identity%20and%20Continuity.pdf, last accessed February 12, 2021; Soheir M. Hegazy, "Cultural Sustainability between Traditional and Contemporary Omani Residences: A Comparative Case Study," *European Journal of Sustainable Development* 42 (2015): 185–194.

52. J. E. Petersen, "The Emergence of Post Traditional Oman, 10, available at: http://www.jepeterson.net/sitebuildercontent/sitebuilderfiles/Emergence_of_Post-Traditional_Oman.pdf, last accessed February 12, 2021; Eickelman, "Kings and People," 51.

53. Sachedina, "Of Living Traces," 7; Amal Sachedina, "The Politics of the Coffee Pot: Its Changing Role in History-making and the Place of Religion in the Sultanate of Oman," *History and Anthropology* 30(3) (2019): 233–255.

54. Oman Cultural Club, Home Page, 2021, available at: https://culturalclub.org/?page_id=29, last accessed February 12, 2021.

55. "Founder Message," *Bait al-Zubair*, 2019, available at: https://www.baital-zubair.com/bait-al-zubair-2/founder-message, last accessed February 12, 2021.

56. Hassan al-Shukaili, "The Perception of Locals Toward Museums sector in Sultanate of Oman," MA thesis, Newcastle University, 2017, 47–54; White, "The Relationship between Museum Architecture, Exhibits and Audience,",422.

57. White, "The Relationship between Museum Architecture, Exhibits and Audience," 398.

58. *The National Museum, Sultanate of Oman: The Building and Collections* (London: Scala Arts & Heritage Publishers, 2019), 22.

59. "Home," *Knowledge World*, 2017, available at: https://www.pdo.co.om/knowledgeworld/pages/default.aspx, last accessed June 3, 2021.

60. "Speech of His Majesty on the Occasion of the 29th National Day," November 18, 1999, 402; Mohamed Berianne, *Tourism, Culture and Development in the Arab Region: Support Culture to Develop Tourism, Developing Tourism to Support Culture* (Paris: UNESCO, 1999), 15.

61. Ministry of Tourism, "Marketing," *Oman Tourism*, 2016, available at: https://www.omantourism.gov.om/wps/portal/mot/tourism/oman/home/ministry/about/marketing/!ut/p/a0/04_Sj9CPykssy0xPLMnMz0vMAfGjzOItvc1dg-40MzAz8fZzMDTyDQz0Mg92djC1czfULsh0VAXHoBBU!, last accessed May 25, 2021.

62. Sultanate of Oman, Ninth Five Year Plan, 2016–2020, 70

63. National Records and Archives Authority Oman, "Home Page," 2021, available at: https://www.oman.om/wps/wcm/connect/en/site/home/gov/gov1/gov5governmentorganizations/nraa/nraa, last accessed February 12, 2021.

64. Law of Documents, available at: https://nraa.gov.om/my_uploads/2018/09/al-laiha-al-tanfethia-lqanon-al-wathaiq.pdf, and its amendment, https://nraa.gov.om/my_uploads/2018/09/62-2008-tadel-qanon-al-wathaiq.pdf, last accessed February 12, 2021.

65. "Oman: Restoring Ancient Sites for Generations to Come," *The Nation Press Arab American News Network*, August 4, 2020, available at: https://thenationpress.net/en/news-60350.html, last accessed May 16, 2021.

66. Historic Arms, Exhibitions, and Forts, LLC, "Company History," available at: https://haefoman.com/company-history, last accessed February 12, 2021; "Heritage Weapons Museum to Open in Birkat al-Mouz," *Muscat Daily*, March 31, 2019, available at: https://www.pressreader.com/oman/muscat-daily/20190331/281496457641977, last accessed February 12, 2021.

67. Sultan Qaboos Higher Center for Culture and Science, "Home Page," 2021, available at: https://sqhccs.gov.om, last accessed February 12, 2021.

68. The National Programme for Enhancing Economic Diversification (TAN-FEEDH), "TANFEEDH Handbook," July 2017, available at: https://www.scp.gov.om/PDF/TANFEEDH%20HAND%20BOOK%202017English.pdf; Oxford Business Group, "Oman Launches a 25-Year Tourism Strategy," *The Report: Oman 2017*, available at: https://oxfordbusinessgroup.com/analysis/framing-narrative-government-has-launched-25-year-strategy-sector?fbclid=IwAR2DcYVahxQOMYWDToP6pWKHHgVRwbQmWdsZIHod-xabzxlJkThSU-rU7Uh0; Oxford Business Group, "Development Efforts Focus on 14 Tourism Clusters in Oman," *The Report: Oman 2017*, available at: https://oxfordbusiness-group.com/analysis/key-growth-areas-development-efforts-focus-14-tourism-cluster, all last accessed February 12, 2021.

69. Onn Winkler, "The Birth of Oman's Tourism Industry," *Tourism: An International Interdisciplinary Journal* 55(2) (2007): 229, available at: https://hrcak.srce.hr/24640, last accessed May 15, 2021.

70. "Beauty Has An Address, Video Advertising Campaign by Oman Ministry of Tourism," *Jepretgrafer*, November 18, 2013, available at: https://jepretgrafer.com/2013/11/18/beauty-has-an-address-video-advertising-campaign-by-oman-ministry-of-tourism, last accessed June 3, 2021.

71. Al-Belushi, "Archaeology and Development in the GCC States," 55.

72. "The National Programme for Enhancing Economic Diversification (Tanfeedh)," *Omanuna: The Official Oman eGovernment Services Portal* (2019), available at: https://omanportal.gov.om/wps/portal/index/interact/tanfeedh/!ut/p/a1/hc9Nb4JAEAbg3-KBKzO7UKK9jVrrgobg-oF7MdisqwZZgyj9-aLxYtLq3N7J8yYzoCAFVWSXncmqnS2y_JZVsIoTFrBhjFF7nnwhTUgmxD-hH9BuwbAD-M4Tv-lIXsAB1ZzKMulL4HOOBZChIDHs9mnI2Cx7Aw2_EuCPG0XRMyL35IOyMAq_f9x_gxR0hKJPb9f2nJRVrr21AlXqjS12657JZ-b6vqePp00MG6rl1jrcm1-2MPDv5V2dpTBemzhOMh_RX7j_wyotYVxt-kRFA!!/dl5/d5/L0lKQSEvUUt3SS80RUkhL2Vu, last accessed June 3, 2021.

73. "Speech of His Majesty to the 33rd Session of the General Conference of UNESCO," October 4, 2005, 479.

74. Patrick Boylan, "The Intangible Heritage: A Challenge and an Opportunity for Museums and Museum Professional Training," *International Journal of Intangible Heritage* 1 (2006): 64; Oman: Elements on the Lists, UNESCO Intangible Cultural Heritage, available at: https://ich.unesco.org/en/state/oman-OM?info=elements-on-the-lists, last accessed February 12, 2021.

75. UNESCO, "Oman 2016 Report," available at: https://es.unesco.org/creativity/governance/periodic-reports/2016/oman, last accessed February 12, 2021.

76. Ray Petersen, "Oman Committed to Protect Heritage Sites," *Oman Observer*, September 16, 2019, available at: https://www.omanobserver.om/oman-committed-to-protect-heritage-sites, last accessed February 12, 2021.

77. HH Sayyid Haitham bin Tariq, "Speech at the Opening of the National Museum," available at: https://www.nm.gov.om/en/his-majesty-speech, last accessed February 12, 2021.

78. Kutty, "Oman Across Ages Museum."

79. Ahmed al-Ismaili, "Ethnic, Linguistic, and Religious Pluralism in Oman: The Link with Political Stability," *Al-Muntaqa* 1(3) (2018): 58–73; Franziska Fay, "Young Swahili-speakers in Oman and the 'Zanzibar Diaspora,'" (Lecture, *Leibniz-Zentrum Moderner Orient*, January 14, 2021); Marc Valeri, "Something

Stirring Under the Still Waters of Oman: Tightening the Grip or Revitalizing the Monarchy?" *International Journal of Archaeology and Social Sciences in the Arabian Peninsula* 14 (2007): 105–116; James Worrall, "Oman: The 'Forgotten' Corner of the Arab Spring," *Middle East Policy* 19(3) (2012): 98–115; Thomas O'Falk, "'Controlling the Situation': Oman Leader Quickly Quells Protests," *Al-Jazeera*, June 3, 2021, available at: https://www.aljazeera.com/news/2021/6/3/controlling-the-situation-oman-leader-quickly-quells-protests, last accessed June 3, 2021.

80. Al-Belushi, "Managing Oman's Archaeological Resource"; M. A. K. Al-Belushi, "The Heritage Prospective and Urban Expansion in Capital Cities: Old Defence Sites in Muscat, Oman," *WIT Transactions on the Built Environment* 131 (2013): 551–562; Nasir Saeed al-Jahwari, "Muhadidat al-Turath al-Athari fi Sultanat Oman" ("Threats to Archaeological Heritage in the Sultanate of Oman"), *Sultan Qaboos University Journal of Arts & Sciences* 7(1) (2016): 243–281.

81. Iram Khalil al-Hamdani, "Towards Sustainable Urban Waterfronts in the Middle East: Assessing the Role of Cultural Heritage in the Redevelopment of Port Sultan Qaboos in Oman," MS thesis, Delft University of Technology, 2019.

82. Senija Causevic and Mark Neal, "The Exotic Veil: Managing Tourist Perceptions of National History and Statehood in Oman," *Tourism Management* 71 (2019): 509–511.

83. Amal Sachedina, "Nizwa Fort: Transforming Ibadi Religion through Heritage Discourse in Oman," *Comparative Studies of South Asia, Africa and the Middle East* 39(2) (2019): 328–330; Sachedina, "The Politics of the Coffee Pot," 252.

84. Abdul Sheriff, "Contradictions in the Heritagization of Zanzibar 'Stone Town,'" in Burkhard Schnepel and Tansen Sen (eds.), *Travelling Pasts: The Politics of Cultural Heritage in the Indian Ocean World* (Leiden: Brill, 2019), 221–245.

85. Limbert, *In the Time of Oil*, 24–27.

86. Manuela Guutberlet, "Socio-Cultural Impacts of Large-scale Cruise Tourism in Souq Mutrah, Sultanate of Oman," *Fennia—International Journal of Geography* 194(1) (2016): 46–63; Sebastian Maisel, "Why Not Go to the Museum Today? On Tourism and Museum Preferences in Saudi Arabia," in Karen Exell and Sarina Wakefield (eds.), *Museums in Arabia: Transnational Practices and Regional Processes* (Abingdon: Routledge, 2016), 53–69; Thalia Kennedy, Jo Hargreaves, and Aisha al-Khater, "A Study of Visitor Behavior at the Museum of Islamic Art, Doha," in Karen Exell and Sarina Wakefield (eds.), *Museums in Arabia: Transnational Practices and Regional Processes* (Abingdon: Routledge, 2016), 70–91; Mariam Ibrahim al-Mulla and Karen Exell, "The Museum of Islamic Art, Doha: Constructing a Museum-Minded Community in Qatar," in Karen

Exell and Sarina Wakefield (eds.), *Museums in Arabia: Transnational Practices and Regional Processes* (Abingdon: Routledge, 2016), 92–100; Ali Alraouf, "One Nation, One Myth and Two Museums: Heritage, Architecture and Culture as Tools for Assembling Identity in Qatar," in Pamela Erskine-Loftus, Victoria Penziner Hightower, and Mariam Ibrahim al-Mulla (eds.), *Representing the Nation: Heritage, Museums, National Narratives and Identity in the Arab Gulf States* (New York: Routledge, 2016), 79–94.

87. Of this, only half are students. Sultanate of Oman, "Statistics" (2016), available at: https://www.omantourism.gov.om/wps/portal/mot/tourism/oman/home/media/statistics/!ut/p/a0/04_Sj9CPykssy0xPLMnMz0vMAfGjzOItvc1dg-40MzAz8fZzMDTyDQz0Mg92djC18DfQLsh0VAa6W7js!, last accessed February 12, 2021.

88. Al-Shukaili, "The Perception of Locals Toward Museums," 47–54; Hamed Almuhrzi, Karen Hughes, and Roy Ballantyne, "Exploring Arab and Western Visitors' Interpretive Experiences at an Omani Heritage Site: Does One Size Fit All?" *Journal of Heritage Tourism* 15(2) (2016): 180–199; Causevic and Neal, "The Exotic Veil," 504–517.

89. Limbert, *In the Time of Oil*, 22.

90. Dorr, et al., "Khasab Castle," 285–286, 290.

91. Matthew MacLean, "Time, Space and Narrative in Emirati Museums," in Pamela Erskine-Loftus, Victoria Penziner Hightower and Mariam Ibrahim al-Mulla (eds.), *Representing the Nation: Heritage, Museums, National Narratives, and Identity in the Arab Gulf States* (New York: Routledge, 2016), 210–203; Karen Exell, "Collecting in an Alternative World: The Sheikh Faisal bin Qassim Al-Thani Museum in Qatar," in Karen Exell and Trinidad Rico (eds.), *Cultural Heritage in the Arabian Peninsula; Debates, Discourses and Practices* (Burlington, VT: Ashgate, 2014), 51, 55–58.

92. Al-Busaidi, "The Protection and Management," 44; National Centre for Statistics & Information, "Culture: Visitor Data," 2021, available at: https://data.gov.om/watxbvb/culture, last accessed February 12, 2021.

93. Sachedina, "Of Living Traces," 7–8, 121.

94. Al-Ismaili, "Ethnic, Linguistic, and Religious Pluralism in Oman," 58–73; Fay, "Young Swahili-speakers in Oman"; Valeri, "Something Stirring Under the Still Waters of Oman," 105–116; Worrall, "Oman: The 'Forgotten' Corner," 98–115.

5

STAMPS AS MESSENGERS OF THE RENAISSANCE: THE POSTAL ISSUES OF OMAN DURING THE REIGN OF SULTAN QABOOS

Calvin H. Allen Jr.

In Oman, postage stamps are more than simply little bits of paper used to pre-pay mail delivery and/or to be collected by philatelists (stamp collectors). The topics depicted on these stamps can also play an important role in promoting both the national identity and goals of the state. Such was the case of stamps issued by the Sultanate of Oman postal service during the reign of Sultan Qaboos bin Said Al-Said which were used to reinforce His Majesty's goal of the modernization of the state within the context of its cultural traditions. This chapter provides an overview of Omani stamps issued to 1970, a period characterized by foreign control of the post office from 1864 to 1966, with very few stamps issued during the final years of Said bin Taimur's reign. Attention then turns to a brief transition after 1970 as stamps began to play a prominent role in promoting modernization and national identity. This is then followed by more detailed analysis of specific stamp issues depicting the Sultanate's economic, social, and political progress while at the same time reinforcing Oman's distinctive cultural identity with issues depicting handicrafts, architecture, dress, Oman's maritime tradition, as well as the country's links to its wider Arab and Islamic heritage. Through these stamp issues the Sultanate documented its material progress and rich cultural traditions and publicized the progress of Oman's Renaissance.

During Sultan Qaboos bin Said's nearly fifty-year reign, Oman issued over 800 postage stamps. My interest in those stamps actually pre-dates the ascension of Sultan Qaboos in 1970. Collecting Omani stamps prompted my interest and eventual scholarly specialization on the Sultanate. Don Reid's 1972 article[1] introduced me to how stamps help us to understand the history of a country. Since then, stamps have developed a limited scholarly interest, but several scholars have examined the role that they play in promoting nationalism and cultural heritage. Recent examples of this include the works of Henio Hovo and Maria Zofia Libera.[2] By way of one example among several, Harcourt Fuller[3] provides an excellent case study on postcolonial Ghana's use of stamps in promoting national identity, a process labeled "banal nationalism," by Michael Billig.[4] This chapter provides a case study of how postage stamps publicized the accomplishments of the Omani Renaissance initiated by Sultan Qaboos. In particular, stamps promoted the Sultan's oft-repeated goal of modernizing his country within the context of Oman's cultural traditions. Accordingly, stamps publicizing economic, social, and political progress were interspersed with issues reinforcing Oman's distinctive cultural identity with stamps depicting handicrafts, architecture, dress, maritime traditions, and the country's links to its wider Arab and Islamic heritage. Postage stamps thus served as a messenger to Omanis and the wider world about the achievements of the Omani Renaissance.

Omani Stamps before 1970

The mail service in Oman dates to May 1, 1864, when the first post office opened in Muscat. However, the Omani government did not manage that post office. Instead, Sultan Thuwaini bin Said (1856–1866) granted permission to the British Indian post office to operate the post office, mainly to serve the large Indian merchant community based in the port. After Indian independence, operation of the post office transferred to Pakistani postal authorities, who administered the post office from December 19, 1947 until March 31, 1948. During that eighty-four-year period, the only post office was located in Muscat, the office did not offer delivery service, and it used current Indian and then Pakistani stamps.[5] Those Indian and Pakistani stamps used in Oman can only be identified by a Muscat cancellation stamp (Figures 5.1 and 5.2).

Figure 5.1   **Figure 5.2**

Although the Omani government issued no stamps during the period of Indian/Pakistani postal administration, in 1941 British Indian postal authorities suggested to Sultan Said bin Taimur the possibility of a special issue commemorating the bicentennial of the Al-Bu Said dynasty in Oman in 1944. The original British proposal suggested overprinting current Indian stamps "Muscat" with or without the year "1944." Sultan Said rejected the idea, claiming that it was nothing more than an imitation of stamps from Kuwait and Bahrain (both of which had Indian-administered post offices using stamps overprinted with the country name) and that it raised questions about his independent status. He preferred a special issue with views of Muscat or, failing that, he would accept Indian stamps overprinted, in Arabic only, Al-Bu Said 1363 (the Muslim year). The British accepted the latter and the Al-Bu Said bicentennial stamps went on sale in Muscat (and the post office in Bombay) from November 20 to December 31, 1944 (Figure 5.3).[6]

Figure 5.3

In the midst of the discussions about the Al-Bu Said stamp issue and the Sultan's reluctance about the type of stamp to be issued and its implications for his independent status, Charles Collier, a British entrepeuneur, proposed to Sultan Said the establishment of an independent post office. Collier's pitch to the Sultan focused on his claim that Oman and Tibet were the only independent countries in the world without their own post offices. Collier also tried to entice Sultan Said with the promise of income from the sale of stamps. Despite the appeal to the Sultan's personal concerns about his political status and potential financial reward, he showed no interest in the proposal, and it died.[7] The post office in Muscat continued to use Indian stamps.

In April 1948 the British Postal Agencies in Eastern Arabia began administering the Muscat post office (along with the former Indian post offices in Kuwait, Qatar, Bahrain, and Dubai). Instead of Pakistani stamps, the post office now issued current British stamps overprinted with Indian currency denominations. Kuwait, Bahrain, and, later, Qatar all included the country name on the overprints, but Sultan Said, still asserting his independence but unwilling to take on the expense of running his own post office, refused to have Muscat or Oman added to the overprint. These "Values only Overprints" were valid in all of the British Postal Agency post offices, and, like the Indian and Pakistani stamps that preceded them, those used in Oman can only be identified by the Muscat cancellation (Figures 5.4 and 5.5).[8]

Figure 5.4   **Figure 5.5**

By the early 1950s, Sultan Said began to express interest in issuing his own stamps, although he did not wish to assume the expense of administering the mails. Nothing came of the discussions. By 1960, the British, preparing to withdraw from the Gulf, started pressuring all the British Postal Agencies to assume control of their own post offices and issue stamps. Kuwait (1959), Bahrain (1960), Qatar, and the Trucial States (1961) acceded, but Sultan

Said held out. The British continued to encourage Said to issue stamps, pointing out that "many states used stamps to project an image of themselves to the world," but when each of the Trucial States (Abu Dhabi, Ajman, Dubai, Fujairah, Ras al-Khaima, Sharjah, and Umm al-Qiwain—all now joined in the United Arab Emirates) began issuing stamps in 1963–64, the Sultan argued that since they had issued "their stamps at [British] behest . . . the image of himself that would be presented if he agreed now would be that this was just another Gulf State coming in to line. His Sultanate was not just another Gulf State." Finally, in early 1965 the Sultan agreed to issue his own stamps and manage postal services. Technical problems, including the printing of the new stamps, delayed the transfer until April 1966.[9]

Twelve definitive stamps (regular stamps as opposed to special issues) inscribed Muscat and Oman appeared on April 30, 1966. The lower six values of the set depicted the royal crest (Figure 5.6) and a view of Muscat harbor (Figure 5.7), while the six higher values included images of historic forts in Nakhl, Sama'il, Sohar, Nizwa, Mutrah, and Mirani in Muscat (Figure 5.8). The Sultanate re-issued stamps of the same design in June 1970 when Sultan Said introduced a new currency. The only other stamps issued during the final years of Sultan Said's regime came in January 1969 when a special issue publicized the beginning of oil exports with a set of four stamps (Figure 5.9).

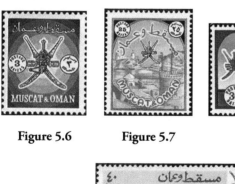

Figure 5.6   **Figure 5.7**   **Figure 5.8**

Figure 5.9

Oman's New Era Begins

Oman's Renaissance commenced on July 23, 1970 when Sultan Qaboos removed his father from power. Given the enormity of Oman's problems, from the war against Communist-inspired insurgents in Dhofar to the almost total absence of any economic and social infrastructure, the new ruler did not focus his immediate attention on postage stamp design. However, on January 15, 1971, the new regime re-issued the Muscat and Oman definitive stamps overprinted Sultanate of Oman (Figure 5.10) as Sultan Qaboos proclaimed to Omanis and the rest of the world the unification of the country.

Figure 5.10

The first new issue came on July 23, 1971 to commemorate National Day (now Renaissance Day with National Day moved to Sultan Qaboos' birthday in November). The four-stamp issue emphasized the differences between old and new Oman with a scene of mud-brick dwellings against a background of new construction, citizens plodding through darkened streets with old-fashioned oil lanterns as opposed to a father and son walking in sunlight, a long line of Omanis awaiting medical treatment and a scene of medical care in a modern clinic, and students seated on the floor of a traditional school and two girl students against a background of a new school building. Two of the stamps also featured images of the new Sultan, one in traditional formal dress and the second in military uniform (Figures 5.11–5.14).

On July 23, 1972 a new set of definitive stamps replaced the old over-printed stamps. The new stamps, similar to the old definitives, depicted various scenes of the country, the three views reproducing 1809 images from British artist Richard Temple's "Sixteen Views of the Persian Gulf." The four

Figure 5.11

Figure 5.12

Figure 5.13

Figure 5.14

lowest values show Mutrah harbor (Figure 5.15), the middle values Shinas (Figure 5.16), and the high values Muscat (Figure 5.17), all emphasizing Oman's maritime tradition. All included the royal crest.

While the new stamps effectively showcased the progress being made in Oman under the new Sultan to the wider world, they could have only a limited impact in Oman because of the limited postal service. When Sultan Qaboos took power in 1970, the country still had only the single post office in Muscat, and the new regime began to expand postal services. New post offices opened quickly in Salalah (1970); Sohar, Sur, Nizwa, Buraimi, and Masirah (1971); Matrah, Rustaq, Khasab, and Taqah (1972); Samail, Ibri, and Mirbat (1973); Mina al-Fahal, Shinas, al-Mudhaibi, and Yanqul (1974); and Seeb,

Figure 5.15

Figure 5.16

Figure 5.17

Musna'a, Bidiya, Diba, and Sadah (1975). By the end of the first five years of the Renaissance, the postal service extended to all regions of the Sultanate.[10]

Special issues during this transition period emphasized education and literacy, among Sultan Qaboos' principal priorities early in his reign. A December 25, 1971 issue commemorating the twenty-fifth anniversary of UNICEF (Figure 5.18) depicted a female Omani child reading. Another stamp followed on January 6, 1972 publicizing International Book Year. This emphasis on education continued into 1974 and 1975 with stamps promoting international and Arab world efforts to eradicate illiteracy (Figures 5.19 and 5.20). Although not specific to Oman, these stamps all served to illustrate Oman's new active role in the world in contrast to its isolation under Said b. Taimur.

| Figure 5.18 | Figure 5.19 | Figure 5.20 |

Promoting the Renaissance

By 1973 stamp issues began to focus much more on progress in the Sultanate while at the same time highlighting the country's heritage and identity. On September 23 a two-stamp issue publicized the opening of the new Ministerial Complex (Figure 5.21), Oman's first modern governmental structure. The four new stamps issued for that year's National Day celebrated transportation in Oman. While one publicized the opening of the new Seeb (now Muscat) International Airport (Figure 5.22), the other three stamps focused on more traditional Omani forms of transportation with sailing ships (country craft, Figures 5.23 and 5.24) and a camel (Figure 5.25).

Figure 5.21

Figure 5.22

Figure 5.23

Figure 5.24

Figure 5.25

These 1973 stamps also began a tradition of including a small portrait of Sultan Qaboos, either in traditional Omani dress or military uniform. Sultan Qaboos' image had been included on the 1971 National Day issue but not on any of the stamps issued thereafter. After 1973 his portrait was included on all National Day issues and special issues related in some way to the military or the police. This inclusion reflected the Sultan's roles as the head of state as well as commander in chief of both the armed forces and police. When the Sultan's portrait appears on stamps, the royal crest, a feature on all stamps during the reign of Said bin Taimur, is sometimes absent (see Figures 5.11, 5.12, and 5.21, above) and sometimes present. However, issues without the royal portrait always include the royal crest, although a series of stamps featuring the *khanjar* (Figure 5.26) mark a notable exception to this rule as it includes neither the Sultan's portrait or the royal crest. Perhaps the *khanjar*, the central feature of the royal crest, served to symbolize the nation.

This balance between modernization and heritage demonstrated in the 1973 stamps continued over the next forty-seven years. Although it had proclaimed the unity of Oman with the January 1971 overprints, the Sultanate possessed little by way of any physical infrastructure that joined the country

Figure 5.26

together. When Qaboos took power in 1970, the only paved highway in the country ran between the ports of Mutrah and Muscat, with badly maintained graveled roads linking the capital to Sohar and Nizwa. National Day in 1976 celebrated road construction nationwide (Figure 5.27) while focusing on the opening of the Seeb–Nizwa dual carriageway (Figure 5.28), while a 1980 National Day stamp featured the Corniche Road in Mutrah (Figure 5.29). Highway construction featured again in 1985 with a view of a flyover (overpass) on a modern highway (Figure 5.30). Then, in 2019, the Sultanate issued two stamps (Figure 5.31) publicizing the opening of the Batinah Expressway, a new superhighway from Muscat to the northern border.

Figure 5.27   **Figure 5.28**   **Figure 5.29**

Figure 5.30   **Figure 5.31**

In addition to a modern highway system, Sultan Qaboos encouraged the development of air travel. Seeb International Airport, featured on the 1973 National Day issue mentioned above, replaced a small facility in Azaiba. The second international airport in Salalah underwent major renovation, as celebrated on a 2015 stamp (Figure 5.32). Then, in 2018, Muscat International Airport began services (Figures 5.33 and 5.34), replacing the dated facilities at Seeb International. National carrier Oman Air, depicted on the 1994 50th Anniversary of International Civil Aviation issue (Figure 5.35), and a 2005 National Day stamp (Figure 5.36) greatly added to international access.

Figure 5.32   **Figure 5.33**   **Figure 5.34**

Figure 5.35   **Figure 5.36**

Highways and airports provided modern solutions to Oman's isolation under Sultan Said bin Taimur, but Omanis had long looked to the sea for connections to the wider world. Oman's maritime heritage dates to ancient times, when it traded such products as copper from around Sohar and frankincense from Dhofar, and many stamp issues reference ships and ports. Development under Sultan Qaboos built on that maritime tradition. Traditional (also referred to as country or native) sailing craft appeared on the 1973 National Day issue mentioned above, and Omani craftsmen produced a wide range of sailing vessels as shown in a historical manuscript (Figure 5.37) and the 1996 eight-stamp set (Figures 5.38–5.45).

Figure 5.37

Figure 5.38

Figure 5.39

Figure 5.40

Figure 5.41

Figure 5.42

Figure 5.43

Figure 5.44

Figure 5.45

Sultan Qaboos further encouraged the sailing tradition with the Sultan Qaboos Sailing Award (Figure 5.46).

Stamps also commemorated the Sultanate's maritime history. A 1981 four-stamp issue (Figure 5.47) celebrated the activities of Sindbad, when a reproduction of a medieval dhow named after the legendary hero of the

Figure 5.46   **Figure 5.47**

Arabian Nights retraced a voyage from Sohar to Canton, China. A 2010 stamp (Figure 5.48) commemorated a similar attempted but failed voyage of the dhow *Jewel* from Muscat to Malaysia. The post office commemorated another famous Omani voyage with stamps in 1986 (Figure 5.49) and 1990 (Figure 5.50) depicting the *Sultana*, which sailed from Muscat to New York carrying an Omani embassy to the United States in 1840, the first such visit by an Arab dignitary to that country. The Royal Oman Navy continues to honor the sailing tradition with the training ship *Shabab*, which serves as a roving ambassador, such as participating in the "Tall Ships" event that marked the centenary of the Statue of Liberty in 1986 (Figure 5.51).

Figure 5.48

Figure 5.49   **Figure 5.50**   **Figure 5.51**

Ships require ports, and these maritime facilities played a prominent role in Omani history and development. As mentioned above, the new definitive stamps issued in 1972 featured the ports of Mutrah, Shinas, and Muscat. Two stamps in 1996 (Figure 5.52) celebrated the ancient port at Sur, long a center of Omani shipbuilding and maritime trade. However, those traditional ports no longer served the needs of a modern country. Mina (Port) Qaboos in Mutrah replaced the old port of Muscat in 1974 (Figure 5.53), and a year later Salalah's new port at Raysut (Figure 5.54) opened. The Sultanate continued to invest in modern port facilities with the opening of the Salalah Container port (Figure 5.55) in 1996, the Oman Drydock Company (Figure 5.56) in 2012, and the major port and logistics complex at Duqm (Figure 5.57) in 2017. These port facilities served to reestablish Oman's central maritime role in the western Indian Ocean region dating from the time

Figure 5.52

Figure 5.53   Figure 5.54

Figure 5.55   Figure 5.56

Figure 5.57

of the "Golden Ages" of Sohar (ninth–twelfth centuries), Qalhat (thirteenth–fifteenth centuries), and Muscat (sixteenth–nineteenth centuries).

Roads, airports, and sea ports link people physically, but aside from two small radio stations in Muscat and Salalah, a telephone exchange limited to Muscat–Mutrah, and a single post office in Muscat, Sultan Qaboos inherited a country totally lacking a telecommunications system. The 1984 National Day issue promoted the expansion of postal services with the opening of the Central Post Office's automatic sorting facility in Seeb (Figure 5.58).

Figure 5.58

Telecommunications expanded rapidly during the renaissance. The 1975 National Day issue publicized the inauguration of Oman Color Television (Figure 5.59), Arabsat (Figure 5.60), the satellite earth station which linked Oman to the wider world for the first time, and a national telephone system (Figure 5.61). The 1976 National Day issue celebrated the opening of a TV station in Salalah (Figure 5.62), and a 1984 National Day stamp depicted a map of the Sultanate's entire telecommunications network (Figure 5.63). Telecommunications development continued to be celebrated with a stamp in 1985 (Figure 5.64) focusing on post and communications, and the 2010 Telecom Day stamp (Figure 5.65) featuring telecommunications activities as depicted by children's art.

Prior to 1970, even with the discovery of oil in 1967, agriculture and fishing provided the principal economic activities for the Omani population. Promotion of the agricultural sector remained a priority under Sultan

Figure 5.59	Figure 5.60	Figure 5.61

Figure 5.62	Figure 5.63	Figure 5.64

Figure 5.65

Qaboos, and agricultural themes appeared regularly on stamps of the Qaboos era, including 1988 and 1989 as Years of Agriculture. The 1975 National Day issue included a stamp featuring wheat farming (Figure 5.66), while mechanization (Figure 5.67) figured prominently in the modernization of agriculture, in contrast to the practice of a bullock-drawn plow prior to 1970 (Figure 5.68). Programs also focused on sustainable agriculture, as depicted on a 2007 stamp (Figure 5.69).

Figure 5.66

Figure 5.67

Figure 5.68

Figure 5.69

Modernization of agriculture did not come at the expense of Oman's agricultural traditions. Dates, in various forms, provided an important source of food for both domestic consumption and export, and 1982 stamps publicized Arab Palm Tree Day (Figure 5.70), while a 2016 stamp celebrated the Omani Date Festival (Figure 5.71). The production and export of frankincense, produced from the sap of a tree native to Dhofar, dates to ancient time and remains an important agricultural product. A 1985 issue featured frankincense production (Figure 5.72), and a 2012 stamp showed the final product and some incense burning in a traditional Omani incense burner (Figure 5.73).

Animal husbandry, especially the raising of sheep and goats, predominated in most of the country and remains important. The Dhofar region, especially the mountainous areas which benefit from greater rainfall than the

Figure 5.70

Figure 5.71

Figure 5.72

Figure 5.73

rest of the country, also supported the raising of cattle (Figures 5.74 and 5.75), which remain important in that area. Stamps issued in 1983 publicized the traditional craft of beekeeping (Figure 5.76).

Agriculture depended on the availability of water, and in ancient times Omanis developed an extensive irrigation system known as *falaj* (pl. *aflaj*) which enabled farmers to draw on underground water sources spread over a

Figure 5.74   **Figure 5.75**   **Figure 5.76**

wide area to water their crops. These *aflaj* remained an important feature of agriculture development and have appeared on several stamps, including in 1987 (Figure 5.77) and 1998 (Figure 5.78–5.79). Several *aflaj*, such as Falaj al-Khatmeen in Birkat al-Mouz (Figures 5.80 and 5.81), Falaj al-Daris in Nizwa (Figures 5. 82–5.84), Falaj al-Muyassar in Rustaq (Figure 5.85), Falaj al-Malki in Izki (Figure 5.86), and Falaj al-Jeela near Sur (Figure 5.87) are considered as being among the greatest examples of this irrigation system. While this traditional water management system remains important, *aflaj*

Figure 5.77 **Figure 5.78** **Figure 5.79**

Figure 5.80 **Figure 5.81**

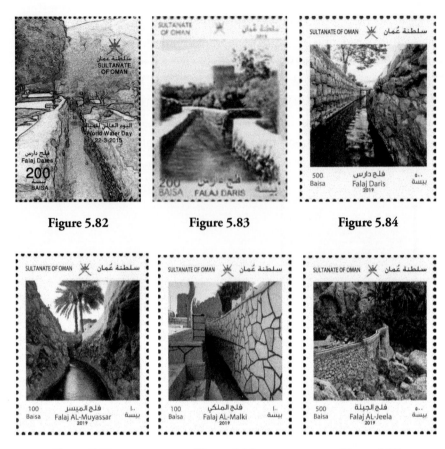

Figure 5.82   Figure 5.83   Figure 5.84

Figure 5.85   Figure 5.86   Figure 5.87

cannot supply all of Oman's water needs. Construction of a water desalination plant (Figure 5.88) was among the first development projects under Sultan Qaboos; a 2004 issue (Figures 5.89–5.90) publicized the development of the Massart and Sharqiyyah water supply projects; and the Arab Water Day issue of 2010 (Figure 5.91) depicts one of the several dams constructed to recharge the Sultanate's depleting aquifers.

In addition to agriculture, prior to 1970 fishing provided an important source of food and income to the Omani population as dried fish were distributed locally and exported. The 1981 and 1989 National Day issues (Figure 5.92–5.93) publicized Oman's fisheries, the stamps contrasting a traditional fishing boat to modern fishing craft. A 1987 stamp commemorated the opening of the Marine Science and Fisheries Center (Figure 5.94).

Figure 5.88

Figure 5.89

Figure 5.90

Figure 5.91

Figure 5.92

Figure 5.93

Figure 5.94

Agriculture and fisheries continued to provide employment for many Omanis after 1970, but oil and other mineral exports remained the principal sources of income for the government. Sultan Qaboos sought both to diversify the petroleum industry and develop other Omani natural resources in order to expand the Sultanate's industrial activities. In 1979, a natural gas plant opened (Figure 5.95), and a 1983 stamp (Figure 5.96) publicized the inauguration of the Mina al-Fahal oil refinery. In 2007. Oman celebrated forty years of oil exports (Figure 5.97). While oil runs the modern economy, in ancient times Oman provided copper throughout the Arabian Sea region. A 1983 stamp (Figure 5.98) publicized the opening of the Sohar copper factory as Oman again became a copper exporter. The Sultanate celebrated 1992 as the Year of Industry (Figure 5.99).

Figure 5.95   **Figure 5.96**   **Figure 5.97**

Figure 5.98   **Figure 5.99**

Just as modernization of infrastructure and agriculture and fisheries did not come at the expense of Omani traditions, Sultan Qaboos encouraged Oman's historical manufacturing activities through promoting handicrafts, culminating with the promulgation of 1994 as Cultural Heritage Year (Figure 5.100). Omani craftspeople produce a wide range of products.[11] Metal workers (Figure 5.101) manufactured objects for daily use such as Oman's distinctive coffee pots (Figures 5.102 and 5.103), platters (Figure 5.104), and incense burners (Figure 5.105), and jewelry has been featured on several stamps (Figures 5.106–5.110). Pottery makers, like

Figure 5.100   **Figure 5.101**

Figure 5.102

Figure 5.103

Figure 5.104

Figure 5.105

Figure 5.106

Figure 5.107

Figure 5.108

Figure 5.109

Figure 5.110

metal workers, historically created a variety of vessels for daily use and storage (Figures 5.111–5.113). Weavers used a variety of fibers, including imported cotton, locally produced wool, and grasses to make blankets, saddle bags, and other decorative items, as well as a variety of mats and baskets (Figures 5.114–5.118). Finally, the halwa maker (Figure 5.119) mixed the juice from dates, honey, spices, and other ingredients together to create Oman's distinctive confection that remains an important accompaniment to the coffee served before each meeting.

Figure 5.111

Figure 5.112

Figure 5.113

Figure 5.114

Figure 5.115

Figure 5.116

Figure 5.117

Figure 5.118

Figure 5.119

In addition to economic development, Oman made tremendous gains in social infrastructure with improvements to education and health services and expanded political participation. Traditional Koran schools (Figure.5 120) provided about the only education for children prior to 1970. Sultan Qaboos' regime expanded that to a modern educational system from elementary through to university (Figure 5.121). The Sultan announced the inauguration of Sultan Qaboos University in 1983 (Figure 5.122), celebrated its opening in 1986 (Figure 5.123), and its twenty-sixth anniversary in 2011 (Figure 5.124). In addition to providing educational opportunities, the Sultanate also initiated efforts to protect its intellectual heritage through efforts to preserve historical manuscripts (Figure 5.125) and documents (Figure 5.126). Healthcare services also expanded throughout the country with clinics and

Figure 5.120   Figure 5.121

Figure 5.122   Figure 5.123   Figure 5.124

Figure 5.125   Figure 5.126

hospitals (Figure 5.127). In developing the final piece of social infrastructure, political participation, Oman's tradition of *shura* (consultation) guided Sultan Qaboos. This process began in 1975 when Sultan Qaboos began his annual meet-the-people tours (Figure 5.128) and continued through the inauguration of the State Consultative Council (Figure 5.129) in 1983.

Figure 5.127   Figure 5.128   Figure 5.129

Reinforcing the Omani Identity

In addition to promoting Sultan Qaboos' goal of balancing modernization within Oman's cultural traditions, stamp issues have also been used to reinforce the Omani identity. National dress represents perhaps the most visible aspect of that identity.[12] A 1987 stamp (Figure 5.130) depicts a family in traditional Omani dress, the males wearing *disdasha*s and the cap known as a *kumma*, the females in the female version of the *dishdasha*, the *waqaya* (a head scarf wrapped around the head or *lahaf* (a head scarf draped over the head), and *sarwal* (pants). Women in national dress appear on many stamp issues, including a 1980 National Day stamp (Figure 5.131) and a 1989 set publicizing regional costumes, including Dhahira (Figure 5.132), Sharqiyah (Figure 5.133), Batinah (Figure 5.134), Interior (Figure 5.135), Dhofar (Figure 5.136), and Muscat (Figure 5.137).

Figure 5.130   Figure 5.131

Figure 5.132

Figure 5.133

Figure 5.134

Figure 5.135

Figure 5.136

Figure 5.137

Men's attire has also appeared on many stamps (Figure 5.138), and the 1989 issue featuring women's costume also included men in regional dress, including Dhahira (Figure 5.139), Sharqiyah (Figure 5.140), Dhofar (Figure.5 141), and Muscat (Figure 5.142). A distinctive feature of male costume is the *khanjar*

Figure 5.138

| Figure 5.139 | Figure 5.140 | Figure 5.141 | Figure 5.142 |

(dagger) worn at the waist during all formal occasions. *Khanjar*s are usually fashioned from silver, and a 1987 stamp (Figure 5.143) shows a *khanjar* maker at work, with a handle traditionally fashioned from rhinoceros' horn, although that practice has ceased. A 2019 set of stamps depicted the four styles of *khanjar*: Batiniya (Figure 5.144), Sa'idiya (Figure 5.145), Suriya (Figure 5.146), and Nizwaniya (Figure 5.147).

Figure 5.143

| Figure 5.144 | Figure 5.145 | Figure 5.146 | Figure 5.147 |

Formal menswear also includes the distinctive Omani turban (*masar*). *Masar*s come in a a variety of colors and designs, and each individual wraps his in a slightly personal style. Sultan Qaboos served as the best model of proper Omani dress. The Sultan, when not shown in military uniform, appeared on many stamps in a variety of *masar* and *khanjar* styles (Figures 5.148–5.150), although the 1995 National Day stamp (Figure 5.151) deserves special note as the Sultan appears in an official al-Said royal family *masar*, a Sa'idiya *khanjar*, and formal black *bisht*.

Figure 5.148   **Figure 5.149**   **Figure 5.150**   **Figure 5.151**

Given Oman's Muslim tradition, drawing, painting, and sculpture have not played an important role in cultural tradition. However, the country does have a vital performance heritage in music[13] and dance, and Sultan Qaboos was an accomplished performer on the Omani oud stringed instrument as well as the Western organ. In 1985, Oman hosted a traditional Omani music symposium, with a stamp featuring drummers (Figure 5.152). Percussion instruments such as the *kasir* and *rahmani* (Figure 5.153) play a central role in traditional music as the main instruments in dance groups. The 2019 traditional music set of stamps also depicted the *barghum* (Figure 5.154), a wind intrument.

Figure 5.152   **Figure 5.153**   **Figure 5.154**

Oman's rich dance tradition includes over 100 different forms and styles with regional variations. The 1999 National Day issue (Figure 5.155) featured the popular *maidan* dance, which includes both men and women. The *razha* traditional battle dance appeared on the 1981 National Day stamp (Figure 5.156). Finally, the *al-'azi* dance (Figure 5.157), on the 2019 traditional music issue, is included on the UNESCO Intangible Cultural Heritage list.

Figure 5.155

Figure 5.156   **Figure 5.157**

Traditional architecture remains Oman's most enduring cultural symbol,[14] and depiction of forts and palaces feature prominently on the Sultanate's stamps throughout the Qaboos era. The eighteenth-century palace at Jabrin holds a high place among Oman's srchitectural wonders. The palace first appeared on a stamp in 1978 (Figure 5.158) and later issues focused on the palace's restoration (Figure 5.159) and its importance as a tourist attraction (Figure 5.160).

Muscat's architectural features appeared on several stamps. Jalali, the sixteenth-century fort built by the Portuguese first appeared on the first issue of Muscat and Oman, then on the 1978 National Day fort series, and then again in a panoramic view of the town (Figure 5.161). Several major restoration projects have taken place in the city, including the Bab al-Kabir gate into the old city (Figure 5.162), and a large gate on the highway between Muscat and Mutrah (Figure 5.163). Bait Faransa (Figure 5.164), the former

Figure 5.158   **Figure 5.159**   **Figure 5.160**

Figure 5.161   **Figure 5.162**   **Figure 5.163**

Figure 5.164

residence of the French consul in Muscat, survived the extensive construction surrounding the palace complex and now houses the Omani French Museum. Matrah Fort (Figure 5.165), the imposing fortress atop the hillside looking overlooking Mina Qaboos, appeared on several stamps, and a 2014 issue (Figure 5.166) featured the Matrah *suq* (market), Oman's largest traditional "shopping center."

Figure 5.165   Figure 5.166

Postal officials honored iconic structures existing throughout the country. The circular fort in Nizwa, an ancient capital of Oman, appeared on two stamps (Figures 5.167 and 5.168), and a 2015 issue recognized the city as a Capital of Arab Culture (Figure 5.169) with one of the stamps depicting Salal mosque. Other stamp issues featured the palaces at Rustaq (Figure 5.170), Sohar (Figures 5.171 and 5.172), Bahla (Figures 5.173 and 5.174), Al-Hazm (Figure 5.175), Khasab (Figure 5.176), and Bait al-Falaj (Figure 5.177), now the home of the Sultan's Armed Forces Museum.

Figure 5.167   Figure 5.168   Figure 5.169

Figure 5.170   Figure 5.171   Figure 5.172

Figure 5.173   **Figure 5.174**   **Figure 5.175**

Figure 5.176   **Figure 5.177**

Oman's Arab and Islamic Identity

Although Omani cultural attributes dominated stamp issues during the reign of Sultan Qaboos, postal authorities also promoted Oman's wider Arab and Muslim identities. A 1979 two-stamp issue (Figure 5.178) publicized Arab achievements, most notably in the sciences; a 1992 stamp (Figure 5.179) publicized publication of Sultan Qaboos' *Encyclopedia of Arab Names*; and in 2009 Oman participated in a pan-Arab joint issue (Figure 5.180) celebrating Jerusalem as a "Capital of Arab Culture." In 2006 and 2015, Muscat and Nizwa received similar international recognition.

Although Oman issued several stamps publicizing its diplomatic ties to the Arab world, it generally avoided using stamps to promote controversial political issues. However, a 2001 stamp demonstrated Omani support of the Palestinian Intifada (Figure 5.181), and a 2020 set, the last issue approved by Sultan Qaboos, proclaiming Jerusalem as the capital of Palestine (Figure 5.182).

Figure 5.178   **Figure 5.179**   **Figure 5.180**

Figure 5.181   **Figure 5.182**

While few issues focused on Oman's Arab heritage, Islam featured prominently on stamps during the Qaboos era. In 2019, Oman commemorated the beginnings of Islam in the Sultanate with a stamp depicting the letter of 629 from the Prophet Muhammad inviting Omanis to become Muslims (Figure 5.183). However, stamps publicizing Oman's Muslim heritage first

Figure 5.183

appeared in 1978 with a stamp (Figure 5.184) publicizing the Muslim pilgrimage (*Hajj*). Five stamps (Figures 5.185–5.189) followed between 1981 and 1986, each depicting various stages of the annual event. A six-stamp issue in 1997 reproduced the earlier stamps. In 1980, the Sultanate marked the beginning of the fifteenth century of the Hegira with two stamps (Figure 5.190). However, Sultan Qaboos' greatest legacy relating to Islam came with the 2002 inauguration of the Sultan Qaboos

Figure 5.184

Figure 5.185

Figure 5.186

Figure 5.187

Figure 5.188

Figure 5.189

Figure 5.190

Grand Mosque (Figures 5.191 and 5.192). An aerial view of the magnificent structure appeared in the Muscat Arab Tourism Capital issue of 2012 (Figure 5.193), and a 2016 issue depicted the mosque's ten *mihrabs* (Figure 5,194).

Figure 5.191

Figure 5.192

Figure 5.193

Figure 5.194

As evidenced above, Omani stamps issued during the reign of Sultan Qaboos bin Said promoted the Sultan's goal of balancing modernization and Oman's cultural traditions. Accordingly, development of a modern transportation system included recognition of the country's strong maritime tradition; agricultural development incorporated traditional crops like dates and frankincense and sought to maintain the ancient *aflaj* system; and modern industrialization paralleled support for handicrafts. Social development emphasized education, while preserving Oman's intellectual heritage, healthcare, and political participation based on the country's tradition of *shura* (consultation). Modernization did not come at the expense of the Omani identity, as stamps promoting costume, music, dance, and architecture all reminded Omanis and displayed to the world what it meant to be Omani. That distinctive identity did not ignore Omanis additional identities as Arabs and Muslims.

Notes

1. Don Reid, "Egyptian History through Stamps," *The Muslim World* 63(3) (1972): 209–229.
2. Henio Hovo, "Posting Nationalism: Postage Stamps as Carriers of Nationalist Messages," in Joan Burbick and William Glass (eds.), *Beyond Imagined Uniqueness: Nationalisms in Contemporary Perspective* (Newcastle upon Tyne: Cambridge Scholars Publishing, 2010), 67–92; Maria Zofia Libera, "The Added Value of the Postage Stamp in Promoting National Cultural Heritage and Identity," in António dos Santos Queirós (ed.), *Examining a New Paradigm of Heritage With Philosophy, Economy, and Education* (Hershey, PA: IGI Global, 2020), 223–231.
3. Harcourt Fuller, "Chapter 2 Philatelic Nationalism," *Building the Ghanaian Nation-State: Kwame Nkrumah's Symbolic Nationalism* (New York: Palgrave Macmillan, 2014), 39–53.
4. Michael Billig, *Banal Nationalism* (London: Sage, 1995).
5. Muscat was one of a number of post offices operated in the Arabian Gulf by the British government in India. For a detailed history of this period in Omani postal history, see Neil Donaldson, *The Postal Agencies in Eastern Arabia and the Gulf* (Batley: Harry Hays, 1975), 19–38. See also Ministry of P.T.T., *The Postal History of Oman 1856–1985* (Muscat: Oman Post, 1985), which includes pictures of all of the Indian and Pakistani stamps that might have been used in Muscat during this period.
6. Calvin H. Allen Jr., "The Al-Bu Sa'id Bicentennial Issue of 1944," *The Arab World Philatelist*, 4 (Spring 1979): 10–12.
7. Coll 20/36 "Muscat: Proposal (by a Mr. C. S. J. Collier) to institute a State Post Office in Muscat," British Library: India Office Records and Private Papers, IOR/L/PS/12/2996, in *Qatar Digital Library*, available at: https://www.qdl.qa/archive/81055/vdc_100000000602.0x00021c, last accessed February 1, 2021.
8. Donaldson, *Postal Agencies in Eastern Arabia and the Gulf*, 189–202.
9. FO 371/104387, "Postal Services 1960," 10; FO 371/156809 "Postal Services 1961," available at: https://www.agda.ae/en/catalogue/tna/fo/371/156809; FO 371/168718 "Post Office 1963," 8, available at: https://www.agda.ae/en/catalogue/tna/fo/371/168718; FO 371/174572 "Post Office 1964," 14, available at: https://

www.agda.ae/en/catalogue/tna/fo/371/174572; FO 371/179827 "Post Office 1965," available at: https://www.agda.ae/en/catalogue/tna/fo/371/179827; FO 371/185382 "Post Office 1966," available at: https://www.agda.ae/en/catalogue/tna/fo/371/185382, *Arab Gulf Digital Archive*, all last accessed February 1, 2021.

10. For the expansion of Omani postal services, see *Postal History of Oman*, 1985; Ministry of Posts, Telegraphs and Telephones, *The Postal History of Oman 1986–1990*, Muscat, 1990; Alistair Gunn and Calvin Allen, *Aspects of Omani Postal History*, 2nd edn. (n.p., 2002); Hatim Al-Attar, *Sultanate of Oman Postal System 1966–2016* (Muscat: Oman Philatelic Association, 2016).

11. On Omani craft traditions, see Neil Richardson and Maricia Dorr, *The Craft Heritage of Oman*, 2 vols. (Dubai and London: Motivate Publishing, 2003).

12. Sarah Malsey, "How Oman's National Dress References the Country's Rich History," *The National News* (UAE), November 18, 2020, available at: https://www.thenationalnews.com/lifestyle/how-oman-s-national-dress-references-the-country-s-rich-history-1.1113063, last accessed February 5, 2021; Aisa Martinez, "Omani Men's National Dress: Displaying Personal Taste, Asserting National Identity," *Ars Orientalis*, 47 (2017), available at: https://quod.lib.umich.edu/a/ars/13441566.0047.013/--omani-mens-national-dress-displaying-personal-taste?rgn=main;view=fulltext, last accessed February 5, 2021.

13. Majid Al-Harthy and Anne K. Rasmussen, "Music in Oman: Politics, Identity, Time, and Space in the Sultanate," *The World of Music*, 1(2) (2012): 9–41.

14. Yaqoub Salim Al-Busaidi, "The Protection and Management of Historic Monuments in the Sultanate of Oman: the Historic Buildings of Oman," *Proceedings of the Seminar for Arabian Studies* 34 (2004): 35–44; Naima Benkari, "Modern Heritage in Oman," in Ugo Carughi and Massimo Visone (eds.), *Time Frames: Conservation Policies for Twentieth-Century Architectural Heritage* (Abingdon: Routledge, 2018), 162–165, available at: https://www.researchgate.net/publication/320445037_Modern_Heritage_in_Oman, last accessed February 5, 2021.

6

FROM THE FIRST RENAISSANCE TO THE SECOND: THE HISTORICAL AND LEGAL BASIS FOR THE SULTANATE

Abdulrahman al-Salimi

Oman's modern renaissance of 1970 was linked to the first Omani Renaissance of Ibadi thought in the nineteenth century. This earlier renaissance was when Oman's Ibadi Sharia (Ibadi Islamic Law; see Chapter 6) was first modernized and adapted for a variety of contexts. It was also in this earlier period when Oman's political system under the Imamate and the Sultanate ruled the country either concurrently or in rotation. There were several links between the traditions of the past and the character of the modern state. Those historic links paved the way for the emergence and evolution of the modern Omani Sultanate that formed under the leadership of Sultan Qaboos. Legitimacy is of major importance in the Ibadi belief system and *fiqh* (jurisprudence) and this is reflected in Oman's history. The legitimacy of the Sultanate is well established on firm legal and historical foundations and sound *fiqh*, or Islamic judicial principles that have played out over centuries of history. Even before the nineteenth and twentieth centuries, and as early as the first Ibadi Imamate (the Imamate of al-Julanda b. Mas'ud in 751 CE), Oman experienced two alternating governing models: sequential and concurrent systems of rule. When either the Imam or the Sultan is the sole ruler, the governing system is sequential. When both the Imam and Sultan share power over different parts of the country (usually with the Sultan in the ports and the Imam in the mountains), the model is concurrent. Over the past two centuries, this shifting between different models has been a feature of Oman's history. Imam Muhammad b. 'Abd 'Allah al-Khalili (1919–1954) existed concurrently with the Sultan. The Imam's successor, Ghālib b. 'Ali al-Hina'i (1954–1957), however, was defeated by the father of Sultan Qaboos, who restored the sequential system.[1] The pattern of Imamate and Sultanate, both concurrent and sequential, has been ingrained in the Omani consciousness for many centuries. The three main features of Omani history have been the interior, usually mountain-based Imamate, and the Sultanate, which has been focused on maritime trade.[2] From 1970 to 2020, Sultan Qaboos started a new era in Omani history, becoming the sole ruler of a united Oman. His legitimacy was confirmed, and oaths of loyalty (bay'a) were pledged to him by former supporters of both the Sultanate and the Imamate systems. Creating coalitions across historic divides and between Imamate and Sultanate, Sultan Qaboos created a foundation of stability and political integration in Oman.

Oman's two political systems—Imamate and Sultanate—coincide in many respects and are in conflict in other ways. Tensions first arose during the time of the first Islamic caliphate—the time of the Rightly Guided Caliphs (632–661 CE)—and the first Islamic empire (the Umayyad Empire, 661–744 CE). Later, since the 1950s, traditional terms such as al-khilafa (the caliphate) and al-mulk al-'adud (kingship) have been supplemented with modern labels. Expressions such as al-daynuna (religiosity) and al-dunyawiyya (secularism), or what the Western tradition describes as conflict between the spiritual power and the temporal power, have become more important. Legitimacy is found not only in religious contexts, but also in effective policies and capable modernization and reasonable governance built on rules that may or may not have a religious origin. Following Western dichotomies of secular and religious, it would be easy to come to the conclusion that the Imamate is a purely religious institution and that the Sultanate is temporal and secular in nature.

In fact, this dichotomy is an oversimplification. Both institutions combined a religious function with a secular one: the mahkumin (ruled), seen first and foremost as a jama'at mu'minin (a community of believers) and only secondly as a jama'at ra'aya (a community of subjects). Thus, the Imamate also had a temporal aspect and the Sultanate also had a spiritual aspect. The distinction between the two was over which of the two aspects was dominant: whether it was mainly religious (Imamate) or mainly temporal (Sultanate). From the installation of the first Imam, it was this characteristic that defined the sequentiality of the two systems and the way they alternated. The *Jahiliyah* (Age of Ignorance before the coming of Islam in the seventh century CE) that preceded it could be regarded as an era of temporal tribal rule, even though local religious traditions were also followed.[3]

One explanation for the rise of the dual Imamate–Sultanate system in Oman was geographical. Being surrounded by the sea on one side and the Empty Quarter desert on the other, Oman's people found themselves compelled to develop their relations with the outside world through seafaring and trade. Just as Herodotus described Egypt as the gift of the Nile, so too can we describe Oman as the gift of the Indian Ocean. From the time the first waves of Arab tribes settled in Oman, tribalism was the dominant force in the mountainous and desert hinterland, whether it was under imamate or sultanate rule, and it provided the motivation that inspired the people to fight all would-be invaders from beyond its borders.[4] This division between outward-facing ports and inward-facing hinterlands fostered duality in the political system: the creation of imamates concurrent with sultanates.

The hinterland has usually also been the more traditional bulwark of Ibadi theology. As they were the scribes and the literate members of the community, Ibadi jurists have also been the chroniclers of the history of Oman. From their more isolated perches in Nizwa, one of the religious centers in Oman, for instance, they have generally shown a preference for an Imamate rather than a kingdom.

This contrasts to the non-Ibadi (Sunni or Twelver Shiite) tradition in which scribes were more closely tied to the Sultans in large cosmopolitan city capitals such as Damascus and Baghdad under the Sunni caliphs, or Isfahan and Tabriz under the Safavids. In the non-Ibadi Islamic world, we find more of a tendency to produce books with titles such as *Mirrors of Kings*, *Advice to Kings*, and *Laws of Sultanic Government*, written by men of letters and jurists, and books on civil politics written by philosophers and scholars such as Al-Mawardi (d. 1058 CE), who wrote the influential Sunni tract, *The Ordinanaces of Government*. In the Sunni context, there is a balance between the books on Sharia politics written by *fuqaha'* and aspects of the Imamate in the writings of theologians.[5]

In Omani and Ibadi history, material on the qualities of the Imamate and how to rule is found more indirectly in jurisprudence and theological literature. We find almost nothing that could be regarded as equivalent to *Mirrors of Kings, Advice to Kings*, or *Laws of Sultanic Government*. Moreover, there is little Ibadi literature on civil politics; instead, we find musings on the deliberations of Ibadi thinkers and the history of the Ibadi Imams.[6] By the end of the eighth century CE, the long struggle waged by the Ibadis in Oman against their Umayyad adversaries in Damascus or the 'Abbasids in Baghdad imbued the Imamate with an egalitarian character and a sense among its followers of the need to fight together in a common cause, as well as a shared sense of responsibility for striving toward their goal of independence. During this period, the electors of the Imam were in three groups: (1) the country's *'ulama'* (Islamic scholars) and *qadi*s (judges); (2) the *shurat*; these were young men who had volunteered for military service to protect the state; and (3) the tribal chiefs. These three social components provided a counterbalance to the authority of the Imam, while he was the state's main source of authority. The *shurat*, being the main source of military power, played a major role in bolstering the commitment to the Ibadi faith and reviving it if it showed signs of flagging, or if the state should fall.[7]

At its height in the eighth century, the traditional Ibadi Imamate in Oman was based on two elements: *'aqd* (contract; literally binding) and *intikhāb* (election). The legitimacy of the premodern, traditional Sultanate, at least before the 1600s, was based upon *taghallub* (power politics) and *'asabiyya qabaliyya* (tribalism). In this respect, we could perhaps describe the history of Ibadi rule in Oman as a non-Khaldunian exception—in principle and at least in some of its periods—it was not based only on overt tribalism or *'asabiyya*.[8] In reality, however, the Imamate required tribal support and sometimes its alliances reflected a degree of tribal partisanship. This is the basis of the Imamate cycle in Omani history: the theory that the fall of an Imamate was generally due to tribal schisms.[9] An Imam could be deposed only on the basis of consensus and he could not be removed arbitrarily. This became a principle of great importance in Ibadi thought: the Imam was not only a religious authority he also had a political, social, and moral position in the community. Any failing on his part would weaken society. Consequently, the Imam's responsibility was defined with the terms *masalik al-din* (ways of religion), *Zuhur* (manifestation), *shira'* (sacrifice of one's life), *difa'* (defence), and *kitman* (secrecy).[10]

Despite the fact that a larger swathe of society was involved in the Imam's election than was normal in other premodern Islamic ruling systems, some Western scholars have been reluctant to describe the Imamate system as being purely imbued with democratic legitimacy. This is either because the practices of *'aqd* /contract and *intikhab* /election were tacitly underpinned by tribal legitimacy, or because the democratic legitimacy was a kind of contractual democracy or contractual legitimacy based upon the Islamic creed according to which the world is divided into Muslims and polytheists; therefore, the Ibadis' inherited their legitimacy on the basis of the declaration *La hukma illā li-Allah* (There is no rule except Allah's), which meant that the implementation of Allah's Sharia according to the Ibadi school was obligatory.[11]

Oman's historians frequently used the term *'adl* (justice) to express the legitimacy of the rule of a particular Imam, and *jawr* (tyranny) or *jababira* or *tajabbur* (arrogance) to indicate that in their view he had lost his legitimacy under the terms of his contract. These jurist-historians tended to contrast the just to the tyrants and described the periods when the Imamate had been replaced by a Sultanate with the theological expression *fatra*, or lacuna, the empty space in Oman's history. For example, the author of *al-Fath al-Mubin* (*The Manifest Victory*)—Ibn Ruzayq (d. 1874)—referred to *sunun fatrat min 'aqdi 'l-Imama* (the years [missing] from the Imamate contract),[12] while Sarhan al-Izkawi (eighteenth century) wrote: ". . . then there were years in Oman in which there was a *fatra* [missing] from the Imamate contract."[13] He uses the same expression again in reference to the Nabhani period (twelfth century–1624): ". . . I did not find the history of a single Imam in these two hundred years and more. Allah knows best that they were *fatra* years [missing] from the Imamate contract."[14]

Nevertheless, not all *fatras* were merely gaps between Imamates. Sometimes, the country was governed by a kind of mixed rule. Ibn Ruzayq writes of a 500-year period in Oman's Middle Ages (eleventh–sixteenth centuries) when "the *ahl al-Istiqama* (People of Uprightness) appointed the Imams and the Nabhanis ruled as kings in part of the land of Oman and the Imams [ruled] in other areas."[15] And according to al-Izkawi:

> I believe that those aforesaid Imams after al-Salt b. Malik did not hold sway over all of Oman, and their Sultan did not exercise complete control over it [either], but they were in some areas and not others, and [enjoyed the allegiance of] one tribe but not another. The people of Oman were not united in word, nor did they agree on [one] Imam after the strife that occurred between them. This was because they exchanged God's Bounty upon them [for something else], so their hearts became disunited.[16]

As these Ibadi jurist-historians indirectly admit, there was in fact more than one type of legitimacy. There was *a priori* legitimacy in which the Imam was chosen in advance by the *ahl al-hall wa'l-'aqd* (People Who Loosen and Bind, i.e., the people qualified to appoint or depose an Imam) and through *ta'aqud* (contract) or *'aqd*; in the view of the Ibadi political *fuqaha'*, this was the ideal type. Then there was legitimacy after the fact; commonly a feature of the Sultanate system, this entailed acquiring legitimacy to rule after taking power by force. However, in cases of *sira hasana* (good conduct) or *sira murdiyya* (satisfactory conduct), a person who had taken power without the prior consent of the subjects would still enjoy true legitimacy—but in its *a posteriori* rather than *a priori* form.

Traditional Legitimacy: Principles and Realities

Ibadi scholars usually see the relationship between ruler and ruled as based upon two principles: values and mechanisms. Thus, Omani historians generally focus on two fundamental values. After his introductory words on the first Omani Imam—al-Julanda b. Mas'ud (r. 749–751),[17] the author of *al-Fath al-Mubin* (*The Manifest Victory*)—refers to the values of *al-'adl wa'l-haqq* (justice and right),[18] *al-haqq wa'l-'adl* (right and justice),[19] *al-'adl wa'l-insaf* (justice and equity),[20] *al-insāf wa'l-'adl* (equity and justice),[21] and *al-haqq wa'l-'adl wa'l-insaf* (right, justice, and equity).[22] Writing about al-Julanda b. Mas'ud, the historian Sarhan b. Sa'id al-Izkawi (eighteenth century) also adds the attribute *ridā* (consent) to these two other values which bestow legitimacy upon an Imam.[23] Although these historians did not use the word *mashru'iyya* (legitimacy), or even *shar'iyya* (legality) like we do today, they used an equivalent word—*sahha* (validity)—which conveyed the same idea—as in their expression *sahhat al-Imama* (the validity of the Imamate). For example, when describing an Imam the author of *al-Fath al-Mubin* wrote that he was: "*'Imām 'adl sahīh al-imāma min ahl al- istiqāma* (an Imam of justice, whose Imamate [was] valid, of the People of Uprightness)."[24] There were also two other key concepts: *'aqd* or *ta'aqud* (contract) and *intikhab* (election) or *istifa'* (choice). Hence, legitimacy was conditional and not absolute. In this connection, and on the basis of his reading of the classical jurisprudential and theological texts on the subject of the Imamate, Wilkinson judges the legitimacy of the Imamate as being based upon two principles: *'aqd* and *intikhab*[25] as opposed to *bay'a* (oath of allegiance), while it appears that the *bay'a* system was the traditional procedure in Oman, it was *bay'a* without the element of compulsion.[26]

Who were the people responsible for choosing the Imam? In principle they were the *ahl al-hall wa'l-'aqd*,[27] whom North African Ibadi and non-Ibadi historians—such as al-Wasiyān (eleventh century) in *Tārīkh al-A'imma*—describe as *Mashāyikh al-Muslimīn* (the Sheikhs of the Muslims). Ibn al-Ṣaghīr (second half of the nineth century) called them *āhl al-Shūrā* (the People of Consultation), and Zakāriyā al-Wārjilānī (late eleventh century) described them in *al-Siyar* (*The Histories*) as *Jamā'at al-Muslimīn min āhl i'l-Kifāya* (The Competent People in the Muslim Community). In practice, however, the Imam tended to circumvent that procedure and resort to negotiation in order to inherit the Imamate and turn it into a kingdom.[28] Although the formal procedure described above represented the ideal, what do the sources tell us?

The American historian Adam Gaiser's study on Ibadi Imamate traditions introduces a note of caution about most secondary, published material on the Ibadi Imamate and the political and Sharia system, which relies largely on official *fiqh* and historical sources. In his review of the primary sources, the Imamate model presented in those books does not necessarily conform to the way the Ibadi Imams were actually chosen.[29] For example, the fall of the first Omani Imamate in 893 CE—at the hands of the 'Abbasids under the leadership of Muhammad b. Thawr—was followed by a period of unrest and intertribal warfare.[30] Subsequently, numerous books were written examining the causes of the Imamate's demise, and a series of debates recorded on the subject were attributed to the Nizwa and Rustaq schools (both cities in Oman). The most reliable of these books was written by Abu Saʿid al- Kadmi (d. *c.* 973), the *Kitab al-Istiqama* (*The Book of Uprightness*), which described the principles, rules, and application of *al-wilayah wa'l-baraʾa* (loyalty and disavowal). It provides the most extensive information about *al-wilayah wa'l-baraʾa* and, in offering a new angle on the relationship between the ruling authority, the people, and the revolutionaries in their demands for rights, describes the views and attitudes of the different parties involved. In doing so, it shows that, despite the values and mechanisms that underpinned it, legitimacy was still threatened by *khilaf* (disagreement), *shiqaq* (schism), and *inqisam* (division). For instance, when examining the mid-seventeenth-century Yaʿariba dynasty (1624–1744), the Ibadi historian Ibn Ruzayq described a conflict over the legitimacy of the Imamate between two Imams—Balʿarab and Sayf—who were brothers: "People disagreed over them; some were with Balʿarab, saying: 'He is the [true] Imam and his brother Sayf is behaving wrongly towards him,' while others said Sayf was the rightful Imam and Balʿarab was not . . ."[31]

With regard to the tribally-based values and mechanisms of legitimacy to rule according to the Imamate system, before the Imam was installed he had to satisfy the conditions laid down by the *ahl al-hall wa'l-ʿaqd* (the people who loosen and bind). One vital condition was that there should be a preliminary contract to which the Imam would be required to adhere, and another condition was that there should be a recognized selection process. On the other hand, in the Sultanate system, in which legitimacy was already assumed, the Imamate system's values and mechanisms for determining legitimacy were usually replaced by another set of values and procedures. Some Omani historians have tried to categorise them: sometimes as *al-jawd wa'l-nasab wa'l-siyasah* (liberality, lineage, and politics), and at other times as *al-karam wa husnu 'l-khuluq* (generosity and good moral behavior), *al-sira al-hasana* (good conduct), or *al-ʿadl* (justice). For example, we find characterisations of this kind in Ibn Ruzayq's assessment of the reign of the Sultan al-Falāh b. Muhsin of the late Nabhanis,[32] and in his overall verdict on the Nabhani period when he classes Imam and just king as being of equal merit.[33]

At times the Imamate embodied an awakening of the conscience or a conscientious objection to injustice or tyranny. According to Ibn Ruzayq: "When the Bani Nabhan's corruption in Oman grew more severe and they

treated the people of Oman in a humiliating manner, the leading men of
Oman joined forces to eliminate injustice, tyranny, and oppression. Seven
years after the death of Mālik b. al-Hawārī they appointed Abu'l-Hasan 'Abd
Allah b. Khamīs b. 'Amir al-Azdī on the fifth day of the month of Ramadhan
in the year eight hundred and thirty-nine (23 March 1435)."[34] Hence, a Sultanate acquired the character of an Imamate. Indeed, on occasion it endeavored to compensate the people of Oman for the injustices they had suffered
under a period of illegitimate rule:

> . . . Then they appointed 'Umar bin al-Khattab b. Muhammad b. Shadhan
> b. Salt al-Yahmadi [r. 1480–1489] to the Imamate. It was he who took pos-
> session of the funds of the Bani Nabhan and released them to the *shurat* who
> were in his entourage; this was because the Muslims came together and looked
> at the bloodshed by the Bani Nabhan and the [funds and] property they had
> seized wrongfully, and they found that it [amounted to] more than the value
> of their property; so the *qadi* ruled that the property should be returned to
> those who had been wronged, and, [in those cases where the rightful owner]
> was not known, [given] to the *Bait al-Mal* (Treasury) or the poor . . .[35]

But did the fact that the Imamate was established on the principles of *'aqd*
and *intikhab* mean that it was a system founded upon democratic legitimacy? There are different opinions on this. In the modern scholar Hussein
al-Ghubash's view, those who say "Yes it was" base their answer upon a
number of democratic paradigms.[36] On the other hand, those who disagree
regard it as a streamlined version of tribal legitimacy inherited from the
old tribal tradition. In any case, according to John Wilkinson, Islamic systems and values differ from those of their European counterparts, while the
Imamate was an institution that clearly represented a partial departure from
the local tribal concepts and their replacement by religious terminology and
principles. At the same time, it was also compatible with the society that had
given birth to it by virtue of the fact that the Imam was the equivalent of
the traditional tribal chiefs, and his authority was based on the community's
democratic choice. If we consider the issue from every possible angle, we
should be able to determine whether or not modern European concepts are
compatible with the Islamic tradition. According to Wilkinson's Eurocentric
view, the way the system operated was only partially democratic because

the leaders were usually elected by a limited number of families with elite status and authority. Even so, any Omani was able to break through the social barriers of the clan system by acquiring knowledge and learning, and thus join the class who elected the Imam—that is, the *'ulama'*—though this channel was only available to an individual and could not be passed on through inheritance. However, even if an individual should succeed in rising above the class into which he was born, as one of those electing the Imam, he would still be aware of the attitudes of his tribe toward the candidates because he would have previously consulted them. Thus, sectional interests and the Imamate system became intertwined, even if the basic framework was a religious one.[37] On the other hand, Ghubash is willing to reshape the concept to bring it into line with the Ibadi experience as well as modern ways of thinking.

Crises of Traditional Legitimacy

How did Ibadi Omanis respond to legitimacy crises? While Ibadi scholars have not come across the words *azmah* (crisis) or *mashru'iyah* (legitimacy) in their traditional literature, we have come across words that convey the same meanings in the books of the old *fuqaha'* and historians who have pondered over the question of the Imamate. For example, in Sarhan al-Izkawi's historical account of the most noteworthy legitimacy crisis in Oman's history at the time of Imam al-Salt bin Malik (r. 851–885) known as Oman's *Harb al-Dakhiliyyah* (Interior War), he uses an expression indicating that there was a legitimacy crisis when the parties concerned failed to choose an Imam as they could not agree on a choice.[38] He describes this crisis with the term *ishtikāl al-āmr* (ambiguity of the affair): Some of them took an ambiguous position on Musa and Rashid.[39] He frequently refers to a particular Imam's legitimacy crisis with the expressions *āshkala amruhu* (his affair became ambiguous)[40] or *ishtabaha amruhu* (his affair became dubious).[41] Ibadi theologians and jurists have described certain chapters of the Imamate using the words *shakk* (doubt) or *waqf* (suspension). Thus, as far as traditional legitimacy was concerned, in the words of Muhammad b. Mahbūb (d. 874)[42] the converse of *yaqīn* (certainty) was *al-ishkal wa'l-shubha wa'l-shakk* (ambiguity, dubiousness and doubt). Generally speaking, most of the problems that arose in Oman during the changeover from Imamate to Sultanate or Sultanate to Imamate—or even from Imamate to Imamate or Sultanate to Sultanate—had the issue of legitimacy hanging over them.

If we look at the history of Oman as a whole, there is a history of legitimacy crisis or crises. According to Ibn Ruzayq, ". . . Then the *'fitnah'* ('sedition'/'civil strife') occurred in Oman and there were many trials and tribulations, [people] differed in their views and there were many [disparate] ways of behavior and statements between them and gossip intensified." He records that in a single year sixteen *bay'a* elections were given to different Imams.[43] Commenting on the tragedies caused by the legitimacy crises, which turned the Imamate into a sport and entertainment, he wrote: "The *'fitnah'* continued to grow among the people of Oman and the sufferings increased."[44]

As Oman's maritime trade with the Far East continued to expand, a significant event in the country's history was the arrival of ships from as far away as China, including the famous admiral Zheng He who arrived on Omani shores in his third and fifth voyages between 1409 and 1419. Nevertheless, and despite apparent prosperity in maritime trade, political stability proved to be elusive due to the proliferation of emirates and statelets along the coastal regions between Hormuz, Sohar, Qalhat, and Mirbat and in the country's interior from Nizwa to Rustaq and Sumail, which generated furious political rivalry without yielding any political benefits. The arrival of the Portuguese in 1507 CE and their occupation of Oman's coastal cities and various locations on the Indian Ocean, including Diu, Goa, Mozambique, and Mombasa, was a major change.[45] By the beginning of the seventeenth century the Indian Ocean region was seeing rapid transformations and a growing rivalry between the two new European interests, represented by the Dutch East India Company and the British East India Company. These new factors not only led to a realignment of the balance of power, they also produced a revolution in the Indian Ocean's maritime trade and helped to transform the states that had been affected by the Protestant Reformation.

At the beginning of the seventeenth century there were also three non-Arab Islamic empires—Ottoman (Sunni), Safavid (Shiite), and Mogul (Sunni)—all of which wielded influence in the Indian Ocean. This situation at the beginning of the seventeenth century coincided with another development in Oman, where the first glimmerings of a nation-state or a national consciousness began to appear. Though Omanis did not describe it as such, some Omani historians began to refer to *āhl 'Umān* (the people of Oman) rather than *āhl al-Istiqāma* (the People of Uprightness) when referring to the choice of Imam Nāsir b. Murshid (r. 1624–1649) by the *ahl al-hall wa'l-'aqd* in alliance with the tribal chiefs. This marked the beginning of modern history not only for Oman, but also for the Gulf and the West Indian Ocean region. Nāsir b. Murshid was able to unite Oman and subsequently the Portuguese were expelled from the region by his successors who succeeded him as Imams of the Ya'arub state (1624–1744). At this time there were signs that the concept of *'aqdī- dīnī* (religious contract) was beginning to be replaced by the notion of *watanī* (national) in the history books when they referred to the contract between ruler and ruled, while references to rule on the basis of the Qur'an, the Sunna and *sīrat al-salaf* (the practice of the forebears) began to give way to the principle of rule on the basis of *makārim al- akhlaq* (noble moral behavior). Moreover, the old opposition forces that used to struggle for control of Oman—such as the Umayyads, the 'Abbasids, the Seljuks, and the Daylamites—disappeared from the scene and the new unity was a classical expression of the balance of power.[46]

The scholar Robert Kaplan writes that Iran and Turkey made an early appearance as nation-states in the Middle East independently of the colonial powers, and that this was the main reason why they are still influential players on the Middle East's political scene.[47] Eugene Rogan observed that from the fall of Baghdad in 1258 CE, Arabs ceased ruling themselves until the creation of the nation-states in the Arab world after the Second World War.[48] Oman, however, was an exception to Rogan's thesis based on Albert Hourani's view of the sources of the Arab *Nahda* (Renaissance) and the changes introduced into Egypt post- Napoleonic occupation between 1798 and 1801 and beyond.[49] Bernard Lewis offers a different angle when he says the Arabs were impotent, and that Napoleon would never have left Egypt if the British had not attacked under the command of Horatio Nelson in 1798. Moreover, he believed that the Arabs were totally dependent upon the West for good or ill.[50]

Oman's national–religious consciousness was distinct from other parts of the Arab world described by Rogan, Lewis, and Hourani. There were two factors in play in Oman: (1) tribal unity and a sense of Omaniness and a resolve to liberate their country; and (2) Oman's territorial expansion beyond its borders to include several Indian Ocean littoral regions from East Africa to the Indian subcontinent and the Gulf. Its growing political power was matched by a flowering of Ibadi learning and a return to the roots of the school's teachings. Rare manuscripts were copied, while scholars sought out the earliest texts and accorded them priority status as authoritative judicial and creedal sources. This helped to protect the Ibadi school from splintering into factions (indeed, the early Ibadi writings had also contributed significantly to the development of Islamic thought in the eighth and ninth centuries). New works were produced on jurisprudence and theology, leading to a reform of the Ibadi tradition of learning—a process that began in the seventeenth century and has continued to the present day.[51] This coincided with a revival in Yemen, during which a clash occurred within the Zaydi community when some of their religious thinkers tried to bring Zaydi thought closer to Sunni teachings. Subsequently, the revivalist movement in the Arabian Peninsula moved to Najd, where a new splinter movement appeared in the Sunni school with the rise of the Wahhabi movement.[52]

The principle of legitimacy continued to evolve after the fall of the Ya'ariba state in 1744 with the arrival of the Persians during the reign of Nadir Shah (r. 1736–1747) and their subsequent occupation of Oman. This was a period of transition in Persian history from the Afsharid dynasty to the Zands—and during this time the Omanis were able to reunite under a new Imam when the Al-Bu Said dynasty was established (1744 to the present day). The founder of the new dynasty—Imam Ahmad b. Said—expelled the Persians from Oman, and in 1775 he launched a campaign in an alliance with the Ottomans to liberate Basra from the Persians.[53] Subsequently, the ruling family discussed the question of legitimacy with respect to Imam Ahmad's sons, who were known to the general Omani public as the sons of the Imam and given the title Sayyid; this had different connotations from the term as it was conventionally used to describe those descended from the line of 'Ali b. Abi Talib and it was different from the Omani title of sheikh. In fact, it was the Omani equivalent of the title emir. Subsequently, the Imam's grandson, Imam Sayyid Said b. Sultan (1804–1856) took the title Sultan. This progression from Imam to Sayyid to Sultan gave the Al-Bu Saids a distinctly higher status in the Omani tribal hierarchy than that of the tribal sheikhs. Moreover, the title Sayyid was not only applied to the ruler, but also—with the force of law—to his family members. In Omani tradition, the Nabhanis had used the titles Sultan and Sayyid.

A fundamental change in the power structure took place when Muscat, a maritime port, became the capital of the country, replacing the old mountainous and landlocked capitals, Nizwa and Rustaq, during the reign of Ahmad b. Said's grandson, Hamad b. Said (r. 1786–1792). By shifting the capital from the interior to the coast, it established Oman's position on the shores of the Indian Ocean. This new access to the outside world also gave his successor— his uncle Sultan b. Ahmad (r. 1792–1804)—an advantage in the exercise of international diplomacy, expanding the country's trade activities, establishing a more effective military balance of power, and concluding international agreements which extended Oman's influence from Bahrain to Baluchistan and from Somalia to Mozambique. During this period Oman conquered the port of Bandar Abbas (which remained under Omani rule from 1794 to 1871) and recovered its scattered possessions in the Indian Ocean formerly held by the Ya'ariba state. According to Nūr al-Dīn al-Sālimī (d. 1914), during the Ya'ariba period the Omani possessions in India, Mombasa, Zanzibar, and elsewhere were ruled by local governors who claimed them as their own personal fiefdoms. Sultan b. Ahmad recovered such territories as he was able to, while the rest were subsequently recovered by his son, Said b. Sultan (r. 1804–1856).[54] Sayyid Said b. Sultan was widely respected and is referred to in some literature as Said the Great; his realm was later divided between his sons, with one of them ruling Oman and another ruling Zanzibar, while its legitimacy as a political entity remained intact. This continued to be the standard model to ensure that the rule continued uninterrupted.[55] The conservative religious–tribal trend and the al-Bu Said's modernizing trend began to evolve in parallel with each other from the middle of the nineteenth century, driven by the traditional-style Imamate revolutions during the period of Imam 'Azzan b. Qays (r. 1868–1871) and the final Imamate period (1914–1952). This feature was particularly apparent in their response to the colonial period, which continued until after the Second World War.

The structure of Omani society changed in the Omani coastal regions and East Africa at a different pace from the social structure in the traditional interior of Oman.[56] In fact, after the First World War a new set of political configurations appeared in more connected, modernized regions of Arabia and Africa for a variety of reasons, including: (1) the Sykes–Picot Agreement; (2) the fall of the Ottoman State in 1924; (3) oil exploration in the Arabian

Peninsula; (4) the rise of the Saudi state under ʿAbd al-ʿAzīz Al-Saʿud; and (5) the arrival of Sir Percy Cox, the British Resident in the Gulf and a pivotal personality in the region; his policies and the policies of his successors planned and shaped the states of the modern Arabian Gulf.[57]

These changes were reflected in the region's rulers and the emergence of what is known today as the nation-state. John Peterson's study of Oman and the changing nature of the state in the Arabian Peninsula and the Gulf, which he compares with the traditional form of government in the region, describes post-traditional and neotraditional structures in the evolution of governance in contemporary Oman.[58] Peterson portrays Oman according to the traditional view of Arabia as a region consisting of nomadic Bedouin and states with settled populations. Yet at the same time he reminds his readers of the early emergence in Oman and Yemen of states with central authorities, noting that the Omani Ibadi and Yemeni Zaidi doctrines added a distinct sense of identity to the two countries' traditions on the question of legitimacy.

The transition of Oman from a traditional entity to a modern nation-state and the shift in the nature of legitimacy from tribal-traditional to nation-state only became apparent during the reign of the father of Sultan Qaboos, Sultan Said bin Taimur (r. 1936–1970). Even so, Oman remained largely unaffected by the major challenges experienced by other Arab states, particularly those around the Mediterranean basin. This was because Oman was independent from direct colonial rule, despite the Treaty of Seeb 1920 with the British, which limited some of Oman's independence and conflicts inspired by nationalism. Oman also differed from the rest of the Arab world because of its Ibadi history as a state with established institutions. The institution of the Imamate, which was abolished in 1952, was the main problem for the country's internal politics and the question of religious legitimacy still appeared to pose a challenge to the framers of Oman's modern political structures.[59]

Sultan Said, was able to consolidate his power and he managed to overcome the disunity of the House of al-Bu Said. The main challenge came from his cousin Ahmad b. Ibrahim (1896–1981) from the line of Qays, son of Imam Ahmad. His branch of the family had posed a threat from their stronghold in Rustaq, and Ahmed was recognized as being descended from Imam ʿAzzan b. Qays, while Sultan Said was descended from Sultan, the son of Imam Ahmad. The problem was resolved when Sayyid Ahmad bin

Ibrahim was appointed Minister of the Interior and the two cousins became partners. This marked the start of a policy in which the allocation of the post of *wali* (local governor) was decided on a tribal basis and a new alliance was established between the tribal chiefs under one umbrella—a system that continued from 1935 to 1952.[60]

The political historian Uzi Rabi characterizes the years from 1955 to 1959 as the time of the unification of the tribes—a period in which Oman was unified and the Al-Jabal Al-Akhdar War and the Imamate came to an end. This was followed by the transition of the state's legitimacy from tribal–religious traditional to institution-based (1960–1964). Then came the beginning of Oman's reincarnation as an oil state when its institutions were updated to bring them into line with modern state systems.[61] On the other hand, describing the real transformation of the concept of the nation-state between 1932 and 1952, the scholars Jones and Ridout pointed out that the Sultanate continued to represent the *Ummah* (nation).[62] It was this notion of tradition and continuity that enabled the ruling authority to maintain its legitimacy before the emergence of the modern state—or what came to be known as the nation-state—at the end of the nineteenth century. National consciousness in Oman was found in histories written by prominent Omanis, many of them descendants of the clerical-jurists of earlier centuries, for example, Nur al-Din al-Salimi (d. 1914) and his son Muhammad (d. 1985) in his *Nahdat al-'Aiyan* and *'Uman Tarikh Yatkalam* (*Oman: History Speaks*), also 'Abd Allah al-Ta'i (d. 1972), *Tarikh 'Uman al-Siyasi* (*The Political History of Oman*). These histories of Oman usually start their accounts deep in pre-Islamic history with the Arab Malik b. Fahm, who is said to have led Yamani tribes into Oman after the collapse of the Ma'rib dam in Yemen (third century BCE). This links the origins of Arabs in Oman to the Qur'an (34:16): "We sent upon them the flood of the dam, and We replaced their two [fields of] gardens with gardens of bitter fruit, tamarisks and something of sparse lote trees."

Malik, with his band of followers, defeated the Persians upon arriving in Oman. Muhammad b. al-Salimi, in contrast, took a broader view, describing the country's geology and the results of archaeological explorations of prehistoric civilizations. Historians, expanding the chronological horizons beyond the Ma'rib dam, note that the name of ancient Oman was Majan and that it was connected with Mesopotamian civilizations.[63] History appeared in the poetry of a new generation of Omani poets such as Abu Muslim al-Bahlani (d. 1920), Muhammad b. Shaykhan al-Salimi (d. 1927), Abu Salam al-Kindi (d. 1960), 'Abd Allah al-Ta'i (d. 1972), and 'Abd Allah al-Khalili (d. 2000). Sulayman al-Salimi (d. 2001) referred to various aspects of the Omani historical experience as an integral part of nationality and identity (see Chapter 11).[64]

In Oman, a Sultanate–nation-state system has remained stable and intact, while other more fragile Arab states were shattered by the impact of modernization. Monarchies in Iraq and Libya, for instance, became nationalist–leftist–military regimes. Countries seeking independence from colonial rule, such as Algeria, were destabilized by the search for a postcolonial identity. Oman's economic transformation, however, coincided with the decline of British hegemony in the region.[65] Through the Protectorate system and the Seeb Agreement, the British had enjoyed strong economic, political, and military influence throughout Arabia (including Oman) for nearly a century. In 1968, the British Prime Minister Harold Wilson announced Britain's fairly abrupt withdrawal from the region. Britain left Aden in 1970, South Yemen was officially declared independent under a Marxist regime, and the British government feared that Oman would fall to Marxism as well. As the time for Britain's departure approached, their fears grew that Sultan Said would be unable to defeat the rebellion in Dhofar, which borders Yemen. British documents expressed the view that "it is probable that Qaboos [the son] would be far preferable to the present Sultan."[66]

The new Sultan based his power on both the promise of change and the maintenance of important institutional continuities. In the Gulf, Oman was unique because of its geographical and social diversity, although in many ways it resembled its neighbors. Unlike the smaller Gulf States, it had a long history as a quasi-national entity and its historical and political experience had been shaped by Ibadism and a legacy of two and a half centuries of Al-Bu Said rule. These factors meant that the country had the potential to develop without losing its stability.

In fact, in terms of governance, and the longevity of its Imamate and Sultanate system Oman has more in common with Morocco than with other Gulf States. The Omani and Moroccan monarchies are traditional ruling dynasties that became states with imperialist support. Jordan was a praetorian monarchy, Saudi Arabia was a product of tribal conquest, and the smaller Gulf States were cities that became states thanks to imperialist machinations and oil.[67]

The Modern Omani Renaissance: Legitimacy under Sultan Qaboos

Although the father of Sultan Qaboos, Sultan Said bin Taimur, took some steps in transforming Oman from a tribal entity to an institution-based state, during the last years of his reign the country suffered from isolation and a lack of modern development. This was further exacerbated by the Communist revolution in the south of Yemen, which led to rising aspirations among the population for a new era.[68] It was felt that after thirty-three years what was needed was a new head of state to take Oman into the modern age and make a clean break with the past. Many Omanis did even not know what the new Sultan looked like before he took power. He had been a cadet at the Royal Military Academy at Sandhurst before undergoing training in Germany with NATO, so that when he arrived in Muscat his photograph was in great demand.[69] On July 23, 1970, Sultan Qaboos bin Said set out his strategy in his first speech, in which he announced the start of a new era of reconciliation: "Yesterday was complete darkness. Tomorrow will be a new dawn for Muscat, Oman, and its people."[70] As well as changing the name of the country from the Sultanate of Muscat and Oman to the Sultanate of Oman, he also changed the country's flag and the composition of the Council of Ministers.[71]

Sultan Qaboos' accession to the throne on July 23, 1970 marked the start of a new era. It was witnessed by Eloise Bosch, an American teacher (American Reform Church) who had lived in Oman since 1955 with her husband, Dr. Donald Bosch. She recalled: "People began to speak of a new Oman full of exciting opportunities and hopes for a brighter future. It seemed as if a tight band round the chest had been removed and people could breathe freely once again."[72] Since the end of the Al-Jabal Al-Akhdar War in 1958 and then the Zanzibar coup in 1962 life for the Omani people had been hard. They were divided. They either lived quiet and simple lives in Oman without education, healthcare, or in a diaspora searching for jobs in the Gulf Arab States to improve their living standards. Meanwhile, other young Omanis were studying in Baghdad, Cairo, Beirut, and Damascus, or had taken up residence in the Communist countries of Eastern Europe. BBC Arabic Radio was the main channel to provide them with news and they were an anxious to hear about Oman's progress. Probably the main challenges concerned conciliation with the Arab states since most of these states had been on bad terms with the previous Sultan; for example, Saudi Arabia, Iraq, Egypt, Syria, and Kuwait had offices of the Imamate of Oman but Oman did not become a member of the Arab League until September 29, 1971. Eventually, however, and despite all the problems the country faced, Omanis came to see Qaboos as their savior and the hope of the country. The amazing process of political and social transformation which ultimately led to the emergence of the unified modern Omani state was no coincidence and it did not occur haphazardly. Instead, Qaboos took prompt steps to outline the basis of his reign's legitimacy in his accession speech as follows:

> I promise you to proceed forthwith in the process of creating a modern government. My first act will be the immediate abolition of all the unnecessary restrictions on your lives and activities. My people, I will proceed as quickly as possible to transform your life into a prosperous one with a bright future. Every one of you must play his part towards this goal. Our country in the past was famous and strong. If we work in unity and cooperation, we will regenerate that glorious past and we will be respected in the world.[73]

Thus, the Sultanate's legitimacy would be based not only on tradition and history, but on the promise of modernization and services. This was new to Oman. While the Imamate and the Sultanate were mainly based on military, religious, or mercantile success or tribal solidarity, the new Sultanate of Qaboos would continue these functions while also providing services for the people from roads to education. The Sultan proclaimed a bold new vision that fundamentally transformed the relationship between the people and the institutions of government. Sultan Qaboos' reign began with a set of promises which amounted to a kind of new contract with two basic objectives: (1) nation-building; and (2) modernization.[74]

At the same time, the Sultanate's new leadership depended to a large extent upon tradition, while incorporating modern cultural features in a model that blended the old with the new and preserved the well-established elements of Omani society and its heritage and customs intact.[75] He modernized the religious establishment to bring it into line with the modern world; the traditional schools were preserved while steps were taken to ensure that the religious institutions did not become involved in the contemporary Islamic revivalist movements; attention was also given to the non-Muslim religions, particularly since Oman had been noted for its religious and ethnic diversity since ancient times. He improved the status of women, women's rights, and the participation of women in the workplace. His policies protected the environment, preventing pollution, and safeguarded Oman's distinctive environmental diversity. He also sought to use legal means to improve workers' rights and promote equality between nationals and foreigners. This led to the creation of the Sultanate's first labor unions. The Gulf States in general still face the problem of inequality between national and foreign labor, but the state's new measures and policies have helped to raise awareness as well as changing the way in which these issues are understood in the region.[76]

Sultan Qaboos' charisma was a major feature of his leadership and a force behind the unification of the state and the nation from the beginning of his rule.[77] The notion that the king was *mahbub* (loved) and *muhab* (revered)— an object of both awe and majesty—was already prevalent. While retaining these traditional features, Qaboos also added a new ingredient with his rousing speeches and annual meet-the-people tours which created a bond between the ruler and the people. Thus, in the updated legitimacy structure the traditions of *shura* (consultation) and *ahl al-hall wa'l-'aqd* were transformed into a *Majlis* (council/parliament) system in the modern sense of the term. *Shura* and *ijmā'* (consensus) were central to Oman's political culture and entailed inviting members of the population to take part in the political process regardless of their status in the community. In fact, this concept of equality is deeply ingrained in the Islamic legal system based on the Qur'an, hadith (traditions and sayings of the Prophet Muhammad), and *ijmā'* which form the foundations of the Sharia, or Islamic law. These elements are defining features of the *majlis* institution. The *majlis*, or council, was historically part of the decision-making process in Oman at both the tribal and village levels. Indeed, consensus is a quintessentially Omani quality.[78] In fact, the concept of *shura* is a far more significant element in Omani political culture than in other political systems in the Islamic Middle East, and Oman's Ibadi traditions provided a historical model. In this unique cultural environment *shura* is an integral part of the decision-making process. The *shura* culture has provided Oman with the basis of its political development, since it is a tradition designed to cater for change and to legitimize change. Dynamic in nature, it is indispensable for the success of any society, particularly a society like Oman's whose leadership appeared to be confronted by insuperable obstacles when Sultan Qaboos assumed power in 1970.[79]

Although the Sultan retained considerable powers in the Constitution, new basic laws expanded citizen participation and the modernization program required cooperation between people and their government. Oman changed from the historical Sultanate and Imamate to one of broader citizen participation characterized by municipal and council elections and underpinned by a number of other historical factors, including the important Islamic concepts of *shura* and *ijma'*. The Ibadi culture of (relative) equality and the respected authority of the tribal system became embodied in the person of the Sultan. All these elements combined to provide a unique road map for political modernisation rooted in the country's heritage and traditional culture.[80]

The Foundations of the New Legitimacy

In 1980, Sultan Qaboos gave an interview with *Time* magazine saying, "I'd like to see us create a democracy for Oman, and I sincerely hope that day is not too far distant." He asserted that he was guiding his people toward it.[81] So when establishing the foundations of the legitimacy of his rule, what were the things Sultan Qaboos sought to avoid?

He did not accept the prevailing model of political legitimacy that existed in the Gulf region; that is to say, the rentier model, in which the regime derives its legitimacy by buying the allegiance of its subjects by distributing the proceeds from the sale of oil—usually unfairly. This model began after the discovery of oil and was encouraged by the colonial powers. Rather than opting for a rentier state, Sultan Qaboos aimed to set up a *dawlat al-qanun* (state governed by the rule of law)—a *Rechtsstaat* (law-based state)[82]—because he saw Oman as being destined to move in another direction, since: "Quite simply, the Sultanate lacked the resources to proceed towards becoming a rentier state."[83]

Sultan Qaboos' decision may well have played in Oman's favor, since it is becoming increasingly clear that for a number of Gulf States oil has turned out to be a curse wrapped in a blessing. As we can see today, those states are trying to replace their current legitimacy based upon subjects living on handouts from the oil revenues with one in which the wealth is produced by the citizens, and this is no easy matter. In fact, the social and political price may be so high as to be destructive.

Sultan Qaboos also sought to avoid a corollary of the rentier model which was also prevalent in the Gulf—the emiri model in which the state's ministerial posts are held by members of the ruling families, who take control of all the state's services and utilities.

As well as avoiding these potential pitfalls, Sultan Qaboos also introduced new machinery to bolster the legitimacy of his rule: a constitution and a state based on the rule of law:

> Royal Decree No. 101/96, issued in 1996, promulgated a constitution for the country. One striking feature of this document is its focus on the word *qanun* (law) which occurs 69 times, so that it may be rightly seen as a law-based constitution in the modern sense of the word and consequently the Highest Law of the Land. This means that none of the powers in the land, including the Sultan and his government, have the authority to change the Law or the Constitution at whim; instead, they are all bound by the procedures laid down in the Constitution. It also makes it difficult for the state's administrative apparatus—the bureaucracy—to issue legislation that is in direct conflict with the Constitution which—rather than any person whoever he may be— is, and will continue to be, the Highest Law of the Land.[84]

One noteworthy feature of the legitimacy mechanism—that is, the Constitution—is Chapter 3, which deals with the citizen's rights and obligations. It guarantees personal freedoms and civil rights, including protection from violation of the sanctity of a person's home, freedom of religion, freedom of opinion, expression and the press, freedom of assembly, and the freedom to form associations.

Article 17: All citizens are equal before the Law:

The Omani Constitution guarantees a broad range of human rights, including civil freedoms and rights, and it prohibits discrimination on the grounds of gender, origin, color, language, religion, sect, or social status. The social obligations include provisions regulating the relationship between the citizen and the state, while it stipulates that the country's political culture shall be based upon the rule of law, including equality before the law, innocence until proven guilty, the right to bodily protection, and the right to a legal defense (including judicial representation).

Although the Constitution states that Islam is the state religion, it explicitly affirms the rights of non-Muslims to observe their religious traditions, including the freedom to practice their religious rites (Chapter 3, Article 28). It also asserts that the rule of law shall be the basis of governance in Oman and that the state guarantees the independence of the judiciary (Chapter 6, Article 60).[85]

The *Majlis* (council/parliament):

According to the Constitution, the *Majlis Oman* (Oman Council) comprises the *Majlis al-Shura* (Consultation Council) and the *Majlis al-Dawla* (State Council), thus combining the directly elected representatives of the people (the *Majlis al-Shura*) with a body of experts and advisors (the *Majlis al-Dawla*). The Sultan announced the establishment the *Majlis al-Istishari li 'l-Dawla* (State Consultative Council) in 1981 as the first step of his program to upgrade Oman's institutions and provide greater opportunities for its citizens to participate in public affairs. Three years later, in 1984, the Council held its first session with forty-five appointed members. Then in 1990, as the Sultanate celebrated the twentieth anniversary of Sultan Qaboos' reign, he announced that the State Consultative Council would become an elected body called the *Majlis al-Shura*, adding that the new Council was designed to be a "ground-breaking experiment and a solid building block for the institution-based state that we are striving hard to consolidate. "[86]

The establishment of this new institution was a turning-point in Oman's modern political history and marked the first of a series of steps paving the way for the creation of a parliamentary system of government. At the same time, this new departure was rooted in tradition and sought to involve those people who were best qualified to represent their electorates. The public response was enthusiastic, as ". . . sheikhs, dignitaries, village leaders and local *'ulama'* were invited to elect educated, open-minded people with the ability to take part in this process."

The *Majlis al-Shura*'s members represented every one of the Sultanate's sixty-one *wilayat*s. With its unique heritage, its unshakeable belief in Allah, and its strong sense of national cohesion, Oman was reborn out of the virtual darkness to become a strong modern state, but also a state firmly rooted in its original culture.[87]

The 2020 Transition

On January 10, 2020, there was a change in the legitimacy of governance in accordance with the Constitution. Sultan Qaboos' will was opened and with his family's consent, power was transferred to his cousin—Sultan Haitham bin Tariq—who became the new Sultan of Oman.

Sultan Haitham will have his own priorities and style of rule. So far, however, he has continued to follow much of the model and roadmap set out by Qaboos; most recently, Sultan Qaboos had transformed the country's politics and the legitimacy of its governance during the Arab Spring of 2011. The role of the state was expanded and the reforms carried out in Oman under Sultan Qaboos were part of a general political plan to be implemented in a number of stages, in direct response to the demands of each successive stage of national development.

Notes

1. J. C. Wilkinson, "Bio-Bibliographical Background to the Crisis Period in the Ibāḍī Imāmate of Oman," *Arabian Studies* 3 (1976): 137–164; Uzi Rabi, "The Ibadhi Imamate of Muhammad bin ʿAbdallah al-Khalili (1920–54): the Last Chapter of a Lost and Forgotten Legacy," *Middle Eastern Studies* 44(2) (2008): 169–188.

2. J. C. Wilkinson, "The Origins of the Omani State," in Derek Hopwood (ed.), *The Arabian Peninsula: Society and Politics* (London: George Allan & Unwin, 1972), 67–68; J. E. Peterson, "Oman's Odyssey: From Imamate to Sultanate," in B. R. Pridham (ed.), *Oman. Economic, Social and Strategic Developments* (London: Croom Helm, 1987), 1–16.

3. J. C. Wilkinson, "The Ibadi Imama," *Bulletin of the School of Oriental and African Studies* 39(3) (1976): 535–551; J. C. Wilkinson, *The Imamate Tradition of Oman* (Cambridge: Cambridge University Press, 1987); Adam Gaiser, "The Ibadi Stages of Religion Re-examined: Tracing the History of the Masālik al-Dīn," *Bulletin of the School of Oriental and African Studies* 73 (2010): 207–222; Adam Gaiser, *Muslims, Scholars, Soldiers: The Origin and Elaboration of the Ibadi Imamate Traditions* (Oxford: Oxford University Press, 2010).

4. J. C. Wilkinson, "A Sketch of the Historical Geography of the Trucial Oman down to the Beginning of the Sixteenth Century," *Geographical Journal* 130(3) (1964): 337–349; J. C. Wilkinson, "The Oman Question: the Background to the Political Geography of South-east Arabia," *Geographical Journal* 137(3) (1971): 361–371.

5. Patricia Crone, "The Kharijites and the Caliphal Title," in G. R. Hawting, J. A. Mojaddedi, and A. Samely (eds.), *Studies in Islamic and Middle Eastern Texts and Traditions in Memory of Norman Calder* (Oxford: Oxford University Press, 2000), 85–91; Patricia Crone, *God's Rule: Government and Islam* (New York and Edinburgh: Columbia University Press and Edinburgh University Press, 2004).

6. Elie Adib Salem, *Political Theory and Institutions of the Khawarij* (Baltimore, MD: Johns Hopkins University Press, 1956), 56.

7. Abdulrahman S. al-Salimi, "Themes of the Ibadi/Omani Siyar," *Journal of Semitic Studies* 54(2) (2009): 475–514; Abdulrahman S. al-Salimi, "Identifying the (Ibadi/Omani) Siyar," *Journal of Semitic Studies* 55(1) (2010): 115–162; Abdulrahman S. al-Salimi, "The Political Organization of Oman from the Second Imamate Period to the Ya 'ruba: Rereading Omani Internal Sources," in Cyrille Aillet (ed.), *L'Ibadisme dans les Societes de l'Islam Medieval* (Berlin: De Gruyter, 2018), 111–124.

8. Muhsin Mahdi, *Ibn Khaldūn's Philosophy of History* (Abingdon: Routledge, 2015), 196–199; Allen J. Fromherz, *Ibn Khaldun, Life and Times* (Edinburgh: Edinburgh University Press, 2011), 140–149; J. C. Wilkinson, *Water and Tribal Settlement in South-East Arabia: a Study of the Aflaj in Oman* (Oxford: Clarendon Press, 1977), 62–64; Thomas Bierschenk, "Religion and Political Structure: Remarks on Ibadism in Oman and the Mzab (Algeria)," *Studia Islamica* 68 (1988): 102–127.

9. Wilkinson, *The Imamate Tradition of Oman*, 91–110.

10. Gaiser, "The Ibadi Stages of Religion Re-examined," 207–222.

11. Wilkinson, *Water and Tribal Settlement in South-East Arabia*, 148–153; Gaiser, *Muslims, Scholars, Soldiers*, 69–96.

12. Humayyid b. Muhammad [b. Ruzayq/Raziq] Ibn Ruzayq, *Al-Fath al-Mubīn fī Sīrat al-Sāda al-Bū Sa'idiyyīn*, ed. 'Abd al-Mun'im'Āmir and Muhammad Mursī 'Abd Allah, 5th edn. (Muscat: MNHC, 2001), 201, 207; trans. G. P. Badger, *History of the Imams and Saiyids of 'Oman from AD 661–1856* (London, 1871) (reprinted New York: Burt Franklin, 1974).

13. Sarhan b. Sa'īd b. Sarhan b. Sa'īd b. Umar al-Sarhani Izkāwī, *Kashf al-Ghumma al-Jami' li- Ākhbār al-Umma*, ed. Muhammad Habshi Sālih et al. (Muscat:

Ministry of Heritage and Culture, 2012), 5:189; E. C. Ross, "Annals of Oman from early Times to the Year 1728 AD," *Journal of the Asiatic Society of Bengal (Calcutta)* 43(2),,Pt 1 (1874): 111–196.

14. Izkāwī, *Kashf al-Ghumma*, 6:19.

15. Ibn Ruzayq, *Al-Fath al-Mubīn*, 219.

16. Izkāwī, *Kashf al-Ghumma*, 5:190.

17. Ibn Ruzayq, *Al-Fath al-Mubīn*, 194.

18. Ibn Ruzayq, *Al-Fath al-Mubīn*, 200; Izkāwī, *Kashf al-Ghumma*, 5:171.

19. Ibn Ruzayq, *Al-Fath al-Mubīn*, 201, 204, 300.

20. Ibn Ruzayq, *Al-Fath al-Mubīn*, 264.

21. Ibn Ruzayq, *Al-Fath al-Mubīn*, 245.

22. Ibn Ruzayq, *Al-Fath al-Mubīn*, 201.

23. Izkāwī, *Kashf al-Ghumma*, 5:162.

24. Ibn Ruzayq, *Al-Fath al-Mubīn*, 211.

25. See Wilkinson, "The Ibadi Imāma," 535–551.

26. Abū Muhammad Nūr al-Dīn 'Abd Allah b. Humayd Al-Sālimi, *Tuhfat al-A'yan bi Sirat Ahl 'Uman*, 2 vols. in one, ed. Abu Ishaq Ibrahim Itfayyish (Cairo: Matabi' Dar al-Kitab al-'Arabi, 1961), 1:269,

27. Wilkinson, "The Ibadi Imama." 535–551.

28. Pierre Cuperly, *Introduction a l'etude de l'Ibadisme et de sa theologie* (Algiers: Office des Publications Universitaires, 1984), 289–309.

29. Gaiser, *Muslims, Scholars, Soldiers*, 144.

30. Izkāwī, *Kashf al-Ghumma*, 5:181.

31. Ibn Ruzayq, *Al-Fath al-Mubīn*, 258.

32. Ibn Ruzayq, *Al-Fath al-Mubīn*, 220–221.

33. Ibn Ruzayq, *Al-Fath al-Mubīn*, 229.

34. Ibn Ruzayq, *Al-Fath al-Mubīn*, 226.

35. Ibn Ruzayq, *Al-Fath al-Mubīn*, 226–227; Izkāwī, *Kashf al-Ghumma*, 6:22–23.

36. See, e.g., example Hussein al-Ghubash, *Oman: the Islamic Democratic Tradition* (Abingdon: Routledge, 2006), 22–40.

37. Wilkinson, "The Ibadi Imama," 545.

38. Wilkinson, "Bio-Bibliographical Background to the Crisis Period in the Ibadi Imamate of Oman," 137–164.

39. Izkāwī, *Kashf al-Ghumma*, 5:196.

40. Izkāwī, *Kashf al-Ghumma*, 5:196.

41. Izkāwī, *Kashf al-Ghumma*, 5:197

42. Izkāwī, *Kashf al-Ghumma*, 5:199–200.

43. Ibn Ruzayq, *Al-Fath al-Mubīn*, 204.

44. Izkāwī, *Kashf al-Ghumma*, 5:177–180; Ibn Ruzayq, *Al-Fath al-Mubīn*, 206.

45. Ralph Kauz, "Omani Ports in Chinese Sources," 57–65; Joao Teles, "China, Oman and Omanis in Portuguese Sources in the Early Modern Period (ca. 1500–1750)," 227–265; Valeria Fioriani Placentini, "The Growth of the Relationships between Oman, the Gulf and the Western Waters of the Indian Ocean. Oman: the Corner-Stone of a Maritime System," 143–184; Eric Staples, "The Formation of Oman's Maritime Power under the Yaariba and Sayyid Said," 185–202; Pius Malekandathil, "From Slumber to Assertion: Maritime Expansion of the Ibadis of Oman and the Responses of Estado da India, 1622–1720," 203–218, all in Michaela Hoffmann-Ruf and Abdulrahman al-Salimi (eds.), *Oman and Overseas* (Hildesheim: Georg Olms Verlag, 2013).

46. S. B. Miles, *The Countries and Tribes of the Persian Gulf* (London: Frank Cass, 1966), 140–142.

47. Robert Kaplan, *The Revenge of Geography* (New York: Random House, 2013), 268–269.

48. Eugene Rogan, *The Arab: A History* (New York: Basic Books, 2009), 13–17.

49. Albert Hourani, *Arab Thought in the Liberal Age* (Cambridge: Cambridge University Press, 1983), chs.1–3.

50. Bernard Lewis, *What Went Wrong? The Clash between Islam and Modernity in the Middle East* (New York: Harper Perennial, 2003), 33.

51. Abdulrahman al-Salimi, "Trends in Religious Reform on the Arabian Peninsula," *HEMISPHERES* (2012), vol. 27.

52. Bernard Haykel, *Revival and Reform in Islam: The Legacy of Muhammad Al-Shawkani* (Cambridge: Cambridge University Press, 2003).

53. Ibn Ruzayq, *Al-Fath al-Mubīn*, 320–321.

54. Al-Salimi, *Tuhfat*, 2:185–186.

55. More details, see Robert G. Landen, *Oman since 1865* (Princeton, NJ: Princeton University Press, 1967).

56. S. N. Eisenstadt, *Tradition, Change and Modernity* (New York: John Wiley, 1973), 4.

57. Philip Graves, *Life of Sir Percy Cox* (Hutchinson: London, 1939); Francis Owtram, *A Modern History of Oman* (London: I. B. Tauris, 2004), 29–50.

58. J. E. Peterson, "Legitimacy and Political Change in Yemen and Oman," *Orbis* 27(4) (1984): 971–998.

59. J. E. Peterson, *The Unification of Oman: Political and Structural Development of Government* (Baltimore, MD: Johns Hopkins University Press, 1973).

60. Dale F. Eickelman, "From Theocracy to Monarchy: Authority and Legitimacy in Inner Oman, 1935–1957," *International Journal of Middle Eastern Studies* 17 (1985): 3–24; J. E. Peterson, "Britain and the Oman War: An Arabian Entanglement," *Journal of Asian Affairs* 63(3) (1976): 285–298.

61. Uzi Rabi, *The Emergence of States in a Tribal Society: Oman Under Sa'id bin Taymur 1923–1970* (Brighton: Sussex Academic Press, 2006), 71–129; P. S. Allfree, *Warlords of Oman* (London: Robert Hale, 1967).

62. Jeremy Jones and Nicholas Ridout, *A History of Modern Oman* (Cambridge: Cambridge University Press, 2015), 99–132.

63. Muhammad b. ʿAbd Allah al-Salimi and Nājī ʿAssāf, *ʿUmān, Tārīkh yatakallam* (Damascus: al-Matbʿa. al-ʿUmūmiyya, 1383/1963), 10–41, commissioned by Sulayman and Aḥmad, sons of Muḥammad al-Sālimī.

64. For further details, see the articles by John C. Wilkinson, "A Historic Perspective on the Nahḍa," 25–34; Angeliki Ziaka, "Redefining Ibāḍī Identity through Religious Discourse in the Time of the Nahḍa," 45–54; Valerie J. Hoffman, "Ibadis in Zanzibar and the Nahda," 129–144; John C. Wilkinson, "Ibāḍism and State Formation in Oman," 163–170, all in Abdulrahman al-Salimi and Reinhard Eisener (eds.), *Oman, Ibadism and Modernity*, Studies on Ibadism and Oman (Hildesheim: George Olms Verlag, 2018); also Abdulrahman al-Salimi, "Bibliographical Dictionary in Oman," in Reinhard Eisener (ed.), *Today's Perspectives of Ibadi History* (Hildesheim: Olms Verlag, 2016), 245–258. Martin Custer, *Al-Ibadiyya: A Bibliography*, 2nd edn. (Hildesheim: Olms Verlag, 2016), 1:508–509; 3:666–668.

65. Joseph Churba, *Conflict and Tension Among the States of the Persian Gulf, Oman and South Arabia* (Alabama, Maxwell Air Force Base, 1971); C. Crouch, "The Jabal Akhdar and Dhofar Wars: A Critical Analysis of Official and Semi-Official Sources," Honours dissertation, University of Western Australia, 1986; J. B. Kelly, *Sultanate and Imamate in Oman* (London: Chatham House Memorandum, 1959); D. de C. Smiley, *"Muscat and Oman," Journal of the United Services Institution* 105(617) (1960): 29–47.

66. Robert Alston and Stuart Laing, *Unshook to the End of Time: A History of Britain and Oman, 1650–1970* (London: Stacey International Publishers, 2012), 254–256.

67. Fred Halliday, "Monarchies in the Middle East: A Concluding Appraisal," in Joseph Kostiner (ed.), *Middle East Monarchies: The Challenge of Modernity* (Boulder, CO: Lynne Rienner, 2000), 289–303. See also Dale F. Eickelman, "Religious Tradition, Economic Domination and Political Legitimacy: Morocco

and Oman," *Revue de l'Occident Musulman et de la Mediterranee* 29 (1980): 17–30.

68. J. E. Peterson, *Oman's Insurgencies: The Sultanate's Struggle for Supremacy* (London: Saqi Books, 2008); Abdel Razzaq Takriti, *Monsoon Revolution* (Oxford: Oxford University Press, 2016).

69. A conversion with the photographer Taghlib al-Barawani.

70. Linda Pappas Funsch, *Oman Reborn: Balancing Tradition and Modernization* (New York: Palgrave Macmillan, 2015), 62; *The Royal Speeches*. 7, Muscat, Ministry of Information, 2015.

71. Ian Skeet, *Muscat and Oman: The End of an Era* (London: Faber & Faber, 1974).

72. Donald Bosch and Eloise Bosch: *The Doctor and the Teacher* (Muscat: Apex, 2000), 61.

73. *The Royal Speeches*, 7, Muscat, Ministry of Information, 2015.

74. Funsch, *Oman Reborn*, 65.

75. See John Townsend, *Oman: The Making of a Modern State* (London, Croom Helm, 1977); Calvin H. Allen Jr., *Oman: The Modernization of the Sultanate* (Boulder, CO: Westview Press, 1987); J. E. Peterson, "Oman: Three and a Half Decades of Change and Development," *Middle East Policy* 11(2) (2004): 125–137.

76. Dale F. Eickelman, "National Identity and Religious Discourse in Contemporary Oman," *International Journal of Islamic and Arabic Studies* 6(1) (1989); Abdulrahman al-Salimi, "The Transformation of Religious Learning in Oman: Tradition and Modernity," *Journal of the Royal Asiatic Society* 21(2) (2011): 147–157; Abdulrahman al-Salimi, *A Comparison of Modern Religious Education in Arabia: Oman and Yemen*, 9 pp., September 2011, available at: www.ijtihadreason.org/articles/modern-religious-education.php.

77. Richard K. Common, "Barriers to Developing 'LEADERSHIP' in the Sultanate of Oman," *International Journal of Leadership Studies* 6 (2) (2011): 215–228.

78. Joseph A. Kechichian, "The Throne in the Sultanate of Oman," in Joseph Kostner (ed.), *Middle East Monarchies: The Challenge of Modernity* (Boulder, CO: Lynne Rienner, 2000), 187–211; Marc J. O'Reilly, "Omani Balancing: Oman Confronts an Uncertain Future," *Middle East Journal* 52(1) (1998): 70–84.

79. Hussain S. Al-Salmi, *Oman's Basic Statute and Human Rights: Protections and Restrictions* (Berlin: Klaus Schwarz Verlag, 2013), 207–221; Jeremy Jones and Nicholas Ridout, *A History of Modern Oman* (Cambridge: Cambridge University Press, 2015), 196–220

80. Hussain S. Al-Salmi, *Oman's Basic Statute and Human Rights*, 105.

81. See at: https://www.csmonitor.com/1980/0320/032051.html.

82. See Harold J. Berman, "The Rule of Law and the Law-Based State (*Rechtsstaat*): With Special Reference to the Soviet Union, in Donald D. Barry (ed.), *Toward the "Rule of Law" in Russia? Political and Legal Reform in the Transition Period* (Armonk, NY: M. E. Sharpe, 1992), 46–47; Nathan J. Brown, *The Rule of Law in the Arab World: Courts in Egypt and the Gulf* (Cambridge: Cambridge University Press, 1997), 242.

83. Calvin H. Allen Jr. and W. Lynn Rigsbee II, *Oman under Qaboos: From Coup to Constitution, 1970–1996* (New York: Routledge, 2013), 226. It is interesting to compare it with Fred Halliday, *Arabia Without Sultans* (London: Penguin, 1974).

84. Allen and Rigsbee, *Oman under Qaboos*, 222–223.

85. Francesca Ersilia, "Religion and Politics in Contemporary Omani Ibadism," 87–96; Adam Gaiser, "The Roots of Religious Tolerance in the Omani–Ibadi Tradition," 297–305, both in Abdulrahman al-Salimi and Reinhard Eisener (eds.), *Oman: Ibadism and Modernity*, Studies on Ibadism and Oman (Hildesheim: George Olms Verlag, 2018).

86. Hussain S. Al-Salmi, *Oman's Basic Statute and Human Rights*, 203–214.

87. Hussain S. Al-Salmi, *Oman's Basic Statute and Human Rights*, 31–33, 70–71.

7

THE INTERPRETATION OF ISLAM
UNDER SULTAN QABOOS

Valerie J. Hoffman

Oman is the only country in the world in which the majority of Muslims, at least by the Omani government's own account, belong to the Ibadi sect of Islam. Ibadism is the only surviving branch of Kharijism, the movement that originated in discontent with the caliphates of 'Uthman (644–656) and 'Ali (656–661). Today Ibadis deny that they are Kharijis because of this appellation's linkage to a long-extinct group that was known for its violence, although there were always moderate Kharijis as well. Ibadism thus represents a third branch of Islam, distinct from Sunnism and Shiism. Ibadis, who number less than 1 percent of the world's Muslims, are found mainly in the Oman and in small pockets in Algeria, Libya, and Tunisia, and among Omani immigrant communities in East Africa. Sultan Qaboos bin Said was himself an Ibadi. His reign from 1970 to 2020 and his program of modernization and social transformation cannot be fully understood without addressing the role of Ibadism in Omani society and history and the interpretation of Islamic thought fostered under his rule.

The original distinctions between the Kharijis, the Shia, and the main body of Muslims, later called Sunnis, concerned the qualifications of the leader of the Muslims (the caliph/*khalifa* or imam). Until the end of the 'Abbasid caliphate (750–1258 CE), Sunnis required that the caliph or imam belong to the Quraysh tribe, but thereafter they accepted any ruler who could unify the majority of Muslims. The Shiites, the partisans of 'Ali, held that the imam must belong to the immediate household or descendants of Muhammad; the Twelver/Imami and Isma'ili branches of Shiism hold that there can only be a single true imam, selected by God. Kharijis held that tribe and lineage have no bearing on the qualifications of the imam, who should be selected in consultation with the leading scholars of the community on the basis of his piety and qualifications for leadership.

Among the distinctive features of traditional Ibadism are a strong insistence on just rule, the requirement to resist injustice, and the permissibility of removing tyrannical rulers whenever possible. Unlike Sunni *ulama'*, who came not only to accept dynastic rule but to make it a religious requirement to obey tyrannical rulers, Ibadi scholars played a role in the selection of the ruling imam and in opposition to injustice. The prioritization of justice over stability has sometimes caused conflict and political upheaval in Ibadi societies. This was particularly evident in the period from the late eighteenth to the early twentieth centuries, when there were numerous uprisings against the rulers of the Busa'idi dynasty, which remains in power in Oman today. One of these uprisings, led by the great Ibadi scholar Sa'id ibn Khalfan al-Khalili, succeeded in overthrowing the reigning sultan in 1868, expelled the Saudi Wahhabis from Omani territory, and installed a pious Ibadi imam, 'Azzan ibn Qays al-Busa'idi, who hailed from the same extended family as the ousted sultan. The sultanate party succeeded in overthrowing the imam in early 1871, with Wahhabi assistance and tacit British approval. The next major uprising, led by the most prominent scholar of modern Oman, Nur al-Din al-Salimi (1869–1914), established the imamate of Salim ibn Rashid al-Kharusi in the Omani interior in 1913, but did not succeed in overthrowing the sultan or conquering the coast. The division between "Muscat," ruled by the sultan, and "Oman," ruled by the imam, remained until December 1955, when Sultan Said bin Taimur reunited Oman under his rule. An initially successful rebellion against the sultan by leaders of the former imamate in June 1957 was quelched by a combined Omani–British force.[1] Nur al-Din al-Salimi's son Muhammad described the conflict between conservative Ibadism and secular government as innate: "The struggle between monarchy and imamate has never ceased, for monarchy loves power, majesty and tyranny, whereas the imamate is imbued with the spirit of the Sharia laws followed by the imams. It is a government built on consultation, the election of a just imam, and conformity to the Sharia."[2]

When Qaboos bin Said ascended the throne in 1970, he faced numerous challenges, including the regrouping of exiled imamate forces, a communist insurgency in Oman's southwestern Dhofar province, and the enormous task of building the infrastructure of a modern nation-state. Despite the agitation of the exiled imamate forces, Qaboos' accession gained the approval of most of Oman's prominent scholars. Through granting amnesty and distributing rewards, including government employment, Qaboos was able to heal the wounds of old ideological divisions. It is a testament to his success in meeting Ibadi standards of justice that Muhammad al-Salimi, who had described the principle of sultanate as inherently opposed to that of imamate, recited a laudatory poem when the sultan visited his hometown in 1979, offering him effusive praise for eliminating injustice, building hospitals and other essential institutions, and preserving Omani heritage.[3]

There are no firm statistics on the percentage of the Omani population that is Ibadi; estimates have ranged from 45 percent to 75 percent. Some researchers estimate that about half the population is Sunni, and there is also a small but important Shiite population. Ibadism has a special connection to the history of Oman, but in the construction of the modern nation-state Sultan Qaboos aimed to win the allegiance of all segments of the population. He charted a path that balanced pride in the Ibadi heritage with a deliberately nonsectarian approach to the teaching of Islam in mosques and schools. Like other states in the region, his regime nationalized, bureaucratized, and regulated religious life in the sultanate.[4] Oman's Ministry of Education developed an Islamic curriculum that avoided all sectarian identities and markers, offering what Dale Eickelman and Marc Valeri have called "generic" Islam.[5] Jones and Ridout, on the other hand, see this as a reflection of a historical tendency toward ecumenism within Omani Islam.[6]

Despite Jones and Ridout's emphasis on historical continuity, there can be no doubt that there have been significant changes in the way Omani Ibadis understand their relationship to non-Ibadi Muslims. Contemporary Omani Ibadis may even be shocked to learn that classical Ibadi sources reserved the epithets "Muslim" and "believer" for pious Ibadi Muslims; non-Ibadi Muslims and unobservant or deviant Ibadis were labeled *kuffar ni'ma*—guilty of the infidelity of hypocrisy or failure to be grateful for God's blessings.[7] It is perfectly true that such labels had little impact on everyday social life and that

Omanis have a culture that values politeness and tolerance, but the change in the way that Ibadis describe their relationship with non-Ibadi Muslims is nonetheless remarkable.[8] When, in 2000, I asked the late Sheikh Salim ibn Hamad al-Harithi, a *qadi* in Mudayrib who preserved the perspective of Nur al-Din al-Salimi, whether Ibadis dissociate from Sunni Muslims, he replied, without hesitation, "Yes." His traditionally exclusive viewpoint did not prevent him from kindly inviting me to have dinner with his daughters; in other words, he exemplified the traditional combination of exclusive theology and inclusive practice. When, a few months later, I posed the same question to the mufti of the Sultanate of Oman, Ahmad ibn Hamad al-Khalili, he replied with a categorical, "No." He went on to say that the differences between Ibadis and Sunnis are insignificant, relegated to secondary issues that do not impede Islamic unity. Having read numerous Ibadi refutations of Sunni doctrine, I pressed him on this. I pointed out that the great Abu Nabhan Ja'id ibn Khamis al-Kharusi (1734/5–1822) had written a *fatwa* in response to a question from an Ibadi about a Sunni friend who was exceedingly devout, pious, and kind. What, asked the Ibadi, is this man's fate in the afterlife? Abu Nabhan's response was uncompromising: regardless of how kind, pious, and good a non-Ibadi Muslim may be, he will inevitably go to hellfire, because his beliefs and practices are faulty. Sheikh al-Khalili was acquainted with this *fatwa* (and prevented me from relating its details in front of our audience), but he said Ibadis no longer believe that, attributing Abu Nabhan's intransigence to the isolation of life in Oman's interior at that time. Social change and historical context influence the interpretation of religion. During the reign of Sultan Qaboos, the interpretation of Islam was adapted to meet the demands of a rapidly modernizing society.

Sheikh Ahmad ibn Hamad al-Khalili, Mufti of the Sultanate

Sheikh al-Khalili has been the most prominent spokesperson in Oman on Islamic issues since Sultan Qaboos appointed him as mufti in 1975. The grandson of a *qadi* in Bahla, Khalili was born and raised in Zanzibar, where he never attended school, but studied with his parents, memorized the Qur'an by age nine, and attended the study circles of several scholars, including those of the Algerian Ibadi scholar, Abu Ishaq Ibrahim Atfiyyash, when he visited Zanzibar. He and his family were forced to leave Zanzibar after the bloody revolution of 1964 and returned to Bahla, where he attached himself to Sheikh Ibrahim b. Sa'id al-'Abri, who became the first Mufti of the Sultanate in 1973. Khalili was appointed Director of Islamic Affairs in the Ministry of Justice, Religious Endowments and Islamic Affairs (later the Ministry of Endowments and Religious Affairs) and was appointed Mufti of the Sultanate upon the death of Sheikh al-'Abri in 1975. In addition to his position as Mufti, he has served as head of the Board of Directors of the Sultan Qaboos Center of Islamic Culture and of the Board of Directors of the College of Sharia Sciences, and also headed the publications and book editing committee in Oman's Ministry of Heritage and Culture. He is a signatory to the Amman Message (*Risalat 'Amman*) of November 2004 that called for tolerance and unity in the Muslim world. This declaration called for the recognition of all the Sunni legal schools, as well as the Ja'fari (Twelver Shiite), Zaydi, Zahiri, and Ibadi schools. It forbade declaring as an apostate anyone who is a follower of the Ash'ari or Maturidi creed, "real Sufism," or "true" Salafi thought, or branding as an unbeliever anyone whom others recognize as Muslims. It also placed stipulations on the issuing of religious edicts. Jordan's King 'Abdullah, who urged this initiative, said it was to proclaim "the Islamic message of tolerance" in response both to intolerance among Muslims and to Islamophobia in the West.[9]

In addition to regular appearances on television and participation in numerous religious and scholarly gatherings, Sheikh al-Khalili is a prolific writer on a broad range of subjects. A frequent topic of his writings and speeches is the necessity of unity among Muslims and the avoidance of intolerance, factionalism, and extremism. This concern is evident even in the titles of some of his publications, such as *Nabdh al-ta'assub al-madhhabi* (Repudiation of Sectarian Factionalism) and *I'adat siyaghat al-umma* (Refashioning the *Umma*). The first of these books is a response to a letter received from a Sunni student in Texas, where Muslims from diverse countries met and prayed together at an Islamic center. They had been very impressed by some of the Ibadi students' knowledge of the Qur'an and had asked them to serve as imams in prayer. Then some new Sunnis came who warned against associating with Ibadis, saying that they are Kharijis. So this young man wrote to Khalili, asking for clarification.

Khalili began by "greeting the noble brother with the greeting of Islam," giving him the full Islamic greeting that a more traditional Ibadi would extend only to an Ibadi affiliate. He expressed sadness over division among Muslims, "which hurts Islam, which God made a single religion." He quotes various Qur'anic verses that affirm that the *umma* is a single community that should not be divided and argues that the unification of ranks in the *umma* is a fundamental requirement of Islam, especially in this time when the global *umma* faces enemies, conspiracies, and diverse threats. "Islam requires every Muslim who believes in God and the last day to strive toward unity and harmony." It is particularly regrettable, he wrote, that those calling for division "are sincere in their work for God and are people of knowledge and virtue."[10]

Khalili then launches into a somewhat revisionist account of the usual narrative of Ibadi origins. He says that the Messenger of God established a system of judgment on the basis of consultation, justice and fairness, staying the hand of the oppressor and giving the oppressed his due. Those Companions who kept to this system followed that way. "That was the Rightly-Guided caliphate, in which there was no distinction between the caliph and anyone else; all the people were equal before the truth. An ordinary person could complain to a judge about the caliph. That was the justice of Islam in the time of the Messenger and the Rightly-Guided Caliphs." But then power was surrendered to people who secretly hated Islam and turned the just caliphate into an oppressive hereditary empire. In other words, Khalili carefully referred to the first four caliphs as "the Rightly-Guided Caliphs" and avoided all mention of previous Ibadi dissociation from 'Uthman and 'Ali, which would offend a Sunni Muslim; in this narrative, the problems started when the Umayyads came to power in 661.[11] His response to the Sunni student is similar to one he gave a reporter in Bahrain in 1997.[12] For selfish reasons, Khalili says, scholars flattered unjust rulers and forged hadiths requiring that unjust rulers be obeyed.

> In this circumstance there were some who called for the truth among the people and called on them to cling to virtue and the principles of the Book and the Sunna that the Messenger brought and applied, as did the Rightly-Guided Caliphs. But tongues wagged against these people and accused them of many things and called them names, so that they were misunderstood among the people. Foremost among those who called on people to follow the way of the Messenger and the Rightly-Guided Caliphs are the Ibadis, who received a great share of the accusations, and who were relentlessly opposed.

"They accused them only of believing in God the Mighty and Praised" (Q 85:8). Those who fought them wanted only to walk in the ways of the oppressors. All this happened after power in the lands of Islam was given to the Umayyads. They were followed by the 'Abbasids, who ruled in the same way. There were numerous battles between these two states and the Ibadis. The Ibadis have been blamed for these, although they kept to the limits and acted according to the Sunna of the Messenger of God and did not go beyond it by a single hair.

Someone might object that I have attacked the Umayyads and blamed them for things of which they are innocent. I would like to assure those who think this that I bear no hatred for the Umayyads for being Umayyad,[13] but I bear hatred for falsehood and injustice. We affiliate with those among the Umayyads who stood up for justice, such as the righteous caliph, the truthful imam, 'Umar b. 'Abd al-'Aziz, may God be pleased with him. We affiliate with him in religion and consider such affiliation nearness to God Most High. But we cite him as proof of the injustice of the [other] Umayyads. He took their wealth and returned it to the public treasury, because they had taken it wrongly and unjustly. If his predecessors had been right, this caliph would have been unjust to take their money. The Ibadis agreed with this just caliph and sent him delegations when they heard of his justice and straightness and virtue. They agreed with him on many matters, but they disagreed with him on very simple, subsidiary matters. Nonetheless, the imam of the Ibadis, Abu 'Ubayda Muslim b. Abi Karima al-Tamimi, said, "If only the people would accept what he says," meaning would that they would agree with him, even in these simple, subsidiary matters on which they disagreed with him; none of them ever wielded a sword in his face. On the contrary, they showed him obedience and called him a just caliph. You will find that the books of the Ibadis are filled with praise for him. This is recorded in the book of Professor Ahmad Amin, *Duha al-Islam*: "They look at personalities in the light of faith, unlike others who look at faith in the light of personalities." He did well in this, although he included them among the Kharijis.[14]

Khalili spoke in a similarly conciliatory fashion in an interview with a reporter from the Bahraini newspaper *Al-Wasat*, who asked him about the origins and distinctive teachings of the Ibadis. Sheikh al-Khalili carefully referred to the first four caliphs as "the Rightly-Guided Caliphs" and avoided all mention of Ibadi dissociation from 'Uthman and 'Ali. When discussing the civil war that tore Muslims apart under the caliphate of 'Ali (656–661), he said that the Ibadis disapproved of those who rebelled against 'Ali, since he was a duly elected imam, and that they also disagreed with subjecting 'Ali's dispute with Mu'awiya to arbitration at the battle of Siffin. In other words, he avoided points that would offend a Sunni Muslim.[15]

Nonetheless, it is interesting to note the non-Ibadi scholars that Khalili invokes in his response to the student in America in order to justify Ibadi rejection of unjust rulers. He calls them "three great scholars who testified to this deviation," and they are none other than Sayyid Qutb, Abul Ala Mawdudi, and Abul Hasan Nadvi. Mawdudi (1903–1979), founder of Jama'at-e Islami in India and Pakistan, denounced the majority of the Muslim elite as un-Islamic (*jahili*). Qutb (1906–1966), a member of the Muslim Brotherhood in Egypt, has often been called the father of modern violent jihadism. He expanded on Mawdudi's notion of the new *jahiliyya* (the Age of Ignorance, a term used to describe Arabia before Islam) to advocate ongoing armed struggle in order to rescue Islam and Muslims from steep moral decay. He called Islam's highest purpose "the liberation of humans from servitude to other humans." Qutb's manifesto, *Milestones*, written in prison during the reign of Gamal Abdel Nasser, "was for jihadis as Lenin's *What Is To Be Done?* was for Communist agitators: a justification and guidebook for revolutionary change."[16] Abul Hasan Nadvi (1914–1999) of India was a member of the puritanical and sometimes violent Deobandi school. In other words, Oman's main spokesman for Islam was explicitly identifying with an Islamist perspective that condemned the majority of the Muslim elite as un-Islamic (*jahili*), an attitude linked to some of the most militant Sunni groups, such as al-Qaeda and ISIS, which Khalili would undoubtedly condemn. But Mawdudi's recital of early Islam, which Khalili quotes at length, is highly supportive of the Ibadi point of view, arguing that *jahiliyya* found its way into Islamic social organization during the caliphate of 'Uthman, because "the caliphate called for expansion and progress due to the rapid expansion of the empire, and the third caliph, who bore the burden of this great work, was not up to the task." So Mawdudi faulted 'Uthman not for immorality, but for incompetence. Mawdudi went on to say:

> 'Ali tried his best to prevent this discord and protect political power for
> Islam from the conquest of *jahiliyya*, but he could not prevent the reactionary

revolution, and lost his life trying. So ended the age of the caliphate according to the way of prophethood. Monarchy took its place, standing on the principles of *jahiliyya* instead of Islam. The greatest defect is that the true nature of the *jahiliyya* was hidden from people, as it took the garb of Islam.[17]

Despite appealing to the authority of Sunni scholars, Khalili decried the falsehoods written by non-Ibadis about the Ibadis; Sunni scholars have accused the Ibadis of the worst crimes of the most violent Kharijis, practices that no Ibadi scholar would condone.[18] Khalili also recalled the rudeness of the Saudi mufti, 'Abd al-'Aziz bin Baz, when Khalili visited the Kingdom of Saudi Arabia in 1986. Khalili writes that he and his party were eager to meet bin Baz and hear what he had to say:

> But we were shocked when he took us into a narrow room and began to advise me concerning the *fatwa*s he had heard from me on matters of the caliphate, on which the Ibadis have a distinct point of view derived from the Book of God and the Sunna of the Messenger. This advice was filled with malignant words; he described the Ibadis as deviants who had gone far from the truth brought by the Messenger.[19]

Khalili replied by politely thanking him for his advice and suggesting that the truth be manifested through calm, purposeful, mutual discussion in whatever place he liked, perhaps in Mecca, and that the discussion be broadcast so people could hear it and know the truth. This bin Baz violently rejected. Khalili writes, "I asked what he wanted. He said, 'I want you to abandon your doctrine and follow ours.'" Bin Baz rejected the idea of a broadcast debate in order to avoid the dissemination of Ibadi "falsehoods."[20] Bin Baz's intransigence led Khalili to deliver a televised rebuttal of Bin Baz's accusations and to write a book defending Ibadi doctrines against accusations of unbelief and deviance.[21]

The most dangerous enemies of this *umma*, said Khalili, are those who strive to divide and dismember it. He refers to the Salafis as *al-Hashwiyya* ("stuffed"), a derogatory term used in Muslim heresiographies and other literature to describe Muslims who adopted an anthropomorphic view of God:

> The worst sin the Ibadis have committed, according to the scales of the Hashwiyya, is that they zealously affirm the transcendence of God Most

High and the unity of this *umma*. The Hashwiyya are enemies of all that. They are the enemies of divine transcendence because they inherited from the Jews the belief that God is like His creation and vigorously spread this belief in all corners of the earth, misleading the people into thinking this is the teaching of the pious first generation of Muslims (*al-salaf al-salih*) and of the Glorious Qur'an and the Sunna of the Prophet, on whom be the best blessing and purest salutations.[22]

Khalili defends Ibadi teaching on the impossibility of seeing God, and cites Sunni authors who condemned the Wahhabis for accusing Muslims of unbelief and allowing them to be killed, plundered, and enslaved. Whereas the Wahhabis accuse the Ibadis of being Kharijis, Khalili says that their violent treatment of other Muslims proves it is they who are the Kharijis. He contrasts the violence of the Wahhabis to the kind and just behavior of various Ibadi imams and cites their defense of Muslim lands from non-Muslim invaders and imperialists.[23]

In a discussion with an unknown Ibadi about Islamic unity, Khalili demonstrated classic Ibadi concerns about unjust rulers and the need to dissociate from them, arguing that religious scholars' support for unjust rulers poses very serious problems for the *umma*. "If the Prophet—on whom be the most noble blessings and peace—announced that he dissociated from anyone who cheats, what about someone who cheats the entire *umma* by imposing unjust burdens on them and robbing them of their legal rights according to his own whims . . .? Shouldn't the entire *umma* dissociate from such a person?"[24] Khalili said that Sunni reformers recognized the truth of this, so the Ibadi stance does not contradict concern for the unity of the *umma*, which concern, he argued, is consistent with Ibadi tradition:[25] when the Ibadi military commander Abu Hamza conquered Medina in 747, he declared that his followers were in unity with all people except idolaters, infidels among the People of the Book, and unjust imams.[26] The *umma* may disagree on subsidiary issues, said Khalili, but this does no harm—indeed, one of the things that distinguishes Islam is that it regards disagreements on such matters as a mercy. The unity of the *umma* is fractured not by insisting on the priority of just government, but when people go to extremes by wrongly insulting other groups.[27]

Khalili pursued this theme further in a book titled *Al-Istibdad: mazahiruhu wa-muwajahatuhu* (*Despotism: Its Manifestations and How to Confront It*), written not in response to attacks on Ibadis, but in response to the denunciation of the Arab Spring uprisings of 2011–2012 by official *'ulama'* in various Arab countries. In this book, which appears to be privately published, the Mufti defends the right of people to demand their rights and attacks unprincipled *'ulama'* who serve the interests of autocratic regimes. Despotism, he argues, has become so pervasive that no other form of rule is accepted, and anyone who questions this is condemned as deviant and heretical and treated without mercy. Is it any surprise, he asks, that when the winds of the Arab Spring blew, *fatwas* were issued against those who protested injustice? The belief that it is proper religion to obey tyrants and be subservient to despots was imposed on the *umma* and inherited generation after generation, ever since the collapse of the rule of the Rightly-Guided Caliphs. In its cunning, this new "orthodoxy" fought Islam with the sword of Islam, whereas "true Islam came to remove from humanity the weight of injustice and the rule of oppressors."[28]

He cites with an attitude of incredulity an Egyptian religious scholar who in 2008 found "Islamic" justifications for then-President Hosni Mubarak to bequeath the presidency to his son. Khalili traces this justification back to the subversion of the caliphate and its transformation into an unjust dynastic monarchy by the founder of the Umayyad dynasty, Mu'awiya ibn Abi Sufyan (r. 661–680). He uses language similar to that quoted earlier to signal that he is not against the Umayyads as a clan and that the Ibadis recognize and affiliate with the Umayyad caliph 'Umar ibn 'Abd al-'Aziz. As in *Wa-saqat al-qina'*, he cites the just and tolerant behavior of various Ibadi imams. He also cites laudatory remarks by non-Ibadis about Ibadi rulers' tolerant policies and their rule based on consultation. He points to the role Ibadi scholars played in exposing the true beliefs of the Wahhabis when they first emerged in the late eighteenth century. In his section on recent Sunni reformers with perspectives similar to those of the Ibadis, he cites not the divisive Mawdudi and Qutb, but a more moderate and widely acceptable figure, the Syrian advocate of pan-Islamism, 'Abd al-Rahman al-Kawakibi (1855–1902), author of *Taba'i' al-istibdad* (*The Nature of Despotism*). Kawakibi was imprisoned for his complaints against the injustices of the Ottoman governor in Aleppo and later moved to Egypt, where he joined the circle of the modernist scholar, Muhammad ʿAbduh.

Sheikh al-Khalili is respected not only in Oman, but internationally. The Tunisian Ibadi scholar Farhat al-Jaʿbiri described him as "a walking encyclopedia" who is sincerely pious. "He is also very popular because he goes out and meets people. The mufti in Egypt doesn't leave his headquarters, whereas Khalili leads the prayer five times a day and he travels everywhere, so the people love him. He goes to console the bereaved, he goes to all events. He has acquired a genuine popularity." He claimed that Khalili does not need to use papers or books, but relies on his memory. "He has impressed people both inside and outside Oman as an exemplary Muslim. He is humble in dress. He went to the Mzab [in Algeria] when Sheikh [Ibrahim] Bayyud [1899–1981] was alive. Sheikh Bayyud said, 'I've never met anyone like him.'"[29] Jaʿbiri also cited an incident at a meeting convened in 1978 to plan the future Sultan Qaboos University in Muscat. A Saudi delegate at the meeting asked the Mufti about the Ibadi perspective on the Companions of the Prophet. "The sheikh gave a beautiful answer. He said, 'The Ibadis have different perspectives on the Companions. Some are severe in their condemnation of some of them, some take a more moderate approach, and another accepts all of them as good Muslims—we have all the viewpoints!' This," said Sheikh Farhat, "had a great effect on me regarding the method of reform." When the time for evening prayer came, Khalili invited the Saudi imam of Mecca to lead them in prayer, to the consternation of an Algerian Ibadi who was present.[30]

Khalili engages in polemic in response to provocations, but his preferred role is that of an enlightened thinker and promoter of Islamic unity. Two scholars at Jordan's Al al-Bayt University, where Khalili serves on the Board of Trustees, wrote a laudatory article on his efforts in promoting pan-Islamic unity and repudiating fanaticism. They note his flexibility and tolerance of those whose doctrines differ from his own. They note that he cites the views of those who disagree with the Ibadis and mentions them with respect. "He believes there can be reconciliation if one removes hatred and tries to understand the views of those who disagree with us and avoid extremism and narrow-mindedness."[31] They also applaud the "realism" of Khalili's ideas on jurisprudence and his insistence that the changing circumstances of life must be taken into consideration when applying Islamic law to modern society; the focus must be on the goals of the Sharia and what is in the best interests of the Muslims, rather than enforcing outdated practices. They quote him as saying that rigidity in interpreting the Sharia is harmful, and that we must use our intellects while engaging in legal reasoning (*ijtihad*). "This is why some *'ulama'* say God's religion revolves around the public good, so wherever the good is found, there is the law of God." However, Khalili draws the line when there is a decisive text from the Qur'an or hadith on a matter.[32]

Not all of Khalili's *fatwas* can be characterized as flexible or liberal. He famously spoke out against the construction of the Royal Opera House in Muscat, urged the government to ban alcohol in Oman, and declared that gyms and health clubs are "dens of vice" that should be shut down or closely watched to prevent abuse. His statement about gyms was prompted by the fact that some of them employ foreign women as masseuses.[33]

Ibadis, like other Muslims, traditionally held the view that People of the Book who do not fight the Muslims must pay the *jizya* tax in a state of humiliation, while unbelievers who fight the Muslims are subject to plunder, enslavement, or death. In his commentary on Nur al-Din al-Salimi's *Ghayat al-murad*, Khalili softens the harshness of this judgment by saying it is reserved for a state of war and implies the capture of prisoners of war, not the perpetuation of slavery or violation of the human right to be free.[34]

Khalili's literary production is so prolific that in 2015 a new publishing house in Muscat was dedicated entirely to his writings: Al-Kalima'l-Tayyiba. His *pièce de résistance*, in both the literal and metaphorical sense of the term, is his fifteen-volume project, *Burhan al-haqq* (*Demonstration of the Truth*),[35] of which fourteen volumes have been published so far. The idea of writing the book, he says, came when he received questions about doctrinal disagreements from some students in Algeria. He decided to write "a comprehensive, definitive (*mani'*) work" on the issues on which the *umma* agreed and disagreed, with an exposition of the arguments used by the different parties, "in order to strengthen the truth, prove the spurious to be false, and to analyze different transmissions (*riwayat*)."[36]

Khalili argues that the *umma* is in urgent need of unification, and that the only way this can be accomplished is through agreement on sound doctrine. He argues that disagreements among the *umma* are caused primarily by the failure to adhere to the teachings of the Qur'an and hadiths that are *mutawatir*.[37] Those who have deviated from the truth, he writes, belong to one of three groups: those who are so attached to the imams of their schools that they fail to turn to the Qur'an and sound Sunna;[38] those who uncritically accept inauthentic hadiths that contradict the teachings of the Qur'an; and those whose embrace of rationalism has led them to reject *mutawatir* hadiths and even to entertain doubts about the Qur'an itself. Khalili insists on the necessity of relying on both the intellect and sound, transmitted texts in the pursuit of truth.

Volume 1 of *Burhan al-haqq* presents arguments for the existence of God drawn from the Qur'an,[39] but draws more extensively on a book published in New York in 1958: *The Evidence of God in An Expanding Universe: Forty American Scientists Declare Their Affirmative Views on Religion*. This work, containing brief chapters by forty American scientists of different specializations, was translated into Arabic and published in Beirut around 1980. In his introduction, the editor argues that monotheism is the original, natural religion of humankind, which became corrupted and degenerated into animism, fetishism, nature worship, idolatry, worship of a human being, deification of the state, and ultimately atheism.[40] Such a viewpoint bears obvious affinities with Muslim belief that Islam is the religion of original human nature (*fitra*), which, in addition to providing scientifically generated arguments for the existence of God, may account for the popularity of this book among Muslims.[41] *Burhan al-haqq* reproduces thirty of the forty chapters of the book verbatim.[42] Volume 2 is dedicated to the attributes of God (attributes of essence and of act, whether the attributes of essence are added to the essence, as some Ash'aris say, or are the essence itself, as the Ibadis and Mu'tazila say). Volume 3 deals with God's speech and the controversy over the createdness or eternity of the Qur'an. Subsequent volumes deal with the questions of whether or not God can be seen, free will versus predestination, the "ambiguous" (*mutashabih*) verses of the Qur'an, what may and may not be said of God, and so on, exhausting all the major questions of theology before going into questions of *fiqh*. The comprehensiveness of his approach is not dissimilar to earlier Ibadi encyclopedic works, but the difference is his desire to appear entirely fair-handed, presenting the arguments of all parties on these questions before analyzing the indications of the Qur'an and sound Sunna. The outcome, of course, is never in doubt: Ibadism provides the most correct teachings, with proper, balanced consideration of textual evidence in the light of rational proof.

Religious Policy of the Sultanate of Oman

The Sultanate of Oman stands out among the Muslim states of the Middle East for its cordial, and even warm, interfaith relations and for the freedom of religion it grants to residents of all faiths. The Busa'idi dynasty has long embraced religious tolerance, which deeply impressed British officials when Omanis ruled the Swahili coast.[43] Sayyid Said bin Sultan (r. 1805–1856), who moved the capital of the Omani empire to Zanzibar in 1832, instructed his governors to respect the religious customs of the people they ruled and prohibited the slaughter of cows in Hindu quarters, out of deference to Hindu religious sensibilities.[44] Barghash ibn Said (r. Zanzibar 1870–1888) approved the building of a huge Anglican cathedral in the center of Zanzibar town, and British and French missionaries were allowed to function freely in non-proselytizing capacities among Muslims.

Sultan Qaboos emphasized the importance of faith in Islam in a speech delivered on November 26, 1975, stating:

> We put the teachings of our religion above all other considerations, and the "message of the mosque" provides the inspiration which guides us through life and illuminates our path. We are resolved to ensure that Islam's radiance fills our minds and souls and casts its light over every part of our land. This is demonstrated by the importance we attach to religion and religious teachings in our educational system—whether in the schools, the barracks or the larger community.[45]

Nonetheless, he inveighed against "factionalism of whatever persuasion," arguing that "obstinacy in religious understanding leads to backwardness in Muslims" as well as violence and tolerance, which contradict Islam, "the religion of liberality."[46] Sultan Qaboos also took pains to promote religious harmony in Oman and in the region.[47] Even Muslim groups are not allowed to proselytize among non-Muslims in Oman. Sultan Qaboos' foreign policy dovetails with his religious policy; Oman has played an important mediating role in regional sectarian disputes and in the negotiations between the United States and Iran that led to the nuclear agreement of 2015.

The Ministry of Endowments and Religious Affairs

In 1997, Oman's Ministry of Justice and Islamic Affairs was renamed the Ministry of Endowments and Religious Affairs, to signal its concern with promoting harmony among all religious groups. The first person to be appointed Minister of Religious Affairs was Abdullah bin Mohammed Al-Salmi, grandson of the great scholar Nur al-Din al-Salimi, who led the rebellion in 1913 that formed an imamate in Oman's interior.[48] According to Angeliki Ziaka:

> The policies that were followed on his behalf strengthened the religious and historical past of Oman and prioritised Ibadism and its historical background—from the early Muslim years until today—with the goal of having this special branch of Islam serve as the religious force responsible for promoting both Omani uniqueness and respect for the other branches of Islam, Sunnis and Shiites, who continue to live constructively within the Sultanate.[49]

In addition to a population that includes all three main branches of Islam, Oman has more than fifty Christian congregations representing different languages and denominations, Hindus and Sikhs are accorded official recognition and have their own places of worship, and smaller religious communities, such as Buddhists, are also free to practice their religion. The Ministry also sponsors, in cooperation with the Reformed Church of America, the Al-Amana Centre, an academic institute that promotes Muslim–Christian cooperation and understanding and introduces delegations of students and officials to Oman's religious and cultural landscape.[50]

In 2003, the Ministry inaugurated a journal titled *Al-Tasamuh* (*Tolerance*), renamed *Al-Tafahum* (*Mutual Understanding*) in 2011. A total of seventy issues of *Al-Tasamuh* and *Al-Tafahum* were published. In the fall 2020 issue, editor Abdulrahman al-Salimi announced that the journal was coming to an end, explaining that the titles of the journal reflected Sultan Qaboos' vision of a human society characterized by intellect, justice, and ethics, implying, though never explicitly stating, that the passing of Sultan Qaboos in January 2020 occasioned the end of the journal.[51] The theme of issue 67 (January 2020) of the journal was Sultan Qaboos' proclamation on human harmony.

The journal described itself as Islamic, but it explicitly promoted a diversity of perspectives, Muslim and non-Muslim, in its coverage of a broad range of subjects. Each issue had a section devoted to a particular theme, containing articles on the subject by diverse scholars. Some authors appeared regularly, especially the Lebanese scholar Ridwan Al-Sayyed, who served as a consultant for the journal. The theme of the first issue of *Al-Tasamuh*, unsurprisingly, was tolerance, and included articles on the subject from numerous philosophical, religious, and historical perspectives, as well as an article by Joseph van Ess on medieval Islamic education, a dialogue with Wilferd Madelung, and an article by the Egyptian scholar Hasan Hanafi on "enlightened Islam." Subsequent themes included the self and the other; current thinking and future transformations; Islamic political thought; language, culture, and identity; reason, justice, and ethics; civil society; freedom and responsibility; modalities of reform; religious pluralism; religion, authority, and the state; civilizations and the arts; global peace and justice; the rights of God and human rights; the concept of social contract; Islam and global mission; the unity of the umma; religious charitable associations; and ethics and the global economic system. In addition to articles discussing the theme of each issue, there are "studies" on a broad range of topics, including history, philosophy, and language, and features on different cities and culture of the Muslim world.

I do not claim knowledge of the publications of all the different ministries of religious affairs in the Muslim world, but I can certainly affirm that the intellectual caliber of this journal far exceeds that of any of the official religious journals of Egypt. I suspect that one would be hard put to find any other official religious publication of its caliber. Although each issue begins with a Qur'anic verse, and the relevance of Islamic texts to the issues at hand is emphasized in many of the articles, the journal is refreshingly devoid of polemic and reflects an impressive diversity of voices from different faiths, philosophies, and regions of the world.

As mentioned earlier, the Minister of Religious Affairs, Abdullah bin Mohammed Al-Salmi, has dedicated his career to the promotion of interfaith understanding. Seven of his lectures were published in Arabic, English, German, Hebrew, and Chinese in a single volume titled *Religious Tolerance: A Vision for a New World*. These speeches took place in diverse venues: Aachen Cathedral in Germany; a meeting of the American Society of Missiology in Illinois; a meeting in Cairo of the Conference on the Islamic Forum; Cambridge University's Inter-Faith Programme; the Centre of Islamic Studies at Oxford University; and the National Defense College of Muscat. In these lectures, Al-Salmi argues that all religions are based on a common foundation of values such as freedom, equality, and tolerance. It is not religion that causes conflicts, he says, but conflicts of interest, power contestations, and power imbalances. He endorses Hans Küng's statement at the Conference on Religions in Chicago in 1991 that there can be no peace between nations without peace between religions, and there can be no peace between religions without dialogue, which must go beyond the Abrahamic religions. Dialogue, says Al-Salmi, will overcome fear and allow for the cooperation necessary for the survival of the planet in today's globalized world.[52] In his lecture at Muscat's National Defense College, he spoke strongly against the politicization of religion or making it the basis of the legitimacy of a political party or state. "The state's body has a highly abrasive digestive system," he said, "which would cause religion to disintegrate and break down."[53] No one should interfere with the beliefs of others, but neither should one react violently to proselytizing efforts. "There should be a reforming effort to instill openness, a balanced and human vision of the religious other," he argues. Belief "should always be an incentive for doing good works" and be based on a system of values that includes human equality, freedom, dignity, and compassion.[54]

Far from ignoring the problems faced by the Muslim world, and the Arab world in particular, in his keynote lecture at the meeting of the American Society of Missiology in Chicago on June 18, 2005, Al-Salmi discussed the crises of identity and politics that produced modern movements of political Islam.[55] Unlike Islamists, who raise fears that Islam is defeated and in danger, Al-Salmi points out that Muslims constitute one-fifth of the world's population, and their numbers continue to grow. The problems that Islamists regard as religious, he says, are actually economic, political, and strategic. The attacks of September 11, 2001 alarmed Muslims all over the world and raised fears for the situation of Muslims in the West and for relations between the Muslim world and the West. Muslim societies are also pluralistic, he pointed out, both religiously and ethnically.[56] He appealed to the United States and the global system to help the Muslim world, and in particular to resolve the Palestinian problem, which he described as "a disturbing, bleeding wound for all of humanity." Wars, he said, are not the answer—after all, the war in Afghanistan produced Bin Laden and Al-Qaeda, and the Iraq war resulted in al-Zarqawi, "and who knows what else." He decried the supposed justification of the invasion of Iraq, the spread of democracy, "which carries no weight in the face of all the bloodshed and destruction."[57] Despite these problems, Al-Salmi said, "We are convinced that the future of at least one-third of humanity depends on this great human experiment, this open society in the United States."[58] Citing Peter Berger's division of the major living religious traditions into three families—those of Semitic origin, those of Indian origin, and those of Chinese origin—Al-Salmi concludes that reason, justice, and morality lie at the heart of all of them, and that a focus on this these elements would "lead us to the heart of our shared humanity."[59]

Although the Sultanate embraces Ibadism as an important part of its cultural heritage, its identity is more firmly oriented toward the sea and the expansive horizon implied by its mercantile culture. This is reflected in many of the cultural programs and exhibits promoted by the Sultanate. Al-Salmi also reflected this orientation when responding to a question about Ibadism posed by a visiting scholar in January 2013. He said, "Ibadism in Oman is different from Ibadism elsewhere, because Omanis are people of the sea."[60] It is somewhat ironic to hear these words from the grandson of Nur al-Din al-Salimi, that uncompromising exemplar of the puritanical Ibadism of the Omani interior. Not only does Sheikh Abdullah's comment imply a modified self-identification in terms of his origins, but it acknowledges that geography influences religious doctrine. Furthermore, he removes the center of Omani Ibadism from its traditional stronghold in the interior, displacing it to the coast, making it a maritime religion that rejects dogmatism and exclusivism and embraces tolerance for all people.

Conclusion

The interpretation of Islam, and religious policy more generally, under the rule of Sultan Qaboos bin Said adapted to a program of modernization and development from 1970 to 2020. The writings of Sheikh Ahmad al-Khalili, Mufti of the Sultanate of Oman, the journal published by the Ministry of Endowments and Religious Affairs, *Al-Tasamuh/Al-Tafahum*, and the published speeches of the Minister of Religious Affairs, Sheikh Abdullah bin Mohammed Al-Salmi, all show how Ibadism was shaped in a general climate of change, reconciliation and oneness inspired by Qaboos' overall policies

and vision. Sheikhs Khalili and Al-Salmi, the two most prominent representatives of Islam in the sultanate, both hail from prominent religious families of Oman's Ibadi heartland, and they are both dedicated to Ibadism, but
they are also, in some ways, a fascinating study in contrasts, beginning with
Khalili's prioritization of sound doctrine as the foundation of Islamic unity,
as opposed to Al-Salmi's statement that power struggles are the cause of conflicts, not religious doctrine. Khalili has devoted his life to the promotion of
Ibadi doctrine and standards of morality, even as he rejected the exclusivism
of classical Ibadism and advocated for the unity of the *umma*. His emphasis
on the priority of morality and justice, so consistent with Ibadi tradition,
led him to find common ground with Sunni Islamists like Mawdudi and
Sayyid Qutb, while waging a prolonged battle against the intolerance and
anti-rationalism of Salafis of the Wahhabi persuasion, whom he derisively
labels *Hashwiyya*. Al-Salmi, on the other hand, has devoted his life to the
promotion of scholarship on Islam and Ibadism, including John Wilkinson's deconstructionist approach to Ibadi origins,[61] and has made interfaith
understanding a personal priority. What these three dimensions of Islamic
interpretation under Sultan Qaboos have in common is a dedication to both
scholarship and social harmony on a national, regional, and global scale. In
a region that is increasingly torn by brutal sectarian violence, Oman presents
a unique balance between religious devotion and social cosmopolitanism; its
people are religiously devout but lack religiopolitical fanaticism, exemplifying
the spiritual courtesy (*adab*) that many Muslims believe to be the hallmark
and heart of Islam.

Notes

1. John E. Peterson, *Oman's Insurgencies: The Sultanate's Struggle for Supremacy*
   (London: Saqi, 2007), 75–182.
2. Muhammad al-Salimi, *Nahdat al-a'yan bi-hurriyyat 'Uman* (Cairo: Dar al-Kitab
   al-'Arabi, n.d.), 149.
3. A video of this presentation may be found at: https://www.youtube.com/
   watch?v=SKxLNXnXcjA, last accessed February 15, 2021.
4. Abdulrahman al-Salimi, "The Transformation of Religious Learning in Oman:
   Tradition and Modernity," *Journal of the Royal Asiatic Society* 21(2) (2011):
   147–157.

5. Dale Eickelman, "Identité nationale et discours religieux en Oman," in *Intellectuels et militants de l'Islam contemporain* (Paris: Seuil, 1990), 117; Marc Valeri, *Oman: Politics and Society in the Qaboos State* (London: Hurst, 2009), 127.

6. Jeremy Jones and Nicholas Ridout, *Oman: Culture and Diplomacy* (Edinburgh: Edinburgh University Press, 2012), 42.

7. I say this based on the reactions of some Omani Ibadis to my discussions of Ibadi doctrine.

8. Cf. Valerie J. Hoffman, "The Articulation of *Ibadi* Identity in Modern Oman and Zanzibar," *Muslim World* 14(2) (2004): 201–216; Valerie J. Hoffman, "Ibadi Scholars on Association and Dissociation, from the Tenth to the Twenty-First Century," in Barbara Michalak-Pikulska and Reinhard Eisener (eds.), *Ibadi Jurisprudence: Origins, Developments and Cases* (Hildesheim: Georg Olms Verlag, 2015), 185–194; Valerie J. Hoffman, "Ibadi Thought in Modern Oman and Zanzibar: An Analysis Drawn from Political Geography," in Yohei Kondo and Angeliki Ziaka (eds.), *Local and Global Ibadi Identities* (Hildesheim: George Olms Verlag, 2019), 177–192.

9. The Amman Message, available at: https://ammanmessage.com/?option=com_content&task=view&id=58&Itemid=42, last accessed February 16, 2021.

10. Ahmad b. Hamad al-Khalili, *Nabdh al-ta'assub al-madhhabi*, Silsilat Muhadarat min ajli fahm sahih li-'l-Islam 10 (Sib: Maktabat al-Damiri, 2010), 5–9.

11. Al-Khalili, *Nabdh al-ta'assub al-madhhabi*, 10–11.

12. Fahd b. 'Ali b. Hashil Sa'di, *Liqa'at fi l-fikr wa-l-da'wa ma'a samahat al-shaykh Ahmad b. Hamad al-Khalili, al-mufti al-'amm li-saltanat 'Uman* (Muscat, 2008), 193–206; cf. Hoffman, "Ibadi Scholars on Association and Dissociation," 190.

13. Meaning that he does not hate them for their clan affiliation.

14. Ahmad b. Hamad Khalili, *I'adat siyaghat al-umma, halqa* 1 (Muscat: Maktabat al-Jil al-Wa'id, 2003), 11–17. Ahmad Amin (1886–1954) was an Egyptian historian. *Duha al-Islam*, first published in 1933–1936, was the second part of his ambitious history of Islamic culture.

15. Sa'di, *Liqa'at*, 193–206.

16. Glenn E. Robinson, *Global Jihad: A Brief History* (Stanford, CA: Stanford University Press, 2021), 7, 14.

17. Khalili, *I'adat siyaghat al-umma*, 18–20.

18. Khalili, *I'adat siyaghat al-umma*, 33–41.

19. Khalili, *I'adat siyaghat al-umma*, 44–45.

20. Khalili, *I'adat siyaghat al-umma*, 45–46.

21. *Al-Haqq al-damigh* (*The Overwhelming Truth*) (Muscat: Maktabat al-Damiri, 1992). Cf. Dale Eickelman, "National Identity and Religious Discourse in Contemporary Oman," *International Journal of Islamic and Arabic Studies* 6 (1989): 1–20.

22. Ahmad b. Hamad al-Khalili, *Wa-saqat al-qina'* (*The Mask Fell Off*) (Seeb: Maktabat al-Damiri, 2010), 16. This book is an edited transcription of a lecture the Mufti gave in response to derogatory comments about Ibadis given in a recorded lecture by a Syrian/Qatari sheikh, 'Abd al-Rahim al-Tahhan.

23. Khalili, *Wa-saqat al-qina'*.

24. Sa'di, *Liqa'at*, 257.

25. Sa'di, *Liqa'at*, 261–263.

26. Sa'di, *Liqa'at*, 256.

27. Sa'di, *Liqa'at*, 256.

28. *Al-Istibdad: mazahiruhu wa-muwajahatuhu* (n.p., 2013), 5–7.

29. Interview by the author with Sheikh Farhat al-Ja'biri in Tunis, February 24, 2020.

30. Interview by the author with Farhat al-Ja'biri in Tunis, February 19, 2020.

31. Muhammad 'Abd al-Karim Muhafaza and Sami Saqr Abu Dawud, "Qira'a fi fikr al-Shaykh Ahmad b. Hamad al-Khalili, al-Mufti al-'Amm li-Saltanat 'Uman," in 'Alyan 'Abd al-Fattah al-Jaludi and Muhammad Mahmud al-Durubi (eds.), *A'mal al-mu'tamar al-'ilmi al-thalith hawla l-tahawwulat fi'l-mujtama' al-'Umani al-hadith wa-l-mu'asir* (Amman: Al al-Bayt University, 2005), 134–137.

32. Muhafaza and Dawud, "Qira'a fi fikr al-Shaykh Ahmad b. Hamad al-Khalili ," 139–140. They cite, among other works of Sheikh al-Khalili, *Manahij al-tashri' al-islami wa-'l-bahth al-'ilmi* (Muscat: al-Matba'a'l-Alamiyya, 2001).

33. Saeed El-Nahdy, "Top Oman Cleric Urges Alcohol Ban, Monitoring Gyms," Associated Press, March 16, 2011, available at: https://www.taiwannews.com. tw/en/news/1544523, last accessed June 17, 2021.

34. *Sharh manzumat "Ghayat al-murad fi nazm al-i'tiqad" li-l-Imam Nur al-Din al-Salimi* (*Commentary on the Poem "The Utmost Aim in Rendering Doctrine into Poetry" by Imam Nur al-Din al-Salimi*) (Muscat: Maktabat al-Jil al-Wa'id, 2003), 171.

35. Ahmad b. Hamad al-Khalili, *Burhan al-haqq fi ta'sil al-'aqida'l-islamiyya wa-dar'i 'l-shubah 'anha bi-'l-adilla'l-'aqliyya wa-'l-naqliyya* (*Demonstration of the Truth in Establishing the Foundation of Islamic Doctrine and Repelling Doubts from it Through Rational and Transmitted Indicators*) (Muscat: Al-Kalima'l-Tayyiba, 2017–).

36. Ahmad al-Khalili, *Fatawa'l-'aqida*, 2:430–431, cited in Sultan b. Mubarak al-Shaybani, *Da'iyat al-kalima'l-tayyiba: al-sira'l-'ilmiyya li-'l-Shaykh al-'Allama Ahmad b. Hamad b. Sulayman al-Khalili, al-mufti al-'amm li-Saltanat 'Uman* (Muscat: Al-Kalima'l-Tayyiba, 2015), 70.

37. I.e., hadiths that have been transmitted by enough different narrators and chains of transmission to be considered authentic.

38. This is a typical Ibadi complaint, especially regarding the Ash'aris, but Khalili cites a startlingly blatant instance of this: the Egyptian scholar Abu'l-'Abbas Ahmad b. Muhammad al-Khalwati al-Sawi (1761–1825), in his gloss on the *Tafsir al-Jalalayn*, wrote, "It is impermissible to follow any school beside the four [Sunni] schools, even if their teaching agrees with what the Companions, sound hadiths, and the text of the Qur'an say. Whoever leaves the four schools has gone astray, and this may lead him to *kufr*, because adopting the apparent meaning of the Book and Sunna is one of the roots of *kufr*." Al-Sawi, *Hashiya 'ala tafsir al-Jalalayn* (Beirut: Dar Ihya' al-Turath al-'Arabi, 1999), 3:10, cited in Khalili, *Burhan al-haqq*, 1:19–20. Khalili also cites the Qatari sheikh 'Abd al-Rahim al-Tahhan, whose criticism of Khalili's earlier work, *Al-Haqq al-damigh*, precipitated the writing of Khalili's most polemical work, *Wa-saqat al-qina'*, as saying, "There is no good in a [verse of the] Qur'an without a *sunna*, and no good in a *sunna* without the understanding of our righteous forebears." A lecture by Tahhan in the UAE, cited in Khalili, *Burhan al-haqq*, 1:21.

39. Al-Khalili, *Burhan al-haqq*, 1:255–280.

40. John Clover Monsma (ed.), *The Evidence of God in an Expanding Universe: Forty American Scientists Declare Their Affirmative Views on Religion* (New York: Putnam, 1958), 12.

41. It was translated by al-Dimirdash 'Abd al-Majid under the title *Allah yatajalla fi 'asr al-'ilm*, ed. Muhammad Jamal al-Din al-Fandi (Beirut: Dar al-Qalam, 1980; reissued 2014). The book is also cited in Mirza Tahir Ahmad, *Revelation, Rationality, Knowledge and Truth*, published on Al-Islam, the official website of the Ahmadiyya Muslim Community, 1997, available at: https://www.alislam.org/library/books/revelation/part_5_section_10.html, last accessed May 29, 2021.

42. Al-Khalili, *Burhan al-haqq*, 1:402–534.

43. William Harold Ingrams, *Zanzibar: Its History and Its People* (London: H. F. G. Witherby, 1931), 191.

44. Ali Muhsin Al-Barwani, *Conflicts and Harmony in Zanzibar (Memoirs)* (Dubai: n.p., 1997), 33.

45. *The Royal Speeches of His Majesty Sultan Qaboos bin Said, 1970–2010* (Muscat: Ministry of Information of the Sultanate of Oman, 2010), 53.

46. *Royal Speeches*, 312–313, speech delivered November 18, 1994.

47. For example, in his speech on November 18, 1992: "We have always adopted in our foreign policy, fundamental and unshakable principles: good neighbourliness,

non-interference in other countries' internal affairs, respect for international law, support of cooperation among states and encouragement of opportunities of dialogue." *Royal Speeches*, 289.

48. I spell His Excellency Sheikh Abdullah's name as he prefers to spell it. Were I to use standard Arabic transliteration, his name would be spelled Abdallah ibn Muhammad al-Salimi.

49. Sheikh Abdullah bin Mohammed Al-Salmi, *Religious Tolerance: A Vision for a New World*, ed. with an introduction by Angeliki Ziaka (Hildesheim: Georg Olms Verlag, 2016), 153.

50. See U.S. Department of State, Office of International Religious Freedom, "2020 Report on International Religious Freedom: Oman," May 12, 2021, available at: https://www.state.gov/reports/2020-report-on-international-religious-freedom/oman, last accessed June 17, 2021.

51. Al-Salimi also noted the significance of the number seventy as a symbol of abundance in Omani culture. Abdulrahman al-Salimi, "Al-Ikhtihlal al-mutafaqam wa-ila ayna yattajh al-'alam?" ("Critical Disorder: Where is the World Headed?), *Al-Tafahum* 70 (2020): 12. We might also note that each issue contained as many as 500 pages or more of scholarly articles, so it was abundant in more ways than one. Abdulrahman is the nephew of Sheikh Abdullah Al-Salmi, the Minister of Endowments and Religious Affairs. Abdulrahman is also grandson of Nur al-Din al-Salimi.

52. Al-Salmi, *Religious Tolerance*, 184, 187.

53. Al-Salmi, *Religious Tolerance*, 244.

54. Al-Salmi, *Religious Tolerance*, 188–189, 224.

55. Al-Salmi, *Religious Tolerance*, 28 (in Arabic); English version, 179, although I use my own translation of the Arabic into English.

56. Al-Salmi, *Religious Tolerance*, 29; English version, 181.

57. This quotation is included in the English version, 183, but does not appear in the Arabic.

58. Al-Salmi, *Religious Tolerance*, 30–31; English version, 183.

59. Al-Salmi, *Religious Tolerance*, 35; English version, 189.

60. I was present at this meeting. I later asked Sheikh Abdullah's permission to quote him.

61. John C. Wilkinson, *Ibāḍism: Origins and Early Development in Oman* (Oxford: Oxford University Press, 2010). Wilkinson says on p. xvi that he wrote this book at the urging of Sheikh Abdullah Al-Salmi and his nephew, Abdulrahman al-Salimi.

8

IN THE MIDDLE OF A REIGN

Mandana E. Limbert

By the mid-1990s, twenty-five years after Sultan Qaboos came to power and in the middle of his reign, the past—and local values associated with it—garnered significant interest for many in Bahla, a medium-sized pre-Islamic oasis town in interior Oman. Townspeople organized and opened a new library for the first time and town elders wrote and copied local histories to disseminate and sell at bookshops in the town *suq*. Such interest in local history did not appear suddenly or out of the blue. International and national attention had already been drawn to Bahla's history. Its citadel had been declared a UNESCO heritage site in 1986, a first on the Arabian Peninsula, and work on it continued through 2012 serving as a daily reminder of ongoing—and regularly challenging—attempts at capturing the town's past. As I have explored elsewhere, plans for national museums (and heritage festivals) as well as concerns about pious learning and practice all helped to direct and encourage attention to how the town and Oman's past more generally should and would be represented.[1]

Even in his first public speech in 1970, Sultan Qaboos invoked history, "Our country in the past was famous and strong. If we work in unity and cooperation, we will regenerate that glorious past." Sultan Qaboos also referenced "customs and traditions" in his 1971 and 1978 national day speeches.[2] Nevertheless, most of the attention in his speeches from the first twenty-three years was directed at ending the Dhofar war, establishing infrastructure associated with a modern state, and entering the world political scene as a respected member and participant. The early 1990s was a turning point, however, with 1993 declared to be the "year of national heritage." The heritage year, however, was postponed until the following year with celebrations in Nizwa marking the occasion. The declarations of national focus on heritage in 1993 and 1994 heightened an already emerging concern about how the past and the values associated with it should be publicly addressed, displayed, and sustained. While studies of national heritage projects are important for understanding state priorities and investments, this chapter focuses on the complex ways those state projects are experienced and understood.[3] In particular, I examine a case of local history work as it manifested in religious knowledge production. As I have also explored elsewhere, Bahlawis in the mid-1990s responded to and experienced state heritage projects in numerous ways, sometimes by remarking on the disconnect between their own memories and the museums that aimed to highlight particular aspects of Oman's past. At other times, and as Dale Eickelman has also argued, projects promoting national identity and enduring values, while aimed at broad and unifying representations, helped to objectify distinctions between religious groups.[4]

By the mid-2010s, the sense of urgency about how the past would be represented had dissipated somewhat. The renovation of the Bahla citadel was complete, national museums had opened to local and foreign tourists, and a state national archive was established with documents available online. Even a project of recalling and labeling street names in Bahla was finished. Thus, while debates and interpretations about life in pre-1970s Oman continued, the sense of urgency about who and how that past might be represented became less acute even if sometimes remaining contentious. Perhaps those accounts sedimented or the lines between the various narrative options became clearer, though never resolved. As scholars of historical memory and representation have long pointed out, however, seemingly resolved silences can present themselves or reappear in unexpected ways.[5]

In Bahla, the 1990s—the middle of Sultan Qaboos' reign—was, thus, a period of inflection when these national heritage projects were the focus of sustained energy. This was a time when the world prior to his rule was still within living memory of the majority of Bahla's residents and the world that was being recalled remained viscerally present. And, not surprisingly, the growing focus on the past was also full of complications, as the postponement of the year of national heritage suggests. First, there were the ongoing questions about who could best recall and relate the past: the youth with their literacy skills garnered from modern state schools or those who came of age prior to 1970, with first-hand experiences and memories of a contentious, and pious, world. Furthermore, there remained the question: who, from among both generations, would be both authentic, authoritative, and, yet, not expose too much? Indeed, some Bahlawis were just as happy to "forget" the tumultuous times "before," either politically or economically. It was sometimes simply better to keep silent about who had supported whom and what families had fought over local power. Yet others, while careful not to glorify the time before, were more nostalgic, emphasizing, for example, the simplicity and non-material values of social life in the past. Second, the time before 1970 was, of course, not homogeneous either. The rule of differing local governors, the relationship of townspeople with the Imamate administration or Sultan Said bin Taimur's government, the lure of jobs in more oil-wealthy sheikhdoms in the Gulf and Saudi Arabia, and the 1964 revolution in Zanzibar certainly all punctuated a seemingly flattened "before." Finally, as being alluded to here, the past was suffused—saturated even—with intense and specific questions about piety. How might righteous values and traditions be sustained in the fast-changing world? What aspects of the past should people emulate and promote? Might attention to the past serve as a subtle critique, intended or otherwise, of the present? Ultimately, the growing attention to heritage and the past was entangled in debates about proper and enduring values as keys to Omani national identity. The establishment of a local library as this chapter explores was a prime example of claims to the legacy of religious knowledge.

Partha Chatterjee once argued (against Benedict Anderson) that non-European nationalisms were not built in modular forms borrowed from Europe. Instead, non-European nationalisms were built in terms of a *difference* from Europe.[6] In particular, anticolonial nationalists in nineteenth-century India, he argued, created their own domain of sovereignty within colonial society—demarcated as "spiritual" or "inner"—and separate from the material domain of the outside, of statecraft, politics, and technology. Protecting the essential "interior" spiritual life not only became the purview of the nationalist elite, but spiritual life itself became the marker of cultural identity, creating, essentializing, and purifying it in the meantime. Certainly, Oman's history is very different from India's. Nevertheless, the process of delineating the distinctiveness of inner, spiritual values that was taking place in Bahla in the 1990s is rather similar. While, for the most part, appreciating the "modern" and "exterior" infrastructural fixings of the new era, inner core values were also being articulated and defined as distinctive. As Omani national sensibilities were being forged and emerging, so too were senses of spiritual inner values as unique and perhaps even sovereign.

At the same time, however, and as I have explored elsewhere, seemingly divided aspects of everyday life (exterior/interior) could never be fully separated: "modern" technology and infrastructure were themselves inseparable from social, legal and ethical values. The library embodied the overlap of these realms. In addition, and as this chapter also examines, the inner and spiritual uniqueness of appropriate life was itself suffused with questions and concerns about how best to live a pious life. In Oman, core values were not only being delineated as unique and distinct, essential and traditional at the emerging national level, but a simultaneous and related process was taking place more locally, both of which seemed to heighten the objectification of religion and tradition themselves. The defining of Omani spiritual life as unique was in process.

In part, what was at a stake was who would serve as the guardians of this inner spiritual life and how knowledge about this realm would be disseminated. In addition, and as Dale Eickelman has also argued as noted above, the process of articulating the uniqueness of Omani heritage and identity—shaping, in the process, an objectification of Ibadi identity itself—emerged not so much in a colonial context as in India, but in response to criticism from a neighboring country.[7] Here, self-definitions were articulated in response to disparaging comments made by the Saudi national mufti, Bin Bazz. The Omani national mufti, Sheikh Ahmed al-Khalili, took to the radio and national television not only defending the branch of Islam dominant in the country, but explaining its uniqueness and distinctiveness. These broad processes of identifying history and values, this chapter highlights, manifest in very local, specific, and complex practices of and debates about heritage and knowledge production.

This chapter, therefore, focuses on one particular project in Bahla in the 1990s: the establishment of a local library and the housing in it of a folder of *fatwa*s, or legal opinions. The establishment of the local library was not a project sponsored or organized directly by the government and the Ministry of National Heritage, though permission was required. Rather, it was a project of a group of male Ibadi residents, known to be pious and scholarly. The group had decided that the town should have a library separate from the state schools, which were inaccessible to most townspeople and which had few of the more sophisticated texts that older residents (high school, college, and beyond) would like to read. The library was also seen as a way to fill gaps in the education system, especially once the Islamic Institutes that had run throughout the country as a compliment to the more "secular" state schools, had closed. When I first arrived in Bahla, the sign for the Islamic Institute, although recently closed, had not yet been removed. While book publishing was expanding significantly at the time and the two bookstores in town sold an assortment of religious texts, most residents traveled to Muscat (or Dubai even) to purchase their books. These books would be held in private homes. The idea for the library was not only to make them more readily available to residents, but to highlight the town's heritage of religious knowledge through the establishment of a publicly recognized institution of religious scholarship and learning. Sultan Qaboos had noted that the celebration of Oman's heritage would not be confined to the reconstruction of its forts and citadels. Townspeople, thus, took it upon themselves to promote this heritage through the founding of the library.

The library, in other words, both promoted local scholarship and religious knowledge as well as highlighted the significance of these values for the town's unique heritage. Within the library and within the work of promoting the heritage of religious knowledge in the *fatwa*s one can also see the forging of new authorities and the focus on particular aspects of personal behavior in the Qaboos era. The 1990s, it should be noted and remembered, was not only a time in the middle of Sultan Qaboos bin Said's reign; it also stood on the eve of our internet age, when *fatwa*s would soon be easily accessed and researched at home rather than in a library, purchased at a bookstore, read in a newspaper, or—as had been practiced previously—

from the direct responses themselves. Yet it was also a time when interest in documenting, compiling, and sharing questions and answers clearly mattered and was perhaps increasing in order to determine what was right and what was wrong. The responses to questions about what was or was not acceptable behavior provided direct and quick guidance for those who may have been unsure for themselves and, it seems, for those especially concerned with the behavior of others. But, housed in the library as they were, the guidance also tied the questions and answers to a heritage of religious knowledge for which towns in interior Oman were famous. How and by whom that heritage would be promoted and authorized, however, was hardly settled.

A group of scholarly men (both elders and those who came of age after 1970), therefore, mobilized and found a small room off the center of one of the town's "old" neighborhoods, *Harat al-Nadwa* (most old neighborhoods have some kind of center with a well, mosque, and meeting room) and began collecting volumes printed from the Ministry of Religious Affairs, along with a small assortment of "acceptable" fiction and VHS tapes of sermons (principally about the brutality of the war in Bosnia). The library was going to be temporary while a larger space was being built, and indeed the shelves of the small room were bursting with the collection. In addition to the texts printed and published by the Ministry of Religious Affairs, however, there was also a folder of *fatwa*s that inevitably drew more attention.

As I explore here, the questions and answers of the *fatwa*s focus overwhelmingly on personal, domestic, and private life. Indeed, the vast majority of the questions pertain to marriage, sex, food, and personal prayer. Even questions about "modern" technology are framed in this collection as what is appropriate for individual and domestic viewing and listening. At the same time, however, some of the questions and answers reveal the uncertainties about the boundaries of personal spiritual life. They reveal too the centrality of on-going concerns about who should have the authority to determine what is proper or appropriate in the first place. These include, for example, questions that highlight differences between generations and legitimate and "illegitimate" religion (i.e., superstition and magic), as well as whether Friday prayers should be performed "these days" (i.e., in the absence of a manifest Imam).

Figure 8.1 Nadwa Library and Rules. © Mandana Limbert 1997.

Though the past with its complicated relationship to Oman's "present" uniqueness is never explicitly evoked in the *fatwa*s, the past as persisting heritage and values was not lost on anyone. It was, it seemed to me, necessary to maintain a tenuous balance of emphasizing the significance of heritage and tradition without invoking what might be perceived as criticism. And, perhaps even more significantly, the past became present through the symbolic frame of highlighting the importance of religious knowledge and promoting particular authoritative voices in the first place. In other words, while the content of the *fatwas* only obliquely reference the past, the establishment of the library and the authority given to the scholars through these *fatwas* affirmed the continuation of scholarly religious traditions and knowledge in a town that was famous for its history as a center for knowledge. At the same time, the new library serving a broader reading public was made possible in an era of expanded publishing and increased literacy. Past and present, proper behavior—normatively framed—and new political–economic conditions all met in the establishment of the library and the collection and content of a pile of *fatwas*.

Scholars in Practice

Several months after I had begun field research in Bahla, a local teacher who had been following my interest in religious knowledge told me that his father-in-law had been instrumental in establishing a library for the town. Girls and women were given permission to use the library for three hours on Friday mornings, ostensibly while boys and men were attending Friday prayer and if their families felt that their help was not required for preparing Friday lunch. I was excited about the prospect of this local library and the possibility of women gathering to find, borrow, and discuss texts and began making my way to the library on as many Fridays as possible. I had already started attending a young women's study group in the same neighborhood and was therefore familiar with it and some of the young women who participated.

Resting on a shelf in a newly established, and temporary, library among the volumes on jurisprudence (*fiqh*) and prophetic biography (*sirat*), was a thin folder. I had noticed young women pulling it down and eagerly leafing through it on Friday mornings and, one Friday, as everyone was busy looking through various books, I asked if I could borrow it and make a copy. The young women were very generous with sharing the folder, which I returned within the week. It turned out to be compilation of approximately sixty hand-written questions from the Wilayat Bahla and Nizwa between 1987 and 1995. The answers were from various scholars, including Sheikh Ahmed al-Khalili, Oman's national mufti.

As Mohammad Khalid Masud, Brinkley Messick, and David Powers once pointed out, while the title of "mufti" has not always been used, the function of authoritative responder to questions of behavior (and even theology) has existed throughout the Muslim world.[8] One way that the work of a scholar who responds to such questions has been seen is as divided between the "private *mufti*" and the "public *mufti*," between the local mufti working in a face-to-face relationship with questioners and the official or formal bureaucratic mufti, working in an office far away. In Oman, the term "mufti" itself came to be used in practice not for local responders to questions, but for someone holding an official state position, while local responders might informally simply be called, "sheikh" or "sheikha."

Indeed, the lack of the use of the title of "mufti" for a local scholar who would issue an opinion was—at first—confusing to me, and others. When I first arrived in Bahla, I naively asked who the local muftis were, expecting that a town with such a great history of scholarly knowledge would surely have many. Not surprisingly, I was met with blank expressions and told that there weren't any. Fortunately, it did not take long for us to realize that in Oman the title "mufti" was reserved for a modern state official and that, otherwise, the function of authoritative answerer of questions—whether written or oral—might have another honorific, a "sheikh," or not have an honorific at all, and simply be someone who others respected for his, or her, piety and, perhaps, even charisma.

In the cases I discuss here, the responder to most of the questions was Oman's national mufti. While his official powers shifted after 1997 with the separation between the Ministry of Justice and the Ministry of Religious Affairs, his moral authority remained significant. On the one hand, he was the quintessential "public mufti," a bureaucratic role established for and within a modern nation-state. On the other hand, as a figure recognized as local—coming from *al-Dakhilyya* itself—he was not completely or only public either. Indeed, his local status was a role that he clearly cultivated as well: he built a house, for instance, at the junction of roads between major towns in the region. In addition, he was also not the only responder to these questions, with other scholars—also sometimes from the area—responding. Some of the *fatwa*s were not signed. While the role of the "mufti" was, therefore, both public and private, so too were the *fatwa*s themselves. The ways in which they were written and compiled reflected both local authority and centralized state power. Thus, in practice, the distinction between public and private roles and practice was, at least at that time and in Bahla, blurred.

Gathered together in a casual folder for locals to read, the *fatwa*s were collected, compiled, and made available outside the official channels of publication, though, of course, those are widely available now as well. This collection outside official channels give them a sense of being particularly authentic, direct, and intimate, as does their hand-written quality. These were questions by neighbors, answered by respected scholars, who may also have been a neighbor and who was also an official. Readers in the library were highly aware of the curated quality of all publications, and certainly this compilation of *fatwa*s was also collected and selected. Nevertheless, with their hand-written quality, and without the formal stamp of approval from any government office, they were understood to be particularly genuine.

This "local" and direct quality is also evident in the fact that only one of the answers was issued on official letterhead from the mufti's office. All of the other responses were written either underneath the note sent or on the back of the same piece of paper. This somewhat informal or personal quality of the responses is, nevertheless, sometimes punctuated with a stamp at the bottom with the official title of "national mufti," but without a state seal or embellishment. These stamps give a sense of officialness, though without any formal flourishes. The seeming informality of the exchanges also suggests that these questions may have been asked and responded to in a local environment, rather than being sent to Muscat and mailed back, though it is impossible to say. To my mind, the condition of the exchange and the collection matter because the direct question and answer—written by hand, with no letterhead, and on the same piece of paper—not only retains a level of intimacy that some have traditionally associated with the work of "private" rather than "public" muftis, but that also suggests the blurring between individual questions about particular, private matters and concerns about expressions of common and public behavior.

Similarly, by compiling these questions and making them available for people in this local library, Bahlawis were interested in shaping authoritative knowledge at the local level in a centralized environment of the library itself. This authoritative, local, and centralized space was made available for literate residents—mostly anyone born after 1970—to access, confer, and presumably to disseminate to fellow residents, many of whom were not literate. These texts could therefore be used to study on one's own, but also to cite in interactions with other people, further guiding proper public behavior. Indeed, the direct, intimate relationships of questions and answers, of authority and immediacy, of generational respect and differences, of local library and national emphasis of scholarly traditions were all at stake in the thin folder and in the organizing of this small library. Taking up the mantle of delineating the particulars of local values and heritage, the library and the *fatwa*s were both part of a broader project of promoting the significance and gaining control of heritage and religious knowledge production in the middle of Sultan Qaboos' reign.

Questions and Questioners

The questions in the *fatwa* folder are mundane ones pertaining to the practicalities and practices of everyday life that people might encounter in their relationships at home and at work. These are not theological or political philosophical questions. Indeed, and not surprisingly perhaps, most of questions address marriage, prayer, gender roles, and even sex. Other questions pertain to appropriate dress, music, gold-wearing for men, banking, photography, meat, relations with other branches of Islam and foreigners, as well as practices that might be considered "customary" or even potentially deemed "innovation" (*bid'a*). In these and the other cases, the questioner often described a particular practice and then asked whether it was acceptable or true (*hadha sahihan?*) or asked—more openly—the mufti's opinion about a particular practice. Is it halal or haram? Or, "please give us a *fatwa* (*iftuna*)."

One could argue that these represent questions of particular concern to residents of *al-Dakhiliyya* in the mid-1990s. Or, perhaps, these were the concerns of the people who compiled them. In either case, included were ongoing questions about marriage and prayer practices (the most personal and "domestic" types of questions that people can have) as well as new experiences of wealth, travel, trade relations, technologies, and interactions with non-Ibadis and non-Muslims. Concern and discomfort with practices that might be deemed innovation (either as old or new practices) permeate the questions. In other words, these might include practices that were associated with older generations ("the past"), but that were being purged from more narrowly defined appropriate religious practice.

Questions about marriage, divorce, and prayer comprise a significant portion of the compiled *fatwas*. Marriage, divorce, sex, and prayer are, in many ways, some of the most private and personal of religious and ritual life, though, of course, prayer, for men, is also public and social. Included are questions about the validity of divorces and whether particular sexual acts require repentance; mistakes a man might make divorcing his wife and intimate sexual concerns become matters of anonymous and public discussion of appropriate piety. At the same time, one recognizes uncertainty about and responses to the promotion of national family planning initiatives and contraception. Indeed, and as Chatterjee similarly highlights in his analysis of nationalist Indian protection of "inner" and "authentic" difference, religion became increasingly confined to domestic worlds.

Other questions about marriage, however, pertain to traditions that younger generations might worry are not quite in accordance with proper practice, highlighting the ways that young, educated children were questioning the authority of their elders. For example, one questioner asks about the preference for not getting married during the period between the two *eids*, or great festivals in the Islamic calendar, which the sheikh dismisses as a pre-Islamic (and ignorant) practice from *jahaliyya*. Generational differences appear in other ways too. One man requests a *fatwa* to confirm that a father cannot take a dowry given to his daughter for marriage. And, in another case, a thirteen-year-old girl complains that her father had signed a marriage contract on her behalf despite her refusal, pleading for a *fatwa* to annul the marriage contract that her father had signed. The mufti advises her to consult a judge immediately. The young girl's ability and confidence to write to a national scholar and question her father's actions not only highlights a level of personal fortitude, presumably supported by a social or academic network, but the directness of the response indicates the seriousness with which this issue was taken and admonished.

A number of the *fatwas* articulate discomfort with "traditional" practices, especially those pertaining to black magic or "superstitious" (*khurafat*) practices, which are dismissed as untrue and antithetical to proper religion. As anyone familiar with the reputation of Bahla would recognize, these questions would be particularly relevant in that context. One questioner explicitly associates these practices with the "elderly in our family" suggesting, again, that the youth—with their "modern" education—understand proper religion, while the elderly do not. It would be a mistake, however, to assume that all the practices deemed innovation were "traditional" or from the past. One questioner, for example, refers to a "new" practice of gathering at the grave of a recently deceased person for the sake of reflection, and this too is deemed innovation.

Concern about proper *Ibadi* practice is not particularly explicit in the questions, though two questions stand out. One case refers specifically to whether a practice is acceptable "in Ibadism." Another, however, is more circumspect, referring not only to a particular heated debate at the time, but specifically to proper practice during "this period (or age)" (*hatha al-ʿasr*), meaning during an era without a manifest Imam. The question refers in passing, therefore, not only to popular discussions among an Ibadi public about the appropriateness or requirement for gathering for Friday prayer, but also to an acknowledgment about the particular circumstances of the historical period for Ibadi practice.

Many of the questions, however, refer to new-found wealth and, in particular, whether it is acceptable for men to wear gold (it is not). But, gold also appears with regard to women who, it is said in a question about *zakat*, have a lot of gold, "as most people these days." The reference to the relative wealth "these days" is echoed in other questions that highlight technologies that people are unsure about, from photography and television to medical transplants and milk banks (for breast feeding). In the cases of photography and television, the responses emphasize that the technologies themselves are not a problem, but if the content is unacceptable, then they should not be watched. Medical transplants and milk banks, however, pose more complicated problems with an acknowledgment that they have their benefits, but the preference is to see them as countering other tenets of respecting the wholeness of the body that humans are given and the concerns about the possibility that milk siblings would not be recognized.

Some of the most vehement positions are taken around music, unless it is "*nasheed*," devotional male acapella, which would not be considered music in the first place. At the time, not only was there more music available because many people had access to satellite television, but there was also a campaign to curb the kind of programs—with music—that state television was producing. Indeed, one questioner asks about state television directly—and pointedly—to which the responder diplomatically recommends that the questioner contact the appropriate ministry. Discussions of music were also common among many of the people I knew, but the association of music with appropriateness was not necessarily understood to pertain specifically to Islam or Ibadism. One young man, for example, was concerned that I would be offended if he listened to music in his car as he drove me to visit his family. In other words, knowing that I was not Muslim or Ibadi did not alter his association of music with potential inappropriateness or a politics of piety, irrespective of specific religious tradition.

There are a few direct additional references to Ibadism in the *fatwa* collection. When Ibadism arises, however, it is mostly to clarify relationships with non-Ibadis, not to understand the particulars of Ibadism per se. In this collection of *fatwa*s, for example, there is a question about whether the marriage of Ibadis to non-Ibadi Muslims is acceptable (yes); whether a man can integrate fully among other Muslims (yes, as long as they do not deny what it "known," though he cannot claim to belong to another genealogy, *nasab*); whether it is acceptable that the imam of a mosque is not a citizen, but is still loved (yes); whether in Ibadism it is acceptable to kiss the forehead of your niece (no, but this has nothing to do with Ibadism); and, finally, how one can practice both *wilaya wa bara'a* (an Ibadi tenet of association and dissociation), while also enjoining the good and forbidding the wrong. That is, the edict to befriend those with whom one can associate and separate from those with whom one differs or disagrees, a core Ibadi tenet, might be seen as rather counter to the more activist tenet of enjoining the good, and forbidding the wrong.

Finally, a number of questions in the folder address the specific question of whether meat imported to Oman or available abroad would be acceptable to eat. Clearly, both the import of frozen meat from abroad and the travel of Omanis to places where acceptable meat might not be readily available were of concern to people. The economy of Oman was obviously changing with new trade agreements for foreign consumer goods making those goods increasingly available: apples from the United States and coffee from Costa Rica were both available locally in Bahla at the time, though neither of these, of course, was of particular concern to people, despite a general preference for domestic produce over "*bahri*," from across the seas. The question of proper slaughter and prayer, on the other hand, were understandably of significant concern in the collected *fatwa*s, especially as frozen meat began to be imported at the time from majority non-Muslim countries (such as Australia). The question was whether this meat should be *presumed* to be forbidden, unless proven otherwise, while meat from a majority Muslim country should be presumed to be acceptable. In another interesting case, and one that was increasingly being faced, a questioner wanted to know whether to eat meat while traveling to a non-Muslim country.

What is striking, however, is not only what people were asking, but to whom they seem to be interested in directing the answers they hoped to receive. While most are not explicit about the ultimate audience of the answers to their questions, a number of questioners are clear. One questioner explicitly states, "Please give us your ruling because I want to battle these superstitions (*khurafat*), especially among the elderly in our family." In another question about meat, we read, "I heard an announcement that came from you, but when I told my family about it, they did not believe me because I could not find the newspaper. I hope that you would clarify this to everyone *in your handwriting*, so that they would believe me."

Or, in another case, a man indicates that he informed a family member that a particular practice (putting stones on a body when it is buried so that it does not flip) is inappropriate but wanted confirmation that he was correct. And, in yet another example, the questioner asks for a particular hadith about the length of a *dishdasha*. It is not clear why the questioner wants the particular hadith, but one could imagine that rather than needing proof for his own sake, he could then quote it when pointing out that someone else's *dishdasha* is too long.

Thus, while some of the questions may have been genuine questions—that is, when an answer is not already known or about an actual case in which a person may be involved—many of the questions are much more vague, or are about practices one could expect that the questioner already knows the answer but wants an external authority's support. In this way, the "private" exchange, with a public figure that is then made semi-public, but intimate in the library, is generally aimed not at understanding what someone should or should not do him or herself (though there are those questions too). Rather, the questions and answers seem to serve as evidence, and particularly as evidence against young people who are being deemed to be acting inappropriately socially (listening to music or wearing gold), or against the elderly whose practices are seen to be based on superstition or *bid'a*.

Answers

The answers to the questions discussed above range in specificity, tone (sometimes exasperated), and, as noted, are from different authorities and scholars. An example of exasperation comes with comments such as, "I have answered this so many times before," or "What do you mean by *jizziyya!!??*," in response to someone who used the term as a way of describing the payments made by foreign workers in the sponsorship system (*kifala*). In this instance, Sheikh al-Khalili seems to have found the analogy between an Islamic legal practice and the sponsorship system absurd and made his disdain known. But he also clearly felt frustrated at having to answer the same questions over and over.

Scholars also respond to questions about permissibility by noting that practices are either *halal* (permissible) or *haram* (forbidden), and often adamantly so. They tend not to use other categories of relative persmissibility such as *wajib/fard* (obligatory), *mustahabb/mandub* (recommended), *mubah* (neutral), and *makruh* (disapproved), though some of the responses suggest disapproval in particular. Certainly, such responses are partly a function of the questions and the kind of activities under consideration. For example, in response to questions about music, of which there are quite a few, scholars are especially absolute. Whereas television, as a form, is considered acceptable (as long as the content is appropriate), music, as noted above, is deemed *haram*, off the bat.

On other occasions, the relative consequence depends not only on content (as with television), but also on intention, *niyya*.[9] Indeed, intention, as scholars of Islamic law have long noted, is significant. That is, if someone's intention is good, but he or she inadvertently does something wrong, then there is no serious problem with the act. At the same time, however, some answers suggest that a person's intentions are less relevant. Since in some circumstances good intentions might lead to problems, those acts should be avoided. One response pertaining to soft drinks that have prizes in their caps raises the point that a behavior that might emulate others with inappropriate intention should also be avoided.

Question: "A man goes to the shop to buy goods for his home and took a cold drink. He discovers that with the cap he wins either 1 RO or can get another drink free. Is this halal or haram?
Answer: If his purpose (*qasid*) in the buying of the drink was to see if he would win, then it is haram—like a lottery. If that was not his intention, I still would not like him to take it just so that he would not copy the path of those with this intention. You must take precautions.

There are two points I wish to highlight here. First, while the questioner—like most of the questioners—only gives the scholar two options for a response (halal or haram), the sheikh's response is less absolute or dichotomous. He first notes that if the intention is to gamble, then, the action is forbidden. However, if not, then he "would not like him to do this." It would be better not to engage in this behavior. And why? It is not because the behavior might lead to habit or support the gambling industry, but because copying the path of those with bad intentions is not good. It is not forbidden, but it is certainly not good.

Other answers are very practical, drawing too on the question of intention. For example, a questioner asks what happens if someone sleeps through the night prayer. The answer is simply that if the person did not intend to sleep through the night prayer, then he should make it up when he remembers. However, he continues, if someone knows that he tends to sleep through the night prayer, then he should have someone wake him up, or get an alarm clock.

In one response about meat from a questioner studying in the United Kingdom, the sheikh notes that meat slaughtered by a Christian or Jewish person is acceptable, if the actual slaughtering is done correctly and even if mentioning God was not performed at the time of the slaughter. The person eating should mention God's name and then eat. A similar practical approach to appropriate behavior is explained with regard to imported meat. One should *assume* that meat is not slaughtered appropriately if it is imported from a predominantly non-Muslim country, unless an investigation has been completed to confirm that the slaughter was done appropriately. Most importantly, however, the sheikh informs the questioner that it is his *personal* responsibility to decide whether he trusts and is comfortable with the information about proper slaughter provided. In other words, while the questioners are searching for absolute responses, which the sheikhs sometimes provide, at other times the responses are not only not absolute, but rely on the context of the situation, intention, and personal judgment.

While the responses to the questions clearly carried authority, and the young women reading them in the Harat al-Nadwa library seemed to take them seriously, never—in my presence—seeming to doubt them, it would be a mistake to presume that all readers of these texts necessarily agreed with them all either. I witnessed numerous women listen to lectures by male scholars in local meeting rooms and then walk away and say that the injunctions for behavior being espoused did not make sense or were too rigid. While listening, the women might appear particularly stern and serious, even wearing socks and gloves for the occasion to ensure that no skin would be evident, signaling through their sartorial display strict interpretations of maintaining separation from men. Afterwards, the same women would, through analogy and through further injunctions, use reason, central to Ibadi thought, to unpack the logic of some determinations and explain to me why the rule outlined for behavior was too rigid and did not make sense according to them and their situations. The authority of the male scholars was not absolute either. In these instances too, the access to modern schools which could have conferred authority onto the younger male lecturers and scholars also did not sway the women.

Conclusions

There is an enormous amount one could say about the *fatwas* and the practices of compiling and sharing them, not to mention the particular occasions during which the questions and answers were asked, answered, read, circulated, and debated. *Fatwa*s are, of course, questions and answers from a particular time, and these were from a period in Sultan Qaboos' reign when attention to

Oman's heritage was increasingly gaining formal and official attention. How such attention resonated locally was complex. One way that the past came to matter was the energy that some townspeople placed in highlighting the significance of scholarly knowledge by organizing a local library in which the folder of *fatwa*s and other texts were placed. The library itself, while promoting a legacy of religious knowledge was also mostly directed at a more literate youth and its rules for access and borrowing, in many ways, like the libraries of the new state schools. At the same time, in highlighting the significance of piety in the contemporary world, these texts both conjured the past and sometimes aimed to correct.

The local library, however, was not the only space where the heritage of religious knowledge was promoted at the time. Lectures, reading groups, Quranic recitation competitions, as well as religious knowledge trivia games were also popular. The popularity of *fatwa*s, however, was particularly widespread. One could argue that such publicly circulating *fatwa*s were popular because they provided immediate answers. The answers were relatively simple ways of receiving instructions about how to be "good" without necessarily having to tackle the vagaries of historical analogies and jurisprudence. As people were traveling to new countries, as new products (from meat to television programs) were being imported and broadcast to Oman, and as newfound wealth (gold and banks) became more common-place, questions and concerns about how to maintain proper piety proliferated. Uncertainty about how to be good as the world transformed was undoubtedly in the air. In the process, the *fatwa*s were centralizing and codifying answers for behavior.

These quick answers by respected authorities to everyday questions that pertain to everyone could also be accessed easily (and even anonymously), providing a guide for how to inhabit and embody good behavior. They might even have been questions and concerns that people, and young women in particular, were embarrassed to ask either friends or their families about, but could read about them here. Newfound access to reading and writing questions enabled new generations of Omanis to participate directly, and with authority, in the articulation of proper behavior. The frankness with which questions of sex were asked also provided, for example, a forum for young women to learn and feel secure, knowing that if they too had questions in the future, there was a space for them to make inquiries.

As I have noted, however, the questions and answers were not solely oriented at a person's uncertainty about their own behavior. Instead, the questions were often directed against the activities that were deemed superstitious or "new" activities that were connected to fashions deemed inauthentic: music, long *dishdaha*s, gold. As such, these *fatwa*s were being used to serve as authoritative evidence to manage other people's social and public behavior, and less because of uncertainty about what might be new. Though, clearly, many of the questions pertain to how to grapple with new products or contexts, it is important to recall that "change" had been happening for years. Indeed, by the time the library was established and the *fatwa* folder was circulating, Sultan Qaboos had already ruled for twenty-five years. This moment was in the middle of his reign.

Thus, rather than being solely (or even primarily) a response to newfound changes, these questions and answers can also be understood as helping to shape and articulate (as Chatterjee and Eickelman suggested albeit in very different ways and in different contexts) the contours of national Omani and local Ibadi uniqueness, as a place and practice of religious knowledge and pious life. In fact, the interest in the library and the *fatwa*s within it, emerged with an increased focus on Oman's heritage and history, not simply as a response to the new but as heritage and the past became increasingly significant for nation-building.

Such attention to religious knowledge, as a link to Oman's heritage, and how it might best be sustained or how it might best be articulated, also of course raised the question of who might best be the guardians and authority of such knowledge. On the one hand, unlike the context of colonial India as explored by Chatterjee, the guardians and producers of this spiritual identity were not Oman's nationalist elite, but rather much more "local" figures. Sheikh al-Khalili's role as authoritative responder and guardian of interpretations and understandings of Ibadism was significant, therefore, not simply because he was a representative of the nation-state, but precisely because he was considered local, emphasizing the ways that the questions and answers were direct, intimate, and even rather unmediated by the state.

Much has changed since the mid-1990s and the middle of Sultan Qaboos' reign. One of the most fundamental transformations being, of course, the introduction of the internet and the explosion of social media, which were just beginning in the mid-1990s. Access to the internet not only transformed library use, introducing the need for computers and lessening the circulation of paper *fatwas*, but raises further questions about the significance of directness, authenticity, and authority in the formation of proper behavior and what it means to be Ibadi. The national *fatwa* telephone hotline and call-center introduced yet another site from which direct, and yet anonymous, questions and answers might be generated, now less associated with the production of local authoritative knowledge or the distinctiveness of the local heritage of religious knowledge.

Notes

1. Mandana E. Limbert, *In the Time of Oil: Piety, Memory, and Social Life in an Omani Town* (Stanford, CA: Stanford University Press, 2010).

2. Ministry of Information. *The Royal Speeches of His Majesty Sultan Qaboos bin Said, 1970–1995* (Muscat: Ministry of Information, 2010).

3. Amal Sachedina, "Nizwa Fort: Transforming Ibadi Religion through Heritage Discourse in Oman," *Comparative Studies of South Asia, Africa and the Middle East* 39(2) (2019): 328–343.

4. Dale Eickelman, "Ibadism and the Sectarian Perspective," in Br. R. Pridham (ed.), *Oman: Economic, Social, and Strategic Developments,* London: Croom Helm, 1987), 31–50; Dale Eickelman, "National Identity and Religious Discourse in Contemporary Oman," *International Journal of Islamic and Arabic Studies* 6(1) (1989): 1–20; Dale Eickelman, "Mass Higher Education and the Religious Imagination in Contemporary Arab Societies," *American Ethnologist* 19(4) (1992): 643–655.

5. Michel-Rolph Trouillot, *Silencing the Past: Power and the Production of History* (Boston, MA: Beacon Press, 1995).

6. Partha Chatterjee, *The Nation and its Fragments: Colonial and Postcolonial Histories* (Princeton, NJ: Princeton University Press, 1993); Benedict Anderson, *Imagined Communities* (New York: Verso Books, 1983] 2006).

7. Eickelman, "Ibadism and the Sectarian Perspective"; Eickelman, "National Identity and Religious Discourse in Contemporary Oman"; Eickelman, "Mass Higher Education and the Religious Imagination in Contemporary Arab Societies" .

8. Muhammad Khalid Masud, Brinkley Messick, and David Powers (eds.), *Islamic Legal Interpretations: Muftis and their Fatwas* (Cambridge, MA: Harvard University Press, 1996); Brinkley Messick, "The Mufti, the Text and the World," *Man* 21(1) (1986): 102–119.

9. Brinkley Messick, "Indexing the Self: Intent and Expression in Islamic Legal Acts," *Islamic Law and Society* 8(2) (2001): 151–178.

9

CONSTITUTIONAL REFORMS DURING THE REIGN OF SULTAN QABOOS

Salim al-Kharusi

The Omani Renaissance transformed more than the visible infrastructure of the Sultanate. It also had a deep impact on the law and on legal structures within the country. This is most apparent in what is called the Omani Constitutional Renaissance, which started in 1996, the middle of Sultan Qaboos' reign. The Omani Constitution that developed is a combination and harmonization of Islamic Sharia as well as modern constitutionalism, based on various models and exisiting constitutions. Sharia (both Ibadi and non-Ibadi) and modern law shaped and inspired the making of the Oman's Constitution during the reign of Sultan Qaboos.

Background to the Omani Constitutional Renaissance

Oman's legal history before the accession of Sultan Qaboos illuminates some of the basic, internal sources of Oman's current constitution. For over a millennium Oman was ruled by the Ibadi tradition.[1] The *Majlis al-Hall wa'l-'Aqd* (the Council to Dissolve and Convene), formulated by religious scholars and tribal leaders, was the primary legal body along with the Imam. Throughout most of Omani history, and with the exception of some of the Nabhani period (1154–1624 CE), this council, or some form of it, had the right to elect imams, the religious head of state, to limit their powers and even to remove them.[2] This role changed after of the death of Imam Ahmad bin Said Al-Busaidi in 1783, the fourth son—Said—of the founder of the present ruling family of Oman, became the head of state despite questions as to his legitimacy. In 1792, he handed over the position as head of state, or Sultan, to his son Hamad, breaking the Ibadi ruling system.[3] This marked the beginning of a period of political conflicts between the imams and the Al-Busaidi monarchs over who had the right to rule. In 1913, there was a revolution in Oman that sought to rebuild the Imamate system. However, as a result, two ruling systems emerged: the Sultan and the Sultanate controlled the ports and coastal areas; the Imam and the Imamate the more isolated interior of the country, especially the mountains.[4] Both systems reached an agreement (Treaty of Seeb) on September 25, 1920 containing obligations for each party, but it did not include details with regard to their borders. In 1954, Sultan Said bin Taimur (1932–1970), the father of Sultan Qaboos, cancelled the agreement after the death of Imam Mohammed Khalili. Disputes between both systems increased.[5] Sultan Said bin Taimur agreed to join with the British in military action with the aim of overthrowing the Imamate in 1964. The Sultan extended his sovereignty to Oman's interior, where oil had been discovered.[6] Nonetheless, the Sultan's authoritarian rule and his efforts to maintain the isolation of the country also put him at odds with his own people and with most of his British consultants and allies. His brother, Sayyid Tariq, the father of the current Sultan Haitham, announced from exile, in 1967, his public opposition to his brother's regime. He proposed a constitution and legal reforms. However, Tariq's effort was not successful insofar as it was not sufficiently supported, neither by the British nor Omani oppositions groups.[7] In 1970, Sultan Qaboos initiated a coup d'état against his father and became the Sultan of Oman.[8]

Therefore, there was no constitution in Oman from when Sultan Qaboos became head of state in 1970 until 1996. Nevertheless, the new Sultan and his government created a legal system, based on other types of legislation and structures for the functioning of the state. In the same way, the British government has never created a single constitutional document. This is Britian's famous "unwritten constitution."[9] However, by the 1990s, the Sultan decided to take a step toward formal constitutionalism and the drafting of a single document. The modern constitutional history of Oman can be divided in four periods as follows: (1) period before the constitution (1970–1996); (2) the introduction of a constitution in 1996; (3) amendments to the 1996 Constitution in 2011; and (4) the introduction of a constitution in 2021.

From 1970 to 1996, Oman was ruled without a constitution. Instead, the legal structure of the Sultanate was based on a collection of laws, decrees, Royal orders, regulations, and formalized tradition. The Sultan's priorities in the early days of his reign were to unite the country, including offering an amnesty to all former opponents, and the removal of various petty restrictions imposed by his father.[10] He also appointed his uncle Tariq as prime minister, and it was he who tried to persuade the Sultan to introduce a constitution establishing a constitutional monarchy.[11] Sultan Qaboos agreed with the idea of eventually introducing a single, formal constitution, but not at that early period for at least three reasons. One reason announced by Sultan Qaboos, was the need to develop the educational system in Oman. He asserted that "You cannot run before you walk," and he believed that the Omani people before anything else wanted "education and health" adding that it:

> . . . would be a mistake, a big mistake. Most of the people do not even know what a vote is . . . In these conditions to draft a constitution, to set up a parliament would be like building a huge dome without either walls or foundations. It might perhaps give a nice impression to the outside world, but it would be nothing but a big show.[12]

Another possible reason was that the introduction of a constitution would complicate the Sultan's efforts to unify the country at that critical time. Sultan Qaboos inherited many challenges from his father. War in Dhofar and opposition from supporters of the Imamate system were immediate concerns.[13] Consequently, the establishment of a formal constitution might have increased challenges to the regime. Making or amending a constitution can sometimes lead to political instability instead of stability.[14] Sultan Qaboos was also aware of the fact that an early constitution could limit the opportunity for pursuing plans to build a modern country based on the needs of the people.[15] Sultan Qaboos made a tour of the major cities every year, to meet tribal leaders, and by using the revenue from oil the Sultan modernized the country and made provision for education, healthcare, employment, and security.[16] Certain laws or Royal orders were specific to certain parts of the country or even to specific relationships and agreements with tribal leaders. Also, before 1996, the legal system was held together by various laws and regulations that the Sultan and his ministers had issued, often in consultation

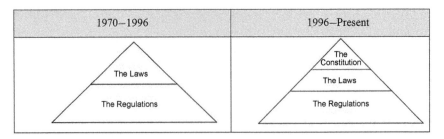

Figure 9.1 Types of legislation and their hierarchy in Oman.

with the people most impacted, to regulate all steps of modernity. There was no higher legislation, namely a constitution, guiding and limiting them as shown in Figure 9.1.[17]

The year 1996 was a watershed in Omani legal history: the Sultan introduced a single formalized document that functioned as the Omani Constitution.[18] In English, it is called The Basic Statute of the State, in Arabic it is *Al-Nizam al-Asasi li l-Dawlah*.[19] Sultan Qaboos followed the approach of not using the Persian word *Dustur* (constitution in English) as was the case in Saudi Arabia. Although their meanings are the same, it is interesting that the drafters avoided using a non-Arabic term for naming such an important and legal document.[20]

The Constitution was created twenty-five years after the Sultan took control of the country, and is the most recent written constitutional document implemented in Arab Gulf countries.[21] Several possible reasons could have driven Sultan Qaboos to adopt the constitution in 1996. One reason is that a succession crisis nearly occurred in the year before the Omani Constitution was to be introduced. In 1995, the Sultan was involved in a car accident in which he and one of his consultants were injured, while a deputy prime minister died. This may have encouraged him to introduce the constitution and fill the gap on the procedure for succession in Oman. Economic necessity may have been another reason which encouraged him to fill a serious gap in Oman's legal system in order to attract investment, build confidence in the system, and protect the interest of investors, especially foreign investors.[22] However, when asked, Sultan Qaboos rejected the reason for the reforms as being related to the accident. In an interview, Sultan Qaboos justified his introduction of a constitution in that year stating:

I had promised on the first day of my rule to create a modern government. But I knew change had to be entered into slowly, very slowly. The level of education had to reach a certain point so that people would know what we were talking about . . . As I approached my silver jubilee, I said to myself this is the time.[23]

The Sultan then described how the constitution had developed, stating:

So, I got together four of my most trusted people—all Omanis, I sat with them and told them exactly what I had in mind. I gave them a year to formulate it in a legal document. Then we had a second review, and then a final session.[24]

The names of the four people, or drafters, who formulated the 1996 Constitution according to the will of Sultan Qaboos have not been revealed to the public. A few months before the adoption of the constitution, the Sultan revealed the existence of the document on his annual tour, but the details were not given to the puplic until the Sultan issued it by Royal Decree No. 30/2016 on November 6, 1996 and published it in the Official Gazette. The Omani Constitution was issued without the participation of a constitutional assembly, or parliament, or by being put to a referendum.[25] Regardless of how the Omani Constitution was adopted, it ushered in a new era for the Omani legal and political systems. As set out in Figure 9.1, it was considered as the supreme legislation of the nation, and any legislation of lower standing (laws or regulations) must be consistent with its provisions.[26] Effectively the introduction of the constitution enhanced the value of the rule of law in Oman.[27]

The preamble of the 1996 Constitution contains three important paragraphs, which define its purposes. The first one states that the Constitution was introduced to maintain the status through *"confirmation of the principles which have guided State policy in various fields during the past period."* The second declares that the Constitution was a further stage *"to create a better future characterized by further achievements for the benefit of the Country and its Citizens."* The third states that the Constitution will *"strengthen Oman's international position and its role in establishing the foundation of peace, security, justice, and cooperation between different*

States and Peoples." More importantly, the introduction of the Omani Constitution addressed many important issues that had not been formally regulated. These included the system of succession; the establishment of Islamic supreme clauses; the definition of the competences of government institutions, including the head of state and the council of ministers; the establishment of new bicameral system of parliament—an elected house *Majlis al-Shura* and an appointed house *Majlis al-Dawla*. There was a new judicial system, a basic framework for the protection of human rights and the creation of a principle guiding state policy and the position of international treaties in the Omani legal system. These issues and others were structured in the 1996 Omani Constitution in seven chapters, as set out in Table 9.1.[28]

Table 9.1 Structure of the Omani constitutions

| Chapter No. | Chapter title | Article No. | | 2021 Constitution |
| | | 1996 Constitution | | |
		Before amendments (1996–2011)	After amendments (2011–2021)	
One	The State and the System of Governance	9	9	12
Two	Principles Guiding the Policy of the State	5	5	5
Three	Public Rights and Duties	26	26	30
Four	The Head of State*	17	17	20
Five	The *Majlis Oman*	1	46	8
Six	The Judiciary	13	13	13
Seven	General Provisions	10	10	10
Total		81	126	98

*There is no title for Chapter Four in the 2021 Constitution, and this chapter is divided into sections, which include titles such as the head of state.

However, some observers argue that the introduction of the 1996 Omani Constitution was only symbolic in character.[29] The executive and legislative authority continued to be mainly in the hands of the Sultan; parliament seemed to be a forum for the exchange of opinions between the government and the people without having any law-making ability or an ability to hold the government accountable.[30] Whilst this argument is both relevant and obvious, it is indicative of an advanced and sophisticated system of Western constitutional process, somewhat removed from the status quo of reality that is reflective of the Omani legal, social, and political environment. Those critics seem focused only on the variables contained in the Constitution that could strengthen or weaken parliamentary powers; they choose not to look at the other variables envisaged by the Sultan that sought to formulate a new broader Omani system, and critics perhaps overlooked that different countries, even in the West, have constitutional arrangements to suit their own circumstances. Sultan Qaboos followed "the step-by-step approach" in formulating the Omani system. He acknowledged this idea in several speeches such as:

> Human experiences have shown and are still showing that the method of abstract imitation is a useless method, and that the method of jumping over practical reality and objective circumstances in any community will always lead to great dangers. For this reason we reject imitation and reject the adoption of the policy of impulsive motion and prefer our factual method of thinking and application. We do not take any step without first studying it, then do so with deep conviction, and then observe the results guided by the principle of responding to the logic of evolution and development in our march forward.[31]

In the early months of 2011, some Omanis felt the influence of the Arab Spring, with the demands of the Omani demonstrators focusing on the idea of "the people want reform of the regime," not on "the people want the fall of the regime" as in Tunis and Cairo.[32] During these events Sultan Qaboos responded to many of the demands of the protestors by issuing several Royal Orders and Decrees.[33] One of which was intended to establish a technical committee of specialists to draft an amendment to the Omani Constitution to grant the Omani parliament legislative and supervisory powers.[34] Two points are worth making; the first is that the names of the committee members and the mechanism of its work were not made public.[35] Second, the committee was to suggest amendments that granted both houses of parliament legislative and supervisory powers, and not just the Elected House as demonstrators demanded. Following the announcement of the results of the *Majlis al-Shura* elections in October 2011, the Sultan issued Royal Decree No. 99/2011, amending some provisions of the Omani Constitution and this can be considered the last phase of constitutional reform under the era of Sultan Qaboos.[36] Regardless of the criticism that the process of amending the Constitution lacked public participation, the amendments were an important achievement.[37] Sultan Qaboos amended the Constitution in order to strengthen the powers of parliament. As shown in Table 9.1, forty-six Articles were amended and added to the chapter on the *Majlis Oman* (the Parliament). Before this reform, only one Article was allocated to parliament and it was then left to the law to define other issues. Al-Kharusi found that the 2011 constitutional amendments extended the involvement of both houses of parliament in the law-making process, as compared with the situation previously. However, a significant finding was that the Sultan Qaboos was still the law-making authority and that both houses of parliament merely had advisory roles. A more significant finding was that a higher number of laws were promulgated without, rather than with, parliamentary involvement for reasons outside the control of parliament.[38]

A year after the death of Sultan Qaboos, his successor, Sultan Haitham, issued a new constitution on January 11. 2021.[39] Therefore, I will use the term "1996 Constitution" issued by Sultan Qaboos, while "the 2021 Constitution" will refer to that issued by Sultan Haitham. At the end of the chapter, I will outline some key similarities and differences between the 1996 and 2021 constitutions in order to recognize the influence of Sultan Qaboos.

Islamic Sharia's Inspiration

A workable constitution needs to relate to the country's cultural heritage, as the French philosopher Montesquieu observed "laws should be so appropriate to the people for whom they are made that it is very unlikely that the laws of one nation can suit another."[40] Such understanding was taken into consideration by Sultan Qaboos, and it is fair to say that he was inspired by Islamic Sharia, which can be seen in the 1996 Constitution. The influence of Sharia can be seen in several areas, including (1) the Islamic features of succession, (2) the Islamic identity of the state, (3) the Islamic philosophy of *shura* (mutual consultation), and (4) Islamic supremacy clause.[41] These four points are worthy of further explanation.

On succession, Article (5) of the 1996 Constitution defined the Omani system of governance as Sultani (royal), and hereditary, which required the Sultan to be selected from amongst the male descendants of Sayyid Turki bin Said bin Sultan, the third grandfather of Sultans Qaboos and Haitham. It also obliged the Sultan to be "a Muslim, mature, rational, and the legitimate son of Omani Muslim parents."[42] In a case where the throne is vacant, the ruling family council was obliged to meet within three days of the vacancy occurring to appoint a successor. If there was no agreement, the defense council together with the chairmen of both houses of the Omani legislature (*Majlis Oman*) and the chairman of the Supreme Court, along with two of his most senior deputies, would install a person nominated by the Sultan in his letter to the Ruling Family Council.[43] In addition to this symbolic role of the chairmen of both houses of the *Majlis Oman* in the succession procedure, the 2011 amendments of the Omani Constitution requires members of the *Majlis Oman* to witness, with the Defense Council, the new Sultan's oath-taking ceremony before he exercises his power.[44] Therefore, the influence of Islam is clear in the requirement of a successor to be Muslim, as other Islamic Gulf constitutions. Because Sultan Qaboos did not have a son, he created a unique succession system compared with other Gulf State monarchies which was a mixture of Islamic views.[45] It was influenced by the Islamic Ibadi traditions arising from the absence of a Crown Prince, which is a matter accepted by some Sunni views.[46] Simultaneously, the succession was influenced by the adoption of an hereditary system—a Sunni view that was not inconsistent with the Ibadi, and Sultan Qaboos benefited from the Ibadi School by the using *shura* in the selection of the new ruler.[47] Under the Imamate system the ruler is chosen by the *ahl al-hall wa'l-'aqd* Council, while the Sultan was chosen by the Royal Family Council.[48] Practically, the succession process was adopted after the death of Sultan Qaboos. The Ruling Family Council agreed on opening sealed envelopes and chose the successor name by Sultan Qaboos in his will. The Ruling Family Council trusted Sultan Qaboos' selection.

Another Islamic influence in the 1996 Constitution is the question of the religious identity of the state. It specified that Oman is an Islamic state and that Islam is the religion of the country.[49] At the same time, however, other religions, such as Christianity and Hinduism, are protected and practiced in the Sultanate. Unlike some Islamic constitutions, it did not mention a specific Muslim school in the clauses of the constitution, although one may argue that Oman is dominated by the followers of the Islamic school of Ibadism and Ibadi people have occupied the presidency of the state throughout Omani history. Notably, this gave an indication of the extent to which the founder of modern Oman, Sultan Qaboos, was tolerant of other opinions if he believed they benefited his country, even if they contradicted the view of the Islamic School he followed. More noticeably, his policy dealt respectfully with other religions. This was a matter not only mentioned constitutionally but applied practically.[50] The issuing of permission by the Ministry of Endowments and Religious Affairs to allow the building of other religious temples is an example of this flexibility and openness.

Some scholars have argued that there was a need to recognize Islam constitutionally in Muslim countries "not only as a religion, but as a political theory and the major source of a legitimization of political power."[51] For this reason, it has been argued that *shura* is the "first theory of democratic government ever known to humanity."[52] Such understanding was not far from the belief of Sultan Qaboos, who acknowledged the high values of the Islamic philosophy of *shura* and followed it in making policy during his tenure as Sultan. Constitutionally, Sultan Qaboos used "*shura*" in the 1996 Constitution in three areas. First, he used "*shura*" in Article (9) as the principle in the system of governance and placed it alongside justice and equality.[53] Unlike some Arab Gulf monarchies (such as Kuwait, Bahrain, and Qatar), Sultan Qaboos avoided using "democracy" in describing the governance system, although Oman has the same traditional monarchy.[54] He wanted to legitimatize the method of governance by connecting it with the idea of *shura*, a notion that had been experienced in Oman for several decades and had become a part of its identity.[55] Nonetheless, there is consistency between *shura* and democracy in terms of offering people the right of political participation.[56] The principle of *shura* was emphasized in the 1996 Constitution in Chapter Two on directive principles and accepted political principles.[57] Interestingly, Article (10) of the 1996 Constitution allowed for a sophisticated structure for *shura* by benefiting from internal and external elements. The internal elements are clear in the clause "Laying suitable foundations for consolidating the pillars of genuine *shura* emanating from the heritage of the nation, its values and Islamic Sharia, and taking pride in his history"; while the external element is "adopting the useful contemporary means."[58] When Sultan Qaboos amended the Constitution in 2011, he highlighted the importance of modernization of *shura* in the preamble to the amendments, stating:

> [O]ur belief in the importance of developing the march of *Shura* in the Country to serve the interests of the Country and Citizens and in confirmation of the importance of the participation of all individuals of Society in the comprehensive development march in line with the requirements of the desired progress.

Second, the 1996 Constitution, like several constitutions in Arab Muslim-majority countries, uses the word *shura* as the name of a house of parliament that can participate in law-making.[59] In general, such a house can be elected (as in Oman), appointed (as in Bahrain and Saudi Arabia), or be a mixture of both methods (as in Qatar).[60] Although the 1996 Constitution established an Appointed House, which can be considered as another attempt at institutionalizing the process of mutual consultation (*shura*), the *Majlis al-Dawla* has been in an equal position with the *Majlis al-Shura* in producing consultation on law-making for the Sultan. However, it is an important to highlight that the design of the 1996 Constitution insofar as it adopts the Islamic theory of *shura mulima* (informative consultation), rather than the theory of *shura mulzima* (binding consultation), means that the final say in law-making, for example, is for the Sultan not for the *Majlis Oman*.[61]

Third, the 1996 Constitution contained ways to ensure that the law was consistent with the requirements of Islamic Sharia. Sultan Qaboos and his drafters were meticulous in choosing terminology in this context. He chose new terms, never used in other Islamic constitutions. Generally, formulation of Islamic supremacy clauses can fall into three categories: the source of law clauses; the repugnancy clauses; and a new proposed category can be called "superior Islamic clauses."[62] Each formulation can lead to a specific meaning. More importantly, the design of the 1996 Constitution in this matter can be located in the third category as Article (4) of the 1996 Constitution, which states that "Islamic Sharia is the basis for legislation." Thus, the 1996 Constitution was a type of constitution that uses the term "Islamic Sharia."[63] Linguistically this term contains all primary and supplementary sources of Islamic Sharia, and therefore it avoids possible criticism directed at constitutions that name specific sources of Islamic Sharia (Saudi Arabia Constitution), or those that refer only to general principles of Islamic Sharia (Egyptian Constitution).[64] Attractively, the term "basis of legislation" seems to be a distinctive linguistic structure that is certainly not used in other Islamic constitutions. It does not reject the probability of benefiting from other sources (like the source of law category and the repugnancy category), but it offers Islamic Sharia a higher ranking over other sources (like the repugnancy category). In other words, it can be said that the design of the 1996 Constitution appeared be appropriate to protect Islamic Sharia as substantive limitation in law-making. However, at the same time, there was an argument for claiming that some Omani laws, during the era of Sultan Qaboos, did not apply Islamic Sharia; for example, the interest on banking loans in commercial law and the non-application of some Islamic punishments for offenses (*hudud*; prescribed punishments) and *qisas* (law of equality or *lex talionis*).[65] Such issues inevitably lead to the question of whether the 1996 Constitution offered enforcement mechanisms for the Islamic supremacy clause. Before looking at these it is worth noting that, in common with institutional schemes to enforce rights in what are called constitutionalism countries, there are, according to Lombardi, three types of method used for interpreting and enforcing Islamic Sharia supremacy clauses as follows: (a) legal method (judiciary); (b) political method (parliament); and (c) hybrid or dialogic method.[66] It is the first method of these that was adopted in Oman, but this is in theory not in practice.[67] In other words, there was no mechanism in practice that could check whether or not Islamic Sharia as a supremacy clause was respected in any law that was issued by Sultan Qaboos.

Modern Constitutionalism

Generally, the processes of constitutionalization may be influenced by local, national, regional, and international factors.[68] It is often thought of as an unfinished process.[69] Sultan Qaboos followed the approach of modern countries in the world in three ways: (1) the design of the Omani political system, focusing on the relationship between the executive and the parliament; (2) the development of the judiciary; and (3) the protection of human rights and freedoms.[70]

Sultan Qaboos was influenced by the international community when constitutionally designing the Omani political system. For example, he borrowed features from three main typologies of political systems: parliamentary (United

Kingdom); presidential (United States); and semi-presidential (France). These three systems are probably representative of systems which exist in a global context.[71] Although the imported features have introduced a modern system for Oman and enhanced political participation, the features of the Omani system cannot be located specifically in any one of the three systems just mentioned. It would appear that Sultan Qaboos borrowed features that he believed to be appropriate for Oman and rejected those he thought inappropriate. Sultan Qaboos, said:

> From the very beginning it was our wish to see Oman embark upon its own enterprise in the field of democratic action.[72]

It is worth noting that the reforms and practices introduced by the Sultan, as shown in Figure 9.2, made the non-elected executive stronger than the *Majlis Oman* (Parliament), which is a feature of the Arab Gulf parliaments, as Parolin claims.[73] The imported features might be said to fall into four areas.

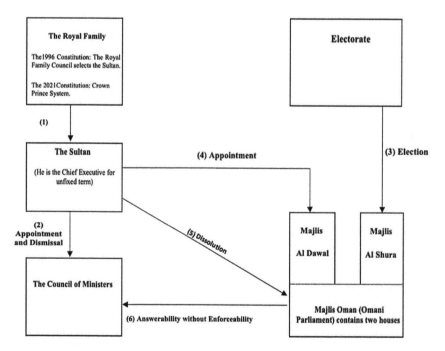

Figure 9.2 Overview of the Omani political system within the 1996 and 2021 Constitutions.

The first relates to the composition of the executive. According to Article (5) of the 1996 Constitution, the Sultan was an absolute monarch for an indefinite term of office (line 1 in Figure 9.2) and this is a feature of the parliamentary system.[74] He defined the composition of the executive as he held the positions of both head of state and head of the executive, and he was the only person able to appoint and dismiss ministers according to Articles (41) and (42) (line 2 in Figure 9.2), which is a feature of presidential system.[75] Interestingly, the 1996 Constitution allowed for a semi-presidential system, where executive authority is shared between the head of state and the head of government.[76] Article (48) of the 1996 Constitution granted the Sultan absolute power to appoint the prime minister by Royal Decree, which also defined the scope of the prime minister's competence. Practically, Sultan Qaboos held the defence, finance, and foreign affairs portfolios.[77] He also held the position of prime minister during his reign except for a few years at the beginning of his power. However, Article (45) of the 1996 Constitution allowed the Sultan not to attend the meetings of the Council of Ministers and authorized him to select whoever he thought appropriate to conduct the meetings if he or his deputy was absent. In all cases, Sultan Qaboos had the power to postpone, amend, or rescind any decisions made by the Council of Ministers whether he attended the meeting or not. The decisions of the Council of Ministers were considered, according to Article (42) of the 1996 Constitution, only as recommendations to the Sultan. A clear example happened in 2014 when the Council of Ministers made a decision to modify a decision of the General Authority for Consumer Protection related to the prohibition of raising prices on some commodities. There was widespread dissatisfaction and members of the elected house widely criticized the decision and attempted to send a letter direct to the Sultan without referring the matter to the Council of Ministers. The demand of the elected house was that the decision should be postponed until such time as economic laws were enacted that could regulate the market (consumer protection law, commercial agencies law, competition and antitrust law).[78] The demand was accepted by the Sultan and the *Diwan* of the Royal court made a statement, which included the words:

> In the context of the supreme concern of His Majesty Sultan Qaboos bin Said
> to be in touch and follow up the needs of his loyal people and the response

of His Majesty for the *Shura* Council's proposal on . . . he gives his order to postpone this decision . . .'[79]

The second area relates to the choice of the structure of parliament. In the 1996 Constitution, Sultan Qaboos adopted a bicameralism formulation for parliament learned from the United Kingdom. According to Article (58) (bis 8) of the 1996 Constitution, the composition of the *Majlis al-Shura* was determined by election and, therefore, the executive was not constitutionally allowed to interfere with the composition of this house (line 3 in Figure 9.2) and this can be seen in the direction of the theory of constitutionalism.[80] However, the *Majlis al-Dawla* became an appointed house with members determined by the Sultan (line 4 in Figure 9.2).[81]

The creation of an Appointed House provided Sultan Qaboos with the opportunity to include representatives from the broader community who had weak representation for one reason or another in the Elected House.[82] For instance, women represented between 18 percent and 16 percent of the membership of the 2011–2015 and 2015–2019 Appointed House, respectively, while women were represented in the Elected House by just 1 percent during the same periods.[83]

The third point is related to parliamentary oversight. Article (58) (bis 19) of the 1996 Constitution allowed the Sultan to dissolve *Majlis Al-Shuar* (line 5 in Figure 9.2).[84] Although this is a common practice in parliamentary and semi-presidential systems, countermeasures such as a vote of no confidence in the executive was not given to the *Majlis Al-Shuar*.[85] Unlike presidential, semi-presidential, and parliamentary systems, the 1996 Constitution, rather subtly, borrowed a pseudo-answerable, or "calling to account" element (line 6 in Figure 9.2); but it fell short of the enforceable aspect: giving account, explained in Table 9.2.[86]

The final point is related to the law-making authority. As stated earlier, the 2011 constitutional amendments made by Sultan Qaboos extend the involvement of both houses of parliament in the law-making process, as compared with the situation previously.[87] The amendment produced a positive reform by forbidding the Sultan to issue any law without parliamentary involvement during ordinary sessions; prior to the 2011 constitutional amendment,

Table 9.2 Overview of accountability mechanisms in three different institutional systems and the Omani system

The Stage of Accountability	Oversight Tools	Parliamentary System	Presidential System	Semi-presidential System	The Omani System
Answerability (Giving Account)	Questions and interpellation	X	(Some)	X	X
	Committees	X	X	X	X
	Special commissions	X	X	X	
	Ombudsman offices	X	X	X	
	Supreme audit institution	X	X	X	X
Enforceability (Holding to Account)	Non-confidence votes	X		X	
	Impeachment		X	X	
	Selection of cabinet	Elected	Ratified	Varies	
	Review of appointment	X	X	X	

the Sultan was able to issue laws without parliamentary scrutiny.[88] However, Sultan Qaboos was the law-making authority and both houses of parliament merely had advisory roles.[89] Despite the fact that Sultan Qaboos created executive and parliamentary institutions, his regime was far from the idea of a Western concept of the separation of powers, especially between legislative and executive authorities.[90] Article (41) of the 1996 Constitution provided the Sultan with a strong position in terms of his role by emphasizing that his orders must be obeyed and were not subject to accountability. It stipulates:

> His Majesty the Sultan is the Head of State and the Supreme Commander of the Armed Forces, his person is inviolable, respect of him is a duty, and his command is obeyed. He is the symbol of national unity and the guardian of the preservation and the protection thereof.

The Appeal Administrative Court considers that the order of the Sultan as legislation must be respected. For example, it states that:

According to Article (41) of [the 1996 Constitution] . . . the High Orders of His Majesty Sultan Qaboos bin Said are binding, enforceable and must be considered as legislation. They cannot not be cancelled or modified except by other the High Orders issued by His Majesty the Sultan. [Therefore], it is not allowed for the government or people disqualify or interpret them in a way make out of their meaning and purpose . . .[91]

When moving to the development of judiciary, it should be acknowledged that there were no formal courts with varying levels of jurisdiction prior Sultan Qaboos' rule. Reconciling disputes were resolving by Islamic judges, tribal leaders, and *waliyes* and they were unfamiliar with what we can describe as current legislation.[92] Sultan Qaboos took many steps to develop the judicial systems in Oman. The dramatic change happened via the 1996 Constitution, and its provisions in this context can be listed into two groups. The first group was related to judicial guarantees and safeguards. For instance, the 1996 Constitution clearly expressed the institutional independence of the judiciary as well as the individual independence of judges, who have the right and the obligation to resolve cases before them according to the law and any interference on their work considered as crime.[93] Additionally, the 1996 Constitution not only stipulated that "litigation is a protected right and guaranteed to all people," but also guaranteed the approximation of judicial bodies to litigants and the speedy settlement of cases.[94] All of these constitutional safeguards are essential for upholding the rule of law and human rights, which are an important element of modern constitutionalism. A second group of articles generally outlined the mechanisms that were needed to implement these safeguards.[95] Therefore, in practice, Sultan Qaboos initiated public prosecution and different types and levels of courts.[96] For instance, he created ordinary courts with three levels (Supreme Court, Appeal Courts and First Instance Courts).[97] Additionally, he established specialized courts such as the Administrative Court and the Military Courts.[98] Furthermore, Artcile (70) of the 1996 Constitution referred to a judicial body that is responsible for reviewing whether laws and regulations are in line with the provisions of the Omani Constitution (called in some systems the Constitutional Court). It stated that:

The Law shall define the judicial body entrusted with the settlement of disputes pertaining to the extent of conformity of laws and regulations with the Basic Statute of the State and that the said laws and regulations do not contradict with its provisions. The Law shall also specify the powers of such judicial body and the procedure which it shall follow.

However, although this body has been theoretically established inside the Supreme Court, in practice it is not operative as previously explained. Despite some reservations, it is fair to say that after the introducion of the 1996 Constitution, Sultan Qaboos attempted to build a new, modern, solid infrastructure for the Omani judiciary and his successors will surely find it easier to develop.[99]

Another influence of modern constitutionalism on the 1996 Constitution is related to the obligation to protection human rights and freedoms.[100] As shown on Table 9.1, the 1996 Constitution included a chapter to deal directly with this issue under the title "Public Rights and Duties," which contains twenty-six Articles including the right to litigation, the right to privacy, religious freedom, and freedom of expression.[101] Human rights protection is also mentioned in other sections, such as the right to participate in public affairs in Chapter One and the right to own property in Chapter Two.[102] Interestingly, some have noted that the 1996 Constitution was influenced by some international human rights instruments, although it has neither signed nor ratified some of them during the period of introduction of that constitution.[103] More specifically, the 1996 Constitution was shaped by the Universal Declaration of Human Rights (UDHR) in twenty-two out of twenty-nine areas, the International Covenant on Civil and Political Rights (ICCPR) in fourteen out twenty-two areas, and from the International Covenant on Economic, Social and Cultural Rights (ICESCR) in six out of ten areas.[104] Possibly some rights and freedoms are not included in the 1996 Constitution to avoid a perceived contradiction with other Islamic values such as gender equality in inheritance, or to avoid contradiction with government's interpretation of rights and freedoms.[105]

In common with a number of constitutions, the 1996 Constitution determined the principles of the rights and freedoms and limit them to be "within the limits of the law" or "specified by law."[106] It is also fair to say that the 1996 Constitution did not include a general Article that states laws must never conflict with the values of rights and freedoms as some constitution do.[107]

However, it has to be remembered that the inclusion of "rights and freedoms" in the constitutional framework was a huge step forward both legally and socially for Omani society during the era of Sultan Qaboos. Omani's enjoyed a huge amount rights and freedoms that never existed before, especially those related to education, healthcare, social protection, and employment.

The 2021 Constitution and Beyond

As shown in Table 9.1, the 2021 Constitution contains seven chapters like the 1996 Constitution. Interestingly, the current Sultan, Haitham, was inspired by Sultan Qaboos. There are similarities between the 1996 and the 2021 Constitutions in several areas. They include the Islamic identity of the state, the Islamic philosophy of *shura* (mutual consultation) and Islamic supremacy clause, public rights and duties, judicial guarantees and their mechanisms, and the Omani political system's design (Figure 9.2 and Table 9.2). However, the 2021 Constitution creates a Crown Prince system to make the succession process clearer and more stable.[108] It also adds a few articles for local administration and monitoring government performance as well as more human rights.[109] In general, most Articles of the 2021 Constitution are based on the 1996 Constitution and this is part of the legacy of Sultan Qaboos and the 1996 document.

Although the 2021 Constitution adds more rights, such as the right to life, a right to human dignity, and intellectual property protection, some rights especially those related to political participation might be enhanced in the future.[110] The Oman Vision 2040, which was created under the era of Sultan Qaboos and has begun to be applied under the era of Sultan Haitham, and states clearly that the power of *Majlis Oman* should be enhanced with the separation of powers within the following years.[111] If this happens, it would make the Omani system more relevant to the values of constitutionalism.[112] The decline of oil production and revenues may make it difficult for Oman to continue with the rentier model, where "the dearth of taxation in rentier states . . . translate[s] into a dearth of political participation."[113] This chapter acknowledges that "the transition from the rule of an individual to limited constitutional government" in Oman can be taken gradually, in stages.[114] Oman Vision 2040 recognizes the importance of the enhancement of political participation. In other words, the Omani Constitution should be redesigned by shifting away from the Islamic theory of *Shura Mulima* (informative consultation) and toward *Shura Mulzima* (binding consultation), which is consistent with the philosophy of constitutionalism. When this suggestion is applied, future research then needs to focus on how this new power can be activated by non-constitutional variables.

Notes

1. For general information about Ibadism, see John C. Wilkinson, *Ibādism: Origins and Early Development in Oman* (Oxford: Oxford University Press, 2010); and Ennami, Amr, Khalifah, *Studies in Ibadism* (Al-Ibadiyah) (Ministry of Endowments and Religious Affairs, Oman, 1971).
2. For a detailed discussion of the Imamate Ibadism in Oman, see Hussein al-Ghubash, *Oman: The Islamic Democratic Tradition* (Abingdon: Routledge, 2006).
3. Ghubash, *Oman*, 68–86.
4. Ghubash, *Oman*, 159–177.
5. Ali al-Rriyami, *Treaty of Seeb*, September 25, 1920 (Daralfarqad, Syria, 2019).
6. Ghubash, Oman, 180–199; Jan Morris, *Sultan in Oman* (London: Arrow Books, 1990).
7. For a detailed discussion of this point, see Basma Mubarak Said, *Constitutional Experience in Oman* (Beirut: Centre for Arab Unity Studies, 2013), 75–96; Khalid M. al-Azri, "Constitutional Reform in Oman: Rights Granted under Reserve," in Rainer Grote and J. Röder Tilmann (eds.), *Constitutionalism, Human Rights, and Islam after the Arab Spring* (New York: Oxford University Press, 2016), 176–178.
8. Dale F. Eickelman, "Kings and People: Oman's State Consultative Council," *Middle East Journal* 38(1) (1984): 51–71 at 53–54.
9. Robert Blackburn, "Britain's Unwritten Constitution," March 13, 2015, available at: https://www.bl.uk/magna-carta/articles/britains-unwritten-constitution, last accessed April 20, 2021.
10. Eickelman, "Kings and People."
11. For more details, see Said, *Constitutional Experience in Oman*, 75–96; al-Azri, "Constitutional Reform in Oman," 176–178; Marc Valeri, "Liberalization from Above: Political Reforms and Sultanism in Oman," in Constitutional Reform and Political Participation in the Gulf (Dubai: Gulf Research Center, 2006), 53.
12. Chris Kutschera, "OMAN : The Death of the Last Feudal Arab State," *Washington Post*, 1970, excerpt, available at: http://chris-kutschera.com/A/Oman1970.htm, last accessed February 2, 2021.

13. Basma Mubarak Said, "The Future of Reform in Oman," *Contemporary Arab Affairs* 9(1) (2016): 49–67 at 50.

14. For more information, see Michele Brandt, Jill Cottrell, Yash Ghai, and Anthony Regan, *Constitution-making and Reform: Options for the Process* (Geneva: Inter-peace, 2011).

15. Al-Azri, "Constitutional Reform in Oman," 167

16. Said, "The Future of Reform in Oman," 50; Valeri, "Liberalization from Above," 227–228; Eickelman, "Kings and People," 53–54.

17. The design of the figure is extracted from Michael Clegg, Katherine Ellena, David Ennis, and Chad Vickery, *The Hierarchy of Laws: Understanding and Implementing the Legal Framework that Govern Elections* (Arlington, VA: International Foundation for Electoral Systems, 2016). However, the content of the figure is formulated according to the Omani legal system.

18. It was issued by Royal Decree No. 30/2016 on November 6, 1996 and published in the Official Gazette No. 587.

19. Al-Azri, "Constitutional Reform in Oman."

20. Salim Al-Shukaili, *The Political and Constitutional System of the Sultanate of Oman* (Muscat: Al-Jeelalwaed, 2018).

21. Other Arab Gulf countries adopted the constitutions as follows: Kuwait 1962, Qatar 1970, UAE 1970, Bahrain 1973, and Saudi Arabia 1992. For more information, see, Nikolaus A. Siegfried, "Legislation and Legitimation in Oman: The Basic Law," *Islamic Law and Society* 7(3) (2000): 359–397 at 386.

22. For more details, see al-Azri, "Constitutional Reform in Oman," 179–180; Said, *Constitutional Experience in Oman*, 112–119.

23. Judith Miller, "Creating Modern Oman: An Interview with Sultan Qabus," *Foreign Affairs* 76(3) (1997): 13–19 at 16.

24. Miller, "Creating Modern Oman," 16.

25. For more discussion about criteria governing the procedure of constitution-making, see Rudiger Wolfrum, "Legitimacy of Constitution-Making Processes," in Rainer Grote and J. Röder Tilmann (eds.), *Constitutionalism, Human Rights, and Islam after the Arab Spring* (New York: Oxford University Press, 2016), 48–51.

26. For more information about types of legislations in Oman, see Salim Al-Kharusi, "Law-Making Authority under the Omani Constitution: Lessons Learned from Constitutionalism and Islamic Sharia," PhD thesis, University of Hull, 2018, 13.

27. For the meaning of the rule of law, see Tom Bingam, *The Rule of Law* (London: Allen Lane, 2010), 37–112; Simon Chesterman, "An International Rule of Law?" *American Journal of Comparative Law* 56(2) (2008): 331–361 at 342.

28. Compiled by the author from the Omani constitutions.

29. For example, see Siegfried, "Legislation and Legitimation in Oman"; Abdullah Juma Alhaj, "The Political Elite and the Introduction of Political Participation in Oman," Middle East Policy 7(3) (2000): 97–110; U. Rabi, "Majlis Al-Shura and Majlis Al-Dawla: Weaving Old Practices and New Realities in the Process of State Formation in Oman," *Middle Eastern Studies* 38(4) (2002): 41–50.

30. Siegfried, "Legislation and Legitimation in Oman," 376–377; Rabi, "Majlis Al-Shura and Majlis Al-Dawla," 46–47.

31. Sultan Qaboos, *The Royal Speeches of His Majesty Sultan Qaboos bin Said* (Muscat: Ministry of Information, 2005), 120.

32. During the Arab Spring in 2011, the Omani regime saw demonstrations the likes of which the country had not seen since the Sultan came to power in 1970. People criticized several issues, including the high unemployment rate; low standard of living; the involvement of long-serving ministers in corruption; the lack of legislative power of the *Majlis al-Shura*; the non-separation between the position of the Sultan and the prime minister, along with the lack of guarantees regarding the separation of three authorities in the Omani Constitution. For more details, see Al-Kharusi, "Law-Making Authority under the Omani Constitution," 6; Valeri, "Liberalization from Above," 225–236; Said, "The Future of Reform in Oman," 56–57. For more information of the Arab Spring, see, e.g., Grote and Tilmann, *Constitutionalism, Human Rights, and Islam after the Arab Spring*.

33. For instance, Sultan Qaboos issued a Royal decree and ordered the employment of 50,000 people, granting monthly fiscal aid for the unemployed, an increase a salary for employees in the executive, and changing a group of ministers. Said, "The Future of Reform in Oman," 56–57; Al-Azri, "Constitutional Reform in Oman," 183; Valeri, "Liberalization from Above," 232.

34. It established by Royal Decree No. (39/2011) in March 12, 2011.

35. Said, "The Future of Reform in Oman," 56–57.

36. Royal Decree No. 99/2011, modifying the Omani Constitution, was issued in October 19, 2011. However, it came into force, according to Article (3), from October 23, 2011, which was the day following its date of publication in the Official Gazette No. 948.

37. For more information about the criticism, see Said, "The Future of Reform in Oman," 57.

38. Al-Kharusi, "Law-Making Authority under the Omani Constitution," 188.

39. The 2021 Constitution was issued by Royal Decree No. 6/2021, January 11, 2021, and published in the Official Gazette No. 1374.

40. Charles de Secondat Montesquieu, *Montesquieu: The Spirit of the Laws*, ed. and trans, Anne M. Cohler, Basia Miller, and Harold S. Stone (Cambridge: Cambridge University Press, 2002), 8.

41. *Shura* means "mutual consultation"—"a process of requesting or offering an opinion on a specific matter with due care and deliberation (such as between the ruler and the ruled) in order to obtain a view or assist in making a decision." This definition is a mixture between several meanings of *shura* which the writer believes come closest to the meaning of *shura*. Gamil Moham-med El-Gindy, "The *Shura* and Human Rights in Islamic Law: the Relevance of Democracy," in Eugene Cotran and Mai Yamani (eds.), *The Rule of Law in the Middle East and the Islamic World: Human Rights and Judicial Process* (London: I. B. Tauris, 2000), 164. See also Fazlur Rahman, "The Principle of 'Shura' and the Role of the Umma in Islam," *American Journal of Islamic Social Sciences* 1(1) (1984): 1–6. The term "mutual consultation" is commonly used in English writing to define the meaning of *shura*. For example, see Muham-mad Shafiq, "The Role and Place of *Shura* in the Islamic Polity," *Islamic Studies* 23(4) (1984): 419–441; Muhammad Nazeer Ka Ka Khel, "The Conceptual and Institutional Development of *Shura* in Early Islam," *Islamic Studies*, 19(4) (1980): 271–282

42. Article (5) of the 1996 Constitution.

43. Articles (5) and (6) of the 1996 Constitution. It should be noted that the 1996 Constitution does not define the composition of the Defense Council. For this reason, Sultan Qaboos issued a Royal Decree forming the Council. For more details, see Royal Decree No. 105/96 about the Defense Council (issued December 28, 1996, published January 1, 1997) Official Gazette No. 590.

44. Article (7) of the 1996 Constitution.

45. Other Gulf States have heirs apparent because of the system of identifying a crown prince, while Oman does not. Abdulhadi Khalaf, "Rules of Succession and Political Participation in the GCC States," in Abdulhadi Khalaf and Giacomo Luciani (eds.), *Constitutional Reform and Political Participation in the Gulf* (Dubai: Constitutional Reform and Political Participation in the Gulf, Gulf Research Center, 2006).

46. Hussain S. Al-Salmi, "Oman's Basic Statute and Human Rights: Protections and Restrictions with a Focus on Nationality, Shura, and Freedom of Association," PhD thesis, University of Manchester, 2011, 90–91; Bekir Ouali Blhaj, *The Imamate under Ibadism between Theory and Practice Compared with Ahlu al-Sunnah wal al-Jamaah* (Tunis: Heritage Society, 2001), 168–169.

47. For more information about the comparison between Ibadism and Sunnism on the Imamate, see Ouali Blhaj, *The Imamate under Ibadism between Theory and Practice*; Ali Al-Abri, *Imamate in Islamic Jurisprudence: a Comparative Study* (Muscat: Al-Dhamri for Publishing and Distribution, 2015).

48. Al Salmi, "Oman's Basic Statute and Human Rights," 51.

49. Articles (1) and (2) of the 1996 Constitution.

50. Article (28) of the 1996 Constitution.

51. Masoud Kamali, "Civil Society and Islam: A Sociological Perspective," *European Journal of Sociology* 42(3) (2001): 457–482 at 457.

52. Bassam Tibi, *The Challenge of Fundamentalism: Political Islam and the New World Disorder*, updated edn. Berkeley: University of California Press, 2002), 174.

53. According to Castelli and Trevathan, the meaning of *shura* is similar to participatory democracy, where the decision is transferred to a local society or where people have equal access to decision-making, regardless of their social standing within a specified society. Mike Castelli and Abdullah Trevathan, "Citizenship and Human Rights in Islamic Education," *International Journal of Children's Spirituality* 13(1) (2008): 85–93 at 91.

54. Article (6) of the Kuwait Constitution; Article (1) of the Bahrain Constitution; and Article (1) of the Qatar Constitution.

55. According to Luciani, one of the motivations for using *shura* in Arab political systems "has to do with the role of religion in politics—because Islam aims at being a political order as well as a personal faith, a clean separation of religion and state is almost impossible." Giacomo Luciani, "Democracy vs. Shura in the Age of the Internet," in Abdulhadi Khalaf and Giacomo Luciani (eds.), *Constitutional Reform and Political Participation in the Gulf* (Dubai: Gulf Research Center, 2006), 283. For more information about the experience of *shura* in Oman, see, Al-Farsi, Sulaiman H., *Democracy and Youth in the Middle East: Islam, Tribalism and the Rentier State in Oman* (I.B. Tauris, London, 2013), p. 140.

56. Unlike democracy, *shura* "was not the result of a battle or the result of a forced outcome necessity, but was rather a divine imposition," as stated in the Qur'an. Nevertheless, *shura* is consistent with the theory of democracy in term of giving people the right of political participation. For more details, see Fahmy Howeidy, "Islam and Democracy," *Contemporary Arab Affairs* 3(3) (2010): 297–333 at 310.

57. Politics, economy, social, culture, and security are areas of principles guiding the policy of the state included in Articles (11)–(14) of the 1996 Constitution.

Directive principles set out the essential objectives that direct and inspire the policy of the state and provide the impetus for reform. For more details of the meaning of directive principles, see Nora Hedlin, "Principles and Cross-cutting Themes," in Markus Böckenförde, Nora Hedling, and Winluck Wahiu (eds.), *A Practical Guide to Constitution Building* (Stockholm: International Institute for Democracy and Electoral Assistance (International IDEA), 2015), 52.

58. Article (10) of the 1996 Constitution.

59. *Majlis al-Shura* was created before the issuance of the 1996 Constitution. It was created by Royal Decree in 1991, replacing a Consultative Council known as the *Majlis al-Stishari lil-Dawla*, which had existed since 1981.

60. Article (58) (bis 8) of the 1996 Constitution; Article (52) of the Bahrain Constitution; Article (68) of the Saudi Arabian Constitution; and Article (77) of the Qatar Constitution.

61. There are two types of *shura* that are relevant to the obligation of rulers to act according to the collective decision of *shura*. The first one is *Shura Mulima* (informative consultation), which means that a *shura* decision is not compulsory; it is more advisory. The second is *Shura Mulzima* (binding consultation), which means that a *shura* decision is obligatory for a Muslim leader to act upon, even if it is contrary to the ruler's view. Some Sunni and Ibadi views are in agreement about the validity of limiting the ruler's power *by Shura Mulzima*, which puts such system in a stronger Islamic position than *Shura Mulima*. For more details, see Al-Kharusi, "Law-Making Authority under the Omani Constitution," 204–215.

62. The terms "the source of law and the repugnancy clauses" are borrowed from Dawood I. Ahmed and Tom Ginsburg, "Constitutional Islamization and Human Rights: The Surprising Origin and Spread of Islamic Supremacy in Constitutions," *Virginia Journal of International Law* 54(3) (2014): 615–696 at 653. See also Kristen Stilt, "Contextualizing Constitutional Islam: the Malayan Experience," *International Journal of Constitutional Law* 13(2) (2015): 407. The source of law category helps to illustrate the position of the clause vis-à-vis its relation to religious requirements among all other sources. It usually states that Islamic Sharia, the principles of Islamic Sharia or Islamic jurisprudence, is/shall be "a" or "the" main source of legislation. For more information, see Al-Kharusi, "Law-Making Authority under the Omani Constitution," 242–246. The repugnancy clauses come in different forms and the commonality of meaning is that it is "constitutionally forbidden to enact legislation that is antithetical to Islam." Dawood I. Ahmed and Moamen Gouda, "Measuring Constitutional

Islamization: The Islamic Constitutions Index," *Hastings International and Comparative Law Review* 38(1) (2015): 1–76 at 14, 47–48. See also, Al-Kharusi, "Law-Making Authority under the Omani Constitution." Some constitutional designs of Islamic Sharia supremacy clauses cannot be located in either of the categories of the source of law or the repugnancy clauses and, therefore, what has been established is a third category called "Islamic superior clauses" which may be a way forward.

63. Such as Article (2) of the Bahrain Constitution; Article (2) of the Kuwait Constitution; Article (1) of the Qatar Constitution; and Article (7) of the UAE Constitution.

64. Article (7) of the Saudi Arabia Constitution and Article (2) of the Egyptian Constitution. There are four primary sources of Islamic Sharia: the Qur'an, the Sunna, *Ijma* (consensus of opinion), and *Qiyas* (Analogy). There are seven supplementary sources of Islamic Sharia; *Maslahah Mursalah* (consideration of public interest), *Sadd al-dharai* (blocking the means), *Istihsan* (equity or favorable construction), *Istishab* (presumption of continuity), *Urf* (custom), *Shar'Man Qablana* (revealed laws preceding to Islamic Sharia), and *Fatwa of Shaba* (the opinion of the Prophet's companion). For more information about the sources of Islamic Sharia, see Mohammad Hashim Kamali, *Principles of Islamic Jurisprudence* (Cambridge: Islamic Texts Society, 1991); Abdul Wahhab Khallaf, *The Roots of Islamic Jurisprudence and Synopsis of Islamic Legislation* (Cairo: Dar Al-Fikr Al-Araby, 1996);, Abdullah Al-Salmi, *Talaat Shams* (Bidiya: Imam Al-Salmi Library, 2010), 92.

65. Al-Azri, "Constitutional Reform in Oman," 73.

66. Lombardi discussed examples of the legal method: Afghanistan, 2004–present;, Egypt, 1980–present; Pakistan, 1977–present; and Iran, 1979–1988. He also reviewed examples of political methods, including Afghanistan, 1923–1967 (and arguably until 2004); Pakistan, 1956–1977; and Sudan, 1988–2005. According to Lombardi, the hybrid or dialogic method is designed to combine important elements of both the political and legal constitutional methods, such as permitting the legislative, under carefully controlled circumstances; to override judicial decisions, as was suggested to change the Egyptian system during a tumultuous period in 2011. Lombardi studied two countries (Pakistan 1952–1953 and Egypt 2012) that experienced proposals to adopt a hybrid method, in which the legislature could override a judicial decision, but this was not put into effect. Also, he discussed Iranian model (1988–present) that approach a unique dialogic model of Islamic review. For more

details, see Clark B. Lombardi, "Designing Islamic Constitutions: Past Trends and Options for a Democratic Future," *International Journal of Constitutional Law*, 11(3) (2013): 615–645 at 623–636.

67. Article (70) of the 1996 Constitution and Articles (10)–(11) of the Judicial Authority Law.

68. Martin Loughlin, "What is Constitutionalisation?" in Martin Loughlin and Petra Dobner (eds.), *The Twilight of Constitutionalism?* (Oxford: Oxford University Press, 2010), 62–68.

69. Clemens Mattheis, "System Theory of Niklas Luhmann and the Constitutionalization of the World Society," *Goettingen Journal of International Law* 4(2) (2012): 625–647 at 627.

70. According to Al-Kharusi, researchers have not yet agreed on a fixed definition of constitutionalism, but the formalistic approach is one way to understand its meaning and thereby it was noted that constitutionalism contains at least six elements: (1) limited government; (2) the rule of law; (3) the obligation to protect human rights; (4) the separation of powers; (5) periodic free and fair elections; and (6) the sovereignty of the people. More importantly, he found that the functional approach to understanding constitutionalism supports practical constitutionalism with the interaction of the cultural, social, political, and historical realities of society. He also argues that the relationship between constitutionalism and the terms the "constitution" and "constitutionalisation." He suggests that "constitutionalism" should be used as a philosophy surrounding the existence of a constitution, but "constitutionalisation" refers to the ongoing process undergone by the legal system of a country in order to attain elements of constitutionalism. Al-Kharusi, "Law-Making Authority under the Omani Constitution," 63–83

71. For more information about parliamentary, presidential, and semi-presidential systems, see John Alder, *Constitutional and Administrative Law*, 10th edn. (London: Palgrave Macmillan, 2015), 165; Richard Albert, "The Fusion of Presidentialism and Parliamentarism," *American Journal of Comparative Law* 57(3) (2009): 536; Bruce Ackerman, "The New Separation of Powers," *Harvard Law Review* 113(3) (2000): 633–729 at 634–664;, Fred W. Riggs, "Presidentialism versus Parliamentarism: Implications for Representativeness and Legitimacy," *International Political Science Review* 18(3) (1997): 253–278 at 257; Robert Elgie, "The Politics of Semi-Presidentialism," in Robert Elgie (ed.), *Semi-Presidentialism in Europe* (Oxford: Oxford University Press, 1999); Cindy Skach, *Borrowing Constitutional Designs: Constitutional Law in Weimar*

Germany and the French Fifth Republic (Princeton, NJ: Princeton University Press, 2009).

71. Riggs, "Presidentialism versus Parliamentarism," 257.

72. Sultan Qaboos, *Speeches of His Majesty Sultan Qaboos bin Said*, 461.

73. Gianluca P. Parolin, "Winter is Coming: Authoritarian Constitutionalism under Strain in the Gulf," in Rainer Grote and, Tilmann J. Roder (eds.), *Constitutionalism in Islamic Countries: Between Upheaval and Continuity* (Oxford: Oxford University Press, 2012), 150.

74. Mark Freeman, "Constitutional Framework and Fragile Democracies: Choosing between Parliamentarianism, Presidentialism and Semipresidentialism," *Pace International Law Review* 12(2) (2000): 253–282 at 262.

75. Freeman, "Constitutional Framework and Fragile Democracies," 263; Cristina Leston-Bandeira, *From Legislation to Legitimation: The Role of the Portuguese Parliament* (London: Taylor & Francis, 2004), 8; Riggs, "Presidentialism versus Parliamentarism," 257.

76. Leston-Bandeira and Norton, *From Legislation to Legitimation*, 9; Robert Elgie, "The Politics of Semi-Presidentialism," in Robert Elgie (ed.), *Semi-Presidentialism in Europe* (Oxford: Oxford University Press, 1999), 13–14; Skach, *Borrowing Constitutional Designs*, 13.

77. Khalaf, "Rules of Succession and Political Participation in the GCC States," 48; Mark N. Katz, "Assessing the Political Stability of Oman," *Middle East Review of International Affairs* 8(3) (2004): 1–10 at 3.

78. *Majlis al-Shura*, "Report on the Activities of Majlis al-Shura's Plenary during the Third Session of Parliamentary Term (2011–15)," *Shura* (2014) August (19), 6–11 at 6.

79. *Majlis al-Shura*, "Report on the Activities of Majlis al-Shura's Plenary during the Third Session of Parliamentary Term (2011–15)."

80. Elections are among the elements of constitutionalism. Mark Tushnet, "Comparative Constitutional Law," in Mathias Reiman and Reinhard Zimmermann (eds.), *The Oxford Handbook of Comparative Law* (Oxford: Oxford University Press, 2006), 1230; Stanley A. De Smith, *The New Commonwealth and its Constitutions* (London: Stevens & Sons, 1964), 106.

81. Article (58) (bis) of the 1996 Constitution.

82. The upper house of parliament exists for many reasons. For more information, see R. L. Borthwick, "Methods of Composition of Second Chambers," *Journal of Legislative Studies* 7(1) (2001): 19–26 at 22; Donald Shell, "The History of Bicameralism," in Nicholas Baldwin and Donald Shell (eds.), *Second Chambers*

(London: Frank Cass, 2013); Meg Russell, "What are Second Chambers For?" *Parliamentary Affairs* 54(3) (2001): 442–458 at 443; Vernon Bogdanor, *The New British Constitution* (London: Hart, 2009), 160–161.

83. Al-Kharusi, "Law-Making Authority under the Omani Constitution," 43.

84. The power to dissolve parliament is usually under the prerogative of the head of state as a way to resolve disputes between the executive and parliament. To exercise this power, some conditions may be requested, including consulting the prime minister or the chairman of the two houses or abstaining from its use at certain times (in Italy during the last six months of the president's term of office or in France in the year after election set off by a dissolution). However, dissolution is not always used to arbitrate on a dispute between these two authorities. For example, in Australia, it is used as an ultimate sanction when the two houses (both elected) are unable to agree upon the contents of a bill. Michel Ameller (ed.), *Parliaments: A Comparative Study on the Structure and Functioning of Representative Institutions in Fifty-five Countries*, new revised edn. (Paris: Inter-Parliamentary Union, 1966), 287.

85. Freeman, "Constitutional Framework and Fragile Democracies," 262; Leston-Bandeira and Norton, *From Legislation to Legitimation*, 8–9; John K. Johnson, *The Role of Parliament in Government* (Washington, DC: World Bank Institute, 2005), 7; Alfred Stepan and Cindy Skach, "Constitutional Frameworks and Democratic Consolidation: Parliamentarianism versus Presidentialism," *World Politics* 46(1) (1993): 1–22 at 3.

86. The concept of accountability consists of answerability and enforceability. Answerability (calling to account) highlights the obligation of the accountee (executive) to inform and to explain its decisions and/or activities to the accountor (parliament). Enforceability (holding to account) highlights the capacity of the accountor (parliament) to impose sanctions on the offending accountee (executive) or, where necessary, to seek remedial action. For more explanation about the two stages of the concept of accountability, see Riccardo Pelizzo and Frederick Stapenhurst, *Government Accountability and Legislative Oversight* (New York: Routledge, 2014), 1–15; Andreas Schedler, Larry Diamond, and Marc F. Plattner, "Conceptualizing Accountability," in Andreas Schedler (ed.), *The Self-Restraining State: Power and Accountability in New Democracies* (Boulder, CO: Lynne Rienner, 1999), 13–18; Derick W. Brinkerhoff, *Taking Account of Accountability: A Conceptual Overview and Strategic Options* (Washington, DC: US Agency for International Development, Center for Democracy and Governance, Implementing Policy Change Project, 2001), 2–3; Greg Power and

Alex Brazier, "Making Government Accountable," *Parliamentary Affairs* 54(3) (2001): 554–559 at 554. Table 9.2 was compiled from Geoff Dubrow, "Systems of Governance and Parliamentary Accountability," in *Systems of Governance and Parliamentary Accountability: A Parliamentarian's Handbook* (Washington, DC: Parliamentary Centre and World Bank Institute, 2002), 23, as improved by Pelizzo and Stapenhurst, *Government Accountability and Legislative Oversight*, 1–15. However, the author of this chapter has added the data related to the Omani system from the 1996 and 2021 Constitutions and the Majlis Oman Law, 2021, Royal Decree 7/2021 (issued January 17, 2021, published January 17, 2021), Official Gazette No. 1375.

87. Al-Kharusi, "Law-Making Authority under the Omani Constitution."

88. For more information, see Articles (28–(29) of Majlis Oman Statute, 1997, Royal Decree No. 86/97 (issued December 16, 1997, published January 3, 1998) Official Gazette No. 614.

89. Al-Kharusi, "Law-Making Authority under the Omani Constitution."

90. For further information about the concept of the separation of powers, see Thomas Nugent (trans. 1752), Montesquieu, Charles de Secondat Baron de, *The Spirit of Laws* (Kitchener: Batoche Books, 2001), 173; B. O. Nwabueze, *Constitutionalism in the Emergent States* (Madison, WI: Fairleigh Dickinson University Press, 1973), 13.

81. Appeal Administrative Court, Case No. 847 of the year (17QS) (June 20, 2017).

92. Al-Salmi, *Talaat Shams*, 90–91.

93. Articles (60) and (61) of the 1996 Constitution.

94. Article (25) of the 1996 Constitution.

95. Articles (61), (62), (64), (66), (67), (68), and (69) of the 1996 Constitution.

96. For more information, see Al-Salmi, *Talaat Shams*, 116–117.

97. Al-Salmi, *Talaat Shams*, 93–100.

98. Al-Salmi, *Talaat Shams*, –103. It should be noted that the Military Courts were created by the Military Justice Law 2011, Royal Decree No. 110/2011 (issued October 24, 2011, published October 29, 2011) Official Gazette No. 949.

99. Sultan Haitham has already started issuing laws to simplify litigation procedures and he has to develop alternative judicial methods. For example, laws to simplify litigation procedures 2021, Royal Decree No. 125/2021 (issued November 12, 2021, published November 22, 2021) Official Gazette No. 1367.

100. Many researchers acknowledge the guarantee of human rights as an element of constitutionalism. For example, see David Feldman, "Constitutionalism, Deliberative Democracy and Human Rights," in John Morison, Kieran McEvoy, and Gordon Anthony (eds.), *Judges, Transition, and Human Rights* (New York: Oxford University Press, 2007), 426; Michel Rosenfeld, "Modern Constitutionalism as Interplay between Identity and Diversity: An Introduction," *Cardozo Law Review* 14(3/4) (1992): 497–532 at 497.

101. Articles (25), (27), (28), (29), and (30) of the 1996 Constitution.

102. Articles (9) and (11) of the 1996 Constitution.

103. Al-Salmi, *Talaat Shams*, 61.

104. Al-Salmi, *Talaat Shams*, 65.

105. One of five reservations made by Sultan Qaboos upon the Convention on the Elimination of all Forms of Discrimination against Women is that "All provisions of the Convention not in accordance with the provisions of the Islamic Sharia and laws in force in the Sultanate of Oman." For more details, see Royal Decree No. 42/2005 Accepting the Sultanate's accession to the Convention on the Elimination of all Forms of Discrimination against Women (issued May 7, 2005, published May 15, 2005) Official Gazette No. 791.

106. Al-Salmi, *Talaat Shams*, 64.

107. Chapter (49) of the Tunisian Constitution.

108. Article (5) of the 2021 Constitution. It should be mentioned that there was some concern about the ability of the Omani system outlined in the 1996 Constitution to be able to cope when faced with the selection of the next Sultan. For more details, see Al-Azri, "Constitutional Reform in Oman," 148.

109. Articles (64) and (65) of the 2021 Constitution.

110. Articles (18) and (38), of the 2021 Constitution.

111. The Oman Vision 2040, 40. It can be found on the Official Website of the Oman Vision 2040, at: https://www.2040.om/Oman2040-En.pdf, last accessed February 13, 2021.

112. Barendt describes the doctrine of the separation of powers as being the "essence" of constitutionalism. Eric Barendt, "Is there a United Kingdom Constitution?" *Oxford Journal of Legal Studies* 17(19) (1997): 137–146 at 141.

113. For more information about rentier states, see Meliha Benli Altunisik, "Rentier State Theory and the Arab Uprisings: An Appraisal," *Uluslararasi Iliskiler* (International Relations) 11(42) (2014): 75–91 at 79

114. Barendt, "Is there a United Kingdom Constitution?"

10

NATION AND STATE IN OMAN: THE INITIAL IMPACT OF 1970

J. E. Peterson

The emergence and consolidation of the Omani state after 1970 can be explained by exploring basic concepts that define the country, nation, state, and government. This approach provides insights into the initial development of the post-1970 Sultanate under Sultan Qaboos. The first few years of the 1970s were pivotal, formative, and transitional. This was the time when Oman changed from being an undefined nation searching for a serviceable state to a new capable state elaborating a cohesive national identity.[1] The new Sultan, Qaboos bin Said, was at the heart of this transformation, stepping into the new experience and role as ruler of a country still divided and fragmented.

The Contemporary Omani Nation

At the root of modern Omani identity lies the concept of the nation, one shared by Omanis from diverse backgrounds. Concepts such as "national origin," "nationality," and "nation-state," were new to the Gulf States and Oman, emerging around the beginning of the oil era in the mid-twentieth century. Their impetus can be termed "legal" rather than "ideological" or "emotional," in that the emergence of these ideas was the consequence of two roughly simultaneous impulses: the consolidation of a primary political role by certain tribes and sheikhly families and the impact of the British. While citizenship or nationality confers Omani legal identity, the sense of who is an Omani and who is not extends well beyond formal citizenship.

There has long existed in Oman a common identity that, although blending into ties beyond the Oman of today, created a sense of being Omani or non-Omani. Over the course of the twentieth century and especially after 1970, this commonality gradually intensified into a fuller feeling of nationalism, of a distinct Omani identity tied to the Sultanate with the Sultan as its symbol. The term "nationalism" has often acquired a rather pejorative connotation, particularly due to its association with the more specific concept of integral nationalism, where individual rights of the citizens are subordinated to the needs of the state, as in the fascist regimes of the twentieth century. The use of the term here, in contrast, relies on the concept of liberal nationalism, whereby a group or groups of people assume a shared identity on the basis of common history, ethnicity, religion, culture, or other self-perceived unity to form a "nation" that ideally is expressed politically within a nation-state. Thus, the emergence of nationalism is a prerequisite for the creation of a nation-state.[2]

What constitutes a nation? Ernst Renan, in his nineteenth-century essay, "Qu'est-ce qu'une nation?" concluded that a nation is based not on racial, ethnic, or language affinities as much as shared memory and forgetfulness.[3] Later, in the 1980s, Benedict Anderson remarked, "Nation, nationality, nationalism—all have proved notoriously difficult to define, let alone to analyse." He goes on to describe the nation as "an imagined political community—and imagined as both inherently limited and sovereign."[4] Eric Hobsbawm notes that just as the concept of a nation is relatively new, its elaboration "must include a constructed or 'invented' component."[5] The traditions that sustain and bind the new nation together not only rely upon "remembered" elements, but also embody newly invented rituals and practices. The development of the Omani "nation" can be described in two ways: as a more amorphous, "traditional," sense of what made the people of Oman distinct from their neighbors; and as a product of more universalist human ideals of the "modern" nation-state.

Conceptions of Oman

Perhaps the most fundamental element of the traditional notion of nation is geography. For centuries before the twentieth century, the essence of Oman was often an amorphous geographical entity with indeterminate borders. An anecdote by geographer and former oil company employee in the Gulf, J. C. Wilkinson, illustrates this point:

> In 1959, when the writer was transferred from Doha to work in Abu Dhabi, he was somewhat surprised when a Qatari remarked to him, "Ah, so at last you've got your wish and you're going to Oman." Shortly after taking up this new appointment, some urgent business arose which required discussion with the Ruler. Inquiries revealed that he was no longer in Abu Dhabi, but had "gone to Oman." Here, at last, seemed to be a perfect excuse for visiting this forbidden land. But it was not to be, because "Oman" turned out simply to be the local name for Sheikh Shakhbut's territory in the so-called "Buraimi Oasis"! . . . [H]ere also the writer was able to talk with those who really knew the area, for the group of men with brightly-coloured head-dresses whom he found waiting in the Sheikh's *majlis* were, it appeared, "visitors from Oman." Some years later when the opportunity did at last come to make the journey along the foot of the mountains southwards from Buraimi, the writer called on one of these "Omanis" at his home at 'Ibri. As he took his leave to carry on towards Nizwa he almost anticipated his host's remark, "Ah, so you're going on to Oman"![6]

Wilkinson's account demonstrates that borders and claims on geography have changed dramatically since the middle of the twentieth century. The idea of Oman geographically was not the same thing as the present nation-state of Oman. Until very recently, that which was regarded as Oman included the Oman Coast, later known, by outside observers, as the Pirate Coast, then the Trucial Coast, and now the United Arab Emirates. But traditionally it did not include the Sultanate's southern region of Dhofar (with its historic links to the eastern regions of what is now Yemen). The melding of Oman with the Sultanate is a recent phenomenon and in some ways is the consequence of the accession of Sultan Qaboos.

Twentieth-Century Nation-building in Oman

The appearance of the Omani nation-state owes much to the creation of the Al-Bu Said state in the eighteenth century. But, more directly, the full formation of the modern Omani state was accelerated with the accession of Sultan Qaboos and the *Nahda* (Renaissance) or *sahwa* (awakening) he set in motion.

This process was comparable to the emergence of the independent emirates of the Gulf around 1971. An important aspect of the change was the creation of a modern national identity coterminous with the Sultanate of Oman.

For Sultan Qaboos and his government to create this national identity among the Omani people, it was first necessary to reconstitute the Sultanate in the 1970s from the foundations laid by their predecessors. Omani culture has revolved around Arabness, Ibadism, tribal affinities, and reactions to outside interference or conquest. A sense of Arab identity has existed perhaps ever since immigrating Arab tribes toppled Persian suzerainty during the Islamization of Oman in the seventh century CE.

Another element of identity in Oman is Ibadi Islam, predominant in Oman since the early Islamic period and given political, as well as religious, representation through the Ibadi Imamate and Ibadi legal structures. Ibadism is distinctive to Oman. Although not all Omanis are Ibadi and there are substantial Sunni and Shiite communities, it is the only country in which Ibadis form a significant part of the population. Doctrinal and practical differences between Ibadis and Sunnis are not substantial, allowing Ibadism to provide a common source of religious and cultural feeling among many Omanis.

A third element is that of tribes, which constituted the constellation of constituencies that formed the backbone of the Ibadi Imamate. Furthermore, Omanis collectively supported broad proto-national responses to invasions by the Portuguese in the sixteenth and seventeenth centuries, by the Persians in the eighteenth century, and by the Wahhabis in the nineteenth century.

At the same time, however, Omani unity was challenged by internal divisions. The political fissure between coast and interior began shortly after the first of the Al-Bu Said rulers was elected Imam in the mid-eighteenth century, even though he did not fulfill the religious requirements of an imam. It only took a few decades for subsequent Al-Bu Said leaders to abandon any pretense of being imams and, equally importantly, move their center to Muscat and their primary objectives to maritime expansion. While some (fitful) authority was exercised over the interior during the nineteenth century—and an interregnum of three years when an imam of a cadet branch of the Al-Bu Said family controlled Muscat—all control over the interior was lost in the early twentieth century. Similar divisions took place in Dhofar with the outbreak of rebellion in the 1960s.

The rulers of Muscat, by now styled sultans, acknowledged the division in their adoption of the name of their dominion as the Sultanate of Muscat and Oman, thus implying a political as well as geographical disconnect between the two. But the people of both coast and interior did not consider themselves Muscati but not Omani or vice versa. It was not until the military deposition of the Imam in the 1950s that the Sultan was able to exercise authority over the core of Oman. Nevertheless, the minimalist government of Sultan Said bin Taimur, his reputation for parsimoniousness and enforced isolation, as well as his absence from Oman in southern Dhofar for the last twelve years of his reign (and his hostile attitude toward the needs of the Dhofari population), did little to advance any sense of national identity.

Contemporary National Identity in Oman

The trappings of contemporary national identity, formal legal citizenship, passports, rights and obligations and legal standing of citizens, and determination of national identity only fully developed after the accession of Sultan Qaboos in 1970. The present Sultanate (i.e., the state of the Al-Bu Said dynasty) encompassed the proto-national identity from its beginning. But its inherent difficulty in doing so was due to conflict with the Ibadi Imam (accompanied by persistent attempts by religious and tribal leaders to restore the Imamate in Oman) and dependence on outside backing.

Even though the present Oman was physically unified during the reign of Said bin Taimur (r. 1932–1970), it was not unified in a coherent national identity until the post-1970 period. In this sense, the reign of Said's son Qaboos, even as it inherited some earlier stirrings, marked the beginning of a true primary national identity, of a sense of nationalism, building on and transforming existing tribal and regional identities. As Ernest Gellner put it, "It is nationalism which engenders nations, and not the other way around."[7]

Several elements were involved in the development of a primary national identity. One of these, aided by Oman's reintegration into the international arena, was the consolidation of a feeling of belonging to a larger Arab and Muslim community, thus reinforcing the connectedness between Omanis of different tribes, regions, or sects, as well as their connections to the wider Arab world and fellow Muslims.[8] Closer to home, the interconnections between the six GCC states helped to build both a commonality and a closer understanding of what it meant to be a citizen in a state. Even the development process contributed. State education and curriculum reinforced the concept of citizenship and belonging, as did state-owned television, radio, and print media. Some scholars have emphasized the deliberate adoption of "identity engineering" to create a unitary and pliable population.[9]

Meanwhile symbols of the state kept focus on a national identification. Soon after Sultan Qaboos' accession, a new national flag was introduced, incorporating the old white flag of the Sultanate and the red flag of the Imamate. Portraits of the Sultan adorned offices and homes throughout the country. Sultan Qaboos' full beard soon gave way to one neatly trimmed and he was frequently portrayed in uniform. This was perhaps not surprising given both his military training and his role as leader of the Dhofar war effort. Nevertheless, it projected a young, competent, and dedicated ruler in sharp distinction from his predecessor. As Muscat built up, an impressive row of government ministries lined the main highway—the tangible manifestation of the power and orderliness of government combined with the modern urban setting of the capital to create national pride. The adoption of a comprehensive corpus of law and a set of regulations emphasized the role of the state in fashioning the new Oman. Omani sports teams wearing the national colors competed in Gulf competitions and farther afield.

From his accession, Sultan Qaboos was enormously popular in the north (Oman) since he embodied change and progress. Additionally, he was regarded by the people of the south (Dhofar) as one of them since his mother was from the Bayt Qatan *jibali* tribe and he was born and raised in Salalah. His visage, visible everywhere, served as a tangible symbol of the growing pride that Omanis felt in their suddenly flourishing country.

The figure of Sultan Qaboos was an important element in the process of strengthening national identity and building a state. Lisa Anderson suggests that "The relative strength of monarchy in the Middle East monarchies [is due] to its affinity with the projects of nation building and state formation . . ."[10] With a weak ruling family and few truly national symbols of unity, the presence and inviolateness of the Sultan was key to rallying public sentiment around Sultan Qaboos. From the beginning, the decision was made that the new ruler should be addressed as "His Majesty" rather than as "His Highness" as his father and grandfather had been. Early discussion even contemplated changing his title from sultan to king.

Certainly, Omanis were sincerely grateful to Sultan Qaboos for the changes sweeping the country: in the early years of his reign, Omanis spontaneously remarked that before Qaboos there was nothing and that everything happened after his accession. This approach was similar to the other Gulf monarchies, where streets, airports, hospitals, and universities bore the names of various senior figures in each family. In Oman, this was directed at only one personality and so there are Port Sultan Qaboos, Madinat Sultan Qaboos, Sultan Qaboos Highway, and other examples with his name.

While Arabic usage pertaining to the ruler retained the adjective "*sultani*," increasingly emphasis was placed on "royal" in English, such as Royal Hospital, Royal Opera House, Royal Guard, Royal Air Force of Oman, and Royal Office. Royal rituals soon became entrenched. The National Day celebrations (Sultan Qaboos' birthday was selected as National Day) included the Sultan's tea party, following the same lines of Queen Elizabeth II's tea party on her birthday. The crossed swords with a *khanjar* (dagger), the traditional "emblem" of the Sultanate, were surmounted by an elaborate crown when used to indicate royal connections. The religious credentials of Sultan Qaboos as national leader were bolstered by the construction of modern Qaboos mosques in towns throughout the country and the erection of the Sultan Qaboos Grand Mosque in the capital.[11]

At the same time as these concepts laid the ground for Omaniness in national identity, simultaneous perceptions were being inculcated of the unique identity of citizens of the Sultanate of Oman. As more Omanis traveled out of the country, their passports, national dress, and accents reinforced their sense of togetherness in the Sultanate. Internal travel and migration for work and education assisted in bringing a new layer of primary identity overlaying tribal and regional identification. As the government provided more services and intruded into people's lives, the sense of common identity deepened.

From another viewpoint, a major push for tourism seems intended, in addition to economic benefits including diversification and employment, to call the Gulf and the world's attention to Oman's attractions. These actions not only boost Oman's competitiveness with the other Gulf States but they also help to redress a lingering resentment by Omanis from the 1970s of how they perceived that other Gulf nationals viewed them.[12] This bonding in national pride is a nation-building exercise too.

The projection of the Sultan as the sole father figure of the country was coupled with his absolute supervision of the apparatus of state, and thus his personal role (either directive or adjucative) in the political and socio-economic development of the country. A regular occasion to connect on a personal level with his people was the meet-the-people tour, an annual occurrence for a few weeks in a selected region of the country—the exercise was abandoned only in the last few years of Qaboos' reign due to the Sultan's health. Even during the 2011 economic protests, the demonstrators empha-sized their loyalty to the Sultan. How much this constituted allegiance to the Sultan as a specific figure and how much to the symbol of the "new" Omani nation-state is an important question.

The New State of Oman

The emergence of Oman's primary national identity after 1970 could not have occurred without the structure of a modernizing state upon which to build it. The previous Omani state, that is, the Sultanate before 1970, pos-sessed the necessary criteria of statehood such as territoriality, formal sover-eignty, an administration even if primitive, and some measure of control—in Weberian terms, "an effective monopoly of legitimate force over a given ter-ritory."[13] But the post-1970 state added depth and new elements of services and legitimacy. The modernizing state involves "the process by which the state not only grows in economic productivity and government coercion, but also in political and institutional power. It is thus closely linked to the process of the bureaucratization and the centralization of the state."[14]

Furthermore, as the theorist S. N. Eisenstadt has written, "The emergence of the first modern states in Europe entailed administrative centralization and relatively clearly defined territorial boundaries. The political community was conceived as autonomous, no longer subsumed under a broader 'religious' canopy. [T]he state was now defined in secular terms . . ."[15] Independence and sovereignty were key components in the development of the nation-state. "The transformation of the basic premises of the social and political order became interwoven with a parallel transformation and institutionalization of the conceptions of sovereignty, of citizenship, of representative institutions, and of accountability of rulers."[16]

It was a long haul from a minimalist to a modernizing state. Oman's independence has been recognized for more than a thousand years, despite having been challenged at times and then falling within the orbit of British India's informal empire. The Ibadi Imams in the mountains could call upon the support of the tribes when external threats appeared. While the Al-Bu Said Sultans in Muscat found it difficult to maintain authority over many parts of the country, they did treat with foreign powers as diplomatic equals and sometimes extended their dominions to overseas territories.

From the beginning of the nineteenth century, Muscat was recognized as their capital apart from a few brief periods. The last armed incursion into Muscat from the interior took place in 1895. Since then, it has been a secure and sovereign base for five sultans. Repeatedly challenged as the voice of the Omani nation, their limitations were epitomized by the inability to fashion a state capable of governing all of Oman. Said bin Taimur was able to assert authority over interior Oman in the 1950s and 1960s but his control over Dhofar steadily decreased. In large part, this was a consequence of his extremely personalized style of ruling and the near absence of any form of viable government.

As there can be no state without a government, the type of government utilized by the state helps to define the viability and effectiveness of the state. In recent history, Oman has produced three types of government: traditional (the Ibadi Imamate and the Al-Bu Said dynasty); neotraditional (the reign of Said bin Taimur); and post-traditional (Qaboos bin Said and Haitham bin Tariq).[17] The minimalist Ibadi Imamate consisted of little more than the figure of the Imam and a small circle of religious advisors. The Imam was generally, except when dynasties appeared, selected and bolstered by the powerful tribal chieftains of the day.

Administration was largely limited to the appointment of *wali*s (personal representatives of the leader in significant settlements) and *qadi*s (Islamic judges), and enforcement depended on the appearance of tribal forces when called upon. The structure of the Al-Bu Said state of the Sultanate was not much more complex, even after the restoration of Sultanate authority over the interior in the 1950s–1960s. There was still no hint of an effective central state or anything beyond bare-bones institutionalization, that is, utilization of long-adopted institutions such as the *wali*s and *qadi*s, the collection of *zakat* (alms-giving), and the employment of a rudimentary guard.

The Al-Bu Said state operated on similar terms to the Imamate as described above, not particularly surprising since the first of the line was an elected Imam and several of his successors claimed the office. The secularization of leadership involved a move from a religious-based Imamate to a kingly dynasty, encouraged at least in part by the diversion of much Al-Bu Said attention abroad. Still, the dynasty's hold over Oman continued to be exercised essentially as it had been under the Imams.

This remained true until the accession of Said bin Taimur as Sultan. In 1929, the British Government of India imposed a four-man council of ministers on the Sultanate with a British financial advisor (the second of whom was the explorer Bertram Thomas) essentially in charge of the state. Upon becoming Sultan in 1932, Said's goal was to restore the "traditional" nature of his rule. This meant both eliminating British interference in the state and restoring Al-Bu Said control over the interior. The first required the eradication of debts owed to the British, which Said managed to do by the end of the Second World War through the application of British war subsidies to outstanding debts and the simple expedient of extreme parsimony in state spending. The second objective had to await the disappearance from the scene of respected Imam Muhammad bin 'Abdullah al-Khalili. The Imam died in 1954 and was succeeded by a weaker Imam dominated by his brother and a strong tribal sheikh.

But regaining actual control over the interior required extraordinary measures. Principal among them was the formation of permanent armed forces, an arrangement alien to Oman. Immediately prior to this development, Sultan Said had permitted an oil exploration team to move into the interior of Oman, accompanied by a protective force for which the company had paid. While Britain set up the Sultan's Armed Forces in 1958, and subsidized and provided the officers for it, it also forced a development subsidy and department on the Sultan. Sultan Said also introduced a new currency to replace the confusing use of the Indian rupee and the Maria Theresa dollar, among others. This was the *riyal sa'idi*, which later was renamed the Omani *riyal*.

By his acceptance and use of these innovations, Sultan Said was no longer a "traditional" ruler. His aim was to preserve the existing traditional society, values, and goals by enhancing or enlarging the capability to control the state and counteract the effect of change. In so doing, however, he altered the nature of the decentralized political system, transforming the basis of authority from traditional to neotraditional.

The emergence of a new Omani nationalism, that is, the creation of a primary national identity, was dependent on the introduction of a new type of state. The state-building that followed the 1970 coup embodied a modernizing emphasis with socioeconomic development and institutionalization of a government as its goals. While the changeover in 1970 was momentous and far-reaching, the result was not a modern state but instead a post-traditional one.

Unlike his father, Sultan Qaboos sought to use his position to change the state and embraced a strategy of modernization. Gradually, Oman became a state like most others around the world. The state's authority was supreme, its leadership was accepted and legitimated internally while external recognition was provided by various bilateral diplomatic ties as well as membership in the United Nations and other global bodies. The country's inhabitants became citizens of a singular entity, the state took charge of distributing oil income, and it adopted the responsibility of providing measures of social welfare for its people. At the same time, oil income and its impact on the economy, politics, and society became and remained the most important factor in determining the path of the sultanate in the half-century after 1970.

The Early 1970s as a Transitional but Formative Period

The accession of Sultan Qaboos bin Said marked the start of the post-traditional period in Omani politics. The new Sultan communicated his vision to his nation in his first radio broadcast on August 9, 1970. He ended the broadcast by reminding listeners of the words he had spoken on his arrival in Muscat: "'the government and the people are one body and if one part fails so will fail the whole body.' Therefore, my brothers, I call upon you to work with us for the future of our country and with God's help we will succeed."[18]

The dramatic changes set in motion by the events of July 1970 had an enormous and wide-ranging impact on the organization of the state and the structure of Oman's government. Most importantly, the political and economic structure of the past was incapable of dealing with new demands and new requirements. The top of Oman's institutional system technically remained the same with a strong Sultan exercising unchallenged power, but the emphasis and vision was transformed almost entirely. A completely new government was necessary, along with a radically different economic system. In large part, the change encompassed an abrupt transformation from a minimalist, that is, decidedly personal, government to a process of institutionalization.

There were two essential aspects to the establishment of the new state: the contrast in personalities between the old and new rulers and the adaptation of old institutions and the creation of new ones. From the very beginning, Sultan Qaboos' role was distinct from that of his father, even though both exercised full authority over the state. Sultan Said sought to be the sole arbiter of matters great and small throughout the state. Orders regarding the affairs of Muscat, the capital, were passed to his cousin, Sayyid Shihab bin Faysal, and he used a more distant relative, Sayyid Ahmad bin Ibrahim, to deal with interior and tribal affairs. F. C. L. Chauncy, his "personal advisor," served (along with the British military secretary) as the liaison with Westerners, such as the commander of the armed forces, the general manager of Petroleum Development Oman (PDO), and the director of the small development department. The handful of Omani and British subordinates of Sultan Said who handled the few government functions extant (such as relations with the tribes, governance of the capital, the minuscule development department, and supervision of Muscat port and customs) quickly retired.

For Sultan Qaboos, the changeover of government in Muscat in 1970 went smoothly. The new Sultan spent the first few weeks carrying out a series of tours around the country to introduce himself to his people, traveling by Skyvan to Nizwa, Suhar, and Bahla and Jabrin. He also toured Muscat and Matrah and made a visit to PDO at Mina' al-Fahl as well as the Sultan's Armed Forces (SAF) headquarters and other units. Further visits by road were made to Izki, Manah, al-Rustaq, al-Sib, al-Suwayq, Barka, and Nizwa.

He also received some of the sheikhs of the Trucial Coast (soon to become the United Arab Emirates), including Abu Dhabi, Dubai, and Sharjah, and other Gulf dignitaries from Kuwait and Qatar. The British special representative in the Gulf and the American consul-general in Dhahran (also accredited to Muscat) stopped in Muscat as well. These visits and meetings served to introduce the Sultan to his people and vice versa, as well as to mark the beginnings of international recognition of the new leader. The visits by the Trucial rulers may have been the last vestigial recognition of the ancient suzerainty of Oman's ruler over all Oman. Sultan Qaboos called for Omanis abroad to return and released prisoners from the fearsome Fort al-Jalali prison before returning to Salalah two weeks after entering Muscat.

A small interim council had been formed immediately after the coup to deal with immediately pressing matters. But the Sultan soon put together a coterie of Omani and expatriate officials and advisors to set forth new state policies and to initiate the ambitious program of socioeconomic development. One of his first actions was to name his uncle, Sayyid Tariq bin Taimur, who had been in exile, as prime minister. Tariq quickly formed a small council of ministers comprised of four members holding the reins for health, education, justice, and the interior. These positions reflected the initial priorities of the fledgling state: two newly prioritized concerns of health and education and two areas of longstanding responsibilities in justice and the interior. The latter two appointees were from the Al-Bu Said family, while the minister for health was a Pakistani-educated Omani medical doctor and education was placed in the charge of a member of the sheikhly family of a prominent tribe of the interior.

The state gradually added government institutions that began simultaneously to carry out the necessary functions of governing and providing services as well as taking the first steps in development. The nucleus of a small bureaucracy was created, relying on Omanis who had gained experience abroad and expatriates from various countries. In short order, government ministries were established mainly to provide a framework for the provision of social services. A health network was established within weeks after the coup and an agency was formed to recruit Omanis for government service.

Other service ministries appeared soon after. These included information, posts, and lands, in addition to education; their ranks were added to existing justice and interior organs. Departments for roads, public works, and labor were established. The duties of the Muscat municipality were expanded. The small existing police force was professionalized and additional security services, such as a royal guard and an intelligence service, appeared.

The *Diwan*, comprising both the Sultan's office and his household, continued uninterrupted from the traditional system into the new one. It contained three important positions: the head of the *Diwan* (who handled ruling family and tribal affairs); the Sultan's equerry (who dealt with political matters); and the aide-de-camp (who organized the royal household and royal establishments). In 1973, the *Diwan* was upgraded to a ministry. It was also during this time that the Royal Guard, the Royal Flight, and the Royal Yacht Squadron emerged as divisions within the *Diwan*. It was not until 1974 that the *Diwan* split according to its two basic functions: the original *Diwan* took care of the royal household, while the *Diwan* for Royal Protocol was formed to handle government matters. A few years later, the Palace Office (later restyled as the Royal Office) was created as a separate organization to deal with political and security concerns.

Two existing institutions provided a basis to build upon at the time of the coup. SAF was a professional light infantry with air and sea wings dating from the late 1950s. Until the late 1960s, all of its officers were British and a high proportion of its ranks were Baluch, either from Oman or from the formerly Omani enclave of Gwadar in Pakistan (returned to Pakistan in 1958). SAF's principal function was of course combat and it had fighting experience during the Al-Jabal Al-Akhdar War of the 1950s and 1960s. From about 1966 until the mid-1970s, it was engaged in a more serious war in Dhofar and underwent considerable expansion.

But SAF also played other roles that supported state formation. Tribesmen from across the Sultanate were recruited and mixed together, broadening horizons of identity. It also provided education and training for its soldiers, skills that were put to good use after 1970. SAF was not only the face of order in northern Oman from the 1960s, but also served as a major means of liaison between people and the government. It was a major source of income via wages for Omani families during a period of poverty. It carried out civil functions such as medical care and transport, and built and maintained roads. Gradually, Omanis replaced British officers and the proportion of Arabs to Baluch steadily increased.[19]

PDO was the other principal pre-1970 institution. At the time of the coup, it was wholly owned by foreign companies, predominantly Royal Dutch Shell, although the government later nationalized 60 percent of the company. From the beginning of exploration, the company provided employment for Omanis although before 1970 this was largely in unskilled jobs.

The company did send small numbers of Omanis to Dubai and the United Kingdom for training as early as the mid-1960s. Like SAF, PDO provided needed income, education, and socialization.[20]

Finding qualified Omanis to fill the growing number of positions was initially difficult due to the state of the education system. Fortunately, a small cadre of Omanis had been educated abroad in defiance of the old Sultan's strictures. Obtaining education in the West was problematic partly because of the lack of money to pay for it, but principally because Western governments did not wish to anger Sultan Said. The oil states of Kuwait and Qatar, as well as Abu Dhabi a little later, provided primary and secondary education to Omanis, as well as places for a few at Kuwait University. Others received education in countries opposed to the Sultanate, as when Saudi Arabia provided for the children of the Oman Revolutionary Movement members (the Imamate group in exile). The Soviet Union and other Communist countries gave scholarships and several of the first ministers in the new state were Russian-educated. Dhufari revolutionaries received basic education at Popular Front schools in South Yemen and university or medical education in the Communist bloc, particularly Cuba.

A few Omanis had held administrative positions in Bahrain, Qatar, and Abu Dhabi, and returned to senior positions. At the same time, the contribution of "Zanzibaris," a broad term encompassing Omanis who had been born in or lived in a variety of East African countries, was welcomed. A majority of these came from Zanzibar itself, landing in Oman either after Zanzibar's anti-Arab revolution in 1964 or after the 1970 Oman coup. Although the native language of most was Swahili, many also spoke English and had received higher education, especially at Makerere University in Uganda.

By 1976, the number of ministries had increased to seventeen: *Diwan* affairs; interior; land and municipalities; *awqaf* (endowments) and Islamic affairs; social affairs and labor; justice; commerce and industry; communications; health; education; information and culture; agriculture, fisheries, petroleum and minerals; public works; foreign affairs; national heritage; youth affairs; and defense.[21] Government employment increased proportionately. The foundations had been laid.

Meanwhile, oil had begun to fuel the economy before 1970, but oil income had barely begun reaching government coffers before the coup. It

was Sultan Said's bad luck that the funds available for even modest development came too late to save him. Nevertheless, he had begun a program of
small projects, including a few schools, eight hospitals, town planning for
Muscat and Matrah along with some small government buildings, electricity
generation and a piped water supply for the capital, work on new roads to
Suhar and Nizwa, and, most notably, a new deepwater port in Matrah that
was completed after his overthrow and ironically named Mina Qaboos (Port
Qaboos).[22]

These ad hoc projects were continued and greatly expanded upon by the
new government. Inescapably, the process of infrastructural and socioeconomic development required planning and implementation, along with a
method for income distribution. Not surprisingly, sophisticated planning
was something for the future. Low absorptive capacity dovetailed with
rudimentary planning. To build schools and health clinics, it was first necessary to engage architects and suitable construction firms. Then it was
necessary to import cement, steel, equipment, and other items. Oman's
single port could not keep up with offloading ships. Once landed, goods
needed to be transported into the interior and remote locations, but this
depended on the construction of viable roads. Once constructed, schools
and clinics needed teachers, doctors, and nurses, nearly all of whom had to
be recruited from abroad and funds found to pay them. There was little in
the way of a master plan to determine which project or which sector was
first in line.

It was not until the massive oil price rise of 1974 that the government
finally had enough income to pursue a planned development agenda more
effectively. Government revenues jumped from OMR 68.6 million in 1973
to OMR 303.2 million in 1974. While the increased income was definitely
welcome, low absorptive capacity meant that 1974 saw a budget surplus of
OMR 116.6 million.[23] Surpluses were recorded for more than a decade for
this reason. The 1970s and the first half of the 1980s constituted the pivotal
decades during which the economic emphasis evolved from haphazard reactions to relatively more sophisticated methodology to sustained planning.
Oman soon became regarded as an example of a rentier state, similar to the
other Gulf States, with its economy and government overly dependent on oil
income. At the same time, however, it seemed to escape the "resource curse,"

which posited that economic distortions inhibited liberalization, increased repression, and discouraged populations from modernizing.[24]

Still, noteworthy accomplishments were recorded during those first years.[25] The figures increased enormously in the following years as government ministries became better staffed and operational, and oil provided greater income.

Another aspect of this period was reconnection with the outside world, ending a long slide into isolation. From the end of the nineteenth century, Oman's foreign relations had deteriorated markedly. Apart from Britain, with whom relations had always been close, the only diplomat resident in Oman pre-1970 was that of India. Relations with the United States (which had commenced in 1833) remained semi-active, while ties to France had lapsed. Oman had been nearly completely cut off from the Arab world and even the Gulf. Sultan Qaboos' 1971 visit to Riyadh marked the establishment of the first official ties between the two countries. The Sultan's attendance at the Shah's 1971 Persepolis celebrations formed the basis for Iran's assistance to the Sultanate in the Dhufar War.

Even more importantly for Oman's position in the global community was its membership of international organizations. Admission to the United Nations and the Arab League had faced some opposition by "progressive" Arab republics, led by Marxist South Yemen, but did not succeeded in blocking the Sultanate. Oman was soon a member of WHO, UNESCO, IPU, and other organizations.

Starting with the early steps taken at the beginning of the 1970s, the specific role and authority of the post-traditional Sultan gradually assumed tangible form. With the resignation of his uncle Tariq as prime minister in 1971, Sultan Qaboos took over that role, adding it to his formal positions of minister of defense, economy, and foreign affairs. He was clearly respected for his seminal role in developing the state and nation of Oman, as well as establishing the Sultanate's reputation as an impartial mediator in regional disputes. In terms of institutionalization, the experience of the early 1970s was a period of trial and error, marked by uncertain steps regarding the establishment and evolution of government machinery.[26] The initial groundwork was laid for the formation of civil society. At the same time, Omani national identity deepened. By the end of the decade or so, a workable pattern had been established that persists until today.

Notes

1. An earlier version of some of these remarks appeared in J. E. Peterson, "Oman: A State Elaborating a Nation," ISPI Commentary, May 16, 2019.

2. For further discussion, see Hans Kohn, *The Idea of Nationalism: A Study in Its Origins and Background* (New York: Macmillan, 1944); Hans Kohn, *The Age of Nationalism: The First Era of Global History* (New York: Harper & Row, 1962); Anthony D. Smith, *Theories of Nationalism* (London: Duckworth, 1971); Ernest Gellner, *Nations and Nationalism* (Oxford: Oxford University Press, 1983).

3. Renan's translated text is reprinted in Alan Dowty (ed.), *The Israel/Palestine Reader* (Cambridge: Polity, 2019), 3–8.

4. Benedict Anderson, *Imagined Communities: Reflections on the Origin and Spread of Nationalism*, rev. edn. (London: Verso, 1991), 3, 5–6.

5. Eric Hobsbawm, "Introduction: Inventing Traditions," in Eric Hobsbawm and Terence Ranger (eds.), *The Invention of Tradition* (Cambridge: Cambridge University Press, 1983), 14.

6. J. C. Wilkinson, *Water and Tribal Settlement in South-East Arabia: A Study of the Aflaj of Oman* (Oxford: Clarendon Press, 1977), 4.

7. Gellner, *Nations and Nationalism*, 54.

8. Smaller variant communities are not excluded but are enfolded into the ethos by extension. Other ethnic groups are incorporated into the matrix of tribal classification, while religious differences are subsumed by policy and tolerance, as shown by the designation of the Ministry of Religious Affairs, not Islamic Affairs. Oman traditionally looked to the Indian Ocean more than it did to the Arab world, and its role as a melting pot is enshrined in its polyglot society with its overseas connections. Undoubtedly, this orientation strongly shapes Oman's relationship to the Arab world today and its interactions with fellow GCC members.

9. "Promotion of the Omani nation has been the occasion to develop what we call identity engineering, in which history, heritage (*turath*) and symbolic references have helped to anchor the awareness of a new political community and to serve the central authority's legitimisation." Marc Valeri, *Oman: Politics and Society in the Qaboos State*, rev. edn. (London: Hurst, [2009] 2017), 109–110.

10. Lisa Anderson, "Absolutism and the Resilience of Monarchy in the Middle East," *Political Science Quarterly* 106(1) (1991): 4.

11. Dawn Chatty covers these developments in detail in her "Rituals of Royalty and the Elaboration of Ceremony in Oman: View from the Edge," *International Journal of Middle East Studies* 41 (2009): 39–58. She concludes that "The sultan

remains the national figure of unity, elaborated out of the wealth of invented ceremonials and created traditions" (p. 54). This process was not unique to Oman of course and was paralleled elsewhere in the Gulf where nation-building was a necessary exercise. For example, Jill Crystal dissects the creation of a national identity in Qatar through the presentation of national symbols, the acquisition of international recognition, and the "invention" of a founding myth. Jill Crystal, *Oil and Politics in the Gulf: Rulers and Merchants in Kuwait and Qatar* (Cambridge: Cambridge University Press, 1990), 162.

12. Author's observations and interviews during the 1970s and beyond. The construction of the impressive al-Bustan Palace Hotel in 1985 to hold Oman's hosting of the GCC summit for the first time and the elaborate expensive preparations for National Day just afterwards were widely seen as Oman's determination to show the outside world how much it had developed since 1970.

13. Guenther Roth, "Personal Rulership, Patrimonialism, and Empire-Building in the New States," *World Politics* 20(2) (1968): 204.

14. Rolf Schwarz, "The Political Economy of State-Formation in the Arab Middle East: Rentier States, Economic Reform, and Democratization," *Review of International Political Economy* 15(4) (2008): 599n1. Or as Joel Migdal has put it, "the image of the state is of a dominant, integrated, autonomous entity that controls, in a given territory, all rule making, either directly through its own agencies or indirectly by sanctioning other authorized organizations—businesses, families, clubs, and the like—to make certain circumscribed rules." In addition to the image, Migdal posits that the state also embraces practices: "The routine performance of state actors and agencies, their practices, may reinforce the image of the state or weaken it; they may bolster the notion of the territorial and public–private boundaries or neutralize them." Joel Migdal, *State in Society: Studying How States and Societies Transform and Constitute One Another* (New York: Cambridge University Press, 2001), 17–18.

15. S. N. Eisenstadt, *Paradoxes of Democracy: Fragility, Continuity, and Change* (Washington, DC and Baltimore, MD: Woodrow Wilson Center Press and Johns Hopkins University Press, 1999), 14–15. But Eisenstadt goes on to contend that "The development in Europe of modern states and collectivities and the transformation of the notion of sovereignty were closely related to changes in the power structure of society, namely, the emergence of multiple centers of economic and political power and the development of some nuclei of distinctive new types of civil society and of public arenas or spheres. The development of multiplicity of centers of power and of the nuclei of civil society was

closely related to the development of a new type of political economy and of new modes of production, namely the market economy, first of commercial and later of industrial capitalism" (p. 16). This also characterizes Oman's stage as one of post-traditionalism.

16. Eisenstadt, *Paradoxes of Democracy*, 24.

17. S. N. Eisenstadt introduced the concept of a scale with "traditional" society at one end and "post-traditional" at the other. See his *Tradition, Change, and Modernity* (New York: Wiley, 1973). I have modified the idea by introducing a "neotraditional" stage, and first presented it in J. E. Peterson, "Legitimacy and Political Change in Yemen and Oman," *Orbis* 27(4) (1984): 971–998.

18. News release by the Government Information Office, August 9, 1970.

19. There is a surprisingly robust literature, including numerous memoirs, on the Al-Jabal Al-Akhdar and Dhofar wars, as well as a number of first-person accounts of activities in SAF by British officers. For a comprehensive history of SAF and the two wars, see J. E. Peterson, *Oman's Insurgencies: The Sultanate's Struggle for Supremacy* (London: Saqi, 2007).

20. For a company-sponsored history, see Terence Clark, *Underground to Overseas: The Story of Petroleum Development Oman* (London: Stacey International, 2007).

21. Sultanate of Oman, Development Council, *First Five-Year Development Plan, 1976–1981*, 8.

22. For a fuller description of the Sultan's development program, see Barbara Wace, "Master Plan for Muscat and Oman," *Geographical Magazine* 41(12) (1969): 892–905. In an announcement of his plans, Sultan Said made the only public pronouncement of his reign in "The Word of Sultan Said b. Taimur, Sultan of Muscat and Oman, about the history of the financial position of the Sultanate in the past and the hopes for the future, after the export of oil" (January 1968), the English version reprinted in John Townsend, *Oman: The Making of a Modern State* (London: Croom Helm, 1977), 192–198.

23. Sultanate of Oman, Development Council, Directorate General of National Statistics, *Statistical Yearbook 1984* (Muscat, November 1985).

24. See Hazem Beblawi and Giacomo Luciani (eds.), *The Rentier State* (London: Croom Helm, 1987); Terry Lynn Karl, *The Paradox of Plenty: Oil Booms and Petro-States* (Berkeley: University of California Press, 1997); Michael L. Ross, *The Oil Curse: How Petroleum Wealth Shapes the Development of Nations* (Princeton, NJ: Princeton University Press, 2012); and the critique of these theories in Matthew Gray, *A Theory of "Late Rentierism" in the Arab States of the Gulf* (Doha:

Georgetown University, Center for International and Regional Studies, 2011), Occasional Paper, No. 7.

25. Measures of the infrastructural accomplishments during the 1970–1973 period can be found in Sultanate of Oman, Ministry of Development, National Statistical Department, *Development in Oman 1970–1974* (Muscat, n.d.), 66–76, and are reproduced elsewhere in this volume.

26. The term "institutionalization" has various specific meanings in social science literature. My use of the term here refers to the transfer of responsibility from the personal rule and control by the Sultan to state agencies and senior officials. A related meaning refers to the development of civil society.

11

LITERATURE IN OMAN DURING THE REIGN OF SULTAN QABOOS

Barbara Michalak-Pikulska

Written cultural and literary life flourished in Oman from 1970 to 2020. While modern Omani writing is grounded in traditions of story-telling and poetry that pre-date this period, increased education, the official promotion of culture and the rise of new technologies and infrastructure has allowed Omanis to express themselves to a much wider public both within Oman and outside its borders. Omani writers grew in fame throughout the Arabic world, and the rest of the world in translation. In 2019, an Omani writer received the internationally esteemed Man Booker Prize. This growing, international acknowledgment of Oman's literary scene was achieved over fifty years of literary development in modern Oman.

Sultan Qaboos' early promotion of education and educational institutions is one major reason for the success of Omani writers and poets. When Sultan Qaboos took power in 1970, apart from the three schools in Muscat and Salalah, there were no cultural and educational institutions. The young, highly educated ruler set the development of education at all levels as his most important priority, which culminated in the opening in 1986 of the University of Sultan Qaboos in Muscat. The founding of the university played a role in the Omani national revival. Earlier, in 1975, Sultan Qaboos founded the Ministry of National Heritage and Culture. The goal was to preserve the rich Omani national heritage and, crucially for the literary scene, to support publications.[1] Cultural and literary clubs arose, for example, *Al-Muntada al-Adabi* (The Literary Club, 1985),[2] *An-Nadi ath-Thaqafi* (The Cultural Club, 1986), *An-Nadi al-'Ilmi* (The Academic Club, 1989), and in 2006 *Al-Jama'iyya al-'umaniyya li-l-kuttab* (Omani Society of Writers and Literati), which is vigorously led by the Omani poet Said as-Saqlawi. These institutions aim to organize cultural and academic events and to cooperate with similar centers in the country and abroad. Since then much attention has been paid to the educational, cultural, and sporting development of Omani youth. For this purpose, the General Organization for Youth Sport and Cultural Activities was established, which supervised events such as poetry competitions, Qur'an recitations, academic conferences, and sporting events. Public libraries, for example, *Maktaba Jami'at As-Sultan Qaboos* (Sultan Qaboos University Library), *Maktaba al-Islamiyya* (The Muslim Library), *Maktaba al-Fanniyya* (The Technical Library), and others were also established. Over the years, the Muscat International Book Fair has attracted a huge number of Omani and Arab publishers.[3]

The founding of the Omani Women's Association (*Jama'iyya al-Mar'a al-'Umaniyya*) by Zamzam Hasan Yusuf Makki in 1970 was an important moment in Omani revival.[4] The association supported the development of education and the fight against illiteracy among women and took care of their participation in cultural and social life. It started publishing the first women's magazine in Oman titled *'Umaniyya* (*Omani Woman*).

The return of many educated Omanis from places such as Kuwait, Zanzibar and India in the 1970s contributed to the development of the country. Omani poet Dr Sa'ida bint Khatir referred to this in her writings:

> We Omanis lived for a long time abroad. We started to return home only when Sultan Qaboos ascended to power. Earlier the difficult conditions of life, together with the absence of educational possibilities, forced our family to leave for Kuwait. When Sultan Qaboos open the borders we returned. The first works I started to write were panegyrics devoted to the beloved homeland. We have all helped to build it. I became the editor-in-chief of the woman's journal *'Umaniyya* (*Omani Woman*) and the chairwoman of the cultural commission in Literary Club (*An-Nadi ath-Thaqafi*).[5]

The press played a tremendous role in the dynamic development of the country. New journalists accelerated the information process by writing about domestic and foreign issues, and at the same time promoted literature and the first Omani authors. The press contributed to the formation of a language capable of articulating new topics related to the dynamic development of the country, dissemination of the concept of freedom, and respect for individual, social, cultural, political, and literary issues. The latter were often edited by poets and writers themselves. The following daily newspapers were founded: *al-Watan* (1971), *'Uman* (1972), *ash-Shabiba* (1983). There were also cultural magazines: *As-Siraj* (1975–1976; 1992–1996), *Al-Ghadir* (1977–1984). The cultural press also created recipients—readers, patriots, and aware citizens of Oman. It was aimed at promoting Oman and performing a cultural mission in the Arab world, as, for example, *Nizwa*, a quarterly magazine that has been published since 1994 and is one of the best-known Omani cultural magazines in the Arab world. Articles on literary and cultural topics have been published there. It promotes the work of talented Omanis. The *Nizwa* magazine builds bridges between the Arab and Western world both at the level of literature and broadly understood culture by presenting events and also brush and stage artists. Since its inception, the Omani press has contributed to the development of Omani heritage and the promotion of cultural and literary publications. Its founder and editor-in-chief is the well-known Omani poet Sayf ar-Rahbi.

Beginnings of Modern Omani Poetry

During a *Nahda* (Renaissance) in contemporary Omani literature beginning in the 1970s, writers returned to the country and played a significant and lasting role in the cultural development of Oman. Omani poets were innovators, introducing new literary genres, especially forms of contemporary poetry—*qasidat an-nathr* (prose poems) and topics related to current sociocultural issues.

'Abd Allah bin Muhammad at-Ta'i (1924–1973) was an icon of Omani *Nahda* (revival, renaissance) in Omani literature. He had a significant impact on later Omani writers and reformers who, like him, actively worked for education and culture in Oman, and the end of his life corresponds with the first, formative years of Sultan Qaboos' reign. He devoted his entire life to building bridges between people, various cultures and literatures, and was involved in politics and diplomacy.

'Abd Allah at-Ta'i wrote many poems, which were collected in three volumes: *Al-fajr az-zahif* (*Creeping Dawn*); *Wida'an ayyuha al-layl at-tawil* (*Goodbye Long Night*); and *Hadi al-qafila* (*The Caravan Guide*).[6] The poems reflect his longing for his homeland while traveling around the Gulf countries and his involvement in the sociopolitical issues of the Arab world, for example, in Palestine or Iraq. In his poetic work, there are features of the renewal of a poem in relation to content and form. The poems are distinguished by thematic diversity, especially those regarding Oman and Sultan Qaboos.

In the ode *'Uman tukhatib wafdaha* (*Oman Addresses the Envoys*) 'Abd Allah bin Muhammad at-Ta'i describes the rule of the new sultan for whom Arab unity is important. At-Ta'i, who spent many years in many Arab countries, praised the young Qaboos for joining tribes and states and building a modern country:

> Qaboos wants to unite all brothers
> Since he took power, there has been a new period in which our hopes could be realized
>
> . . .
>
> Oman rose high because He planned how to build it . . .[7]

'Abd Allah at-Ta'i died on July 18, 1973 in Abu Dhabi at the peak of his creative abilities. However, his works were an inspiration for the exchange of thoughts, dialogue, understanding, and acceptance of other cultures that he met during many journeys to India, Pakistan, and Gulf countries. In this respect, he followed the Omani tradition of maritime travel and openness to many cultures, even as he remained rooted in his Omani origins. At-Ta'i represented a connection to a previous generation of writers. After Sultan Qaboos came to power in 1970, more names appeared on the literary scene, such as Abu Surur Hamid bin 'Abd Allah bin Hamid al-Jami'i from Sama'il and Mahmud al-Khusaybi.

Abu Surur Hamid al-Jami'i (1942–2014) was a prolific writer. He authored several volumes of poems collected in a selection titled *Diwan Abi Surur* (*Selection of Poems by Abu Surur*), dealing with national-patriotic issues (*wataniyyat*); Arabic matters (*qawmiyyat*); and devoted to social brotherhood (*ikhwaniyyat*), social affairs (*ijtima'iyyat*), as well as love (*ghazaliyyat*). From 1973, he worked as a judge in the Ministry of Justice, hence the book on Muslim law *Bughat at-tullab* (*Purpose of Students*) or grammar titled *Ibhaj assudur: Sharh nahwiyya Abi Surur* (*The Joys of Writing: Explaining Abu Surur's Grammar*).

Abu Surur Hamid al-Jami'i was proud of the place where he was born and lived: Sama'il, a town that was an important link on the road between the port of Muscat and the religious capital Nizwa. In the poem *Rawdat al-Albab* (*Garden of Minds*), which was dedicated to his hometown, we find traces of its glory and affirmation of how important it is as a place of culture and history on the map of Oman. The title word *al-Albab* can mean everything that is inside, for example, the heart or mind because Sama'il is inside him and is an inseparable part of the poet. He describes his hometown in this way:

> This is Sama'il, full of traces of her glory
> You made Oman proud and you are the axis around which everything revolves[8]

Abu Surur has devoted a lot of classical poems to the homeland, its history and glory. In the poems *'Uman al-madi wa at-tarikh* (*Old-Time Oman*) or *Majd 'Uman* (*The Glory of Oman*) you can admire Oman over the centuries of various historical events. He is proud of his country and being an Omani. He is not worried about the future of the country, because he believes that it will develop perfectly thanks to young Omani people. In his introduction to *Diwan Abi Surur* (*Selection of Poems by Abu Surur*), Yahya al-Lizami wrote, "Abu Surur is a national and all-Arab poet, and in his poetry tradition is intertwined with innovation."[9]

Mahmud al-Khusaybi (1927–1998) also came from Sama'il. He went to Kuwait, where he worked in various positions in education. Then he returned to Oman after Sultan Qaboos came to power and worked for the Ministry of Information. He wrote mainly panegyrics for his beloved Oman, and in honor of Sultan Qaboos. Al-Khusaybi created in his poems a portrait of an ideal, strong, just, brave, respectful, and loving ruler. At the same time, he is a determined politician and brave soldier, the personification of Oman's majesty, which leads to the well-being and happiness of the Omani people.

Mahmud al-Khusaybi considers himself a representative of the Omani paying tribute to Sultan Qaboos in the poem *Qulu li-sultan al-bilad* (*Tell the Sultan of the Country*):

Tell Him: we are with You	We give our souls to You
Go to the horizon	And all will hasten after You[10]

The poets mentioned here praised Sultan Qaboos for his bravery, nobility, generosity, justice, and munificence, and also for watching over the security of Oman. They consider the period of his rule as a golden age in the history of the country, for which all Omanis were grateful. They set him up as a role model for the Middle East region.

Omani Poetry at the Turn of the Century

The 1990s saw the full blooming of the Omani modernization project, both economic and sociocultural. A whole host of new names appeared in that decade in the literary arena, among them the following deserve attention: Sa'id as-Saqlawi, Sa'ida bint Khatir al-Farisi, and Sayf ar-Rahbi. Their poems are written mainly in the free verse form (*taf'ila*) and in prose poem (*qasidat an-nathr*), and sometimes classical form (*'amudi*).

Sayf ar-Rahbi (b. 1956) is a citizen of the world after numerous and many years of travel in Damascus, Algiers, Beirut, London, and Paris. In the 1990s, he returned to Oman to play a significant role in literary life. He is the editor-in-chief of one of the most important cultural and literary magazines in the Arab world, *Nizwa*. At the same time, he took the lead in publishing books on world literature, culture, and philosophy, such as *Dhakirat ash-shatat* (*Distraction Memory*), in 1991, or *Hiwar al-amkina wa al-wujuh* (*Dialogue of Places and Faces*), in 1999.

Sayf ar-Rahbi leads a generation of Omani poets. He published many volumes of poetry, for example, *Ajras al-qati'a* (*Parting Bells*, 1984), *Ra's al-musafir* (*Head of a Traveler*, 1986), *Rajul min ar-Rub' al-Khali* (*A Man from the Rub' al-Khali Desert*, 1994), *Mu'jam al-jahim* (*Hell's Dictionaries*, 1996), *Yadd fi akhir al-'alam* (*A Hand at the End of the World*, 1998), and *al-Jundi al-ladhi ra'a at-ta'ir* (*A Soldier Who Saw a Bird in a Dream*, 2000). He moves away from the classical *qasida* in favor of poetic prose (*qasidat an-nathr*). Ar-Rahbi's innovation lies in the verbal connection of different meanings, creating images of our world filled with unknown sounds and mysterious thoughts.

Ar-Rahbi is a keen observer of the world. In poems he creates his own world, whose message is often difficult and incomprehensible in reception. It seems that in the poem *Safarun* (*Travel*) he refers to his travels around the world as a tireless wanderer, but he always returns to his homeland:

> In these distant spots
> Deserted even by a wolf's howling
> I saddle the light of a candle
> And Travel.[11]

In the poetry volume *Manazil al-khutwa al-ula* (*First-Step Homes*), published in Cairo in 1993, Sayf ar-Rahbi refers to his own childhood and family history. He is impressed by the surroundings, nature, and simple life, expressing enjoyment that he has returned to the bosom of his homeland. Images related to beloved places are reflected in the poem *Qasidat hubb ila Matrah* (*Love Poem for Matrah*):

> When I lay on your coast for the first time
> resembling a heart whose beats are lanterns
> The flocks of these lighthouses graze on your mountains
> Across the sea.[12]

Sayf ar-Rahbi as a wanderer through life and the world expresses his own views on universal issues. As a sensitive individual, he feels great responsibility not only for himself but also for others, which is reflected in the poems of the volume *Al-Jabal al-akhdar* (*The Green Mountain*):

> So this is the green mountain
> She was not the ruler of the foothills of snow
> but the crown of escaping space
> And the pearl of presence.[13]

Mountain or mountains appear in many poems by Sayf ar-Rahbi. They become apparent even in the titles of poetry volumes, for example, *Al-Jabal al-akhdar* (*The Green Mountain*), published in Damascus in 1981, or *Jibal* (*Mountains*), published in Beirut in 1996. The mountain symbolizes mysticism, wisdom, lofty thoughts, a place of meditation, his homeland, and at the same time loneliness, it is the border between the visible and invisible world symbolizing the deeper truth about man, and his true nature. This meaning fully corresponds to the content of the poems by ar-Rahbi, in which the mountain is a symbol of existence because it is "the crown of space and the pearl of presence." The poems by Sayf ar-Rahbi are brief, powerful, and expressive. They are accompanied by loss and loneliness in the modern world. He developed his own individual form of sincere feelings and passions. In his poems he referred to and used to return to his homeland.

Sa'ida bint Khatir al-Farisi is another Omani poet of this generation. Born in Sur in 1956, she obtained her PhD from Cairo University in Literary Criticism in 2002, taking up the topic of women's poetry in the Gulf. She returned to Oman with her family from Kuwait after Sultan Qaboos came to power. Since then, she has worked for an Omani institute for culture and literature. She is the author of many volumes of poetry, including *Maddun fi bahr al-a'maq* (*The Tide in the Heart of the Sea*, 1986), *Ughniyat li-l-tufula wa al-khudra* (*Songs for Childhood and Greenery*, 1991), *Ilayha tahuj al-huruf* (*Letters Make Pilgrimages to Her*, 2003), *Wahdak tabqa salat yaqini* (*You Alone Remain the Prayer of my Confidence*, 2005), *Mazaltu amshi 'ala al-ma'* (*I Have Not Stopped Walking on Water*, 2009), and *Awraq min bayni ath-thuqub* (*Papers Between Holes*, 2018).

She possesses a special gift of observing the surrounding reality. She shows civilizational changes that took place not only in Oman, but also around the world. In this enormous machine of changes, she does not lose herself, her role as a woman and mother. She lives her dreams that reflect her sensitivity. There are many personal references in her poetry. In the poem titled *Umuma* (*Motherhood*) she describes the moments of childbirth extremely emotionally. On the one hand, she is accompanied by joy and enormous happiness, and, on the other hand, she is overwhelmed by fear of the future.

Women have always been a topic taken up by poets. Women were assigned different roles in men's lives depending on culture and religion. In this case, a female poet writes about a woman. Sa'ida bint Khatir al-Farisi presents the dilemmas of a woman over forty in the poem *Ba'd al-arba'in* (*Over Forty*). For an Arab woman, she emphasizes the needs of a mature woman:

Please keep your hands off . . .
Go to the veils of the heart
Move them aside and then fondle the pores of the soul

. . .
A woman in her forties
Needs a light touch
She needs a knight to talk to her with the tongue of water
and the singing of lovers

. . .
A woman in her forties
Needs a rose shade
And a heart that smells of tenderness
With a prophetic pulse.[14]

In another poem titled *Ana man akun* (*Who am I*), Sa'ida is against the aging process due to the sight of a gray hair on her head. The poem resembles a monologue and is characterized by numerous rhetorical questions. The poet is terrified by the impending process of growing old and dying. Nevertheless, she humbly accepts the laws that govern the world:

Are you laughing?!
At our combs
Mirrors
Oils
And the jasmine flower potion.[15]

Sa'ida al-Farisi tells us about the feelings of mature women, their need for more tenderness and love on the part of their partner. The desires of the lyrical subject are clearly felt: better intimacy with the partner. She dreams of love, she is full of longing, anticipation and hope that this love will come and last. In her poem *Dabbur* (*Wasp*) she writes:

I swear, that before your transformation
you were a bee
And that's why you knew that a source of spring honey
Is on the edges of my mouth
I wasn't surprised
When you built there your beehive.[16]

The poem exposes love as a timeless feeling that gives meaning to human life, and the desire to acquire it is a strong and out of control feeling. Without love, when crossing a certain age barrier, a woman feels an inner emptiness and loneliness. Her work is a strong voice of a modern Omani woman, proclaiming publicly her emotions, fully aware of the value her own feelings.

Saʿid as-Saqlawi (b. 1956) plays a significant role in Omani literary life. He has been managing the literary club—*Al-Jamaʿiyya al-ʿumaniyya li-l-kuttab wa-l-udaba'* (Omani Society of Writers and Literati)—in Muscat for years. But after all, he is the author of several volumes of poetry, such as *Tarnimat al-amal* (*The Hymn of Hope*, 1975), *Anti li qadar* (*You are my Fate*, 1985), *Ajnihat an-nahar* (*The Wings of Day*, 1999), *Nashid al-ma'* (*Water Song*, 2004), *Wasaya Qaid al-Ard* (*The Commandments of Qaid al-Ard*,[17] 2015). His poetry is distinguished by clarity of meaning as well as rhetorical figures and images.

On the cover of *Ajnihat an-nahar* (*The Wings of Day*) Ahmad Kashak wrote: "This volume presents a broad look coming from the heart of a poet who loves his country and his belonging to Arab people."[18] A good example of his poetry could be the poem *Tawajjus* (*Apprehension*), in which Saʿid used the ship of which he himself is a captain as a means of transport. He feels safe on it and is free to choose its direction, time, purpose, and space. The poet deliberately uses the local term *badan*, which is the type of Omani ship, to emphasize his national identity:

> I am the Omani *badan* (ship)
> Which never becomes weakened by exhaustion;
> Despite wind, current and storm
> Travel pulls me by force toward itself
> Without fear or caution
> My sail is determined faith
> Danger disappears in its presence
> And my anchor is history and example.[19]

Literature does not give a clear answer to the question about our destiny. Man feels the fear of loneliness and death. People, preoccupied with themselves, do not notice when somebody is dying nearby. Men of letters in different countries understand it differently. Saʿid as-Saqlawi in the poem *Aqdar* (*Fate*) speaks of a destiny that is inevitable for man, from which one cannot escape and no one is able to change. The lyrical subject submits to this destiny. Every day is important to him. Something begins and something ends every day, although not always as we want it to:

> No holiday is coming
> Not a single day prevent it
> Everyone will meet his death
> in the orbits of destiny.[20]

The ultimate result of human fate is death. This path leads through fear and the painful feeling of passing that each person strives in solitude. After the death of Sultan Qaboos, the poem *Ya sayyid al-hubb al-kabir* (*Oh Lord of Great Love*) by Sa'id as-Saqlawi appeared in the newspaper *Al-Watan* on January 23, 2020, being a panegyric, elegy (*marthiya*), in honor of the ruler:

> You taught us that deeds are goals,
> Which rise to heaven with a wise thought
> . . .
> As soon as you say something, your homeland will follow your words
> Because the promised achievements are already facts
> . . .
> God has placed in you a paradise of His love
> You filled the hearts of people with even greater love.[21]

In another poem written in honor of Sultan Qaboos by as-Saqlawi, *Wafa' wa 'Irfan* (*Memorial of Gratitude and Fidelity*), the poet emphasizes love for his homeland and nation. He believes that although the Sultan has physically passed away, he remains forever in the hearts and thoughts of Omanis:

> We will testify, in front of God
> That you relinquish the oath
> Fulfilled the promise,
> Undertake our renaissance
> You justly strived to sign our pride
> You writhed
> You bequeathed
> Ruled

Amended fairly
You implanted goodness
We, thus, harvested, gaiety
You give away your life for us
Adorning us overtly and in covertly
Your good behavior, we follow
A father
Elevated us above the sky
In eminence and dignity
O' Almighty, Lord of the Universe and mankind
Qaboos is between your Merciful Hands
Qaboos, the love of the populace
Wrap him with Your soothing serenity
Harbor him into Your advocacy
Shed Your Light upon thee
Shower upon him Your Divinely Bounties
O' God
O' God
O' God.[22]

Qaboos enjoyed a high degree of popularity. Saʿid as-Saqlawi feels proud to be an Omani and his poetry is full of love for the country. At the same time, he deals with sociocultural and historical matters in his poems.

Elegies (*marthiya*) written by Omani poets in honor of Sultan Qaboos after his death on January 10, 2020 are characterized by stylistic and thematic diversity. The full picture of the great ruler and the patriotic feelings were recorded in the poems of such poets as, for example: Hilal bin Sayf ash-Shiyadi and his poem *Ansaka? (Will I Forget You?)*;[23] ʿAbd al-Halim al-Badaʿi in the poem *ad-Dars al-baligh (Eloquent Lesson)*;[24] Ahmad bin Hilal al-ʿAbri in the poem *Raya al-amjad (Sign of Glory)*;[25] and Shumaysa an-Nuʿamaniyya in her poem *Wadaʿan ya Abi (Father Goodbye)*.[26]

Poetry of The Twenty-first Century

The next generation of contemporary Omani poets, born after the 1950s represents a different way of thinking. They write their works mainly in the form of free verse (*tafʿila*) and in poetic prose (*qasidat an-nathr*). Their works are endowed with sensitivity, expressing the pain of existence much more strongly. They struggle with existential fears and doubts about the rightness of choices characteristic of the present time. They use the experiences of precursors, but they also continue their topics related to love, patriotism, or traditional values tied to their natural environment. This gives them a basis for analyzing their own soul. Their creative loneliness is sometimes the price for saving their inner freedom and independence. They observe and describe those who cannot find their place in their contemporary reality. However, they want their poetry to be welcomed and appreciated like their predecessors.

Hasan al-Matrushi was born in the coastal town of Shinas in 1965. His first volume of poetry titled *Fatima* (*Fatma*) dealing with human topics, was published in 1996. Another volume of poetry containing romantic and patriotic pieces written in *taf'ila* form was published in 1997 under the title *Qasam* (*The Oath*). In 2008, he published in Beirut the volume *'Ala as-Safh iyyah* (*On that Mountain Side*).

The poem titled *Andalus tukhabbi' shalaha al-'arabi* (*Andalusia Hides its Arabic Shawl*) deserves reader attention. The poet refers to the Arab heritage in Spain and the symbolic meaning of Andalusia, which still remains in the memory of Arabs due to writers such as Ibn Zaydun (d. 1071 CE).

> I was walking . . . I saw Andalusia hiding its Arabic shawl
> Under the bush in the soul
> How many times they passed, her tramp poet continued to mumble
> . . .
> Why, the longer the evening, the more often
> Angels crowded on the terraces of Andalusia,
> And the spaces narrowed in front of Ibn Zaydun?[27]

Hasan al-Matrushi's poems have a wide thematic spectrum, ranging from love poems to patriotic and historical ones. There is also a mystical and religious element in the works. 'Awad Muhammad al-Luwayhi (b. 1976), received a BA in Arabic Philology from Sultan Qaboos University in 2001 and an MA in Linguistics in 2011 from the Australian National University. Since 2003, he has been working as a cultural researcher at the Literary Forum at the Omani Ministry of Heritage and Culture in Muscat. He has published the following volumes of poetry: *Ka'inat az-zahira* (*Midday Creatures*), 2006; *Al-Miyah takhun al-birak* (*Water Betrays a Pond*), 2013;

Al-'Atma tahrub min zilaliha (*Darkness Escapes from its Own Shadows*), 2018; and *Basira wa hasa* (*Vision and Stones*), 2018. In addition, he has published many stories, articles, and poems in Omani newspapers and magazines. The poem *Al-Atfal* (*Children*) comes from the volume *Ka'inat az-zahira* (*Midday Creatures*):

> . . .
> The children are crying in the darkest of nights
> From the brutality of mothers
> They stuffed their bones
> Underneath plastic skins
> Then fell asleep
> The birds strike their throats with hammers of water
> The children return to their mothers' bosoms
> Leaving their names behind
> Their eyelids, drowned in the milk of whiteness, are stitched
> With butterflies' scream.[28]

The idea of the poem *Al-Atfal* (*Children*) was to depict the world of childhood and its fragility. Thus, the title appears in the plural, but this plural is not based on designation. Children flee from one fate to another without names, without anyone recognizing them or paying attention to them. Here, it is not necessary that childhood be a stage, but rather a state of non-recognition of their being. Confusion is evident in the images presented in the poem.

There is no doubt that 'Awad Muhammad al-Luwayhi's main work is to search for his own voice on the level of the poetic sentence and the artistic treatment of the poem in terms of meaning and visual image. His main effort was to popularize and escalate the details of everyday life. He is not afraid of a poetic world that humanizes assets and creates worlds paradoxical to the natural world. Then he is keen to go beyond his experience in terms of dealing with various topics in every poetry collection of his. Throughout the collection *Ka'inat az-zahira* (*Midday Creatures*) the reader can touch new poetic images, short and condense language which deal directly with different objects. Childhood scope played an important role in imaginary worlds of the poems, giving various approaches to the existence question and to investigating the meaning of being a human in modern era.

Badriyya Muhammad ʿAli al-Badri was born in Muscat in 1975, five years after Sultan Qaboos came to power. She published the following novels: *Ma waraʾ al-faqd* (*What's Beyond Loss*), 2015; *al-ʿUbur al-akhir* (*The Last Crossing*), 2017; and *Zill hirmafruditus* (*The Shadow of the Hermaphrodite*), 2018. Moreover, she published a book of poems in literary language titled *Wadin ghayr zi buh* (*Mysterious Valley*) in 2018, and a volume of poetry in dialect *Aqrab li-talwiha qasida* (*Closer to the Notes of Qasida*) in 2019.

The poet carefully observes the surroundings in which she comes to live, and then introduces them in her work. She devotes a lot of space in her work to feelings: love, in the poem *La uhibbu ash-shiʾr* (*I Don't Like Poetry*); alienation, in *Li-l-mawqid hataba* (*Like Wood for the Fireplace*); loneliness, in *Baʿidan: Yughanni al-wahidu ghiyabahu* (*Far Away, a Loner Sings His Absence*). In the latter, the poet talks about her life and that of her generation, which has a sense of alienation and loneliness, clearly pointing to the need for warm relations with the environment.

> The loner sings his absence
> Like a lily that covers itself in winter
> It hides the secret of seduction in the snow
> Heat is nil
> There is no hand
> There are no tears
> . . .
> He sleeps like a stranger
> He searches at night
> particles of something
> what will hug him.[29]

The poems from the volume *Wadin ghayr zi buh* (*Mysterious Valley*) show the loneliness or alienation that are signs of our times. Her generation is going through a period of disintegration of traditional family ties and interpersonal relations in Arab society. Selfishness and indifference to the concerns of others became common. You can be lonely by choice or rejection, often unaware of your family or surroundings. The poet often experiences internal tears, self-doubt, and fear.

The new generation of poets renewed the language of poetry, which became an instrument of communication on the emotional and intellectual levels. Moreover, they expanded the subject of poems to include matters concerning the meaning of life, transience, loneliness, alienation, as well as seeking and improving oneself in the contemporary world.

Prose Writing in Modern Oman: The First Generation

The development of prose in Oman was, like poetry, an expression of the enormous cultural and social changes instigated by Sultan Qaboos and the Omani Renaissance starting in the 1970s. Just as he excelled in poetry, the renaissance man, 'Abd Allah bin Muhammad at-Ta'i also paved the way for the development of modern Omani prose. He was a pioneer of the novel in the Gulf area, and his work had a huge impact on future generations in Oman. The novel *ash-Shira' al-kabir* (*The Great Sail*) was written to comfort the hearts of his compatriots, being proud of the history of Oman. He wanted to show the strength of unity at the level of Oman but also at that of the Arab world.[30]

The action in the second novel, titled, *Mala'ikat al-jabal al-akhdar*[31] (*Angels of the Green Mountains*) takes place during the reign of Sultan Said Ibn Taimur and refers to the succession movement led by Imam Ghalib bin 'Ali and his brother in 1954–1959, which ended with the Sultan's success in unifying the country and extending his authority over it.[32] For 'Abd Allah at-Ta'i history consists of facts that can form the basis of a novel, hence the novel is an attempt to penetrate historical processes and show certain human attitudes.[33] At-Ta'i's texts were to testify to his contemporary times. They were not only to inform but also to educate. He systematized knowledge of all the contemporary literature of the Gulf that he had known.

One of the followers of 'Abd Allah at-Ta'i, Ahmad az-Zubaydi (b. 1945), after studying in Cairo and working in Damascus, returned when Sultan Qaboos took power to support the development of contemporary literature. He published a collection of short stories, titled *Intihar Ubayd al-'Umani* (*Suicide of Omani Ubayd*, 1985), which depict Oman undergoing changes on various sociocultural levels during the reign of Qaboos. The author clearly emphasizes that from a backward and very divided country, Oman opens up to the world while preserving its own cultural heritage. The aforementioned poet Mahmud al-Khusaybi writes about the changes not only in Oman, but also in other Arab countries in the 1970s in the collection of short stories, titled *Qalb li-l-bay'* (*Heart for Sale*, 1983). In his works, we can see topics related to the impact of the discovery of oil on the lives of the inhabitants of the Gulf. The hero of the short story *Tabakhkhar al-ahlam* (*Dreams are Over*) has been fishing for pearls all his life. With the discovery of oil and artificial pearls, this profession has ceased to be profitable, hence the hero of the story earns his living by teasingly telling about the times that have already passed. Al-Khusaybi also makes efforts to defend women by recognizing their role and position in society, for example, in the short story *Su'ad* (the heroine's name). The first Omani short stories are simple in form and literal in content, and their authors become reliable witnesses of their era and the social changes taking place in the country.[34]

The 1980s brought a definite development of Omani prose, both in content and form. Su'ud bin Sa'd al-Muzaffar (b. 1953), studied in Kuwait before returning to Oman. He started his literary activity by writing short stories, brought together in the collection *Yawm qabla shuruq ash-shams* (*The Day Before Sunrise*),[35] in which he explicitly refers to the social situation in Oman before Qaboos' rule. The writer shows the malfunctioning of a country in which poverty, fear, violence, and backwardness reigned, but there is hope in the title "sunrise" which refers to the coming of the young sultan's rule. Al-Muzaffar emphasizes the element of emigration and Westernization in the short story *Hayat rubbama haditha* (*Life May be Modern*). He points to generational differences in the approach to everyday life and tradition, which is emphasized in the short story *Nihayat jil* (*End of Generation*). Another collection, titled *Wa ashraqat ash-shams* (*And the Sun Rose*),[36] is a presentation of the situation in Oman after Qaboos took power. At the news of the changes and reforms of the new sultan many educated Omanis decided to return to the country and support the young ruler. These returns were not always easy because much had to be changed, especially to undertake the education of society. The word *shams* (sun) appears in the titles of both collections of short stories, which seems to refer to Sultan Qaboos and the arrival of a new beginning that came after he took power. The sun is here to symbolize life, happiness, and freedom.

Su'ud bin Sa'd al-Muzaffar was the first such prolific Oman novelist. He published many novels, of which—in the context of the development of the homeland—the novel *Al-mu'allim 'Abd ar-Razzaq* (*'Abd ar-Razzaq the Teacher*)[37] deserves attention. The writer takes up the subject of educating society to combat prejudices. This applies to people whose soul is taken away. They die in a mental sense and, although they live in a physical sense, they belong neither to the world of the living nor to that of the dead. They are called *maghasib*.[38] And just such a hero is Rashid, who, like many others in the village, fell into the hands of the enchanter Haykal. The second thread of the novel describes the strange reactions of the villagers after the arrival of the educated engineer Salih, who, by building a road, wants to make changes not only in the village, but above all to the mentality of its inhabitants. The novel illustrates the prejudices and superstitions rooted in the countryside and their negative impact on people's lives.

In the context of views on the family and the role of women, the novel *Rajul wa imra'a* (*Man and Woman*)[39] deserves the attention of the reader. Su'ud al-Muzaffar presents male–female relations with foreigners in contemporary Omani society. He describes social changes taking place under the influence of visitors from other countries representing different cultures, religions, and speaking different languages. The writer also presents the new way of thinking of the newcomers, which has an irreversible impact on the native inhabitants of Oman. A similar topic is raised in the novel *Rimal wa jalid* (*Sand and Ice*),[40] which shows a materially and mentally heterogeneous society after 1970. The cultural differences of the man, an Arab, and a European woman do not allow them to communicate. Sand refers to the desert, traditions, and Arab society, and ice is the loneliness and coldness of the West. In turn, the novel titled *1986* (*The year 1986*)[41] warns against the country's dependence on foreign labor, which in consequence may lead to the danger that Omanis will become a minority in their own country. The other novel, titled *Rijal min Jibal al-Hajar* (*Men of the Stone Mountains*),[42] shows the changes associated with the rapid material advancement of a poor society and how it affects the behavior and mentality of the characters in the novel. The poor heroes, thanks to their cleverness and favorable circumstances, had achieved financial success, which did not bring them happiness. They did not understand and accept some social changes.

The action in all al-Muzaffar's novels takes place in Oman. The writer has comprehensive knowledge about the country and tries to present the most important problems faced by Omani society. His books reflect the views and dilemmas of the younger generation. And his goal is to serve the country.

Sayf bin Sa'id as-Sa'di (b. 1967) belongs to a generation of writers already educated in Oman. In his stories and novels, he imitates the theme and style of Su'ud al-Muzaffar. And so Ahmad, the main character of the novel *Kharif az-zaman* (*Autumn of Time*),[43] after arriving in the town of Al-Batina, meets the engineer Salim who wants to introduce modern irrigation methods. His commitment to the introduction of modernity in the village, however, meets with great social resistance. The author sketches the transformation of the hero in an interesting way, who after the death of the engineer takes the initiative and introduces many modern solutions. This novel is also a panegyric in honor of Sultan Qaboos, who instilled in the Omanis a sense of unity in the pursuit of the development of the homeland and the unification of the tribes inhabiting Oman. This sense of unity is also portrayed in the novel *Jirah as-sinin* (*Painful Years*).[44] In addition, social changes are shown here, for example, leaving villages in order to get a job in cities since the current life as a farmer is a series of hardships and poverty.

Hamad Khamis an-Nasiri (b. 1964) is a writer who has contributed greatly to the development of new prose forms. He published two collections of short stories: *Awja' min az-zaman al-madi* (*Wounds of old Times*),[45] where he describes the realities of urban and rural life; and *Al-layla al-akhira* (*The Last Night*),[46] where he deals with the topic of marriage. The author shows different psychological types of young people forced to enter into traditional marriages. This applies to both men and women; for example, in the short story *al-Maqsum* (*The Fate of Life*) the hero forces his sister to marry a man she does not love, even though "the groom" is divorced twice already. In addition, an-Nasiri presents various types of heroine who experience turbulent feelings, but also those prone to self-reflection; for example, in the short story of *Al-Aqdar* (*Destiny*), in which a sterile wife herself advises her husband to choose another wife. However, over time, it turned out that the latter is infertile too.

Hamad Khamis an-Nasiri is also the author of the novel *Sa'ati la tazal taduqq* (*My Watch is Still Ticking*),[47] which also refers to changes in the countryside and difficult conditions that force the hero's family to move, ending with the death of his son. In turn, in the novel *Ma'sat fi al-madina* (*Tragedy in the City*),[48] moving from the village to the city and a desire for quick enrichment leads to prostitution of the heroines against their will. Ultimately, the novel ends tragically with the revenge of the girls and the murder of the man who forced them into prostitution. The novel *Niran qalb* (*Fire of the Heart*)[49] is even more dramatic because the heroine contracts HIV and dies of AIDS.

The writers publishing in the 1970s and 1980s tried to be involved and sensitive to changes that had taken place in the country. In many prose works, we are faced with the phenomenon of multiple forms serving to convey one content. We find a reference or praise to Sultan Qaboos, whom the Omani admired and considered to be the driving force that led to the unification of the tribes. The writers try to present the ways of thinking and the mentality of their heroes following the changes that took place after Sultan Qaboos came to power. While describing the image of Oman they use simple forms of expression so that they are understandable to everyone.

In the end of the twentieth century, Omani prose dealt mainly with existential topics, especially the existence of man in the modern world. These works are often a jumble of random images and associations. An example of this is the collection of short stories *Sa'at ar-rahil al-multahiba* (*Exciting Travel Time*)[50] by Muhammad Al-Qurmuti (b. 1955). His innovative stories are steeped in surrealism, in which the hero is sentenced to wandering on the borderland of waking and sleeping. He suffers so much that he wants to die to become free. The narrative is conducted in an uncontrolled manner through a stream of associations. Despite the tips, the reader who meets the characters of Cinderella or Solomon has a problem in understanding these hallucinations of the hero. The absurdity reigns in content and construction. The author wants to influence many senses, playing with sound, light, and ending with smells. Silence also plays a role, thanks to which you can look into your own soul. Descriptions are conducted in a poetic language with numerous metaphors and rhetorical figures. The work of Al-Qurmuti is the beginning of a new order, or rather creative disorder, in Omani prose,[51] which has found many followers.

Other writers remained devoted to traditional symbols and scenes in their stories: the sea and the palm tree. Hamad Rashid bin Rashid (b. 1960) is the author of a collection of short stories titled *Zagharid as-sahil* (*Horses Neighing*).[52] He is a keen observer of social changes in Oman, and a feature of his writing is a short, almost reportage imaging of the issue using a beautiful poetic language. In the story *Farhat al-luqya* (*Joy of Meeting*), he describes the joy of the Omani people on returning to their families after a long separation, at the same time depicting their hard work, worries, and small moments of joy at sea, which is their eternal ally by giving them work, food, and rest. The Omani heritage is also a desert where palm trees grow. The writer illustrates the special relationship with them in the short story *An-nakhla as-saghira* (*Little Palm*). The hero on the eve of leaving this world is worried about the fate of the palm trees, so he explains to his grandson that all the goods of this world will pass away and the palm trees will remain to feed and shelter the inhabitants. The title palm is a symbol of intergenerational bond. Hamad Rashid bin Rashid is part of the development of a new writing style in Oman through the simplicity and conciseness of single-threaded novellas.

The New Narrative Generation

Badriyya ash-Shahhi (b. 1971) is the author of the first novel written by an Omani woman, titled *At-tawaf haythu al-jamr* (*Circling Around the Embers*).[53] The novel has not only a social but also a historical dimension. The author took up the theme of love in it, because the heroine escapes to Zanzibar from an unwanted marriage. However, her chosen path is complicated by the events resulting from her lack of independence and life experience, so she decides to marry a sailor who, unfortunately, is soon killed. This makes Zahra decide to go to the countryside. There, she employs the brave and beautiful Munira, who is her opposite. Unfortunately, her dreams of the freedom to choose a partner do not come true. The end of the novel is open and causes many thoughts related to the social situation of an Arab woman. This novel supports women in their fight for freedom, and its author paved the way for the development of the creativity of other Omani writers.

Jukha al-Harthi (b. 1978), who won the Man Booker Prize in 2019, is the author of both short story collections and novels, such as *Manamat* (*Dreams*),[54] and *Sayyidat al-qamar* (*Ladies of the Moon*).[55] The first novel relies on modernist techniques such as fragmentation of time, coupled with an allusive language rich in Sufi associations, to delve into the experience of a female protagonist living through contemporary social transformation. The second novel deals with change in Omani society over the past century, seen through the prism of the sensitive subject of slavery and the status of former slaves in Oman, in addition to other themes such as love, gender, marriage, patriarchy, and identity.[56] The novel *Sayyidat al-qamar* (*Ladies of the Moon*) was on the list of the six best novels in the international competition International Prize for Arabic Fiction in 2011. Translated into English by Marilyn Booth under the title *Celestial Bodies*,[57] it was recognized by the Man Booker International Prize 2019 as the first best translated novel to English. Jukha al-Harthi's latest novel is titled *Naranjah* (*Bitter Orange*).[58] It is the story of an Omani girl studying in Great Britain. The emerging London theme seems to be symbolic to show young people from different countries and the problems they face while studying abroad. The main theme of the novel is a return to the past, memories of the family home and grandmother, whom the heroine could not help leaving to study. Eventually, the woman passed away, as did the orange tree she planted in front of her house when she was young. The novel is dominated by sadness, pain, and regret.

Zuwayna al-Kalbani (b. 1970) also enjoys considerable achievements in prose writing. In her novels, she uses narrative techniques that allow her to cross the border between reality and fiction. In the first novel, published in 2011, titled *Thaluth wa ta'wiza* (*Trinity and Talisman*),[59] she deals with the Gulf War and its impact on the psyche of the characters. Another novel, *Fi kahfi junun tabda' al-hikaya* (*In the Grotto of Madness the Story Begins*),[60] is also psychological, showing characters representing different cultures who share the desire to live according to their own rules. With the novel titled *Al-Jawhara wa al-qabtan* (*The Jewel and the Captain*),[61] the author is part of the first historical novels initiated by 'Abd Allah at-Ta'i. She describes the journey of a faithful copy of the ninth-century ship called *Jawharat Muscat*, referring to the history of Oman and showing sea trade relations with China and the countries of East Asia. This theme is an opportunity to present the hard work of the multinational and multireligious ship's crew, their feelings, and dreams. In the last novel, titled *Arwah mushawwasha* (*Confused Souls*),[62] published in 2017, the author takes up the difficult topic of mental disorders.

Badriyya Muhammad 'Ali al-Badri (b. 1975), published two social and moral books, which end with the tragic death of the heroes: *Ma wara' al-faqd*

(*What's Beyond Loss*), and *al-'Ubur al-akhir* (*The Last Crossing*). However, it was her last novel, titled *Zill hirmafruditus* (*The Shadow of the Hermaphrodite*),[63] which appeared in 2018, that brought her fame and the main prize in 2019 for the best novel published in Oman. This is the story of Su'ad, who has been trying to establish her identity since her birth. The novel deals with a very rare issue in Arab writings, it is the subject of sexual identity. The heroine talks about her physical and mental suffering, her life in a simple rural Omani society, which does not tolerate this type of otherness. Su'ad in her deliberations brings up many topics, such as abandoned children, personal freedom, and many others. She talks about this life from the cradle to the age of twenty-five. The heroine, feeling not very feminine, undergoes plastic surgery to accentuate her femininity at the urging of her friend Olivia. However, she is surprised to discover that she has a different inner side that has a passion for Olivia just as a man feels for a woman. Su'ad began to analyze her love story with her boyfriend and found that she had not felt any desire at the time. Under the influence of her thoughts, she decided to change her gender and turn from a woman to a man. Will she be accepted by society? She could not answer this question since she could not find the courage and strength to inform her family about her decision, especially as they did not recognize her when she had come to them as a man. The author describes not only the psychological state of the protagonist and the internal conflict she is experiencing, but also takes up the issue of the right to freedom of the individual. The question of social acceptance is left open.

Mahmud ar-Rahbi (b. 1969) made his debut in 1998 with a collection of short stories titled *Al-lawn al-bunni* (*Brown Color*).[64] The title reflects the presence of the brown color in all aspects of life, starting with the skin color of the Omanis. The collection includes stories and observations from the author's childhood, memories from the cities of Matrah or his hometown of Surur. The next collection of short stories, *Sa'at zawal* (*The Hour of Passing Away*),[65] and the latest, published in 2020, *Thalath qisas jabaliya* (*Three Mountain Stories*),[66] draw themes from ethnographic wealth and Omani tradition, as well as from world heritage, crossing the barriers of time and geography. In the title part of the collection, Mahmud ar-Rahbi uses stories belonging to universal human heritage, for example, the story of a giant who came out of a bottle and then returned to it because of his stupidity; the story of a faithful man who sold his years of worshiping God for a sip the water given to him by the Devil; and the story of a noble man who wanted to commit suicide because of despair over life. The author modified the stories by changing some details to give them the spirit appropriate to the era in which his collection of stories was created. The stories are characterized by an irony related to social and political realities.

Mahmud ar-Rahbi is also the author of many novels, including *Kharita al-halim* (*A Map of the Dreamer*),[67] whose protagonist embarks on a journey to New Zealand as a teacher of Islamic law. In the novel, we see a juxtaposition of Western civilization with the Arab culture and traditions of Islam through the interaction of the protagonist with those around him. The author presents the life of the local people as free from anxiety and focused on tolerance, which is the basis of all relationships. The hero's stereotypical beliefs that Westerners do not believe in God and do not respect religion change over time. The author emphasizes that the strength of Western civilization results not only from its own historical experience, but also from its constant striving to improve the level of science. Ar-Rahbi's latest novel, *Awraq al-gharib* (*The Alien's Diaries*),[68] is set in Matrah. It is a story of a young Egyptian, who was employed in a KFC restaurant, described in his memoirs. It realistically reflects the difficult living and working conditions of "Aliens" in the Gulf countries.

The diversity, innovation, and expressiveness of Omani narrative forms initiated by 'Abd Allah at-Ta'i are now flourishing in Oman. This high level of cultural expression, increasingly recognized by the literary world outside Oman, reflects the social, educational, and economic developments initiated after the accession Sultan Qaboos. The writers analyzed the human psyche, created a type of hero corresponding to their present reality, who represents social ideas. The dynamically developing novel writing draws themes from the history, tradition, and experiences of individuals, contributing to the presentation of important contemporary phenomena that have appeared in social life.

Conclusions

Both poetry and prose developed greatly under Sultan Qaboos (1970–2020). Omani writers referred to patriotic themes in their works, emphasizing their love and commitment to the development of their homeland, especially in social and historical novels. At the same time, not every work is nationalistic. Independent and creative thinking has flourished: an advanced literary arena of Oman, that shows innovations in psychological surrealism.

Under the rule and sponsorship of Sultan Qaboos and the patronage of his government, as well as under the civic life of clubs, journals, and writers, Omani cultural life has abounded in cultural events scattered throughout the country, not just in Muscat. An-Nadwah Library in Bahla, Sheikh Muhsin Zahran Library in Al-Hamra', Sur Library in Sur City, As-Salimi Libray in Badiyyah, Dar Al-kitab Library in Salalah, or Bayt Az-Zubayr all host writers and discussions. The cultural and literary movement has also developed in private literary salons of cultural influencers such as Sa'ida bint Khatir al-Farisi, Fatima Al-'Iliyani, Majlis Al-Khalili, and Majlis Qahtan Al-Busa'idi. Virtual internet salons, for example, *Masa'at Thaqafiyyah* (Cultural Evenings), as well as through traditional and electronic newspapers and magazines have fostered creative talent. *Al-Tafahum* (*Mutual Understanding*) magazine and cultural supplements to newspapers remain popular venues for literary output. There is also an increasing awareness of literature online. This vibrant and self-sustained interest in literature and creativity in Omani literary life has roots in the changes initiated by Sultan Qaboos and the people of Oman from 1970 to 2020.

Notes

1. The *Journal of Oman Studies* was founded by the Ministry of National Heritage and Culture in 1975 to publish academic articles on archeology, history, and natural history.
2. The first evidence of club activities were published in *Al-Muntada al-Adabi. Fi'aliyat wa manashit* (The Literary Club. Events and Activities).
3. Organized for first time in 1992 by the Ministry of Heritage and Culture.
4. Compare Barbara Michalak-Pikulska, *Modern Poetry and Prose of Oman 1970–2000* (Krakow: Enigma Press, 2002), 11–19.
5. On the basis of an interview carried out by Barbara Michalak-Pikulska with Sa'ida bint Khatir al-Farisi in Muscat. Sa'ida bint Khatir al-Farisi (b. 1956), woman pioneer when it comes to literary and cultural activities in Oman. She is the author of such volumes of poetry as: *Maddun fi bahr al-a'maq* (*The Tide in the Heart of the Sea*) and *Ughniyat li-t-tufula wa al-khudra* (*Songs for Childhood and Greenery*).

6. 'Abd Allah bin Muhammad at-Ta'i, *al-A'mal ash-shi'ariyya* (Amman: Dar al-Fada'at, 2016).

7. 'Abd Allah bin Muhammad at-Ta'i, *'Uman tukhatib wafdaha*, in *al-A'mal ash-shi'ariyya* (Amman: Dar al-Fada'at, 2016), 171.

8. Hamid bin 'Abd Allah bin Hamid al-Jami'i, *Rawdat al-Albab*, in *Diwan Abi Surur* (Sama'il: Maktabat al-Firdaws 1998), 1:305.

9. Yahya bin 'Abd Allah al-Lizami, *Diwan Abi Surur* (Sama'il: Maktabat al-Firdaws 1998), 1:32.

10. Mahmud al-Khusaybi, *Qulu li-sultan al-bilad*, in *Awraq min shajarat al-majd* (Muscat: Matba' ash-Sharqiyya 1987), 107–108.

11. Sayf ar-Rahbi, *Safarun* in *Mu'jam al-jahim. Mukhtarat shi'ariyya* (Cairo: Dar Sharqiyyat li-l-nashr wa-t-tawzi', 1992), 307.

12. Sayf ar-Rahbi, *Qasidat hubb ila Matrah*, in *Mu'jam al-jahim. Mukhtarat shi'ariyya* (Cairo: Dar Sharqiyyat li-l-nashr wa-t-tawzi', 1992), 131.

13. Sayf ar-Rahbi, *Al-Jabal al-akhdar*, in *Mu'jam al-jahim. Mukhtarat shi'ariyya* (Cairo: Dar Sharqiyyat li-l-nashr wa-t-tawzi', 1992), 41.

14. Sa'ida bint Khatir al-Farisi, *Ba'd al-arba'in*, in *Ma zaltu amshi 'ala al-ma'* (Cairo: Shams li-l-nashr wa-t-tawzi', 2009), 37–40.

15. Sa'ida bint Khatir al-Farisi, *Ana man akun*, in *Maddun fi bahr al-a'maq* (Ruwi: Matba'a al-'alamiya, 1986), 59.

16. Sa'ida bint Khatir al-Farisi, *Dabbur*, in *Ma zaltu amshi 'ala al-ma'* (Cairo: Shams li-l-nashr wa-t-tawzi', 2009), 104.

17. Sayf bin Sultan Ya'rubi (1692–1711), known as Qaid al-Ard.

18. Ahmad Kashak, *Ajnihat an-nahar* (Muscat: Matba' an-Nahda, 1999), back cover of the book.

19. Sa'id as-Saqlawi, *Tawajjus*, in *The Awakening of the Moon: A selection of Poems*, trans. A. Al-Shahham and M. V. Mcdonald (Muscat: Shariqa Matabi' Al-Batinah, 1996), 27.

20. Sa'id as-Saqlawi, *Aqdar*, in *Ma tabqa min suhuf al-wajd* (Beirut: Al-Markaz ad-Dawli li-khadamat ath-Thaqafiyya, 2020), 7–8.

21. Sa'id as-Saqlawi, *Ya sayyid al-hubb al-kabir*, in *Al-Watan*, Muscat, January 23, 2020, No. 13204, vol. 49, 27.

22. Sa'id as-Saqlawi, *Wafa' wa 'Irfan*, in *'Alam ath-thaqafa*, trans. Dr. Naimah Al-Ghamdi, available at: http://www.worldofculture2020.com/?p=21476.

23. Hilal bin Sayf ash-Shiyadi, *Ansaka?* in *Al-Watan*, Muscat, January 20, 2020, No. 13201, vol. 49, supplement Culture and Art.

24. 'Abd al-Halim al-Bada'i, *ad-Dars al-baligh*, in *Al-Watan*, January 27, 2020, No. 13206, vol. 49. 23, supplement Culture and Art.

25. Ahmad bin Hilal al-'Abri, *Raya al-amjad*, in *Al-Watan*, January 27, 2020, No. 13206, vol. 49, 23, supplement Culture and Art.

26. Shumaysa an-Nu'amaniyya, *Wada'an ya Abi*, in *Al-Watan*, January 28, 2020, No. 13207, vol. 50, 23, supplement Culture and Art.

27. Hasan al-Matrushi, *Andalus tukhabbi' shalaha al-'arabi*, in *'Ala as-Safh iyyah* (Beirut: Al-Intishar al-Arabi, 2008), 50–51.

28. 'Awad al-Luwayhi, *Al-Atfal*, in *Ka'inat az-zahira*, 2nd edn. (Muscat: Bait al-Ghisham li-l-nash wa-t-tarjama, 2014), 10–12.

29. Badriyya al-Badri, *Ba'idan: Yughanni al-wahidu ghiyabahu*, in *Wadin ghayr zi buh* (Sharjah, 2018), 20.

30. 'Abd Allah bin Muhammad at-Ta'i, *ash-Shira' al-kabir*, in *Sardiyyat* (Amman: Dar al-Fada'at, 2016), 193–330.

31. 'Abd Allah bin Muhammad at-Ta'i, *Mala'ikat al-jabal al-akhdar*, in *Sardiyyat* (Amman: Dar al-Fada'at, 2016), 115–192.

32. Barbara Michalak-Pikulska and Wail S. Hassan, "Oman," in *The Oxford Handbook of Arab Novelistic Traditions* (Oxford: Oxford University Press, 2017), 359–360.

33. Compare Michalak-Pikulska, *Modern Poetry and Prose of Oman 1970–2000* (Krakow: The Enigma Press 2002), 160–163.

34. Compare Michalak-Pikulska, *Modern Poetry and Prose of Oman 1970–2000* (Krakow: The Enigma Press 2002), 169–174.

35. Su'ud bin Sa'd al-Muzaffar, *Yawm qabla shuruq ash-shams* (Muscat: Al-Matabi' al-'alamiya, 1987).

36. Su'ud bin Sa'd al-Muzaffar, *Wa ashraqat ash-shams* (Muscat: Al-Matabi' al-'alamiya, 1988).

37. Su'ud bin Sa'd al-Muzaffar, *Al-mu'allim 'Abd ar-Razzaq* (Muscat: Matabi' an-Nahda, 1989).

38. Sing. *maghsub*, pl. *maghasib*, meaning enchanted, possessed, kidnapped, and used by a shaman. Then abandoned in the mountains or in a cemetery. Considered dead to relatives and friends and only a sorcerer knows their whereabouts. It refers to superstitions and local beliefs.

39. Su'ud bin Sa'd al-Muzaffar, *Rajul wa imra'a* (Muscat: Matabi' an-Nahda, 1990).

40. Su'ud bin Sa'd al-Muzaffar, *Rimal wa jalid* (Muscat: Matba' al-alwan al-haditha, 1989).

41. Su'ud bin Sa'd al-Muzaffar, *1986* (Muscat: Khadamat al-I'lan as-sari', 1993).

42. Su'ud bin Sa'd al-Muzaffar, *Rijal min Jibal al-Hajar* (Muscat: Matba' al-bustan, 1995).

43. Sayf bin Sa'id as-Sa'di, *Kharif az-zaman* (Muscat: Al-Matabi' al-'alamiya, 1990).

44. Sayf bin Sa'id as-Sa'di, *Jirah as-sinin* (Muscat: Al-Matabi' al-'alamiya, 1989).

45. Hamad Khamis an-Nasiri, *Awja' min az-zaman al-madi* (Muscat: Matabi' an-Nahda, 1989).

46. Hamad Khamis an-Nasiri, *Al-layla al-akhira* (Muscat: Matabi' an-Nahda, 1989).

47. Hamad Khamis an-Nasiri, *Sa'ati la tazal taduqq* (Muscat: Matabi' an-Nahda, 1990).

48. Hamad Khamis an-Nasiri, *Ma'sat fi al-madina* (Muscat: Matabi' an-Nahda, 1991).

49. Hamad Khamis an-Nasiri, *Niran qalb* (Muscat: Matabi' an-Nahda, 1993).

50. Muhammad Al-Qurmuti, *Sa'at ar-rahil al-multahiba* (Muscat: Matba' al-alwan al-haditha, 1988).

51. Compare Michalak-Pikulska, *Modern Poetry and Prose of Oman 1970–2000* (Krakow: The Enigma Press 2002), 228.

52. Hamad Rashid bin Rashid, *Zagharid as-sahil* (Muscat: Dar jarida 'Uman li-s-sahafa wa-n-nashr, 1990).

53. Badriyya ash-Shahhi, *At-tawaf haythu al-jamr* (Beirut: Al-mu'assasa al-'arabiyya li-l-dirasat wa-n-nashr, 1999).

54. Jukha al-Harthi, *Manamat* (Beirut: Al-mu'assasa al-'arabiyya li-l-dirasat wa-n-nashr, 2004).

55. Jukha al-Harthi, *Sayyidat al-qamar* (Beirut: Dar al-Adab, 2010).

56. Barbara Michalak-Pikulska and Wail S. Hassan, "Oman," in *The Oxford Handbook of Arab Novelistic Traditions* (Oxford: Oxford University Press 2017), p. 367.

57. Jukha al-Harthi, *Celestial Bodies* (Dingwall: Sandstone Press, 2018).

58. Jukha al-Harthi, *Naranjah* (Beirut: Dar al-Adab, 2016).

59. Zuwayna al-Kalbani, *Thaluth wa ta'wiza* (Beirut: Mu'assasa al-'arabiyya li-l-dirasat wa-n-nashr, 2011).

60. Zuwayna al-Kalbani, *Fi kahfi junun tabda' al-hikaya* (Beirut: Mu'assasa al-'arabiyya li-l-dirasat wa-n-nashr, 2012).

61. Zuwayna al-Kalbani, *Al-Jawhara wa al-qabtan* (Muscat: Dar Al-Ghasham li-l-nashr wa-t-tarjama, 2014).

62. Zuwayna al-Kalbani, *Arwah mushawwasha* (Beirut: Mu'assasa al-'arabiyya li-l-dirasat wa-n-nashr, 2017).

63. Badriyya al-Badri, *Zill hirmafruditus* (London: Dar 'Arab, 2018).

64. Mahmud ar-Rahbi, *Al-lawn al-bunni* (Damascus: Al-Mada, 1998).

65. Mahmud ar-Rahbi, *Sa'at zawal* (Amman: Dar Fada'at, 2012).

66. Mahmud ar-Rahbi, *Thalath qisas jabaliya* (Amman: Al-Jama'iyya al-'umaniyya li-l-kuttab wa-l-udaba' bi-ta'wun ma' Al-an nashirun wa muwaza'un, 2020).

67. Mahmud ar-Rahbi, *Kharita al-halim* (Baghdad-Beirut: Manshurat al-Jamal, 2010).

68. Mahmud ar-Rahbi, *Awraq al-gharib* (Cairo: Dar al-'Aynayn, 2017).

12

PUBLIC HEALTH AND THE OMANI RENAISSANCE

Sean Foley

As it is well known that a healthy mind is in a healthy body, health should be a right of every citizen. Since July 1970, we have decided to attach high priority to the development of the health of the Omani people.

> Sultan Qaboos bin Said, Speech for Omani National Day, 1975[1]

Islam encourages the prevention of all diseases.

> Dar al-Ifta' (Oman's Fatwa Office),
> "Fatwa: The Role of Islam in Preventing AIDS"[2]

In the early 1970s, Oman was among the poorest and most isolated states in the Middle East; some dubbed it the "Tibet of Arabia." The country's deprivation was clearest in the poor state of public health: most Omanis did not live into their fifties, while morbidity and mortality rates were among the highest in the region.[3] There were fewer than 100 doctors for a nation of 723,000 people, with appalling death rates in overcrowded hospitals—a reflection of the fact that many Omanis were often very sick when they reached medical care, much of which was situated a significant distance from their homes.[4]

In contrast, by the year 2000, life expectancy had increased to 72, while the World Health Organization (WHO) classified the Sultanate's healthcare system as one of the best in the world.[5] While important gaps remain between different regions of the country in access to healthcare, there is little question that the country has made tremendous progress overall since the late Sultan Said bin Qaboos assumed the throne in 1970 and created the Omani Ministry of Health (MOH).[6] Under direction from Sultan Qaboos, that ministry has built, from nearly scratch, a model national healthcare system while also combating malaria and other communicable diseases. Indeed, the Sultan publicly promoted the MOH's work, insisting during his five decades on the throne that access to quality healthcare was a right that should be enjoyed by everyone—from Omanis residing in the wealthiest neighborhoods of Muscat to Bedouins living in the poorest and most remote areas of Dhofar's interior.[7]

Throughout that time, the ministry has benefited from generous official support and its work with domestic and international partners, including Oman's Ibadi religious elites. The Omani manual on communicable diseases features a *fatwa* (Islamic legal opinion) on Ebola by Assistant Grand Mufti Sheikh Kahlan al-Kharusi, which calls on Allah "to ward off every plague."[8] The Grand Mufti, Sheikh Ahmed b. Hamad al-Khalili, has been similarly committed to public health, calling on Omanis to refrain from smoking and to practice strict safety protocols during the Covid-19 pandemic. The pictures of him modelling social distancing and receiving the Covid-19 vaccine on Twitter have reinforced the public outreach campaigns of the MOH.

Those campaigns have played a key role in the country's response to the pandemic, with messages targeted at Omanis and expatriates in multiple languages.[9] They also built on three principles that Qaboos promoted while he was Sultan: (a) Islam can confidently and independently interact with modernity; (b) the nation's religious leaders must be cognizant of contemporary issues and speak about them as part of their ministry; and (c) it is better to prevent illnesses from emerging through vaccines and other preventative measures than it is to treat them after they had spread.

This chapter explores the improvement in public health in the Sultanate throughout the Omani Renaissance, building on the insights of Jeremy Jones, Nicholas Ridout, Marc Valeri, and others. I focus on how Qaboos, religious scholars, and some health professionals have used Islam and modern medicine and science to promote public health and their agendas for reform—often blurring the distinctions between these fields of knowledge. Their approach in many ways mirrors that of Qaboos, who stressed that it was essential for Oman's government and for Islam to respond to the needs and realities of the contemporary world, including healthcare.[10] To illustrate my chapter's argument, I draw on a variety of documents that medical professionals and others use to study the Sultanate's healthcare system, along with sources that have yet to be used as extensively to date in works on public health in Oman: Islamic legal opinions, Qaboos' speeches, social media posts, the reports written by tobacco executives on Oman, and film. Ultimately, I stress that two factors played a critical role in the success of the Sultanate's approach to healthcare over the last half century: (a) Qaboos' prioritization of public health and vision of Islam; and (b) the ability of Omanis to transcend the types of oppositional forces that are assumed to exist between Islam and modern fields of knowledge.

The State of Omani Healthcare before the 1970s

In July 1970, Sultan Qaboos came to power in Oman, bringing an end to what Michael Hudson has dubbed "one of the most successful and resolute efforts by any ruler to prevent modernization."[11] That program had been so successful that Oman was known as the "Tibet of Arabia."[12] It was no accident that Wendell Phillips, the famous U.S. archaeologist, titled his book about living in Oman and interacting with its people and leaders during the 1950s *Unknown Oman*.[13]

A decade after Phillips was in Oman, there were just 5 miles (8 km) of paved road in a vast country that extended over 120,000 square miles (roughly 311,000 square kilometers). Although oil had been both discovered and exported since the 1960s, Oman's gross domestic product (GDP) stood at just $256 million in 1970.[14] The GDP per capita was only $343 in 1970—a fraction of Kuwait's at $3860, and only a third of neighboring Saudi Arabia's in 1970.[15] What's more, Qaboos' father and predecessor, Said bin Taimur, had failed to suppress a rebellion in Dhofar while creating a stifling social environment in which he had banned private cars, forbidden anyone from wearing sunglasses, and jailed anyone caught playing music or smoking in public. Upon taking power, Qaboos lifted these restrictions while initiating a new reform program meant to win the war in Dhofar, while at the same time improving the country's economy and addressing areas of Omani life his father had long overlooked. Qaboos identified education and healthcare as the twin "national pillars" for his development strategy.[16] Both became core national priorities. Qaboos had ample reason to do so as Taimur had devoted few resources to these two sectors, largely leaving them to others. There were just three schools, which served boys only.

During his time in Oman, Phillips was struck by the poor state of healthcare, devoting an entire chapter of *Unknown Oman* to disease and healthcare in the country in the 1950s. In the chapter, he discusses how Omanis used a variety of techniques, including branding each other with hot irons, to address the many illnesses present in Sultanate, including common childhood diseases, intestinal worms, respiratory ailments, malaria, syphilis, and trachoma.[17] He also describes a case where a ten-year-old boy in Muscat, whose father prevented him from being vaccinated, lost his sight after contracting smallpox.[18] Others observed similar conditions. In 1958, a British colonel, upon his arrival in Oman, observed that Muscat was in "a deplorable shape," adding that he had "seen what could be done [for modern healthcare] in Hadhramaut . . . with a revenue about half of what the Sultan of Muscat drew in custom duties."[19] Yet, here, he concluded, "there are no medical services at all."[20]

Twelve years after the colonel made those comments, little had improved. The Omani government paid only 534,282 riyals for health and had just thirteen doctors on salary and just twelve hospital beds. The one modern hospital in the country, a twenty-nine-bed facility built by Petroleum Development Oman (PDO), was restricted to the company's employees and their families.[21] That budget and its restrictions, reflected the core priorities of Taimur, who once observed:

> We don't need hospitals here. Oman is a very poor country which can only support a small population. At present, many children die in infancy and so the population does not increase. If we build more clinics, many more will survive. To what end, to starve?[22]

For ordinary Omanis, there were few viable options. Since 1910, there had been the British-administered Muscat Charitable Hospital, a facility of only fifteen beds.[23] But in March 1970, the British government announced that it would no longer finance the facility.[24] That left the American Mission Hospital. For many decades, a skeleton staff of American missionary doctors and nurses, aided by Omani assistants and Indian nurses, attended to the sick in the 100-bed facility in Mutrah, not far from Muscat.[25] Among the most famous of the missionaries was Donald Bosch, who was awarded the Order of Oman in 1972—the highest honor that can be awarded to a civilian.[26]

That honor reflected the hours of tireless work that he and his colleagues devoted to their patients where conditions were difficult at best. At times there were goats and other animals in the hallways. There was also no electricity and air conditioning—creating significant hazards for surgery and for patients and hospital staff alike during the summer. The hospital was often so crowded that two patients shared a bed, with others cooking meals in the corridors and "sleeping in odd corners."[27] Death rates in the hospital were appallingly high, in large part because many patients arrived at the hospital already extremely sick, having traveled four days or more to reach Mutrah from the interior.[28] There they often faced lines that were hundreds long. Still, the American Mission Hospital, in 1969, "saw 51,836 patients as out-patients, admitted 2,566, and operated on 2,385."[29]

Those numbers reflected the vast need for medical care. In 1958, a British official with nearly two decades of experience in the region, expressed his astonishment at the conditions in the Sultanate, noting "had never seen a people so poverty-stricken or so debilitated with disease capable of treatment and cure."[30] "A visitor to the hinterlands in the 1950s," Fred Halliday reported, 'In the village of Oman there is often not a single healthy inhabitant in sight.'"[31] As Valeri starkly notes, "Pneumonia proved usually fatal for Inner Oman inhabitants because the journey to Mutrah by donkey took so long."[32]

Not surprising the morbidity and mortality rates in Oman were some of the highest in the region—in part earning the country the moniker the "Sick Man of the Gulf."[33] In 1970, according to a 2010 article drawing on MOH statistics, "one out of every eight infants born alive died before reaching their first birthday, and one out of every five died before reaching the age of 5 years."[34] The infant mortality rate was 152 per 1,000 births.[35] In 1975 alone, there were 103 cases of acute poliomyelitis, 102 cases of tetanus, and 43 cases of diphtheria.[36] Other diseases were no less prevalent. In 1975, there were more than 16,000 cases of measles, 14,000 cases of mumps, and 13,000 cases of pertussis.[37]

Those Omanis who survived into adulthood rarely made it into their fifties. Many of those who did suffered from other serious diseases. "Out of every three people in the population, one had an episode of malaria, and out of every thousand persons, thirty were reported to be infected with trachoma, eight with pulmonary tuberculosis, and six with hepatitis."[38] Many Omanis were devastated by these diseases, unable to support themselves or their families. This problem was so acute that Omanis created scores of *waqfs* (pious endowments) to help aid with leprosy and other similar diseases. Present throughout the Sultanate, the *waqfs* used the proceeds from agricultural properties along with the future proceeds from the sale of white lands, or undeveloped urban land in prime locations, to help the sick and indigent in Oman.[39]

The Dhofar Rebellion and Healthcare

No matter how generous those *waqfs* were to ordinary Omanis, they were not enough to address the country's health challenges, especially in Dhofar. There people "lived without any encounter with modern medicine, relying instead on traditional remedies and rituals."[40] British diplomatic documents from the era point this out clearly.[41] Recognizing this need, the Dhofar Liberation Group (DLG) employed modern healthcare to promote their cause against the Omani Sultan—building healthcare centers and training medical professionals in some of the southern mountainous region's poorest areas.[42]

We can also see that rhetoric clearly in *The Hour of Liberation Has Arrived*, the 1974 documentary directed by Lebanese filmmaker Heiny Srour.[43] Throughout the film, Srour, then a PhD student at the Sorbonne, focused on everyday healthcare.[44] In a sketch opening the film, the narrator condemns Taimur "for imposing underdevelopment" on the people of Dhofar while banning "schools, roads, shops, and medical care."[45] In a later sketch, the narrator praises the DLG for improving sanitation and healthcare in Dhofar—despite its limited resources. In particular, the narrator notes the DLG's success in combating a series of horrific diseases that had plagued the region: dysentery, malaria, trachoma, and tuberculosis. But the narrator seems to admit there are challenges and the DLG's efforts are not comprehensive. In fact, he still calls on the nations of the wider Arab world to send as many doctors as possible, for the situation remains extremely desperate.[46]

As the camera shows a man sticking a syringe into a man lying prostrate in a small tent, the audience is told that there is not a single doctor in Dhofar and a shortage of medicines. Just six first-aid volunteers reportedly address the medical needs of everyone in rural and urban areas. Sometimes people in the region must travel vast distances just to be seen. One man is said to have walked nearly 249 miles (400 km) on foot through regions without any roads to get assistance from the DLG's medics for trachoma. By the time he arrived at a place where the medics were providing care, the narrator concludes, it was too late to reverse the progress of the disease.[47]

These and other images from *The Hour of Liberation Has Arrived*, especially the iconic one of a female DLG soldier, helped to make the film a critical success when it was shown in Europe, the United States, and around the world. Notably, that success was harnessed for public health too. The DLG used showings of the film to fundraise and secure supplies for its medical facilities in Dhofar.[48]

The DLG's rhetoric and its ability to fundraise using the film reveal how important it was that Qaboos had already made healthcare a signature national priority. Having taken power and driven out the DLG, the Sultan wanted to clearly lay out his dedication to the health of Omanis throughout the Sultanate, including Dhofar. Such institutional work already occurred in 1970. By 1976 a final decisive victory by the Omani government and allies over the DLG allowed the region to be folded into a larger national project of healthcare development. During the final years of the war in Dhofar, British military engineers fought Dhofar's rebels while building medical clinics and other civilian infrastructure in the region—a program that was designed to help to counter rebel propaganda and aided Oman's success in winning the war in 1976.[49]

Omani Public Health under Qaboos

In one of his first actions in August 1970, Qaboos issued a decree founding the MOH, which officially came into existence in 1971. The ministry launched the first of successive five-year plans in 1976 and oversaw an increase in healthcare spending.[50] In 1970, Oman spent 534,282 riyals on healthcare. Two years later that figure had risen to 4.44 million riyals. Those funds led to an increase in the number of doctors from 13 to 63 and beds from 12 to 562.[51] The MOH also incorporated Bosch and his missionary hospital into Oman's healthcare system. From the start, the MOH benefited from technical assistance from both the British government and the WHO, which has regularly praised the Omani government's efforts on healthcare and has a branch office in the Sultanate.

As the MOH expanded its operations, the ministry enjoyed the strong public support of the Sultan. Throughout the 1970s, he "proudly reported on the progress made in establishing new hospitals, clinics and health centers"[52] in the speeches that he gave on Omani National Day.[53] In these annual speeches, Qaboos often presented his national vision while unveiling new policies. Among the most important of these speeches was the one that he gave in 1975, in which he asserted that every citizen has the right to healthcare. He also detailed the measures that his government had taken since July 1970 to improve the medical system, including opening 13 hospitals, 11 health centers, and 3,400 dispensaries throughout Oman. All of these facilities, he added, "are outfitted with the latest equipment" and staffed by trained medical professionals.[54]

During the speech, Qaboos also voiced a guiding principle of public health that not only marked a sea change from earlier eras, but would also impact the nation well into the twenty-first century. "Since prevention is better than cure," the Sultan explained, his government had provided generous resources for "preventive medicine and immunization against infectious diseases." Oman's youth, he continued, had been prioritized, with "periodic vaccinations that helped reduce the incidence of infectious diseases and improved the health of schoolchildren."[55]

At the same time, Qaboos promised that existing clinics and hospitals throughout the country were to be expanded and supplemented with new facilities. He provided especially detailed information about upcoming upgrades to Dhofar's hospital while promising the war-ravaged region that a new facility with 300 beds would be built there soon. He also reiterated his commitment to Omanization generally and in the healthcare sector, noting that 228 young Omanis were being trained at home and abroad in different medical specialties. In addition, he noted that Omanis now had access to specialized care in mental illness, skin diseases, hearing, neurosurgery, thoracic surgery, and plastic surgery within the Sultanate. And if a specific medical specialty did not exist in the country, he continued, his government would import qualified doctors or arrange for Omanis to get their care overseas.[56]

Although Qaboos did not stress the nation's medical system as prominently in the Omani National Day speeches that he gave after 1980,[57] his government continued to invest heavily in public healthcare which benefited from government oil revenues. Despite the heavy burdens of combating the rebellion in Dhofar,[58] Oman's national GDP grew from $260 million riyals in 1970 to $6.34 billion riyals in 1980.[59] Although Oman's population grew by a third in the 1970s, GDP per capita income also rose from $343 riyals in 1970 to $5,284 riyals in 1980.[60] Over the next thirty years, the economy continued to grow, and, in 2016, Oman's GDP had reached $173.1 billion riyals and its GDP per capita was $43,700 riyals, the thirty-fifth highest in the world in 2016.[61]

Those funds permitted the MOH to build facilities from Muscat to Mudayy, including a twenty-four-bed hospital on Masirah Island, one of the "most remote" regions in the Sultanate.[62] Conveys were also sent deep into Dhofar's interior to bring healthcare to the Bedouin communities. When the Harasiis, a camel and goat herding community in Dhofar, asked why they should be vaccinated against a set of common childhood diseases being targeted by the WHO, Omani officials were clear: "the Sultan of Oman wishes to see all Omanis immunized against these diseases."[63] Thanks in part to these efforts, Oman, as early as the 1980s, was becoming a country whose healthcare system increasingly resembled that of Kuwait and the other oil-producing nations that were sufficiently more advanced when Qaboos staged his coup. In 1986, the country spent nearly 90 million Omani riyals (approximately $233 million) annually on healthcare, permitting Muscat to employ 1,096 doctors and provide access to 3,348 hospital beds.[64] In 1990, Sultan Qaboos officially opened the University Hospital at Sultan Qaboos University,[65] which he had promised, during his Omani National Day speech in 1988, "would ensure an unprecedented level of available care" in the country.[66] A quarter of a century later, Oman boasted sixty-six public and private hospitals with state-of-the-art medical technology.[67] A new $1 billion International Medical City is now under construction in Salalah, Dhofar's largest city.[68]

Today, there is an extensive network of public and private healthcare facilities of various sizes in the country. Together these facilities help to provide near universal primary care to the entire country—upholding the promise Qaboos made in his Omani National Day speech in 1975 and fulfilling a central pillar of Oman's Basic Law, effectively the Sultanate's constitution. In the document, which was first promulgated in 1996 and amended in 2011, the state guarantees healthcare to all Omani citizens, while assuming responsibility for maintaining public health and preventing disease.[69] As part of achieving that goal, the government has continued to import scores of doctors from overseas while educating Omanis at the medical school at Sultan Qaboos University along with the Omani Medical College, a private university affiliated with West Virginia University.[70]

Those facilities and the staff they have trained have had an impressive impact on the daily lives of Omanis. The nation's infant mortality rate had dropped by the 2000s to 10.2 per 1,000 births, while the under-five mortality rate had dropped by 94 percent since the 1970s—a number that the WHO observed was "one of the fastest drops in infant mortality on record."[71] The government has also made significant investments in immunizations. Consequently, cases of measles fell from 39,000 in 1981 to 317 in 1987, while pertussis dropped from 2,700 cases in 1982 to just five in 1987.[72] As a British doctor noted in 1987, the Omani rates of immunizations were better than those of the United Kingdom.[73]

Oman has made similarly impressive progress with other communicable diseases. While malaria was widespread in the 1970s and there were 32,720 cases in 1990, there were less than a thousand cases in 2008. The number of cases of pulmonary tuberculosis has declined from 6,000 in 1975 to just 217 cases in 2007.[74] Even larger declines were witnessed in hepatitis and trachoma: "5,000 cases of hepatitis and 24,000 of trachoma were reported in 1975 compared to 772 and 72 cases, respectively, in 2008."[75]

Some diseases have been effectively eliminated. There have been no reported cases of poliomyelitis since 1993.[76] Leprosy in Oman has declined to one case per 100,000 people. That number is low enough that the disease is no longer considered a public health problem in the country—a sea change for a bacterial infection that was once a prominent part of public life throughout every region of the country. Indeed, the situation could not have been more different than the one that Phillips had seen decades earlier when he wrote *Unknown Oman*.

Smoking, Religion, and Public Health

From the early 1980s, however, doctors and senior health officials recognized that rising rates of smoking could decimate the Sultanate's rapid modernization, its healthcare system, and its progress in combating disease generally. A decade earlier, tobacco executives had targeted the Sultanate and several other oil-exporting states in the Middle East as new markets. In their eyes, smoking was, in the words of one executive, a "necessary evil"[77] of the Sultanate's program of modernization and rising dependence on foreign workers.

Their view was supported by detailed studies of young Omanis[78] and the rising number of cigarettes imported and sold in the country. Between 1972 and 1980, the number of imported cigarettes jumped from 157 million cigarettes[79] to a billion cigarettes a year by 1980.[80] Over the next two decades, imports skyrocketed to over 16 billion pieces a year,[81] representing 7 percent of Oman's total trade.[82] While many of the cigarettes entering Oman were re-exported to Iran, which had banned Western cigarettes following the 1979 Islamic Revolution, ever more people within the Sultanate were taking up smoking.

Despite the threat posed by cigarettes and smoking, Omani government policy on smoking only began to shift in the 2000s after Al-Khalili fully joined the public debate on smoking in Oman, arguing decisively in Arabic and in English that smoking was inconsistent with Islam. His decision built on a consensus among Muslim scholars that smoking was *haram* (forbidden) along with a powerful new force in the country—namely, urban educated Omanis, who were a natural market for tobacco companies while also being the core base of support for the Grand Mufti's vision of Islam and society. They, along with the Omani government, would increasingly seek his support on medical-related issues.

When Al-Khalili was appointed Grand Mufti in 1975 at the age of 33, he was not a prominent figure and focused largely on the apolitical aspects of the Omani–Ibadi tradition.[83] For instance, in 1987, he stated that smoking and tobacco were unlawful, "arguing that Islam forbids everything which causes damage to body, mind or health and prohibits everything which causes financial burdens or undermines one's honor."[84] "If it is proved that tobacco causes cancer," he continued, "a smoker will be equal to a person who takes poison."[85] In other words, Al-Khalili is suggesting that a smoker could be analogous to a person using poison to commit suicide—both of which are clearly prohibited by the Qur'an and hadith (sayings of the Prophet Muhammad) from Bukhari.[86]

Initially, these types of argument did not resonate with Omani society, and, by his own admission, there was little interest in his speeches. This dynamic began to change in the 1980s with the intersection of two key events. The first was Al-Khalili's public defense, in 1987, of Omanis and their faith against the charge made by Sheikh Abdul Aziz ibn Abdullah bin Baz (Ibn Baz), a leading Saudi cleric and scholar, that Ibadis were infidels. As Dale Eickelman has argued, the Grand Mufti's defense endeared him to a rising generation of educated professionals.[87] They were the first large group of Omanis to complete both secondary and university education, a key pillar of the state's post-1970 program of modernization.[88]

Their vision of Islam also conformed to the one Qaboos had voiced in public since he had ascended to the throne in 1970. In his public remarks, the Sultan often quoted scripture and linked Islam to key national priorities along with the broader national program of renewal and renaissance under his leadership.[89] He stressed that Islam was compatible with the modern world, arguing it stood for "tolerance, morality, openness . . . knowledge and thought."[90] At the same time, Qaboos argued that there were aspects of contemporary life that were "morally and physically damaging" to Omani society and could hinder the Sultanate's ability to maintain its traditions—unless its religious figures understood the pressures and problems of modern life.[91] Consequently, in his 1977 Omani National Day Speech, the Sultan called for the inclusion of secular subjects in religious training "in order to produce mature teachers of Islam."[92] These types of religious teachers, the Sultan argued, would be "familiar with the ways of modern society and will be qualified to provide our people[93]—especially our young people—with the moral and spiritual guidance they must have."[94]

The Sultan's approach worked well. The Omani professionals who came of age in the 1980s were the type of young people who Western tobacco companies usually convinced to become loyal smokers: they were better educated in modern subjects and wealthier than earlier generations of Omanis. But these Omanis were also better educated in their faith and eager to engage the Mufti and the wider world on critical cultural and social questions. By the 1990s, the sheikh, whose rhetoric used Islamic discourse to address these questions, had firmly established himself as a respected national leader with a wide following among an increasingly literate young society—just as Qaboos hoped he and other religious leaders would do.[95]

It is in this context that we should evaluate his decision in the late 1990s and the twenty-first century to issue multiple *fatwas* on smoking, the first of which was a summary verdict issued in 2000 in conjunction with Islamic scholars around the world, but is a recognizably Ibadi document. The second, which is in Arabic, is a bit longer. But both decisions build on the logic of his 1987 decision on smoking along with *Ijma* (the consensus of Islamic scholars on a given topic) and *Qiyas* (analogy using hadith). As Valarie Hoffman-Ladd has shown, these two concepts, both of which are core parts of Islam's legal tradition, were also central to the thinking of Abu Muslim Al-Bahlani[96]—a leading poet and modern scholar of Ibadi Islam.[97]

Notably, Al-Khalili opens his first opinion by stating that there is widespread consensus among Muslims that their faith prohibits smoking, because "it is well known that smoking causes cancer and cardiovascular diseases and seventy ailments."[98] This fact allows Al-Khalili to turn to analogy, a more powerful weapon that was not available to him in 1987.

Within this framework, smoking is analogous to a person committing suicide—an act he shows that is prohibited by the Qur'an: "Do not kill yourself for God almighty is most merciful to you."[99] He then cites two hadith to reinforce his argument. In the first one, the Prophet Muhammad condemns those who commit suicide to eternal hell.[100] In the second, He condemns committing suicide by poison: "One who sips poison will eternally sip poison on the day of final judgement."[101]

But Al-Khalili does not limit his argument to the finer points of Islamic law and modern science and seeks to make a larger point: smoking corrupts society by eroding the moral fabric governing everyday human life. In the first opinion, he stresses how smoking wastes money and negatively affects innocent non-smokers through second-hand smoke.[102]

Al-Khalili built on these arguments in a third opinion issued in 2013 titled "smoking is the plague of plagues."[103] Throughout, he draws on science and Islamic jurisprudence to challenge the morality of Egyptian medical professionals along with an Islamic jurist who had refused to label smoking as inconsistent with Islam. While he does not name the jurist, Al-Khalili says that the scholar headed the most prominent Islamic institution in the world, undoubtedly Al-Azhar in Cairo, Egypt. One person who fits this description is Sheikh Muhammad Sayyid al-Tantawi. He was the Grand Imam of Al-Azhar from 1996 to 2010 and did not view smoking as *haram*. For instance, he noted on his weekly television show in Saudi Arabia in 1988 that: "I am unable to equate the smoking of cigarettes with the drinking of a glass of alcohol. Alcohol is clearly forbidden and only God can forbid things. It may well be that it is better not to smoke and to give it up, but it is not a sin in the sense as is drinking alcohol."[104]

Whether or not Al-Khalili meant Al-Tantawi, the argument of his *fatwa* is clearly aimed at this type of argument. In the opening, he argues that the number of deaths linked to smoking has increased exponentially and is expected to do so in the future, reaching 10 million annually, a number that outpaced the deaths caused by either illicit drugs or the acquired immunodeficiency syndrome (AIDS). He also observes that smoking causes strokes, heart disease, liver disease, and other deadly maladies. Mirroring the arguments he made in his 2000 *fatwa*, Al-Khalili concludes that smoking is a form of self-poisoning, an act that is clearly a sin, just as forbidden as drinking alcohol under Islamic law. In a nod to his earlier writings, he cites the same Qur'anic passages and hadith that he did in his 2000 decision, including the warning that those who drink risked being condemned to the fire of hell.

These types of warnings—when paired with increasing tobacco cessation campaigns in the private and public sectors—have had an effect. In 2017, an article on cigarettes and Oman's public health system in the *Oman Medical Journal* observed that the country has the "lowest tobacco use among the GCC states and the Eastern Mediterranean region."[105] The country had witnessed a significant shift since the 1990s.

"This *Fatwa* Allowed for Flexibility to Proceed"

By the time that article was published, Omani physicians had already partnered with the Grand Mufti to investigate how he and other religious leaders could help the country's medical system improve public health. In 2012, for instance, Sultan Qaboos University Hospital hosted "The First Medical and Theological Seminar." The one-day conference discussed how Sharia

(Islamic law) could inform how physicians and topologists approach a variety of medical issues: abortion, genetic disorders, resuscitation, and patients with chronic diseases. Among those who attended were Al-Khalili and physicians from the hospitals of the Health and Defense ministries along with the Royal Oman Police Hospital.[106]

Those discussions built on the role that the Mufti had played in addressing smoking and other public health threats, including communicable diseases such as HIV-AIDS. That disease appeared in the Sultanate in 1984, thanks in part to contaminated blood transfusions imported from overseas along with overseas travels and exchanges.[107] In response, Oman adopted a comprehensive national response featuring public education, free treatment, and other mitigation measures.[108] Again, Al-Khalili and his colleagues have filled a key public role by issuing judicial opinions responding to society's basic questions about the disease and how those infected with it should interact with the rest of society.

Among the most important of these questions have been could a married couple, one of whom has AIDS, cohabitate? Could Omanis infected with AIDS study, work, and interact with others in society? In responding to these questions, Al-Khalili and his colleagues blended basic science and advice on AIDS with injunctions drawn from Islam, such as the avoidance of disease. They even advise HIV-infected individuals to protect their sperm from infecting others. But what is most striking is the simple standard he calls on his fellow Omanis to use with those infected with AIDS and similar diseases: does an action infect others or transmit the disease? If the answer is yes, then the infected individual must avoid others. Otherwise, he or she may freely interact with others and is accountable to the same Islamic principles and rules as anyone else.[109] Similar advice is provided for how to address pregnancies in HIV-infected women: will the mother pass on HIV to her unborn child?[110]

Al-Khalili and Oman's other religious scholars have also found themselves playing a key role in acute, short-term public health emergencies. A good example was when an Ebola outbreak in 2014 and 2015 spread very rapidly in West Africa, a region with deep ties to Oman. Not only do many Omanis frequently travel to and from the region, but there are many students and workers in the Sultanate who are West African. As officials in the MOH undertook exercises and worked on a strategy to protect Oman from Ebola, they realized that Omani funeral rites could serve as a mechanism to spread the disease.[111] Those rights, which are tied to the Sharia, call on relatives of a deceased person to pray for and to wash the deceased at close quarters in his or her home—a dangerous task for anyone handling a person who has died from Ebola: the disease can be spread easily via contact with infected bodies, body fluids, contaminated clothing, and other personal items.[112]

Because there was little in the published medical literature that addressed the issue, Dr. Hilal bin Saif Mohammad al-Hishami, an MOH communicable diseases specialist, requested a special *fatwa* on the matter from Al-Kharusi, again, the Omani Assistant Grand Mufti. Today, an English-language version of the *fatwa* is prominently featured on the MOH's website along with other documents, most of which are in English as well. This was likely a reflection of the fact that Omani doctors are educated in English and have worked alongside English-speaking foreigners in Oman's medical system.

The three-page *fatwa*, which is written on the official letterhead of the Grand Mufti, reads far more like an official business memorandum, complete with an "RE:" line. It is also addressed to Al-Hishami. Al-Kharusi does not directly cite Qur'anic passages or hadith, instead, he cites, only once and briefly, the view of "some" unnamed Muslim scholars. Still, he adopts much of the style as Al-Khalili, seeking multiple avenues by which Omanis can reconcile their Islamic principles with science. To do that, he grounds his argument in two guiding principles. First, all Muslims "deserve to be washed, enshrouded, prayed for, and buried in accordance with Islamic teaching."[113] Second, he notes, Islamic law takes "exigency" into consideration and "one of its high objectives is to save lives and preserve souls."[114]

Throughout the rest of the document, the Assistant Grand Mufti utilizes these principles to provide the ministry with multiple and detailed approaches to how medical professionals should bury those who have died from Ebola and counsel their grieving families. These approaches include holding small funerals behind glass barriers where trained staff would wash the body with disinfectant or even cancelling a funeral and praying for the deceased in absentia. "We agree with you," Al-Kharusi reiterates at the end of the document, "on the importance of sensitizing the community about preventative measures, and the necessary ways and means to cope with the disease." Ultimately, he calls on "Allah to ward off every plague, and to ordain health, safety and well-being for everyone."[115]

That work proved to be immensely valuable to Omani public health. As senior MOH officials noted in the *Journal of Infection and Public Health* in 2016, Al-Kharusi's *fatwa* "allowed" the "flexibility" for them "to proceed based on a medical assessment of the risk of infection transmission" for anyone who had perished of Ebola or other highly infectious diseases.[116] MOH officials then developed new guidelines by which trained healthcare workers would disinfect and transport the dead body to a grave that is at least 6.5 feet (2 meters) deep. Only after the grave had been covered would a prayer ceremony occur with a limited number of people related to the deceased.[117]

Overall, Al-Kharusi's *fatwa* allowed the nation's medical professionals to address a serious challenge to Oman's public health in a manner that respected the country's traditions and values, and, even more importantly, was likely to be accepted as legitimate by most of the people. The document also showed the wisdom of Qaboos' decision, made decades earlier, to promote a vision of Islam compatible with the contemporary world while insisting that Omani religious leaders be well versed in modern subjects. Through his *fatwa*, the Oxford-educated Al-Kharusi had shown, to paraphrase the Sultan, that he was "familiar with the ways of modern society" and "qualified to provide" the "moral and spiritual guidance" that his fellow citizens needed in a time of crisis.[118] In short, Al-Kharusi was fulfilling his monarch's vision for how a religious leader should serve the nation in the contemporary world.

Covid-19

Al-Khurusi's skills along with the new regulations unveiled in his *fatwa* would become even more important a few years later with the rise of Covid-19. The first cases of the virus in the Sultanate appeared in February 2020, only weeks into the new reign of Sultan Haitham, who had succeeded Sultan Qaboos in early 2020. A month later the Sultan formed a supreme committee to direct the country's response to the pandemic at home and abroad. In short order, the committee implemented a series of measures meant to curb the spread of the virus, including closing non-essential businesses, mosques and other houses of worship, schools, and all international borders. The borders between states in Oman were closed as well.[119]

While Omani authorities accelerated programs promoting Omanization in the medical system during the pandemic,[120] they initially made Covid-19 tests and treatments free and accessible to everyone residing in Oman, including the vast expatriate population.[121] Those policies toward non-Omanis built on published studies and the recommendations of public health professionals. In an article published in the June 2020 issue of the *Oman Journal of Medicine*, a group of five doctors and senior MOH officials stressed the urgent need for measures "to protect and reduce transmission and symptom progression of COVID-19 in vulnerable populations, including among both elderly people and foreign-born individuals living in crowded housing."[122] In addition, the MOH used its social media accounts to disseminate information in a variety of Asian, Middle Eastern, and Western languages.[123] There have even been tweets in sign language.[124]

Oman's Muslim clerics reinforced these messages broadly, mirroring the type of public health messages that they had given in the past. In an interview with the *Times of Oman* in April 2020, Al-Kharusi called on Muslims to perform their prayers at home during Ramadan while always listening to the advice of doctors, reminding them that they could fast after Ramadan if needed. At the same time, he reminded readers that fasting, provided a person is healthy, has been scientifically proven to aid the body's immune system.[125]

Al-Khalili reinforced Al-Kharusi's words on social media and in his writing. On Twitter, the Mufti called on everyone to adhere strictly to new safety regimes, adding "men and women, to safeguard themselves, their families, their communities, and their nation, should refrain from getting together with others."[126] He also called on Omanis "to ward off the effects of the pandemic by committing to the safety norms."[127] During Eid, Al-Khalili, on his Twitter account, called on Muslims to exchange congratulatory messages by phone or text while refraining from holding large gatherings.[128]

Other Twitter accounts associated with the Mufti, such as @kaleematayba, featured pictures of the Mufti practicing social distancing[129] along with messages reminding Omanis to be safe.[130] One of these tweets even had a picture of a red prohibition over a picture of two hands griped in a handshake with the message that Omanis should refrain from shaking hands to protect their health.[131] Those accounts also promoted a *fatwa* that Al-Khalili wrote about the virus in April 2020 that worked to contextualize the virus for Omanis, providing them with an Islamic vision for the spread of the virus in the contemporary world and how they could harness their faith to combat it. Although the *fatwa* was not dated, it drew on many of the same type of sources that the Mufti's other *fatwa*s on public health have, such as the Qur'an and hadith, while discussing both international relations and the dangers of smoking.[132]

As media reports from the time noted, Al-Khalili's words carried weight, not only among other clerics but also among ordinary Omanis, such as Sleyyem Khalaf, an ordinary government employee, who told the *Muscat Daily* that he was closely following the Mufti's words on Covid-19.[133] This advice proved critical, especially in the early stage of the global pandemic during the summer of 2020 when the Sultanate's success at combating the spread of the virus stood out regionally and internationally, especially in comparison with nations with higher per capita incomes and far more outwardly robust healthcare systems.[134] In addition, Al-Kharusi's *fatwa* on burying victims of Ebola allowed Oman to avoid a contentious question that troubled Muslim societies in Africa and Asia in 2020—namely, how to safely bury individuals who had died of Covid-19 while respecting Muslim burial principles.[135]

A year later the Sultanate's leaders continued to utilize the same integrated public health strategy to deal with the pandemic, which had killed just over 2,000 Omanis, about 46 per 100,000 people—a number that is lower than that of many wealthy Western nations.[136] Oman's medical professionals have prioritized preventative medicine and vaccines, following the model Qaboos first championed in the 1970s. Muscat was one of the first governments to join the Covid-19 Vaccines Global Access (or COVAX), the global coalition working with the WHO to equitably distribute Covid-19 vaccines.[137] Thanks in part to that partnership, by April 2021, more than 90 percent of healthcare workers in Oman were vaccinated, with detailed plans ready to vaccinate 70 percent of the country's population by late 2021.[138] Religious leaders have consistently lent their credibility to these initiatives, again just as Qaboos would have hoped. Al-Khalili signed an Organization of Islamic Cooperation *fatwa* urging the world's Muslims to take Covid-19 vaccines in late February 2021,[139] while social media publicized his decision to be vaccinated in early March 2021.[140] During his media appearances, Al-Kharusi has fielded questions about Covid-19 and the vaccines that combat it, employing scientific data to support his religious arguments. For instance, when he was asked on TV in April 2021 whether inoculation interfered with fasting during Ramadan, the Assistant Mufti answered that it did not, adding that he regularly checked studies on AstraZeneca and Pfizer—the two Covid-19 vaccines being used in the Sultanate.[141]

Conclusion

One of Qaboos' earliest actions upon taking power in 1970 was to create the MOH. Over the following decades, his government sought to use the country's wealth from oil to address the widespread deficiencies in healthcare while eliminating the diseases that had long plagued Omanis. While the system faces a number of key regional and other challenges,[142] the Sultanate's response to the Covid-19 pandemic during the year after Qaboos' death suggests that the investments that he and others made in healthcare and medicine during the Omani Renaissance have yielded positive results.

Throughout that era, Qaboos stressed that Islam is not only consistent with modernity, but that religious leaders should also be fluent in contemporary ideas and subjects—a framework that we can see clearly in the works of Omani jurists on public health. During that time, they have not treated modern medicine or science as competing sources of knowledge with Islam—as many argue they are. Instead, Al-Khalili and others have used the insights of science and medicine as potent tools to reinforce their arguments, grounded in Islam, aimed at Oman's transforming society. There has been a burgeoning audience in the Sultanate for a vision of Islam fully compatible with modernity, including modern medicine and science.[143] Within this sociocultural context, it is just as reasonable to use a scientific study to justify observing Qur'anic injunctions during Ramadan as it is to secure a *fatwa* to implement scientifically-sound procedures to combat a communicable disease.

The refusal of Omanis to treat Islam and modernity as separate and competing forces in some ways mirrors Martin Luther King Jr.'s insight in the 1960s on how "integration" and "desegregation" might work in American society. "It is not either/or," King once explained, "it is both/and."[144] The key thing to understand is that however much logic may constantly cry "foul," an entity that appears to be contradictory to another entity may neither eliminate its opposite nor force it into some sort of new "synthesis." It may exist alongside it in a not necessarily harmonious, ongoing balance.

"The test of a first-rate intelligence," F. Scott Fitzgerald observes in *The Crack Up*, "is the ability to hold two opposing ideas in mind at the same time and still retain the ability to function."[145] "One should," he adds, "be able to see that things are desperate yet be determined to make them otherwise."[146] For decades, Omanis have implicitly followed Fitzgerald's advice, drawing on Ibadi Islamic jurisprudence and modern medicine and science to make a desperate public health situation better. Through their actions, these Omanis have, to paraphrase the great American writer, seen "the improbable, the implausible, often the 'impossible,' come true."[147]

Notes

1. Ministry of Health, Sultanate of Oman, *The 8th Five-Year Plan For Health Development (2011–2015)* (Muscat: Ministry of Health, 2010), 4, available at: http://staging.nationalplanningcycles.org/sites/default/files/country_docs/Oman/five_year_plan_for_health_development_2011-2015.pdf, last accessed May 23, 2021.

2. "Fatwa: Dawr as-Islam fi al-Wiqaya min marad al-Aids" ("Fatwa: The Role of Islam in Preventing AIDS"), Dar al-Iftaʻ, available at: https://iftaa.om/fatwa_dis-462-1914.html#content, last accessed February 23, 2021.

3. Jeremy Jones and Nicholas Ridout, *A History of Modern Oman* (Cambridge: Cambridge University Press, 2015), 162.

4. Richard Smith, "Health Service Profiles: Oman: Leaping Across the Centuries," *BMJ* 297 (6647) (August 20–27, 1988), 540.

5. Yahya M. al-Farsi and Shahid M. al-Balushi, "Go Lean, Get Leaner: The Application of Lean Management in Omani Healthcare," *Sultan Qaboos University Medical Journal* 18(4) (2018): 431; Ajay Tandon, Christopher J. L. Murray, Jeremy A. Lauer, and David B. Evans, "Measuring Overall Health System Performance for 191 Countries," *World Health Organization*, available at: https://www.who.int/healthinfo/paper30.pdf, 18, last accessed February 23, 2021.

6. Marc Valeri, *Oman: Politics and Society in the Qaboos State* (London: Hurst, 2017), 80.

7. Ahmed al-Mandari, "Oman," in Jeffrey Braithwaite, Yukhiro Matsuyama, Russel Manyon, and Julie Johnson (eds.), *Healthcare Reform, Quality and Safety: Perspectives, Participants and Partnerships in 30 Countries* (New York: Routledge,

2016), 47; Dawn Chatty, "Rejecting Authenticity in the Desert Landscapes of the Modern Middle East: Development Processes in the Jiddat il-Harasiis, Oman," in Sherine Hafez and Susan Slyomovics (eds.), *Anthropology of the Middle East and North Africa: Into the New Millennium* (Bloomington: Indiana University Press, 2013), 154.

8. Sheikh Kahlan al-Kharusi, "Fatwa on How to Deal with Those Who Die of Ebola," April 2, 2015, available at: https://www.moh.gov.om/documents/236878/0/Fatwa+communicable+diseases/1f352660-b26a-4b95-82dd-2e2b2e9e09ea, last accessed February 23, 2021.

9. For example, see Omani Ministry of Health, Twitter post, July 8. 2020, 12:01 am, available at: https://twitter.com/OmaniMOH.

10. Linda Pappas Funsch, *Oman Reborn* (New York: Palgrave Macmillan, 2015), 71; Carol Riphenburg, *Oman: Political Development in a Changing World* (Westport, CT: Praeger, 1998), 91–92.

11. Michael Hudson, *Arab Politics: The Search for Legitimacy* (New Haven, CT: Yale University Press, 1977), 207.

12. Funsch, *Oman Reborn*, 49.

13. During his time in Oman, Phillips developed close ties with Sultan Said bin Taimur. In the opening page of *Unknown Arabia*, Phillips writes that the text is "In Honor of His Majesty Sultan Said bin Taimur Abul Said." Wendell Phillips, *Unknown Oman* (London: Longman, 1966), V.

14. MEED Editorial, "Reflecting on 40 Years of Sultan Qaboos' Rule," *Middle East Economic Digest*, July 20, 2010, available at: https://www.meed.com/reflecting-on-40-years-of-sultan-qaboos-rule, last accessed February 23, 2021

15. Data on GDP per capita in this era is drawn from data available at https://www.macrotrends.net, last accessed February 1, 2021.

16. Funsch, *Oman Reborn*, 89.

17. Phillips, *Unknown Oman*, 60–69.

18. Phillips, *Unknown Oman*, 61.

19. John Townsend, *Oman: The Making of a Modern State* (New York: St. Martin's Press, 1977), 147.

20. Townsend, *Oman*, 147.

21. Smith, "Health Service Profiles: Oman," 541.

22. Valeri, *Oman: Politics and Society in the Qaboos State*, 63. For their part, Jones and Ridout challenge Valeri's framework, arguing that Taimur was planning on building more hospitals in 1970. Jones and Ridout, *A History of Modern Oman*, 164.

23. Christopher Grant and Nayil al-Kindy, "Surgery in Oman," *Archives of Surgery* 140(1) (2005): 22, available at: https://jamanetwork.com/journals/jamasurgery/fullarticle/508280, last accessed February 24, 2021.

24. Hugh Arbuthnott, Terence Clark, and Richard Muir, *British Missions around the Gulf, 1575–2005: Iran, Iraq, Kuwait, Oman* (Folkstone: Global Oriental, 2008), 244.

25. Smith, "Health Service Profiles: Oman," 541.

26. "Renowned Surgeon Bosch Passes Away," *Khaleej Times*, February 9, 2012, available at: https://www.khaleejtimes.com/region/renowned-surgeon-bosch-passes-away, last accessed February 23, 2021.

27. Donald Bosch and Eloise Bosch, *The Doctor and the Teacher: 1955–1970: Memoirs of Dr. Donald and Eloise Bosch* (Lexington, KY: Apex, 2000), 19.

28. Bosch and Bosch, *The Doctor and the Teacher*, 19.

29. Smith, "Health Service Profiles: Oman," 540.

30. Townsend, *Oman: The Making of a Modern State*, 147.

31. Fred Halliday, *Arabia Without Sultans*, rev. edn. (London: Saqi, 2001), 275.

32. Valeri, *Oman: Politics and Society in the Qaboos State*, 63.

33. Funsch, *Oman Reborn*, 49, 189.

34. Moeness M. Alshishtawy, "Four Decades of Progress: Evolution of the health system in Oman," *Sultan Qaboos University Medical Journal* 10(1) (2010): 12, available at: https://www.ncbi.nlm.nih.gov/pmc/articles/PMC3074664, last accessed June 4, 2021.

35. The World Bank, "Infant Mortality Rate per 1,000 live births: Oman," available at: https://data.worldbank.org/indicator/SP.DYN.IMRT.IN?locations=OM, last accessed February 23, 2021.

36. Alshishtawy, "Four Decades of Progress," 18.

37. Alshishtawy, "Four Decades of Progress," 19.

38. Alshishtawy, "Four Decades of Progress," 12.

39. "Fatwa: Hukm bay'a al-Waqf wa Naqlihi 'an Mawdi'hi" ("Fatwa: Ruling on the Selling of Waqf and Moving it from its Location"), Dar al-Ifta', available at: https://iftaa.om/fatwa_dis-617-3687.html#content, last accessed February 23, 2021. For more on the issue of white lands in the Gulf, see Mamdouh Shouman, "Deserts in the City: White Land and Regime Survival in the Gulf," PhD dissertation, Georgia State University, 2017), available at: https://scholarworks.gsu.edu/political_science_diss/46, last accessed February 23, 2021.

40. Abdel Razzaq Takriti, *Monsoon Revolution: Republicans, Sultans, and Empires in Oman 1965–1976* (Oxford: Oxford University Press, 2013), 44.

41. See Joint Intelligence Staff HQ British Forces Gulf, "Possible Effects of RAF Sallah Arising from Threats to the Sultan in Dhofar," January 20, 1969, 163–170, available at: https://www.agda.ae/en/catalogue/tna/fo/1016/804/n/165, last accessed February 23, 2021.

42. Khalid M. al-Azri, *Social and Gender Inequality in Oman: The Power of Religious and Political Tradition* (New York: Routledge, 2012), 101.

43. Heiny Srour, *The Hour of Liberation Has Arrived*, directed by Heiny Srour, Dhofar, Oman, 1974, Film.

44. Srour, *The Hour of Liberation Has Arrived*.

45. Srour, *The Hour of Liberation Has Arrived*.

46. Srour, *The Hour of Liberation Has Arrived*.

47. Srour, *The Hour of Liberation Has Arrived*.

48. Takriti, *Monsoon Revolution*, 242.

49. Walter C. Ladwig III, "Supporting Allies in Counterinsurgency: Britain and the Dhofar Rebellion," *Small Wars & Insurgencies* 19(1) (2008): 72.

50. Alshishtawy, "Four Decades of Progress," 12.

51. Smith, "Health Service Profiles: Oman," 540.

52. Joseph A. Kéchichian, "A Vision of Oman: State of the Sultanate Speeches by Qaboos bin Said, 1970–2006," *Middle East Policy* 15(3) (2008): 115.

53. Omanis celebrate their national day annually on November 18—the date of Qaboos' birthday and the day that Imam Sultan bin Saif, in 1650, led a rebellion that expelled the Portuguese from Oman and its ports.

54. Sultan Qaboos, "Khatab Sahab Aljalalat ila as-Sha'ab 26-11-1975" ("His Majesty's Speech to the People"), available at: https://bit.ly/2RLrHkZ, last accessed May 24, 2021.

55. Sultan Qaboos, "Khatab Sahab Aljalalat ila as-Sha'ab 26-11-1975."

56. Sultan Qaboos, "Khatab Sahab Aljalalat ila as-Sha'ab 26-11-1975."

57. Kéchichian, "A Vision of Oman," 116.

58. Al-Azri, *Social and Gender Inequality in Oman*, 103.

59. Dudley, "Reflecting on 40 Years of Sultan Qaboos' Rule."

60. Dudley, "Reflecting on 40 Years of Sultan Qaboos' Rule."

61. Central Intelligence Agency, s.v. "Oman," available at: https://www.cia.gov/the-world-factbook/countries/oman, last accessed February 23, 2021.

62. Kéchichian, "A Vision of Oman," 116.

63. Chatty, "Rejecting Authenticity," 154.

64. Smith, "Health Service Profiles: Oman," 540.

65. Sultan Qaboos University Hospital, "Iftah Mustashfa Jam'at Sultan Qaboos" ("Opening of Sultan Qaboos University Hospital"), YouTube video, 1:00 min,

July 14, 2020, available at: https://www.youtube.com/watch?v=h5DoRPLtrjQ, last accessed May 27, 2021.

66. Kéchichian, "A Vision of Oman," 116.

67. Funsch, *Oman Reborn*, 96.

68. "$1bn International Medical City to Open in Oman," *Asian Healthcare and Hospital Management*, available at: https://www.asianhhm.com/projects/international-medical-city-open-oman, last accessed February 23, 2021.

69. Funsch, *Oman Reborn*, 96.

70. Grant and Al-Kindy, "Surgery in Oman," 23.

71. Allen G. Hill, Adaline Z. Muyeed, and Jawad A al-Lawati (eds.), *The Mortality and Health Transitions in Oman: Patterns and Processes* (Muscat: WHO Regional Office for the Eastern Mediterranean and UNICEF, 2000), available at: https://www.unicef.org/french/evaldatabase/files/2000_Oman_health_transition_rec_347399.pdf, 2.41, last accessed February 23, 2021.

72. Smith, "Health Service Profiles: Oman," 541.

73. Smith, "Health Service Profiles: Oman," 541.

74. Alshishtawy, "Four Decades of Progress," 19.

75. Alshishtawy, "Four Decades of Progress," 19.

76. Alshishtawy, "Four Decades of Progress," 18.

77. Bisharah Baroudi, "META Priorities 1992–1993," Dubai 1991, 3, available at: http://industrydocuments.library.ucsf.edu/tobacco/docs/skmv0196, last accessed February 23, 2021.

78. Brown and Williams International Marketing Research Department, *The 1979 Oman Basic Survey: Project #1979–6* (Louisville, KY: Brown and Williams, 1979), 55, https://www.industrydocumentslibrary.ucsf.edu/tobacco/docs/#id=gncd0138, date accessed February 23, 2021.

79. P. N. Lee, *Cigarette Consumption in Various Countries: A Summary of Maxwell's Data by Country: 1960–1977* (London: n.p., 1979), 62, available at: http://industrydocuments.library.ucsf.edu/tobacco/docs/qfbb0196, last accessed February 23, 2021.

80. Philip Morris International, *Philip Morris International Fact Book* (London: n.p., 1983), 16, available at: http://industrydocuments.library.ucsf.edu/tobacco/docs/pzgl0000, last accessed February 23, 2021.

81. Anonymous, *Iran*, 2000, 11, available at: https://www.industrydocumentslibrary.ucsf.edu/tobacco/docs/#id=nghk0189, last accessed February 23, 2021.

82. Oleh Havrylyshyn and Peter Kunzel, *International Monetary Fund Working Paper: Intra-Industry Trade of Arab Countries: An Indicator of Potential Competitiveness* (Washington, DC: International Monetary Fund, 1997), 10, available

at: http://www.imf.org/external/pubs/ft/wp/wp9747.pdf, last accessed February 23, 2021.

83. Al-Azri, *Social and Gender Inequality in Oman*, 104.
84. Tobacco Information Center, "Communication-The Grand Mufti Speaks on Smoking," *Infotopics* 6(7) (July 31, 1987), 31, available at: https://www.industrydocumentslibrary.ucsf.edu/tobacco/docs/#id=gsjw0117, last accessed February 23, 2021.
85. Tobacco Information Center, "Communication," 31.
86. Tobacco Information Center, "Communication," 31.
87. Dale Eickelman, "National Identity and Religious Discourse in Contemporary Oman," *International Journal of Islamic and Arabic Studies* 6(1) (1989): 1–4.
88. Eickelman, "National Identity and Religious Discourse in Contemporary Oman," 1–4.
89. Kéchichian, "A Vision of Oman," 130–131.
90. Arabia Felix, *Quotes of His Majesty Sultan Qaboos*, available at: https://www.oman.de/en/society/governance/quotes-of-qaboos, last accessed May 26, 2021.
91. Sultan Qaboos, Speech on the Occasion of the 7th Omani National Day, November 18, 1977, available at: https://www.educouncil.gov.om/en/sultan_detail.php?scrollto=start&id=160, last accessed May 27, 2021.
92. Sultan Qaboos, Speech on the Occasion of the 7th Omani National Day.
93. Qaboos was not the only person raising these concerns in the 1970s. As Yasmin Moll observers in her 2020 article in the *International Journal of Middle East Studies* about the rise of Islamic media, Muhammad Qutb, Sayyid Qutb's younger brother, noted, in 1976, that many young people were turning away from Muslim media because it was too narrowly about "Islam" and not about the problems facing them in the contemporary world. To remedy this problem, Qutb called for the creation of "programming that was Islamic without a single Qur'anic verse quoted, prophetic saying narrated, or pious practice exhorted." "Islamic media," he concluded "could be Islamic without being about Islam." Yasmin Moll, "The Idea of Islamic Media: The Qur'an and the Decolonization of Mass Communication," *International Journal of Middle East Studies* 52 (2020): 624.
94. Qaboos, Speech on the Occasion of the 7th Omani National Day.
95. Eickelman, "National Identity and Religious Discourse in Contemporary Oman," 3–4.
96. Abu Muslim Al-Bahlani was the nickname for Nasir b. Salim b 'Udayyam al-Rawahi (d. 1920).

97. Valerie Hoffman-Ladd, *The Essentials of Ibadi Islam* (Syracuse, NY: Syracuse University Press, 2012), 75.

98. A. B. H. al-Khalili, "Islamic Ruling on Smoking," in Dr. M. H. Khayat (ed.), *Islamic Ruling on Smoking* (Alexandria: World Health Organization, Regional Office Eastern Mediterranean, 2000), 91, http://applications.emro.who.int/dsaf/dsa46.pdf, date accessed February 23, 2021.

99. Al-Khalili, "Islamic Ruling on Smoking," 91.

100. Al-Khalili, "Islamic Ruling on Smoking," 91.

101. Al-Khalili, "Islamic Ruling on Smoking," 91.

102. Al-Khalili, "Islamic Ruling on Smoking," 91.

103. Sheikh Ahmed al-Khalili, "At-Tadkhin Afat Wa Ay Afata!!" ("Smoking is the Plague of Plagues"), March 9, 2013, available at: https://iftaa.om/artical_dis-392-110.html, last accessed February 20, 2021.

104. Abdullah Borek, "Smoking and Religion: The Position of Islam Towards Smoking." Speech given to INFOTAB Workshop, Málaga, Spain, October 19, 1988, available at: http://industrydocuments.library.ucsf.edu/tobacco/docs/njyp0193, last accessed February 21, 2021.

105. Jawad al-Lawati, Ruth M. Mabry, and Zakiya Q. Al-Busaidi, "Tobacco Control in Oman: It's Time to Get Serious!" *Oman Medical Journal* 32(1) (2017): 3, available at: https://www.ncbi.nlm.nih.gov/pmc/articles/PMC5187396, last accessed February 23, 2021.

106. "1st Medical & Theological Seminar in SQU to Open tomorrow," *Oman News Agency*, October 3, 2012, available at: https://www.thefreelibrary.com/1st+Medical+%26+Theological+Seminar+in+SQU+to+Open+tomorrow-a0304291281, last accessed June 1, 2021.

107. Lucy Ashton, "Oman: Sisters Live with HIV for 20 Years," UNICEF: Oman at A Glance, November 14, 2005, available at: https://uni.cf/3sdaTQK, last accessed February 23, 2021; Valeri, *Oman: Politics and Society in the Qaboos State*, 80.

108. Salah T. al-Awaidy and Adithya Sharanya, "Successes and Challenges of HIV/AIDS Program in Oman: 1984–2015," *Oman Medical Journal* 34(1) (2019): 1–9, https://www.ncbi.nlm.nih.gov/pmc/articles/PMC6330192/, date accessed February 25, 2021.

109. "Fatwa: Huquq al-Musab bi Marad al-Aids" ("Fatwa: The Rights of Those with Aids"), available at: https://iftaa.om/fatwa_dis-462-1913.html#content, last accessed February 23, 2021.

110. "Hukm al-Haml li-Al-Mar'a al-Musab bi al-Aids" ("Ruling on Pregnancy for Women with AIDS"), available at: https://iftaa.om/fatwa_dis-462-1910.html#content, last accessed February 25, 2021.

111. Seif S. al-Abri, Amal S. al-Maani, Idris al-Abaidani, Mamoun Elsheikh, and Nicholas J. Beeching, "Letter to the Editor: Ebola preparedness in Oman: An Experience from the Middle East," *Journal of Infection and Public Health* 9 (2016): 200–201, available at: https://www.sciencedirect.com/science/article/pii/S1876034116000137?via%3Dihub, last accessed February 25, 2021.

112. Kathryn G. Curran, James J. Gibson, Dennis Marke, Victor Caulker, John Bomeh, John T. Redd, Sudhir Bunga, Joan Brunkard, and Peter H. Kilmarx, "Cluster of Ebola Virus Disease Linked to a Single Funeral—Moyamba District, Sierra Leone, 2014," *Centers for Disease Control and Prevention, Morbidity and Mortality Weekly Report* 65(8) (March 4, 2016): 202–205, available at: http://bit.ly/2OYEQ8R, last accessed February 23, 2021.

113. Al-Kharusi, "Fatwa on How to Deal with Those Who Die of Ebola," 201.

114. Al-Kharusi, "Fatwa on How to Deal with Those Who Die of Ebola," 201.

115. Al-Kharusi, "Fatwa on How to Deal with Those Who Die of Ebola," 201.

116. Al-Abri et al., "Letter to the Editor: Ebola preparedness in Oman," 201.

117. Al-Abri et al., "Letter to the Editor: Ebola preparedness in Oman," 201.

118. Al-Kharusi has an MA and a PhD in religious studies from Oxford University. Sultanate of Oman Education Council, *Symposium on the Role of Endowment in Supporting and Funding Education*, October 23, 2019, Kempinski Hotel, Muscat, 4, available at: https://www.educouncil.gov.om/symposium/downloads/pub3.pdf, last accessed May 29, 2021.

119. "Oman Takes Tough Measures to Combat Coronavirus," *Times of Oman*, March 17, 2020, available at: https://timesofoman.com/article/2925874/Oman/Government/Coronavirus-Supreme-Committee-takes-key-decisions, last accessed February 23, 2021.

120. Samuel Kutty, "Omanisation in Medical Jobs on the Rise," *Oman Daily Observer*, July 10, 2020, available at: https://www.omanobserver.om/omanisation-in-medical-jobs-on-the-rise, last accessed February 23, 2021.

121. "Covid-19 Test, Treatment Free for Expats: Health Minister," *Oman Daily Observer*, April 9, 2020, available at: https://www.omanobserver.om/covid-19-test-treatment-free-for-expats-health-minister, last accessed February 23, 2021.

122. Faryal Khamis, Badria al-Rashidi, Ibrahim al-Zakwani, Ahmed H. al-Wahaibi, and Salah T. al-Awaidy, "Epidemiology of Covid-19 Infection in Oman: Analysis of the First 1304 cases," *Oman Medical Journal* 35(3) (2020), available at: http://www.omjournal.org/IssueText.aspx?issId=2597, last accessed February 23, 2021.

123. For example, see these Tweets in Bengali, Hindi, and Urdu: Omani Ministry of Health, Twitter posts, July 8, 2020, 12:01 a.m.; Omani Ministry of Health, Twitter post, June 20, 2020, 8:17 a.m.; Omani Ministry of Health, Twitter post, June 20, 2020, 8:13 a.m.; Omani Ministry of Health, Twitter post, May 30, 2020, 2:30 a.m.; Omani Ministry of Health, Twitter post, May 22, 2020, 11:48 a.m.; Omani Ministry of Health, Twitter post, May 22, 2020, 11:48 a.m.; Omani Ministry of Health, Twitter post, May 14, 2020, 2:34 a.m.; Omani Ministry of Health, Twitter post, May 2, 2020, 2:03 a.m.; Omani Ministry of Health, Twitter post, April 22, 2020, 2:03 a.m.; Omani Ministry of Health, Twitter post, March 22, 2020, 3:09 a.m., all available at: https://twitter.com/OmaniMOH.

124. Omani Ministry of Health, Twitter post, January 27, 2021, 12:00 a.m., available at: https://twitter.com/OmaniMOH.

125. Times News Service, "Don't Fast if Infected by the Virus: Oman's Assistant Grand Mufti," *Times of Oman*, April 21, 2020, available at: https://timesofoman.com/article/dont-fast-if-infected-by-the-virus-omans-assistant-grand-mufti, last accessed February 23, 2021.

126. Ahmed H. Al-Khalili, Twitter post, May 10, 2020, 1:10 p.m., available at: https://twitter.com/AhmedHAlKhalili.

127. Al-Khalili, Twitter post, May 10, 2020, 1:10 p.m.

128. Ahmed H. Al-Khalili, Twitter post, May 23, 2020, 8:28 a.m., available at: https://twitter.com/AhmedHAlKhalili.

129. Kaleematayba, Twitter post, April 28, 2020, 12:48 p.m., available at: https://twitter.com/kaleematayba.

130. Kaleematayba, Twitter post, April 17, 2020, 10:21 a.m., available at: https://twitter.com/kaleematayba.

131. Kaleematayba, Twitter post, April 21, 2020, 9:01 a.m., available at: https://twitter.com/kaleematayba.

132. Kaleematayba, Twitter post, April 13, 2020, 8:58 a.m., available at: https://twitter.com/kaleematayba.

133. Shaddad al-Musalmy, "Adhere to Instructions on COVID-19: Grand Mufti," *Muscat Daily*, May 12, 2020, available at: https://muscatdaily.com/Oman/386645/Adhere-to-instructions-on-COVID-19:-Grand-Mufti-, last accessed February 23, 2021.

134. Zainab al-Nasseri, "WHO Hails Sultanate's Fight against Covid-19," *Oman Observer*, June 23, 2020, available at: https://www.omanobserver.om/who-hails-sultanates-fight-against-covid-19, last accessed February 23, 2021.

135. Lauren Frayer, "Coronavirus is Changing the Rituals of Death," April 7, 2020, avail-able at: https://www.npr.org/sections/goatsandsoda/2020/04/07/828317535/coronavirus-is-changing-the-rituals-of-death-for-many-religions, last accessed May 31, 2021; Michael Sullivan, "Fearing Infection Some in Indonesia Refuse Nearby Burial of Covid19 Victims," May 1, 2020, available at: https://www.npr.org/sections/coronavirus-live-updates/2020/05/01/848956806/fearing-infection-some-in-indonesia-refuse-nearby-burial-of-covid-19-victims, last accessed May 31, 2021; Abidemi Emmanuel Omonisi, "How the COVID-19 Pandemic is Changing Africa's Elaborate Burial Rites, Mourning and Grieving," *Pan African Medical Journal* 35 (Supp. 2) (2020), available at: https://www.ncbi.nlm.nih.gov/pmc/articles/PMC7875800, last accessed June 1, 2021.

136. Johns Hopkins University Coronavirus Resource Center, *Mortality Analysis*, avail-able at: https://coronavirus.jhu.edu/data/mortality, last accessed May 29, 2021.

137. "Oman to Receive More than One Million Covid-19 Vaccines," *Times of Oman*, April 15, 2021, available at: https://timesofoman.com/article/100301-oman-to-receive-more-than-one-million-covid-19-vaccines, last accessed May 29, 2021.

138. "Oman to Receive More than One Million Covid-19 Vaccines"; Gavin Gibbon, "Oman to Vaccinate 1.5m against Covid-19 by the end of June," *Arabian Business*, May 9, 2021, available at: https://www.arabianbusiness.com/healthcare/463184-oman-to-vaccinate-15m-against-covid-19-by-the-end-of-june, last accessed May 29, 2021.

139. Organization of Islamic Cooperation's International Fiqh Academy, *Final Statement and Recommendations of the Medical Fiqh Symposium: Shariah Rulings regarding the Use of Covid-19 Vaccines, their Purchase and the Financing of their Distribution with Zakat funds*, February 22, 2021, 7, available at: https://www.iifa-aifi.org/wp-content/uploads/2021/03/IIFA-Symposium-on-Anti-Covid-19-Vaccines-Feb-2021-3.pdf, last accessed May 30, 2021.

140. Oman News, Twitter post, March 1, 2021, 8:11 a.m., available at: https://twitter.com/OMNNews/status/1366390635142463499, last accessed May 25, 2021.

141. "Ma Hakm Altat'aim biliqah Karona fi nahar Ramadan?" *Shabiba*, April 4, 2021, available at: https://bit.ly/3fzPQUE, last accessed May 25, 2021.

142. One of those challenges is difference in medical care between Muscat and other regions. For more on these challenges, see Valeri, *Oman: Politics and Society in the Qaboos State*, 80.

143. Eickelman, "National Identity and Religious Discourse in Contemporary Oman," 1–4.

144. Rufus Burrow, *Extremist for Love: Martin Luther King, Man of Ideas and Nonviolent Social Action* (Minneapolis: Fortress, 2014), 42.

145. F. Scott Fitzgerald, *The Crack Up*, ed. Edmund Wilson, reprint edn (New York: New Directions Publishing, 2009), 69.

146. Fitzgerald, *The Crack Up*, 69.

147. Fitzgerald, *The Crack Up*, 69.

13

BEYOND THE HORIZON AND BACK: THE SULTAN QABOOS SCHOLARSHIP

Jody Pritt

From the start of his reign in 1970, Sultan Qaboos bin Said prioritized education for all citizens. His establishment of Oman's first national university in 1986, Sultan Qaboos University (SQU), was a major pillar of Oman's modernizing *Nahda* or "Renaissance." Sultan Qaboos also created an external scholarship program under the authority of the newly created Department of Knowledge. The scholarships "aimed to send young Omanis to various countries for their higher education."[1] As a result, Oman was able to educate Omanis in different cultural, economic, and social contexts around the world. That international exchange helped to transform the perspectives of those Omani students, their families, and those they knew or employed. Beneficiaries of Sultan Qaboos' study abroad scholarships returned to Oman with cosmopolitan perspectives and technical competencies that were necessary to support the development of a renewed society in the Sultanate.

Skills development and labor force growth are often highlighted as necessary steps in Oman's move to nationalize its oil industry and move away from a reliance on foreign partnership and toward an independent business model. Study abroad opportunities also increased a sense of independence and a reinforced national identity. Research has demonstrated that there are few other experiences, outside study abroad, that produce such transformational benefits.[2] This chapter compiles the results of a series of interviews of Omanis who received the scholarship. It focuses on the experiences they had and the skills they gained while studying outside Oman. The interviews also inquire into subsequent reintegration, after the scholarship, into Omani society. Woven throughout are recollections of Qaboos' Renaissance in students' reflections on their lived experiences.

The Interviews

I spoke to five Omani nationals at length about their experience abroad and its impact on their lives after returning to the Sultanate for this chapter. All five interviewees were benefactors of the Sultan Qaboos scholarship program. They studied in the United States and Australia before returning to the Sultanate after graduation. For their privacy, names and specific study locations have been changed.

Mouna studied in the United States in the early 1980s and is notably one of the first scholarship recipients to do so. From a Bedouin family, she had not encountered foreigners before her sojourn. Initially, her family had intended for her to study closer to home, potentially in the United Arab Emirates; however, while discussing options with an advisor at the Ministry of Higher Education, she was convinced to study in the United States. After graduating, Mouna returned to Oman and worked in the public sector until retirement.

Jamal studied both in the United States and in Australia. In 2006, he traveled to Australia to study at the graduate level. This was his first study abroad opportunity and the experience encouraged him to do so again in the United States. His experience in Australia was made possible through a Sultan Qaboos scholarship, so the interview focused on that experience. He returned to Oman afterwards and has worked in various educational roles since.

Alma studied in the United States in a Master's program in 2013 after many of her family members had earned their undergraduate degrees abroad. She was hesitant at first, having grown up in a family where only her brothers or male cousins had gone abroad, so as she stated, "it was a very bold move." Upon graduation from Sultan Qaboos University, Alma endeavored to experience a Western classroom, something none of her female relatives had done. Since returning to the Sultanate, she has been working in the private sector.

Hana graduated from an American university in December 2019. Initially, she had hoped to study business but changed to hospitality management because she is interested in strengthening tourism development in Oman. The youngest of the interviewees, Hana stated that she went to the United States with an intention to be involved on campus and to experience the American lifestyle beyond just her academic work. She returned to Oman in early 2020 and is seeking employment in the tourism sector.

Hakim studied accounting in the United States starting in 2005. He was the first in his family to study outside Oman. While seeking admission to Sultan Qaboos University, Hakim learned that he was eligible to apply for one of the Sultan's study abroad scholarships and did so understanding the unique opportunity that this could be for him. Upon graduating, Hakim returned home and worked in the public sector before transitioning to a position in private industry.

The subjects' varied backgrounds and the timing of their experiences abroad afforded ample opportunity for reflection. Interview questions were chosen to spur the process of meaning-making through that reflection. While each experience was unique, three notable overarching themes emerged.

New Experience of Independence

An initial theme that revealed itself across all interviews was the experience of independence for the first time. Mouna remembers her study abroad experience as the first time in her life that she dealt with money on her own. At that time in the early 1980s, the Ministry of Higher Education would deposit an entire year's salary and stipend into the student's bank account. Coming from a Bedouin background, Mouna had never been responsible for her own money; however, she does credit her upbringing with her ability to be very conservative with her newfound income to the point that she had built up quite some savings upon returning to Oman. "Even this sense of independence and confidence that I have now, and the strength that I have now I don't think would be this strong if it was not for my experience in the U.S."

Independence did not suit Alma very well in the beginning. Before leaving for the United States, she excitedly daydreamed about having her own apartment and her own space; however, she was filled with fear during the first few nights in her new apartment. This was not because she feared being in a new place but because she had, until that point, never spent one night in a bedroom alone. "I slept with the lights on the whole time during those first few nights. That experience was just so strange. I wasn't necessarily scared, I think I was just, you know, a new person in a new situation." Ultimately, Alma found living alone empowering, stating, "it made me a stronger person. You know I can take anything basically."

Hana also wanted to go to the United States to experience independence. "I just wanted to be like 100 percent independent because, yeah, I grew up most of my life, like my mom doing everything for us." Hana settled into her newfound independence easily in the United States. She proudly discussed how, during her time in the United States, she became a sort of unofficial mechanic using internet videos to learn how to change the oil in the car she drove, something which her family and friends in Oman now find very impressive.

Jamal didn't go abroad specifically to gain independence, but rather to "change and be challenged." He too found that the experience of being independent is strikingly highlighted in his memory of his time abroad.

Prior to going to the United States, Hakim had only been to surrounding countries such as the UAE and Bahrain. "I didn't even consider traveling before." He believes his time abroad helped him to understand his ability to be independent in whatever he is hoping to do.

On "Being Omani"

The second theme that emerged from the discussions was that of being Omani. By being Omani, the interviewees did not mean literally, in the sense of holding an Omani passport, but having a heightened self-consciousness of their national identity. All five interviewees discussed at great length what it meant to represent the Sultanate while they were abroad. None of the interviewees had expected this experience prior to their departure.

Hakim said, "I had never really watched television or paid attention to the news, so all I knew of America was that it was like France, or at least that's what I thought, so when I landed in the States, I was quite taken aback." Mouna said she had never even heard of the United States before arriving in a small rural southern town to start her undergraduate studies.

Jamal certainly knew of Australia, but was very surprised at the number of Australians he encountered who had not heard of Oman. It was, after all, 2010. Hana was shocked to discover that this was still the case as late as 2019.

Hana considers herself a social butterfly, but when she arrived in the United States and began interacting with her counterparts in the classroom, she was surprised to learn that very few of her classmates knew about Oman. She took on a volunteer position in an international student speakers program on campus where she reflects on that experience saying, "students there had never heard of Oman, so it was my obligation to show my country to them."

Alma found Americans to be very dismissive of her Middle Eastern background. Having many close friends and family who studied abroad, she felt equipped to do so herself, choosing an academic program that closely aligned with her professional goals but never giving any thought to the social interactions she might experience. "It turned out to be a real challenge," she recalled having constantly to dispel stereotypes about the Middle East while also educating her classmates on Oman. This experience led her to critically examine her own identity, but, ultimately, she found that examination healthy. "[It] make[s] you rethink everything, and you don't just take things for granted and that made me really, you know, grateful for everything like my upbringing and my culture and my country."

All five interviewees felt that they were not simply representing Oman but embodied the very spirit of being the country itself. When asked if they felt that they were playing the part of an unofficial ambassador, their experiences seemed to encapsulate more than a superficial tie to their homeland, but rather a deep, personal connection to their homeland that affected every detail of their experience abroad.

Most interviewees spoke to the resilience that this experience required. Alma's comment is exemplary, "it was hard to contextualize every conversation with a briefing over where I was from, and my background." But upon reflecting on that piece of her personal experience abroad, Alma stated definitively, "it made me a stronger person. I can basically take anything now." Hana remembered being flummoxed at having to defend women's rights in Oman to her American classmates and surprised that she would have to explain the fact that Oman is not an impoverished country. "I had to explain to them what I think and like, put them to the defensive side of me for the rest of the time." But she also recounted the experience as making her more understanding of different perspectives when she said it "gave me access to seek growth about myself and others."

Jamal found the experience of defending Oman "a bit daunting," but said that it sparked a desire within him to teach others about Oman. He discussed how framing and reframing his experience as an Omani in Australia drew him closer to Western counterparts saying "living the life, the daily life, the lived experience of [a] Western person, or Western culture was different, and it made me realize there are different experiences in the world and different ways to be." Jamal believes this experience contextualized his lived experience as an Omani more accurately. Seeing Oman through this new lens led him to gain a renewed idea of what his relation as an Omani was to the world beyond his country and ultimately led him to see "there are different ways to do things but my place in the world is as an Omani."

Hakim found it particularly interesting when he witnessed the Omanis on his campus come together as a unified group, even if they did not necessarily all get along, in order to showcase their culture in a positive light to their American classmates. "It is weird, in a way, because we are not perfect. Maybe we fight, or don't get along well together, but when you go out of the country, we are united and stronger, and we want to show a good image of the country."

Mouna elegantly summed up the experience of being an Omani expat by reminiscing about a time when a classmate asked her if Oman was in New Mexico. "I was Oman. It was nice though because for the first time, they knew somebody who comes from that region, and I felt that I am the ambassador of Oman. I was very proud to be Oman for them."

Connecting the Experience to Qaboos' Vision

All five interviewees stated that they believe that if it were not for the Sultan's scholarship program and his emphasis on education for all Omanis, they would not be the people they are today. Mouna, one of the first female Omani students to benefit from the study abroad scholarship program, understands that Qaboos always emphasized equal access to education for girls and women. "From the beginning, from day one, His Majesty made it a point that girls should go to school. Initially, when His Majesty came [to power], he used to give families with little girls money so that they would not give their daughters for marriage and instead send them to school." As she discussed how she believes equality between men and women in Oman is certainly a distinction, she noted, "our population was very small, so we did not have the luxury of inequality." She again confirmed that she believes her confidence and independence as a successful woman in Oman is due to Qaboos' vision. "I think this is what His Majesty wanted us to have as Omanis; strong independence, and a sense of pride in Oman, and exposure to other cultures." Upon returning to Oman, Mouna courageously asked her father to move to Muscat where she worked for a major NGO that was assisting in the development projects happening at the time.

Hana's experience is tied directly to Qaboos' vision. "[His Majesty] just taking everyone out of their comfort zone and sending them to different countries and opening them up to a different perspective so they can learn and bring all of that progress they got from the outside back to Oman." She extrapolated further, noting Qaboos' focus on investing in the younger generations of Omanis. "It's smart because he invested in the youth, and having them going out and studying, I feel his investment is coming back now as we give back to the country." Hana hopes to work in the hospitality industry to continue moving the Sultanate forward.

Jamal often used Qaboos' speeches as a point of reference in his graduate studies but worried that he was received as being inauthentic. "It was really a struggle for me to know how to frame it." At the time of the interview, Jamal was examining and questioning the motives of His Majesty in providing opportunities for Omanis to study abroad. He questioned, "are we conscious that we are part of a bigger plan to connect the world to Oman and Oman to the world?"

Alma was quite intentional when considering how she would apply her experience studying abroad upon her return home. "I, especially in my last year, always had in mind that I really wanted to bring this experience back to Oman. I wanted to be an example for my younger siblings and that's due to his [Qaboos'] vision of, you know, developing more women and supporting women. I think that's why he started the whole thing to begin with." Alma believes she has so far been successful in parlaying her graduate degree into a management position in corporate Oman, but she also believes the experience has played a role in her personal development. She has a social circle beyond her Omani family and routinely blends the two. She often challenges her traditional father but does so in a way that leads him to support her decisions, even when those decisions do not align with his wishes.

Alma believes Qaboos' own time abroad lent force to his vision for his study abroad scholarship program. Alma started to get emotional when considering that connection. "I think because of the fact that he experienced studying abroad first hand and he saw how much of a change that made, that you know, now that he has died, for him to think of his citizens and give them this opportunity, I don't know, it's the most selfless thing."

Hakim connects the experience with his current wishes for Oman. He questions how those who studied abroad are currently working to help further the country's agenda will use their knowledge. "My wish for the younger generation is to not think in terms of consumerism but to be innovative and be part of the productive people in the Sultanate." He links the intentions of Qaboos' scholarship program to that wish. "I think he saw this more in the vision of that program than it may appear because he himself studied abroad in the U.K. and he saw the benefits personally, and he knew that this experience will benefit and teach Omani people as a whole and that they will change the country to the present." Hakim expressed his gratitude for being able to connect his experience abroad with the vision of Sultan Qaboos in a way that he had not considered previously. At the end of the interview, he simply stated, "Thank you. This is emotional but thank you. His Majesty had a vision of creating a diverse population to help move the country forward."

Conclusion

Though the specific experiences of each of the interviewees were different, each of their reflections brought forth themes of study abroad outcomes that they carry into their experiences as Omani nationals. Their experiences with independence led to a newly established comfort in taking on leadership roles not only in their professional lives, but also in their personal communities. For example, though Mouna has retired, she continues to apply her experience from abroad by providing private consulting to young women in Oman, helping them to develop their own leadership skills and their business acumen. She also now counsels her daughter who is studying abroad and is the first Omani on her own college campus, on representing the entire country as an international student. "History repeats itself," said Mouna proudly.

After having been rather shy and naturally soft spoken, Hakim is very active in a professional public-speaking club attributing his time abroad as the cause of the bravery necessary for such activity. He also applies his experience abroad to his professional life when interacting with expatriate co-workers in Oman. "Now I am able to relate to knowing how they are far away from their family. I sympathize with them more."

Their renewed sense of national identity and pride has helped them to seek opportunities to be more directly involved in the improvement of various facets of their communities in Oman. This wish goes beyond simply contributing to the labor force in their respective field to furthering and fostering new initiatives that bolster development and innovation. Hana hopes to work in the tourism and hospitality sector specifically by applying sanitation and food handling safety that she learned while studying in the United States, while Alma is working in the private sector to develop alternative forms of renewable energy by investing in solar energy infrastructure.

All five interviewees continue to connect their experience abroad with the vision set forth by Sultan Qaboos and are now finding ways in which to apply that vision to the renewed vision being established by His Majesty Sultan Haitham bin Tariq Al-Said. In his own quest to ensure that others have access to the same experiences from which he benefited, Jamal's professional work assists Omani youth in forging their own educational paths that lead to study abroad opportunities both in high school and college.

Study abroad opportunities are a common means to bolster the skills of a population, but the additional benefits of international study often play a more comprehensive role in the home society's development. According to the current Omani Cultural Attaché to the United States, "it is truly a learning experience that transcends boundaries by aiming at contributing to increasing your competency in your field of study, but also, in a wider context, at contributing to the development of society."[3] While understanding the necessity of educating the population is not an original insight of Qaboos, he did from the beginning understand the benefits that accrue beyond skill development that come with international study. He had himself benefited from an international education and understood the enormous advantages of the experience, especially when envisioning a dynamic, modern society on the Arabian Peninsula.

Notes

1. Council of Higher Education, "Higher Education in the Sultanate of Oman," available at: https://www.educouncil.gov.om/en/page.php?scrollto=start&id=17, last accessed December 26, 2020.
2. M. Dwyer and C. Peters, "The Benefits of Study Abroad," *Transitions Abroad* 27(5) (2004), available at: https://www.transitionsabroad.com/publications/magazine/0403/benefits_study_abroad.shtml, last accessed January 17, 2021.
3. Embassy of Oman, Cultural Division in Washington, DC, available at: https://www.culturaloffice.info/homeenglish, last accessed December 26, 2020.

14

MUSCAT AND SULTAN QABOOS: THE OMANIZATION OF MUSCAT AND THE MUSCATIZATION OF OMAN

Javier Guirado Alonso

After 1970, Oman began a rapid economic and institutional modernization process. Over the first decades of Sultan Qaboos' reign, Greater
Muscat came to embody modernity, heritage, and the demographic diversity
of Oman. Muscat was the face of the new, inclusive state. Muscat became
an integral part of Qaboos' nation-building program, a source of legitimacy
for his rule, and the urban representation of the state he embodied. Viable
modernization required sustainable urbanization. Both rested on three main
pillars: infrastructure, politics, and culture, a model to be reproduced in other
urban centers across the country.

Starting in the 1970s, a growing number of Omanis from different ethnic and religious affiliations were attracted to Greater Muscat, making the
administration in Muscat and throughout the country more representative
and diverse. At the same time, new infrastructure and economic developments in Muscat during the 1970s and 1980s created a gravitational shift
in the political economy of Oman after Qaboos took office. The Seeb International Airport or Mina Qaboos (Qaboos Port) not only symbolized the
development of the country; major infrastructure projects also established a
dialogue between the Indian Ocean maritime tradition of the Sultanate and
the Arab component of Omani identity. Similarly, culture was institutionalized in projects like the Omani Museum, which provided a national narrative

for the new Oman. The impact of these transformations in the urban sphere shows the extension of the Oman Renaissance in Muscat, and how it established a new relation between state, city, and resident.

Muscat also allowed Oman to reach out to the wider Arabic-speaking world, creating links with major metropolitan centers in the region. Cairo, as the most populous and important urban center of the time, focused in earnest on changes in Muscat. The new Sultan and his government eagerly presented a new vision for Oman and its capital to reporters in Egypt. From there, news of Oman's progress spread throughout the Arabic-speaking world.

All Roads Lead to Muscat

The ascent to the throne of Sultan Qaboos in July 1970 gathered wide media coverage outside Oman. In Egypt, with one of the most important media industries in Arabic at the time, periodicals reproduced Qaboos' inaugural speech. Reporters conducted a number of interviews with the Sultan or with some of the members of his government during the first years of his rule. On September 20, 1971, the magazine *Rose al-Youssef* highlighted Qaboos' commitment to form a government with "the adequate people, from inside or outside, which was prohibited in Oman," meaning that the ban on foreigners had come to an end.[1] A few days later, Sheikh Saud bin Ali Al-Khalili,[2] Omani Minister of Education, visited Cairo for a meeting with other ministers of education, and was interviewed by journalist Mohamed Selhani. He was asked about plans to develop inner Oman, which had suffered from long-term stagnation. "Our plan in the interior," he replied, "is to build our country and deliver a decent living to all the people, something that can only be done by making the people take responsibility in its important construction," and ultimately leading to "a stable democratic rule in our country."[3] The words of Al-Khalili not only highlighted the central role that the modernization of infrastructure would have, but also the will to incorporate the population into these developments.

Infrastructure centered around Muscat played a key role, and its development was so quick that as early as 1971, journalist Mohammed Selhani talked about the "miraculous" Qaboos, or "the road of a thousand miles,"[4] referring to the road projects that were under construction. In fact, the connection between Muscat and the rest of the country was central, and as stated by Thuwaini bin Shihab Al-Said, personal representative of Sultan Qaboos, "the most important new road is the road between Muscat and Mutrah and between Muscat and Seeb, its length being of about 75 kilometers, and from there to the al-Batinah coast . . . and there is another one from Muscat to the interior."[5] Modernization in Oman went in hand with urbanization, but the growth of Muscat and its transformation into a modern metropolis also required huge investment in connections within the city itself, on the one hand, but also with the rest of the country, on the other.

The importance that road infrastructure had in the modernization of Oman gains special relevance if put side by side with the descriptions of Oman before 1970. In this sense, American archaeologist and oil entrepreneur Wendell Phillips described Muscat in the 1960s as a poorly connected and poorly developed port, prisoner of its geography:

> Muscat has no amenities or natural resources and has been unkindly referred to as "the abomination of desolation" and as a "mirror image" of Aden as regards its dependence on the sea. It has been likened to a fjord embosomed in precipitous towing sterile mountains of igneous rock which almost completely enclose the city. Although only two passes, to the south and west, offer convenient entrance or exit through these natural fortifications, Muscat is, nevertheless, the principal window through which Oman sees the world; "this window opens outwardly and not inwardly . . . Muscat has one foot in Arabia and the other in India," for the *suq*, "market," is dominated by shrewd and enterprising Indian merchants (mostly from Bombay) who are called banyani by the local Arabs.[6]

Philips labelled Muscat's relation with the sea as a burden, leading to a lack of integration with the rest of the country and even the rest of the world.[7] Although some developments like the pavement of the road between Muscat and Mutrah in 1967 had been accomplished by Sultan Said, Sultan Qaboos took development to another level. Phillips was describing a city with very few modern amenities and poorly developed, defined by its geographical circumstances and lacking a specific identity. Even if his account shows a prejudiced and questionable view, the transformation the city experienced after 1970 incorporated a series of developments that established the amenities that Wendell Phillips did not see or criticized, enhanced its Arab character, and overly incorporated it into the world after decades of isolation.

With the accession of Qaboos, a ban on foreigners that was installed by Sultan Said bin Taimur was lifted. Many Omanis that went into exile before 1970 were welcome to come back. Qaboos promised them industries and jobs, and certain convictions from the time of Said were forgiven.[8] Similarly, one of the early priorities of his rule was to create public institutions dealing with social services, such as the ministries of Health, Education and Public Works, and the jobs associated with these organizations were largely occupied by returning Omanis. They were mostly Zanzibaris, whether they were originally from the island or Omanis who had remained there after Zanzibar became a separate Sultanate in 1856.[9]

In line with this increased engagement with the exterior, Oman joined the United Nations and the Arab League in 1971. This sudden internationalization required space and amenities for diplomats, businesspeople, United Nations workers, and a host of international dignitaries who visited Oman through its gateway—Muscat. The 1970s were a decade of frantic activity in the Sultanate. While during the rule of Sultan Said only an Indian diplomatic mission and a British honorary consul were admitted, after Qaboos took over the country changed this policy completely. Using a historic building, the United States housed its embassy in Mutrah Port, part of Greater Muscat, in 1973, putting it close to the center of commerce and activity. In the meantime, the country pursued frantic diplomatic activity, opening offices across the world, particularly in the Arab countries. In 1972, Thuwaini bin Shihab Al-Said visited Saudi Arabia, Lebanon, Syria, and Egypt to appoint ambassadors.[10] Similarly, Sultan Qaboos and top officials claimed their participation in the Palestinian cause and stated that unity against Zionism meant unity between all the peoples in Oman.[11] By the end of the 1970s, Muscat had become an established, international Arab capital.

Muscat also became much more integrated, creating and linking together a "greater Muscat" of the many neighborhoods surrounding the old capital city. Before the 1960s and 1970s there had been much more of a distinction between Muscat and Mutrah and other surrounding ports and cities. Greater Muscat included quarters and suburbs into its geographical limits, such as Muhallat Banyan, chiefly inhabited by Indian merchants; Wadi al-Aur, mostly a Baluchi quarter; Ajam, with a large population of Persians; or Muhallat as-Suq, which combined many races and Arab tribes.[12] At one point, British officials even argued that Nizwa could potentially be a better capital because of its religious leverage in the Imamate and to calm the upheavals that had been taking place in in the second half of the 1950s.[13] Muscat's advantages and position as an international port outweighed the advantages of Nizwa and its historic claims. To this day, however, Nizwa is still a prominent center—the "capital of the interior of Oman." The *ad-Dakhiliyah* governate of which Nizwa is the capital, literally translates to "the interior" of Oman.

While the social make-up of the population in old Muscat (the area around the palace) was diverse, the port of Mutrah (just to the east of the old city of Muscat and accessible mainly by dhow before the building of the connecting road), sprawling around the next bay, was even more cosmopolitan. Mutrah had three times the population of old Muscat.[14] In Mutrah there were Arabs, Baluchis, Africans, Persians, and Indians, as well as other occasional traders that came from other parts of the Indian Ocean or the world that characterized it as a port city. The Baluchi community, famous for their military prowess, was represented. There were also very distinctive groups such as the Alawati, Indians who were originally Ismailis but converted to Shiism in the mid-nineteenth century, who even resided in their own walled area in Mutrah called Sur al-Lawatiyya. Considered alone, and not a part of Greater Muscat, Mutrah was, in fact, the largest town of coastal Oman during much of the nineteenth and twentieth centuries. It held the most thriving commercial activity.[15] Interestingly, access from Mutrah to inner Oman was much easier than was the case from old Muscat—of course, this made protecting Muscat from raids much easier.

While Mutrah was the economic center, old Muscat (which was the urban area between al-Jalali and al-Mirani forts and around al-Alam Palace) retained its prestige as the seat of political power. With the arrival of Qaboos, Muscat became "Greater Muscat" and the urban area of the capital city was expanded, incorporating into the metropolitan area not only Muscat and Mutrah, but also other previously well-distinguished towns in the area such as Seeb that were now more easily accessible thanks to the infrastructure developments. The incorporation of all these previously separate towns and ports into a single metropolitan area, Greater Muscat, gave the new capital city its characteristic polycentric layout, establishing an urban paradigm in Oman that echoed the relation between the Sultan and the rest of the country. The urban

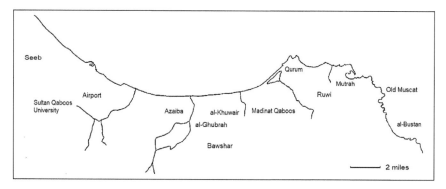

Figure 14.1 Map of Greater Muscat. The metropolitan area includes a number of towns and new urban developments between old Muscat (east) and Seeb. Drawn by author.

development of Muscat served as an image of the modernization process that Oman witnessed during the 1970s and after, incorporating a number of ethnic and religious communities into a single unity under the umbrella of the Sultan (Figure 14.1).

In this sense, Salalah became a Muscat in Dhofar, a regional center and a replication of the successful modernization model pursued in the capital. While Salalah during the time of Said bin Taimur served as a place of solace for the Sultan, far from Muscat and its political atmosphere, with Qaboos, investment in medical facilities, education institutions, or projects such as the Raysut Port, which by the 1970s handled over 250,000 tons of shipping per year, meant that the new Oman implied an ample and far-reaching process of urbanization throughout the country. "Salalah itself now boasts one of the largest and most modern hospitals in the world while schools, housing developments, shops and power plants seem to spring up overnight."[16]

Pauline Searle, who visited Oman in the late 1970s, found a rapidly developing country. In terms of agricultural development, which particularly affected areas in the south, the modernization program achieved important victories in Nizwa and Sohar, but mostly in the Batinah and Rumais areas. The approach focused on preserving the social patterns of Oman rather than substituting them with new practices, even if new crops were introduced and foreign experts visited the areas all the time. "Since 1970 the aim of the Agricultural Department has been more to help the smaller farmer and its Bedu counterpart to improve on his present methods rather than to try and force new ideas upon him."[17] As for the fisheries, the government commissioned Mardela International Ltd, Del Monte International, and FMC International to carry out developments in facilities, techniques, and productivity.[18] Military development affected Muscat and its naval power in particular. The country expanded its fleet, notably with ships like the 1,000-ton royal yacht *Al-Said*, with a fleet that not only fought the Dhofar War, but also aimed at controlling illegal immigration and smuggling along the coasts of Oman. Qaboos formalized the ways to enter the country and took control of the economy, fiscalizing or eliminating informal economies in Oman. Naval bases were established at Mukallah (Muscat Harbor), Bandar Jiseh (south of Muscat), in Dhofar, and in Musandam, a strategic enclave of Oman at the Strait of Hormuz.

The flip side of this development, especially in its maritime aspects, was the effect it had on previous forms of living that largely relied on informal trade with small vessels generically referred to as dhows. These vessels are particularly fit for the type of coasts that Phillips described in his account of Muscat, but that also applied to an important part of the Omani seashore and had represented over the nineteenth and twentieth centuries a way to evade and benefit from the maritime regulations and demands that the European empires had in the region.

In this sense, Mina Qaboos (Qaboos Port), in Mutrah, a project that had been started by Sultan Said bin Taimur in 1967 but that was not officially inaugurated until 1974 by Sultan Qaboos, played a central role in the modernization and policing of the Omani shores. Before it was finished, "*dhows* anchored immediately off the town; a lesser number unloaded their cargoes at Muscat, two miles east of Mutrah. Today [1980] *dhows* use Mutrah exclusively since the former port of Muscat is now a naval base."[19] Dhow routes were also fundamental for trade between the Gulf sheikhdoms due to the lack of viable land routes, and their use saw its heyday in Oman in the early 1970s due to the flow of oil revenue, which had only started to be exploited in the late 1960s. Nevertheless, developments in Muscat, Mutrah, and Dhofar led to a sharp decline in dhow trade that also spread to other ports, even those that were not subject to so much attention in the modernization program. Related industries like dhow-building were also affected and by the end of the 1970s all these livelihoods became more of a practice related to heritage rather than commerce. The new ports welcomed larger boats and steamships that carried bigger loads and were easier to track.[20] Mina Qaboos, for instance, in the late 1970s "handled well over a million tons of shipping and the amount is increasing all the time,"[21] and only a few hundred dhows were arriving in Omani ports, much less than only a decade earlier.

Besides roads, ports, and maritime trade, other developments that led to better connections included the new Seeb International Airport, only a few miles far from Muscat, which replaced the largely outdated installations of Bait al-Falaj. The new airport included a 3,000-meter runway and held a Concorde trial flight in August 1974 as a demonstration of its state-of-the-art facilities. Similarly, telecommunications, post offices, and information services like radio (1970) and TV (1974) were established, whose goals included fighting the propaganda that stations like Radio Aden were spreading, particularly in Dhofar.[22]

Urban transformations followed the proliferation of these services, such as the construction of Radio City in Muscat in 1974, or the development of Ruwi in 1977, a suburb which became a crucial business district of the capital. The Muscat municipality, on the other hand, was established in 1972 and incorporated Old Muscat, Mutrah, Ruwi, Bausher, Seeb, and its suburbs. From being a relatively small port city, under the rule of Qaboos, Muscat was in the process of being transformed into a modern metropolis that served as the capital of a country that was taking off in terms of development. Therefore, more government offices were needed and some facilities that were initially defined for educational or residential purposes were soon required for government use. Other complexes, like the *mujamma'*, between Ruwi and Mutrah, held offices for more than one ministry before further developments were carried out.[23]

The Omanization of Politics in Muscat

One of the key aspects of modernization concerns control by a central authority over territories and the peoples who inhabit them. As seen, maritime trade was one of the realms in which this control and policing were established after 1970, but Omani politics also witnessed a similar process in the same time period. The Omani modernization that Qaboos represented, nevertheless, had very unique features caused by relations between the vernacular institutions that were already in place, particularly in the interior of the country, and the new, central authorities that aimed to represent the interests of all Omanis from the capital. The form of the post-1970 Sultanate was also a primary matter of concern for the British, who advocated for these programs of reform.[24] The *Omanization* of Muscat meant that inner Oman increasingly permeated politics in Muscat, transforming its political landscape and its character as a port city that mostly looked outwards into the capital of the whole of Oman.

Conversely, the Omani government at the local and regional level remained largely untouched, since Qaboos did not want to cause upheaval in the existing networks of loyalty, particularly in the interior. The country had three governorates (Muscat, Dhofar, and Masandam) and five regions (al-Batinah, al-Dhahira, al-Dakhiliya, al-Sharqiya, and al-Wusta), each of which included a variable number of *wilayat*. Qaboos also showed continuity with governors and *wali*s, who in a number of cases remained the same or were close to the previous leaders. *Wali*s were appointed directly by the Sultan, many of them being selected from the local branch of the Al-Bu Saidi or from the local tribes, establishing a political connection between regional and national government, or, in other words, an explicit connection between Muscat and the rest of the country. The *wali* was also connected to a number of local sheikhs representing the tribe or branch that inhabited a ward of the *wilaya*. The main function of the *wali* was to serve as an interlocutor of the central government in a given region. Together with the *qadi*, an Islamic judge, they represented the main forms of political power throughout the country, providing a sense of continuity in institutional terms and also allowing a certain degree of independence.[25] They were the personal manifestation of the web of institutional connections centered around Muscat. This web, however, still allowed for regional concerns to be expressed and heard, as shown by the example of a sardine fishermen from Sohar who directed a collective petition to the Sultan to overrule an unfavorable regulation on fishing rights imposed by the *wali*. Such types of contestation were not common in Oman, and most collective demands were expressed through other associational institutions, most notably along tribal lines or through the sheikh of the district, a non-official title assigned to a respected elder in a given area.[26]

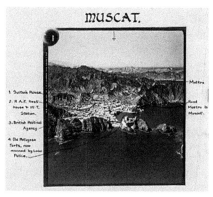

Figure 14.2 Black-and-white aerial photographs of Mutrah (*left*) and Muscat (*right*) in 1939. Source: Qatar Digital Library/British Library, IOR/R/15/6/384, f 139 1 and 2 Public Domain.

The way the fisherman acted, nevertheless, showed how the role of the *wali* as a link between the central power in Muscat and other parts of the country was contested at times, but at the same time it reveals that the relation with the authority of Sultan Qaboos in Muscat was not only acknowledged, but invoked through other mechanisms.

The figure of the *wali* started to lose its importance early on. In 1973, the municipality system began to spread across Oman and its functions were expanded with the reform of the land law in 1979. Similarly, law enforcement responsibilities were not part of the *wali*'s duties, but of the Royal Omani Police, controlled from Muscat.[27] Qaboos, then, maintained a system of government that was already in place before his tenure, but also spread the footprint of Muscat politics into parts of the country that had previously been largely disconnected from the central authorities—the relation between policing and urbanization was a central component of the Omani modernization.

In a similar fashion, scholars have detailed how Sultan Qaboos gradually incorporated most of the families that held power in the Imamate, such as the Al-Khalili, installing them in government and working with them in a broad and inclusive modernization project. This strategy was also employed to incorporate former members of insurgent movements in Dhofar, such as Yussef bin Alawi, who was named Minister of Foreign Affairs in 1982, or Salim al-Ghazali, who held a number of cabinet posts since the 1970s. The political landscape of Muscat was attracting Omanis of all kinds, coming from all parts of the country. The success of Qaboos' strategy to incorporate all the territories of inner Oman into the political umbrella of the new Sultanate relied on the preservation of existing informal social systems and their actualization in light of the new political officers that were being deployed to these areas. Besides larger towns like Nizwa, Bahla, Izki, or Rustaq, the territories of inner Oman follow a rationale under which a territory (*dar*) is ruled by one sheikh.[28] Qaboos tried "to embody the role of the nation's tribal sheikh; he has thus taken care to spread the idea that there is an unofficial way available to address complaints or requests directly to him, bypassing the modern administrative ways."[29] The *tamima*s, sheikhs whose political authority covered several branches of a tribe and who acted as the main interlocutors between the authorities and members of the tribe, were also largely respected. Keeping this system in place allowed Qaboos to connect Muscat with the rest of the country without upending local structures of authority.

One of the resources used by Qaboos to make his figure closer to all Omanis was the *al-jawla al-sanawiyya*, a journey across the country held as an open parliament with the people of each region, a performance of closeness to the common Omani. It is, in fact, a reinterpretation of the tradition in which Muslim princes visit their territories, thus also building a bridge with the notion of the Imamate. This was, therefore, a way to keep and renew the allegiances of the notables to Qaboos, which by evoking religion brought back the importance of Ibadism to legitimize his rule. While power was being centralized in the new Muscat, Qaboos recovered an Islamic practice that brought his authority, geographically sited in the capital, to the whole country, particularly in a context in which the monarch serves as a unifying element for a largely heterogeneous population.[30]

The impact of the development of water supplies was also particularly relevant in terms of social and political structures in the interior of Oman. The social order in place in areas like Nizwa or Rustaq was heavily influenced by the *falaj* (pl. *aflaj*), the irrigation systems that watered the region. Wilkinson shows how these systems of underground channels, originally introduced by Persians in pre-Islamic times, related to the social structure of most of inner Oman.[31] Rabi also argues that the *aflaj* were an infrastructural origin for the values of wealth-sharing that Ibadism defines, and also the urban landscape of towns in which this system is the source of water.[32] Land ownership and water resources were frequently centered around a few tribesmen of religious lineage, who also tended to live closer to the areas in which the *falaj* entered the town. The market is frequently on the other side of the village, in an area where slaves used to live before the abolition of slavery.[33]

Tribal lineage and religious authority bear a relationship that defines the social structure of Ibadi inner Oman. The fact that Qaboos relied on Ibadism as one of his legitimation tools, where many of the inhabitants of the coastal areas that formed the old Sultanate of Muscat were Sunni or Shia, shows his commitment to incorporate the region into the national narrative of the new state. The political maneuvering that maintained tribal and Ibadi structures while incorporating developments in infrastructure, education, and health services follows a similar strategy. Ibadi forms of government can be understood as the religious translation of tribal social and political structures. More specifically, Ibadism tries to keep one of the fundamental principles of Islam, arguing that "an Imam should rule with the counsel and consent of the public. In practical terms, selection was in the hands of the senior *'ulama'* (Islamic clerics) and tribal notables, those with the ability to translate the community's will and give it voice."[34] Yet British interference and the arrival of oil wealth upset some tribes in a way that threatened the relative stability that was in place. For this reason, Qaboos kept tribal and Ibadi institutional arrangements and incorporated the territory into the rule of Muscat in order to handle these allocations in the form of investment and the development of projects that not only improved the standard of living of all Omanis, but also showed that the central authority shared the wealth of the land and fostered an understanding based on consensus, one of the key mandates that the Ibadi ruler has to follow.

The Omani Museum and the Cultural Narrative of Oman

The modernization program of Sultan Qaboos also had a cultural component. The Omani Museum was deliberately established in Muscat as an expression of its role as a cultural capital as much as a political and economic center. Inaugurated in 1974 in Qurum, a newly developed neighborhood that is part of Greater Muscat, it came before the new Oman National Museum of 2013, providing a close testimony of the cultural policies that were being deployed in the early years of Qaboos' tenure. Qurum emerged in the 1970s in the recently formed Greater Muscat. Qurum was and is still known as a diplomatic quarter, but it does not bear the cultural and historical significance of areas like old Muscat or Mutrah. Sultan Qaboos, therefore, decided to place a crucial cultural institution such as a national museum in a newly developed quarter as part of his modernization plan, populating newly developed areas of Greater Muscat with institutions that spoke about a narrative of tradition.

This approach is in contrast to the skyscrapers that have been favored in other cities in the Gulf, such as Kuwait, Doha, or most notably, Dubai.[35] In Muscat, the preferred attitude towards landscape has been preservation and not dizzy modernization. In fact, as an example, the height of buildings in Muscat is limited to a maximum of 10–12 stories depending on the type of building, and with very few exceptions to this rule.[36] With such regulations, the skyline of Muscat embraces the view of its mountainous surroundings, crucial to understanding the country and the relations between coast and hinterland. Similarly, the chronological aspect of this traditional modernization is also in contrast to other cities in the Gulf. While in the 1970s many of the newly independent states were eager to develop cultural institutions to promote local identities (the Dubai Museum in 1971, or the Qatar National Museum of Doha in 1975), the erection of high-rise glass skyscrapers became a commonplace from the 1990s. In Oman, this fever never took over, and the approach toward modernity and heritage that the 1974 Omani Museum represented remained the standard in the Sultanate in terms of policy, despite the fact that the museum was ultimately closed and substituted by a new facility in the more historically significant old Muscat.[37]

The Omani Museum collection was displayed on two stories. The first one showed an introductory section, and rooms for ancient history, land and peoples, and research and new acquisitions, while the second floor included space for Islamic heritage, contemporary art, Omani arts and crafts, and an armory. Although it was closed later on, the museum was one of the first national museums in the Gulf that started to proliferate in the 1970s, and the first item in a landscape of museums and cultural institutions that started to populate Oman from the ascent of Sultan Qaboos to the throne, such as the National Museum (1978), the Natural History Museum (1986), the Armed Forces Museum (1988), or the Omani French Museum (1992).

One of the main goals of the museum was to incorporate a complex heritage into the idea of the Omani nation-state as one of the key components of Qaboos' modernization program. "Attention to the preservation of the original Omani heritage increases day after day," the documents of the museum state, leading to the establishment of a series of research and cultural institutions whose "goal is to revive this heritage and reveal its various aspects inside and outside Oman."[38] The museum emphasized the multifaceted social and cultural fabric of the country, incorporating this diversity into a state institution and placing it at the forefront of the character of Oman. Also, the project brought to Muscat a number of artifacts and pieces from all parts of the country, thus making the capital part of the symbolic space of all Oman in terms of heritage.

One goal of the museum is to link the city of Muscat and the rest of the country. The section devoted to land and people pays particular attention and space to the Jabal Akhdar mountain range, which lies close to Nizwa, the historic capital of inner Oman. The region had witnessed a series of upheavals against the authority of the Sultan of Muscat in the late 1950s, something that was ultimately settled with the aid of the United Kingdom. The Omani Museum describes in detail the rich natural resources of the Jabal Akhdar, specifically its pomegranates and roses.[39] As for Muscat, the Omani Museum states that it has "reached the pinnacle of its glory under the rule of the Al-Bu Saidi," a family that "has ruled Oman since 1841,"[40] a claim that leaves behind the often tense relations between the Imamate of Oman and the Sultanate of Muscat, or particularly relevant historical events like the Treaty of Seeb in 1920, which established a separate rule for both regions. The historical narrative of Sultan Qaboos during his first years, then, argues that the rule of the Al-Bu Saidi has been continuous since the mid-nineteenth century. An important section of the museum is also devoted to the industry of sea trade. The coastal cities of Oman have been a key historical participant in the Indian Ocean route, and have a history of contact with a number of empires and trade. The museum shows the influence of the Portuguese in shipbuilding, the trade relations with China and the different type of vessels that are usually labeled as dhows, such as the *boum*, the *sambuk*, or the *jelbut*.[41] Other aspects of heritage are highlighted in the museum: religion, forts and military constructions, and arts and crafts. Ibadism also occupies an important part of the museum, focused on the quality and dignity of Ibadi mosques in different parts of the country. Regarding military construction, the Rustaq fort, located in one of the historical capitals of inner Oman, is featured in detail, and the section treating arts and crafts pays special attention to Sohar, gold, jewelry for men and women, and *khanjar*s, the traditional Omani dagger.[42] In the same way that the museum collected artifacts from throughout the unified Sultanate, the city of Muscat tied the Sultanate together economically, bureaucratically, and socially.

Conclusion

Muscat embodies the unique modernization program of Sultan Qaboos and Oman. Rather than forcing centralization, Muscat linked regions together as the hub of a new system of roads, hospitals, and schools. Instead of forcing compliance to Muscat, or to destructive modernization, the capital became a heterogenous city that linked the past to present and region to center. It also became a cultural, social, and economic center, encouraged by the Sultan, but also as a result of natural growth. Incorporating elements of Ibadism, tribal loyalties, and the investment of the newly arrived oil revenues into infrastructure and social services, Muscat is now connected to the rest of Oman, to the Indian Ocean, and the wider world.

Notes

1. Muhammad Selhani, "'iadat bina' shamilat fi sultanat 'uman," *Rose al-Youssef*, September 20, 1971. Translations by the author unless stated.
2. Sheikh Saud bin Ali Al-Khalili also founded in 1977 the Al-Taher conglomerate, which aggregates companies in the petroleum industry, construction, engineering, trading, and real estate, and the first Islamic bank in Oman, Bank Nizwa.
3. Muhammad Selhani, "intilaq nahw al-haqi wa al-'adl fi sultanat 'uman," *Rose al-Youssef*, September 27, 1971.
4. Muhammad Selhani, "awal khatwah ila altariq," *Rose al-Youssef*, October 3, 1971.
5. Fuad Said, "mustashar as-sultan qaboos yatahadath ila al-musawwar," *al-Musawwar*, March 10, 1972.
6. Wendell Phillips, *Unknown Oman* (Beirut: Libraire du Liban, 1971), pp. 8–10.
7. A number of works have challenged this vision, usually under the conceptual framework of *new thalassology*, which understands the ocean as a space

of connection and not of separation. Vid. Janet Abu-Lughod. *Before European Hegemony: The World System A.D. 1250–1350* (Oxford: Oxford University Press, 1989); Matthew Hopper. *Slaves of One Master: Globalization and Slavery in Arabia in the Age of Empire* (New Haven, CT: Yale University Press, 2015); or Johan Mathew. *Margins of the Market: Trafficking and Capitalism Across the Arabian Sea* (Berkeley: University of California Press, 2017).

8. J. E. Peterson, "Oman: Three and a Half Decades of Change and Development," *Middle East Policy* 11(2) (2004): 127.

9. Peterson, "Oman."

10. Peterson, "Oman"; Fuad Said. "mustashar as-sultan qaboos yatahadath ila al-musawwar," *al-Musawwar*, March 10, 1972.

11. Muhammad Selhani, "intilaq jadidah nahw al-mustaqbal fi sultanat 'uman." *Rose al-Youssef*, February 28, 1972.

12. Heinz Gaube, "Muscat and Mutrah," in Abdulrahman Al-Salimi and Eric Staples (eds.). *The Ports of Oman* (Hildescheim: Georg Olms Verlag, 2017), 147–148.

13. U.K. military operations in Muscat and Oman, Code BA file 1195, papers 28–47, U.K. National Archives, Foreign Office, FO 371/140168 (1959).

14. Ian Skeet, *Muscat and Oman: The End of an Era* (London: Faber & Faber, 1974), 53.

15. John Gordon Lorimer, *Gazetteer of the Persian Gulf, Oman and Central Arabia* (Calcutta: 1908–1915), 1197–1198.

16. Pauline Searle, *Dawn over Oman* (London: George Allen & Unwin, 1979), 131–132, 138.

17. Searle, *Dawn over Oman*, 133.

18. Searle, *Dawn over Oman*, 134.

19. Martin, Esmond Bradley. "The Decline of Omani Dhows," *The Great Circle* 2(2) (1980): 77.

20. Bradley. "The Decline of Omani Dhows," 82.

21. Searle, *Dawn over Oman*, 137.

22. Searle, *Dawn over Oman*, 138.

23. J. E. Peterson, *Historical Muscat* (Leiden: Brill, 2006), 23.

24. HMG's policy towards the Sultanate of Oman, U.K. National Archives, Foreign and Commonwealth Office, FCO 8/1680 (1970), 12–35.

25. Calvin Allen, *Oman under Qaboos: From Coup to Constitution 1970–1996* (London: Frank Cass, 2000), 44–46.

26. Fredrik Barth, *Sohar: Culture and Society in an Omani Town* (Baltimore, MD: Johns Hopkins University Press, 1983), 125.

27. Allen, *Oman under Qaboos*, 47

28. Dale Eickelman, "From Theocracy to Monarchy: Authority and Legitimacy in Inner Oman, 1935–1957," *International Journal of Middle East Studies* 17(1) (1985): 6.

29. Marc Valeri, *Oman: Politics and Society in the Qaboos State* (Oxford: Oxford University Press, 2009), 173.

30. Valeri, *Oman: Politics and Society*, 174.

31. J. C. Wilkinson, *Water and Tribal Settlement in South-East Arabia: A Study of the Aflaj of Oman* (Oxford: Clarendon Press, 1977).

32. Uzi Rabi. *The Emergence of States in a Tribal Society: Oman under Saʾid bin Taymur, 1932–1970* (Brighton: Sussex Academic Press, 2006), 14.

33. Eickelman, "From Theocracy to Monarchy," 8.

34. Rabi, *The Emergence of States in a Tribal Society*, 18–20.

35. Yasser Elsheshtawy, *Dubai: Behind an Urban Spectacle* (London: Routledge, 2009).

36. Law on the Protection of National Cultural Heritage, Ministry of Heritage and National Culture, Muscat, 1980, 18

37. National Museum of Oman, see at: https://www.nm.gov.om/en/home.

38. *Al-mathaf al-ʿumani. dalil mujaz lil-zaayirin* (Muscat: Ministry of Information and Culture, 1977), 7.

39. *Al-mathaf al-ʿumani. dalil mujaz lil-zaayirin*, 12

40. *Al-mathaf al-ʿumani. dalil mujaz lil-zaayirin*, 19.

41. *Al-mathaf al-ʿumani. dalil mujaz lil-zaayirin*, 20.

42. *Al-mathaf al-ʿumani. dalil mujaz lil-zaayirin*, 28–29.

15

DUQM AND SALALAH: OMAN'S PORTS AND SPECIAL ECONOMIC ZONES

Jeffrey R. Kinnier

The development of seaport infrastructure in Oman during the fifty-year reign of Sultan Qaboos was a result of his government's vision and strategic planning. Seaport development reflects Oman's engagement with broader international trends such as globalization. Local and geopolitical forces both within the jurisdiction of Oman, as well as beyond the Sultan's scope of influence, have shaped seaport initiatives. Exemplifying this are the Omani port cities of Duqm and Salalah, with their associated Duqm Special Economic and Salalah Free Zones. These two seaports represent Oman's increasing engagement with global trade through the reign of Sultan Qaboos 1970–2020.

Salalah, the largest city and traditional capital in the Dhofar Governate, is located on Oman's southeastern coast of the Arabian Sea. Today it is a containerized seaport for supplies and manufactured goods, ranking it among the top fifty worldwide.[1] The seaport's affiliated Salalah Free Zone offers an extensive range of trading, storage, assembly, and transit services. Duqm is a new, but growing, port city on Oman's mid-Arabian Sea coast. The recent Duqm Special Economic Zone is poised for significant growth. Duqm is to the east of Salalah in the Al-Wusta Governate, a natural port and accessible to major shipping lanes. Over the past fifty years, both Duqm and Salalah and their opportunity zones were designed and developed to provide trade services to the western Indian Ocean world, and beyond.

Sultan Qaboos' record reflects his ability to inspire Oman's citizenry and produce positive results, while also timing his government's efforts to the identified opportunities and adjusting to the vicissitudes of his era. Sultan Qaboos communicated his strategy to the Omani people using Annual Speeches of His Majesty before the Council of Oman, and through regular decrees. "In the name of God, the Compassionate, the Merciful," or a similar refrain, introduced and permeated his words of purpose, encouragement, enthusiasm, and direction.[2] Addressing specific endeavors, such as education, employment, development, international affairs, tourism, or infrastructure, Sultan Qaboos consistently based his message on God's love, and the responsibility of both citizen and state to work in harmony toward continued progress to achieve the goals of Oman's Renaissance. The plans and programs were inspired by four fundamental principles: the development of human resources; the development of natural resources; the building of infrastructure; and the establishment of state institutions to accomplish the mission.[3] The seaport development of Salalah and Duqm has engaged these four principles.

Salalah before 1971

"As you will see from your files the provision of port facilities has been the Cinderella of the Civil Development Budget for the last five years."[4] This mid-1960s characterization of Muscat's silted up harbor reflected the backwardness and isolation of Oman's basic infrastructure. This condition was indicative of the similar lack of investment and development Dhofar had experienced under Qaboos' predecessor, a factor in the insurrection in this governate against the Sultanate of Oman beginning in 1965. Sultan Qaboos, in his first National Day Speech of 1971, called the building process an exacting one, with much hard work and sacrifice needed to overcome the obstacles and difficulties before Oman.[5]

Known for its ancient and medieval trade in frankincense, Salalah in the 1960s was off the radar of most global commerce, and its port facilities were an extension of its original early common era Khor Rori and Al-Badid ports. These ports were sparingly modified for the arrival of occasional steamship services in the nineteenth century, but were silted over and limited in functionality.[6] Prior to 1970, break-bulk cargo ships were moored in the sea near

Salalah, and goods arrived to and from the Governate of Dhofar through rudimentary infrastructure. Break-bulk shipping, or loose cartons stowed directly in the ship's hold, had declined dramatically worldwide as the process of containerization grew; just prior to Qaboos' ascension, break-bulk cargo carriage began shifting to this more efficient process.[7] The advent of containerization, the use of large metal standard containers stacked onto "container vessels," revolutionized ocean transportation globally, after a gradual, sporadic start in U.S. domestic ports in the 1950s.[8] The transition moment from break-bulk cargo to container carriage was the mid-1960s, when the first transatlantic container services, utilizing standard containers of 20- and 40-ft lengths, coupled with standardized lashing systems, commenced (1 TEU = 20-ft container equivalent; a 40-ft container is equal to 2 TEUs).[9]

With the end of Sultan Said bin Taimur's reign in 1970, Oman's transition toward modernity was dramatic, not just in the capital Muscat, but also in Salalah.[10] Qaboos invested in Dhofar to win the hearts and minds of the Dhofaris, to break them away from the Yemeni-led, Soviet Union-inspired and supported revolution, upon his ascension. Through a combination of military success, funding from the U.K. government and British banking sources, a strong anti-communist and radical Islamist stance, and a rigorous focus on employing Dhofar Omanis in infrastructure, Oman's government, with assistance from international partners including the British, ended the insurrection by the middle of the 1970s. Dhofar was fully incorporated into the Sultanate of Oman. Qaboos' timing was propitious.

Salalah: The Turnaround, 1971–1990

"In the history of world trade there has probably never been an upheaval quite so sudden and so sharp as that in the Middle East in the last five years."[11] This report of 1977 characterized the recent years of war, oil embargo, and price surge in the Middle East as catalysts for the economic boom among the Gulf region nations. The boom resulted in increased import demand for consumer, manufactured, and infrastructure-related goods, amid chaotic delays caused by the sub-par ocean, surface, and air logistic capabilities throughout the Gulf neighborhood. Oman, new to the oil production arena, experienced a 733 percent increase in imported value in this short period, comparable in growth rate to its neighbors.[12]

Sultan Qaboos' strategy from the mid-1970s positioned the port at Salalah as a major component in the Indian Ocean trade route system. Salalah would establish a strong position as a transshipment seaport, attractive due to location and planned infrastructure and poised to capture a major role in the global containerization trade route realignment just underway. Salalah was to also serve as the gateway and main national load center for southern Oman. The first infrastructure accomplishment related to Salalah, commencing in 1971, was investment in its local Raysut Port, as planned for in Sultan Qaboos' first budget. By 1973, with measurable progress recorded, Sultan Qaboos addressed the improving port in his annual National Day Speech.[13] This modernization effort advanced the current conditions reflective of nineteenth-century standards, improving upon capabilities for handling break-bulk shipments, but not containers.[14] This was followed by a Phase Two project which yielded an annual capacity of 1 million metric tons of break-bulk cargo, as planned for in Oman's first Five-Year Development Plan. This initial five-year outlook included a "very ambitious, balanced, and studied plan based on utilizing the various resources of society in order to reach the target of the economic development . . . and formed a higher council of economic development under our presidentship."[15] This initial plan was to be revised and proclaimed every five years thereafter and incorporated into Twenty-Year Visions.

Between 1975 and 1980, the Phase Two project of Raysut Port development advanced at the cost of $129 million. These enhancements were but a down payment on the future plans for Salalah. They were also a catch-up action to other ports in the Indian Ocean arena. The subsequent five-year plans progressively launched Salalah on its aggressive growth trajectory.[16] The plans were adjusted during the 1980s, impacted by regional conflicts, oil price declines, and recession effects on Gulf shipping, slowing the initial progress in the development of Salalah's Raysut Port, and Oman generally.[17] But the plans were never abandoned.

Building the seaport alone was not the endgame. Oman created the foundation for nurturing and supporting private productive, state-run and joint ownership enterprises beyond shipping, and the extraction and export of oil. According to one analysis from the 1980s, Sultan Qaboos and his ministers avoided many of the expensive mistakes made by Mexico, Venezuela, and other more advanced nations suddenly inundated by petrodollars. They did not try to "buy" an industrial base overnight, but rather developed it with private sector engagement.[18] This infrastructure effort characterized the strategic balance of Sultan Qaboos' state leadership engagement and the encouragement of market capitalism, serving both domestic and international goals.

An early and sustained component of Qaboos' strategy was to creatively use the limited liability corporation (LLC) as the favored manner for business organization. LLCs allowed for investors to own a company which became a building block for a larger combination of investors; a combination where the Governate of Oman provided overall direction. Two examples of the LLC structure offer insight to the Omani strategy. Seven Seas Group LLC, the well-known and renowned group, was incorporated in 1984 and steadily grew into a large collection of LLCs with diverse operations. Similarly, Modern Shipping Services LLC, of the Seven Seas Group of Companies, was established in 1995 and is considered one of the pioneering shipping companies in Oman.[19]

Salalah: Catching Up with Other Ports, 1991–2000

During the late 1980s and throughout the 1990s three developments beyond the control of Oman were shaping the ocean trade business: containerization, as described above; the evolution of large, globalized public and private shipping, seaport management and investment organizations of northern European and Asian ownership; and the emergence of supply-chain management and its impact on ocean carriers, trade-lane management, and seaports.[20] By the early 1990s, containerized cargo had been adopted worldwide, and from this point onwards rapid acceleration in both the number and size of container vessels occurred.[21] By the 1990s, container lines Maersk Sealand, MSC, Coscon, APL, and Evergreen, with their developed trade-lane networks, were important to the next stages of development of Salalah.[22] Finally, during this period the business science of supply chain management solidified. With globalization as the catalyst, and lowered impediments brought about by trade liberalization agreements around the world, supply chain management became a powerful driver in economic expansion, and, by extension, the strategic development of seaport cities, their surrounding environments, and their infrastructures. The challenge for Oman was to make certain the seaport investments made were synchronized with this new trade-lane and port management reality by offering a more comprehensive package.

Oman's opportunity zones in Salalah, and later in Duqm, were developed to attract national and international investment through the use of tax exemptions, relaxed regulations, and ownership control of up to 100 percent, and applying the real estate concept of usufruct. By the 1980s, there was traction: Raysut Cement Company in Salalah, and the Rusail Industrial Estate outside Muscat, where small factories assembled water pumps, air conditioners, car batteries, furniture, and other items once imported from abroad.[23] It was the intent of Sultan Qaboos' government to replicate this Rusail activity in the free zones of Salalah and ultimately Duqm.

By the mid-1990s, three berths had been constructed at Raysut Port, cementing Salalah at center stage of Oman's strategy to spur economic development. This strategy was implemented via joint government–private infrastructure investments, highlighted by the Maersk–Sealand and APM Terminal Ports Agreements of 1996 and 1997. The Sultanate of Oman, Maersk Line and APM, coupled with private institutions, agreed to jointly invest in the development of Raysut Port's new world class container terminal, inaugurated in November 1998. These investments established Raysut Port as a container transfer location on the wider global transportation network, and in 1999 the seaport set a world record for productivity with more than 250 berth moves per hour.

In 2000, Salalah Port LLC was named as the joint government–private entity assuming control of Raysut Port, eliminating full government ownership while retaining substantial influence. This public–private mixed consolidation of port activities in Salalah was further strengthened that same year, when bunkering (full-service ship maintenance and fueling services) facilities reached completion, and the soon to be operational general cargo terminal came under Salalah Port LLC management.[24]

Salalah: Staying Competitive, 2001–2020

By 2002, volumes in the Salalah Port container terminal exceeded design capacity for the first time.[25] This would recur, tempered by continued efficiency gains. Fortunately, Oman continued to act, anticipating growth, and by 2003 Salalah's expansion project for two new berths and a new breakwater gained approval. That same year 2 million TEUs transited through Salalah Port's facilities. Productivity in unloading and uploading full containers continued to set efficiency records, and the three-berth capacity success led to plans for fourth and fifth berth additions, completed by 2007. With the fifth berth fully operational by 2008, more than 3 million TEUs processed through Salalah Port facilities that year. Concurrently, Salalah Port's capabilities in handling break-bulk, bulk (grains, coal, etc.), and project cargo (including large equipment and infrastructure building materials) also expanded. Raysut Cement, the joint government–private enterprise constructed as a productive industrial component of the greater Salalah zone, required better cargo-handling capabilities. The Salalah Port entity responded by constructing the general cargo terminal in 2002, supported by additional material-handling equipment at berth-side. This action fed the infrastructure projects in Oman's coastal points and hinterlands. Commencing from an already growing volume of 800,000 tons annually by 1998, Salalah Port handled 1.7 million tons of break-bulk, bulk, and project cargo in 2002. By 2008, this volume doubled to 3.4 million tons, and in the next decade more than doubled again to 7.2 million tons. This occurred despite global economic headwinds during this period, contradicting the global trends of break-bulk contraction.[26]

The addition of a free trade zone was an elemental component of the strategy. Oman positioned the Salalah Free Zone as an attractive location for chemicals, manufacturing, assembly, and raw and refined material processing. The Salalah Free Zone, established by decree in 2006 and owned by the Omani government, was a free trade zone for infrastructure and support services in trading, distribution, warehousing, manufacturing, assembling, processing, packaging, and logistics companies.[27] In 2008, the Oman–US Free Trade Agreement was signed to attract U.S. investment to the Salalah Free Trade Zone. The agreement encouraged Omani manufacturing, stipulating that 35 percent of the volumes exported to the United States from the Salalah zone was of local origin. This effort bolstered the Omani economy, encouraging the employment and management of Omani nationals as part of the Omanization program.[28] Examples of companies formed during this period are Sea Land Shipping & Logistics Services LLC and Seven Seas Shipping & Logistics LLC.[29] These organizations, built on the limited liability model, joined logistics and port services companies brought under one umbrella in the following decade.

By the 2010s, Salalah Port was handling Panamax generation vessels (Panama Canal suitable), positioning it to process most of the world's container-carrying capacity. The year 2011 brought the implementation of the new Twenty-Year Vision Plan (2011–2030), and with it an impact on Salalah Port. The master plan envisioned Salalah Hub, including a railway connection and distribution center.[30] The next year witnessed the authorization of the greatly expanded general cargo terminal (GCT), coupled with new bulk-handling equipment.[31] This expansion plan involved capacity for handling over 6 million tons of liquid products such as natural gas.[32] Parallel to this development, in 2012, Salalah Port's handling capacity increased to 20 million tons per year of dry bulk commodities; The results were impressive and led to further development.[33]

In 2016, Salalah Port contracted with Cavotec SA to install eight vessel floatation and security units on the new berth number six at the container terminal to secure ships during the monsoon season. This was completed in time for Salalah to attain the highpoint of 3.9 million TEUs processed in 2017.[34] In 2020, Salalah Port launched its connectivity to the proposed national rail network. The multibillion-dollar railway project, conceived as part of the wider Gulf Cooperation Council (GCC) rail network, will open up prospects for freight forwarding through Salalah Port.[35]

In 2020, the last year of Sultan Qaboos' reign, Salalah Port accommodated 122 weekly arrivals of container vessels.[36] Maersk alone accounted for twenty-three of these port callings per week.[37] However, Salalah still faces the challenge of efficiently handling the Super-Post-Panamax vessels, especially the Very Large Container Vessel Class (VLCV), suitable for only fifty seaports globally. *Business Gateway* reported in 2019 that Salalah requires significant investment to meet these new demands and the Tanfeedh Initiative of Oman's government was tasked with the upgrade, which remains in process.[38] The National Program for the Promotion of Economic Diversification and Implementation (the Tanfeedh) was a component of the 2016–2020 Five-Year Plan.[39]

The development of Salalah Port over the fifty years of Sultan Qaboos' reign, while impacted by events beyond his scope of influence, held to the four fundamental principles of human and natural resource, infrastructure and state institution enhancement, under the umbrella of God's love. Upon his passing, Qaboos' leadership, vision, and results positioned Salalah Port and Oman to compete in the twenty-first century, bringing the private sector to the forefront in creating sustainable employment opportunities to the Omani citizenry.

From Undeveloped Land to Production: Duqm Port

The 2000s also saw the rapid evolution of Duqm's seaport development. The Port of Duqm Company comprised a joint 50/50 venture between the Consortium Port Antwerp (CAP) and the Government of the Sultanate of Oman. As evident in other arrangements the Omani government made with international sources, the relationship with CAP allowed for world class guidance from Europe's second largest port management organization. Critically, the engagement with CAP served as an excellent source for investment in Duqm's development, while maintaining the Sultanate's direct influence.

The development of the Duqm Port was led by the Special Economic Zone Authority of Duqm (SEZAD), the oversight management arm of the Omani government. SEZAD had responsibility for the planning and construction of the city of Duqm, including the seaport and the special economic zones within it.[40] SEZAD also led the build-out of the special economic zone in Duqm, accommodating assembly and supply-chain enhancements for potential local and international companies. SEZAD was the driver of Duqm as Oman's Seafront Industrial Complex, a critical component of Oman's Vision 2040 goal. Sultan Qaboos assigned Haitham bin Tariq Al-Said as head of the Oman Vision 2040 Committee in 2016, tasked with a plan deliverable by 2019.[41] This committee's mission statement, the foundation for the future five-year plans for Oman, recognized that the economy and society must no longer rely on non-renewable resources, but on innovation and knowledge. Investments in opportunities triggered by regional and international dynamics, and based on eight drivers, including infrastructure and logistics enhancements, were the way forward.[42] The key to maintaining this strategic direction and the emphasis on youth set by the ninth Five-Year Development Plan was the need to develop dynamic leaders with new competencies. Leaders functioning in an integrated institutional and economic framework, supporting the Oman Vision 2040 imperatives of preserving environmental sustainability, establishing modern infrastructure, and an integrated physical system, were of paramount importance.[43]

Seeking to gain better control of the logistics aspect and profits of its seaports, the government formed ASYAD (Arabic proper name meaning versality, enthusiasm, creativity) in 2016. ASYAD was the centerpiece of Oman's ambition to reclaim its 2,000-year-old regional trade leadership position and establish the country as one of the world's top ten logistics hubs by 2040. ASYAD Group brought together sixteen logistics companies and joint ventures under one entity, improving performance, creating efficiencies, and offering economies of scale. The group included three deep ports (Sohar, Duqm, and Salalah) and three free zones supporting Oman's five airports, a new rail network, and a world class road network.[44] Oman's recently developed Banyan Customs System allowed for ASYAD to handle customs transactions electronically and served as the cornerstone to the Muscat Compact of 2019. This agreement linked Oman to global customs systems.[45] AYSAD offered Oman an opportunity to provide training and employment opportunities for Omani youth, an issue highlighted by Oman in response to the Arab Spring. In August 2012, the Sultan announced a royal directive mandating the speedy implementation of a national job creation plan for thousands of public and private sector jobs.[46] Given the large population of youth in Oman (44 percent under age 15), continued focus on providing for education, jobs, and career growth was a domestic challenge for the country.[47] In 2012, Sultan Qaboos declared that both the private sector and individual Omanis needed to work harder to create jobs and accept them, respectively.[48] The Sawaed Initiative underway in Duqm, Salalah, and Sohar since 2016 encourages young Omanis to study logistics operations to build a versatile workforce for this lucrative and sustainable career path.[49]

China's 2013 strategic plan to expand its power globally was institutionalized in the Belt and Road Initiative (BRI). This movement set to spread China's economic might to regions where it was either vulnerable to competing Western military or economic interests, using trade and the economic soft influence of funding.[50] The BRI allowed the Sultanate to utilize an alternate avenue for development expertise and financial backing, without jeopardizing Oman's relationship with the West. Thus, Western companies such as Maersk and APM were selectively utilized in the initial development of container capabilities in Salalah, while the BRI was of more initial impact in the subsequent development of Duqm, reflecting Oman's strong emphasis on neutrality and the ability to thread the diplomatic needle.[51]

By 2018, the Port of Duqm was positioned to play a key role as a catalyst in the commercialization of the vast mineral resources of the Al-Wusta region. An example was the liquified natural gas plant's first phase, completed in 2018. Another area of development was the Special Economic Zone of Duqm, designed for supply chain-related activities such as assembly, light manufacturing, and free trade mingling of products for either export of Omani finished goods or for manipulated materials or products. Included in this economic zone was the China Oman Industrial Park, where the financial and development expertise of the BRI is in full swing today. Oman Wanfang, the master developer of the China–Oman Industrial Park in Duqm, commenced ten projects in 2018 worth $3.2 billion, with twenty-five more in the pipeline for completion by 2028–2030.[52] By 2019, China had provided several training courses in a diverse range of topics for nearly 400 Omanis, free of cost.[53] In the second quarter of 2021, the first industrial investment implemented will be operational: Duqm Hongtong Piping LLC's plant is to commence production with an eye on domestic, regional, and international markets.[54] Also in mid-2021, Duqm is poised to manufacture transit buses within the SEZAD, with locally and internationally sourced components.[55]

The evolving port at Duqm is a manifestation of Oman's strategy to turn its eastern coast into the entrepot for the interior of the Arabian Peninsula. Tied into the global logistics network, linked via road and rail infrastructure to Oman's hinterland and to points throughout the GCC, Duqm is an important catalyst for Oman's 2040 Vision. Duqm will serve as a departure point for exports from the surrounding area of central and northern Oman, and the Arabian Peninsula and beyond. Duqm is being developed as a neutral business site, where trade and naval support operations from all nations are welcomed, but where political differences are neutralized under tight security. Duqm's Arabian Sea location is suitable for avoiding potential conflicts inherent in the Strait of Hormuz; it is also well located to support the efforts against piracy impacting Arabian Sea trading nations and companies.[56] In mid-2021, Duqm launched its full bunkering and support apparatus.[57]

Another feature of Duqm Port is its capabilities which were built and planned to handle large-proportioned project cargo. Duqm is the only port in Oman capable of handling such cargos, and other ports of the GCC are unable to receive and transport project cargo overland into Oman.[58] Duqm Port is designed as both an origin/destination and point of transshipment, but is a nascent participant as of 2021. Because Super post-Panamax container vessels, representing the largest container ships and tankers in the world, can dock at Duqm, the port is well situated for expansion.[59]

Duqm Port's ongoing development reflects Sultan Qaboos' commitment to provide sustainable employment for Oman's citizens through public–private engagement. The state institutions built during his reign produced both economic growth and a renewed focus on social improvement. Oman will benefit from the dual track of natural resource extraction and sustainable economic development not linked to oil and gas. Duqm Port has adhered to Qaboos' four fundamental principles.

Positioned for the Future

Although challenges remain, the Government of Oman under the leadership of Sultan Qaboos built a sustainable infrastructure to meet its ultimate goals as stated in the Five-Year Development and Twenty-Year Visions plans. Among the variables impacting Oman's desired outcomes are local and global economics; geopolitical considerations within the GCC; the surrounding western Indian Ocean world and beyond; the evolution of the ongoing Omanization project and responses to local social pressures; and the differentiation of Oman through both actual growth and comparative position. But the potential end game, the anticipated social and economic results, could be significant once these ports are at their full capacity.

Analysis of data from the United Nations Conference on Trade and Development (UNCTAD), supplemented by World Bank data, covering the period 2003–2019, confirms Oman's results in seizing the opportunity reins during the fifty years of Sultan Qaboos' rule to engage with the broader global economy and, more specifically, with the globalization of its infrastructure. Container port traffic data confirms the first thirty years (1970–2000) of infrastructure modernization cemented the position of Oman as the number three GCC seaport host, measured by throughput, behind the UAE and Saudi Arabia. By 2000, Salalah Port had established itself as an important factor in the trade network of global logistics firms, and the plans for Duqm were well underway.[60] Importantly, UNCTAD's data from its Liner Shipping Connectivity Index, with 2004 as its baseline, vindicates Oman's strategy and implementation during the first thirty years.[61] But the infrastructure strategy did not propel Oman demonstrably beyond regional or global trends.[62] Salalah's current inability to efficiently process the Very Large Container Vessel class is a potential drag on future progress.

However, Sultan Qaboos' strategy created the path forward. Oman's neutral and diplomatic approach helped global trade. Regionally, good relationships with GCC partners, and the resulting rail and road program connecting the seaports and hinterland, once completed, should be a major advantage for Oman. Assuming the continuation of the Banyan Customs System and its coordination with those of the region, combined with the cost and time efficiencies anticipated and Duqm and Salalah's geographic advantages, Oman is poised to benefit from growth throughout the region. Oman's perpetuating good relationships with India, the European Union, and the United States, while taking measured advantage of the Chinese presence, is of strategic importance. "We currently live in a world of overlapping policies and interests, but our international cooperation is in line with the Sultanate's higher interests and in line with our contribution to the establishment of world security and prosperity."[63] Omanization, the encouragement of local economic actors and Omani ownership and business ventures, exemplified in the Sawaed project to build a logistics and supply chain expertise among its citizenry, will likely continue to be a focus of infrastructure plans in the future.

Notes

1. Lloyds List website, *One Hundred Ports 2020*, available at: https://lloydslist. maritimeintelligence.informa.com/one-hundred-container-ports-2020, last accessed January 2021. Salalah ranked No. 44 in container tonnage in 2020, No. 51 in 2019. World Shipping Council website, available at: https://www. worldshipping.org/about-the-industry/global-trade/ports, last accessed November 2020. Salalah ranked No. 53 in 2015.
2. Oman Ministry of Information website, available at: https://www.mol.om/His-Majesty-Speech, last accessed April 2021, Sultan Qaboos Speech of October 12, 2004.
3. Sultan Qaboos Speech of October 1, 2005.

4. Arabian Gulf Digital Archive, available at: https://www.agda.ae/en/catalogue/tna/fo/1016/94, last accessed September 2020. Letter to British Consulate General, Muscat, from E. A. W. Bullock, Esq., Ministry of Overseas Development, London.

5. Oman Info website, *The Royal Speeches*, 16, available at: https://www.OmanInfo.om, last accessed February 2021.

6. Arabian Gulf Digital Archive, available at: https://www.agda.ae/en/catalogue/tna/fo/1016/94, last accessed September 2020. The recorded notes of the UK political agent Chauncy's description of his visit to Salalah in April 1950 offers a snapshot of the rudimentary capability of the Raysut port of this era. "Next morning, therefore, two shoxe bonts each rowed by six men, and somewhat rezeritable for the fact that their planks were sewn together with string and lined with skin, care at 9:30 a.m. to take off Woods-Ballard and me and the luggage." They were rowed to the beach after spending 24 hours offshore.

7. World Shipping Council website 2020, available at: https://wwwworldshipping.org/Glossary-of-Industry-Terms, last accessed November 2020.

8. Brian Slack and Antoine Fremont, "Fifty Years of Organizational Change in Container Shipping: Regional Shift and the Role of Family Firms," *GeoJournal* (2009): 23–24. Also see, Edward G. Hinkelman, *Dictionary of the International Trade: Handbook of the International Trade Community* (Novato: World Trade Press, 1999). Containerization refers to the technique of using a box-like device in which a number of packages are stored, protected, and handled as a single unit in transit. Advantages of containerization include: less handling of cargo, more protection against pilferage, less exposure to the elements, and reduced cost of shipping.

9. Slack, "Fifty Years of Organizational Change."

10. Frauke Heard-Bey, "Inside Oman," in *Abu Dhabi, the United Arab Emirates and the Gulf Region: Fifty Years of Transformation* (Göttingen: Gerlach Press, 2017). "In the 1960s Oman was a closed country to the extent that archaeologists working near the Buraimi oasis on a site near Hili in Abu Dhabi territory could not inspect tumuli . . . a mile from Oman, for fear of being shot at."

11. Michael Baily, "The Great Freight Race," *The Times*, October 28, 1977, 2. For contemporary reporting on the surge in imports and resulting clogging of the Gulf ports, the poor inland infrastructure, and the role of private entities in charting the corrective course, see Hilaire Gomer, "Middle East: Harbours to Match the New Riches," *The Times*, November 22, 1977, 31.

12. Gomer, "Middle East: Harbours to Match the New Riches," between 1971 and 1974.

13. Oman Info website, *The Royal Speeches*, 27.

14. Salalah Port website, 2020, available at: https://salalahport.com.om, last accessed July 2020. Between 1971 and 1974, even as it fought the insurgency, the government of Oman invested $11.5 million to deepen this port as a first phase to accommodate vessels with drafts up to 13 ft,.

15. Oman Info website, *The Royal Speeches*, 36.

16. Salalah Port website, 2020, available at: https://salalahport.com.om, last accessed July 2020. Between 1981 and 1982, Phase Three of Raysut Port established a container terminal equipped with a 35-ton gantry crane, costing $9 million, and supporting the government's second five-year plan to further the country's economic growth via international maritime transportation.

17. A. R. Walker, "Recessional and Gulf War Impacts on Port Development and Shipping in the Gulf States in the 1980s," *GeoJournal* 18(3) (1989): 273–284.

18. Mark N. Katz, "A New Dawn?" *Wilson Quarterly* 11(1) (1987): 64–77.

19. Sealand of Oman website, 2020, available at: https//:www.sealandoman.com/about-us; also About us: Sea Land Shipping, available at: sealandoman.com, last accessed October 2020. The current chairman, His Highness Sayyid Shihab Bin Taraq Al-Said is an important member of the ruling Royal family of the Sultanate of Oman. Also see Modern Shipping Services LLC, website, available at: http://modernshipping.com, last accessed December 2020.

20. B. Slack, "Pawns in the Game: Ports in the Global Transportation System," *Growth and Change* 24 (1993): 379–388. There is noteworthy dialogue on this subject. Also see Cesar Ducruet and Sung-Woo Le,. "Frontline Soldiers of Globalization: Port City Evolution and Regional Competition," *GeoJournal* 67(2) (2009); T. Heaver, "The Implications of Increased Competition for Port Policy and Management," *Journal of Maritime Policy and Management* 22(2) (1995): 125–133; Michael Field, "Rivalry between States Leads to Lack of Cooperation and Wasteful Development," *The Times*, December 16, 1970, 3; T. Notteboom and W. Winkelmans, "Structural Changes in Logistics: How do Port Authorities Face the Challenge?" *Maritime Policy and Management* 28(1) (2001): 71–89; T. Notteboom and Jean-Paul Rodrigue, "The Future of Containerization: Perspectives from Maritime and Inland Freight Distribution," *GeoJournal* 74(1) (2009): 10.

21. Notteboom and Rodrigue, "The Future of Containerization," 10.

22. A. Fremont, "Global Marine Networks: The Case of Maersk," 15 (2016): 431–442, available at: https://www.sciencedirect.com/science/article/pii.

This essay offers the story of Maersk during the above referenced transitional period. Also see Slack and Fremont, "Fifty Years of Organizational Change," 23–34.

23. Katz, "A New Dawn?" 64–77. Usufruct is the legal right granted by the land and facility owner conferring complete use of the property for a set, and usually very long period, paying only fees and taxes. The advantage for international entities was the ability to invest over the long term without real estate purchase and ownership responsibilities.

24. Salalah Port website, 2020, available at: https://salalahport.com.om, last accessed July 2020.

25. Salalah Port website, 2020.

26. Salalah Port website, 2020.

27. Zawya website, 2020, available at: https://zawya.com/mena/en/company/Salalah_Free_Zone, last accessed December 2020.

28. Salalah Port website, 2020, available at: https://salalahport.com.om, last accessed July 2020. Also see Oman Ministry of Information website, available at: https://www.mol.om/His-Majesty-Speech, last accessed April 2021. Speech of November 11, 2008.

29. Sealand of Oman website, available at: https://www.sealandoman.com/about-us, last accessed October 2020. Sea Land Shipping & Logistics Services LLC, an Oman headquartered shipping agency and logistics company, was established in 2008 and belongs to the Seven Seas Group family. Similarly, Seven Seas Shipping & Logistics LLC was established in 2009 to take care of the freight forwarding activities of the shipping division and represented FedEx Trade Network in Oman.

30. Salalah Port website, 2020, available at: https://salalahport.com.om, last accessed July 2020. Also, food reserve and processing centers among warehousing and other logistics facilities, and liquid storage along with dedicated facilities aimed to accommodate small- and medium-sized entrepreneurs.

31. Salalah Port website, 2020.

32. Salalah Port website, 2020.

33. Salalah Port website, 2020. Upon becoming operational in 2015, a more than doubling in non-containerized volume occurred, and Salalah Port's break-bulk, bulk, and project cargo by 2018 reached 16.2 million tons. The sixth berth addition, and its accompanying material-handling investment, supplemented this increased volume processed in the new deep-water general cargo and liquid-bulk terminal. This trend of general cargo expansion continued to buck global

trends. Finally, 2018 brought plans for the container terminal to add 3 million TEUs to capacity.

34. Salalah Port website, 2020. Cavotec was installing sixteen additional units on berths three and four at the container terminal by 2017.

35. Salalah Port website, 2020. As a superhighway for rail-based freight, the network was planned to enhance connectivity between Salalah and the major population centers and markets of the GCC. When the network comes into service, Salalah has the potential to become a major gateway for the GCC for fast moving consumer goods and other high-value commodities. Salalah Port anticipates a significant upsizing of their capabilities as a liquid hub serving the markets of the East and India.

36. ASYAD website, 2020, available at: https://www.asyad.om/freight/direct-lines-to-Oman, last accessed December 2020.

37. Maersk website, 2020, available at: https://www.Maersk.com, last accessed November 2020.

38. *Business Gateways News* website, 2020, available at: https://businessgateways.com/news/2019/05/13/Upgrade-key-to-attracting-mega-container-ships, last accessed November 2020.

39. The Business Year Oman website, 2020, available at: https://www.thebusinessyear.com/Oman-2019/development-plan/inside-perspective, last accessed December 2020.

40. Kaori Sugihara, "Varieties of Industrialization: An Asian Regional Perspective," in Tirtankar Roy and Riello Giorgio (eds.), *Global Academic History* (New York: Bloomsbury Academic, 2010). The "Seafront Industrial Complex" embodies the development and enhancement of seaports beyond import–export activities. This model led to the successful development of north, eastern and southeastern Asian seaports; these seaports have successfully linked the oceanic and hinterland elements. SEZAD was accountable for the Duqm Industrial Land Company (DILC), the emerging site of planned manufacturing, natural resource collection, and enhancement. The DILC was responsible for developing the 2,000 hectares (4,949 acres) set aside for heavy manufacturing and petrochemical developments, located near the Duqm refinery for oil extraction.

41. Yoel Gozanky and Efraim Halevy, "The End of the Qaboos Era," Institute for National Security Studies, 2020. Haitham was ultimately named Qaboos' successor.

42. Oman Vision 2040 website, available at: https://www.2040.om/wp-content/uploads/2020/12/Oman2040-En.pdf.2020, last accessed January 2021.

43. Business Year Oman website, 2020, available at: https://www.thebusinessyear. com/Oman-2019/development-plan/inside-perspective, last accessed December 2020.

44. ASYAD website, 2020, available at: https://www.asyadgroup.com?about-us, last accessed November 2020.

45. ASYAD website, 2020, video on Logistics Services in Duqm.

46. Anthony Cordesman, Max Markusen, and Eric P. Jones, "Oman: Stability and Instability in the Gulf Region in 2016," Center for Strategic and International Studies (CSIS), 2016.

47. United Nations Office for the Coordination of Humanitarian Affairs website. available at: https://unocha/oman, last accessed November 2020.

48. Oman Ministry of Information website, available at: https://www.mol.om/His-Majesty-Speech, last accessed April 2021. Speech of November 12, 2012.

49. ASYAD Group website, 2020, available at: https://www.asyadgroup.comabout-us, last accessed November 2020.

50. Camille Lons, Jonathan Fulton, and Naser Al-Tamimi, "China's Great Game in the Middle East," European Council on Foreign Relations, 2019. The BRI in the Middle East is well discussed among scholars and practitioners. Also see Muhammad Abbas Hassan, "Growing China–India Competition in the Indian Ocean," *Strategic Studies* 39(1): (2019), Institute of Strategic Studies; Daniel J. Kostecka, "Places and Bases: The Chinese Navy's Emerging Support Network in the Indian Ocean," *Naval War College Review* 64(1) (2011).

51. Times of Oman website, 2021, "Oman's Balanced Foreign Policies Praised by Chinese Ambassador," available at: https://timesofoman.com/article/100236-omans-balanced-foreign-policies-praised-by-chinese-ambassador, last accessed October 7, 2021.

52. Oman Observer website, 2021, available at: https://www.omanobserver.om/3.2-billion-invested-industrial-park, last accessed November 2020. The first ten planned projects ran the gamut from a building materials marketplace to production plants for methanol, electricity, desalination, and bromine. Also planned are factories for non-metallic composite pipes used in oilfields, solar panels and equipment, high-mobility utility vehicles, oil and gas fields, and even a five-star hotel in Duqm.

53. Oman Observer website, 2021, available at: https://www,omanobserver.om/more-chinese-firms-eye-industrial-park-in-duqm, last accessed January 2021.

54. Oman Observer website, 2021, available at: https://www.omanobserver. om/first-manufacturing-project-of-china-oman-industrial-complex-set-for-q2-launch, last accessed February 2021.

55. Times of Oman website, 2021, "Bus Manufacturing Plant to Start Production Soon in Oman," available at: https://timesofoman.com, last accessed April 2021.

56. Port of Duqm website, 2020, available at: https://www.portofduqm.om, last accessed August 2020.

57. Times of Oman website, 2021, "Pact Signed to Operate, Maintain Bunker Terminal Facility in Duqm Port," available at: https://timesofoman.com/ article/100413-pact-signed-to-operate-maintain-bunker-terminal-facility-in-duqm-port, last accessed October 7, 2021.

58. Times of Oman, "Pact Signed to Operate, Maintain Bunker Terminal Facility in Duqm Port."

59. Times of Oman, "Pact Signed to Operate, Maintain Bunker Terminal Facility in Duqm Port." With depths of at least 18 meters (58 ft) guaranteed through the approach to the wharf, the initial port arrangement at Duqm is positioned to accommodate twenty-first-century commerce.

60. UNCTAD website, available at: https://unctadstat.unctad.org, last accessed October 2020. Also see World Bank website, available at: https://databank. worldbank.org/databases, last accessed October 2020.

61. UNCTAD website. Oman's score of 24.6/100 in 2004 improved to 52.0/100 by 2019. This score performance, compared with the UAE's 39.0/100 (2004) and 71.5/100 (2009) results, and those of Saudi Arabia's 36.2/100 (2004) and 63.0/100 (2009), indicate that Oman remained competitive with the other two GCC container seaport powerhouses (consistently these three represent 92–94 percent of container activity in the GCC).

62. UNCTAD website. Between 2000 and 2019, Oman's container traffic grew by a multiple of 4.27, compared with Saudi Arabia's 5.9 and the UAE's 3.79. Further, Oman's growth multiplier trailed the GCC's average of 4.64, India's 6.96, and South Asia's 6.6, but was higher than Egypt's 3.88, or the global volume multiplier of 3.54.

63. Oman Ministry of Information website, available at: https://www.mol.om/His-Majesty-Speech, last accessed April 2021. Speech of November 11, 2008.

16

GREENING OMAN: ISLAMIC ENVIRONMENTALISM, SUSTAINABLE DEVELOPMENT, AND POST-OIL FUTURES

Maria F. Curtis

We, in the Sultanate of Oman, through our deep personal interest and the directives we have given our Government to act in concert with neighboring countries, are making energetic efforts to protect our environment and territorial waters from pollution and other problems. We hope that world detente and the positive trend being pursued in settling serious problems will permit us to work together, regardless of ideologies and selfish national interests, to address the environmental and development-related issues which face us in a spirit of reconciliation, amity and peace so as to secure a healthy life for ourselves and the generations to come.[1]

Sultan Qaboos, The Earth Summit Conference,
UNCED, Rio de Janeiro, Brazil June 3, 1992[2]

The discovery of oil in Oman in 1964 contributed to unprecedented change and development, resulting in a demographic shift from a largely agrarian, rural village society to increased urbanization around Muscat, and a transformation of the human relationship to land and resources. Policy-making was an act of "*Omanibalancing*"; incorporating a regional oil and gas economy, forward-thinking sustainability built on Qur'anic precepts, and "Omani ecocultural spirituality."[3] During his fifty-year reign, His Majesty Sultan Qaboos bin Said Al-Said safeguarded Oman's many environmental assets through national initiatives, thus laying the foundation for enduring policy that cultivated a spirit of ecological appreciation that remains part of contemporary Omani cultural identity. The young Sultan Qaboos began leading his country during the dawning of the global ecological movement, ascending to power just two years before the first United Nation's Conference on the Human Environment in Stockholm in 1972.[4] Oman's consistent engagement in international discussions around environmental regulations and protocols can be seen in its evolving domestic agenda and institutions. The modern Omani Renaissance occurred with environmental preservation in mind and the involvement of a vast cadre of stakeholders seen across such varied domains as K-12 through university education, governmental and non-governmental agencies, national architectural style, wildlife preservation, resource and habitat conservation, agricultural advancement, regional beautification projects, and international ecotourism initiatives. Oman has been carefully shaping its policy in tandem with a "moral and scientific obligation" to modernize at a measured and reasoned pace.[5]

This chapter uses the term *greening* to describe Oman's environmental policies, initially conceived by Qaboos, that manifest in new ways among generations educated in institutions he helped to establish.[6] Further, the term underscores the growing voices from the Muslim world calling for a "green *din*" (*din* means "religion" in Arabic), while invoking humanity's responsibility to protect the planet and its living creatures as set forth in the Qur'an.[7] Greening recalls the *aflaj* irrigation system in *Jabal al-Akhdar*, the Green Mountains, which continues to release water in accordance with centuries' old indigenous notions of the just distribution of finite resources.[8] The urgency of Sultan Qaboos' priorities anticipated the environmental degradation seen today as well as a growing Islamic ecological paradigm, a green *Nahda* (Renaissance).[9] In Arabia, a region of the world that "contributes to approximately 25% of the world's oil production and holds 40% of the world oil reserves," and accounts for 50 percent of the Arabic-speaking world's and 8 percent of global carbon emissions, Oman has remained committed to charting a greener path.[10] Mitigating climate change and creating smarter, more sustainable cities is of increasingly critical importance given accelerating global carbon emissions.[11]

Figure 16.1 Al-Jabal Al-Akhdar terrace gardens and *aflaj* irrigation.
Source: Badar Ali Al-Yazeedi.

Oman's Environmental Record over Five Decades

Oman formally embarked on protecting resources and wildlife in 1974 with the Law Monitoring Marine Pollution, and by establishing its Office of Environmental Conservation, the first of its kind in the Arab world. Sultan Qaboos emphasized building a diversified economy in the National Development Strategy (1976–1995), encouraging the development of the public sector from the earliest days of the Sultanate's oil and gas production. The drafting of some sixteen royal decrees and the ratification of international conventions concerning environmental protections preceded Oman's formal constitution promulgated in 1996, later revised in 2011.[12] This "conservation of the environment, its protection and the prevention of pollution" is enshrined in Article 12 of the Constitution.[13]

Week-long educational and awareness programs were launched in the mid-1970s to cultivate a sense of pride and kinship with the natural environment. The Ministry of Regional Municipality, and Environment and Water Resources worked with the Ministry of Education to deliver a bilingual Arabic–English environmental awareness curriculum to school-age children.[14] Qaboos stressed close cooperation between different ministries to share in the charge of educating the public; "Article (6): The Ministry shall disseminate environmental knowledge education and awareness among all sectors of the Community. The responsibility for conservation and preservation of the environment is the duty of all whether individually or in groups."[15]

The tumultuous ecological times in which Sultan Qaboos began as a new leader served to heighten his ecological preoccupations. In 1979, the First World Water Conference was held, and the Three Mile Island nuclear accident occurred in New York. Halfway around the world, the Omani Council for the Conservation of Environment and Prevention of Pollution was formed by royal decree 68. The Marine Pollution Monitoring Law and the Law of the Natural Protected Areas and National Parks soon followed.

Legislative momentum continued with Oman's accession to the International Convention for the Regulation of Whaling (1980), and a number of important decrees focused on the sea, including the Fishing and Protection of Water Wealth Law.[16] In 1982, just a year after Oman joined the GCC, it became the first country in the region to create a comprehensive environmental policy, and, in 1984 the Ministry of the Environment was born.[17] In 1985, the same year that scientists reported a tear in the Earth's ozone layer, the Omani Ministry of Water Resources was established, as was the Oman Company for Marine Pollution Protection in response to an oil tanker accident that destroyed sea life and left crude residue on Muscat's shorelines.[18] Coastal development and pollution dealt a heavy blow to Oman's coastal environments. Oil and tar pollution on beaches from illegal ship discharge at sea, the mining of sand for construction projects, new roads, disposal of fish in market areas, and improper waste disposal have further threatened already delicate areas.[19] The Ministry of Regional Municipalities and Environment has developed a multipronged approach to resolving these concerns.[20] To prevent oil spillage, a dumping center for oil tankers was created. Beaches were protected by forbidding sand extraction and the dumping of trash. The 1980s were devoted largely to establishing limitations for shipping, whaling, and fishing, and concluded with Oman's ratification of the United Nations Convention on the Law of the Sea (1989).

Sultan Qaboos attended the UNESCO meeting in Paris in 1989, and later launched the UNESCO Sultan Qaboos Prize for Environmental Preservation, representing the first global environmental prize given from the Arab world.[21] The award offers an annual prize of $60,000, and recognizes initiatives around the world. Oman has harnessed its domestic vision to leverage science diplomacy in a larger diplomatic context.[22]

The 1990s pivoted from marine conservation to a greater focus on ecosystems. From 1994 to 1996, Oman ratified the Convention on Biological Diversity, modified the Law of the Natural Protected Areas and National Parks, and amended the Environmental Protection and Pollution Control Law. It continued to take part in international discussions with the Implementation Agreement of Part Eleven of the United Nations Convention on the Law of the Sea. Legislation around food security was ratified in the Global Plan of Action for the Conservation and Sustainable Utilization of Plant Genetic Resources for Food and Agriculture, and later the System Prevention and Protection of Agricultural Wealth. The midpoint of Sultan Qaboos' reign was a watershed year for Oman with the drafting of its first Constitution. When the Kyoto Protocol was adopted in 1997, Sultan Qaboos was awarded the International Union for Conservation of Nature (IUCN) John C. Philips Prize in recognition of efforts to protect and conserve Oman's resources and heritage. Important legislation continued aiming to stop desertification, to create the Damaniyat Nature Preserve, and turtle reserves.[23] Oman inaugurated the celebration of what is effectively its second national day, January 8, as Omani Environment Day.

In the first two decades of the new millennia, new legislation, ratification, and membership of international organizations expanded. Sultan Qaboos defined sustainable development as "[l]inking environmental conditions with planning and development policy in order to satisfy needs and aspirations of the present generation without endangering future needs and requirements."[24] In 2000, Oman joined the Tuna Fisheries Organization in the Indian Ocean, created the Law of Agricultural Quarantine, and the Law on Protection of New Plant Varieties. Oman sought membership in the Regional Commission for Fisheries in 2001, and drafted the Law on Conservation of the Environment and Prevention of Pollution. In 2003, laws on Nature Reserves and Wildlife Conservation, and Pastures and Animal Resources Management Law were created. Oman signed the International Treaty on Plant Genetic Resources for Food and Agriculture and drafted the Law on Veterinary Quarantine.

The Environment Society of Oman (ESO), an NGO supported by Qaboos and other royal patronage, was established in 2004 to "protect Oman's natural heritage and influence environmentally sustainable behavior through education, awareness and conservation."[25] The ESO continues to play a vital role in voicing ecological concerns, and produces research that drives legislation and expands scientific knowledge. In 2006, the Oman Botanic Garden was created as a site of preservation, conservation, and education.

The Ministry of the Environment was reorganized as the Ministry of the Environment and Climate Affairs (MECA) in 2007 to address urgent climate concerns. The period between the early 1970s until 2007 dealt largely institutional foundations, while later shifting to a national strategy to fight climate change and reduce greenhouse gases by implementing the United Nations Environment Program.[26] The International Plant Resources Institute (Biodiversity International) was founded in 2007, and Oman thereafter joined the International Trade Treaty on Endangered Species of Animals and Plants. Two years later, the Protection of the Breeds' Rights in New Varieties of Plants Law was created. Oman adopted provisions of the United Nations Convention on the Law of the Sea Concerning Conservation and Management of Straddling Fish Stocks and Highly Migratory Fish Stocks (2007), adopted the International Trade Treaty on Endangered Species of Animals and Plants (2007), and joined the Near East Plant Protection Organization (2014).

Under the direction of the Ministry of Agriculture and Fisheries Wealth, the Oman Animal & Plant Genetic Resources Center (OAPGRC) was founded to "review opportunities in conservation and maintenance of globally significant genetic resources".[27] The OAPGRC strategy report identifies new areas of research and policy and reiterates the "moral and scientific duty" of conserving microbial diversity in Oman's desert sands, soils, and marine environments.[28] In 2015, an Intergovernmental Panel on Climate Change (IPCC) was formed in conjunction with greater data collection on carbon emissions, and increased precision in interagency collaboration. In 2019, Oman signed the Paris Agreement on Climate Change, and announced the final two nature preserves of the twenty that Sultan Qaboos established.

This summary attempts to capture the breadth and scope of policy and law as it unfolded over time under Qaboos. Sultan Haitham reconfigured Oman's ministries early in his reign, and the Ministry of Environment and

Climate Affairs was reorganized as the Environment Authority in August 2020.[29] What began as Sultan Qaboos' aspirations for Oman's green *Nahda* in the early 1970s has grown into an infrastructure built on an education system that raised a generation of citizens who embody the notion that ecological conservatism is the responsibility of all. Oman's approach toward managing resources preceded by nearly four decades the 2015 Islamic Declaration on Climate Change, regarded as a new environmental awakening among Muslim-majority countries.[30]

Environmental Sustainability and Stewardship in Ibadi Islam

Omanis are taught from the time they are small to appreciate natural resources, and to feel responsible for the natural world. Scholars have described "Omani indigenous ecocultural spirituality" as "intertwined with religion inspired by the Qur'an and the Prophet Muhammad's teachings, conveying, in part, a sense of ethical duty toward the more-than-human world."[31] Villagers who still tend family farms speak of their animals as children, and palm trees as family members for whom they are responsible (*amana*) and equal members of a shared community (*'umma*).

There is debate in the "green *din*" (green religion) literature as to whether Islamic ecological movements are reinvigorating older Qur'anic teachings, or if concepts like *mizan* (balance and sustainability) and *khalifah* (stewardship) are being recast in a modern ecological frame.[32] It is clear from recent featured Ibadi *fiq* theological lectures that sustainability and stewardship are central to the Ibadi-lived tradition. Following several decades of thought on the environment, a sermon delivered by Hatim Al-Abdissalaam from Be'ah during Ramadan in 2021, addressed the topic "How Islam Perceives Food Waste." He explains that "This is not the month of feasting; this is the month of fasting," and that "Allah does not love those who are selfish, those who are extravagant and take more than they actually need." He explained that Ramadan is a time of self-control and to identify with those who have little, and concluded that to experience the true meaning of Ramadan, one must take only what is truly necessary, leaving resources for those less fortunate. He extended this argument to the mandate to protect the Earth in a spirit of *khalifah*, which gives resources for the needy while preserving the Earth and reducing food waste, a leading contributor to carbon emissions.

The Qur'an states that land and its protection by humans is a sacred duty, and the Earth ('ard) is mentioned nearly five hundred times.[33] The concept of the *khalifah* (Surah 2:30) asserts the responsibility of stewardship.[34] Within the Islamic perspective on the environment, *al-hima*[35] is understood as the portion of available land and resources conserved for the sake of future generations to ensure that living creatures and species are not imperiled. *Al-hima* as an idea that challenged pre-Islamic practices of claiming and using land, insisting that some land could not be privately owned if they contributed to a larger public good. The Prophet Muhammed challenged excessive land grabs and resource monopolies even as he ruled over an important agricultural oasis in Madina and encouraged trade through Mecca.

Ibadi Islam's high regard for environmental sustainability (*mizan*) and stewardship (*khalifah*) converge in perhaps an unexpected place, the Oman Holding Company for Environmental Services, or Be'ah.[36] A government-owned company charged with "leading change in the waste management sector," it invites Omanis to take part in "Conserving Our Beautiful Oman" through programming and educational materials featured on their official website. Be'ah authored a report on the marked decrease in food waste seen in Ramadan in 2020 due to Covid-19 restrictions on large gatherings, citing that in 2019 Omanis wasted some 13,000 tons of food in the first ten days of Ramadan alone, enough to feed some 374,135 people.[37] Be'ah launched a social media campaign entirely around preventing food waste during Ramadan 2021. The month-long campaign combined lectures in Arabic and English with Islamic scholars, public service announcements on the dangers of Covid-19 face masks to birds and other animals, cooking tips from Omani chefs, and featured Mother Khawla, an elderly Omani grandmotherly cultural hero figure sent from the past to teach young Omanis "*ma yajouz!!*," or, "don't waste!"

Mother Khawla wears traditional Omani clothes while waving her hennaed hand and sometimes wielding a traditional date reed palm broom as a comical instrument for spanking naughty children. She cautions against straying from traditional Omani values and urges children to practice resourcefulness. Her voice haunts the conscience of a young man in a grocery aisle, prompting him to unload some items from his shopping cart. She whispers, "don't waste!" over a food-loaded morning *suhour* table when a couple remembers to be thankful for all their blessings. In a more dramatic skit a young wife is unable to control her desire to put food out and is whisked from her Western-style dining table into the past, falling abruptly into Mother Khawla's traditional *majlis* dining area. She is reminded of the important role of monitoring and planning household consumption practices as a way to uphold traditional Omani Ibadi values as she is returned back to her own table in the present. Here, preventing food waste is not an extension of women's domestic work, but is exalted as a critical endeavor to saving the planet, one individual act at a time.

Saving Oman's Rare, Threatened, and Endangered Species

The ethical balance between economic development and stewardship resonates in Oman's laws protecting water, animals, rare and endangered plant and animal species, and land. Environmental concerns must always be balanced by the need for human development and there have been some costs to Oman's modernization. For example, as construction in the lush Dhofar region in the south expands, particularly in infrastructure projects like highways and the Duqm port, care has been taken to guard species of plants and trees in the Oman Botanic Garden. This is one example of Oman's approach to weaving together conservation and development.

Sultan Qaboos defined wildlife as "All kinds of living organisms such as plants, animals, bacteria, fungi and others exist within or outside their habitat."[38] The ecosystem also includes soil, which should be protected against all manner of soil degradation, whether from the removal of trees, shrubs, roots, or grass.[39] Oman has been committed to conserving its unique ecology by safeguarding roughly 20 percent of the country into three subcategories of ecological reserves: nature reserves, scenic reserves, and resource reserves.[40] By 1995, there were some eighty-three natural, scenic, and resource reserves that encompassed all of Oman's diverse geographical landscapes, including mountain ranges, desert, *wadi* or oasis villages, rocky coastlines, and sand beaches.[41] Qaboos declared nature conservation areas as: "Areas designated for the conservation of one or more species of wildlife particularly endangered ones whose removal, hunting, transporting or damaging is prohibited. These areas shall also include archeological sites or natural sceneries and public natural parks".[42] Oman has established a corps of rangers that patrol protected spaces, and who work in cooperation with local people to identify and prosecute offenders, to address livestock loss from endangered predatory species, and create means to keep agricultural sites protected for farmers while still protecting would-be endangered foraging species. Environmental inspectors were "appointed by the Minister to enforce" provisions, regulations, and decisions.[43] Fines and penalties are stiff, ranging in severity in relation to infractions, with prison sentences for those who "corrupt or spoil" conservation areas or wildlife.[44]

Nature reserves are created with the intention of preserving endangered species of plants and animals by safeguarding the complete ecosystems in which they live.[45] Scenic reserves include both protected species and the landscapes where they live while also protecting villages and vernacular architecture that are a part of these landscapes.[46] Here, traditional architecture is seen as critical as it is linked to older human relationships to the land that were less degrading to the environment. While new buildings may be constructed, they must share common features with existing architecture externally. Internally, as long as buildings are still deemed safe for habitation, modern appliances and styles are at the discretion of homeowners. Although archeological sites and traditional architecture are classified among Oman's environmental treasures and are a part of the UNESCO intangible world heritage sites, preservation and who benefits appears to be uneven.[47] Criticism has been leveled at the manner in which different groups and regions benefit from such initiatives. Food ecotourism in Dhofar capitalizes on frankincense and the region's other unique foods.[48] Resource reserves include areas where further studies will identify sites containing important resources or endangered species.[49]

There are many endangered and protected species in Oman including Oman's infamous hawksbill and green turtles which nest most notably Masira Island and Ras al-Hadd.[50] Studies by the World Wildlife Federation and the World Conservation Union (IUCN) have documented five species of turtles that are threatened by predatory animals and humans alike. Human consumption of turtle eggs is a practice existing some 7,000 years in the region.[51] Tourism and urbanization threaten sea turtle populations, and great efforts are made to limit tourist presence in nesting areas while leveraging sustainable ecotourism.[52] Ecotourism near turtle nesting areas is strictly monitored, and numbers of visitors are permitted based on the particular presence of turtles and their nesting periods.[53]

Still more rare in Oman is the elusive Arabian Leopard which roams the mountainous regions of Musandam province in the far north and the Dhofar province bordering Yemen.[54] In 1976, a ban on hunting the Arabian Tahr brought it "back from extinction."[55] Other endangered mammals include the Arabian Oryx, mountain gazelles, ibex, large Caracal lynx, and the sand cat.[56] These animals and the ecosystems they inhabit are what remains of the time when the Arabian Peninsula was a savannah, dating back some 12,000 years.[57] Detailed studies on other near-threatened species such as the Sooty Falcon, demonstrate that animals living in more urban and unprotected areas may face food scarcity and food stress which stunts growth, ultimately impacting their ability to thrive and reproduce.[58]

Sultan Qaboos convened, encouraged, and sponsored a number of seminars and summits nationally and internationally, and brought Oman's concern for larger global environmental degradation into conversation with organizations like the International Maritime Organization for the Protection of the Marine Environment, the International Union for the Conservation of Nature and Natural Resources, and the World Wildlife Fund, to name but a few.[59] The White Oryx, with the help of the WWF and support from Sultan Qaboos, was brought back from extinction when pairs were collected from zoos in the United States.[60] Today their sanctuary is on the UNESCO's World Heritage List.

Conclusion

The early articulation of ecological preservation found in Sultan Qaboos' writings and decrees constitutes a narrative of sustainable stewardship that is in contrast to other nations in the region.[61] The Oman 2020 plan envisioned an Oman built on sustainable economics and a modern efflorescence built on a strong governmental and ecological foundation. The United Nations ESCWA data on Oman's key environmental performance indicators demonstrate increased data collection in critical areas in the 1990s. Like all other countries in the region, Oman has seen increases in greenhouse and methane emissions and municipal waste generated in growing, urban areas.[62]

Because of economic reliance on extracting and producing hydrocarbons (crude oil, natural gas, and liquified natural gas), the GCC is among the highest contributors to CO_2 emissions in the world.[63] The industry contributes to high living standards, which then leads to higher consumption patterns with increased population in urban centers such as Muscat, where nearly half the population now resides. The construction industry alone accounts for some "40% of entire produced energy, and in recent years all GCC countries have begun to implement greener building codes."[64] Between 2006 and 2013, Oman's economy grew by 71 percent and the population increased by 16 percent, with continued growth in construction predicted to spike in the coming years. The Research Council was established to create new, greener forms of building and housing.[65] The Oman Green Building Council (OGBC), established in 2012 to support the new eco-construction movement, reports that the transition to green building from conventional building practices has been slow. Oman ranks seventh in the world in gypsum deposits, a primary ingredient in drywall used in new building production.[66] It is unclear how mining for gypsum and balancing greener construction can be resolved. As yet, there remains work to be done in defining terms and baseline expectations for what constitutes green and eco-friendly building.[67] Other reports indicate while the Omani public is highly receptive to green technologies like solar and wind, the lack of legislation in these areas has been a setback for widescale adoption.[68]

Sultan Qaboos' passing in 2020 coincided with the unveiling of the ambitious Oman Vision 2040 plan, for which Sultan Haitham has been largely credited. The 2040 "Moving Forward with Confidence" aims to increase Oman's standing in the global Environmental Performance Index by raising it to among the top twenty countries in the world and by increasing the non-oil share of the GDP to 90 percent.[69] This passing the torch of sustainable development was memorialized in a story covered in the Omani press of Sultan Haitham bin Tariq planting a frankincense tree in Salalah, whereby his planting of the iconic tree recalls the focus on the natural world during Sultan Qaboos' era.[70] The Oman Vision 2040 has integrated more data from world environmental rankings and has set specific goals for how to improve its green record, thus, making Oman's goals more concrete, realistic, and realizable.

The 2040 Oman Vision Plan indicates specific measures needed to realize Sultan Qaboos' green *Nahda*. Oman has been called "a life-size environmental laboratory."[71] The greening of Oman has become an important facet of its larger foreign policy objectives, adding to its already well-established

Figure 16.2 Sultan Haitham planting a frankincense tree at Royal Razat Farm, Salalah, Oman.

diplomatic record.[72] Sultan Haitham bin Tariq echoed Sultan Qaboos' vision, asserting that the "optimal and balanced use of land and natural resources and the protection of the environment to bring about food, water, and energy security" are among Oman's top concerns.[73]

The Ministry of Environmental and Climate Affairs became the Environmental Authority in 2020, however, its mandate appears to be much as it was before.[74] The Oman Vision 2040 similarly lays out a renewed plan for protections including biodiversity, a green and circular economy, renewable resources, food and water security, and ecological awareness around the long-term consequences of increased consumption.[75] The Sultan Qaboos Cultural Center in Washington, DC, working in partnership with the Omani Embassy in the United States and the *Diwan* in Oman, has organized conferences on the circular economy (2018) and on environmental sustainability and stewardship (2019), bringing Omani decision-makers into conversation with emerging practitioners leading clean disruption.[76]

The Oman Vision 2040 explicitly refers to the transition towards a decentered, post-oil economy:

> Some might think that oil wealth, bestowed by God upon the Sultanate, is the main reason behind achievements made thus far. However, facts indicate that financial resources alone were not enough ... If oil loses some of its global glow, the will and determination of the Omanis will increase in defending these achievements and will continue the process of modernization and building for future generations.[77]

Sultan Qaboos imparted in a generation the idea that everyone can and must not only care for the environment, but go further to demonstrate commitment to innovative solutions to contemporary crises. As the world has moved squarely into the Anthropocene, the drive to combat climate change is only more pressing.[78] Today the region synonymous for carbon emissions is now heavily investing in solar power development and carbon capture and storage capabilities.[79] Sultan Qaboos' legacy endures, and his efforts to instill an ecological ethos in his people will drive Oman towards 2040 and beyond.

Notes

1. Sultanate of Oman, Ministry of Environment and Climate Affairs, Environment and Authority, Historical Background.
2. The United Nations Conference on Environment and Development (UNCED), 1992.
3. Marc J. O'Reilly. "Omanibalancing: Oman Confronts an Uncertain Future," *Middle East Journal* 52(1) (1998): 70–84. For discussion of *mizan* as balancing "the material and immaterial worlds" (*dunya* and *din*), see Saleem Ali, "Reconciling Islamic Ethics, Fossil Fuel Dependence, and Climate Change in the Middle East," *Review of Middle East Studies* 50(2) (2017): 172–178. For more on "indigenous Omani" ecospiritual worldview, see Maryam Alhinai and Tema Milstein, "From Kin to Commodity: Ecocultural Relations in Transition in Oman," *Local Environment* 24(12) (2019): 1085.
4. United Nations Conference on the Environment, June 5–16, 1972, Stockholm, Sweden. John McCormick, *Reclaiming Paradise: The Global Environmental Movement* (Bloomington: Indiana University Press, 1989).
5. OAPGRC Strategy 2012: "Transforming Genetic Resources in Value".

6. Mohamed R. Hassanien, "Greening the Middle East: The Regulatory Model of Environmental Protection in the United States–Oman Free Trade Agreement: A Legal Analysis of Chapter 17," *Georgetown International Environmental Law Review* 23 (2010): 465.

7. Erdur Oğuz, "Reappropriating the 'Green': Islamist Environmentalism," *New Perspectives on Turkey* 17 (1997): 151–166; Ibrahim Abdul-Matin, *Green Deen: What Islam Teaches about Protecting the Planet* (Oakland, CA: Berrett-Koehler Publishers, 2010).

8. Ian B. Oliver, "Oman Botanic Garden: A Unique Desert Botanic Garden in the Making," Desert Plants 1(30) (2014): 9–18. For descriptions of Oman in the nineteenth century, see Samuel B. Miles, "Across the Green Mountains of Oman," *Geographical Journal* 18(5) (1901): 465–498. On the Oman Botanic Garden project, see Annette Patzelt et al., "The Oman Botanic Garden," *Sibbaldia: International Journal of Botanic Garden Horticulture* 6 (2008): 41–77. *Aflaj* in Omani village cultural life, see Alhinai and Milstein, "From Kin to Commodity," 1084.

9. See Mohd Marsuki's study on "The Practice of Islamic Environmental Ethics: A Case Study of Harim and Hima," PhD dissertation, University of Wales Trinity Saint David, 2009, 208–222; Md Saidul Islam, "Old Philosophy, New Movement: The Rise of the Islamic Ecological Paradigm in the Discourse of Environmentalism," *Nature and Culture* 7(1) (2012): 72–94; Alhinai and Milstein, "From Kin to Commodity," 1085–1087.

10. Esmat Zaidan et al., "Sustainable Development in the Arab World: Is the Gulf Cooperation Council (GCC) Region Fit for the Challenge?" *Development in Practice* 29(5) (2019): 670–681. Oil and gas reserves and emissions from the GCC, see Mouyad Alsamara et al., "The Environmental Kuznets Curve Relationship: A Case Study of the Gulf Cooperation Council Region," *Environmental Science and Pollution Research* 25 (2018): 33183–33195.

11. See Ahmed Mushtaque and B. S. Choudri, "Climate Change in Oman: Current Knowledge and Way Forward," *Education, Business and Society: Contemporary Middle Eastern Issues* 5(4) (2012): 228–236. On documented climate change, see A. Alruheili, *An Approach to Resilient Strategic Planning in the Face of Climate Change: A Case Study of Oman* (ProQuest Dissertations Publishing, 2017). For examples of carbon capture, see Tariq Umar, "Frameworks for Reducing Greenhouse Gas (GHG) Emissions from Municipal Solid Waste in Oman," *Management of Environmental Quality: An International Journal* 31(4) (2020): 945–960. Sabah A. Abdul-Wahab et al., "CO_2 Greenhouse Emissions

in Oman over the Last Forty-Two Years," *Renewable and Sustainable Energy Reviews* 52 (2015): 1702–1712.

12. Royal Decrees and ratified conventions can be found on the Ministry of Higher Education, Research and Innovation website. Calvin H. Allen and W. Lynn Rigsbee, *Oman under Qaboos: From Coup to Constitution, 1970–1996* (London: Frank Cass, 2000); Austin Bodetti, "Oman Blazes a Trail for Environmentalism in the Arab World," *Lobe Log*, December 15, 2018; Sultanate of Oman Environmental Authority, Historical Background.

13. On Sultan Qaboos' role in formulating the Omani Constitution, see Chapter 9 in this volume by Salim al-Kharusi, "Constitutional Reforms during the Reign of Sultan Qaboos."

14. Abdullah Ambusaidi and Ahmed Al-Rabaani, "Environmental Education in the Sultanate of Oman: Taking Sustainable Development into Account," in Neil Taylor, Michael Littledyke, Chris Eames, and Richard K. Coll (eds.), *Environmental Education in Context* (Leiden: Brill Sense, 2009), 37–50.

15. Ambusaidi and Al-Rabaani, "Environmental Education in the Sultanate of Oman," 8.

16. Territorial Sea, the Continental Shelf and the Exclusive Economic Zone (RD 15/1981); Accession to the International Treaty for the Prevention of Marine Pollution from Ships (RD 25/1981); Accession to the Convention on the Prevention of Marine Pollution (RD 26/1981); Issuance of the Sea Law (RD 35/1981).

17. Agnes Guirindola-Astolfi, "Sustainable Development in Oman: A Timeline," (2017).

18. Sameen Ahmed Khan, "Legacy of the UNESCO Sultan Qaboos Prize for Environmental Preservation," in Reggie Paredes (ed,), *A Closer Look at Climate Change* (New York: Nova, 2018), 65–81 at 66. Guirindola-Astolfi, "Sustainable Development in Oman"; Royal Decree 63/85. Kellie Pendoley, "Oil Spills in Oman: Environmental Protection, Planning and Response Case Study," n.d.

19. Pendoley, "Oil Spills in Oman," 39.

20. Sultan Qaboos, Royal Decree No. 114/2001 Issuing the Law on Conservation of the Environment and Prevention of Pollution, issued 28 Shaban 1422 AH, November 14, 2001. This Royal decree mentioned and expanded upon earlier decrees.

21. Khan, "Legacy of the UNESCO Sultan Qaboos Prize," 66; Mahmood Al-Abri, "The Role of UNESCO in Sustaining Cultural Diversity in the Sultanate of Oman, 1970–2020," PhD dissertation, 2020.

22. Hani Albasoos and Musallam Maashani, "Oman's Diplomacy Strategy," *International Journal of Research in Business and Social Science* 9(2) (2020): 152–163.

23. Royal Decrees 5/1996; 23/1996; 25/1996.

24. Royal Decree 114/2001, Law on Conservation of the Environment & Prevention of Pollution, Ch. 1, 3.

25. ESO, available at: http://www.eso.org.om/index/list.php?categoryId=289.

26. UNESCO Sultan Qaboos Award, 2017, 51.

27. OAPGRC, Foreword, 2.

28. OAPGRC, Foreword, 6.

29. Sultanate of Oman Environment Authority, Overview.

30. For more on Islamic environmentalism, see Ali, "Reconciling Islamic Ethics"; Islamic Declaration on Climate Change.

31. Alhinai and Milstein, "From Kin to Commodity," 1085–1086.

32. See, e.g., Tarik M. Quadir, *Traditional Islamic Environmentalism: The Vision of Seyyed Hossein Nasr* (Lanham, MD: UPA, 2013), who argues that Islam offers a model for environmental ethics, and Richard C. Foltz (ed.), *Environmentalism in the Muslim World* (New York: Nova Science Publishers, 2005). Foltz argues that most writing Islamic ecotheologians is "highly apologetic," xxi.

33. Islam, "Old Philosophy, New Movement," 77.

34. Ali, "Reconciling Islamic Ethics," 175.

35. H. Kilani et al., "Al-Hima: A Way of life," International Union for Conservation of Nature, West Asia Regional Office, Amman, Jordan, and the Society for the Protection of Nature in Lebanon, Beirut, Lebanon. 2007.

36. Be'ah, About Us, available at: https://www.beah.om/About-Us/be-ah. The Qur'an mentions *mizan* in Surah 42:17; Surah 55:7–9, and Surah 57:25.

37. Be'ah, "COVID-19 Lockdown Limits Food Waste", available at: https://www.beah.om/Media/News/Be%E2%80%99ah-receives-OFA-and-Omani-Fandom-League-mem-(5).

38. Sultan Qaboos, Royal Decree No. 114/2001, 4.

39. Royal Decree No. 114/2001, 10.

40. "Oman: Environment and Ecology; Omani Conservation Laws Protect Flora, Fauna, and Even Architecture," *The Washington Report on Middle East Affairs*, 08, 1995, 52.

41. "Oman: Environment and Ecology,", 52.

42. Sultan Qaboos, Royal Decree No. 114/2001, 4.

43. Royal Decree No. 114/2001, 5.

44. Royal Decree No. 114/2001, 12–14.

45. B. S Choudri et al., "An Overview of Coastal and Marine Resources and their Management in Sultanate of Oman," *Journal of Environmental Management and Tourism* 7(1) (2016): 21–32.

46. Noor Hanita Abdul Majid et al., "Vernacular Wisdom: The Basis of Formulating Compatible Living Environment in Oman," *Procedia-Social and Behavioral Sciences* 68 (2012): 637–648.

47. Dawn Chatty, "Heritage Policies, Tourism and Pastoral Groups in the Sultanate of Oman," *Nomadic Peoples* 20(2) (2016): 200–215.

48. Debra J. Enzenbacher, "Exploring the Food Tourism Landscape and Sustainable Economic Development Goals in Dhofar Governorate, Oman," *British Food Journal* 121(6) (2019): 1897–1918.

49. Sultan Qaboos, Royal Decree No. 114/2001, 5.

50. See Royal Decree No. 114/2001, App. 1 and 2, for lists of endangered animals, 15–16. See "Oman: Environment and Ecology," 52,

51. France Bequette, "Environment-Friendly Oman," *UNESCO Courier* 48(4) (1995): 39; John G Frazier et al., "Remains of Leatherback Turtles, Dermochelys Coriacea, at Mid-Late Holocene Archaeological Sites in Coastal Oman: Clues of Past Worlds," *PeerJ (San Francisco, CA)* 6 (2018): e6123–e6123.

52. Mariam Al-Busaidi et al., "Sea Turtles Tourism in Oman: Current Status and Future Prospects," *Tourism and Hospitality Research* 19(3) (2019): 321–336.

53. Bequette, "Environment-Friendly Oman," 39.

54. Marcelo Mazzolli, "Arabian Leopard, Panthera Pardus Nimr, Status and Habitat Assessment in Northwest Dhofar, Oman: (Mammalia: Felidae)," *Zoology in the Middle East* 47(1) (2009): 3–11.

55. "Oman: Environment and Ecology," 52.

56. David L. Harrison, "The Mammal Fauna of Oman," *Journal of Oman Studies* 6 (1980): 329.

57. "Oman: Environment and Ecology," 52.

58. Michael J. McGrady et al., "Sooty Falcon Falco Concolor Reproduction and Population Dynamics on the Islands in the Sea of Oman," *Ibis (London, England)* 159(4) (2017): 828–40 at 835.

59. "Oman: Environment and Ecology," 52.

60. James Andrew Spalton et al., "Arabian Oryx Reintroduction in Oman: Successes and Setbacks," *Oryx* 33(2) (1999): 168–175; Bequette, "Environment-Friendly Oman," 39.

61. Royal Decrees, Oman Portal.

62. United Nations ESCWA Data Portal, available at: https://data.unescwa.org/portal/e28b867b-13b6-4d97-ad5e-85264879c2ef.

63. Mohamed S. Saleh and Chaham Alalouch, "Towards Sustainable Construction in Oman: Challenges & Opportunities," *Procedia Engineering* 118 (2015): 177–184.

64. Saleh and Alalouch, "Towards Sustainable Construction in Oman," 178.

65. A. H. Al-Badi et al., "Assessment of Renewable Energy Resources Potential in Oman and Identification of Barrier to their Significant Utilization," *Renewable and Sustainable Energy Reviews* 13(9) (2009): 2734–2739.

66. Rosario Shireen M. and C. R. Rosario, "Sustainability of Omani Raw Gypsum Pricing with Reference to Asian Regional Competition," *World*, 2(3) (2018): 4

67. Mohamed S. Saleh and Chaham Alalouch, "Towards Sustainable Construction in Oman: Challenges & Opportunities," *Procedia Engineering* 118 (2015): 177–184 at 184.

68. Syed Arshad and Maria Petrou, "Major Projects: Environment Risks in Oman: Overview," Thomas Reuters Practical Law.

69. Oman Vision 2040, "Moving Forward with Confidence," 10.

70. "HM Sultan Haitham Plants Frankincense Tree in Salalah*," Muscat Daily News*, September 18, 2020.

71. Bequette, Environment-Friendly Oman," 39.

72. Joseph A. Kechichian, *Oman and the World: The Emergence of an Independent Foreign Policy* (Rand Corporation, 1995).

73. Oman Vision 2040, 39.

74. The Sultanate of Oman Environment Authority, "Overview."

75. Oman Vision 2040, 38.

76. SQCC, Annual Conference held at the University of Houston-Clear Lake, "UHCL-SQCC Energy and Environmental Stewardship: Oman and the U.S.," 2019; SQCC, Annual Conference held at Arizona State University, "Promoting Economic Development via Entrepreneurship and Innovation: Oman and the U.S.," November 1, 2018.

77. Oman Vision 2040, 45.

78. Christopher J. Preston, "Beyond the End of Nature: SRM and Two Tales of Artificity for the Anthropocene," *Ethics, Policy & Environment* 15(2) (2012): 188–201.

79. A. H. Al-Badi et al., "Sustainable Energy Usage in Oman: Opportunities and Barriers," *Renewable and Sustainable Energy Reviews* 15(8) (2011): 3780–3788; Mohammed Albadi et al., "Enhancing Electricity Supply Mix in Oman with Energy Storage Systems: A Case Study," *International Journal of Sustainable Engineering* (2020): 1–10.

References

Abdul-Matin, Ibrahim. *Green Deen: What Islam Teaches about Protecting the Planet* (Oakland, CA: Berrett-Koehler Publishers, 2010).

Abdul-Wahab, Sabah A., Yassine Charabi, Rashid Al-Maamari, Ghazi A. Al-Rawas, Adel Gastli, and Keziah Chan, "CO_2 Greenhouse Emissions in Oman over the Last Forty-Two Years: Review," *Renewable and Sustainable Energy Reviews* 52 (2015): 1702–1712.

Ahmed, M. and B. S. Choudri, "Climate Change in Oman: Current Knowledge and Way Forward," *Education, Business and Society: Contemporary Middle Eastern Issues* 5 (2012): 228–236.

Alhinai, Maryam and Tema Milstein, "From Kin to Commodity: Ecocultural Relations in Transition in Oman," *Local Environment: International Journal of Justice and Sustainability* 24(12) (2019): 1078–1096.

Alsamara, Mouyad, Zouhair Mrabet, Ali Salman Saleh, and Sajd Anwar, "The Environment Kuznets Curve Relationship: A Case Study of the Gulf Cooperation Council Region," *Environmental Science and Pollution Research* 25 (2018): 33183–33195.

Al-Abri, Mahmood, "The Role of UNESCO in Sustaining Cultural Diversity in the Sultanate of Oman, 1970–2020," PhD dissertation, Bangor University, 2020.

Al-Alawi, Khatir Mohd Said, "Food Security Approach in Sultanate of Oman," *Food Security: Global Trends and Perspective*, Report of the 32nd Afro-Asian Rural Development Organization (AARDO) (2010): 239–250, available at: https://aardo.org/aardohomepage/PDF/Reca.pdf#page=240.

Albadi, Mohammed, Abdullah Al-Badi, R. Ghorbani, A. Al-Hinai, and Rashid Al-Abri, "Enhancing Electricity Supply Mix in Oman with Energy Storage Systems: A Case Study," *International Journal of Sustainable Engineering* (2020): 1–10.

Al-Badi, A. H., A. Malik, and A. Gastli, "Assessment of Renewable Energy Resources Potential in Oman and Identification of Barrier to their Significant Utilization," *Renewable and Sustainable Energy Reviews* 13(9) (2009): 2734–2739.

Al-Badi, A. H., A. Malik, and A. Gastli, "Sustainable Energy Usage in Oman: Opportunities and Barriers," *Renewable and Sustainable Energy Reviews* 15(2) (2011): 3780–3788.

Albasoos, Hani and Musallam Maashani, "Oman's Diplomacy Strategy: Maneuvering Tools to Face Regional Challenges," *International Journal of Research in Business and Social Science (2147–4478)* 9 (2020):152–163.

Ali, Abdullah Yusuf, *The Qur'an: A Translation*, 7th U.S. ed. (Elmhurst, NY: Tahrike Tarsile Qur'an, 2001).

Ali, Saleem H., "Reconciling Islamic Ethics, Fossil Fuel Dependence, and Climate Change in the Middle East," *Review of Middle East Studies* 50(2) (2017): 172–178.

Al-Ismaily, Said, Anvar R. Kacimov, Ali Al-Maktoumi, and Hamad Al-Busaidi, "Progressing from Direct Instruction to Structured and Open Inquiry-Based Teaching in a Bachelor of Soil Sciences Program: Experience at the National University in Oman," *Journal of Geoscience Education* 67(1) (2019): 3–19.

Al-Kalbani, Abeer Ali Abdullah, "Household Food Security in Oman: The Role of Women Consumers," PhD dissertation, University of York, 2017.

Allen, Calvin H. and W. Lynn Rigsbee, *Oman under Qaboos: From Coup to Constitution, 1970–1996* (London: Frank Cass, 2000).

Al-Mayahi, Ahmed, Said Al-Ismaily, Tarig Gibreel, Anvar Kacimov, and Ali Al-Maktoumi, "Home Gardening in Muscat, Oman: Gardeners' Practices, Perceptions and Motivations," *Urban Forestry & Urban Greening* 38 (2019): 286–294.

Alruheili, A., *An Approach to Resilient Strategic Planning in the Face of Climate Change: A Case Study of Oman* (ProQuest Dissertations Publishing, 2017).

Ambusaidi, Abdullah and Ahmed Al-Rabaani, "Environmental Education in the Sultanate of Oman: Taking Sustainable Development into Account," in Neil Taylor, Michael Littledyke, Chris Eames, and Richard K. Coll (eds.), *Environmental Education in Context: An International Perspective on the Development Environmental Education* (Leiden: Brill Sense, 2009), 37–50.

Ansari, Iram and Jacqueline McGlade, "Omanisation, Youth Employment and SME Firms in Oman," *The Future of Labour Market Reform in the Gulf Region: Towards a Multi-Disciplinary, Evidence-Based and Practical Understanding* (2018): 55.

Arshad Syed and Maria Petrou, "Major Projects: Environment Risks in Oman: Overview," Thomas Reuters Practical Law, available at: https://uk.practicallaw.thomsonreuters.com/w-008-2712?transitionType=Default&contextData=(sc.Default)&firstPage=true.

Barstow, D. and E. Geary (eds.), *Blueprint for Change: Report from the National Conference on the Revolution in Earth and Space Science Education* (Cambridge, MA: Technical Education Research Center, 2002).

Benison, Georgina, "Sleepwalking into and Environmental Catastrophe," *Oman Daily Observer*, June 28, 2020, available at: https://www.omanobserver.om/article/12300/Oman/sleepwalking-into-an-environmental-catastrophe.

Bequette, France, "Environment-Friendly Oman," *UNESCO Courier* 48(4) (1995): 39–41.

Bodetti, Austin, "Oman Blazes a Trail for Environmentalism in the Arab World," *Lobe Log*, December 15, 2018, available at: https://lobelog.com/oman-blazes-a-trail-for-environmentalism-in-the-arab-world/#:~:text=Sultan%20Qaboos'%20support%20for%20the,an%20environmental%20ministry%20in%201984.

Busaidi, Mariam Al-, Shekar Bose, Michel Claereboudt, and Manjula Tiwari, "Sea Turtles Tourism in Oman: Current Status and Future Prospects," *Tourism and Hospitality Research* 19(3) (2019): 321–336.

Chatty, Dawn, "Heritage Policies, Tourism and Pastoral Groups in the Sultanate of Oman," *Nomadic Peoples* 20(2) (2016): 200–215.

Choudri, B. S., Mahad Baawain, and Mushtaque Ahmed, "An Overview of Coastal and Marine Resources and their Management in Sultanate of Oman," *Journal of Environmental Management and Tourism* 7(1) (2016): 21–32.

Environmental Society of Oman, see at: http://www.eso.org.om/index/list.php?categoryId=289.

Enzenbacher, Debra J., "Exploring the Food Tourism Landscape and Sustainable Economic Development Goals in Dhofar Governorate, Oman," *British Food Journal* 121(6) (2019): 1897–1918.

Erdur, Oğuz, "Reappropriating the 'Green': Islamist Environmentalism," *New Perspectives on Turkey* 17 (1997): 151–66.

Foltz, Richard C. (ed.), *Environmentalism in the Muslim World* (New York: Nova Science Publishers, 2005).

Frazier, John G., Valentina Azzarà, Olivia Munoz, Lapo Gianni Marcucci, Emilie Badel, Francesco Genchi, Maurizio Cattani, Maurizio Tosi, and Massimo Delfino, "Remains of Leatherback Turtles, Dermochelys Coriacea , at Mid-Late Holocene Archaeological Sites in Coastal Oman: Clues of Past Worlds," *PeerJ. (San Francisco, CA)* 6 (2018): e6123–e6123.

Guirindola-Astolfi, Agnes, "Sustainable Development in Oman: A Timeline," (2017), available at: https://sustainableoman.com/wp-content/uploads/2017/09/Timeline-2.pdf.

Harrison, David L., "The Mammal Fauna of Oman," *Journal of Oman Studies* 6 (1980): 329.

Hassanien, Mohamed R., "Greening the Middle East: The Regulatory Model of Environmental Protection in the United States–Oman Free Trade Agreement: A Legal Analysis of Chapter 17," *Georgetown International Environmental Law Review* 23 (2010): 465.

Hussain, Sadiq and Thuwayba Albarwani, "Leadership for Sustainability Perceptions in Higher Education Institutions in Oman," *Management in Education* 29(4) (2015): 151–157.

Islam, Md Saidul, "Old Philosophy, New Movement: The Rise of the Islamic Ecological Paradigm in the Discourse of Environmentalism," *Nature and Culture* 7(1) (2012): 72–94.

Islamic Declaration on Climate Change, available at: https://www.ifees.org.uk/about/islamic-declaration-on-global-climate-change.

Kechichian, Joseph A., *Oman and the World: The Emergence of an Independent Foreign Policy* (Rand Corporation, 1995).

Kilani, H., A. Serhal, and O. Llewellyn, "Al-Hima: A Way of Life," International Union for Conservation of Nature, West Asia Regional Office, Amman, Jordan, and the Society for the Protection of Nature in Lebanon, Beirut, Lebanon, 2007.

Khan, Sameen Ahmed, "Legacy of the UNESCO Sultan Qaboos Prize for Environmental Preservation," in Reggie Paredes (ed.), *A Closer Look at Climate Change* (New York: Nova Publishers, 2018), 65–81.

Kotagama, H., H. Boughanmi, S. Zekri, and S. Prathapar, "Food Security as a Public Good: Oman's Prospects," *Sri Lankan Journal of Agricultural Economics* 10(1) (2009): 61–74.

Kotagama, Hemesiri, Salwa Abdullah Nasser Al-Jabri, Houcine Boughanmi, and Nejib Guizani, "Impact of Food Prices, Income and Income Distribution on Food Security in Oman," in *Environmental Cost and Face of Agriculture in the Gulf Cooperation Council Countries* (Cham: Springer, 2014), 145–161.

Majid, Noor Hanita Abdul, Hokoi Shuichi, and Nozomi Takagi, "Vernacular Wisdom: The Basis of Formulating Compatible Living Environment in Oman," *Procedia-Social and Behavioral Sciences* 68 (2012): 637–648.

Marsuki, Mohd Zuhdi Bin, "The Practice of Islamic Environmental Ethics: A Case Study of Harim and Hima," PhD dissertation, University of Wales Trinity Saint David, 2009.

Mazzolli, Marcelo, "Arabian Leopard, Panthera Pardus Nimr, Status and Habitat Assessment in Northwest Dhofar, Oman: (Mammalia: Felidae)," *Zoology in the Middle East* 47(1) (2009): 3–11.

Mbaga, Msafiri Daudi, "Alternative Mechanisms for Achieving Food Security in Oman," *Agriculture & Food Security* 2(1) (2013): 1–11.

McCormick, John, *Reclaiming Paradise: The Global Environmental Movement* (Bloomington: Indiana University Press, 1989).

McGrady, Michael J., Waheed A. Al-Fazari, Mansoor H. Al-Jahdhami, Malcolm A. C. Nicoll, and Madan K. Oli, "Sooty Falcon *Falco Concolor* Reproduction and Population Dynamics on the Islands in the Sea of Oman," *Ibis (London, England)* 159(4) (2017): 828–840.

Megdiche-Kharrat, Fairouz, Mohamed Moussa, and Hichem Rejeb, "Aflaj Water Management in Oman: The Case of Falaj Al-Khatmeen in Birkat Al-Mouz, Wilayat Nizwa," *Water and Land Security in Drylands* (Cham: Springer, 2017), 119–128.

Miles, Samuel B., "Across the Green Mountains of Oman," *Geographical Journal* 18(5) (1901): 465–498.

Muscat Daily News, "Converting Mosques into Green Buildings Powered by Solar Energy," April 1, 2021.

Muscat Daily News, "HM the Sultan Plants Frankincense Tree in Salalah," September 18, 2020.

Mushtaque, Ahmed and B. S. Choudri, "Climate Change in Oman: Current Knowledge and Way Forward," *Education, Business and Society: Contemporary Middle Eastern Issues* 5(4) (2012): 228–236.

Oliver, Ian B., "Oman Botanic Garden: A Unique Desert Botanic Garden in the Making," *Desert Plants* 1(30) (2014): 9–18, available at: https://repository.arizona.edu/handle/10150/622040.

Oman Animal & Plant Genetic Resources Center, Ministry of Higher Education, Research and Innovation, available at: https://oapgrc.gov.om/Pages/General.aspx.

Oman Animal and Plant Genetic Resources Center (OAPGRC) Strategy 2012: "Transforming Genetic Resources in Value," available at: https://oapgrc.gov.om/Documents/OAPGRC%20Strategy%202012.pdf.

"Oman: Environment and Ecology; Omani Conservation Laws Protect Flora, Fauna, and Even Architecture," *The Washington Report on Middle East Affairs*, 08, 1995, 52.

Oman Vision 2040, "Moving Forward with Confidence," available at: https://www.2040.om/Oman2040-En.pdf.

O'Reilly, Marc J., "Omanibalancing: Oman Confronts an Uncertain Future," *Middle East Journal* 52(1) (1998): 70–84.

Patzelt, Annette, Leigh Morris, Laila Al-Harthi, Ismail Al-Rashdi, and Andrew Spalton, "The Oman Botanic Garden (1)," *Sibbaldia: International Journal of Botanic Garden Horticulture* 6 (2008): 41–77.

Pendoley, Kellie, "Oil Spills in Oman: Environmental Protection, Planning and Response Case Study," available at: https://www.researchgate.net/profile/Andrew-Morgan-26/publication/292984377_Oil_Spills_in_Oman_Environmental_Protection_Planning_and_Response_Case_Study/links/56b3e10308ae636a540d202a/Oil-Spills-in-Oman-Environmental-Protection-Planning-and-Response-Case-Study.pdf . No date.

Prathapar, S. A., M. Ahmed, S. Al-Adawi, and S. Al-Sidiari, "Design, Construction and Evaluation of an Ablution Water Treatment Unit in Oman: A Case Study," *International Journal of Environmental Studies* 63(3) (2006): 283–292.

Preston, Christopher J., "Beyond the End of Nature: SRM and Two Tales of Artificity for the Anthropocene," *Ethics, Policy & Environment* 15(2) (2012): 188–201.

Quadir, Tarik M., *Traditional Islamic Environmentalism: The Vision of Seyyed Hossein Nasr* (Lanham, MD: UPA, 2013).

Shireen, Rosario, M. and C. R. Rosario, "Sustainability of Omani Raw Gypsum Pricing with Reference to Asian Regional Competition," *World*, 2(3) (2018): 4.

Saleh, Mohamed S. and Chaham Alalouch, "Towards Sustainable Construction in Oman: Challenges & Opportunities," *Procedia Engineering* 118 (2015): 177–184.

Spalton, James Andrew, S. A. Brend, and M. W. Lawrence, "Arabian Oryx Reintroduction in Oman: Successes and Setbacks," *Oryx* 33(2) (1999): 168–175.

SQCC, Annual Conference held at Arizona State University, Promoting Economic Development via Entrepreneurship and Innovation: Oman and the U.S., November 1, 2018, available at: https://na.eventscloud.com/ehome/index.php?eventid=360714.

SQCC, Annual Conference held at the University of Houston-Clear Lake, UHCL-SQCC Energy and Environmental Stewardship: Oman and the U.S., 2019, available at: https://www.uhcl.edu/human-sciences-humanities/centers-initiatives/sqcc.

Sultan Qaboos, Royal Decree No. 114/2001, Issuing the Law on Conservation of the Environment and Prevention of Pollution, issued 28 Shaban 1422 AH, November 14, 2001.

Sultanate of Oman Environment Authority, *Overview*, available at: https://www.ea.gov.om/en/the-authority/about-authority/overview/?csrt=12659532194701563580 .

Sultanate of Oman Ministry of Environment and Climate Affairs, Environment Authority (MECA), *Overview*, available at: https://www.meca.gov.om/en/the-authority/about-authority/overview/?csrt=2054419265376204794.

Sultanate of Oman Ministry of Environment and Climate Affairs, Environment Authority (MECA), *Historical Background*, available at: https://www.meca.gov.om/en/the-authority/about-authority/the-founder-of-environmental-work/?csrt=2054419265376204794, last accessed March 2, 2021.

Sultanate of Oman Royal Decrees, Oman Portal, available at: https://www.omanportal.gov.om/wps/wcm/connect/EN/site/home/gov/gov1/gov7royaldecrees.

Umar, T., "Frameworks for Reducing Greenhouse Gas (GHG) Emissions from Municipal Solid Waste in Oman," Management of Environmental Quality 31(4) (2020): 945–960.

United Nations Conference on the Environment (UNCED), June 5–16, 1972, Stockholm, Sweden, available at: https://www.un.org/en/conferences/environment/stockholm1972.

United Nations Conference on Environment and Development (UNCED), June 3–14, 1992, Rio de Janeiro, Brazil, available at: https://www.un.org/en/conferences/environment/rio1992.

United Nations Economic and Social Commission for Western Asia (ESCWA), Data Portal, available at: https://data.unescwa.org/portal/e28b867b-13b6-4d97-ad5e-85264879c2ef.

UNESCO Sultan Qaboos Prize for Environmental Preservation, program brochure, 2017, available at: https://en.unesco.org/sites/default/files/bro2017e.pdf.

Zaidan, Esmat, Mohammad Al-Saidi, and Suzanne H. Hammad, "Sustainable Development in the Arab World: Is the Gulf Cooperation Council (GCC) Region Fit for the Challenge?" *Development in Practice* 29(5) (2019): 670–681.

17

OMANI PEACEMAKING AND MIDDLE EAST CRISES IN THE 2010s: SULTAN QABOOS' LAST DECADE

Juan Cole

The Sultanate of Oman under the rule of Sultan Qaboos (r. 1970–2020) developed a culture of peacemaking and mediation over the five decades of his rule.[1] Oman's geographical position on the edge of the Arab world abutting the Strait of Hormuz, its good relations with both Saudi Arabia and Iran, the diversity of its population (with significant Baluch, South Asian, and African minorities), and the adherence of many of its people to Ibadi Islam (i.e., neither Sunni nor Shiite), all contributed to this potential for a role as mediator. The personality and convictions of Sultan Qaboos himself, however, were central to the development of the country's eirenic foreign policy. Although it is a member of the Gulf Cooperation Council (GCC) that groups the Arab Gulf oil monarchies, including Kuwait, Bahrain, Qatar, the United Arab Emirates and Saudi Arabia, established in 1981 to counter Iran's rising power, Oman has steadfastly pursued an independent foreign policy.

In the second decade of the twenty-first century, Oman played a mediating role in three big crises wracking the Middle East. These included US–Iran relations, the Saudi and UAE war on Yemen, and the Qatar Crisis that began in 2017. In each instance, Oman offered a neutral ground on which conflicting sides could meet, and it exercised its good offices in carrying proposals from one side to the other. Oman's mediation efforts initially succeeded with regard to the Obama administration and Iran, but faltered once the Trump administration breached the Joint Comprehensive Plan of Action (JCPOA), Iran Nuclear Deal. In Yemen, Oman kept lines open to all of the belligerents, and facilitated transfer and medical treatment of POWs, but Sultan Qaboos was unable during his last years to bring the sides together for serious negotiations. The rise of extremism in neighboring Mahra province threatened to embroil Oman itself in the conflict. With regard to the Qatar blockade in 2017–2021, Oman supported the mediation efforts of Kuwait and also made its own efforts. Oman's own mediation between Qatar, on the one hand, and Saudi Arabia and the United Arab Emirates, on the other, from 2017 forward may have smoothed the rough edges of the conflict and helped to pave the way, along with Kuwait and Washington, for its resolution at al-Ula in January 2021.

When big world powers mediate a dispute, they have the advantage of wealth and military power that dwarfs the two parties that they are attempting to conciliate. They can thus use money to pacify the belligerents, or credibly threaten them with their surplus military force if they prove recalcitrant. Even small countries such as Saudi Arabia and Qatar can mediate, not on the basis of military power or threatened coercion but on that of their vast wealth, which they can use as a carrot for the parties in conflict.[2] Thus, Saudi Arabia ended the Lebanese Civil War in 1989 with the Ta'if Agreement, after which it rewarded the former warring parties with substantial investment in the country. Qatar mediated between Hezbollah and the Lebanese establishment in 2008, also deploying the carrot of wealth transfers. Interventions with the aid of wealth and power are classed as "active mediation" by theorists of peacemaking.[3]

As a country of some 3 million citizens and 2 million expatriates that is not nearly as wealthy, per capita, as some of its neighbors, Oman was not always in a position to pursue either sort of intervention in Middle East disputes. Sultan Qaboos led Oman through several military conflicts and Oman's military more than holds its own. Benefiting from training with British and U.S. forces, it has participated in the Gulf War coalition; the Omani armed forces are well-respected throughout the region.[4] Although the UAE and other Gulf states are increasing their investments, it could be claimed that only Saudi Arabia, with its far larger population, surpasses Oman in terms of military readiness. Even so, Oman's military, including its navy, which has played an important role in securing waterways, is mainly meant for defensive purposes, to maintain the integrity of the Sultanate within current maritime and territorial boundaries. Instead of relying on overwhelming military or financial power, Oman participates in what political scientists call "quasi-mediation" or "passive mediation efforts." Degang Sun and Yahia Zoubir explain, "This type of mediator acts without seeking to dominate; to follow rather than to lead; to partake in the revision of the agenda rather than setting it; and, to encourage conflict de-escalation in lieu of determinedly engaging in conflict resolution."[5] Sultan Qaboos offered neither external military might nor large sums of money to participants in a dispute, but rather a discreet venue for parties to meet and a framework for contacts and de-escalation. It was precisely his lack of an ability to intervene that made his court in Muscat attractive to participants in some sorts of dispute. The relative secrecy in which consultations could be held in Oman, far from the prying eyes of the international press, meant that talks could be opened with the enemy without fear of losing face or looking desperate. This chapter will examine the successes and failures of each of these quasi-mediation attempts by Oman and the reasons for them. It will also consider the importance of the existence of a back channel that is low-key and discrete in the search for ways of negotiating a way out of intractable conflicts.

Iran

Former Secretary of State John Kerry wrote about the importance of Omani mediation with Iran in his memoir *Every Day is Extra*. When he was still chairman of the Senate Select Committee on Foreign Affairs, he met Salem al-Ismailly, an emissary of Sultan Qaboos. In 2009, three American hikers in Iraqi Kurdistan were captured by the Iranian government and imprisoned on espionage charges. The first to be released was Sarah Shourd, a journalist, who on her arrival in Muscat in September 2010 thanked her "good friend Salem al-Ismailly" for his role in securing her freedom.[6] Oman had taken the lead in negotiating the release of the three young people, and Sultan Qaboos appears to have personally paid a $450,000 ransom for each of them, which was deposited in the Muscat branch of Iran's Bank Melli. Because of U.S. sanctions, no American could have transferred this money to Tehran, so the sultan's magnanimity was crucial. Each of the three made a public appearance in Muscat on being released, to underscore the key role Oman had played in rescuing them from the notorious Evin prison.[7]

Al-Ismailly came out to see Kerry in Washington to discuss Shourd's release. Although they talked about the need to secure the liberty of the two other hikers, Shane Bauer and Josh Fattal, Kerry revealed that the Sultan's envoy quickly moved beyond the hostage issue to that of Iran's nuclear enrichment program. Kerry and President Barack Obama came to understand that Oman shared the U.S. concern about the possible ultimate weaponization of Iran's program, and that Muscat believed it could bring the United States together with Iran for talks to forestall it. Kerry wrote that the Omanis had "proven their bona fides," recalling his conviction regarding Iran that "we needed greater insight into their thinking." The then senator began secretly speaking regularly to al-Ismailly by telephone.[8]

Some fifteen months after Shourd's release, Kerry flew to Muscat and was welcomed to the palace on December 8, 2011. President Obama had asked him to go. Kerry wrote, "I had never met Sultan Qaboos, but I knew his reputation as a thoughtful interlocutor with good relations on both sides of the region's sectarian divide and as a leader who had taken his country from dirt roads to modernity."[9] The sultan engaged in a pleasant and wide-ranging conversation with the senator on a veranda overlooking the Gulf, then over "a spectacular Middle East feast" Sultan Qaboos told Kerry that "he believed there was a real opportunity at hand" in Iran because Iran's clerical leader, Ali Khamenei, had transferred authority over the nuclear issue to the Ministry of Foreign Affairs, taking it away from hard-liners on the National Security Council. Kerry took the insight back to the White House and the Secretary of State.[10]

Obama and his foreign policy principals decided that the United States would need to meet face to face with the Iranians and agreed that Sultan Qaboos should be asked to go to Tehran to seek such a meeting. Kerry returned to Muscat on January 3, 2012 and secured an agreement on the part of the Sultan to make a visit to the Iranian Supreme Leader Khamenei to assess the possibility that the Iranians would be willing to negotiate in good faith. What Qaboos discovered encouraged the Obama administration to go forward. The president decided that the Muscat back channel should be pursued, and later in 2012 dispatched Secretary of State Hillary Clinton's chief of staff, Jake Sullivan and National Security Council staffer Puneet Talwar to Oman to meet Iranian officials. As Kerry told the story, this first contact did not produce progress, since the U.S. envoys wanted a complete end to enrichment, whereas the Iranians wanted to accept virtually no restrictions on their nuclear program. Sullivan and Talwar had been sent because it was felt too potentially explosive to send a higher-ranking delegation, lest word of the meeting should leak. One of the virtues of Oman as a site for such contacts, however, is that it is does not have the high profile of, say, Dubai, in U.S. and European journalism, and the sultan's own officials practiced complete discretion.[11]

There was little further movement in 2012, as the Obama team campaigned for re-election. Behind the scenes, Obama had decided to tap Kerry as Secretary of State in his second term. After he won in November, and after Kerry was sworn in on February 1, 2013, Obama and Kerry decided to try again, retaining Oman as their back channel. Crucially, the Iranian rebuff in early 2012, and extensive consultations with the other members of the UN Security Council and with European allies had convinced them that the only path to a successful negotiation lay in accepting a continuing Iranian civilian nuclear enrichment program.[12] Hard-line Iranian president Mahmoud Ahmadinejad was coming to the end of his second and final term, and it was not clear who would succeed him. Still, the Obama administration did not feel they could put off making further contact.

Kerry had asked career Foreign Service official William Burns to serve as deputy secretary of state and sent him to Muscat to meet with the Iranians. The United States was substantially elevating the level of its delegation and hoped it would encourage the Iranians to do so as well. In early March, Burns and others met with Iranian Deputy Foreign Minister Ali-Asghar Khaji, and tried to make clear that the Obama administration had turned a corner and had decided to accept in principle that Iran would continue its enrichment activities as long as they remained civilian. The Iranians found the U.S.formulation so vague that they wondered if they should bother with any further meetings. According to Trita Parsi, Sultan Qaboos then met with Khaji and attempted to convince him that the Americans had been quite explicit. Khaji said he wanted it in writing. The United States refused to write any such letter to Iran at that point, but Sultan Qaboos saved the day by suggesting that Washington simply write to him with these representations. He would then quote the American letter in his own correspondence with Tehran. The centrality of the Omani role in mediating between these two delegations, who entertained the severest suspicions of one another, was thus underlined.[13]

After the presidential election in Iran was won by pragmatic centrist Hassan Rouhani, who appointed Mohammad Javad Zarif as his foreign minister, the scene was set to go forward. Obama sent Rouhani an encouraging letter, and it was reinforced when Sultan Qaboos flew to Tehran soon thereafter. For his part, Khamenei reassured Washington through the Sultan of his commitment to the negotiations.[14] Burns met again with Iranian officials in August 2013, in Muscat, and Kerry wrote that his deputy felt there was progress toward dialogue. The U.S. team held six more meetings with the Iranians in Muscat that summer and fall, with the U.S. participants being Burns, National Security Adviser Jake Sullivan, and NSC staffer Puneet Talwar. Iranian officials confirmed that these preliminary talks had the full backing of Ayatollah Khamenei.[15] After the meeting of the UN General Assembly in September, the Obama administration finally informed the other members of the Security Council as well as European allies about their talks with Iran. Kerry says that they were angered that the United States had not informed them of its acceptance of some level of Iranian enrichment, a major change of policy, and that they had not been read into the back channel discussions.[16] They were, however, heartened that there was now the prospect of negotiations with Iran by the P5 + 1 (the Security Council plus Germany, which informally represented the European Union). That is, other world capitals breathed a sigh of relief that the United States had finally understood that it was impractical to demand a complete cessation to Iranian enrichment.

The Geneva negotiations stretched through 2014. By late in that year, the P5 + 1 appear to have felt that they were getting close to an agreement but needed to escape the spotlight that the press had shone on Geneva. On November 9–10, 2014, Kerry, Zarif, and Catherine Ashton (the European Union High Representative of the Union for Foreign Affairs and Security Policy) met at the al-Bustan Hotel in Masqat with the aim of doing a deal within thirteen days. Iran's IRNA news service observed that it was the first time that such a high level, open meeting had been held in any of the Gulf

Cooperation Council (GCC) states.[17] Zarif met with the deputy foreign minister of Oman on the sidelines, suggesting more than a hosting role for the Omani government. He admitted that the thirteen-day deadline for a comprehensive agreement was unlikely to be met, given that the several issues being treated in the talks were interrelated. He was confident, however, that some progress would be made. Sayyid Abbas Araghchi, Iran's chief nuclear negotiator, said in an interview from Muscat:

> If there is real political will on the other side, there are solutions. The proposals and ideas that have been put forward, especially by Iran, have the capacity to reach an acceptable solution and agreement. If there really is the political will, this opportunity can be taken advantage of. We will be at the negotiating table until the last moment, and we believe that an agreement can be reached before November 24, at least on the big question and the main issues.[18]

The meeting in the end went poorly. The United States wanted to allow Iran only 1,500 centrifuges, not the 9,000 on which Iran insisted. Iran wanted all U.N. sanctions lifted as soon as the deal was signed, rather than after a long period of scrutiny. Kerry and Zarif at one point fell to shouting angrily at one another.[19] These heightened tensions indicated how close the two sides were to a final agreement, such that each final detail took on heightened significance. In the wake of the apparent failure at Muscat, Omani foreign minister Bin Alawi was again dispatched to Tehran, likely in the hope of smoothing over bad feelings.[20]

The JCPOA was ultimately agreed upon on July 14, 2015. It aimed at limiting Iran to a breakout period of at least one year. The deal was designed such that, should the Iranian leadership ever decide to attempt to construct a nuclear weapon, it would take them a year to do so on the basis of their existing civilian uranium enrichment program. The JCPOA limited the number of centrifuges that Iran could operate and forced Tehran to cast their stockpile of low enriched uranium (LEU) in a form that could not be used for bomb construction. Iran had to give up its plan to build a heavy water reactor, which could theoretically be used to harvest fissile material. Iran would also be subject to regular inspections by the International Atomic Energy Agency of the U.N. In return, the U.N. Security Council sanctions imposed in 2007 because of Iran's nuclear enrichment program would be completely lifted, and the United States would rescind its own severe unilateral sanctions.[21]

In fact, Iranian purchases of U.S. civilian airliners and other commercial initiatives were blocked by the Republican Congress in Obama's last years. In May 2018, his successor, Donald J. Trump, breached the JCPOA and imposed a wide-ranging financial blockade on Iran that devastated even its ordinary petroleum exports and even rendered making a transaction with the country's central bank a terrorism offense.[22]

In 2021, the administration of Joe Biden determined to re-enter the JCPOA. If the nuclear issue between the United States and Iran can more permanently be resolved, it will be a major plus for peace in the Middle East. Any such achievement will owe a great deal to Sultan Qaboos, who unfortunately passed away at a time when relations between Washington and Tehran were at their nadir. Kerry himself perhaps provided us with the best conclusion to this episode. He wrote of the importance of the Omani back channel, "Ultimately, the Iranians had to trust that the United States wasn't going to be the spoiler of the talks—that we were as serious as anyone about getting a deal—and we had to get the same sense of certainty with respect to the Iranian position. The back channel had enabled our two nations to reach a baseline of good faith."[23]

Yemen

Yemen's civil war of the 1960s between nationalist forces and those supporting Zaydi Imam Yahya was won by the nationalist officers. In 1978, Ali Abdullah Saleh, one of the officers, came to power as dictator. He allowed a weak parliament to be elected in the 1990s, but for most practical purposes he ruled Yemen until 2012. He was forced out of office by the Arab Spring youth protests of 2011, which were joined by some opposition parties, including the Helpers of God (Ansar Allah) or Houthis, who hailed from the Zaydi Shiites of Sa'deh. Under the auspices of the United Nations and the GCC (especially Oman and Qatar), Saleh signed a power transfer agreement in November 2011, pledging to step down by February 2012. Yemen then held a national referendum in which there was an 80 percent turn-out and which selected Saleh's vice president, Abdurabbuh Mansour Hadi as president. Between 2012 and 2014, Mansour Hadi oversaw a long drawn out and contentious political process aimed at moving to new parliamentary elections and a new constitution. Oman supported these efforts via the GCC, which offered donations of oil supplies and payments to ransom Europeans taken hostage.[24]

The reconciliation process was interrupted in September 2014, when the Houthis, possibly in covert collusion with Saleh and his forces, abruptly took control of the capital, Sana'a. They initially maintained that their security control of the capital would not interfere with the functioning of the Mansour Hadi government. In January 2015, however, they began attempting to assert direct control and Mansour Hadi resigned and fled to the southern port city of Aden. The Houthis, allied with parts of the Yemeni military still loyal to Saleh, then attempted to expand their rule down to Aden.[25]

Saudi Arabia and the United Arab Emirates viewed the Houthis as a cat's paw of Iran, though this interpretation is overblown. The Helpers of God movement was an indigenous protest, in part against Saudi proselytizing of Zaydis in an attempt to make them into hard-line Sunni Salafis, proselytizing that Saleh had authorized in return for Saudi monetary aid. The Zaydi branch of Shiite Islam differs in most respects from the Twelver Shiism of Iran, lacking ayatollahs and respecting the Sunni caliphs. Iranian support for the Houthis grew over time, but it remained negligible in monetary terms, though it did include some rockets. There was never any evidence that Iran had any command and control over the Ansar Allah cadres. Most Houthi weapons were American and were looted from Yemeni Army arms depots with the help of military loyalists of the deposed Saleh, who tacitly allied with the Houthis.

On March 22, 2015, the then Saudi Arabian Minister of Defense Mohammed bin Salman, in conjunction with the United Arab Emirates and some other allies, launched an air war on the Houthis that they called Operation Decisive Storm.[26] Sultan Qaboos firmly refused to join the war, and instead his officials cultivated contacts with both sides in the conflict and aimed at arriving at a formula for its swift resolution. Omani government sources told *al-'Arabi al-Jadid* (*The New Arab*) in April that the Sultanate was conducting contacts with regard to the Yemen crisis and hinted at a "welcome in Muscat of a number of personalities concerned."[27] These parties allegedly included Riyadh, and Oman's first hope was to arrange for a truce, given heavy Saudi bombing of targets in Yemen. Muscat hoped that the truce could lead to a permanent ceasefire that would permit a return to talks in a third country acceptable to all parties. The Omanis then hoped that the Houthis and Saleh's forces could be persuaded to withdraw from Yemen's cities in favor of forces loyal to the legitimate president, Mansour Hadi. They envisaged new parliamentary elections and a new government of national unity in which all factions would participate. In this scenario, the Houthis would have to return Yemeni military facilities and demobilize, transforming themselves into a civilian political party rather than a militia.

Neither side in the war, however, was ready for serious negotiations. Joint Houthi and Saleh forces marched south to take Aden, depriving Mansour Hadi of his capital a second time. Since the air war could not hope to take territory, the United Arab Emirates landed troops and fought alongside Mansour Hadi loyalists in what was left of the divided Yemeni military, and succeeded in retaking Aden and expelling the Houthis in July 2015. Mansour Hadi's forces, with help from the United Arab Emirates and the rest of the Saudi-led coalition, marched north to establish positions in the south of the city of Taiz and the port of Hodeida, but over the succeeding four years failed to dislodge the Houthis from them or significantly to weaken the Houthi control over the north.[28]

In 2015, Oman pursued low-key diplomacy, allowing Houthi delegates to meet with Iranian Foreign Minister Mohammad Javad Zarif in Muscat, and also hosting Houthi representatives with Saudi and U.S. officials.[29] At the same time as it attempted to facilitate diplomacy, Oman faced the threat of the instability in Yemen spilling over onto western Oman. Al-Qaeda in the Arabian Peninsula and the Islamic State group were active in Mahra in southeastern Yemen and sometimes used Omani territory for transit. Oman attempted to intervene in the vacuum and organize Mahra tribes to curb the extremist groups. It also faced the threat of increased Saudi and United Arab Emirates military hegemony in Mahra. Riyadh eyed the province's Nishtun Port for a pipeline that would allow Saudi petroleum to reach the Arabian Sea without having to go through the Strait of Hormuz, where Iran had a substantial naval presence. Mutahhar al-Sufari, a Yemeni analyst, told the Anadolu Agency that Oman viewed increased Saudi and UAE hegemony in Mahra as a threat to its security interests, and had organized tribesmen and demonstrations to oppose it.[30] Throughout the Yemeni war, Oman was on the edge of intervention in southeastern Yemen, which had the potential for compromising its stance of neutrality.

Oman attempted, not always successfully, to remain an important interlocutor for the warring parties even after formal negotiations opened in Geneva under the auspices of the United Nations. One such meeting scheduled to be held in June 2018 in Geneva had to be canceled because the Houthi delegation said they could not get a guarantee that they could leave Yemen for Switzerland and return. They had been expected to depart Sana'a airport in an Omani plane, but the Saudi-led coalition that controlled Yemen's airspace would not permit the flight. The sponsors of the U.N. conference asked Oman to attempt to secure such assurances for the Houthi delegation. Agence France Presse asserted that Oman gained trust in mediating on Yemen precisely because it maintained its neutrality in the Qatar crisis (see below).[31]

Oman was not, however, trusted by Saudi Arabia, the newspapers of which alleged that Sultan Qaboos was allowing Houthi leaders freely to move from Yemen to Oman and to travel for consultations with Iran and Lebanon's Hezbollah. Riyadh apparently refused to guarantee the safety of the Oman Airlines plane on which the Houthis had planned to fly to Geneva because the Saudis rejected the demand that it not be searched, and because they suspected it would also be used to transport wounded Houthi commanders for treatment. The editor of *Riyad al-Yawm* (*Riyadh Today*), Sami al-'Uthman, asked on Twitter in September, 2018, whether Oman's "support" for the Houthis amounted to a declaration of war on Saudi Arabia and the UAE. Omani analysts implicitly lambasted such views as an attempt to conscript Oman into either the Saudi or the Iranian camp, something Muscat insisted on avoiding.[32] In contrast, the Mansour Hadi government in Aden denied any Omani tilt to the Houthis and praised the neighboring country for its consistent neutrality. Transportation Minister Salih al-Jabwani described Oman as having "clean hands."[33] The difference in attitude shows that whereas the Saudis hoped to win by main force, the Mansour Hadi government was aware of its weakness and of the likelihood that it would ultimately need a mediator to negotiate with the Houthis.

Oman forged ahead with its efforts, and in December 2018 the Saudi-led coalition delivered wounded Houthi POWs to Oman for treatment after U.N.

mediation. Omani Foreign Minister Yusuf bin 'Alawi said in 2019, "The truth has become clear to everyone, and it is that the war in Yemen offers no benefits at all and was the result of miscalculations." He added that the conflict stemmed from a lack of mutual trust: "They do not trust one another, and restoring confidence depends on the efforts expended by the United Nations." He pledged Oman's support to these U.N. initiatives to restore peace and stability to the region.[34]

In 2019, Muscat became a de rigeur stop for politicians seeking the role of peace-maker, from British Foreign Secretary Jeremy Hunt to U.N. special envoy Martin Griffiths. In mid-September 2019, Sultan Qaboos called on the warring Yemeni sides to negotiate a peace. By September 22, 2019, a delegation from the recognized government of Mansour Hadi, led by Vice President Ali Muhsin al-Ahmar, was in Muscat, demonstrating the eagerness with which local actors embraced Oman's mediating role. A few days later, bin 'Alawi welcomed U.S. Assistant Secretary of State for Middle East Affairs David Shanker and U.S. Deputy Assistant Secretary of State for Iran, Iraq, and Regional Multilateral Affairs Timothy Lenderking, and underlined Oman's willingness to play the role of mediator in the Yemen conflict. On October 3, the U.N. special envoy on Yemen, Martin Griffiths, met with Houthi leaders in Muscat. On October 12, bin 'Alawi met with Saudi Defense Minister Khalid Bin Salman, and said afterwards that he hoped that a settlement in Yemen could reached soon.[35]

One of Oman's tasks was simply to keep lines of communication open between the Houthis and their various enemies and to seek limited quasi-mediation successes. One of these was the release, in October 2020, by the Helpers of God of two American hostages. In return, the United States and its allies permitted some 200 wounded Houthis to return to Sana'a; they had been stranded in Muscat since U.N. intercession had led the Saudi-led coalition to release them to Sultan Qaboos.[36]

Oman's quasi-mediation efforts had little impact on the course of the war, but did allow the Americans, for instance, who backed the Saudi-led war until Joe Biden became president in early 2021, to have a back channel to the Houthis. It also allowed the Mansour Hadi government to talk to Sana'a without risking a loss of face or the fury of its own partisans. The full story of such Houthi talks in Muscat, including with Saudi Arabia itself, is difficult to tease out precisely because discretion was the value-added of Oman-sponsored such contacts. The Oman channel permitted some hostage crises to be resolved, some wounded fighters to receive medical attention, some POWs to be repatriated. As such, it served the purpose for which the Sultanate established it.

Qatar Crisis

On June 5, 2017, Saudi Arabia, the UAE, Bahrain, and Egypt abruptly imposed a blockade on Qatar, cutting it off from overland food imports and denying its aircraft air traffic control and the use of their airspace. They may have considered a military invasion, but were deterred by Turkey. President Trump supported the move, accusing Qatar of supporting terrorism, though without supplying any details for this allegation. Trump's own cabinet members, Secretary of State Rex Tillerson and Secretary of Defense James Mattis disagreed with the president and gave Qatar support behind the scenes, gradually convincing Trump to repair relations with Emir Tamim Bin Hamad Al-Thani. Qatar leased the crucial al-Udeid Air Force base to the United States, where some 12,000 U.S. military personnel are stationed and from which sorties were flown against ISIL and the Taliban. Tillerson came to the Department of State from ExxonMobil, which has gas operations in Qatar (and which Doha offered to expand). The boycotting quartet presented Doha with a thirteen-point ultimatum demanding, among other things, that it cut off relations with Iran, close the Turkish military base, cut off relations with the Muslim Brotherhood (which the boycotters viewed as a terrorist organization), close down the Al-Jazeera satellite news channel, pay reparations to the blockading states for the harm Qatar had allegedly caused them, and open its books so that its neighbors could monitor its finances.[37]

Riyadh and Abu Dhabi were able to bring Bahrain along, but Kuwait and Oman declined to join the blockade, decisively weakening the initiative. The independent Arab Gulf think tank *SASA Post* noted that Oman announced its neutrality in the conflict on the level of politics, but at the same time refused to join in the boycott or to cut diplomatic relations with Doha.[38] The "neutrality" of Sultan Qaboos, however, seemed to favor Qatar, inasmuch he openly defied Saudi Arabia and the UAE, actively supporting the breaking of the economic isolation imposed on Qatar. They note that Saudi officials had for some time expressed displeasure at what they saw as the maverick policies of Oman with regard to Iran, Iraq, Syria, and Yemen, which they saw as harming the joint interests of the GCC by violating the body's consensus on these issues. They report that Sultan Qaboos had begun to fear that eventually he might also fall victim to the fury of the Riyadh–Abu Dhabi axis within the GCC if the Qatar precedent held. Moreover, that President Donald Trump had initially supported the blockade on Qatar and echoed on Twitter the false charges against Doha of supporting terrorism had shaken the Sultan and his circle. Oman had good relations with the United States and saw Washington as proffering it a security umbrella, but they had suddenly realized that the United States under Trump could not be depended on for the country's security. The obvious influence the Saudis and the UAE had with the Trump administration through his son-in-law Jared Kushner's close friendships with crown princes Mohammed bin Salman and Mohammed bin Zayed raised the specter that they might be able to ruin Muscat's relations with Washington if Sultan Qaboos did not fall in line and cut off Iran and Qatar. Still, the long-serving monarch stood his ground.

The blockade of Qatar by the quartet violated basic principles of Omani statecraft, but also raised the specter of a concerted campaign of regime change within the GCC that threatened the Al-Sabah in Kuwait and the Al-Said in Oman as much as it did the Al-Thani in Qatar. Sultan Qaboos could not help but remember when, in 2011, his security officials had discovered a UAE espionage ring operating in his country. Indeed, unconfirmed reports circulated in March 2019, that two Emirati officers had been tried in Muscat on charges of spying.[39]

Oman broke the blockade by offering Qatari shipping use of its territorial waters, and giving Qatar Airways access to its airspace, which aided it in reaching its Africa destinations.[40] Moreover, right from the beginning of the crisis, Oman and Qatar advertised increased commercial ties as a way of signaling that the organization had split over the Saudi and UAE boycott, even if the precise sums of Oman–Qatar trade were not very consequential. Already in July, Oman announced enhanced economic cooperation with Qatar, in a clear attempt to offset the blockade.[41] In June, a delegation of 140 Qatari businessmen traveled to Muscat to kick off talks. The announcement issued a month later envisioned a rise of bilateral trade from $815 million a year to $1.6 billion, most of it driven by an increase in Qatari imports, including of food and building supplies. Likewise, the Qatari private sector had, by June 2017, invested nearly $200 million in 148 Omani companies, while the Qatari state had invested $4 billion in Oman. These enterprises included the Ras al-Hadd eco-tourism complex and an automobile assembly plant in Duqm. As for Omani investments in Qatar at that time, some 115 completely Omani-owned companies were operating in Qatar, along with 106 joint Omani–Qatari enterprises, capitalized at $116 million. Qatar announced incentives for Omani entrepreneurs to invest in the blockaded country, saying that they would be given the same prerogatives as Qatari businessmen.

A year and a half later, in December 2018, the economies of the two small Gulf states were even more strongly intertwined.[42] Before the boycott, a third of Qatari food imports had come overland through Saudi Arabia or via the UAE's Jabal Ali Port. In the aftermath of the blockade, Qatar turned to Iran and Pakistan for food, but also to imports through Oman's ports, Salala and Sohar.[43] Purchases of Omani fish soared, and the state-owned Qatari al-Hasad commercial fishing company had $138 million worth of investments in Oman. Qatar turned to Oman for greater food security, investing not only in fisheries but also in poultry farms. The Hisad corporation bought a 33 percent share in al-Safa' li al-Aghdhiya, considered the biggest poultry company in Oman, producing 44 million birds a year in 2018, with big expansion plans. By late 2018, the number of Qatari companies selling in Muscat had jumped to 240, and Doha's annual "Made in Qatar" commercial exhibition was for the first time in 2018 held in Muscat. Most often based in Doha, it had been held abroad before, but only in Riyadh and Dubai. Oman had emerged as the biggest market for Qatar's non-hydrocarbon exports, a trade worth some $225 million per month in 2018. By 2019, some 513 joint Omani–Qatari companies were active in both countries, with 361 of them based in Qatar.[44] Oman had already been eager to diversify its economy away from dependence on hydrocarbons, and ironically enough the Qatar crisis gave a fillip to these efforts.

With regard to diplomacy, journalist Hamoud Bin Ali al-Tawqi argues that Muscat strongly supported the mediation efforts of Emir Sabah al-Ahmad al-Jaber al-Sabah, given Sultan Qaboos' similar commitment to the "One Gulf House," that is, the nearly forty-year experiment of the GCC.[45]

One vehicle for this ongoing diplomatic initiative was the annual GCC summits, which continued to be held despite Qatar's absence, where Kuwait and Oman sought to mediate among the parties. Oman hoped that its steadfast commitment to a resolution would signal that it was time to end the crisis and that Qatar was an inseparable part of the GCC. The leaders of both countries faced an active public on Twitter, where impassioned citizens, as well as trolls and bots, waged a vicious propaganda war using smear tactics that made the resolution of the crisis even more difficult. This battleground impelled the militaries and intelligence agencies of the concerned parties to form electronic warfare units, according to al-Tawqi. He warned that these social media battles were making a resolution of the crisis more difficult.

In 2019, Oman took the chairmanship of the GCC, and sought to use this bully pulpit to bring an end to the blockade. In January 2019, Omani Foreign Minister Yusuf bin 'Alawi came to Doha with a proposal for reducing tensions short of ending the crisis.[46] He met with Qatar's ruler, Emir Tamim Bin Hamad Al-Thani, as well as with the Qatari minister of defense. Muscat proposed that the boycotting quartet drop their thirteen demands of Qatar and restore diplomatic relations, even if they did not immediately compromise on their economic sanctions. He went on to share the proposal with each of the other four GCC states. Journalist Anwar al-Khatib reported in *al-'Arabi al-Jadid* (*The New Arab*) that a drag on this effort was the secretary-general of the GCC, Abdullatif bin Rashid Al-Zayani, a Bahraini who strongly supported the boycott.

In the absence of movement on the diplomatic front, through the rest of 2019 Oman reinforced its military cooperation with Qatar. In September, Qatari Minister of Defense Khalid Bin Muhammad al-'Atiyya met with his counterpart, Badr Bin Sa'ud Al-Busaidi at the Bayt al-Falaj Air Force base.[47] This meeting had been preceded by a number of other lower-level military contacts that year. Although the communiques issued in the aftermath were maddeningly vague, it seems clear that both states remained wary of being treated as Bahrain had been in 2011, when Saudi Arabia and the UAE led a small invasion of Bahrain to help put down the Arab Spring youth revolt, which had become in their eyes entangled with popular Shiite politics.

In January 2020, Sultan Qaboos died and was succeeded by Sultan Haitham bin Tariq Al-Said, who improved relations with the UAE somewhat.

He appointed Badr Al-Busaidi as the new foreign minister, who had better relations with the UAE than had his predecessor, Yusuf bin 'Alawi. Nevertheless, Sultan Haitham was by May continuing his cousin's quiet diplomacy in the hope of resolving the Qatar crisis, continuing the policy of strongly supporting Kuwaiti initiatives.[48]

Through 2020, the coronavirus pandemic and resulting low oil prices took a severe toll on Oman's finances, and there was a danger that it might have to turn for help to the blockading quartet and so might lose its stance of neutrality. Simeon Kerr at the *Financial Times* reported that Muscat took out a $2 billion bridge loan in 2020 from a consortium of which the UAE's leading private lender was a part and was exploring other financial support from the wealthier Gulf states. One way for Qatar to help Oman remain neutral was to do matching funds. In October 2020, Qatar provided Oman with $1 billion in direct financial support to help cover its increasing budget deficit, depositing the money directly into the central bank.[49] That Oman might become closer to the UAE out of need for loans and investment, however, possibly strengthened its ability to help negotiate an end to the crisis.

As the Trump administration prepared to exit after Joe Biden's triumph at the polls in November 2020, special envoy for Middle Eastern affairs Jared Kushner appears to have become especially eager to bring the Qatar crisis to a close. Kushner and Secretary of State Mike Pompeo had for some time recognized that the blockade had divided the GCC in a way that made it impossible for Washington to deploy the organization in its quest to isolate Iran. For instance, the denial of air space rights to Qatar Air by Bahrain and the rest of the quartet forced the airline to depend on Iran, and on air traffic control at Shiraz. Qatar paid Iran $122 million a year for overflight rights, at a time when the Trump administration had been attempting to strangle the Iranian economy with its maximum pressure campaign. Qatar and Oman both routinely offered congratulations to Iran every February 1, for instance, on the anniversary of the Iranian Revolution. Qatar's dependence on Iran made it impossible for Doha to take a hard line against Tehran even if the Al-Thanis had desired to do so, which they did not.

On December 16, the Emir of Qatar, Tamim Bin Hamad Al-Thani, abruptly visited Muscat for consultations on ending the crisis, and it was thought that Sultan Haitham was mediating with Riyadh and Abu Dhabi alongside the Kuwait efforts.[50] Kushner then pushed Saudi Arabia and the UAE hard on accepting Kuwaiti mediation, efforts that Oman had also steadfastly backed. It may be that Kushner and Pompeo hoped that a united GCC would be able more effectively to pressure the incoming Biden administration against simply restoring the 2015 Iran nuclear deal, which had been widely despised in the Arab Gulf. After a good deal of arm-twisting by Washington, on January 5, 2021, the GCC met at al-Ula and the boycotting countries agreed to end the blockade and restore full diplomatic relations. Oman's refusal to join the attempt to isolate Qatar, its loud signaling of its determination to continue economic integration with the peninsula, and its backing for the Kuwait mediation efforts, all contributed to the failure of the Saudi–UAE plan to reduce Doha's autonomy.

Oman's low-key attempts at quasi-mediation in Sultan Qaboos' last decade made a palpable contribution either to reducing tensions in the Gulf or at least to keeping crucial lines of communication open among enemies. With regard to the blockade of Qatar in 2017–2021, Oman refused to cut off diplomatic or economic relations with Doha. Indeed, Sultan Qaboos determinedly expanded both, sending a loud message to crown princes Mohammed bin Salman and Mohammed bin Zayed of Saudi Arabia and Abu Dhabi, respectively, that he would not join the boycotting quartet. It was unlikely that Muscat's opposition to the blockade of Qatar was, however, entirely selfless, inasmuch as a successful Saudi–UAE disciplining of Doha for its independent foreign policy and commitment to a free Arab press might well have been a harbinger for a similar imposition of constraints on Oman itself. The Sultanate played a small role in helping Qatar to survive the blockade by offering use of its airspace for Qatar Airway's flights to Africa, offering use of its container ports to replace those of the UAE, and pursuing mutual investments and business enterprises. Surely, however, the symbolic solidarity Sultan Qaboos offered the young, untested Emir Tamim bin Hamad was more important. In addition to supporting Kuwaiti mediation efforts, Oman deployed its chairmanship of the GCC in 2019 to engage in quasi-mediation between Riyadh and Doha. Oman's stance was consistent with the country's long history of maintaining neutrality and cultivating ties with countries that had poor bilateral relations, and offering its good offices for the resolution of outstanding disputes.

The account of former Secretary of State John Kerry of Sultan Qaboos' efforts to act as a go-between for Washington and Tehran over the latter's nuclear enrichment program makes it crystal clear that Oman played much more than the passive role of host. Sultan Qaboos intervened on more than one occasion to revive the talks when they faltered because of mistrust or misunderstandings. Since for fear of loss of face, the United States could not put in writing its acceptance of the Iranian enrichment program, it became crucial that President Obama could, in contrast, put that pledge in a letter to Sultan Qaboos, who could in turn share it with Ayatollah Khamenei. The United States could not send a diplomat to Tehran to meet with Khamenei and make an estimation of his openness to serious talks, but Sultan Qaboos could do so and report his impressions back to Washington. That the latter had gained the trust of Kerry was also crucial. The Sultan's demeanor of dispassionate neutrality impressed both Kerry and Khamenei and engendered trust. Oman could offer nothing of tangible value to the United States or Iran, which dwarfed the small Gulf state in every way. It could, however, offer an out-of-the way venue for the gradual building of mutual trust between the Americans and the Iranians. William J. Burns later wrote, "I met with Oman's shy and reclusive monarch on a number of occasions. Full of wise insight and quiet dignity, the sultan's perspective and advice were always well informed, independent, and pragmatic."[51] In this episode, Sultan Qaboos and his officials took the art of quasi-mediation to its highest level, preparing the way for the ultimately successful talks in Geneva.

The Yemen Civil War proved a much less promising arena for efforts at mediation, given the entirely uncompromising posture of the belligerents. The Houthis spoke of taking all of Yemen and then going on to Riyadh to overthrow the House of Saud. The Saudis and the UAE dismissed the Helpers of God as terrorists and puppets of Iran. The two fought a years-long brutal war on land and in the air that left little taste for compromise. Oman's insistence on remaining open to visits by the Houthis at least allowed it to help settle some issues with prisoners of war and hostages, both between Saudi Arabia and the Houthis and between the Houthis and the United States. Oman also used its good offices, and perhaps some funding, to ensure that the neighboring Yemeni province of Mahra organized to combat al-Qaeda in the Arabian Peninsula and other extremists and to prevent Yemen-based extremism from spilling over into Oman. After the Sultan's death, when the Biden administration took charge of U.S. foreign policy and sought to end the ruinous Yemen War, Washington took advantage of the previous Omani efforts at mediation by meeting with the Houthis in Muscat and providing them with a copy of the U.S. initiative for a settlement in Yemen.[52] Sultan Qaboos' policies thus have the potential to continue to yield peace dividends.

Notes

1. Jeremy Jones and Nicholas Ridout, *A History of Modern Oman* (Cambridge: Cambridge University Press, 2015); Jeremy Jones and Nicholas Ridout, *Oman, Culture and Diplomacy* (Edinburgh: Edinburgh University Press, 2012).

2. Mehran Kamrava, "Mediation and Qatari Foreign Policy," *Middle East Journal* 65 (2011): 539–556.

3. Khurram Abbas, "Passive Mediation in Persian Gulf Conflicts: An Analysis of Pakistan's Peace Initiatives," *Asian Journal of Middle Eastern and Islamic Studies* 13(4) (2019): 604–620.

4. For more on British training of Omani forces, see the speech by Lord Astor at: https://www.gov.uk/government/speeches/2011-11-25-sultan-of-oman-s-armed-forces-association-annual-dinner.

5. Degang Sun and Yahia Zoubir, "China's Participation in Conflict Resolution in the Middle East and North Africa: A Case of Quasi-Mediation Diplomacy?" *Journal of Contemporary China* 27(110) (2018): 224–243 at 224; see also Abbas, "Passive Mediation."

6. John Kerry, *Every Day is Extra* (New York: Simon & Schuster, 2019), 487.

7. Jones and Ridout, *A History of Modern Oman*, 244.

8. Kerry, *Every Day is Extra*, 488.

9. Kerry, *Every Day is Extra*, 489.

10. Kerry, *Every Day is Extra*, 489–90; Trita Parsi, *Losing an Enemy* (New Haven, CT: Yale University Press, 2017), 164–169.

11. Kerry, *Every Day is Extra*, 494–495; Parsi, *Losing an Enemy*, 169–173.

12. Kerry, *Every Day is Extra*, 495–496.

13. Parsi, *Losing an Enemy*, 194–195.

14. Parsi, *Losing an Enemy*, 217–218

15. Arshad Mohammed and Parisa Hafezi, "U.S., Iran held secret talks on march to nuclear deal," Reuters, November 24, 2013, available at: https://www.reuters.com/article/us-iran-nuclear-bilateral/u-s-iran-held-secret-talks-on-march-to-

nuclear-deal-idUSBRE9AN0FB20131124; Kerry, *Every Day is Extra*, 496; Parsi, *Losing an Enemy*, 219.

16. Kerry, *Every Day is Extra*, 497.

17. "Sayih-'i rawshan-i hastih-'i: Iran dar Masqat," IRNA, November 12, 2014, available at: tinyurl.com/3o5fuguw.

18. "Sayih-'i rawshan-i hastih-'i: Iran dar Masqat."

19. Parsi, *Losing an Enemy*, 265.

20. "Bin Alavi chih payami bih Tehran khvahad avard?" *Diplumasi-yi Iran*, November 14, 2014, available at: https://tinyurl.com/229aswbb

21. Milena Sterio, "President Obama's Legacy: The Iran Nuclear Agreement," *Case Western Reserve Journal of International Law* 48(1/2) (2016): 69–82; Arun Vishwanathan, "Iranian Nuclear Agreement: Understanding the Nonproliferation Paradigm," *Contemporary Review of the Middle East* 3(1) (March 2016): 3–22; Parsi, *Losing an Enemy*, chs. 14–15.

22. Juan Cole, "Missed Opportunities: The Trump Administration, Iran, and the Coronavirus Pandemic," *Gulf Insights* No. 31, Qatar University Center for Gulf Studies, June 2020, available at: https://www.qu.edu.qa/static_file/qu/research/Gulf%20Studies/documents/Gulf%20Insights%2031.pdf.

23. Kerry, *Every Day is Extra*, 497.

24. Abdullah Baabood and Ahmed Baabood, "Omani and Qatari Roles in the Yemen Crisis," in Stephen W. Day and Noel Brehony (eds.), *Global, Regional, and Local Dynamics in the Yemen Crisis* (New York: Palgrave Macmillan, 2020), 165–178 at 168–169.

25. Luca Nevola and Baraa Shiban, "The Role of 'Coup Forces,' Saleh, and the Houthis," in Stephen W. Day and Noel Brehony (eds.), *Global, Regional, and Local Dynamics in the Yemen Crisis* (New York: Palgrave Macmillan, 2020), 233–252.

26. Bruce Riedel, "Saudi Arabia's Role in the Yemen Crisis," in Stephen W. Day and Noel Brehony (eds.), *Global, Regional, and Local Dynamics in the Yemen Crisis* (New York: Palgrave Macmillan, 2020), 115–130.

27. Salim al-Juhuri, "Al-Yaman wa malamih wasata 'Umaniyya: Hudna fa-hiwar fa-intikhabat wa mu'tamar li al-manihin," *al-'Arabi al-Jadid*, April 8, 2015, available at: https://tinyurl.com/y4kp9qxg; Baabood and Baabood, "Omani and Qatari Roles," 169.

28. Noel Brehony, "The UAE's Role in the Yemen Crisis," in Stephen W. Day and Noel Brehony (eds.), *Global, Regional, and Local Dynamics in the Yemen Crisis* (New York: Palgrave Macmillan, 2020), 131–147.

29. Baabood and Baabood, "Omani and Qatari Roles," 169–170.

30. Mohammed Alragawi, "Saudi Arabia, Oman, Compete for Control in Yemen's Mahra," *Anadolu Agency*, January 5, 2021, available at: tinyurl.com/4i3ijt3s.

31. Tahir Hani, "Ma huwa dawr saltana 'Uman fi al-malaff al-yamani?" AFP, June 9, 2018, available at: https://tinyurl.com/y7q46ubn.

32. "'Uman fi marma 'niran' sahifa sa'udiyya," *al-Jazira*, September 24, 2018, available at: tinyurl.com/1nluv40g.

33. "Mas'ul Yamani: al-'Umaniyyun nuzaha'," *Athir*, January 2, 2020, available at: tinyurl.com/otxmajhz.

34. "Mas'ul Yamani yatahaddath 'an dawr saltanat 'Uman fi al-harb 'ala Yaman," *Watan al-Dabur*, January 1, 2020, available at: tinyurl.com/tr432v9o.

35. "Masqat, 'Jinif al-'Arab,' rasul 'al-tahdi'a," *Andadolu Agency*, November 14, 2019, available at: tinyurl.com/3acfdq43.

36. "Ba'd najah wasata al-saltana: wusul 200 Yamani ila al-San'a," *Nabd*, October 14, 2020, available at: tinyurl.com/3abhuhp6.

37. Kristian Coates Ulrichsen, *Qatar and the Gulf Crisis: A Study of Resilience* (Oxford: Oxford University Press, 2020); Mahjoob Zweiri, Md. Mizanur Rahman, and Arwa Kamal (eds.), *The 2017 Gulf Crisis: An Interdisciplinary Approach* (Singapore: Springer Nature Singapore, 2021); Juan Cole, "David and Goliath: How Qatar Defeated the Saudi and UAE Annexation Plot," *The Nation*, February 16, 2018.

38. "La aman li al-jiran aw al-halif al-amriki . . . al-'ilaqat al-'umaniyya al-qatariyya 'ala jabal mashdud," *SASA Post*, July 24, 2019, available at: https://www.sasa-post.com/diplomatic-relation-between-oman-and-qatar.

39. "Anba' 'an muhakamat dubat imaratiyyin fi 'Uman bi tuhmat al-tajassus," *al-'Arabi al-Jadid*, March 11, 2019, available at: https://tinyurl.com/y6fcjr6f.

40. Giorgio Cafiero and Theodore Karasik, "Yemen War and Qatar Crisis Challenge Oman's Neutrality," *Middle East Institute*, July 6, 2017, available at: https://www.mei.edu/publications/yemen-war-and-qatar-crisis-challenge-omans-neutrality.

41. Muhammad Azwin, "Tasa'ud watira al-ta'awun al-iqtisadi bayn Qatar wa 'Uman," *al-Jazira*, July 20, 2017, available at: https://tinyurl.com/y523kbfc.

42. Ali Shakir, "Qatar wa 'Uman . . . 'Ilaqat iqtisadiyya qawiyya wa tawassu' bi al-istithmar," *al-Jazira*, December 16, 2018, available at: https://tinyurl.com/y6lasfd7.

43. For Iran, see Mehran Hagirian, "Iran's Pragmatic Foreign Policy in Response to Regional Crises: The Case of the Blockade against Qatar," in Mahjoob Zweiri,

Md. Mizanur Rahman, and Arwa Kamal (eds.), *The 2017 Gulf Crisis: An Interdisciplinary Approach* (Singapore: Springer Nature Singapore, 2021), 171–288 at 278–284.

44. "La aman li al-jiran aw al-halif al-amriki," *SASA Post*.

45. Hamoud Bin Ali al-Tawqi, "al-Diblumasiyya al-'Umaniyya wa hall al-azma al-khalijiyya," *al-Ru'ya*, January 14, 2019, available at: https://tinyurl.com/y6am8wh5.

46. Anwar al-Khatib, "Saltanat 'Uman tu'rid masa'iha li hall al-azma al-khalijiyya," al-'Arabi al-Jadid, January 13, 2019, available at: https://tinyurl.com/y5no2xyd.

47. "Qatar wa 'Uman . . . al-'ilaqat tata'zzaz bi al-tafahumat al-'askariyya," al-Jazira, September 29, 2019, available at: https://tinyurl.com/y3r3wdvn.

48. "Al-Diblumasiyya al-'Umaniyya tataharrak li inqadh al-khalij," *al-Watan*, May 18, 2020, available at: https://tinyurl.com/y3k9mqf5.

49. Simeon Kerr, "Oman gets $1 bn. In aid from Qatar," *Financial Times*, October 28, 2020, available at: https://www.ft.com/content/8ba9e58f-3c66-45f3-8417-0cb39f3a9083.

50. "Oman tusharik fi al-wasata bayn al-Su'udiyya wa Qatar," *al-'Arab*, December 16, 2020, available at: https://tinyurl.com/yxr7u5o7.

51. William J. Burns, "The Death of a Temperate Leader in an Intemperate Region," *The Atlantic*, January 13, 2020, available at: https://www.theatlantic.com/ideas/archive/2020/01/sultan-qaboos-oman/604807.

52. "Oman Brings into the Open its Mediation on Yemen," *The Arab Weekly*, March 31, 2021, available at: https://thearabweekly.com/oman-brings-open-its-mediation-yemen.

18

"FRIEND TO ALL, ENEMY TO NONE": OMAN'S QUIET DIPLOMACY SINCE 1970

Francis Owtram

As Qaboos' coffin was carried into Muscat in January 2020 on the same military vehicle that had brought him into the capital city in 1970, the world had good cause to reflect on the implications of the passing of this ruler of five decades. His long rule was marked by Omani facilitation of dialogue between states and parties locked in diplomatic tension or all-out conflict and war. Muscat was a conduit for communication between Iran and Iraq during the Gulf War, Israel and the Palestinians, combatants in the Yemen War, and the United States and Iran. Helping first to secure the release in 2011 of American hikers held by Iran, Oman subsequently facilitated secret meetings in Muscat between American and Iranian officials during the Obama presidency which eventually led to the Joint Comprehensive Plan of Action (JCPOA), otherwise known as the Iran nuclear deal. In his five decades in power Sultan Qaboos carefully developed a strategy for managing Oman's exposure to the swirling currents of regional conflicts through his foreign policy, in ways calculated to support his state's survival. In so doing, Oman's foreign policy has been seen as quite distinct, several terms have been used to try and capture its essence: independent, neutral, particularistic, pragmatic, balanced. In the implementation of this policy Oman has been a facilitator and sometimes perceived as a mediator between groups in conflict. This approach has been continued under Sultan Haitham who succeeded his cousin in January 2020. Hence, this chapter uses "since

1970." It is this aspect of Oman's foreign policy—Oman's quiet diplomacy—that is the focus of this chapter. Avoiding conflict or taking sides in wars (such as between Iran and Iraq or in Yemen) Oman's foreign policy of even-handedness is such that the Sultanate has frequently been referred to as "the Switzerland of the Middle East."[1]

This chapter has fairly limited aims: it uses the conceptual framework of "quiet diplomacy" to characterize an aspect of Oman's foreign policy that has been evident since 1970, and most unambiguously since Qaboos established himself after the end of the Dhofar War. It is not intended as an attempt to offer a comprehensive account of Omani foreign policy or international relations. Neither is intended as analysis of Oman's foreign policy from the various theoretical perspectives offered in the academic discipline of International Relations (IR), to which I will return briefly later in the chapter.

Whilst Oman would seem to be a very good example of the conduct of "quiet diplomacy," there has been relatively little written explicitly placing Omani diplomacy in this framework. Jeremy Jones has penned a short piece titled "Oman's Quiet Diplomacy," which succinctly surveys some key details without outlining the essential features of this phenomenon in its wider sense.[2] This chapter therefore offers a more expanded version of what has been written and at the same time contextualizes this aspect of Omani diplomacy in a category ("quiet diplomacy") that has been more broadly applied in instances of conflict resolution between states and within states (intra-state conflict).

Quiet Diplomacy as a Conceptual Category

For our purposes I find writings by former diplomats Craig Collins and John Packer useful for identifying the essential features of "quiet diplomacy."[3] In one of the publications (2005) they write under the auspices of the "Initiative for Conflict Prevention through Quiet Diplomacy," which highlights how significant this concept is for practitioners in diplomacy, peace-building, and conflict resolution.[4] In terms of categorization of this framework, it is noted by Dr. David A. Hamburg that "quiet diplomacy" is a subcategory of "preventive diplomacy":

> Preventive diplomacy is the range of peaceful dispute resolution approaches mentioned in Article 33 of the UN Charter when applied before a dispute crosses the threshold to armed conflict. It has many forms and methods. "Quiet

diplomacy" is a notable one . . . Quiet diplomacy can address both basic and proximate causes of conflict. In the process, it can help to create mechanisms that enhance dialogue and cooperation among different groups and therefore encourage future management of disputes through peaceful means.[5]

Concerning the definition of quiet diplomacy for Collins and Packer "At the nexus of international affairs and violent conflict, quiet diplomacy generally describes confidential, non-coercive assistance of an impartial third party who seeks to create conditions in which disputing parties can address—and ultimately resolve—their differences before they lead to violence or recur (where there may already have been violence)."[6] They go on to note that a range of tools and techniques can be deployed as part of quiet diplomacy: facilitation, mediation, conciliation, good offices, special envoys, adjudication, and arbitration.[7] According to Collins and Packer facilitation "describes third-party engagement which provides a forum, space and environment conducive to dispute settlement. Other facilities and services may be provided as appropriate, notably communications. Such provision may be minimal or substantial depending on the situation, and (most importantly) the will of the parties."[8] A further point they make is that experience has shown that by tempering confrontational approaches and enhancing receptiveness to peaceful solutions quiet diplomacy can home in on both the "root" and "proximate" causes of inter- and intra-state tensions.

In relation to the above three salient points can be made which will be evidenced in the following section. First, as we shall from see the record of Omani quiet diplomacy, it has often been deployed after a dispute has crossed the threshold to armed conflict, not just before the outbreak of hostilities. Second, Omani quiet diplomacy usually takes the form of facilitation rather than mediation. Indeed, it has been noted that Omani officials, having provided a meeting space for disputants, will even step out of the room lest they become embroiled in the details of others' disputes or appealed to by one side or the other, which would compromise Oman's independent position. Omani quiet diplomacy has both helped to bring about ceasefires and provided a platform by which longer lasting peace agreements may be struck. The ability to offer channels of communication stems from a fundamental premise of Omani diplomacy which is to avoid ever publicly taking sides in disputes thus allowing it to play the role of a good faith broker. It is in this regard that Oman has often been called "the Switzerland of the Middle East." Thus, there is never a severing of diplomatic relations, channels of communication are maintained, there is a willingness to listen and talk, and a neutral stance is cultivated which allows the practice of "backchannel diplomacy." Or as Jeremy Jones and Nicolas Ridout put it, in Omani foreign policy "a principle that communication is better than severed or non-existent relations tends to prevail."[9] We now turn to the record of Oman's quiet diplomacy since 1970.

Oman's Quiet Diplomacy since 1970

This section surveys the record of Oman's quiet diplomacy since 1970; in doing it so will cover this aspect of Oman's foreign policy in relation to the Arab–Israeli conflict, the Iran–Iraq War, the United States and Iran, the Yemen conflict since 2014, and the Qatar crisis.

We will turn later to some consideration of different explanations for Oman's quiet diplomacy. The specialist on modern Oman, Marc Valeri, provides an initial context that is helpful to frame the issue:

> The Omani authorities have always perceived political instability in the Gulf and Western Asia as a factor threatening Oman's internal stability. This perception of political vulnerability in a region disrupted by regional convulsions explains Omani pragmatism in the international arena, leading it to emphasize underlying geo-strategic realities and promote consensus-oriented solutions.[10]

We should also be cognisant that "friend to all" is not a complete characterization of Omani foreign relations for the whole period covered in this chapter. Likely due to the struggle against the ideology and military forces of the Popular Front for the Liberation of Oman and the Arabian Gulf (PFLOAG) in the Dhofar War there was an initial reluctance to engage with certain states. For example, as Valeri points out, "despite the historical connections between Oman and East Africa, Muscat waited until 2005 to establish official diplomatic relations with Tanzania, out of dislike for the latter's 'African socialism' ideology."[11]

Related to this, and as a necessary historical contextualization, it is important to note that Oman's quiet diplomacy did not really start until the end of the Dhofar War in 1975. During the Dhofar War Oman's foreign policy was mostly geared toward securing international recognition for the Sultanate of Oman (in 1970 Qaboos changed the name of the state from the Sultanate of Muscat and Oman) and obtaining aid and support for the fight against PFLOAG. By the end of the Dhofar War Qaboos had consolidated his power both against the forces of PFLOAG and established his pre-eminence over his uncle, Tariq bin Taimur, who resigned as prime minister in 1972.[12] He had also started to extricate himself from the dominance of the British officials who de facto ran the Dhofar War and the Omani state in the early to mid-1970s.[13] Referring to this period and drawing on some British and American archival sources, Gardner outlines an argument that Qaboos sought to progressively enhance his independence from British officials and secure his place against his uncle Tariq bin Taimur.[14] British officials felt that Tariq was "too independent" and less willing to accept British advice than Qaboos. The Arab–Israeli conflict was one of the first areas of the nascent Omani quiet diplomacy.

Oman and the Arab–Israeli Conflict

Oman was the only Arab state that did not break off relations with Egypt because of the Camp David Agreement between Egypt and Israel in 1978. Indeed, Qaboos welcomed the 1979 Egypt–Israeli Peace Treaty and did not participate in the 1979 Arab League summit that expelled Egypt. Oman has maintained informal contacts and relations with Israel over the years, even while supporting the Palestinian cause. Issues of water conservation in the Middle East became an issue around which Muscat was able to deploy its subtle diplomacy during the time of the Oslo peace process.[15] In April 1994, Muscat hosted the Water Resources Working Group, which gave a framework for contacts with Israel and eventually resulted in Middle East Desalination Research Center being established in Muscat.

A similar process of using technical problems as an avenue for building contact seemed to be at play a quarter of a century later. In October 2018, shortly after the visit by President Mahmood Abbas to Muscat, there followed a visit of Israel Prime Minister Binyamin Netanyahu, for talks with Qaboos. The joint Israeli–Omani communiqué mentioned some prospects for peace; it was also announced that Israel's transportation minister would take part in an international event in Oman concerning a railway project to connect Haifa with the Gulf States via Jordan. In June 2019, Omani even-handedness was displayed when Oman announced that it intended to establish an embassy in Ramallah in the Occupied Palestinian Territories. For Kristian Coates Ulrichsen, Oman was "characteristically attempting to play its unique hand of diplomatic cards to reverse the recent escalation of tensions between Palestinians and Israelis, while also demonstrating its independence and commitment to advancing dialogue and compromise between regional actors."[16] Following the Abraham Accords Peace Agreement in August 2020, Oman has so far not joined the UAE, Bahrain and Sudan who have by the Accords formally and publicly established diplomatic relations with Israel.[17] The statement released by the Ministry of Foreign Affairs reflects Oman's careful approach, under which an accord with Israel would require Tel Aviv to agree to the Arab Peace Initiative. Thus, ". . . this new strategic path taken by some Arab countries will contribute to bringing about a peace based on an end to the Israeli occupation of Palestinian lands and on establishing an independent Palestinian state with East Jerusalem as capital." Coates Ulrichsen argues that it is the Iranian factor that is key: Oman has always been the Gulf Cooperation Council (GCC) state that has most taken into account Iranian security considerations, and for Iran the Abraham Accords are perceived as a threat to their security; indeed, the visit of Netanyahu to Muscat occasioned a rare criticism of Oman from Iran.

Oman, Iran, and the United States

The Shah of Iran sent troops to help Qaboos in his fight against the revolutionaries in Dhofar, and in 1976 Qaboos convened a meeting of the foreign ministers of the Gulf States (the six Gulf monarchies, Iraq, and Iran) to consider a regional security policy. With the overthrow of the Shah in 1979 and the establishment of the Islamic Republic of Iran it might have been thought almost impossible to maintain Omani–Iranian relations. Indeed, although it now tends to be stated almost as self-evident that Oman never decisively takes sides in conflicts, there was a moment at the outset of the Iran–Iraq War when it almost did. A few days after Iraqi troops crossed into Iran, Qaboos decided he was going to make Omani facilities at Seeb and Masirah airports available to Iraqi forces to attack Bander Abbas, one of Iran's most important ports. Qaboos had been irritated by Khomeni's call for revolution in the region. Had Oman implemented this decision, the ramifications could have been extensive, impacting that most sensitive issue of international freedom of movement through the Strait of Hormuz and possibly exposing Oman to Iranian retaliation.[18] In the end, a delay in the arrival of Iraqi forces who were then concealed in the Sultan's Muscat guest house, prevented this from happening. Also, Washington had made clear that if Iran retaliated against Oman because of this operation, the U.S. Navy would not come to the defense of Oman.[19]

In any case, cooler heads prevailed, and the ruction of the Iranian Revolution was soon smoothed over in Omani–Iranian relations based on geostrategic realities. Valeri puts it well:

> Less inclined than his GCC counterparts to see in his domestic Shia minority as a Iranian Trojan horse, Qaboos did not break diplomatic relations with Iran after the 1979 Iranian revolution. He considered that he had no interest in presenting Iran as the sole source of regional tensions, because such an attitude could not lead to long-term stability and mutual cooperation.[20]

At the 1981 summit that established the GCC, Oman supported the creation of an organization for mutual security between the Arab Gulf monarchies in tandem with a close relationship with the United States, but the Sultanate opposed the GCC being turned into an anti-Iranian organization. In 1987, Qaboos' special representative helped to ease the path for diplomatic contacts between Iran and Iraq, and later Oman sought to persuade Tehran to agree to the U.N. resolution to end the war. Also in that year Muscat offered to be a go-between as an aid to the improvement of U.S.–Iran relations. Oman hosted a meeting in 1991 which led to the restoration of Saudi–Iranian diplomatic relations. Since the 1990s, ministerial visits have taken place on a regular and frequent basis, and in 2009 Qaboos paid a three-day visit to Iran. Both countries worked on development of gas fields and other economic matters. Oman became was an intermediary in securing the release of a U.S. national in Iran as well as Iranian nationals held in Britain and the United States. It was these nurtured contacts that allowed Oman to negotiate the release of the American hikers held in Iran.

This was to bear fruit in November 2013 when the JCPOA between Iran and the P5+1 (the five permanent UN Security Council members plus Germany) over Iran's nuclear program was quickly agreed in Geneva.[21] It subsequently emerged that secret talks had taken place in March 2013 in Muscat between Iranian and U.S. officials. These and further talks had laid the groundwork for the swift conclusion of a deal in Geneva. This was a high point of Omani diplomacy which Sayyid Badr Albusaidi described as a historic win-win.[22] Although viewed with suspicion by several Arab Gulf states, by persuading the United States and Iran to engage in dialogue, Oman was able to ensure free and safe passage through the Strait of Hormuz and reduce the possibility of a war breaking out, forcing it to choose sides. However, the advent of the Trump administration posed new challenges for Omani quiet diplomacy.

"Confrontation is not in the interest of any of the parties involved," the Omani minister responsible for foreign affairs declared on May 18, 2018 in a press release in response to President Donald Trump's announcement that he was withdrawing from the JCPOA. Oman had tried to maintain a balance between Iran and the Sunni Arab Gulf States but the U.S. withdrawal from the nuclear agreement had potentially put Oman in a difficult position in the escalating tensions. Therefore, Oman welcomed the advent of the Biden administration which declared "America is back." There has followed a renewed U.S. willingness to reinstate the JCPOA and eschew overt confrontation with Iran over its nuclear program and in Yemen.

Oman and the Yemen War

Since the outbreak of the Yemen War in 2014, Oman has consistently offered to facilitate talks between the conflicting parties, acutely aware that instability in Yemen can easily transfer into Oman through the shared border. Thus, Muscat was proffered as a meeting place for the U.N. Special Envoy for Yemen Martin Griffiths to convene talks with relevant parties (the Houthis decided not to attend). In September 2019, in an interview conducted at the United Nations, Yusuf bin Alawi, then Minister Responsible for Foreign Affairs, clarified the Omani role in connection with the Yemen conflict—a statement which incidentally also sums up Oman's role over four decades in connection with peace-building and conflict resolution: "Oman will assist.

We are not playing the role of mediator. What we choose for ourselves is the role of facilitator."[23]

President Trump, following an Israeli world view, had seen the hand of Iran in Yemen and backed without reservation the Saudi bombing offensive; to Omani dismay the Houthis were designated a terrorist organization by the Trump administration, which made the facilitation of peace initiatives more difficult. Again, Oman was pleased that this designation was revoked by the Biden administration, and it remains to be seen whether the Omani offer of facilities for talks will be taken up. The ethos of this facilitative approach is followed to the extent that Omani officials will leave the room once parties brought there by Omani back-channel diplomacy have taken their seats. However, this Omani role in the Yemen conflict has sometimes been viewed with suspicion by its Gulf neighbors. Saudi Arabia and the United Arab Emirates, under their crown princes and de facto rulers, Mohammed bin Salman and Mohammed bin Zayed, have engaged in an attempted restructuring of the region, and have made no great secret of their suspicion of Oman's independent foreign policy which refuses to align with their anti-Iran coalition. It remains the case that Oman will do its utmost to promote a peaceful resolution of the conflict which threatens the stability of the Dhofar region and indeed Oman. It is impossible to compartmentalize the security and stability of the Gulf region and Arabian Peninsula as the Qatar crisis demonstrated.

Oman and the Qatar Crisis

As scholar of Gulf diplomacy Abdullah Baabood put it, Oman's neutral position in the dispute was "textbook Omani foreign policy."[24] Baabood offers a succinct and inciteful analysis referencing the role of Oman's quiet diplomacy in this conflict as in many before and is therefore quoted at length here:

> The Sultanate has long pursued an independent foreign policy stance and has avoided falling into any particular faction or political bloc—maintaining friendly relations with neighbors and favoring non-interference in the internal affairs of other states as well as respect for international law, conventions and customs. As a result, Oman has not sided with any party of the conflict despite enjoying a close relationship with Qatar. Doha at first looked to their counterparts in Muscat to mediate the row, and Oman initially agreed. But recognizing the sensitivities, Oman realized that it

cannot play the role of principal mediator. The Sultanate chose to maintain its position of impartiality and non-interference—reverting to its typical strategy of supporting mediation and pursuing quiet diplomacy to bring the two sides together toward reconciliation. This approach explains why Oman's foreign affairs minister, Yusuf bin Alawi bin Abdullah, recently met with Qatari officials both in Doha and Muscat to discuss bilateral relations, regional developments, and, significantly, Oman's support for Kuwaiti- and US-led mediation efforts.[25]

In the end all this bore fruit (quite possibly helped by the end of the Trump administration) when at the 41st GCC summit in January 2021 the leaders of the GCC states signed the "security and stability" agreement. However, the underlying tensions remain, so it is quite possible that discord will break out again. Although Oman benefited financially and economically from the dispute due to increased use of its ports, it sees the dangers for regional stability if the dispute festers. It will be a test for Omani quiet diplomacy to prevent a reoccurrence or indeed to resolve it should such a dispute surface again. This section has reviewed Oman's quiet diplomacy since 1970 in several highly significant conflicts; we now turn to how this policy might be explained.

Contending Explanations of Oman's Quiet Diplomacy

The purpose of this section is to flag up (rather than analytically assess and fully articulate an argument) different candidate explanations for Oman's quiet diplomacy. Sayyid Badr Albusaidi, Minister of Foreign Affairs, offered the following observation in February 2021:

> I send you greetings from Oman, the land of peace. I say that because I always believed throughout my life, throughout my career and working life, that one should lead by example, and peace building has to start from within first, and this is exactly what Oman did fifty years ago, and managed to forge not just peace within itself, but with all its neighbours and with the rest of the world, to a position where now, if you look at the map of the world, this is the one country that has no political problem with anybody on that map.[26]

The respected scholar Anoushirivan Ehteshami comments that Oman has an "extraordinary ability to talk to governments of any colour."[27] Different explanations have been posited as to what lies beneath these public state-ments and communications. As Calvin Allen notes: "Most nation-states in the world have two forms of foreign policy, the rhetorical that involves lofty statements of intent, and the reality which involves the actions taken by the country's leadership. Oman is no exception."[28] For Edwin Tran there is a rational calculation behind the policy of "friend to all":

> Oman's foreign policy is simple. It must maintain its appearance as a coun-try focused on mediation and negotiation to gain international approval. This ensures a significant amount of security for the country should any acts of regional aggression occur. Oman accomplishes this by placing itself firmly in the international community while avoiding any hard alignments regionally . . . it is important to recognize that Oman's rhetoric here is more than just words. Throughout the course of history, Oman has exemplified this geopolitical strategy by maintaining an image of moderation and peace propagation, acts that are key in securing its own international security.[29]

In similar vein but also identifying a cultural factor, Roby Barrett notes that "Oman has traditionally pursued policies that have enhanced its value to powerful interests in the region, thus shoring up its security. It has practiced a calculated even-handedness among the players . . ."[30] Jeremy Jones sees part of this emphasis on mediation and negotiation (whilst maintaining a low profile) as stemming from Oman's Ibadi culture, which he argues follows Frederick Barth's notion of an "ideology of politeness."[31] Abdullah Baabood contends that this policy of quiet diplomacy is part of Oman's "indepen-dent foreign policy" which stems from its culture and national interest.[32] In contrast, Nora Ezzat argues against a culture-based interpretation and pre-fers a historical–institutional approach.[33] This explains Omani foreign policy through the structural factors of the history of the Sultanate as it arose in conditions of British supremacy in the Indian Ocean and a weak connection with the postcolonial Arab world. The transformations brought about by oil brought it back into contact with its Gulf neighbors, but without removing its earlier perception of its role and place in the region.

Marc Valeri observes that Oman has assiduously retained a close relation-ship with the core Western power, the United States, as a security guarantor, whilst also balancing this relationship with other Western and global powers.[34]

Further, through its policy of not taking sides in regional conflicts combined with its facilitation of dialog between fractious states and groups, it does not expose itself to the risks of incurring dangerous enmities and accrues political capital on which it can call if trouble brews. A broader theoretical framework developed by Raymond Hinnebusch and Anoush Ehteshami has argued for a "combined" or "complex" theoretical approach in order to understand and explain the international politics of the Middle East and the foreign policies of Middle East states.[35] Furthermore, Almezaini and Rickli have developed a framework for analysis for the foreign and security policies of the small Gulf States, and Baabood's chapter in their collection is an essential starting point for any consideration of Omani foreign policy.[36]

It is important to note that there is this body of literature that aims to analyze and explain the dynamics of Omani foreign policy and foreign relations from the extant concepts of the discipline of International Relations, including such fields of academic inquiry as the foreign policies of small states, security studies, and international political economy.

Conclusion: Oman's "Quiet Diplomacy," 1970–2020

The record of Omani quiet diplomacy in conflict resolution and peace-keeping since 1970 is extensive. Oman is in a "tough neighborhood." In recent years, as the de facto rulers of Saudi Arabia and the United Arab Emirates have sought to reshape the region's political landscape they have been irritated with Oman's independent foreign policy, and it has been suggested that they have promoted a narrative that "as Oman is not with us, it is against us." Accordingly, analysts have questioned whether opportunities will be used to see if Oman can be drawn closer into their orbit. Sultan Haitham has set out his stall to continue maintaining a neutral and independent position, but questions remain as to whether Oman's economic vulnerabilities exacerbated by the pandemic will be used to influence the Sultanate's foreign policy stance.[37]

In a turbulent region, even if, as it might be argued by some, it forms part of a strategy for state survival and maintenance of the rule of the Al-Bu Said, Sultan Haitham's continuation of Oman's facilitation of quiet diplomacy between parties is welcome news indeed. When conflict breaks out it is not the leaders instigating the conflicts who suffer, rather, it is the people— the ordinary men, women, children, and families—who experience the devastating effects of silent missile attacks, cluster bomb destruction of their schools and hospitals, the relentless onslaught of proxy militias, and destitution brought on by embargoes. Sultan Haitham's continuation of the quiet diplomacy of Sultan Qaboos cannot be understated as a contribution to the mitigation and management of tensions in the Middle East and, hopefully, in time the peaceful and just resolution of the conflicts that threaten to tear the region apart.

Notes

1. Simon Kerr, "Switzerland of the Middle East: Economic Crisis Threatens Oman's Neutrality," *Financial Times*, October 19, 2020.
2. Jeremy Jones, "Oman's Quiet Diplomacy," NUPI Paper, June 4 , *Norwegian Institute of International Affairs*, 2015, available at: https://www.nupi.no/en/Publications/CRIStin-Pub/Oman-s-Quiet-Diplomacy, last accessed October 22, 2021.
3. Craig Collins and John Packer, *Options and Techniques for Quiet Diplomacy* (Stockholm: Folke Bernadotte Academy, 2005); Craig Collins and John Packer, "Quiet Diplomacy: Preventing Conflict through Discreet Engagement," in Stefan Wolff and Christalla Yakinthou (eds.), *Conflict Management in Divided Societies: Theories and Practices* (Abingdon: Routledge, 2012).
4. Collins and Packer, *Options and Techniques for Quiet Diplomacy.*
5. Collins and Packer, "Quiet Diplomacy," 9.
6. Collins and Packer, "Quiet Diplomacy," 100.
7. Collins and Packer, *Options and Techniques for Quiet Diplomacy*; Collins and Packer, "Quiet Diplomacy," 105–108.
8. Collins and Packer, "Quiet Diplomacy," 106.
9. Jeremy Jones and Nicholas Ridout, *Oman: Culture and Diplomacy* (Edinburgh: Edinburgh University Press, 2012), 244
10. Marc Valeri, "Oman's Mediatory Efforts in Regional Crises," in Expert Analysis, Norwegian Peacebuilding Resource Centre, March 2014
11. Marc Valeri, "Oman," in Christopher Davidson (ed.), *Power and Politics in the Persian Gulf Monarchies* (London: Hurst, 2011), 106.
12. See Abdel Razzaq Takriti, *Monsoon Revolution: Republicans, Sultans, and Empires in Oman, 1965–1976* (Oxford: Oxford University Press, 2013); Majid Al-Khalili, *Oman's Foreign Policy: Foundation and Practice* (Westport, CT: Praeger Security International, 2009).
13. Francis Owtram, *A Modern History of Oman: Formation of the State since 1920* (London: I. B. Tauris, 2004; Francis Owtram, "A Close Relationship: Britain

and Oman since 1750," *Qatar Digital Library*, December 11, 2014, available at: https://www.qdl.qa/en/close-relationship-britain-and-oman-1750, last accessed October 22, 2021; Takriti, *Monsoon Revolution*.

14. Nikolas Gardner, "The Limits of the Sandhurst Connection: The Evolution of Oman's Foreign and Defense Policy, 1970–1977," *Journal of the Middle East and Africa* 6(1) (2015), available at: https://www.tandfonline.com/doi/abs/10.1080/21520844.2015.1028850.

15. Jones and Ridout, *Oman: Culture and Diplomacy*, 236–240.

16. Kristian Coates Ulrichsen and Giorgo Cafiero, "Oman's New Embassy in Palestine," *Middle East Institute*, August 12, 2019.

17. Coates Ulrichsen and Cafiero, "Oman's New Embassy in Palestine."

18. See Edwin Tran, "In the Lion's Den: Oman's Foreign Policy, Part 1," *International Review*, December 6, 2018; Kambiz Fattahi, "The Oman Scare: The Untold Story of Oman's Almost Strike on Iran," September 27, 2018

19. Fattahi, "The Oman Scare."

20. Valeri, "Oman's Mediatory Efforts in Regional Crises."

21. Jones, "Oman's Quiet Diplomacy," 2015.

22. Tran, "In the Lion's Den."

23. *Al-Monitor*, "Oman Minister Describes Role as 'Facilitator' of Diplomacy in Turbulent Region," September 26, 2019.

24. A. Baabood, "Oman and the Gulf Diplomatic Crisis," Foreign Policy Trends in the GCC States, Oxford Gulf and Arabian Peninsula Studies Forum, Autumn 2017, 30–31.

25. Baabood, "Oman and the Gulf Diplomatic Crisis," 31.

26. Atlantic Council, 2021.

27. In comments made at a webinar of the Anglo-Omani Society, "Oman's Foreign Policy: A Forward Look," July 6, 2020, available at: https://www.youtube.com/watch?v=q-o5791bGqE.

28. Calvin Allen and Lynn Rigsbee, *Oman under Qaboos: From Coup to Constitution, 1970–1996* (London: Frank Cass, 2000), 180

29. Tran, "In the Lion's Den."

30. Barrett, "Oman's Balancing Act," 2015.

31. Jones and Ridout, *Oman: Culture and Diplomacy*; Jones, "Oman's Quiet Diplomacy," 2015.

32. Abdullah Baabood, "Oman's Independent Foreign Policy," in Kalid S. Almezaini and John-Marc Rickli (eds.), *The Small Gulf States* (New York: Routledge, 2017).

33. Noha Ezzat, "Oman: Institutional Genealogy of an Exceptional Foreign Policy," *Global Policy Journal*, IMEIS 2019 Conference Proceedings, University of Durham, June 2019.
34. Valeri, "Oman."
35. Raymond Hinnebusch *The International Politics of the Middle East*, 2nd edn. (Manchester: Manchester University Press, 2015); Raymond Hinnebusch and Anoushiravan Ehteshami, *The Foreign Policies of Middle East States*, 2nd edn. (Boulder, CO: Lynne Rienner, 2014); Raymond Hinnebusch and Anoushiravan Ehteshami, "Foreign Policymaking in the Middle East: Complex Realism," in Louise Fawcett (ed.), *International Relations of the Middle East*, 5th edn. (Oxford: Oxford University Press, 2019), 249–270.
36. See Baabood, "Oman's Independent Foreign Policy."
37. See Francis Owtram, "Oman after Qaboos: Continuities, Challenges and Choices," LSE Middle East Centre, 2020; Francis Owtram and Malak Hayek, "Oman in the COVID-19 Pandemic: People, Policy and Economic Impact," LSE Middle East Centre blog, July 23, 2020.

References

Abouzzhour, Yasmina, "Neutral Oman is Clear Winner of Gulf Crisis and Resolution," January 20, 2021, Brookings Institution, available at: https://www.brookings.edu/opinions/bdc-snapshots-neutral-oman-is-clear-winner-of-gulf-crisis-and-resolution.

Albusaidi, Badr bin Hamad, "Small States' Diplomacy in the Age of Globlization: An Omani Perspective," in G. Nonneman (ed.), *Analyzing Middle East Foreign Policies and the Relationship with Europe* (Abingdon: Routledge, 2005).

Al-Khalili, Majid, *Oman's Foreign Policy: Foundation and Practice* (Westport, CT: Praeger Security International, 2009).

Almezaini, Khalid S. and Jean-Marc Rickli, *The Small Gulf States: Foreign and Security Policies Before and After the Arab Spring* (Abingdon: Routledge, 2017).

Al-Monitor, "Oman Minister Describes Role as 'Facilitator' of Diplomacy in Turbulent Region," September 26, 2019, available at: https://www.al-monitor.com/originals/2019/09/interview-oman-foreign-minister-bin-alawi-iran-syria-israel.html.

Allen, Jr., Calvin and W. Lynn Rigsbee, *Oman under Qaboos: From Coup to Constitution, 1970–1996* (London: Frank Cass, 2000).

Anglo-Omani Society, "Oman's Foreign Policy: A Forward Look," webinar July 6, 2020, available at: https://www.youtube.com/watch?v=o5791bGqE.

Anglo-Omani Society, "Oman Outlook 2021: Domestic and Foreign Policy," webinar January 21, 2021, available at: https://www.youtube.com/watch?v=C5jC-V1cfAA.

Atlantic Council, "A Conversation with HE Sayyid Badr Al-Busaidi, Foreign Minister of Oman," February 11, 2021, available at: https://www.youtube.com/watch?v=1nj8xbM7450.

Baabood, A., "Oman's Independent Foreign Policy," in Kalid S.Almezaini and John-Marc Rickli (eds.), *The Small Gulf States* (New York: Routledge, 2017), 107–122.

Baabood, A., "Oman and the Gulf Diplomatic Crisis," Foreign Policy Trends in the GCC States, Oxford Gulf and Arabian Peninsula Studies Forum, Autumn 2017, 30–31, available at: https://www.oxgaps.org/files/commentary_-_baabood.pdf.

Barrett, Roby, "Oman's Balancing Act in the Yemen Conflict," Middle East Institute, June 17, 2015, available at: https://www.mei.edu/publications/omans-balancing-act-yemen-conflict.

Business Year, The, "Friends to All, Enemy to None," Oman 2020, available at: https://www.thebusinessyear.com/oman-2020/friends-to-all-enemy-to-none/focus.

Castelier, Sebastian, "Everyone Will Lose Fearing New Gulf War: Oman Doubles Down Diplomacy 2017," *Middle East Eye*, available at: https://www.middleeasteye.net/news/everyone-will-lose-fearing-new-gulf-war-oman-doubles-down-diplomacy.

Castelier, Sebastian, "Oman's Foreign Policy after Sultan Qaboos," *Al-Monitor*, March 13, 2020, available at: https://www.al-monitor.com/originals/2020/03/oman-foreign-policy-gulf-sultan-qaboos-haitham.html#ixzz6qmOFBzXK.

Coates Ulrichsen, Kristian, "Can Kuwaiti Mediation and Omani Facilitation Support Ending Yemen's War?" May 6, 2020, available at: https://sanaacenter.org/publications/analysis/9900.

Coates Ulrichsen, Kristian and Giorgo Cafiero, "Oman's New Embassy in Palestine," *Middle East Institute*, August 12, 2019, available at: https://www.mei.edu/publications/omans-new-embassy-palestine.

Coates Ulrichsen and Giorgo Cafiero, "Oman Plays It Safe on Israel," *Middle East Institute*, October 27, 2020, available at: https://www.mei.edu/publications/oman-plays-it-safe-israel.

Coates Ulrichsen, Kristian and Giorgo Cafiero, "Yemen War: How US and Oman are Finding Common Ground," March 4, 2021, *Middle East Eye*, available at: https://www.middleeasteye.net/opinion/yemen-war-how-us-and-oman-are-finding-common-ground.

Cohen, Billy, "The Country that Never Takes Sides," *BBC*, July 21. 2017, available at: http://www.bbc.com/travel/story/20170717-the-country-that-cant-choose-a-side.

Collins, Craig and John Packer, "Quiet Diplomacy: Preventing Conflict through Discreet Engagement," in Stefan Wolff and Christalla Yakinthou (eds.), *Conflict Management in Divided Societies: Theories and Practices* (Abingdon: Routledge, 2012).

Collins, Craig and John Packer, *Options and Techniques for Quiet Diplomacy* (Stockholm: Folke Bernadotte Academy, 2005).

Davidson, Christopher, *Power and Politics in the Persian Gulf Monarchies* (London: Hurst, 2011).

Due-Gundersen, Nicolai, "The Two Sultans of Oman: From Qaboos to Haitham bin Tariq' Albawaba," February 19, 2000, available at: https://www.albawaba.com/opinion/two-sultans-oman-qaboos-haitham-bin-tariq-1340223.

Ezzat, Noha, "Oman: Institutional Genealogy of an Exceptional Foreign Policy," *Global Policy Journal*, IMEIS 2019 Conference Proceedings, University of Durham, June 2019, available at: https://www.globalpolicyjournal.com/sites/default/files/pdf/Beaujouan%20-%20GCC%2C%20Evaluation%2C%20Lessons%20Learned%20and%20Future%20Prospects%20%28PDF%29_0.pdf.

Fattihi, Kambiz, "The Oman Scare: The Untold Story of Oman's Almost Strike on Iran," September 27, 2018, available at: https://www.wilsoncenter.org/blog-post/the-oman-scare-the-untold-story-omans-almost-military-strike-iran.

Fawcett, Louise (ed.), *The International Relations of the Middle East*, 4th edn. (Oxford: Oxford University Press, 2019).

Gardner, Nikolas, "The Limits of the Sandhurst Connection: The Evolution of Oman's Foreign and Defense Policy, 1970–1977," *Journal of the Middle East and Africa* 6(1) (2015), available at: https://www.tandfonline.com/doi/abs/10.1080/21520844.2015.1028850.

Hinnebusch, Raymond, *The International Politics of the Middle East*, 2nd edn. (Manchester: Manchester University Press, 2015).

Hinnebusch, Raymond and Anoushiravan Ehtesham, *The Foreign Policies of Middle East States*, 2nd edn. (Boulder, CO: Lynne Rienner, 2014).

Hinnebusch, Raymond and Anoushiravan Ehteshami, "Foreign Policymaking in the Middle East: Complex Realism," in Louise Fawcett (ed.), *International Relations of the Middle East*, 4th edn. (Oxford: Oxford University Press, 2019), 249–270.

Jones, Jeremy, "Oman's Quiet Diplomacy," NUPI Paper, June,4, *Norwegian Institute of International Affairs*, 2015, available at: https://www.nupi.no/en/Publications/CRIStin-Pub/Oman-s-Quiet-Diplomacy, last accessed October 22, 2021.

Jones, Jeremy and Nicholas Ridout, *Oman: Culture and Diplomacy* (Edinburgh: Edinburgh University Press, 2012).

Kerr, Simon, "Switzerland of the Middle East: Economic Crisis Threatens Oman's Neutrality," *Financial Times*, October 19, 2020, available at: https://www.ft.com/content/2fac87cf-3ed4-4d3e-9ee9-280734d323f9.

Owtram, Francis, *A Modern History of Oman: Formation of the State since 1920* (London: I. B. Tauris, 2004).

Owtram, Francis, "Oman after Qaboos: Continuities, Challenges and Choices," LSE Middle East Centre, January 24, 2020, available at: https://blogs.lse.ac.uk/mec/2020/01/24/oman-after-qaboos-continuities-challenges-and-choices.

Owtram, Francis and Malak Hayek, "Oman in the COVID-19 Pandemic: People, Policy and Economic Impact," LSE Middle East Centre blog, July 23, 2020, available at: https://blogs.lse.ac.uk/mec/2020/07/23/oman-in-the-covid-19-pandemic-people-policy-and-economic-impact.

Owtram, Francis, Annemarie Profanter, and Elena Maestri, "Oman, No Security for the Migrant Health Workers," openDemocracy.com, July 23, 2020, available at: https://www.opendemocracy.net/en/north-africa-west-asia/in-oman-no-security-for-the-migrant-health-workers.

Takriti, Abdel Razzaq, *Monsoon Revolution: Republicans, Sultans, and Empires in Oman, 1965–1976* (Oxford: Oxford University Press, 2013).

Tran, Edwin, "In the Lion's Den: Oman's Foreign Policy, Part 1," *International Review*, December 6, 2018, available at: https://international-review.org/in-the-lions-den-omans-foreign-policy-part-1.

Valerie, Marc, "Oman's Mediatory Efforts in Regional Crises," in Expert Analysis, Norwegian Peacebuilding Resource Centre, March 2014, available at: https://ore.exeter.ac.uk/repository/handle/10871/14682.

Valeri, Marc, *Politics and Society in the Qaboos State*, 2nd edn. (London: Hurst, 2017).

Valeri, Marc, "Oman," in Christopher Davidson (ed.), *Power and Politics in the Persian Gulf Monarchies* (London: Hurst, 2011), 135–160.

INDEX

Note: n indicates note, *f* indicatse figure, *T* indicates table